The Hellenistic philosophers

VOLUME I

Study of the Stoic, Epicurean and sceptical schools of philosophy has been hampered by the inaccessibility and difficulty of the surviving evidence. To help students and scholars, Anthony Long and David Sedley have compiled a comprehensive sourcebook, which makes the principal texts available to the widest audience since classical antiquity. The material is organised by schools, and within each school topics are treated thematically, thus providing the reader with immediate access to all the central concepts and the controversies they aroused in their historical context.

In this book the authors present the texts in their own new translations, and these are accompanied by a philosophical and historical commentary designed for use by all readers, including those with no background in the classical world. With its glossary and set of indexes, this volume can stand alone as an independent tool of study. (Details of the Greek and Latin originals are available to specialists in a companion volume.)

The collection should be invaluable to students and teachers of Greek thought in departments of philosophy and classical studies. No knowledge of Greek or Latin is required.

The Hellenistic philosophers

VOLUME 1
Translations of the principal sources with philosophical commentary

A. A. LONG
Professor of Classics, University of California, Berkeley

D. N. SEDLEY
Professor of Ancient Philosophy, University of Cambridge,
and Fellow of Christ's College

CAMBRIDGE
UNIVERSITY PRESS

Published by the Press Syndicate of the University of Cambridge
The Pitt Building, Trumpington Street, Cambridge CB2 1RP
40 West 20th Street, New York, NY 10011–4211, USA
10 Stamford Road, Oakleigh, Melbourne 3166, Australia

First published 1987
Reprinted 1988 (twice), 1990, 1992, 1995, 1997

Printed in Great Britain at the University Press, Cambridge

British Library cataloguing in publication data

The Hellenistic philosophers.
Vol. I: Translations and commentary
1. Philosophy, Ancient
I. Long, A. A. II. Sedley, D. N.
180′.938   B171

Library of Congress cataloguing in publication data

Long, A. A.
The Hellenistic philosophers.
Bibliography.
Includes indexes.
Contents: v. 1. Translations of the principal
sources with philosophical commentary.
1. Philosophy, Ancient—Addresses, essays, lectures.
I. Sedley, D. N. II. Title.
B505.1.66   1986   186   85–30956

ISBN 0 521 25561 9 hardback
ISBN 0 521 27556 3 paperback

SE

For D. J. FURLEY

Contents

Contents

Preface

This work is a collection and discussion of the primary sources for Hellenistic philosophy. By presenting the material both in its original languages and in translation, we aim to give classicists and philosophers direct access to the surviving evidence on the Stoics, Epicureans, Pyrrhonists and Academics, whose thought dominated philosophy in the three centuries after the death of Aristotle in 322 B.C. There has been a remarkable upsurge of interest in these philosophies over the last few decades, but up to now the original texts have not been collected in any single book with the comprehensiveness and detail we have sought to provide.

In its scope and purpose our book closely resembles G. S. Kirk, J. E. Raven, and M. Schofield, *The Presocratic Philosophers* (ed. 2, 1983), but we divide the material between two volumes. Vol. 1 is entirely in English, offering translations of texts, accompanied by philosophical commentary. It is presented in a manner which we hope will make it usable by those with no historical background in the classical world. With its glossary and set of indexes, it is designed to be entirely self-sufficient. But the expectation is that our classical readers will use it in conjunction with vol. 2. This latter supplies (sometimes in longer excerpts) the texts translated in vol. 1, together with critical apparatus, information on their original contexts, supplementary commentary on technical matters and points of detail, and some additional texts.

The surviving record of Hellenistic philosophy, though extensive, varies greatly in quality and reliability. Only a small fraction of it reports the original words of the philosophers themselves (see Introduction, section 3). For the rest, we are dependent upon odd sentences, often quoted out of context, the writings of later sceptics, Stoics and Epicureans, and the sympathetic, or more often hostile, summaries composed by numerous other authors. In selecting from all this material, our guiding principles have been historical authenticity and philosophical interest. The evidence we present on each topic is what we judge to be the best that survives. On some topics – for instance Stoic ontology – the selection was relatively easy since the complete record on this material is exiguous. In other cases - for instance Stoic ethics – the surviving evidence is much fuller and more accessible. Here our selection of passages should help the reader to isolate the salient doctrines in many similar texts that we omit.

The format of the work is as clear as we have been able to make it without prejudicing the authentic nature of the material. Even so, we recognize that it will impose certain demands on any careful reader. Just within vol. I it will be necessary to move constantly back and forth between texts and commentary of each single section, and strongly advisable to follow up the cross-references given in the commentary. We regard these latter as a crucial feature of the book, since one part of a philosophy is frequently illuminated by reference to another, or by comparison with the rival doctrine of another school. At the same time, we emphasize that this is a *source*book. We intend the commentary to play a role strictly subordinate to that of the texts and translations, and we would respect the decision of any reader or class-instructor to work purely with the texts, by-passing our commentary altogether. What it offers is orientation and exposition, especially of the more demanding material, where we include suggestions and interpretations of our own without, in many cases, any claim that these are orthodox. We hope that these comments will clarify the central philosophical issues even where the position we adopt is novel or controversial. Some sections of the book seemed to need briefer comment than others because the texts largely spoke for themselves. Hence the length of our commentary should not be regarded as a measure of our own interest in each topic.

Throughout our preparation of this book we have had to balance the practical restrictions on its size against our wish to do justice to numerous individuals, both ancient and modern, and the range of subjects studied by Hellenistic philosophers. The decision to proceed school by school, and not for example topic by topic or philosopher by philosopher, is one which we took early and have never regretted. But it has sometimes led us to emphasize the unity of school doctrines, especially Stoic, where there is a good case for singling out two or more divergent strands within the apparent consensus. Readers will find no separate treatments of Aristo, Cleanthes, Panaetius, Posidonius, or even Chrysippus himself. However, our commentary does frequently discuss their divergences, and, more important, a reader interested in chasing up the work of an individual can very well do so by consulting the *Index of philosophers* appended to vol. I.

Again, we have had to be ruthlessly selective about 'non-standard' Hellenistic philosophers. Ideally we would have devoted much space to Cynics, Cyrenaics, Megarians, Dialecticians, and others who exerted a formative influence on Hellenistic philosophy; to the Hellenistic Peripatos; to individualistic Academics like Philo of Larissa and

Antiochus; and to post-Hellenistic philosophers like Epictetus and Sextus Empiricus who are powerful adherents of Hellenistic schools. As it is, we have had to content ourselves with bringing these in, if at all, only where they can be perceived as contributing to the debates in which the principal schools were engaged, or as reliable spokesmen for them.

Scepticism does much to lend Hellenistic philosophy its distinctive colouring, and we have tried to give it due emphasis. Appropriately, the period is made to open with Early Pyrrhonism and to close with The Pyrrhonist Revival. We had originally planned that this latter should fully represent the sceptical philosophy of Sextus Empiricus, despite his post-Hellenistic date. In the event, however, shortage of space, combined with a few historical misgivings, led us to treat the founder of that philosophy, Aenesidemus, as virtually the sole spokesman for late Hellenistic Pyrrhonism. Aenesidemus is an impressive figure, whose work cannot be easily appreciated without being isolated from that of his later adherents. As for the principal Academic sceptics, these are better represented than a glance at the Contents might suggest. In addition to our coverage of their own philosophical positions in **68–70**, their individual criticisms are worked into many of the Stoic sections, where, indeed, they are often most at home: see especially **28, 37, 39–41, 64.**

As with individuals, so too with schools we have had to confine our treatment to those topics in which issues central to the history of philosophy are raised. Science is featured in our book only as philosophy of science or as cosmology integral to the general world-view of a school. Astronomy, physiology, rhetoric, grammar, and aesthetics are subjects to which Hellenistic philosophers, especially Stoics, made important contributions. We have not attempted to deal more than incidentally with these, on which much primary work remains to be done.

We have profited enormously from the wealth of scholarship devoted to Hellenistic philosophy in the last hundred years, and more especially in the last twenty, but found that any serious discussion of these studies in vol. 1 would have expanded it to an unacceptable size. We have therefore, with regret, restricted such discussion to points of detail in the vol. 2 notes. What we offer instead is, at the end of vol. 2, an annotated bibliography, arranged topic by topic, which will help readers to judge the tendency of our commentary and its relation to other studies. (The model for this, which we gratefully acknowledge, is J. Barnes, M. Schofield and R. Sorabji, *Articles on Aristotle*, London 1973–7.)

This sourcebook is the product of joint-authorship, not parallel authorship. Each section was of course initially the work of one or other of us, but we have intervened heavily in each other's sections, sometimes rewriting parts. Every issue, whether of interpretation or of policy, has been resolved by discussion between us. Thus we jointly accept responsibility for the entire book. However, for those curious to distinguish the separate strands, *primary* authorship of the sections was as follows.

A.A.L.: **1–3, 21–2, 26, 31, 33–4, 39–41, 43–9, 51–3, 56–61, 63–9.**
D.N.S.: **4–20, 23–5, 27–30, 32, 35–8, 42, 50, 54–5, 62, 70–2.**

Although planning of these volumes goes back to the middle 1970s, systematic work on them lasted from 1979 to 1986. During that time, we have incurred numerous debts of gratitude, of which the following deserve special mention. We were fortunate to have the superb research assistance of Hayden Ausland, Dirk Obbink, Allan Silverman and Steve White, all of whom, in addition to their tireless labour on relatively routine matters, provided us with searching criticisms and invaluable suggestions. Individual sections were read and commented on by Jonathan Barnes, Myles Burnyeat, Fernanda Decleva Caizzi, Richard Davies, Michael Frede, Brad Inwood, Jim Lennox, Geoffrey Lloyd, Malcolm Schofield, Richard Sorabji, and Robert Wardy, and we greatly appreciated their advice. Others to whom we have turned with profit for expert advice on individual points include Catherine Atherton, Francesca Longo Auricchio, Nicholas Denyer, Tiziano Dorandi, Adele Tepedino Guerra, Jim Hankinson, Michael Inwood, E. J. Kenney, A. C. Lloyd, and Margie Miles. In the planning of the book we have been helped by the ideas of David Furley, Pauline Hire, Ian Kidd, Susan Moore, and above all Jeremy Mynott, whose brainchild the entire project is. Valued assistance with the preparation of the manuscript has been rendered by Sandra Bargh, Yvonne Cassidy, Sylvia Sylvester, and Andrea Shankman. And we thank Candace Smith very warmly for the drawing on p. 4 – her advice about it, as well as its eventual execution.

A further debt of gratitude must be recorded here. Karlheinz Hülser has been preparing a magnificent collection, *Die Fragmente zur Dialektik der Stoiker* (= *FDS*), and was kind enough to provide us with pre-publication drafts. We have found his work immensely helpful in preparation of this sourcebook. We regret that our policy of very limited cross-reference to collections of fragments has prevented our providing *FDS* numbers in vol. 1 for those of our texts which also appear in his collection (a few of these are noted in vol. 2, however).

For research resources, we thank the Institute for Advanced Study, Princeton, whose generous grants of membership (A.A.L. in 1979, D.N.S. in 1982) provided ideal conditions for the furtherance of the project; and the Universities of Liverpool, California, and Cambridge, and Christ's College Cambridge, for research grants. We are also grateful to Robinson College Cambridge for a bye-fellowship awarded to A.A.L. in 1982, and to the University of California at Berkeley for a visiting professorship awarded to D.N.S. in 1984: these afforded us the rare luxury of extended collaboration in the same geographical location without our usual dependence on the post and the telephone.

The two volumes are dedicated to David Furley, who has taught us both so much about Greek philosophy, and whose own publications provide a model of clarity and incisiveness which we fear will be only palely reflected in what follows.

Berkeley, April 1986   DAVID SEDLEY
                                                          TONY LONG

Introduction

1 THE SCHOOLS

If Aristotle could have returned to Athens in 272 B.C., on the fiftieth anniversary of his death, he would hardly have recognized it as the intellectual milieu in which he had taught and researched for much of his life. He would have found there new philosophies far more diverse and more self-consciously systematic than those on offer in his own day. Some of the central issues, and much of the technical terminology in which they were being discussed, would have seemed unfamiliar.

How had this change come about? Aristotle might have perceived it as one aspect of the radical transformations effected throughout the greater part of the known world by the conquests of his delinquent pupil Alexander the Great. Alexander's hellenization of the east Mediterranean and beyond had generated a new excitement about Greek culture among people with primarily non-Greek backgrounds. For those who were attracted by Greek philosophy in particular, Athens was their natural Mecca, both because it still housed the schools founded by Plato and Aristotle, and because such literary masterpieces as Plato's Socratic dialogues, which will have afforded many their first taste of the subject, lent Athens an unfading glamour as the true home of philosophical enlightenment. Thus in the new Hellenistic age philosophy flourished at Athens as never before. And many of her new breed of philosophers hailed from the eastern Mediterranean region.

In the mean time the city of Alexandria, founded by Alexander in Egypt, was becoming a rival cultural centre, thanks largely to the generous patronage offered by its rulers the Ptolemies. Philosophy itself could not flourish under such patronage, and Athens remained uneclipsed as the philosophical centre of the Greek world. But the drift of other intellectuals to Alexandria had a crucial effect. Plato's Academy and Aristotle's school in the Lyceum had been research centres in the broadest sense. Plato's colleagues and disciples had included many of the leading mathematicians of the day, and the Lyceum had housed, in addition to philosophy in the modern sense, scholarly and scientific research on almost every conceivable topic. Few readers will need

I

reminding, for example, of Aristotle's own seminal contributions to zoology, political history and literary theory. Now, however, such disciplines were finding a new home in Alexandria. The result was that philosophy became for the first time pared down to something resembling the specialist discipline which it is today.

Whether Plato and Aristotle had meant to create philosophical *systems* at all is far from clear. But in the new era a philosophy was above all an integrated system for the complete understanding of the world's basic structure and man's place in it. One's choice of philosophical allegiance, it was assumed, would radically affect one's whole outlook on life.

Had Aristotle's ghost in 272 paid a nostalgic visit to the Lyceum, just outside the eastern city wall (see topographical sketch, p. 4), the effects of this philosophical revolution would have struck him with particular poignancy. His old associate, and successor as head of the Peripatetic school, Theophrastus, was fifteen years dead. With him had died the last representative of Aristotle's own encyclopaedic conception of philosophy. Many of the school's adherents had drifted away to Alexandria, and even its library had been shipped abroad by Theophrastus' heir. Aristotle's own most technical philosophical work (the school texts by which we know him today) was, it seems, relatively little circulated or discussed. As for Theophrastus' successor as head of the school, Strato, he was a highly original physical theorist, but even by the standards of the day a narrow specialist in his field. The Peripatetic school maintained a low profile, at least in philosophy, until the end of the Hellenistic period (officially dated to 31 B.C.), even though the Roman imperial era which followed was to be to a large extent dominated by the revival of Aristotelianism.

If we imagine Aristotle continuing his tour, at the central agora just a kilometre away from his own school he would have found the scene very different. Here stood the Stoa Poikile, or 'Painted Colonnade', in which a thriving philosophical group met daily to discuss and teach. They were popularly known as the Stoics, or 'the men from the Stoa', and their system, Stoicism, was already the dominant philosophy of the day. Thanks in part to the immense intellectual prestige that it had acquired, it was by now the source of much of the technical terminology and conceptual equipment with which doctrinal debates were being framed. Its founder, Zeno of Citium, now aged 62, had arrived in Athens as a young man from his native Cyprus, a new recruit to Hellenism, eager to learn philosophy in the public gymnasia, walks and colonnades which Socrates himself had once frequented. Philosophy in Athens was always a supremely public affair, and in concentrating their activities on the agora the Stoics were likely never to be far from the public eye.

Zeno's most stalwart colleague, and eventual successor on his death in 262, was Cleanthes, whose own contributions to Stoicism lay especially in the areas of theology and cosmology. Not all members of the School were entirely orthodox, however, and the ethical heterodoxy of the Stoic Aristo will be receiving particular attention in our book. The most important of all the Stoics, Chrysippus, was at this date an eight-year-old boy at Soli, on the shores of the east Mediterranean. In the period roughly from 232 to 206 he was to hold the headship of the school, and to develop all aspects of Stoic theory with such flair, precision and comprehensiveness that 'early Stoicism' means for us, in effect, the philosophy of Chrysippus. The individual contributions of these and other Stoics can be explored through the *Index of philosophers* at the end of this volume (see especially Sphaerus, Diogenes of Babylon, Antipater, Panaetius, Posidonius).

The Stoics held no monopoly on the agora and its environs. This was one area towards which any philosopher staying at Athens could be expected to gravitate. Aristotle's ghost might have encountered there some curiously familiar types, and perhaps some curiously unfamiliar. One omnipresent figure since the mid-fourth century had been that of the itinerant Cynic, whose main tenets would be the absolute self-sufficiency of virtue and the total inconsequentiality of all social norms, physical comforts, and gifts of fortune. In a way the greatest triumph of Cynicism was its formative influence on the work of Zeno, whose first philosophical training had been with the Cynic Crates. However, orthodox Stoicism subtly modified the ethical extremism of the Cynics, so as to retain an integral role for the conventional values which Cynicism rejected out of hand (see **58–9**, and **67A–H** for some Cynic elements in early Stoic political theory).

Others whom he might well have observed there include Cyrenaics, Dialecticians and Megarians – schools whose contributions to Hellenistic philosophy may be explored through our *Index of philosophers* – and Timon of Phlius, chief propagandist for the sceptic guru Pyrrho, whose philosophy both opens and closes our book.

The nostalgic tour might have been completed with an excursion beyond the Dipylon Gate to the north-west, to visit the Academy, where a century earlier the young Aristotle had himself sat at the feet of Plato. On the way he might just have noticed an enclosed garden – *the* Garden, as it was known. It was the property of Epicurus, whose philosophy occupies a large share of our book. His was certainly the most inward-looking of the philosophical schools, avowedly shunning all political involvements and concentrating on the proper functioning of its own philosophical

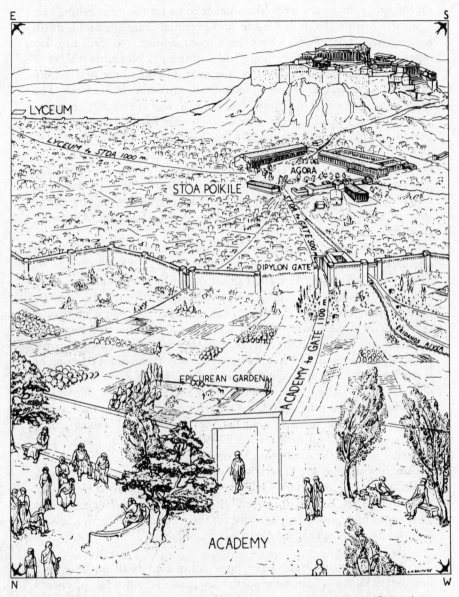

E · S · N · W

LYCEUM

LYCEUM to STOA 1000 m.

AGORA

STOA POIKILE

DIPYLON GATE

ACADEMY to GATE 1100

EPICUREAN GARDEN

ERIDANOS RIVER

ACADEMY

The philosophical schools of Hellenistic Athens: locations and distances. © Candace H. Smith 1987

community within the Garden and of similar movements elsewhere. Even so, it is no accident that he had set up his main school at Athens, the hub of philosophical activity. Originally, presenting himself as a follower of the early atomist Democritus, he had established branches of his school at two locations in the eastern Aegean area. But in 306 he had made the decisive move to Athens, where he set up what was to become and remain his school's headquarters. The Stoa and the Academy were located within easy reach (see the topographical sketch, p. 4), and we need not doubt that Epicurus was as keen as his rivals were to have a finger on the philosophical pulse of Athens. In numerous ways, as our book will seek to bring out, Stoicism and Epicureanism appear to have developed in polar opposition to each other.

Arriving finally at the Academy itself, Aristotle might have suffered his most severe shock of all. Its recently appointed head, Arcesilaus, was admittedly a dedicated Platonist. But his Platonism was modelled above all on what we know as the early dialogues of Plato, those in which Socrates is portrayed as constantly questioning the tenets and assumptions of those more opinionated than himself, and exposing their fragility and inconsistency. Doctrinal Platonism, stemming from Plato's later work, had survived for many years after its author's death. Even in the last years of the fourth century the young Zeno had studied a version of it under the then head of the Academy, Polemo, and that was the principal route by which Platonic doctrine was to acquire a foothold in Hellenistic philosophy. But in the Academy itself it had little momentum left, and it was Arcesilaus' reversion to the critical dialectic of Plato's early work that was now at last rejuvenating the school. Under his leadership the 'New Academy' gained the status of the chief sceptical school, and throughout the Hellenistic age every new generation of Stoics was subjected by it to the most searching critiques. Its greatest head, Carneades, was to dominate the philosophical scene in the mid-second century B.C. He was not only an influential critic of Chrysippean Stoicism, but also a brilliantly original philosopher in his own right. It was not until the first century B.C. that the Academy entered a new decline, finally falling apart in doctrinal disarray (see **68, 71**).

What was a 'school'? Not, in general, a formally established institution, but a group of like-minded philosophers with an agreed leader and a regular meeting place, sometimes on private premises but normally in public. School loyalty meant loyalty to the *founder* of the sect – Zeno for the Stoa, Epicurus for the Garden, Socrates and Plato for the Academy – and it is in that light that the degree of intellectual independence within each school must be viewed. It was generally thought more proper to present new ideas as interpretations or developments of the founder's views than as criticisms of him. It was thus to the great advantage of the Stoics that Zeno had left many issues unclarified or unsettled, and of the Academics that Plato's dialogues were open to a variety of interpretations. Epicurus, on the other hand, had spelled out his system with immense precision, leaving relatively few issues to his successors for genuinely open debate (e.g. **21A 4**; **22O**). The virtually unquestioned authority of the founder within each of the schools gave its adherents an identity as members of a 'sect' (*hairesis*), readily recognizable by their labels 'Stoic', 'Epicurean', 'Academic', or 'Pyrrhonist'.

2 THE SYSTEMS

There is little point in trying to supply summaries of Academic and Pyrrhonian scepticism. Neither school would even have welcomed the attribution of a 'system'. The nature of their philosophical enterprise will emerge more effectively from a study of the texts themselves (especially **1–3, 39–41, 64, 68–72**). But in the case of Epicureanism and Stoicism the material is so extensive and wide-ranging that some readers may find the following very brief overviews helpful.

Epicureanism consists of three principal divisions: physics (**4–15**); epistemology, or 'canonic' (**16–19**); and ethics (**20–5**).

The physical theory is developed out of intuitively primary first principles. All that has independent existence is body, which is shown to consist of an infinity of atomic particles, and infinite space, much of it void. Secondary properties do exist too, but parasitically on these. Our world, like literally countless others, is the accidental and transient product of complex atomic collisions, with no purposive origin or structure, no controlling deity. And the soul, itself a complex atomic conglomerate, perishes with the body. With these conclusions, physics can eliminate the psychologically crippling fear of divine intervention in this life and retribution in the next.

Cognitive certainty is attainable through the senses, combined with a set of natural conceptions and intuitions. Using these tools, we can infer with varying degrees of certainty the hidden nature of things. The formal dialectical techniques of Plato and his successors are unnecessary to the enterprise.

Despite our ultimately atomic construction, we are genuinely autonomous agents, capable of structuring our own lives in accordance with the one natural good, pleasure. Epicureanism's means of teaching us to maximize the pleasantness of life include eliminating fears of the unknown; recognizing the utility of mutual benefits and non-aggression; and mapping out the natural limits of pleasure, any attempt to exceed which is merely counterproductive. The tranquillity of Epicurean enlightenment, complemented by a few simple enjoyments and underpinned by friendship with others of the same persuasion, can emulate even the paradigmatic bliss of the divinities we worship.

Unlike Epicureanism, the Stoic system is not a linear development from first principles, but a self-supporting edifice in which no plank is unambiguously prior to any other (cf. **26**). Our detailed organization of the material in **26–67** makes no special claims of authenticity. Overall it does correspond roughly to the official Stoic tripartition into logic (**27– 42**), physics (**43–55**), and ethics (**56–67**), but what we call 'ontology' (**27– 30**) probably combines material from physics and from logic.

To exist is to be a body. But all matter is totally imbued with an intelligent force called variously 'god' or 'reason', or, at another level of analysis, 'breath'. Our world, a unique, finite, and eternally recurrent organism, is thus itself coextensive with god, and in a way *is* god. Its rationality is manifested in its moral perfection as a unified organism, the appearance of imperfection only arising when the parts are viewed in isolation. Every detail is predetermined by a causal nexus called 'fate', so that human moral responsibility has to be understood as not entailing genuinely free choice of action. Individual goodness and happiness consist in the wise man's perfect concord with the preordained scheme of things. All other objects and states which are conventionally prized, such as wealth and health, are morally 'indifferent'. We should, generally speaking, seek them, but not as ultimate objectives, just as natural guidelines for our fully developed end of 'living in agreement with nature'. The hope of such moral improvement rests in particular on the primarily intellectual nature of our morally bad states, or 'passions': as false *judgements*, they are capable of being modified by reason. Even so, the Stoics often set such high standards for their idealized wise man as to leave the impression that individual goodness is barely attainable.

The understanding of the world requisite for moral virtue demands rigorous philosophical methodology. The true dialectician is an expert at division, definition, and the complex logical analysis of arguments. He can also evaluate the epistemic status of his premises, being an expert on all 'impressions' of the way things are. There are many grades of these, but only one species of impression has the cognitive certainty on which it is safe to build a proof.

Readers who feel the need for a more extensive general survey could consult

> A. A. Long, *Hellenistic philosophy* (London, 1974; ed. 2, London, Berkeley and Los Angeles, 1986);
> F. H. Sandbach, *The Stoics* (London, 1975);

and the translations in the Loeb Classical Library series of Cicero's philosophical works (especially *On ends, Academica, On the nature of the gods, On fate*) and of Lucretius.

Books bearing on specific topics and usable by the non-specialist include

> D.J. Furley, *Two studies in the Greek atomists* (Princeton, 1967)
> A. A. Long (ed.), *Problems in Stoicism* (London, 1971)
> J.M. Rist (ed.), *The Stoics* (Berkeley, Los Angeles and London, 1978)
> J. Barnes, M. Burnyeat, M. Schofield (edd.), *Doubt and dogmatism* (Oxford, 1980)
> M. Burnyeat (ed.), *The skeptical tradition* (Berkeley, Los Angeles and London, 1983)
> J. Annas, J. Barnes, *The modes of scepticism* (Cambridge, 1985)
> M. Schofield, G. Striker (edd.), *The norms of nature* (Cambridge and Paris, 1986)

An extensive bibliography is appended to vol. 2.

For the most relevant texts of the forerunners to Hellenistic philosophy, we recommend

> G. S. Kirk, J. E. Raven, M. Schofield, *The Presocratic philosophers* (ed. 2, Cambridge, 1983; referred to as KRS in this volume);
> Plato, *Protagoras, Gorgias, Meno, Phaedo, Republic, Euthydemus, Phaedrus, Timaeus, Theaetetus, Sophist, Philebus, Laws* 10;
> Aristotle, *Nicomachean ethics, Physics* 2, 4 and 6, *On generation and corruption, Metaphysics* 12, *On the heaven, Posterior analytics, De interpretatione, Topics, On soul*.

3 THE EVIDENCE

Epicurus and Chrysippus wrote, between them, works amounting to more than a thousand books (i.e. scrolls of papyrus). So the total literary output of Hellenistic philosophy must have run into many thousands of books. From these, all that survive intact are three epitomes and a set of maxims by Epicurus, and a hymn by Cleanthes. We are also fortunate to possess the brilliant Epicurean poem of the Roman writer Lucretius, a number of Latin works by Cicero presenting outlines of the main Hellenistic philosophies, and the writings of a few post-Hellenistic philosophers who were adherents of Hellenistic schools. All our other evidence is, to a greater or lesser degree, fragmentary. Philosophers' views are summarized or quoted, normally out of context, by later writers who are as often as not their declared enemies.

(Some information on these can be found in our *Index of sources*.)

Consequently Hellenistic philosophy is a jigsaw. Our primary object has been to assemble, if not a complete, at least a plentiful set of pieces, grouped according to the general area of the jigsaw to which they belong. Our commentary suggests how some of the precise joins might be effected, with the warning that the fit may not always be exact. Since the reconstruction of one part of the jigsaw will as often as not depend on that of other parts, readers are urged to follow up the cross-references supplied in the commentary and to make regular use of the additional information available in the four indexes.

The sources selected represent a wide range of literary genres, both Greek and Latin. If our style of translation does less than justice to some of these genres, it is because we have felt the interests of the book to be better served by technical clarity than by literary fine tuning. For example, many verse passages will scarcely be distinguishable from prose. And where a Latin author is Latinizing Greek philosophical terminology we have felt at liberty occasionally to base our translation less directly on his precise words than on the Greek terms which we take them to represent. This policy serves the interests of terminological consistency, and should, in conjunction with the glossary at the end of vol. 1, make more manageable the reader's task in negotiating the technical vocabulary of the period.

Texts are marked by capital letters **A**, **B** etc. within each section. Occasionally one or two extra texts are added at the end of the corresponding section of vol. 2, and these are marked by lower-case letters. The vol. 2 passages also sometimes extend beyond the translated portions, the additional words being marked by small print.

Within the translations, square brackets, [ ], contain our own glosses; angle brackets, < >, contain words judged to have fallen out of the texts. All numbered subdivisions within the translations are our own.

The systems of reference to texts are explained in the *Index of sources* at the end of this volume. We have also supplied many of the passages with their equivalent numbers in certain standard collections of fragments – works which will be found listed at the end of the same index. But we have not been entirely thorough or systematic. The main point has been to facilitate the task of readers using this book in conjunction with other studies which refer to those collections. We have therefore only supplied those references which we believe will be helpful in this regard, often omitting them when the two corresponding passages coincide only partially. Thus the absence of such a cross-reference should not be taken as an indication that the passage in question is missing from the relevant collection.

Translations and commentary

Early Pyrrhonism

1 Scepticism

A Diogenes Laertius 9.61–2 (Caizzi 1A, 6, 7, 9)

(1) Pyrrho of Elis was the son of Pleistarchus, as Diocles also records. According to Apollodorus in his *Chronicles*, he was first a painter, and was instructed by Bryson son [or pupil?] of Stilpo, as Alexander says in his *Successions*. Later he studied under Anaxarchus and accompanied him everywhere, with the result that he even associated with the Naked Philosophers in India and with the Magi. (2) In consequence he seems to have practised philosophy in a most noble way, introducing that form of it which consists in non-cognition and suspension of judgement... (3) For he would maintain that nothing is honourable or base, or just or unjust, and that likewise in all cases nothing exists in truth; and that convention and habit are the basis of everything that men do; for each thing is no more this than this. (4) He followed these principles in his actual way of life, avoiding nothing and taking no precautions, facing everything as it came, wagons, precipices, dogs, and entrusting nothing whatsoever to his sensations. But he was looked after, as Antigonus of Carystus reports, by his disciples who accompanied him. Aenesidemus, however, says that although he practised philosophy on the principles of suspension of judgement, he did not act carelessly in the details of daily life. He lived to be nearly ninety.

B Diogenes Laertius 9.63–4 (Caizzi 10, part, 28)

(1) He [Pyrrho] used to go off by himself and live as a recluse; and he rarely made an appearance to his household. This he did because he had heard an Indian reproach Anaxarchus with the remark that he would not be able to teach anyone else to be good while he paid court to kings. He was always in the same mental state, so that even if someone left him in the middle of his talking, he would complete the conversation to himself... (2) When once discovered talking to himself, he was asked the reason, and said that he was practising to be virtuous. No-one belittled him in arguments, owing to his ability to discourse at length and to respond to questioning. This explains why even Nausiphanes as a young man was

keen on him. He used to say, at any rate, that it was Pyrrho's character one needed to get but his own doctrines; and he would frequently say that Epicurus also admired Pyrrho's lifestyle and was always asking him about Pyrrho.

C Diogenes Laertius 9.66–7 (Caizzi 15A, 16, 20, part)

(1) When he [Pyrrho] was once scared by a dog that set on him, he responded to criticism by saying that it was difficult to strip oneself completely of being human; but one could struggle against circumstances, by means of actions in the first instance, and if they were not successful, by means of reason. When a wound he had was treated with disinfectants, surgery and cautery, it is said that he did not even frown . . . (2) Philo of Athens, who became a pupil of his, used to say that he referred above all to Democritus, and secondly to Homer as well, whom he admired, constantly quoting, 'As is the generation of leaves, so too is that of men' [*Iliad* 6.146] . . . and that he also used to cite . . . all the lines which point to the inconsistency of men and their futility and childishness.

D Sextus Empiricus, *Against the professors* 7.87–8

A good many people . . . have said that Metrodorus, Anaxarchus and Monimus abolished the criterion [of truth] – Metrodorus because he said 'we know nothing, nor do we even know just this, that we know nothing'; and Anaxarchus and Monimus, because they compared existing things to stage-painting and took them to be like experiences that occur in sleep or insanity.

E Diogenes Laertius 9.60

On account of the impassivity and contentment of his life Anaxarchus was called the 'happiness man'; and he was able to induce moderation in the easiest possible way.

F Aristocles (Eusebius 14.18.1–5; Caizzi 53)

(1) It is supremely necessary to investigate our own capacity for knowledge. For if we are so constituted that we know nothing, there is no need to continue enquiry into other things. Among the ancients too there have been people who made this pronouncement, and Aristotle has argued against them. (2) Pyrrho of Elis was also a powerful spokesman of such a position. He himself has left nothing in writing, but his pupil Timon says that whoever wants to be happy must consider these three questions: first, how are things by nature? Secondly, what attitude should we adopt towards them? Thirdly, what will be the outcome for those who have this attitude? (3) According to Timon, Pyrrho declared

that things are equally indifferent, unmeasurable and inarbitrable. (4) For this reason neither our sensations nor our opinions tell us truths or falsehoods. Therefore for this reason we should not put our trust in them one bit, but we should be unopinionated, uncommitted and unwavering, saying concerning each individual thing that it no more is than is not, or it both is and is not, or it neither is nor is not. (5) The outcome for those who actually adopt this attitude, says Timon, will be first speechlessness, and then freedom from disturbance; and Aenesidemus says pleasure. (6) These are the main points of what they say.

G Diogenes Laertius 9.76 (Caizzi 54, part)

As Timon says in his *Pytho*, the expression ['no more'] signifies 'determining nothing, and suspending judgement'.

H Diogenes Laertius 9.104–5 (including Caizzi 55, 63A)

(1) We [later Pyrrhonists] affirm the appearance, without also affirming that it *is* of such a kind. We too [i.e. like the doctrinaire philosophers] perceive that fire burns; but we suspend judgement about whether it has an inflammable nature ... Our resistance (so they say) is confined to the non-evident accompaniments of appearances. For when we say the picture has projections, we are indicating the appearance. But when we say that it does not have projections, we no longer state what appears but something else. (2) That is why Timon too says in his *Pytho* that he has not departed from normal practice. In his *Images* as well he makes a similar point: 'But the appearance prevails everywhere, wherever one goes.' (3) And in his writings *On sensations* he says: 'That honey is sweet I do not affirm, but I agree that it appears so.'

I Sextus Empiricus, *Against the professors* 11.140 (Timon fr. 844, Caizzi 64)

... nothing exists which is good or bad by nature, 'but these things are decided on the part of men by convention', as Timon says.

J Cicero, *Tusculan disputations* 5.85 (Caizzi 69L)

These opinions [Stoic, Epicurean etc.] are the ones that have some solid foundation; for those of Aristo, Pyrrho, Herillus and some others have faded away.

K Seneca, *Natural questions* 7.32.2 (Caizzi 71)

So many schools of philosophy pass away without a successor. The Academics, both old and more recent, have left no representative. Who is there to hand on the teachings of Pyrrho?

☐ For the Hellenistic philosophers Pyrrho occupies a position that is comparable, in many respects, to that of Socrates in relation to the philosophy of the fourth century B.C. Old enough to join Alexander the Great's expedition to India (**A** I), Pyrrho was already an established figure when Epicurus, Zeno and the Academic Arcesilaus were developing their philosophical identities. Epicurus is said to have admired his lifestyle (**B 2**), his ethical position was likened to the doctrine of the early Stoic Aristo (**2F–H**), and contemporaries named him a progenitor of Academic scepticism (**68E 2, F**). When Aenesidemus seceded from the Academy in the first century B.C., out of disquiet over its dogmatic tendencies, he represented his independent philosophical affiliation as a revival of Pyrrhonism (see **71–2**). The life and thought of Socrates had been similarly catholic in the variety of philosophy it stimulated, and in similar ways. If the solitary Pyrrho (**B** I) differed sharply from the gregarious and talkative Socrates, both men made their dominant impression by personality and way of life rather than by writing books or constructing systematic doctrines, leaving it to their followers to develop and systematize the theoretical foundations of their lifestyles.

Anything approaching a historical portrayal of Pyrrho the man is even harder to recover than with Socrates. Yet allowing for the credulity and embellishment of Hellenistic biography, testimonies such as **A 4** and **C** I should be treated as indicative of an imperturbability in Pyrrho that observers found genuinely extraordinary. (Aenesidemus' more circumspect Pyrrho, **A 4** second part, is perhaps unduly toned down; see **71** commentary.) The wise man whose self-mastery in all circumstances is a paradigm of happiness was a concept of pre-eminent appeal to the Hellenistic schools. Pyrrho in this regard was foreshadowed by Diogenes the Cynic, himself a way-out representative of a Socratic posture; and Timon's polemics against the pretentiousness of other philosophers (see **3**) draw on Cynic style and language.

What makes Pyrrho's recipe for happiness distinctive and seminal is its emergence from a totally negative position concerning objective values and accessibility to truth (**A 3**). The key passage on this 'scepticism' is **F**. Here, though at third-hand, we are given a report on the foundations of Pyrrho's philosophy by his chief disciple and spokesman, Timon. The report is prefaced by a statement from Aristocles, its source, that Pyrrho belonged to an earlier line of philosophers who disclaimed human capacity for knowledge. However, as we proceed to Timon's reported comments (**F 3–5**), we see that this cognitive incompetence is not attributed, as in Democritus for instance (KRS 552–4), to a weakness in our faculties as such, but to 'how things are by nature'. The reason why 'neither sensations nor opinions tell us truths or falsehoods' (**F 4**) appears to be grounded in the 'indifferent, unmeasurable and inarbitrable' nature of things, quite independently of ourselves. Pyrrho on this evidence denies access to truth or falsehood as a consequence of a claim that the world itself lacks any determinable character: either there are no facts, or if there are, they are not the sorts of things that are even in principle available to cognition.

Notice that Pyrrho is not credited with saying that sensations and opinions, though they may be true or false, cannot be known as such. He does not alert us, as later sceptics do, to the unavailability of an agreed criterion of truth. That strategy is quite compatible with, and regularly associated with, the assumption that some of our experience, if we did but know it, has a hold on objective reality (cf. **70A**; **69D**). Pyrrho's inference from the world's indeterminability is much stronger, denying truth or falsehood to *any* sensations or opinions. We are to take it that indeterminability really is the nature of things, and that this proposition, unlike any other judgement we may make about the world, falls outside the exclusion of truth or falsehood (contrast Aenesidemus in **71C 6–8**). This exclusion then provides the grounds for the modal statement (**F 4**) that we should not rely on sensations or opinions in characterizing things, but instead use utterly non-committal and impartial language about anything: 'it no more is than is not, or it both is and is not, or it neither is nor is not'. Unlike a balance which inclines one way or the other, when utilized for weighing items, the Pyrrhonist's attitude, in relation to anything that confronts it, is one of 'speechlessness' or equipoise; and this equipoise constitutes 'freedom from disturbance' (**F 5**).

That every word of this report takes us back to Pyrrho, or even to Timon, can scarcely be assumed. It seems, none the less, to be remarkably uncontaminated by the centuries of intervening philosophy, and sufficiently different from later Pyrrhonism to be taken as the stance of Pyrrho and Timon themselves. On this construal Pyrrho's scepticism was not simply the outcome of equally-balanced and undecidable disagreements between philosophers (as suggested by Aenesidemus, **71A 1**), but the response to a metaphysical thesis, concerning the nature of things. How he defended such a view, we are not told (but see vol. 2 note on **F**). His mentor Anaxarchus, and the sceptical Cynic Monimus, are both said to have likened existing things to 'stage-painting', i.e. illusions (**D**). Anaxarchus was one of those fourth-century atomists who appear to have extended Democritus' reservations about the cognitive reliability of the senses to a general kind of scepticism. The most famous dictum of these later atomists, that of Metrodorus who preceded Anaxarchus, anticipates Arcesilaus in its inclusion of our own ignorance as something that we do not know (**D**, cf. **68A 3**). But Metrodorus and, presumably, Anaxarchus were willing to make use of atomism as an explanatory hypothesis. Pyrrho, on Timon's testimony (**2C**), was serenely unconcerned with every form of speculation.

Through Anaxarchus Pyrrho will also have been acquainted with the 'freedom from disturbance' and moderation that were central to Democritean ethics; and Anaxarchus himself was renowned for the same qualities (**E**). Thus Pyrrho's philosophical pedigree, though insufficient to reconstruct his own reasons for the world's indeterminability, does at least indicate appropriate influences on his position and its ethical outcome. (Note Timon's favourable description of Democritus, **3J**.) Nor should we exclude the attractive Indian sages (**A 1**) from making a salient contribution. Indian thought at this period seems to have developed some kind of scepticism about phenomena, which was linked to the desirability of equanimity.

The recommendations of **F**, covering the attitude appropriate to an indeterminable world, can also be described as 'suspension of judgement' (**A 2**, **G**). Timon insists that this does not involve the Pyrrhonist in differing from convention in his responses to 'appearance' (**H 2**, cf. **A 3**, **I**). Here we seem to glimpse the beginnings of the tendency to turn 'what appears' into the practical guide for living (see **71A**, **B**, **D 2**, with commentary, for Aenesidemus' specification of this criterion). Timon's agreement that honey appears sweet (**H 3**) registers the Pyrrhonist's profession that complete indifference to the nature of things is quite compatible with having normal sense experiences. What he suspends judgement about is the 'non-evident', as later Pyrrhonists put it (**H 1**).

Why going along with appearances should yield tranquillity is a question for our next section. As to Pyrrho's scepticism, the Greek term's connotations of critical enquiry, and the modern notion of reasonable doubt, are out of place. Unlike the later Pyrrhonist, who exploits disagreements, pitting one opinion against another or advancing his own counter-arguments, Pyrrho himself seems to have needed no reassurances that his negative thesis concerning truth and cognition will stand its ground. At the same time, he may be thought to have acknowledged the need for an effort of will, and reinforcements by reasoning, in order to act consistently without commitment to the objective goodness or badness of any situation he confronted (cf. **C 1**).

In assessing the general tendency of his scepticism, the concern with outlawing objective values should be noted (**A 3**, **I**). We hear nothing about any interest in the standard epistemological puzzles debated between Academics and Stoics (cf. **40**), like the problem of discriminating between identical-looking eggs or the straight stick that appears bent in water.

Pyrrho, though publicized by Timon within his own lifetime or soon after, founded no school. For Cicero, contemporary with Aenesidemus, he is merely a figure from the past (**J**). By Seneca's time the Pyrrhonist revival was well under way (see **71–2**), but apparently not widely known in Rome (see **K**).

2 Tranquillity and virtue

A Aristocles (Eusebius 14.18.17; Timon fr. 782, Caizzi 57, part)

[Timon says] Truly, no other mortal could rival Pyrrho.

B Aristocles (Eusebius 14.18.19; Timon fr. 783, Caizzi 58, part)

This is what Timon also says about Pyrrho: 'Such was the man I saw, unconceited and unbroken by all the pressures that have subdued the famed and unfamed alike, unstable bands of people, weighed down on this side and on that with passions, opinion and futile legislation.'

C Diogenes Laertius 9.64 (Timon fr. 822, Caizzi 60)

Moreover, Pyrrho had many admirers of his unconcernedness, so that Timon speaks of him thus in his *Pytho* and in his *Silloi*: 'O old man, O Pyrrho, how and whence did you discover escape from servitude to the opinions and empty theorizing of sophists? How did you unloose the shackles of every deception and persuasion? You did not trouble to investigate what winds prevail over Greece, from whence all things arise and into what they pass.'

D Diogenes Laertius 9.65, Sextus Empiricus, *Against the professors* 11.1, 1.305 (Timon fr. 841, Caizzi 61A–D, part)

[Timon says] This, O Pyrrho, my heart yearns to hear, how on earth you, though a man, act most easily and calmly, never taking thought and consistently undisturbed, heedless of the whirling motions and sweet voice of wisdom? You alone lead the way for men, like the god who drives around the whole earth as he revolves, showing the blazing disk of his well-rounded sphere.

E Sextus Empiricus, *Against the professors* 11.19–20 (Timon fr. 842, Caizzi 62)

In regard to the nature and existence of what is good, bad and indifferent, we have quite enough battles with the doctrinaire philosophers. But with respect to their appearance we are in the habit of calling each of them good or bad or indifferent, just as Timon too seems to indicate in his *Images*, when he says: 'Come, I will speak a word of truth, as it appears to me to be, who have a correct yardstick: the nature of the divine and the good always consists in what makes a man's life most equable.'

F Cicero, *Academica* 2.130 (Caizzi 69A)

[Speaker: Cicero on behalf of the New Academy] Aristo, after he had been a pupil of Zeno, established in practice what Zeno proved in theory – that nothing is good except virtue and nothing is bad except what is contrary to virtue. On his estimation, the intermediates contain none of those differences of value which Zeno wanted. For Aristo the highest good is not to be moved to either side in these things, which he calls 'indifference'. Pyrrho, on the other hand, held that a wise man is not even aware of them, which is called 'impassivity'.

G Cicero, *On ends* 2.43 (Caizzi 69B, part)

Since Aristo and Pyrrho thought that these [i.e. 'the primary things in accordance with nature', see **58**] were of no account at all, to the extent of saying that there was utterly no difference between the best of health and the gravest illness, arguments against them rightly stopped a long time ago. For the effect of their wish to make virtue on its own so all-embracing was to rob virtue of the capacity to select things, and to grant it nothing either as its source or its foundation; consequently they undermined the very virtue which they embraced.

H Cicero, *On ends* 4.43 (Caizzi 69C, part)

[Speaker: Cicero on behalf of Antiochus] So in my opinion all those people are mistaken who have said that living honourably is the highest good, but some more so than others: Pyrrho above all certainly, since, having posited virtue, he leaves nothing at all to seek after. Next Aristo . . .

I Athenaeus 337A (Timon fr. 845, Caizzi 65)

Timon quite splendidly said: 'Desire is absolutely the first of all bad things.'

J Sextus Empiricus, *Against the professors* 11.164 (Timon fr. 846, Caizzi 66, part)

[Timon says of the Pyrrhonist] He will not decline nor will he choose.

☐ The extent of Timon's canonization of Pyrrho emerges clearly here (**A–E**). If **E** is 'Pyrrho's' answer to 'Timon's' question in **D**, all five passages agree in portraying Pyrrho as the unique paradigm and guide of the best human life. The main purpose of Timon's *Silloi*, 'lampoons', was caricature of doctrinaire philosophers (see **3**), who were represented in part of the poem as fighting each other in a Trojan war of words. **A**, a parody of Odysseus (*Iliad* 3.223), implies that Pyrrho's astounding tranquillity puts him above and beyond all philosophical controversy. His equipoise is then illustrated from a moral viewpoint (**B**) and from the context of scientific speculation (**C**), while both themes are combined in **D**.

What sets Pyrrho apart from the general run of people is his utterly consistent immunity to opinion on anything whatever. This equipoise (cf. **1F 5**) enables him to remain quite indifferent to 'the passions, opinions and futile legislation' that 'weigh down' the opinionated masses, whatever their status, and cause them to veer hither and thither in response to their unfounded judgements about the world (**B**; cf. **1C 2**). Timon's language and thought here reflect Cynic moralising, which preached against the 'trumpery' of popular Greek morality and contemporary institutions. Such attack on the 'conceit' of intellectuals was a marked feature of Timon's *Silloi*; he probably saw a close similarity between the Cynic contempt for 'empty opinion', and Pyrrho's refusal to admit any natural basis for the values and beliefs characteristic of his day. But neither Pyrrho nor Timon can have endorsed the Cynic doctrine that there is a natural life, discoverable by reason. What reason discloses to Pyrrho is the absence of any reason for saying 'this rather than that'. Hence the Pyrrhonist, having undermined the foundation for all preferences, 'will not decline nor will he choose' (**J**). This outcome of his scepticism might also be described as a lifestyle so equable that it is altogether without desire. So it comes as no surprise that Timon ranked desire, which presupposes strongly held value judgements, as 'absolutely the first of all bad things' (**I**).

A critic, however, might press Timon to clarify his grounds for calling anything bad (cf. **1I**); and the same question arises in reference to 'the nature of the divine and the good' (**E**), which, on the most plausible reading of a difficult text, is said 'always to consist in what makes a man's life most equable'. Are we to take these as doctrinaire pronouncements, like that of the world's indeterminability (**1F 3**), which fall outside the exclusion of truth and falsehood? Conceivably Pyrrho thought that the relation between goodness and equability was one that transcended the inarbitrability of everything, given the rationality of such a disposition for confronting such a world. But it seems better to take **E** and **I** as descriptions of 'what appears' to the Pyrrhonist, in the light of his negative characterization of all access to objective discriminations. In **E** Timon is careful to preface the (i.e. 'Pyrrho's'?) 'correct yardstick' – the identification of divine and good with the constituents of equability – by reporting 'a word of truth, *as it appears to me to be*'. The Pyrrhonist is as entitled as anyone else to tell us how things appear to him (cf. **1H**), and to guide his life accordingly. He is also entitled to invite those who accept his indeterminable world to draw from it the same practical inferences that he does, and to describe the resulting mental state in the conventional language of approval (cf. Sextus Empiricus' gloss on Timon's lines in **E**). Having arrived at equipoise, he finds himself giving supreme value to everything that enables him to maintain this state. As for his particular actions, he can go along with any conventions that appear to him compatible with non-commitment to their truth or value. Equipoise, not opinion or preference, is the yardstick he consistently employs.

In Cicero (**F–H**) Pyrrho is credited with a position on 'virtue' almost identical to that of the deviant Stoic, Aristo. Unlike his master Zeno, Aristo admitted no objective differences of value between anything except virtue and vice. In particular, he totally rejected the natural 'preferability' of health to sickness etc. (see **58F**), and specified as his account of the end, total indifference to everything intermediate between virtue and vice (**58G**). The general Stoic concept of 'indifferent' was sometimes explained by the 'no more' formula beloved by early and later Pyrrhonists (cf. **1F 4, G**): 'wealth and health no more do benefit than they harm' (**58A 5**). There is plainly, then, some overlap with the Pyrrhonian scope of indifference. But even Aristo's stricter use of the term scarcely justifies assimilation to Pyrrho. For Aristo virtue and vice are determinate moral dispositions, based upon the perfection and imperfection of reason in its conformity or lack of conformity to nature. Pyrrhonian equability, if describable as virtue, derives its *subjective* value from his scepticism, and not from any theory about human nature and the rational.

Cicero in fact has nothing to say on Pyrrho's scepticism, but this does not make his evidence completely worthless. It registers the recognition that Pyrrho was principally remembered, before the first-century B.C. Pyrrhonist revival, as a remarkably austere moralist. If that too is a distortion, it at least has the merit of focusing upon the core of Pyrrho's significance, so far as we can recover this. The 'impassivity' of a Pyrrhonian sage (**F**), and still more the lifestyle of Pyrrho himself, could serve later Sceptics when they defended the possibility of a life without belief (see **71**).

And not just Sceptics. Epicurus, one of Pyrrho's admirers (**1B 2**), also promises freedom from disturbance (cf. **21B 1**; **25B**), and identifies the 'empty desires' which originate from 'empty opinion' as principal threats to its realization (see **21B 1, E 3, G 4, W, X**). The Stoic sage, like the Pyrrhonist, does not opine (cf. **40D 1**; **41C 1–5, D 2, G**), and the passions, from which he is totally free, are false opinions or mistaken judgements, on Chrysippus' analysis (**65B–D, K, L**). But Stoic and Epicurean checks on unfounded opinion have nothing to do with scepticism. Unlike the Pyrrhonist, Epicureans and Stoics posit 'criteria of truth' which give their wise man cognitive access to the real nature of things (see **17**; **40**). The primacy of epistemology in these philosophies, and its foundation in sense-perception, can be viewed as a determined effort to reject just such sceptical challenges as the paralysing Pyrrhonian thesis, 'neither our sensations nor our opinions tell us truths or falsehoods' (**1F 4**).

3 Timon's polemics

A Diogenes Laertius 9.111 (Timon fr. 775)

There are three books of the *Silloi*, in which Timon, adopting the stance of a sceptic, insults everyone and spoofs the doctrinaire philosophers in the form of parody. The first book has him as the narrator, while the second and third are in the style of a dialogue. He appears questioning Xenophanes of Colophon about each philosopher, and Xenophanes responds to him. In the second book he deals with the older philosophers, and in the third with the later ones . . . The first book covers the same subjects, except that the poem is a monologue. It begins like this: 'Tell me now, all you busybody sophists.'

B Aristocles (Eusebius 14.18.28; Timon fr. 785)

Human windbags, stuffed with empty conceit.

C Sextus Empiricus, *Against the professors* 9.57 (Timon fr. 779)

< Foremost of all early > and later sophists, not lacking clarity of speech or vision or versatility, Protagoras. They wanted to make a bonfire of his writings, because he wrote down that he did not know and could not observe what any of the gods are like and whether any of them exist, completely safeguarding his honesty.

D Diogenes Laertius 2.107 (Timon fr. 802)

But I do not care for these wafflers, nor for any other [Socratic], not for Phaedo, whoever he was, nor for quarrelsome Eucleides, who implanted a frenzied love of contentiousness in the Megarians.

E Diogenes Laertius 4.42 (Timon fr. 808)

Having spoken thus, he [Arcesilaus] plunged into the crowd of bystanders. And they like chaffinches round an owl gawped at him, showing up his vanity because he pandered to the mob. There's nothing big in this, you miserable fellow. Why do you give yourself airs like a fool?

F Diogenes Laertius 7.15 (Timon fr. 812)

And I saw a greedy old Phoenician fisherwoman [i.e. Zeno of Citium] in her dark conceit seeking after everything; but her wicker basket, small as it was, is gone; and she had less intellect than a string of twaddle.

G Diogenes Laertius 5.11 (Timon fr. 810)

Nor [do I care for?] Aristotle's painful futility.

H Diogenes Laertius 9.23 (Timon fr. 818)

And I saw mighty Parmenides, high-minded and not prone to common opinions, who removed thought-processes from the deception of appearance.

I Diogenes Laertius 9.25 (Timon fr. 819)

And I saw Zeno [of Elea], unfailingly powerful with his two-edged tongue, who trapped everyone, and Melissus, superior to many illusions and vanquished by few.

J Diogenes Laertius 9.40 (Timon fr. 820)

Such was Democritus, wise shepherd of discourses, hesitant conversationalist, among the first I recognized.

K Diogenes Laertius 10.2 (Timon fr. 825)

The latest of the natural philosophers [Epicurus] and the most shameless, who came from Samos, the schoolmaster's son, the least educated of creatures.

☐ Timon of Phlius was Pyrrho's leading disciple. His record of his master's life and thought was probably the principal source of the Hellenistic biographers, and the literary foundation for the renewal of Pyrrhonism initiated by Aenesidemus (see **71**). From biographical reports (see Diogenes Laertius 9.109–15), and the evidence of his own writings, Timon, unlike Pyrrho himself, emerges as a leading member of the Hellenistic intelligentsia. In Athens, where he spent his later life, he was acquainted with Lacydes, Arcesilaus' successor as head of the sceptical Academy (see **68C 2**). His writings, even in their highly fragmentary state, display detailed knowledge of most leading philosophers, past and present, and the brilliance of his parodies attests to his literary accomplishment. In the absence of any books by Pyrrho, Timon gave an account of his way of life, theorized about the foundations of Pyrrho's philosophy, and used satirical verse to portray the main Greek philosophical tradition as a complete aberration from the enlightenment represented in Pyrrho.

This last point was the theme of the *Silloi* (see **A**), from which **B–K** preserve direct quotations. Their literary form was Homeric parody, a Cynic device. Timon seems to have drawn particularly on the early books of the *Iliad* and book 11 of the *Odyssey*, where Odysseus conjures up the shades of his dead companions. The *Iliad* provided ample scope for picturing philosophical disputes as battles, while the *Nekuia* (*Odyssey* 11) was apt for describing philosophers of the past. The pretentiousness of philosophers in general was emphasized (cf. **B**), and our selection includes tart comments on Aristotle (**G**), Socratic, especially Megarian, philosophers (**D**), Arcesilaus (**E**), the Stoic Zeno (**F**), and Epicurus (**K**). Thus the emergent scepticism of the Academy was treated no more sympathetically than the leaders of the other Hellenistic schools, probably because Timon saw little in common between the Academic practice of argument *contra* every thesis, as the basis for suspension of judgement (see **68**), and Pyrrho's tranquil indifference (but cf. **68E 2**).

But if no mortal could rival Pyrrho (**2A**), a few philosophers of the past were complimented in the *Silloi* for their anticipations of his scepticism. We have already commented (in **1**) on the Democritean background of Pyrrhonism; Timon's favourable assessment of the Eleatic tradition (**H, I**) as well as Democritus himself (**J**) accords with the modern belief that atomism developed as a constructive rejoinder to Parmenides, who had denied any cognitive content to 'appearances'. Parmenides, in his turn, was traditionally regarded as the follower of Xenophanes, the inventor of *Silloi*, to whom Timon gave a special role in his revival of this genre (see **A**). Finally, Protagoras' famous scepticism about the gods won him an honourable mention (**C**). Thus Timon provided Pyrrho with a philosophical pedigree which would illuminate his position within the mainly doctrinaire tradition.

Little is known about any contribution by Timon to philosophical debates, but cf. vol. 2 on **l** and **m**.

Epicureanism

PHYSICS

4 The principles of conservation

A Epicurus, *Letter to Herodotus* 38–9

(1) Having grasped these points, we must now observe, concerning the non-evident, first of all that nothing comes into being out of what is not. For in that case everything would come into being out of everything, with no need for seeds. (2) Also, if that which disappears were destroyed into what is not, all things would have perished, for lack of that into which they dissolved. (3) Moreover, the totality of things was always such as it is now, and always will be, (4) since there is nothing into which it changes, (5) and since beside the totality there is nothing which could pass into it and produce the change.

[handwritten margin note: nothing comes from nothing]

B Lucretius 1.159–73

(1) For if things came into being out of nothing, every species would be able to be produced out of everything, nothing would need a seed. (2) Men, to start with, would be able to spring up out of the sea and scaly fish from the land, and birds hatch out of the sky. Cattle and other livestock, and every species of wild animal, would be born at random and occupy farmland and wilderness alike. Nor would the same fruits stay regularly on the same trees, but would change over: all trees would be able to bear everything. (3) In a situation where each thing did not have its own procreative bodies, how could there be a fixed mother for things? (4) But since in fact individual things are created from fixed seeds, each is born and emerges into the realm of daylight from a place containing its own matter and primary bodies; (5) and the reason why everything cannot come into being out of everything is that particular things contain their own separate powers.

[handwritten margin note: everything d/n come from everything]

C Lucretius 1.225–37

(1) Besides, if time totally destroys the things which it removes through old age, and consumes all their material, from where does Venus bring back living creatures, each after its species, to the daylight of life? Or

from where, thereafter, does the creative earth nourish them and make them grow by supplying each species with its food? From where do internal springs, and rivers flowing from afar, replenish the sea? From where does the aether feed the stars? (2) For infinite time past ought to have consumed those things whose body is perishable. (3) But if in that expanse of time past there have been bodies out of which this sum of things is reconstituted, they are indeed endowed with an imperishable nature. (4) Therefore it cannot be that all things are reduced to nothing.

Imperishable nature

D Lucretius 1.670–1

death changes

For if something changes and leaves its boundaries, that is immediately the death of the thing that it previously was.

☐ Epicurus launches his physical theory from the three principles set out in **A**. Their object is to establish the existence of a permanent and unchanging pool of constituents for the world.

The first two principles, that nothing comes into being out of nothing and that nothing perishes into nothing, had a long history in Greek thought, starting from their canonization by Parmenides in the early fifth century, and had been fundamental to Democritus' atomism (cf. **44D–E** for a Stoic use of them). The defence of the first (**A**, **B**) takes the form of *modus tollens* ('if *p* then *q*; but not-*q*; therefore not-*p*'), with the major premise 'If things came into being out of nothing, everything would come into being out of everything.' This may appear a *non sequitur*, until it is seen that 'out of' is being used in two different senses. The meaning must be 'If things came into being from a prior state of absolute non-existence, they might come into being under any conditions whatsoever.' These conditions are then listed by Lucretius (1.174–214) as place of generation (see **B**), time of generation, duration of generation, nutrition, limit of growth, and soil conditions for crops. The main thrust of the argument is that to assert generation *ex nihilo* is to abandon the principle of sufficient reason with respect to generation, with unacceptable consequences. (Cf. Parmenides, KRS 296,9–10, perhaps the only part of Parmenides' arguments against generation and destruction that Epicurus respects.)

The second principle (**A 2, C**) is defended on more directly empirical grounds: if things perished into nothing, destruction would be, what it is seen not to be, an instantaneous and effortless process (Lucretius 1.217–24, cf. 238–49), and in the infinity of past time matter would have disappeared altogether (see **A 2, C**); besides, the natural cycle of life shows that one thing's 'death' contributes to another's growth, and therefore cannot be literal annihilation (1.250–64).

In **A 4–5** two proofs are offered for the unchanging character of the totality of things (literally 'the all'; 'the universe' is sometimes a convenient translation). The first has usually been interpreted, according to the most natural meaning of the Greek (as of the English), as denying that there is anything that the universe could still *become* – anything, that is, which it has not already become. But the apparent symmetry between the two proofs suggests that 'into' should have the same sense in **A 4** as in **A 5**, where it must bear a literal spatial sense; and Lucretius (2.304–8 = **e** in vol. 2, and **14H** 1) presents what seems to be the same argument in literal spatial terms throughout. It may be best to understand **A 4** in the sense 'since there is nothing into which it *passes and thus* changes' – a possible Greek usage but admittedly a slightly strained one.

What is the nature and scope of the claim made here? In another context, once the nature of the universe has been established, the same argument can be put to work by Lucretius to show that the behaviour patterns of atoms never change (**e** in vol. 2); and the two conditions of change ruled out in **A 4** and **A 5** can be specified as further space for the universe to expand into, and external matter to enter it (**14H** 1). However, at this early stage in Epicurus' exposition the point made must be an entirely general one. It is not, of course, that the universe undergoes no internal change of any kind; yet to guess that Epicurus is restricting its immutability to this or that aspect, for example to its shape or to the laws that govern its behaviour, might seem gratuitous. The vital clue is provided by the immediately following announcement that the totality of things is bodies and void (**5A**). This implies that the aspect of the totality of things currently under discussion is *what it consists of*, and in such a context to call it unchanging must simply be to say that, for the reasons given in **A 4** and **5**, no ingredients can be added or subtracted. This is anyhow the natural implication of saying that the 'totality' or 'sum' of things is invariable – a meaning which the more stylish translation 'universe' masks. On this interpretation, **A 3–5** in no way prejudges the next question, what the totality does in fact consist of. It merely clears the ground by showing that whatever the answer is, it is true for all time.

Thus change by generation, destruction, subtraction and addition have now been ruled out. It could be objected that Epicurus has overlooked another possible source of change in the basic stock of ingredients: one thing might become another thing. Epicurus would almost certainly dismiss this as a case of the existent perishing into the non-existent: see **D**, a favourite dictum of Lucretius, and compare the words of the fifth-century Eleatic Melissus (KRS 537), 'If it changes, the existent has perished and the non-existent come into being'. It must be admitted, however, that none of the recorded Epicurean arguments for the principle 'Nothing perishes into nothing' is valid against 'perishing' in this extended sense.

5 The basic division

A Epicurus, *Letter to Herodotus* 39–40.

(1) Moreover, the totality of things is bodies and void. (2) That bodies exist is universally witnessed by sensation itself, in accordance with which it is necessary to judge by reason that which is non-evident, as I said above; (3) and if place, which we call 'void', 'room', and 'intangible substance', did not exist, bodies would not have anywhere to be or to move through in the way they are observed to move. (4) Beyond these [i.e. body and void] nothing can even be thought of, either by

bodies & void

imagination or by analogy with what is imagined, as completely substantial things and not as the things we call accidents and properties of these.

B Lucretius 1.419–44

(1) The totality of things, then, in so far as it exists *per se*, has a nature made up out of two things: there are bodies, and void in which these are located and through which they move in their various directions. (2) That body exists is declared by universal sensation itself, in which our confidence must be securely based at the outset; otherwise we shall not have a standard against which we can confirm by the mind's reasoning anything concerning the non-evident. (3) Then again, if place and room, which we call 'void', did not exist, bodies would not have anywhere to be located, nor anywhere at all to move to in their various directions, as I proved to you a little earlier. (4) Beyond these there is nothing which you can call distinct from all body and separate from void, to play the role of a third discovered substance. (5) For whatever will exist will have to be in itself something with extension, whether large or small, so long as it exists. (6) If it has tangibility, however light and faint, it will extend the measure of a body and be added to its sum. (7) Whereas if it is intangible, and hence unable to prevent anything from moving through it at any point, it will undoubtedly be the emptiness which we call void. (8) Moreover, whatever exists *per se* will either act upon something, or itself be acted upon by other things, or be such that things can exist and happen in it. (9) But nothing that lacks body can act or be acted upon, nor can anything except void and emptiness provide place.

only bodies can act and be acted upon

C Aetius 1.20.2 (Usener 271)

Epicurus says that the difference between void, place and room is one of name.

void = place = room

D Sextus Empiricus, *Against the professors* 10.2 (Usener 271)

Therefore one must grasp that, according to Epicurus, of 'intangible substance', as he calls it, one kind is named 'void', another 'place', and another 'room', the names varying according to the different ways of looking at it, since the same substance when empty of all body is called 'void', when occupied by a body is named 'place', and when bodies roam through it becomes 'room'. But generically it is called 'intangible substance' in Epicurus' school, since it lacks resistant touch.

☐ **A** follows on directly from **4A** in Epicurus' exposition: now that the totality of things has been proved invariable, its constituents can be identified as body and void. Lucretius' account corresponds to it closely in **B** 1–4, and in **B** 5–10 expands on it with argument for the exhaustiveness of the body–void dichotomy.

The first argument for this, **B** 5–7, takes as its premise that only that which is spatially extended exists (**B** 5). This must in the context be understood as 'three-dimensionally extended'. Epicurus seems in **B** 5–7 to be relying on an old argument of Zeno of Elea's (KRS 316) that something sizeless could not exist since when *it* was added to something else *nothing* would be added to that thing. From this premise Epicurus proceeds to a dilemma: either this extended thing is tangible or it is intangible. If it is tangible (**B** 6), it will, when added onto a quantity of body, increase it (this further exploits the argument of Zeno of Elea mentioned above). The implicit conclusion is that the thing in question must then itself be body, and this follows provided we assume a further premise, that if a quantity of body is increased by addition that which has been added to it is itself body. The argument continues: if, on the other hand, the extended thing in question is intangible (**B** 7), being unable to resist moving bodies it will allow them to pass through – precisely the function of void.

In this way body and void are turned into express contradictories by appeal to their contradictory definitional attributes, tangibility and intangibility respectively (cf. **7A** 3). The second argument **B** 8–9 (cf. **14A** 7) is perhaps less successful because it appeals to an alternative pair of defining attributes – the power to interact and the power to house things which interact – which are not in themselves contradictories. Although Epicurus is clearly committed to the mutual exclusiveness of body and void, it is widely held that he compromises his position by failing to distinguish void from place, i.e. unoccupied space from space occupied by body. The charge rests on what appears to be good evidence, for example **A** 3, **B** 1 and 3 and **10A** 5. Nor can he be defended simply by the observation of some scholars that, since atoms are in constant motion through space and it is only on the macroscopic level that things seem stationary, there is strictly speaking no occupied space (see **11**). The laws of atomic motion cannot be assumed at this early stage, since they themselves follow from the proof of the existence of void; and besides, the language of **A** 3 makes it plain that Epicurus *is* including occupied as well as empty space, and that the occupants he has in mind are phenomenal bodies, not atoms.

But if Epicurus conflates the notions of void and place, what mistake is involved? Partly, it may be thought, that occupied space can hardly be regarded as a second constituent of the universe on a par with the bodies which occupy it, whereas the void intervals between these bodies clearly can be; partly too that his task of proving the existence of void, which his opponents denied (see **6**), cannot be equated with that of proving the existence of occupied place, which was uncontroversial.

However, there is no simple oversight here, but a doctrine carefully evolved to cope with conceptual difficulties already raised by Aristotle (for Epicurus' use of Aristotle, *Physics* IV in evolving his void doctrine, cf. **11**) and still kept in play by sceptics in the Hellenistic age. In arguing against the existence of void in *Physics* IV, Aristotle observes that void is thought of by its proponents as a place which is sometimes empty and sometimes filled, so that 'void', 'plenum' and 'place' are all names for one and the same thing, though under different definitions (IV.6 = **e** in vol. 2). He later argues that since a cube entering void could not displace it, the void must remain and become coextensive with it; and he brings out some of the conceptual difficulties which this would raise (IV.8 = **f** in vol. 2).

Epicurus' problem, then, is to explain what happens to void when it is approached by body. He was familiar with Plato's law that anything which is approached by its own opposite must either withdraw or perish (Plato, *Phaedo* 102d ff.; the same principle is invoked by Lucretius 1.760–2), but neither alternative proved very palatable in the case of void. It cannot withdraw because it lacks the power, characteristic of body, to act or be acted upon (cf. **B 9, 14A 7**). Nor can it perish, since that would violate the principles of conservation (**4**). It must therefore remain; and the paradox raised by Aristotle has somehow to be disarmed. This is done, as **D** clearly demonstrates, by inventing the name 'intangible substance' (literally 'intangible nature') for space in the broadest sense, whether occupied or not, and explaining 'void', 'place' and 'room' as being merely the terms by which we actually refer to it in specific contexts: 'void' when it is unoccupied, 'place' when it is occupied, and 'room' when bodies move through it (this last definition is backed up by an etymological association of *chōra*, 'room', with *chōrein*, 'go', here translated 'roam'). All three are extended yet intangible, and thus qualify as 'intangible substance', the true contradictory of 'tangible' body. When bodies pass into it or out of it, it remains unaffected in all but name (cf. **C**). In **A 3** Epicurus seems to announce that he will use its various names indifferently, probably in order to emphasize that the difference between them is one of context, not of essence. True to his word, he does elsewhere fluctuate in his usage between 'void' (e.g. **10A**), 'place' (*On nature* 34.14.9) and 'intangible substance' (**18C 2**) without apparent distinction, although 'void' gets most emphasis.

We can now see that Epicurus is wise not to single out void in the strict sense of unoccupied space as the second permanent constituent of the world alongside body; for unoccupied space is not permanent, but can turn into occupied space at any time. By choosing instead space in the broadest sense – a notion which he is, arguably, the first ancient thinker to isolate – he ensures the permanence of his second element. By his range of alternative names for it he stresses that at least some of it is occupied and at least some unoccupied; and his proofs of its existence (**A 3, B 3**) confirm that this is so.

This leaves his account with a paradox of its own: although body and space are in some way mutually exclusive substances, some parts of space are occupied by body. Body and space are not, then, coordinate ingredients – the bricks and mortar of the universe, as it were. Epicurus is careful, for example, never to call space an element (cf. **18C 2**). It provides bodies with location, with the gaps between them, and with room to move, but it cannot itself be part of a compound object. The opening assertion of **A 1** means only that body and space are the only two orders of reality required to account for the universe. All other candidates – properties, time, facts etc. – can be written off as parasitic properties of body (see **7A**). Space alone cannot, because it exists even where body does not.

Many of the concepts and principles underlying this discussion recur in the Stoic treatments of body (**45**) and place (**49**).

6 Proof of the existence of void

A Lucretius 1.334–90

(1) So there exists intangible place, void and emptiness. Otherwise there would be no way in which things could move. For that which is the function of body, to hinder and block, would be there to affect everything at all times; so that nothing would be able to move forward, since nothing would start the process of giving way. But as it is, we see before our eyes many things moving in many different ways, through seas, lands and the lofty skies. If void did not exist, these things would not just be deprived of their restless motion: they would never have come into being at all, since matter would everywhere be jammed solid and at rest. (2) Besides, however solid things may be thought to be, you can see that their bodies are porous from the following facts. In rocks and caves the liquid moisture of water seeps through and everything weeps with an abundance of drops. Food spreads itself throughout animals' bodies. Trees grow and in season pour forth their fruits because their food spreads throughout them from the tips of their roots up, through their trunks and through all their branches. Voices permeate walls and fly across between closed houses. Brittle cold penetrates to the bones. There is no way in which you could see this happen without the existence of voids for the individual bodies to pass through. (3) Next, why do we see some things exceed others in weight without being larger than them? For if there is as much body in a ball of wool as there is in lead, they ought to weigh the same, since the function of body is to push everything down, while the nature of void on the contrary remains weightless. It naturally follows that what is equally large but seems lighter reveals that it contains more void, while by contrast what is heavier announces itself as containing more body and much less void. Naturally, then, the thing we call void, which we are seeking with keen reasoning, *is* mingled with things. (4) On this topic, I am compelled to forestall a fiction of some people, in case it leads you away from the truth. These people say that the waters give way to the pressure of scaly fish and open liquid paths because the fish leave places behind them into which the waters which give way can flow; and that this is also how other things can move in relation to each other and change place, even though everything is full. You can see that the theory in its entirety has been accepted on false reasoning. For which way, after all, will the scaly fish be able to move forward unless the waters have provided space for them? And which way, moreover, will

the waters be able to retreat, when the fish will be unable to move? Therefore either we must deny motion to all bodies, or we must say that void is mingled with things and provides each thing with the beginning of motion. (5) Finally, if two broad bodies, which have come together, quickly spring apart, it is of course necessary that air come to occupy all the void created between them. Now however fast the currents with which the air converges from all sides, it will still be impossible for the entire space to be filled at one and the same time. For it must occupy each successive place before the whole space is occupied.

☐ At least one of the following must be false: (a) Some things move; (b) nothing can move without void; (c) void does not exist. The fifth-century Eleatic philosophers, who originated this debate, rejected (a). The majority of Greek philosophers, from Empedocles on, rejected (b), defending instead the theory of *antiperistasis*, or 'reciprocal replacement', which Lucretius outlines and condemns in **A 4**. The atomists are almost the only ancient thinkers known to have retained both (a) and (b) and denied (c), as Lucretius explicitly does in **A 1**, and Epicurus in **5A 3** above. The existence of void is established before the atomic nature of body (see **8**) – necessarily since the body-void dualism is a premise in the proof of atomism (**8B 1–2**). If the order could have been reversed, **A 4**'s unsatisfactory disproof of *antiperistasis* might have looked less vulnerable, since that theory tended to rely on the assumption that matter was infinitely divisible and hence totally flexible. A world of atoms without void would indeed be rigid to the point of immobility.

The supplementary empirical proofs in **A 2–3**, based on the phenomena of permeation and relative weight, might also look more convincing if atomism were already assumed; since without that assumption permeation could be attributed to the total interfusion of substances, and relative weight to the interactive powers of the four elements (both Stoic views, see **47–9**).

Epicurus (**5A 3**) and Lucretius seem to regard the dependence of motion on void as conceptually indubitable. (A later Epicurean attempt, reflected in **18G 5**, to give it a direct empirical basis suffers from the weakness that the 'empty' spaces which permit motion at the phenomenal level are not 'void' in the technical sense at all.) **A 5** is misleadingly presented by Lucretius as an argument coordinate with **A 1–3**. In fact it is best read as a proof, not of the regular admixture of void in compound bodies, but of the *possibility* of the existence of void, in refutation of those from Melissus onward who had argued that void was a logically incoherent notion. As such, it is a brilliant success.

For further relevant texts, see **5B 3**; **18A 3–4**, **F 3**.

7 Secondary attributes

A Lucretius 1.445–82

(1) Hence no third *per se* substance beside void and bodies can be left in the sum of things, neither one that could fall under our senses at any time nor

one that anyone could grasp by the mind's reasoning. (2) For all things which are spoken of you will find to be either fixed attributes of these two or accidents of them. (3) A fixed attribute is that which can at no point be separated and removed without fatal destruction resulting – as weight is to stones, heat to fire, liquidity to water, tangibility to all bodies, and intangibility to void. (4) By contrast slavery, poverty, wealth, freedom, war, peace, and all the other things whose arrival and departure a thing's nature survives intact, these it is our practice to call, quite properly, accidents. (5) Time, likewise, does not exist *per se*: it is from things themselves that our perception arises of what has happened in the past, what is present, and further what is to follow it next. It should not be conceded that anyone perceives time *per se* in separation from things' motion and quiet rest. (6) Moreover, when people say that the rape of Helen and the defeat in war of the Trojan tribes *are* facts, we must be careful that they do not force us into an admission that these things exist *per se* on the ground that the generations of men of whom they were accidents have by now been taken away by the irrevocable passage of time. For all past facts can be called accidents, either of the world or of actual places. And besides, if there had been no matter for things, and no place and space, in which all events occur, never would that flame kindled deep in Paris' Phrygian heart and fanned with love through Helen's beauty have ignited the shining battles of savage war, nor would that wooden horse by giving birth to its Grecian offspring at dead of night have set fire to the citadel undetected by the Trojans. Thus you can see that it is fundamental to all historical facts not to exist *per se* like body, and not to be or to be spoken of in the way in which void exists, but rather in such a way that you can properly call them accidents of body and of the place in which all events occur.

B Epicurus, *Letter to Herodotus* 68–73

(1) Now as for the shapes, colours, sizes, weights, and other things predicated of a body as permanent attributes – belonging either to all bodies or to those which are visible, and knowable in themselves through sensation – we must not hold that they are *per se* substances: that is inconceivable. Nor, at all, that they are non-existent. Nor that they are some distinct incorporeal things accruing to the body. Nor that they are parts of it; but that the whole body cannot have its own permanent nature consisting *entirely* of the sum total of them, in an amalgamation like that when a larger aggregate is composed directly of particles, either primary ones or magnitudes smaller than such-and-such a whole, but that it is only in the way I am describing that it has its own permanent nature consisting of the sum total of them. (2) And these things have all their own individual ways of being focused on and distinguished, yet

with the whole complex accompanying them and at no point separated from them, but with the body receiving its predication according to the complex conception. (3) Now there often also accidentally befall bodies, and impermanently accompany them, things which will neither exist at the invisible level nor be incorporeal. Therefore by using the name in accordance with its general meaning we make it clear that 'accidents' have neither the nature of the whole which we grasp collectively through its complex [of attributes] and call 'body', nor that of the permanent concomitants without which body cannot be thought of. (4) They can get their individual names through certain ways of being focused on, in concomitance with the complex, but just whenever they are each seen to become attributes of it, accidents being impermanent concomitants. (5) And we should not banish this self-evident thing from the existent, just because it does not have the nature of the whole of which it becomes an attribute – 'body', as we also call it – nor that of the permanent concomitants. Nor should we think of them as *per se* entities: that is inconceivable too, for either these or the permanent attributes. But we should think of all the accidents of bodies as just what they seem to be, and not as permanent concomitants or as having the status of a *per se* nature either. They are viewed in just the way that sensation itself individualizes them. (6) Now another thing that it is important to appreciate forcefully is this. We should not inquire into time in the same way as other things, which we inquire into in an object by referring them to familiar preconceptions. But the self-evident thing in virtue of which we articulate the words 'long time' and 'short time', conferring a uniform cycle on it, must itself be grasped by analogy. And we should neither adopt alternative terminology for it as being better – we should use that which is current – nor predicate anything else of it as having the same essence as this peculiar thing – for this too is done by some – but we must merely work out empirically what we associate this peculiarity with and tend to measure it against. After all, it requires no additional proof but merely empirical reasoning, to see that with days, nights, and fractions thereof, and likewise with the presence and absence of feelings, and with motions and rests, we associate a certain peculiar accident, and that it is, conversely, as belonging to these things that we conceive that entity itself, in virtue of which we use the word 'time'.

C Sextus Empiricus, *Against the professors* 10.219–27

(1) Epicurus, as Demetrius of Laconia interprets him, says that time is an accident of accidents, one which accompanies days, nights, hours, the presence and absence of feelings, motions and rests. For all of these are accidents belonging to things as their attributes, and since time accompanies them all it would be reasonable to call it an accident of

accidents. (2) For – to start at a slightly earlier point so as to make the account intelligible – it is a universal principle that of things that exist some are *per se* while others are viewed as belonging to *per se* things. What exist *per se* are things like the substances, namely body and void, while what are viewed as belonging to *per se* things are what they call 'attributes'. (3) Of these attributes some are inseparable from the things of which they are attributes, others are of a kind to be separated from them. Inseparable from the things of which they are attributes are, for example, resistance from body and non-resistance from void. For body is inconceivable without resistance, and so is void without non-resistance: these are permanent attributes of each – resisting of the one, yielding of the other. (4) Not inseparable from the things of which they are attributes are, for example, motion and rest. For compound bodies are neither always in ceaseless motion nor always at rest, but sometimes have the attribute of motion, sometimes that of rest (although the atom in itself is in everlasting motion, since it must approach either void or body and if it should approach void it moves through it because of its non-resistance, while if it should approach body it ricochets and moves away from it because of its resistance). (5) Hence the things which time accompanies are accidents – I mean day, night, hour, presence and absence of feelings, motions and rests. For day and night are accidents of the surrounding air: day becomes its attribute because of its illumination from the sun, while night supervenes because of its deprivation of illumination from the sun. And the hour, being a part either of day or of night, is also an accident of the air just as day and night are. And co-extensive with every day, night and hour is time. That is why a day or a night is called long or short: we pass through the time which is an attribute of it. As for presence and absence of feelings, these are either pains or pleasures, and hence they are not substances, but accidents of those who feel pleasant or painful – and not timeless accidents. In addition, motion and likewise rest are also, as we have already established, accidents of bodies and not timeless: for the speed and slowness of motion, and likewise the greater and smaller amount of rest, we measure with time.

D Polystratus, *On irrational contempt* 23.26–26.23

(1) Or do you think, on the basis of the foregoing argument, that someone would not suffer the troubles which I mention but rather would make it convincing that fair, foul and all other matters of belief are falsely believed in, just because unlike gold and similar things they are not the same everywhere? (2) After all, it must stare everybody in the face that bigger and smaller are also not perceived the same everywhere and in relation to all magnitudes . . . So too with heavier and lighter. And the

same applies also to other powers, without exception. For neither are the same things healthy for everybody, nor nourishing or fatal, nor the opposites of these, but the very same things are healthy and nourishing for some yet have the opposite effect on others. (3) Therefore either they must say that these too are false – things whose effects are plain for everyone to see – or else they must refuse to brazen it out and to battle against what is evident, and not abolish fair and foul as falsely believed in either, just because unlike stone and gold they are not the same for everybody . . . (4) Relative predicates do not have the same status as things said not relatively but in accordance with something's own nature. Nor does the one kind truly exist but not the other. So to expect them to have the same attributes, or the one kind to exist but not the other, is naive. And there is no difference between starting from these and eliminating those and starting from those and eliminating these: it would be similarly naive to think that since the bigger and heavier and sweeter are bigger than one thing but smaller than another, and heavier, and likewise with the other attributes, and since nothing has the same one of these attributes *per se* as it has in relation to something else, in the same way stone, gold and the like ought also, if they truly existed, to be gold in relation to one person while having the opposite nature in relation to another; and to say that, since that is not the case, *these* things are falsely believed in and do not really exist.

☐ **A** follows immediately on **5B**, and has the object of dismissing any candidates for *per se* existence beyond body and space. Permanent attributes, accidents, time, and facts about the past are all therefore argued to be parasitic on body and space. In **B** the original context and emphasis are different: Epicurus is at pains to say in just what way the first three of these do exist; and the passage comes after, and presupposes, his accounts of the atomic structure of body and the difference between primary and secondary qualities (**12** below). **C** is in effect a commentary on **B**, by the first-century B.C. Epicurean Demetrius of Laconia.

(There has been much confusion over the term 'attributes', *sumbebēkota*. These are usually taken, on Lucretius' evidence, to be only permanent attributes. But in **C** Demetrius, an expert in Epicurean textual exegesis, makes it quite clear that 'attributes' are the genus of which 'accidents' and 'permanent attributes', or 'permanent concomitants', are the species; and Epicurus' own usage in **B** seems fully consistent with this. Therefore, unless Lucretius has misunderstood his Greek source, his *coniuncta*, translated here as 'fixed attributes' in **A 2–3**, must be his rendering of what Epicurus calls 'permanent attributes'.)

At a basic level of analysis, the permanent attributes of a body are tangibility, shape, size and weight, these being essential to it *qua* body (compare the Stoic analysis, **45**). At the macroscopic level, they can include secondary qualities like its temperature or colour, in so far as these are essential to it under some phenomenal aspect (**A 3, B 1**). Heat is essential to fire, for example, and colour to visible body – although neither of these is an attribute of the underlying atoms themselves (see **12**). A body is, in a way, just a 'complex' of permanent attributes.

This means not that they are its material constituents (**B 1**), but that the characterization of what it is is determined by the sum of its permanent attributes – in other words, they are its *conceptual* parts (**B 2**, cf. **B 3**). A body is a complex of tangibility, weight, size and shape; a man is a complex of (presumably, cf. **19F**) animal, rational, mortal, etc.

Accidents, non-essential attributes (**A 4**), exist only at the phenomenal level, not at the atomic level (**B 3**), and are intrinsically observer-dependent (**B 4–5**). Democritus had for these reasons denied their reality (KRS 549), and part of Epicurus' purpose in **B 5** is no doubt to resist that conclusion: see also **12** and **16**. An argument for this is supplied by the third-century B.C. Epicurean Polystratus (**D**), who subsumes observer-dependent attributes under the broader heading 'relative' (**D 2–3**), then shows excellent reasons why the relative, albeit different in status from the *per se*, is not in consequence any less real (**D 3–4**). Indeed, such a degree of reality does Epicurus assign to one class of accidents, mental states, that he even seems to grant them their own independent causal efficacy: see **20**. All the more reason to stress, as he does in **B 5**, that they are not separable *per se* entities.

[margin note: relative & accidents not entities*]*

Time is a special case (**A 5**, **B 6**, **C 1** and **5**), being discernible not in bodies themselves but in certain of bodies' accidents, typically motion and rest. Paradoxically, it is something self-evident, yet can only be understood by 'analogical reasoning' – first drawing directly on experience to collect an appropriate set of accidents, then abstracting time as the common measure of them all (**B 6**). Since it depends for its existence on the bodies whose motion etc. it measures, it certainly cannot exist *per se*. Demetrius' attempt (**C 1** and **5**) to extract from **B 5** the precise metaphysical status of time clearly relies on Epicurus' description of time as 'a certain peculiar accident' associated with days, motions, etc. (viz. their respective durations), plus the status of days, motions etc. as themselves accidents of body.

[margin note: Demetrius stole Epicurus' shit (accidents motion + time)*]*

In **A 6** Lucretius is apparently replying to the following challenge, whose source is unknown. Everything that exists is, according to the Epicureans, either a *per se* entity or an attribute of a *per se* entity. Now facts about the past certainly exist: it *is*, after all, a fact that the Greeks conquered the Trojans. But they can hardly exist as attributes of *per se* entities, since the *per se* entities in question – Agamemnon, Helen etc. – themselves no longer exist. It follows that facts about the past must themselves exist as *per se* entities. This conclusion need not be read as somebody's own philosophical doctrine. Rather, it is an anti-Epicurean consequence drawn from Epicurean premises for dialectical purposes, and to which the Epicureans owe a reply. That reply is that there *is* still something in existence *per se* for such facts to be attributes of, namely the places in which they occurred, and, more specifically, the body and space that once constituted Paris, Helen, Troy etc.

[margin note: something for pasts to be attr. of*]*

8 Atoms

A Epicurus, *Letter to Herodotus* 40–1

(1) Moreover, of bodies some are compounds, others the constituents of those compounds. (2) The latter must be atomic [literally 'uncuttable']

and unalterable – if all things are not going to be destroyed into the non-existent but be strong enough to survive the dissolution of the compounds – full in nature, and incapable of dissolution at any point or in any way. The primary entities, then, must be atomic kinds of bodies.

B Lucretius 1.503–98 (with omissions)

(1) First, since we have found a vast difference between the twin natures of the two things – body, and the place in which everything happens – each must in itself be absolute and unmixed. For wherever there is the empty space which we call void, there no body exists, while wherever body is in occupation, there the emptiness of void is totally absent. Therefore the first bodies are solid and without void . . . (2) These can neither be dissolved when struck by external blows, nor be dismantled through internal penetration, nor succumb to any other kind of attack, as I proved to you a little earlier. For we see that without void nothing can either be crushed, broken or cut in two, or admit moisture, permeating cold or penetrating fire. These cause the destruction of all things, and the more void each thing contains the more it succumbs to internal attack from them. So if the first bodies are solid and without void, as I have taught, they must necessarily be everlasting. (3) Besides, if matter had not been everlasting, everything would before now have been totally annihilated, and all the things which we see would have been regenerated from nothing. But since I have taught earlier [**4B–C**] that nothing can be created from nothing and that what has been generated cannot be reduced to nothing, there must be principles with imperishable body, into which everything can be dissolved when its final hour comes, so as to ensure a supply of matter for the renewal of things. The principles, then, are solid and uncompounded, and in no other way could they have survived the ages from infinite time past to keep things renewed . . . (4) Furthermore, since things have a limit placed on their growth and lifespan according to their species, and since what each can and cannot do is decreed through the laws of nature, and nothing changes but everything is so constant that all the varieties of bird display from generation to generation on their bodies the markings of their own species, they naturally must also have a body of unalterable matter. For if the principles of things could in any way succumb and be altered, it would now also be uncertain what can and what cannot arise, and how each thing has its power limited and its deep-set boundary stone, nor could such a long succession of generations in each species replicate the nature, habits, lifestyle and movements of their parents.

☐ The existence of atoms, i.e. of physically indivisible particles of matter, follows from (**B** 1) the mutual exclusiveness of body and void, plus (**B** 2) the dependence of a body's divisibility on void gaps within it. Note that **B** 1 is misleadingly worded by Lucretius. At first he makes it appear that body and *place* are mutually exclusive, which they are not in the required sense, since all body is coextensive with place (**5** above). But as he goes on he corrects the picture, relying on the proper premise that body and *empty* space, or void, cannot be coextensive.

How do **B** 1 and **B** 2 jointly yield atomism? The point is that whatever the degree of admixture of body and void it can never amount to total interpenetration. Hence a process of division must eventually arrive at portions of body containing no void. (If an opponent were to ask if this division process might not instead continue for ever without result, Epicurus might have to fall back on his theory of minima – see **9** below.)

The existence of atoms is required (**A** 2, **B** 3–4) (a) so that body should not be fragmented to infinity and so annihilated beyond recall, in contravention of the second principle of conservation (**4**), and (b) so that there can be something enduring at the microscopic level to correspond to and explain the marked regularities of nature at the macroscopic level. For (b), cf. Newton, *Opticks*, 260: 'While the particles continue entire, they may compose bodies of one and the same nature and texture in all ages; but should they wear away or break in pieces, the nature of things depending on them would be changed.'

9 Minimal parts

A Epicurus, *Letter to Herodotus* 56–9

(1) Furthermore, we must not consider that the finite body contains an infinite number of bits, nor bits with no [lower] limit to size. (2) Therefore not only must we deny *cutting* into smaller and smaller parts to infinity, so that we do not make everything weak and be compelled by our conceptions of complex entities to grind away existing things and waste them away into non-existence, (3) but also we must not consider that in finite bodies there is *traversal* to infinity, not even through smaller and smaller parts. (4) For, first, it is impossible to conceive how [there could be traversal], once someone says that something contains an infinite number of bits or bits with no [lower] limit to size. (5) Second, how could this magnitude still be finite? For obviously these infinitely many bits are themselves of some size, and however small they may be the magnitude consisting of them would also be infinite. (6) And third, since the finite body has an extremity which is distinguishable, even if not imaginable as existing *per se*, one must inevitably think of what is in sequence to it as being of the same kind, and by thus proceeding forward in sequence it must be possible, to that extent, to reach infinity in thought.

(7) As for the minimum in sensation, we must grasp that it is neither of the same kind as that which admits of traversal, nor entirely unlike it; but that while having a certain resemblance to traversable things it has no

distinction of parts. Whenever because of the closeness of the resemblance we think we are going to make a distinction in it – one part on this side, the other on that – it must be the same magnitude that confronts us. (8) We view these minima in sequence, starting from the first, neither all in the same place nor touching parts with parts, but merely in their own peculiar way providing the measure of magnitudes – more for a larger magnitude, fewer for a smaller one.

(9) This analogy, we must consider, is followed also by the minimum in the atom: in its smallness, obviously, it differs from the one viewed through sensation, but it follows the same analogy. For even the claim that the atom has size is one which we made in accordance with the analogy of things before our eyes, merely projecting something small onto a large scale. (10) We must also think of the minimum uncompounded limits as providing out of themselves in the first instance the measure of lengths for both greater and smaller magnitudes, using our reason to view that which is invisible. (11) For the resemblance which they bear to changeable things is sufficient to establish this much; (12) but a process of composition out of minima with their own movement is an impossibility.

B Lucretius 1.746–52

(1) [Proponents of the four-element theory are mistaken] secondly in that they place absolutely no limit on the cutting up of bodies and no end to their fragmentation, (2) and no minimum in things, even though we see that final extremity of each thing which to our senses seems to be a minimum – from which you can guess that the extremity which invisible things possess is the smallest thing in them.

C Lucretius 1.599–634

(1) Then again, seeing that there is always a final extremity of that body which is below the threshold of our senses, it is presumably partless and of a minimal nature, and never was or could be separated by itself, since its very existence is as a part of something else: it is one part, the first, and is followed by similar parts in sequence, one after another, filling out the nature of the body in dense formation. Since these cannot exist by themselves, they must stick together inextricably. (2) Therefore the primary particles are solid and uncompounded, being tightly packed conglomerations of minimal parts, not composed by assembling these but rather gaining their strength through being everlastingly uncompounded. Nature is still preventing anything from being prised away or subtracted from them, but preserves them as seeds for things. (3) Besides, unless there is going to be a minimum, the smallest bodies will consist of infinitely many parts, since half of a half will always have a half

and there will be nothing to halt the division. In that case, what is the difference between the universe and the smallest thing? None. For however utterly infinite the whole universe is, the smallest things will nevertheless consist equally of infinitely many parts. Since true reasoning protests against this and denies that the mind can believe it, you must give in and concede the existence of those things which possess no parts and are of a minimal nature. Since these exist, you must admit that those things too [the atoms] are solid and everlasting. (4) Finally, if nature the creator of things were in the habit of forcing everything to be resolved into its minimal parts, she would by now be unable to renew anything out of them, because things which are not swollen by any parts cannot possess the properties required in generative matter – the variety of connexions, weights, blows, conjunctions and motions which are responsible for everything that happens.

☐ **A** is the principal text on Epicurus' doctrine of minimal units of magnitude, with a brief echo in **B**. **C** belongs to Lucretius' arguments for the existence of atoms (immediately following **8B**): his use of the theory of minima for this end is methodologically questionable, but the passage still provides valuable evidence about the theory itself.

The atomism of the fifth century B.C. originated at least partly as an answer to certain of Zeno of Elea's paradoxes, which drew absurd consequences from the supposition that a finite magnitude contains an infinite number of parts: the whole magnitude, being the sum of an infinity of parts, must be infinitely large; and motion over any finite distance is impossible because it requires traversing separately each of its infinity of component distances (KRS 316, 318). Although Leucippus and Democritus almost certainly intended their atomism as a rejection of Zeno's infinite divisibility premise, it is doubtful whether their atoms were indivisible in anything more than a physical sense. Since the atoms varied in shape and size, they can hardly have been considered 'theoretically' indivisible, or partless. They were simply too solid to *break* into their parts. This way of answering Zeno can still find sympathy today among those who feel that the Zenonian division process becomes futile once magnitudes smaller than one electron are reached; but it invites the retort that such particles, even if physically indivisible, still *contain* an infinity of smaller magnitudes, and hence are theoretically or conceptually divisible into them. Even Aristotle, for all his astute criticisms of the atomists, is little clearer on this distinction, and it is probably Epicurus' arguments in **A 1–6** that provide the first clear recognition of it (echoed in **B**).

Atoms, literally 'uncuttables', are physically indivisible, and 'cutting' to infinity is to be denied for reasons connected with the conservation of matter: so Epicurus says at **A 2**, directly recapitulating his earlier argument of **8A**. But now he adds a new principle. A finite magnitude does not even *contain* infinitely many parts (**A 1**). The kind of divisibility now being denied is not 'cutting' to infinity, as in **A 2**, but 'traversal' to infinity (**A 3**): in a finite magnitude one could not even traverse an infinite series of smaller constituent magnitudes. This is subsequently taken to mean that there is an absolute minimal unit of magnitude, 'the minimum in the atom' (**A 9**). All larger magnitudes, including atoms themselves, consist of a finite number of these minima.

The Zenonian nature of the arguments for their existence is plain. If a magnitude contained an infinite number of parts, first, traversal would become impossible (**A 4**), and second, the magnitude would be infinitely large (**A 5**). These appear to be the two Zenonian arguments mentioned above. Third, by thinking your way along the magnitude you would, impossibly, 'reach infinity in thought' (**A 6**) – complete an infinite series of mental operations, count to infinity. This is a reading of Zeno's dichotomy argument against motion which, whether or not historically accurate, was current in Epicurus' day (see the pseudo-Aristotelian treatise *On indivisible lines* 968a18 ff.). A fourth argument in the same vein is preserved at **C 3**: on the assumption of infinite divisibility, size could not be a function of the number of parts (a consequence readily accepted by the Stoics, see **50C 2–3**).

A 7–8 exploits an analogy between the real minimum and the smallest sensible magnitude. Lucretius (**B 2**) uses this analogy as an independent proof of the *existence* of real minima, but this does not appear to be Epicurus' own intention in **A**. The wording at the opening of **A 9** suggests rather that the existence of minima has already been proved at **A 1–6**, and in **A 9–11** the job of the analogy is clearly to explain their nature and how they function mathematically within larger magnitudes. This reading makes the best sense of Epicurus' methodological comparison in **A 9** of the use of analogy in establishing that atoms have size: the existence of atoms (see **8**) is not proved by analogy, but, once it has been proved, analogy with the sensible is used to work out their properties (**12**).

The analogy, which can in all essentials be found recurring in Hume (*Treatise of human nature*, II), is between the actual minimum ('the minimum in the atom') and 'the minimum in sensation'. The latter will be a vanishingly small dot, one so placed that at any greater distance it would be altogether invisible. As such, it is seen as extended yet partless (**A 7**): to be seen at all it must occupy *some* area of your field of vision, yet no *part* of it can be discriminated because any part smaller than the whole would be below the threshold of perception.

In **A 8** the ingenuity of the parallelism becomes apparent. Aristotle had argued in *Physics* VI.1 (= **d** in vol. 2; followed by the Stoics, **50C 6**) that a magnitude could never be composed of partless constituents, because these could never be in contact with each other. Contact, he explains, must be of whole to whole, part to whole, or part to part; but the first would make the partless entities completely coextensive, while the second and third are ruled out precisely because of their partlessness. The analogy of the sensible minimum gives Epicurus his answer to Aristotle. For sensible minima are seen *neither* as fully coextensive ('in the same place') *nor* as touching part to part – the possibility of part-to-whole contact is not considered, in view of the equal size of the minima – yet they do somehow combine to make larger magnitudes. That is, any other perceived magnitude can be analysed into an exact number of perceptible minima, such that when you run your eye along it you see these one by one in sequence. The Greek word for 'providing the measure of . . .' in **A 8** and **10** implies that a minimum is an exact submultiple of any larger magnitude, as indeed it must be: when the magnitude is divided into minima there could not be a fraction of a minimum left over. All this applies not just to apparent minima at the macroscopic level but also, *mutatis mutandis*, to actual minima at the microscopic level (**A 9–11**).

The analogy yields the result that Aristotle's list of the ways in which magnitudes can combine is not exhaustive. Sensible minima provide us with a further way, 'their own peculiar way' (**A 8**), and since we can actually perceive this way of combining we can imagine it, Epicurus would say, and hence also transfer it in thought to the minimum in the atom. Epicurus is ostensibly entitled to this conclusion, whether or not he goes on to analyse what the 'peculiar way' amounts to. But if the text does contain such an analysis, it may be located in the expression 'in sequence' (**A 8**; cf. **A 6**, **C 1**). For Aristotle, two items 'touch' if their boundaries coincide, but can be 'in sequence' provided only that there is nothing of the same kind between them. Now if Epicurus is here choosing to answer Aristotle in his own terms, he may be *conceding* that minima never 'touch' – far from having boundaries which might coincide, they are treated by him as themselves being boundaries, as we shall see – but still insisting that they can be 'in sequence'. That is, two minima can be so placed that there is no third minimum between them. (Aristotle, *Physics* VI.1, = **d** in vol. 2, had denied this, but his argument only works for unextended partless items like points and moments.) Since of course there could not be a gap between them of *less* than one minimum, they will be perfectly adjacent, without 'touching' in Aristotle's technical sense.

In **A 11** all the characteristics of the sensible minimum so far described are said to be transferable *mutatis mutandis* to actual minima. The latter are to be imagined as vanishingly small dots of magnitude into which larger magnitudes like atoms can be conceptually analysed. It may be guessed that these dots have no shape of their own, just as sensible minima could have no sensible shape; for it would be hard for them to have a shape without thereby having discriminable parts. But note too that in order to be component parts of atoms they must be assumed to exist in three dimensions, a feature less obviously attributable to the perceptible minimum.

The final claim at **A 12**, which is exploited by Lucretius in **C**, is the one respect in which the analogy is said not to hold. Real minima cannot exist as separate entities, move around, and enter into combinations with each other. Sensible minima presumably can – e.g. falling specks of dust viewed at a suitable distance. Real minima, on the other hand, are to be thought of as the 'limits' of larger magnitudes (**A 10**, cf. **A 6**), and this implies their inseparability from those magnitudes (**C 1**). But why introduce this restriction, rather than allow that at least some atoms consist of just one minimal part?

In looking for Epicurus' motivation it is worth noticing **A 12**'s emphasis on the impossibility of minima with their own motion. Aristotle (*Physics* VI.10 = **e** in vol. 2) had argued that something partless could not be in motion, except incidentally to the motion of a larger body. It could never in itself be traversing any boundary between places, since to do so would require its having one part of itself on one side of the boundary and one on the other, and that is ruled out by its partlessness. It may only possess motion derivatively, by courtesy of a larger body's motion. Thus strictly speaking it is never true that 'the central point on this train is now moving from England into Scotland', since the point, being partless, must be either wholly in England or wholly in Scotland; it is only by courtesy of the fact that the entire train is now moving from England into Scotland that the same can be said of any point on it. The same will apply to partless *magnitudes*, if, as Epicurus holds, there are such things. Minima could never move by themselves, but only by courtesy of the motion of the atoms to which they belong. (See further, **11**.)

The introduction of atomic quanta of magnitude is not unique to Epicurus. The Platonist Xenocrates and Diodorus Cronus had both already developed comparable theories, and Diodorus' exploration of the consequences for motion may have influenced Epicurus' later work (see **11**). One further consequence should be the falsity of conventional geometry. If, for example, the perfect geometrical square could exist, its side and diagonal would be incommensurable – incompatibly with the theory of minima, in which, as we have seen, all magnitudes share a common submultiple. There is good historical evidence that Epicurus accepted this consequence (Cicero, *Academica* 2.106 and *On ends* 1.20, = **f** and **g** in vol. 2), but none that he worked out in detail an alternative geometry.

10 Infinity

A Epicurus, *Letter to Herodotus* 41–2

(1) Moreover, the totality of things is infinite. (2) For that which is finite has an extremity, and that which is an extremity is viewed as next to some further thing. Therefore having no extremity it has no limit. And not having a limit it would be infinite [literally 'unlimited'] and not finite. (3) Indeed, the totality of things is infinite both in the number of the bodies and in the magnitude of the void. (4) For if the void were infinite but the bodies finite, the bodies would not remain anywhere but would be travelling scattered all over the infinite void, for lack of the bodies which support and marshal them by buffering. (5) And if the void were finite, the infinite bodies would not have anywhere to be.

B Lucretius 1.958–97

(1) The totality of things is not limited in any direction. (2) For if it were, it would have to have an extremity. Now it is a visible fact that nothing can have an extremity unless there is something beyond it to limit it – so that the same can be seen to be true beyond the reach of this kind of sense-perception. But since, as it is, it must be admitted that there is nothing outside the totality of things, it has no extremity and hence no limit or boundary. Nor does it make any difference what part of it you stand in: so true is it that wherever someone goes to take up position, he is leaving

the universe just as infinite in all directions. (3) Besides, supposing for the moment that the totality of room is finite, if someone at the very edge ran up to its outermost frontier and hurled a flying javelin, do you prefer that after being hurled with great force the javelin should go in the direction in which it was aimed and fly far, or do you think that something can obstruct and block it? You must concede and choose one of the two answers, and either one cuts off your escape and forces you to admit that the universe stretches without end. For whether there is something to obstruct it, to prevent it travelling in the direction of aim, and to station itself as a limit, or whether it is carried outside, what it started from was not the limit. I shall pursue you in this way, and wherever you place the outermost frontier I shall ask what is the outcome for the javelin. It will turn out that a limit cannot exist anywhere, and that the availability of flight will delay escape for ever. (4) Besides, if the totality of room in the whole universe were enclosed by a fixed frontier on all sides, and were finite, by now the whole stock of matter would through its solid weight have accumulated from everywhere all the way to the bottom, and nothing could happen beneath the sky's canopy, nor indeed could the sky or sunlight exist at all, since all matter would be lying in a heap, having been sinking since infinite time past. But as it is, the primary bodies are clearly never allowed to come to rest, because there is no absolute bottom at which they might be able to accumulate and take up residence. At all times all things are going on in constant motion everywhere, and underneath there is a supply of particles of matter which have been travelling from infinity.

C Epicurus, *Letter to Herodotus* 60

(1) Moreover in speaking of the infinite we must not use 'up' or 'down' with the implication that they are top or bottom, but with the implication that from wherever we stand it is possible to protract the line above our heads to infinity without the danger of this ever seeming so to us, or likewise the line below us (in what is conceived to stretch to infinity simultaneously both upwards and downwards in relation to the same point). For this [i.e. that there should be a top and bottom] is unthinkable. (2) Therefore it is possible to take as one motion that which is conceived as upwards to infinity, and as one motion that which is conceived as downwards to infinity, even if that which moves from where we are towards the places above our heads arrives ten thousand times at the feet of those above, or at the heads of those below, in the case of that which moves downwards from where we are. (3) For each of the two mutually opposed motions is none the less, as a whole, conceived as being to infinity.

☐ In **A** and **B** the Epicureans defend the infinity of the universe, which the atomists and others had proclaimed in the fifth century, but which had been abandoned by Plato and Aristotle in the fourth. For the Stoic view, see **49**. For Epicurus' conception of space, see **5**. For the infinite number of worlds, see **13A, D**. For the infinity of time, in retort to Plato's apparent claim in the *Timaeus* that time only began with the orderly motion of the heavens, see **13G 4**.

C (a controversial text, which has been construed and translated in other ways than the above) is probably an attempt to justify Epicurus' view that even in an infinite universe there is a single direction 'down' in which all bodies tend by virtue of their own weight (see **11**). Up and down need not be determined by relation to an absolute top or bottom, which in an infinite universe are both equally unthinkable (cf. **A–B**, especially **B 4**). Rather they are to be thought of by relation to our own viewpoint in any single chosen place ('in relation to the same point', **C 1**), 'up' being the rectilinear trajectory travelling from our feet to our head and beyond, and 'down' that travelling from our head to our feet and beyond. Their infinite extension is not jeopardized by the arbitrariness of their starting-point. Our 'upward' line, for example, may pass through numerous alternative starting-points, namely the viewpoints of inhabitants of other worlds vertically above ours; but none of these constitutes its terminus, and it must still be conceived as infinite (**C 2–3**).

11 Atomic motion

A Epicurus, *Letter to Herodotus* 43–4

(1) The atoms move continuously for ever, some separating a great distance from each other, others keeping up their vibration on the spot whenever they happen to get trapped by their interlinking or imprisoned by atoms which link up. (2) For the nature of the void brings this about by separating each atom off by itself, since it is unable to lend them any support; (3) and their own solidity causes them as a result of their knocking together to vibrate back, to whatever distance their interlinking allows them to recoil from the knock. (4) There is no beginning to this, because atoms and void are eternal.

B Lucretius 2.80–124

(1) If you think that the primary particles can stand still, and can thus initiate motions of things from scratch, you are wandering far from true reasoning. (2) For since they wander through void, they must necessarily all be borne along either by their own weight or, if it should so happen, by the impact of another. (3) For as a result of their frequent high-speed collisions they recoil suddenly in opposite directions – not surprisingly, given that they are entirely hard with their solid weights and unobstructed by anything from behind. (4) And to see more clearly that all particles of matter are being tossed about, remember that in the

totality of the universe there is no bottom and that the primary bodies have nowhere to stand still, since room has no limit or boundary and I have shown at length and proved with conclusive argument that it stretches measureless in all directions. Since that is established, naturally the primary bodies are granted no rest throughout the depths of void. (5) But rather they are driven in continuous and varied motion, and some after being squeezed together rebound over great intervals, while others are tossed about over short spaces from the impact. (6) And whichever ones are in a denser aggregation and rebound over small intervals from that impact, held back by the interweaving of their own shapes, these form the strong roots of stone, the brute bulk of iron, and the like. Those others which go on wandering through the great void, few and far between, and recoil and rebound a long way over great intervals, these supply the thin air for us and the sun's brilliant light. In addition many wander through the great void, which have been rejected by compounds and have also failed to gain admittance anywhere and harmonize their motions. (7) Of this fact, as I have recounted it, there is a pictorial representation regularly present and taking place before our eyes. Take a look where the sun's rays weave their way in and pour their light through a darkened room. You will see many tiny bodies intermingling in many ways throughout the empty space right there in the light of the rays, and as if in everlasting combat battling and fighting ceaselessly in their squadrons, driven by frequent meetings and separations. So you can conjecture from this what it is like for the primary particles of things to be for ever tossed around in the great void. To some extent something small can give a model of great matters, and the traces of their preconception.

C Lucretius 2.142–64

(1) Here now, Memmius, is a brief account from which you may know the speed which the particles of matter possess. (2) First, when dawn spreads new light over the earth, and the various birds flying about the pathless woods through the soft air fill the place with their flowing voices, we see it plainly revealed to all how suddenly the risen sun at such a time regularly swamps all things and clothes them with its own light. And yet the heat and calm light which the sun emits does not travel through empty void, and so is compelled to go more slowly as it beats its way through the waves, so to speak, of the air; nor do the particles of heat travel individually, but in interlinked aggregations. Hence they are simultaneously retarded by each other and obstructed from outside, and are thus compelled to go more slowly. (3) But when the solid and uncompounded primary particles travel through empty void, and are both unimpeded from outside and, being such a unity of its own parts, borne hurtling onward in their one initial direction of movement, they

must naturally be of supreme swiftness, and travel much faster than the sun's light, and traverse many times the extent of space in the same time as the sunlight takes to cross the sky.

D Epicurus, *Letter to Herodotus* 46–7

(1) Moreover, the lack of obstruction from colliding bodies makes motion through the void achieve any imaginable distance in an unimaginable time. (2) For it is collision and non-collision that take on the resemblance of slow and fast. (3) Nor, on the other hand, does the moving body itself reach a plurality of places *simultaneously* in the periods of time seen by reason. That is unthinkable. (4) And when in perceptible time this body arrives in company with others from some point or other in the infinite, the distance which it covers will not be one from any place from which we may imagine its travel. (5) For that will resemble [cases involving] collision – even if we do admit such a degree of speed of motion as a result of non-collision. (6) This too is a useful principle to grasp.

E Epicurus, *Letter to Herodotus* 61–2

(1) Moreover the atoms must be of equal velocity whenever they travel through the void and nothing collides with them. (2) For neither will the heavy ones move faster than the small light ones, provided nothing runs into them; nor will the small ones move faster than the large ones, through having all their trajectories commensurate with them, at any rate when the large ones are suffering no collision either. (3) Nor will either their upwards motion or sideways motion caused by knocks [be quicker], or those downwards because of their individual weights. For however far along either kind of trajectory it gets, for that distance it will move as fast as thought, until it is in collision, either through some external cause or through its own weight in relation to the force of the impacting body. (4) Now it will also be said in the case of compounds that one atom is faster than another, where they are in fact of equal velocity, because the atoms in the complexes move in a single direction even in the shortest continuous time, although it is not single in the periods of time seen by reason; but they frequently collide, until the continuity of their motion presents itself to the senses.

F Simplicius, *On Aristotle's Physics* 938,17–22 (Usener 277)

For unless every magnitude were divisible, it would not be possible for the slower always to move less distance than the faster in equal time; for that which is atomic, and that which is partless, are traversed by the faster in the same time as they are by the slower. For if the slower takes a longer time, in the equal time it is going to traverse a distance smaller than the partless. That is why Epicurus' school holds that all things move at the same speed through the partless places, lest their atoms be divided and thus no longer atoms.

G Simplicius, *On Aristotle's Physics* 934,23–30 (Usener 278, part)

That this obstacle which he [Aristotle] has formulated is itself not entirely beyond belief is shown by the fact that despite his having formulated it and produced his solution, the Epicureans, who came along later, said that this is precisely how motion does occur. For they say that motion, magnitude and time have partless constituents, and that over the whole magnitude composed of partless constituents the moving object moves, but at each of the partless magnitudes contained in it it does not move but *has* moved; for if it were laid down that the object moving over the whole magnitude moves over these too, they would turn out to be divisible.

[margin note: time having partless constituents]

H Lucretius 2.216–50

(1) On this topic, another thing I want you to know is this. When bodies are being borne by their own weight straight down through the void, at quite uncertain times and places they veer a little from their course, just enough to be called a change of motion. (2) If they did not have this tendency to swerve, everything would be falling downward like raindrops through the depths of the void, and collisions and impacts among the primary bodies would not have arisen, with the result that nature would never have created anything. (3) But if anyone should suppose it possible that heavier bodies, by virtue of their faster travel in a straight line through the void, should land from above on lighter ones and in that way produce impacts capable of leading to creative motions, he is departing far from true reasoning. For whatever things fall through water and thin air must necessarily fall at a speed proportionate to their weight, since the body of water and the rarefied substance of air cannot impede everything equally, but succumb and yield faster to heavier things. But the emptiness of void, by contrast, can nowhere and at no time stand up to anything, but must constantly, as its nature demands, give way. Through the passive void, consequently, all things must travel at equal speed, regardless of differences in weight. Hence it will never be possible for the heavier ones to land from above on the lighter ones and by themselves produce impacts resulting in the variety of motions through which nature does her work. (4) Thus it follows once again that the bodies must veer off a little – no more than one minimum, lest we seem to be inventing oblique motions and be refuted by the facts. For we see it as plain and obvious that weights when hurtling downwards have no intrinsic power to travel obliquely. But who in the world can see that

they do not swerve from their straight trajectory *at all*? [continued at **20F**]

□ One of the two primary causes of an atom's motion is its own weight (**E 3, H**), which manifests itself as a natural tendency to move downwards except in so far as it is diverted by collisions. The existence of a single universal direction 'down' is taken by Epicurus as a datum of experience (cf. **10C**). He was aware of the rival Aristotelian theory, that falling objects are in fact tending towards the centre of a spherical earth, but had to reject it because he could not see how in an infinite and undifferentiated space one point could possess this special status of centrality (Lucretius 1.1050–1113: for the Stoic rehabilitation of the theory, see **49I**).

The other primary cause of an atom's motion is the impact of collision with other atoms (**A** 1, 3, **B, E** 3–4, **H** 2–3), which can propel it in any direction whatever. What collisions cannot do is halt an atom altogether: all atoms are in motion at all times (**A, B**; **7C** 4), because the void which surrounds them can offer no resistance, and collisions will result in nothing more than a change of direction. Hence even a stationary solid body consists of moving atoms, although their motion consists of rapid vibration within a closely interlocking formation (**A** 1, **B** 6).

The non-resistance of void has two further consequences. Aristotle in *Physics* IV.8 (215a24–216a21) had argued that the speed of moving objects is determined by the ratio of their weight to the density of the medium: hence the idea of void as a medium is absurd, he alleged, since where the medium has zero density objects will move at a speed which stands in no ratio whatever to any finite speed; moreover, all will move at equal speed. Epicurus' theory accepts the Aristotelian premise but tries to accommodate the resulting difficulties. First, atoms move through void (the only thing available for them to move through) at a speed which, though not of course infinite (**D** 3), is *unimaginable* in relation to any phenomenal motion through a resistant medium. That is, either the distance is imaginable but the time taken to traverse it unimaginably short (**D** 1); or the time is long enough to be observed but the distance traversed unimaginably large (**D** 4). This is because we can only imagine it in terms of familiar phenomenal motions, which are slowed down by collisions with the medium (**D** 5); the fastest such motion is that of sunlight, but atomic speed is vastly in excess of that (**C**) – 'as fast as thought' (**E** 3; cf. **15A** 4).

Second, atoms do indeed all move at equal speed, regardless of their weight (**C** 1–3, **H** 3). But it is not the absurdity which Aristotle thought it: **E** 4. Phenomenal bodies are not required to move at the same speed as their constituent atoms, because the atoms are in complex patterns of motion within them. During an imperceptibly brief period of time, the atoms will all be moving at uniform high speed in different directions; but over even the shortest observable passage of time (this seems the best way to understand 'the shortest continuous time', **E** 4: cf. **D** 3–4) their overall tendency will be in one direction only. That tendency yields the corporate motion of the compound body, whose speed can vary (**D** 2; cf. the variable overall motion of a swarm of insects each of which is flying a zigzag course at uniform velocity).

Some further features of Epicurus' theory of motion are absent from his *Letter to Herodotus*, which is probably a comparatively early work written around the time of his arrival in Athens. They may reflect subsequent developments in his thought, or in that of his colleagues, particularly under the influence of Diodorus Cronus, who was active in Athens and had a theory of minimal partless units of magnitude not unlike Epicurus' own (on which see **9**).

Aristotle (*Physics* VI. 10 = **9e** in vol. 2) had pointed out that something partless could never in itself be 'moving': if it is to get from *AB* to *BC* it must either still be at *AB* or already be in *BC*: not having parts, it can at no time be partly in *AB* and partly in *BC*. Either, then, it moves only incidentally to the movement of a larger body – as Aristotle would himself want to say that, for example, an extensionless point on a moving body moves – or we will have to say, impossibly, not that it 'is moving' but only that it 'has moved'. The latter alternative, Aristotle claims, would imply that time consists of partless 'nows' and motion of 'jerks': thus in each successive 'now' a partless entity could occupy a fresh position, but would never be in transition between the two positions. There is no sign in the *Letter to Herodotus* that Epicurus was prepared to accept the staccato motion theory for his partless minima (some have seen the imperceptibly short times at **D 3** and **E 4** as indivisible 'nows', but nothing in those passages requires such an interpretation), and he appears instead to have chosen the first Aristotelian alternative, that what is partless can only move incidentally to the motion of a larger body, the atom (see **9A 12** and commentary). But if **G** is to be believed, at some later stage the Epicureans did come to accept in addition the staccato motion theory. What were the reasons for this development? One was probably the influence of <u>Diodorus</u>, who had himself <u>adopted just that same theory</u> (see **i** in vol. 2) as part of his own doctrine of minimal units. In defence of it, Diodorus argued at length that logically it is quite respectable to assert 'it has moved' while denying that 'it is moving' was ever true: thus, he observed, 'Helen had three husbands' is true, while 'Helen has three husbands' was never true. This encouragement from a professional logician may have emboldened the Epicureans to question Aristotle's condemnation of the staccato thesis. In addition, Diodorus' formulation drew attention to the need (if only for the sake of consistency) to divide space as well as body into minimal units; and that realization would have shown Epicurus the inadequacy of the 'incidental motion' solution. Even an atom composed of many minima would, as a whole, have to move not less than one minimum of space at a time. Thus its motion could not fail to be staccato. Strange though this theory of motion may look, for anyone puzzled by Zeno's question how motion is possible through an infinitely divisible continuum (cf. **9A 3–4**) it might well seem the lesser of two evils.

Moreover, such an analysis had at least one independent attraction. From Aristotle's work in *Physics* VI.2 it had emerged that differences of speed depend on the infinite divisibility of time and magnitude; and it seemed to follow that a theory of indivisible magnitudes would have to dispense with real differences of speed. For example, in the time taken by a moving object to traverse one minimal unit of space, a slower moving object would, impossibly, have to

[margin annotation: infinitely divisible continuum "staccato"]

traverse less than one minimal unit. According to **F**, the Epicureans invoked precisely this reasoning in support of their thesis of equal speed in atomic motion. That the Diodorean analysis could be used to vindicate a thesis already proven on independent grounds (**E**) must have made it almost irresistible to the Epicureans.

Finally, **H** testifies to a further refinement of the atomic motion theory which is not yet present in the *Letter to Herodotus* but which is widely reported, and ridiculed, as Epicurus' own doctrine. Atoms travelling through space are primarily propelled by their own weight and by the effect of collisions, but in addition they are capable of an entirely undetermined 'swerve'. All sources are agreed that the swerve is by exactly one minimum (e.g. **H 4**; **18G 6**; **20E 2**; for the theory of minima, see **9**), and this should probably be interpreted as follows. An atom's basic tendency is to travel in a straight line until it is in collision. That line itself has a thickness of one minimum (nothing thinner being conceivable), and adjacent to it run a number of other parallel lines. At any time or place in its travel the atom may spontaneously shift to one of these adjacent trajectories. Its overall motion is likely to remain *virtually* rectilinear, so there should be no resultant chaos at the macroscopic level. Nevertheless the system is, in this minimal degree, indeterministic.

The enormous current interest of this theory arises from the fact that, however preposterous, it is to a large extent true. In quantum physics it is now widely agreed that there is a degree of indeterminacy in the behaviour of sub-atomic particles. The philosophical implications of this fact lie especially in its possible bearing on free will. In the present context the swerve theory is invoked to solve a problem of Epicurus' own making: given the equal speed and natural downward motion of atoms, how can collisions between them ever have started (**H 2–3**)? One might wonder whether this problem was sufficiently grave in itself to demand so drastic a solution – one which Epicurus' opponents rushed to deride as 'motion without a cause' (e.g. **20E 2**). When he wrote the *Letter to Herodotus*, at any rate, he was content with the more economical answer that, given the infinite past existence of atoms and void, there was *no* first collision (**A 4**). This raises the suspicion that it was his subsequent well attested concern about the autonomy of responsible agents that led him to the theory, and that it was then with hindsight grafted onto the existing cosmological system. On this ground, the main discussion of the swerve will be found in **20**, on 'free will'.

12 Microscopic and macroscopic properties

A Epicurus, *Letter to Herodotus* 55–6

(1) We must not adopt, either, the view that every size is to be found among the atoms, lest it be contested by things evident. (2) On the other hand, we must suppose that there are *some* variations of size, for this addition will yield better explanations of the events reported by our feelings and senses. (3) But the existence of *every* size is not useful with

respect to the differences of qualities. Indeed, we ourselves ought to have experienced visible atoms, and that is not seen to happen, nor is it possible to conceive how a visible atom might occur.

B Epicurus, *Letter to Herodotus* 42–3

(1) In addition, these bodies which are atomic and full, from which compounds are formed and into which they are dissolved, have unimaginably many differences of shape. For it is not possible for as many varieties as there are to arise from the same shapes if these are of an imaginable number. (2) For each species of shape, also, the number of atoms of the same kind is absolutely infinite; but in the number of their differences they are not absolutely infinite, just unimaginably many, if one is not going to expand them to absolute infinity in their sizes too.

 atoms have many shapes

C Lucretius 2.478–531

(1) Having explained this, I shall go on to attach to it a point which depends on it for its proof: that the primary elements of things have a finite range of different shapes. (2) Should this not be so, it will again necessarily follow that some seeds have infinite bodily extension. For within one and the same narrow compass of a given body there cannot be much variety of shapes. Say, for example, that atoms consist of three minimal parts or a few more. Well obviously, when you have taken all these parts of one body, positioned them top and bottom, swapped left with right, and in short tried every permutation to see what shape of the whole body each arrangement yields, should you want to vary the shapes further you will have to add more parts. And the next stage will be that, should you want to vary the shapes even further, the arrangement will require more parts in just the same way. Thus a consequence of adding new shapes is bodily increase. So there is no way in which you can suppose the seeds to have infinitely many differences of shape, lest you force some to be immensely huge, which I have already explained above to be unacceptable. (3) You would find, too, that exotic garments, glowing Meliboean purple dyed with the colour of Thessalian shells, and the golden generations of peacocks bathed in their smiling charm, would by now lie neglected, outshone by some new colour appearing in things. The fragrance of myrrh would lie in disrepute, as would the taste of honey. And the melodies of swans and the intricate string music of Apollo would likewise have been outshone and silenced. For one thing would constantly be arising to eclipse the others. And in the same way all things would be able to change in the reverse direction for the worse, just as I have said they could change for the better. For one thing would also in the reverse direction be more revolting than all the rest for nose, ears, eyes and the mouth's taste. Since this is not so, but the totality of things is

proof can variety of sizes

held in check at either end of the scale by the assignment of a fixed limit, you must admit that matter also has a finite number of different shapes. (4) Again, from fire right down to the icy frosts of winter is a finite passage, and in the reverse direction it is measured in the same way. For all heat, cold, and lukewarm temperatures, making up the whole range in succession, lie in between. Therefore they are generated with a finite range of differences, since they are marked off by two points, one at either end of the scale – hemmed in by fire at one end and stiff frost at the other. (5) Having explained this, I shall go on to attach to it a point which depends on it for its proof: that the primary elements of things, within each group of the same shape as each other, must be called infinitely many. For since there is a finite variety of shapes, it is necessary that those of a single shape be infinitely many. Otherwise the totality of matter must be finite, which I proved not to be the case when I showed in my poem that particles of matter from the infinite permanently maintain the totality of things with a continuous succession of impacts from all sides.

D Epicurus, *Letter to Herodotus* 54–5

(1) Moreover, the atoms themselves must be considered to exhibit no quality of things evident, beyond shape, weight, size, and the necessary concomitants of shape. (2) For all quality changes. But the atoms do not change at all, since something solid and indissoluble must survive the dissolution of the compounds to ensure that the changes are not into, or out of, the non-existent, but result from transpositions within many things, and in other cases from additions and subtractions of certain things. (3) Hence those things which do not admit of [internal] transposition must be indestructible, and must lack the nature of that which changes. And their own peculiar masses and shapes must survive, since this is actually necessary. (4) After all, also in familiar objects which have their shape altered by shaving, it can be ascertained that in the matter which undergoes change, as it is left, shape remains whereas the qualities do not remain but vanish from the entire body. (5) So these properties which are left are sufficient to bring about the differences of the compounds, given the necessity for *some* things to be left and not be destroyed into the non-existent.

E Lucretius 2.730–833 (with omissions)

(1) Come now, mark what I say, the fruit of my pleasant labours – that you should not suppose those white objects which you see before your eyes as white to consist of white primary particles, or those which are black to be the product of black seeds, or that objects dyed any other colour exhibit it because their particles of matter are imbued with the same colour. For particles of matter have absolutely no colour, whether

like or unlike that of the objects. (2) You are quite wrong if you think that
the mind cannot be focused on such particles. For given that those who
are blind from birth and have never seen the sun's light nevertheless from
their first day know bodies by touch without any association of colour,
you can be sure that our mind too can form a preconception of bodies
without any coating of colour. In fact, we ourselves sense as colourless
everything that we touch in blind darkness . . . (3) Besides, if the primary
particles are colourless, and possess a variety of shapes from which they
generate every kind of thing and thus make colours vary – since it makes
a great difference with what things and in what sort of position the
individual seeds are combined and what motions they impart to each
other and receive from each other – it at once becomes very easy to
explain why things which a little earlier were black in colour can
suddenly take on the whiteness of marble, as the sea, when its surface has
been churned up by great winds, is turned into waves whose whiteness is
like that of gleaming marble. All you need say is that what we regularly
see as black comes to appear gleaming white as soon as its matter is mixed
up, as soon as the ordering of its primary particles is changed, as soon as
some particles are added and some subtracted. But if the sea's surface
consisted of blue seeds, there is no way in which they could turn white.
For things that *are* blue could never change to the colour of marble, no
matter how you were to jumble them up . . . (4) Moreover, the tinier the
pieces into which any object is shredded, the more you can see the
gradual disappearance and blotting out of its colour. This happens, for
example, when purple cloth is pulled apart into little pieces: when it has
been dismantled thread by thread, the purple and the scarlet colour, by
far the brightest there is, is completely wiped out. So you can tell from
this that fragments breathe away all their colour before they are reduced
to the seeds of things.

F Lucretius 2.381–407

(1) It is very easy, with the mind's reasoning, for us to work out why the
fire of lightning flows with much more penetration than the fire which
we produce from torches here on earth. All you need say is that the
lightning's fire up in the sky is finer and consists of smaller shapes, and
hence passes through passages through which this fire which we produce
from logs and torches cannot pass. (2) Besides, light passes through horn,
while rain water is rejected by it. Why, unless the particles of light are
smaller than those which make up water's nourishing draught? (3) And
however instantaneously we see wine flow through a sieve, olive oil, by
contrast, is sluggish and takes its time. This is naturally either because it
consists of larger elements; or because they are more hooked together
and entangled, with the consequence that individual primary particles

55

good tastes =
round particles

bad taste =
hooked particles

cannot be so immediately separated and flow individually through each thing's passages. (4) A further point is that the liquids of honey and milk, when taken by mouth, are pleasant to the tongue's sensation, while, by contrast, foul wormwood and pungent centaury twist up the mouth with their repellent flavour. Thus you can easily recognize that those things which can have a pleasant effect on the senses consist of smooth round particles, while by contrast all those which seem bitter and harsh are joined and interwoven with more hooked particles, and for that reason tend to make violent inroads into our senses, and to wrench our body when they enter it.

☐ In determining the range of properties to be attributed to atoms, Epicurus' principal criterion is the need to explain the phenomenal properties of things. But two further methodological considerations are analogy with the perceptible, and the theory of minimal parts.

Atoms must possess the primary physical properties of shape, size and weight, together with such further properties as shape entails (**D** 1) – e.g. the possession of parts? That these are inseparable concomitants of all body (**7B** 1) is learnt through the analogy of perceptible bodies (**9A** 9).

we can only
"surface" of objects
rather than
colorless atoms

Democritus had put no upper limit on the possible size of atoms (KRS 561). Epicurus rejects this (**A**), but his argument is puzzling, since it assumes that if atoms were large enough they would be visible – contrary to his theory that vision is caused by effluences of atoms *from the surface of* the perceived object (**15A**) and to his insistence that atoms are colourless (**E**). At best, a large atom might render itself 'visible' only to the extent of blotting out whatever was behind it.

finite size =
finite shapes

A consequence of this revision is that, although the number of atoms is infinite (**10A** 3–4), the number of different atomic shapes is finite (**B, C**). From any given number of minimal parts (on which see **9**), only a finite number of atomic shapes can be constructed, because one minimum can only be adjacent to another by standing directly alongside it: being partless, it cannot be half-way or one-third of the way along it. The consequences can be appreciated by comparing the task of producing designs on a sheet of graph paper by filling in whole squares. Only a finite number of designs will be possible, and further diversification will eventually require the purchase of a larger sheet of graph paper. At **C** 2 we have an essentially similar argument, to the effect that, given an upper limit to the size of atoms, there can only be a finite range of shapes.

An infinite range would have the additional consequence of obliterating the limits which are seen to circumscribe all natural processes, since for any phenomenal predicate *F*, however *F* a thing became, there would always be the possibility of some further variety of atom turning up to produce something still *F*-er (**C** 3–4). Nevertheless, by the same criterion of explanatory force, the vast variety of phenomenal explananda requires that the range of atomic variety be, at least, 'unimaginably' large (**B**).

Although the primary properties of shape, size and weight must belong to atoms *qua* body, all secondary properties are absent from them. These, the phenomenal properties ('qualities', as Epicurus loosely terms them in **D**) of colour, flavour etc., are 'accidents' which exist only at the macroscopic level (**7B 3**). The distinction between primary and secondary properties is one which Epicurus inherited from Democritus, but a difference of motivation is evident. Democritus banned secondary properties from his atoms on the grounds that they were unreal – nothing more than arbitrary and subjective constructions placed by the sense-organs on what were really just amalgams of atoms and void (KRS 549). Epicurus, as part of his rearguard action against Democritean scepticism, defends their reality (**7B 1–5**), but keeps the atoms free of them on the grounds of the enormous explanatory power that this confers on the system: **E3**. Further arguments in favour of the colourlessness of atoms – such as that at **D 4** and **E 4**, and the appeal to non-contestation (see **18**) at **E 2** – may be thought of as ancillary to this consideration. **F** exemplifies other explanatory functions of atomic shape and size (cf. also **11B 6**).

[margin, handwritten] atoms only have primary properties

13 Cosmology without teleology

A Epicurus, *Letter to Herodotus* 45

Also, the number of worlds, both of those which are similar to this one and of those which are dissimilar, is infinite. For the atoms, being infinitely many as has just been proved [**10A**], travel any distance; and the atoms of a suitable nature to be constituents of a world or responsible for its creation have not been exhausted on one world or on any finite number of worlds – neither worlds which are like ours nor worlds of other kinds. Therefore there is nothing to prevent there being an <u>infinite number of worlds.</u>

B Epicurus, *Letter to Pythocles* 88

A world is a certain envelopment of a heaven. It envelops celestial bodies, an earth, and the whole range of phenomena. It is cut off from the infinite, and terminates in a limit which is either rare or dense, on whose dissolution all its contents will undergo a collapse. It has its <u>terminus either in something revolving or in something stationary,</u> which has its outer perimeter round, triangular, or of whatever other shape. All are possible; for they are contested by none of the things evident in this world, in which we cannot discover a terminus.

[margin, handwritten] no terminus known

C Epicurus, *Letter to Herodotus* 73–4

(1) In addition to what was said earlier, we must suppose that the worlds, and every limited compound which bears a close resemblance to the things we see, has come into being from the infinite: all these things, the larger and the smaller alike, have been separated off from it as a result of individual entanglements. (2) And all disintegrate again, some faster some slower, and through differing kinds of causes.

[margin, handwritten] worlds came into being from infinite; all disintegrate again

D Lucretius 2.1052–1104

(1) Now it is not to be thought at all likely, when there is an infinity of empty space in every direction and countless seeds flying through the depths of the universe with their varied, everlasting and restless motion, that this is the one world and heaven to have been created, and that all those particles of matter outside it do nothing . . . (2) Moreover, nothing in the universe is the only one of its kind to be born and to grow, as opposed to belonging to some species, with many members of the same kind. Focus your mind first on animals. You will find that the wild beasts of the mountains, the human race, the speechless swarms of scaly fish, and all flying creatures, have such an origin. Therefore we must likewise admit that heaven, earth, sun, moon, sea, and all other existing things, are not unique but, rather, countless in number. After all, these are just as much products of birth, just as much awaited by the deep-set boundary stone of life, as any of the prolifically reproducing species in our world. (3) Provided you fully understand this, nature is at once revealed as rid of haughty overlords, the free autonomous agent of everything, without the gods' participation. For I appeal to the holy hearts of the gods, in their tranquil peace, leading their life of calm serenity. Who is capable of ruling the totality of the measureless, of holding in his hands and controlling the mighty reins of its depths? Who could turn all those heavens at the same time? Who could warm all those bountiful earths with celestial fires? Or be present everywhere at all times to darken the earth with clouds, to shake the calm sky with thunder, to despatch thunderbolts (often rocking his own abodes with them!) and to withdraw to the wilds and furiously hurl his weapon (which often misses the guilty and wipes out the innocent!)?

E Lucretius 4.823–57

(1) One mistake in this context, which I am determined you should shun and take precautions to avoid, is that of supposing the clear lights of the eyes to have been created in order that we might see; that it is in order that we might be able to take lengthy strides that the knees and hips can be flexed above their base of feet; and again that the forearms were jointed to the powerful upper arms, and hands supplied on either side, as our servants, in order that we could perform whatever acts were needed for living. All other explanations of this type which they offer are back to front, due to distorted reasoning. (2) For nothing has been engendered in our body in order that we might be able to use it. It is the fact of its being engendered that creates its use. Seeing did not exist before the lights of the eyes were engendered, nor was there pleading with words before the tongue was created. Rather, the origin of the tongue came long before

speech, ears were created long before sound was heard, and all our limbs, in my view, existed in advance of their use. Therefore they cannot have grown for the sake of their use. (3) By contrast, fighting out battles with bare hands, mutilating limbs, and staining bodies with blood, existed long before shining weapons began to fly. Nature compelled men to avoid wounds before the time when, thanks to craftsmanship, the left arm held up the obstructing shield. Presumably too the practice of resting the tired body is much more ancient than the spreading of soft beds; and the quenching of thirst came into being before cups. Hence it is credible that these were devised for the sake of their use, for they were invented as a result of life's experiences. (4) Quite different from these are all the things which were first actually engendered and gave rise to the preconception of their usefulness subsequently. Primary in this class are, we can see, the senses and the limbs. Hence, I repeat, there is no way you can believe that they were created for their function of utility.

[margin note: utilities created before use.]

F Lucretius 5.156–234 (following **23L**)

(1) Now to say that they [the gods] conceived the wish to create a world wonderful in nature for the sake of men, and that for that reason the gods' work is praiseworthy, so that it is proper for us to sing its praises and consider that it will be everlasting and imperishable, and that it is wrong that what was built by an ancient plan of the gods for the sake of mankind, in perpetuity, should ever be disturbed from its foundations by any force, or assailed with words and turned upside down – to elaborate such a fiction, Memmius, is folly. (2) For what profit could imperishable and blessed beings gain from our gratitude, to induce them to take on any task for our sake? What novelty could have tempted hitherto tranquil beings, at so late a stage, to desire a change in their earlier lifestyle? For it is plainly those who are troubled by the old that are obliged to delight in the new. But where someone had had no ill befall him up to now, because he had led his life well, what could have ignited a passion for novelty in such a person? (3) Or again, what harm would it have done us never to have been born? Did our life lie in darkness and misery until the world's beginning dawned? Although anyone who has been born must wish to remain in life so long as the caresses of pleasure hold him there, if someone has really never tasted the passion for life and has never been an individual, what harm does it do him not to have been created? (4) Also, from where did the gods get a model for the creation of the world, and from where was the preconception of men first ingrained in them, to enable them to know and see in their mind what they wished to create, or how did they come to know the power of the primary particles and what they were capable of when their arrangement was altered, if nature itself did not supply a blueprint of creation? (5) For so many primary particles

[margin note: existence of earth and man]

have for an infinity of time past been propelled in manifold ways by impacts and by their own weight, and have habitually travelled, combined in all possible ways, and tried out everything that their union could create, that it is not surprising if they have also fallen into arrangements, and arrived at patterns of motion, like those repeatedly enacted by this present world. (6) On the other hand, even if I were ignorant what the primary constituents of the world are, I would still dare to assert, from the very working of the heavens, and to prove from many other things, that the world's nature is certainly not a divine gift to us: it is so deeply flawed. First, of all that is covered by the heaven's vast expanse, mountains and beast-infested forests have appropriated a greedy share. It is occupied by rocks, vast swamps, and sea, which keeps the coastlines of the lands far apart. Of nearly two-thirds of it mortals are robbed by scorching heat and constant falls of frost. What farmland is left nature would use its force to smother with brambles, but for the resistance of human force . . . Besides, why does nature sustain and multiply on land and sea the dreadful hordes of wild beasts? Why do the seasons bring diseases with them? Why is untimely death rife? (7) A child, when nature has first spilt him forth with throes from his mother's womb into the realm of light, lies like a sailor cast ashore from the cruel waves – naked on the ground, without speech, helpless for life's tasks. And he fills the place with his miserable wailing, not without justification, in view of the quantity of troubles that lie ahead for him in life! On the other hand, the various domestic and wild animals grow without the need for rattles, for the smiles and broken speech of a nurse, and for different clothes to fit the different seasons. Nor, moreover, do they need weapons and high walls to protect their possessions, since the earth itself and creative nature supply all their wants in plenty.

G Cicero, *On the nature of the gods* 1.18–23

[Speaker: the Epicurean Velleius] (1) Listen to no ungrounded and fictitious doctrines: no creator and builder of the world like the god from Plato's *Timaeus*; no prophetic hag like the Stoics' Providence . . .; no world which is itself an animate, sentient, spherical, glowing, rotating god. These prodigies and marvels are the work of philosophers who dream, not argue. (2) By what kind of mental vision could your Plato have envisaged that great building enterprise by which he has god construct the world? What were the building techniques, the tools, the levers, the machines, the labourers, for such an enterprise? How were the air, fire, water and earth capable of complying with and obeying the architect's wishes? . . . To crown it all, having introduced a world which was not merely born but virtually hand-made as well, he said that it would be everlasting. Do you suppose that this man had so much as

sipped at the cup of natural philosophy – that is, of the rationale of nature
– when he thinks that something with an origin can be everlasting? What
compound is not capable of dissolution? What is there that has a
beginning and no end? (3) As for your [the Stoics'] providence, Lucilius,
if it is the same thing as this, I repeat my earlier question about the
labourers, the machines, and the entire planning and execution of the
project. If it is something different, why did it make the world
perishable, and not everlasting, as the Platonic god did? (4) A question for
both of you [Plato and Stoics] is why the world-builders suddenly
appeared on the scene, after sleeping for countless centuries. For if there
was no world, it does not follow that there were no centuries. By
'centuries' here I don't mean the ones which are made up by the number
of days and nights as a result of the annual orbits. Those, I concede, could
not have been produced without the world's rotation. But there has been
a certain eternity from infinite time past, which was not measured by any
bounding of times, but whose extent can be understood, because it is
unthinkable that there should have been some time at which there was no
time . . . (5) Was it for the sake of men, as you [the Stoics] are in the habit
of saying, that all this world was assembled by god? For wise men? In that
case this massive feat of world-building was accomplished for just a
handful of people. For foolish men? But, first, god had no reason to do
the bad a favour. And second, what did he achieve, seeing that all fools
are beyond doubt utterly wretched, above all because they are fools (for
what can be called more wretched than folly?), but also because there are
so many disadvantages in life that, whereas the wise mitigate them with
compensating advantages, fools can neither evade those still to come nor
bear those which are present.

H Cicero, *On the nature of the gods* 1.52–3

[Speaker: the Epicurean Velleius] (1) We can rightly call this god of ours
blessed, and yours [the Stoics'] extremely overworked. For if the world
itself is god, what can be less tranquil than rotating about an axis without
a moment's break at the heaven's amazing speed? And yet nothing is
blessed if it is not tranquil. Or if god is some being within the world, there
to rule, to control, to maintain the orbits of the heavenly bodies, the
succession of seasons, and the variations and regularities of things, to
watch over land and sea and guard men's well-being and lives, he is surely
involved in a troublesome and laborious job. We, on the other hand,
place the blessed life in peace of mind and in freedom from all duties. (2)
For the man to whom we owe all our other teaching taught us too that
the world is the product of nature, that there was no need for it to be
manufactured, and that so easy was that process, the one which you call
impossible without divine expertise, that nature will make, is making,

and has made infinitely many worlds. Just because you don't see how nature can do this without some mind, finding yourselves unable to work out the denouement of the argument you resort, like the tragedians, to a *deus ex machina*.

I Lucretius 5.837–77

(1) At that time [in the world's infancy] the earth tried to create many monsters with weird appearance and anatomy – androgynous, of neither one sex nor the other but somewhere in between; some footless, or handless; many even without mouths, or without eyes and blind; some with their limbs stuck together all along their body, and thus disabled from doing anything or going anywhere, from avoiding harm or obtaining anything they needed. These and other such monsters the earth created. But to no avail, since nature prohibited their development. They were unable to reach the goal of maturity, to find sustenance, or to copulate. For we see that creatures need the concurrence of many things in order to be able to produce and spread their progeny. First, there must be food. Second, a way for the procreative seeds in their bodies to flow out, released from their limbs. And third, in order that male and female can have intercourse, they must both have the equipment for indulging in the shared pleasure. Many animal species must have become extinct at that time, unable to produce and spread their progeny. (2) For whatever creatures you see breathing the air of life, their kind has from the start been preserved and protected by its cunning, its courage or its speed: and there are many too which have survived by being commended to our protection, thanks to their usefulness to us. First, the fierce lion species has been protected by its courage, foxes by cunning, deer by speed of flight. On the other hand dogs, light-sleeping and faithful, all the varieties of beasts of burden, wool-bearing sheep, and the horned herds of cattle, have all come under the protection of men, Memmius. For these, having by their own wish avoided the wild beasts and sought peace, have found food in plenty, supplied without any labour on their part: it is how we reward them for their usefulness. (3) But those which nature did not endow with any of these advantages, and which were thus unable either to live on their own resources or to perform some service to us in return for which we might allow their species to feed under our protection and be safe, these presumably lay as the prey and pickings of other creatures, all of them hampered by their fateful handicaps, until nature reduced their kind to extinction.

J Simplicius, *On Aristotle's Physics* 371,33–372,14

(1) Thus Empedocles says that under the rule of Love parts of animals first came into being at random – heads, hands, feet, and so on – and then

came into combination: 'There sprang up ox progeny, man-limbed, and the reverse' (obviously meaning 'man progeny, ox-limbed', i.e. combinations of ox and man). And those which combined in a way which enabled them to preserve themselves became animals, and survived, because they fulfilled each other's needs – the teeth cutting and grinding the food, the stomach digesting it, the liver converting it into blood. And the human head, by combining with the human body, brings about the preservation of the whole, but by combining with the ox's body fails to cohere with it and perishes. For those which did not combine on proper principles perished. And things still happen in the same way nowadays. (2) This doctrine seems to be shared by all those early natural philosophers who make material necessity the cause of things' becoming, and, among later philosophers, by the Epicureans. Their mistake, according to Alexander, springs from the supposition that all things that come into being for some end come into being through decision and reasoning, coupled with the observation that natural things do not come into being in that way.

☐ Epicurean cosmology is devoted to the elimination of groundless fears (**25B**), notably of death and of the divine. This requires explanations in purely physical terms for a range of phenomena, from minds to magnets, which had become standard in cosmological treatises. Readers interested in pursuing this topic would do well to read widely in Lucretius' poem. Here, however, apart from the topics of celestial phenomena (**19**), god (**23**), and death (**24**), covered elsewhere, we restrict our discussion mainly to the Epicurean defence of a mechanistic world view, in defiance of the Platonist teleological view which in the Hellenistic period was taken up by the Stoics (**54**).

On the mechanistic view of world-formation, see **C, F 5, H 2** and **11H**, and for the opposition on this issue between Epicureans on one side and Platonists and Stoics on the other, cf. **G–H; 54L–M**. Much effort on the part of the Epicureans goes into combating the idea, common to both Platonists and Stoics, that the world is governed by divine providence. Note the following grounds of dissent.

(a) Argument from the infinity-of-worlds thesis (**A, D, H 2**). This inheritance from Epicurus' atomist forerunners is not in the extant texts used, as one might have expected, to question the *anthropocentric* teleology of his opponents. Instead it is made the basis of doubt as to how even a divine ruler could have sufficient powers to control the entire universe (**D**).

(b) God's nature. God, Epicurus maintains, is thought of as an imperishable and blessed being, and this is simply incompatible with the stresses and strains of world administration (**H 1; 23B–E**). One might discern here a variation on Aristotle's theme, taken further by his successor Theophrastus, that since god's activity must be the best it cannot include any interest in the sublunary world.

(c) Why should god have chosen to create the world (**F–G**)? This breaks down into several more specific questions. Why sooner rather than later (**G 4**, cf. **F 2**? How can he have been motivated by benevolence towards non-existent beings (**F 2–3**)? How could he have sufficient powers (**G 2**)? From where did he get the preconception of the objects he was to create (**F 4**)? This last challenge may sound surprising, but should be read as a response to Plato's story in the *Timaeus* that a divine craftsman created the world and its contents in the likeness of the eternal Forms. Since Epicurus, as an empiricist, self-consciously replaces Forms with empirically derived 'preconceptions' (see **17**, commentary), he feels a reasonable doubt as to how the idea of a thing could pre-exist the thing itself (cf. **19B 4**).

(d) Animal nature (**E**). To regard the functional character of animal parts as evidence of design is to rely on a false analogy with artefacts. Artefacts are devised to fulfil *pre-existing* functions (e.g. cups for drinking) of which nature has already supplied the model. The function of natural organs themselves cannot have been similarly preconceived in advance of the organs' existence.

(e) The existence of evil is incompatible with anthropocentric providence (**D 3**, **F 6–7**). For the Stoic side of this debate, see **54O–U**.

So much for the negative aspect of Epicurus' case. But how does he himself hope to explain non-teleologically the *prima facie* evidence of design in the world? Does he have any inkling of the modern evolutionary alternative? His theory, such as it is, takes on the challenge at three levels: the world, animal nature, and human institutions.

That worlds capable of supporting life should come into and pass out of existence by mere accident is seen as relatively straightforward. The Stoic insistence on the laughable improbability of such flukes occurring (**54M**) is well countered by appeal to the infinity of the universe: **F 5**, cf. **H 2**. As for the existence of regularity and fixed laws in nature, including the continuity of species, these are explained by the existence of immutable atoms in a determinate range of shapes and sizes: **8B 4**; **12C 3**.

Animal evolution is a trickier topic. Originally, Epicurus holds, a vast number of species were thrown up at random, of which only the fittest survived: **I**; cf. **J** for the origins of this idea in the work of the fifth-century B.C. physicist Empedocles. The various functions of their limbs and organs were not intrinsic to them, but were worked out by practice (**E**: anyone unimpressed by this claim might pause to reflect on the astonishing dexterity with the feet developed by people born without arms).

But how are we to reconcile **E**, with its assertion that each animal part pre-existed its function, with the argument at **19B 1–2** for the natural origin of language, which exploits the premise that young animals are already instinctively aware of the powers of their various parts, even before they are ready to use them? The evidence for such instincts provided the teleology lobby with one of its best arguments (cf. Galen, *On the use of parts*; also **57C**), and the anti-teleologist Epicurus might have been expected to find them an embarrassment. The likeliest explanation is that in Epicurus' view an animal species' nature can be *changed* by the lessons of the environment: see **19A 1**. All we need hypothesize for him in order to make this plausible is a belief in the inheritance of acquired characteristics, a belief widely held in antiquity and long after. He could then maintain that the original members of each species (the subject of **E**) had to learn to use their bodily equipment from scratch, but that what they learnt was inherited by their descendants, thus becoming part of each species' nature. For example man was originally solitary by nature, but since expediency has turned him into a social being (**22J–K**) the drive to communicate has become instinctive to him (**19B 2**). A similar story might be developed about the faithful natures of dogs on the basis of **I 2**.

Such human institutions as language, law, and the use of fire were also often seen as divine benefactions (cf. **19C**). Here the Epicurean reply consists mainly in careful naturalistic accounts of their origins in terms of the promptings of circumstances (**E3**; **19A 1**; cf. **19A–C** for language, **22J–N** for law).

We have mentioned the Platonists and Stoics as the Epicureans' opponents on this issue. Aristotle is often taken to be another. But the target is very evidently a creationist doctrine, such as was certainly embraced by the Stoics, and also by Plato, at least on a literal reading of his *Timaeus*, but was emphatically denied by Aristotle. Certainly Epicurus must disagree with Aristotle's belief in the eternity of the world, in its hierarchical structure, and in the eternal fixity of species. But such dissent is not prominent in the texts, and on most of the issues emphasized there he and Aristotle could happily agree: in particular, that art is posterior to nature, and that although each animal species, at least as it is now constituted, functions from birth in a goal-directed way, there is no deliberate design in nature. Unless Epicurus simply neglected Aristotle's contribution (always a possibility, and apparently what Alexander in **J 2** suspects), it may be safer to suppose that, when confronted with the challenge of Plato's wholesale teleology, he was inclined to regard Aristotle as an ally.

14 Soul

A Epicurus, *Letter to Herodotus* 63–7

(1) The next thing to see – referring it to the sensations and feelings, since that will provide the strongest confirmation – is that the soul is a fine-structured body diffused through the whole aggregate, most strongly resembling wind with a certain blending of heat, and resembling wind in some respects but heat in others. But there is that part which differs greatly also from wind and heat themselves in its fineness of structure, a fact which makes it the more liable to co-affection with the rest of the aggregate. (2) All this is shown by the soul's powers, feelings, mobilities and thought processes, and by those features of it whose loss marks our death. (3) We must grasp too that the soul has the major share of responsibility for sensation. On the other hand, it would not be in possession of this if it were not contained in some way by the rest of the aggregate. And the rest of the aggregate, having granted this responsibility to the soul, itself too receives from the soul a share of this kind of accidental attribute – though not of *all* those which the soul possesses. (4) That is why when the soul has been separated from it the rest of the aggregate does not have sensation. For we saw that it does not have

this power as its own intrinsic possession, but grants it to a second thing, which shares its moment of birth and which, by means of the power brought to perfection in it, instantly produces the accidental property of sensation as a result of the process and bestows it both on itself and, as I said, on the rest of the aggregate, owing to their contiguity and co-affection. (5) Hence too the soul, so long as it remains in [the rest of the aggregate], will never lose sensation through the separation of some other part: whatever of the soul itself is destroyed too when all or part of the container disintegrates will, so long as it remains, have sensation. But the rest of the aggregate, when either all or part of it remains, does not have sensation following the separation of however many atoms it takes to make up the nature of the soul. (6) Moreover, when the whole aggregate disintegrates the soul is dispersed and no longer has the same powers, or its motions. Hence it does not possess sensation either. For it is impossible to think of it perceiving while not in this organism, and moving with these motions when what contains and surrounds it are not of the same kind as those in which it now has these motions. (7) Another point to appreciate is this. The 'incorporeal', according to the prevailing usage of the word, is applied to that which can be thought of *per se*. But it is impossible to think of the incorporeal *per se* except as void. And void can neither act nor be acted upon, but merely provides bodies with motion through itself. Consequently those who say that the soul is incorporeal are talking nonsense. For if it were like that it would be unable to act or be acted upon in any way, whereas as a matter of fact both these accidental properties are self-evidently discriminable in the soul.

B Lucretius 3.136–76

(1) My next point is that the mind and the spirit are firmly interlinked and constitute a single nature, but that the deliberative element which we call the mind is, as it were, the chief, and holds sway throughout the body. It is firmly located in the central part of the chest. For that is where fear and dread leap up, and where joys caress us: therefore it is where the mind is. The remaining part of the spirit, which is distributed throughout the body, obeys the mind and moves at its beck and call. (2) The mind by itself possesses its own understanding and its own joys while nothing is affecting either the spirit or the body. And just as, when our head or eye is hurt by an attack of pain, the agony is not shared by our whole body, so too the mind sometimes itself suffers pain or waxes with joy while the rest of the spirit throughout the limbs and frame is receiving no new stimulus. But when the mind is affected by a more powerful fear we see the whole spirit throughout the limbs share its sensation, with sweat and pallor arising over the whole body, the tongue crippled and the voice

choked, the eyes darkened, the ears buzzing, the limbs buckling – indeed, we often see men collapse through the mind's terror. From this anyone can easily tell that the spirit is interlinked with the mind: when it is impelled by the mind's power it immediately hurls the body forward with its own impact. (3) This same reasoning proves the nature of the mind and spirit to be corporeal. For when it is seen to hurl the limbs forward, to snatch the body out of sleep, to alter the face, and to govern and steer the entire man – and we see that none of these is possible without touch, nor touch without body – you must surely admit that the mind and spirit are constituted with a corporeal nature. Besides, you can see that the mind is affected jointly with the body and shares our bodily sensations. If the frightful force of a spear, when it penetrates to wrench apart the bones and sinews, fails to strike at life itself, there nevertheless follows relaxation and an agreeable descent to the ground, and on the ground a turmoil which develops in the mind and at times a half-hearted will as if to rise. Hence the nature of the mind must be corporeal, since it suffers under the impact of corporeal spears.

C Aetius 4.3.11 (Usener 315)

Epicurus [said that the soul is] a blend consisting of four things, of which one kind is fire-like, one air-like, one wind-like, while the fourth is something which lacks a name. This last he made the one responsible for sensation. The wind, he said produces movement in us, the air produces rest, the hot one produces the evident heat of the body, and the unnamed one produces sensation in us. For sensation is found in none of the named elements.

D Lucretius 3.262–322

(1) The primary particles of the elements so interpenetrate each other in their motions that no one element can be distinguished and no capacity spatially separated, but they exist as multiple powers of a single body. Just as, familiarly, in any animal flesh there is odour and a certain heat and flavour, and yet between them these go to make up a single mass of body, so too heat, air and the unseen force of wind when mixed form a single nature, along with that mobile power which transmits the beginning of motion from itself to them, the origin of sense-bearing motions through the flesh. (2) For this substance lies deeply concealed, deeper than anything else in our body. It is, moreover, the very spirit of the entire spirit. Just as the power of the mind and that of the spirit, interspersed in our limbs and entire body, lie hidden because compounded out of tiny particles few and far between, so too this nameless power, made of minute particles, lies hidden, and is moreover the very spirit of the entire spirit and holds sway throughout the body. (3) In a similar way wind, air

and heat must so interact in their mixture throughout the limbs, with one deeper than the others and one more prominent, as to be seen to constitute between them something unitary, lest in separation from each other the heat, the wind and the power of air destroy and dissipate sensation. (4) The mind also has that kind of heat which it takes on when it boils with anger and the eyes shine with a fiercer flame; it has plenty of cold wind, the companion of fear, which excites fright in the limbs and rouses the frame; and it has that state of the still air which is found in a tranquil chest and in a calm face. But there is more heat in those with fierce hearts and angry minds which easily boil over in anger. A prime example is the lion, which regularly bursts its chest with roaring and groaning and cannot contain the billows of rage in its chest. But the cold mind of stags is more windy, and quicker to rouse through their flesh those chilly gusts which set the limbs in trembling motion. The nature of cattle, on the other hand, is characterized more by calm air. Neither does ignition by the smouldering brand of anger ever overexcite it and cloud it with blind darkness, nor is it transfixed and numbed by the icy shafts of fear. It lies midway between stags and fierce lions. (5) Likewise the human race. Even though education may produce individuals equally well turned out, it still leaves those original traces of each mind's nature. And we must not suppose that faults can be completely eradicated, so that one man will not plunge too hastily into bitter anger, another not be assailed too readily by fear, or the third type not be over-indulgent in tolerating certain things. There are many further respects in which men's various natures and characteristic behaviours must differ, but I cannot now set out their hidden causes, nor can I find enough names for all the shapes of primary particles from which this variety springs. But there is one thing which I see I can state in this matter: so slight are the traces of our natures which reason cannot expel from us, that nothing stands in the way of our leading a life worthy of the gods.

E Lucretius 4.877–91

(1) Now I shall tell you – and you mark what I say – how it comes about that we can take steps forward when we want to, how we have the power to move our limbs, and what it is that habitually thrusts forward this great bulk that is our body. (2) First, let me say, images of walking impinge on our mind and strike it, as I explained earlier [**15D 7–8**]. It is after that that volition occurs. For no one ever embarks upon any action before the mind first previews what it wishes to do, and whatever it is that it previews there exists an image of that thing. (3) So when the mind stirs itself to want to go forwards, it immediately strikes all the power of the spirit distributed all over the body throughout the limbs and frame: it

is easily done, because the spirit is firmly interlinked with it. (4) Then the spirit in turn strikes the body, and thus gradually the whole bulk is pushed forward and moved.

F Lucretius 3.417–62

(1) Come now, so that you may be able to recognize that animals' minds and flimsy spirits are subject to birth and death, I shall continue to set down verses worthy of your standing in life, the product of long searching and agreeable toil. See that you couple both under a single name: when, for example, I proceed to speak of 'spirit', proving that it is mortal, assume that I mean 'mind' as well, inasmuch as they constitute between them a unity and an interlinked entity. (2) First, since I have proved that it is a delicate construction of minute bodies, and made of much smaller primary particles than the flowing liquid of water or cloud or smoke – for it is far more mobile, and moves under the impact of a more delicate cause, seeing that it is moved by *images* of smoke and cloud, as when subdued in sleep we see altars breathe out their heat skywards and emit smoke: for these are undoubtedly images which travel to us – now then, given that when vessels are smashed you see the liquid flow away on all sides and disperse, and that cloud and smoke disperse into the air, you should believe that the spirit too is scattered, perishes much faster, and is quicker to disintegrate into its primary particles, once it has been separated from a man's limbs and taken its leave. After all, seeing that the body, which serves as its vessel, if it is shattered by something or made porous by loss of blood from the veins, cannot hold it together, how could you suppose that the spirit can be held together by any air, which is more rarefied than our body and less capable of holding it together? (3) Furthermore, we perceive that the mind is born jointly with the body, grows up jointly with it, and ages jointly with it. For just as infants walk unsteadily with a frail and tender body, so too their accompanying power of mental judgement is tenuous. Then when they have matured to an age of robust strength, their judgement is greater and their mental strength increased. Later, when their body has been battered by time's mighty strength and their frame has collapsed, its strength blunted, then their intelligence hobbles, their tongue rambles, their mind totters. Everything fails and deserts them at the same time. Therefore it is consistent also that the whole substance of the spirit should disintegrate like smoke into the lofty air, since we see that they are born jointly, jointly grow up, and, as I have shown, simultaneously weary with age and crack up. (4) Also, we see that just as the body itself undergoes dreadful diseases and harsh pain, so too the mind undergoes bitter cares, grief and fear. Hence it is consistent that it should also share in death.

G Lucretius 3.624–33

Besides, if the nature of the spirit is immortal and it can have sensation when separated from our body, we must presumably equip it with the five senses. There is no other way in which we can imagine souls wandering below in Acheron. That is why painters and earlier generations of writers have presented souls as equipped with senses in this way. But neither eyes nor nose nor even hand can exist for the spirit in separation. Nor can tongue or ears. Therefore spirits cannot by themselves have sensation or exist.

H Lucretius 3.806–29

(1) Besides, all things that endure for ever must either, through having a solid body, repel impacts and allow nothing to penetrate them which might separate their tight-fitting parts from within, for example the particles of matter whose nature we proved earlier [**8B**]; or be able to endure through all time because they are free from blows, like void, which remains untouched and is quite unaffected by impact; or again because there is no place available around them such that the things might be able to disperse into it and disintegrate, in the way that the totality of totalities is everlasting and has no place outside it into which things might escape nor bodies which might burst into it and disintegrate it with the strength of their impact. (2) But if the reason for holding it immortal should rather be that it is permanently protected from things which affect life – either because things hostile to its survival do not reach it at all, or because those which reach it are somehow repulsed before we can feel their ill effects – <that is contrary to the evidence. > For quite apart from the fact that it suffers in tandem with bodily disease, things often arrive to torment it about the future, to keep it sick with fear, and to exhaust it with cares. And even when its misdeeds are past it suffers remorse for its sins. Think too of the mind's own peculiar affliction of madness, and its forgetfulness; think of its submergence in the black waters of lethargy.

☐ 'Soul' (*psuchē*) is a term whose breadth varies sharply in Greek usage. At its widest, notably in Aristotle, it embraces the entire range of vital functions of any living thing, plants as well as animals. At its narrowest, as in Plato's *Phaedo*, it is a largely intellectual force, housed in the animal body but ultimately separable from all bodily functions and sensations. Epicurus' conception of it falls midway between these two extremes, very much like that of the Stoics (see **53**). For him the soul's primary functions are consciousness in all its aspects – especially sensation, thought and emotion (e.g. **A 2–6**, **B 1–2**) – and the transmission of impulses to the body (**B 3**, **E**). Of these, thought and emotion are localized in the 'mind', which in common with most ancient philosophers Epicurus argued to be in the chest, the apparent seat of emotion (**B** 1; cf. **65H** for the Stoics). The other functions belong to the 'spirit', which extends throughout the body and interacts closely with the mind, although the mind retains enough independence to count as a distinct entity (**B** 2). Thus these two parts of the soul fulfil more or less the roles which subsequent physiology has assigned to the brain and nervous system respectively. Epicurus has *prima facie* an Identity Theory of mind – that is, he identifies it with a physical portion of the body – although we will see an important qualification to this in **20** below.

That the soul cannot survive the body's death is the single most important upshot of the analysis. (**A** 6 and **F–H** exemplify the Epicurean defence of this conclusion, although ideally the 28 such arguments at Lucretius 3.417–829 should be read in their entirety. For the ethical implications of the doctrine, see **24**.) To this end two main theses must be established.

The first is that the soul is corporeal. Plato, like many since, had regarded its incorporeality as an essential condition of its separability from the body. The main ground offered by the Epicureans for its corporeality is its ability to interact with the body and to be affected jointly with it (**A** 7, **B** 3; cf. **45C** for the same argument in Stoicism). The elaboration of the soul's physical composition can be thought of as subservient to this consideration, its importance lying mainly in its demonstration of the *possibility* of a physicalist analysis. This may explain Epicurus' own reticence about the details at **A** 1–2, when selecting what he sees as the cardinal features of the theory.

For fuller information we must rely on the reports in **C** and **D**. The soul is a 'blend' of four substances – heat, air and wind, plus a fourth consisting of immensely fine atoms, which is 'nameless' in that it is the dominant component of no phenomenal substance after which it might be named. The technical implication of 'blend', which Lucretius is struggling to convey at **D** 1–3, seems to be that rather than consisting of juxtaposed portions of heat, air etc. the mixture is one in which the individual atoms of the four substances are separated and recombined into an entirely new kind of substance. Although in this sense it is more than the sum of its parts, the soul does manifest certain powers of its individual ingredients. Heat accounts for the bodily warmth characteristic of life (**C**), and, when it predominates in the soul, for hot temper (**D** 4–5). Wind, with its agitation and coldness, propels the limbs (**C**), and when present in excess causes fear and flight (**D** 4–5). (Epicurus' word for wind, *pneuma*, is also the term used by the Stoics for the warm 'breath' which they hold to be the stuff of the soul – see **53**.) Air, that is calm air, which must consist of the same atoms as wind in different patterns of behaviour, accounts for bodily rest (**C**), and, when predominant, for tranquillity of character (**D** 4–5). Finally, the 'nameless' ingredient has to be so subtle in texture and so mobile as to initiate in the spirit as a whole the motions which transmit sensation (**D** 1–2), since the other three ingredients manifestly lack this capacity in themselves (**C**).

The second thesis which helps to underpin the mortality arguments is that of the extreme functional interdependence of soul and body. Sensation is the soul's sphere of responsibility, but it is the body that 'grants' it that responsibility, i.e. provides a suitable locus for the activity (**A** 3). And once this has happened, as it does in the very process of birth (**A** 4), sensation becomes a *joint* activity of both soul and body (**A 3–4**), despite an important asymmetry between their respective roles (**A 5**). It is neither, for example, merely the eyes that see, nor merely the soul which sees through the eyes (cf. Lucretius 3.350–69 = **j** in vol. 2). Such proofs of the soul's mortality as **A 6** and **G** rely heavily on this thesis.

A physicalist analysis like that proposed by Epicurus easily invites the charge of reducing the human mind to a mechanism. Some, for example, have read **E**'s account of human action as deterministic in tendency: the mind is struck by images of walking (for the cumbersome process by which imagination is held to employ images arriving from outside the mind, invoked also at **F 2**, see **15D**), which cause it to decide to walk, whereupon it initiates the action of walking. But this is a misreading. The passage is concerned purely with the physical stages of the process, and these quite properly include the focusing of the mind on the image of the action in question as a necessary precondition of our deciding whether to perform it (**E 2**). There is no suggestion that the volition is itself nothing more than a mechanical stage in the process, and Lucretius' reticence on any physical analysis of it may suggest otherwise. Similarly at **D 5**, where he recognizes that human character is to a large extent physically determined, he is at pains to stress the power of reason to counteract the effects of our chemical make-up. How the Epicureans could hope to exempt volition and reason themselves from mechanistic determinism is a further question, which will be examined in **20**. There we will also glimpse Epicurus' defence against another familiar challenge to the physicalist analysis of mind, that it is incapable of accounting for the subjective aspects of consciousness.

15 Sensation, imagination, memory

A Epicurus, *Letter to Herodotus* 46–53

(1) Moreover, there are delineations which represent the shapes of solid bodies and which in their fineness of texture are far different from things evident. For it is not impossible that such emanations should arise in the space around us, or appropriate conditions for the production of their concavity and fineness of texture, or effluences preserving the same sequential arrangement and the same pattern of motion as they had in the solid bodies. These delineations we call 'images'. (2) [= **11D**] (3) Next, that the images are of unsurpassed fineness is uncontested by anything evident. Hence they also have unsurpassed speed, having every passage commensurate with themselves, in addition to the fact that infinitely many of them suffer no collision or few collisions, whereas many, indeed infinitely many, atoms suffer immediate collision. (4) Also that the creation of the images happens as fast as thought. For there is a continuous flow from the surface of bodies – not revealed by diminution in their size, thanks to reciprocal replenishment – which preserves for a long time the

positioning and arrangement which the atoms had in the solid body, even if it is also sometimes distorted; and formations of them in the space around us, swift because they do not need to be filled out in depth; and other ways too in which things of this kind are produced. (5) For none of this is contested by our sensations, if one is considering how to bring back self-evident impressions from external objects to us in such a way as to bring back co-affections too. (6) And we must indeed suppose that it is on the impingement of something from outside that we see and think of shapes. (7) For external objects would not imprint their own nature, of both colour and shape, by means of the air between us and them, or by means of rays or of any effluences passing from us to them, (8) as effectively as they can through certain delineations penetrating us from objects, sharing their colour and shape, of a size to fit into our vision or thought, and travelling at high speed, with the result that their unity and continuity then results in the impression, and preserves their co-affection all the way from the object because of their uniform bombardment from it, resulting from the vibration of the atoms deep in the solid body. (9) And whatever impression we get by focusing our thought or senses, whether of shape or of properties, that is the shape of the solid body, produced through the image's concentrated succession or after-effect. (10) But falsehood and error are always located in the opinion which we add. (11) For the portrait-like resemblance of the impressions which we gain either in sleep or through certain other focusings of thought or of the other discriminatory faculties, to the things we call existent and true, would not exist if the things with which we come into contact were not themselves something. (12) And error would not exist if we did not also get a certain other process within ourselves, one which, although causally connected, possesses differentiation. It is through this that, if it is unattested or contested, falsehood arises, and if attested or uncontested, truth. (13) This doctrine too, then, is a very necessary one to grasp, so that the criteria based on self-evident impressions should not be done away with, and so that falsehood should not be treated as equally established and confound everything. (14) Hearing too results from a sort of wind travelling from the object which speaks, rings, bangs, or produces an auditory sensation in whatever way it may be. This current is dispersed into similarly-constituted particles. (15) These at the same time preserve a certain co-affection in relation to each other, and a distinctive unity which extends right to the source, and which usually causes the sensory recognition appropriate to that source, or, failing that, just reveals what is external to us. (16) For without a certain co-affection brought back from the source to us such sensory recognition could not occur. (17) We should not, then, hold that the air is shaped by the projected voice, or likewise by the other things classed with voice. For the air will be much less adequate if this is an effect imposed on it by the voice. Rather we should hold that the impact which occurs inside us when we emit our voice immediately squeezes out certain particles constitutive of a wind current in a way which produces the auditory feeling in us. (18) We must suppose that smell too, just like hearing, would never cause any feeling if there were not certain particles travelling away from the object and with the right dimensions to stimulate this sense, some kinds being disharmonious and unwelcome, others harmonious and welcome.

B Lucretius 4.230–8

Besides, since a given shape handled in the dark is recognized to be the same one as it is seen to be in clear daylight, touch and sight must be moved by a similar cause. Thus if in the dark we probe and are moved by what is square, what will the square thing be which in the light can impinge on vision, if not its image? Hence it can be seen that the cause of vision lies in the images, and that without these nothing can be seen.

C Lucretius 4.256–68

(1) One thing in this matter which should not be thought puzzling is why, although the images which strike the eyes cannot be seen individually, the objects themselves are perceived. (2) For also when wind beats on us little by little, and when bitter cold creeps on us, we do not normally feel every separate particle of that wind and that cold, but rather the combination of them, and we see on those occasions an effect in our body just as if some object were beating us and imparting to us a sensation of its bodily mass from outside. (3) Furthermore, when we knock a stone with our finger we are *touching* its external outermost colour, but what we are *sensing* with our touch is not that but rather the actual hardness deep down within the stone.

D Lucretius 4.722–822

(1) Come now, hear what things move the mind, and learn briefly the source of the things which enter the mind. (2) The first point is this: that many images of things wander variously in every direction. They are delicate and easily join together in the air when they meet, like spider's web or gold leaf. For they are, indeed, much more delicate-textured than the ones which fill the eyes and stimulate vision, seeing that they penetrate the body's openings, arouse the delicate substance of the mind within us, and stimulate its sensation. (3) That is why we see Centaurs, the bodily forms of Scyllas, the dog-faces of Cerberus, and the likenesses of those who have met their death and whose bones are in the ground. For images of every kind travel everywhere, some of which spontaneously form in mid-air, while others are those which come off various things,

and those made when these things' shapes combine. For certainly the image of a Centaur does not arise from a living one – there never was such a species of animal – but when the images of a horse and a man have accidentally met they easily and immediately stick together, as I said previously, owing to their fine nature and delicate texture. Others of this type are created in the same way. (4) Because, as I showed earlier, their extreme lightness makes their travel so mobile, it is easy for any one fine image to arouse our mind with a single impact. For the mind is itself delicate and extraordinarily mobile. (5) That this happens as I say it does you can easily tell as follows. In so far as what we see with the mind is similar to what we see with the eyes, it must come about in a similar way. Well, since I have proved that it is by means of whatever images stimulate my eyes that I see, say, a lion, you can now tell that the mind is moved in a similar way through images of lions and equally through the others it sees, no less than the eyes except in that what it discerns is more delicate. (6) And when sleep has relaxed the limbs the mind stays awake in just the same way, except that these same images which stimulate our minds while we are awake do so to such an extent that we seem to see beyond all doubt someone who has departed this life and is dead and buried. The reason why nature compels this to happen is that all the bodily senses are suppressed and at rest throughout the limbs and cannot convict falsehood with the true facts. Moreover, the memory lies in slumber and does not protest that the man whom the mind thinks that it sees alive is long dead. (7) This matter raises many questions, and there is much that we must clarify if we want to expound the facts clearly. The first question is why each person's mind immediately thinks of the very thing that he has formed a desire to think of. Do the images observe our will, so that as soon as we form the wish the images impinge on us, whether our desire be to think of sea, land or sky? Are assemblies, parades, parties and battles all created and supplied by nature on demand, and in spite of the fact that everything which the minds of other people in the same place are thinking of is quite different? A further question is, what about our seeing in our dreams the images rhythmically going forward and moving their supple limbs, when they fluently swing their supple arms in alternation and before our very eyes replicate the gesture with matching foot movements? No doubt the images are steeped in technique, and have taken lessons in wandering to enable them to have fun at night-time! (8) Or will this be nearer the truth? Because within a single period of time detectable by our senses – the time it takes to utter a single sound – there lie hidden many periods of time whose existence is discovered by reason, it follows that everywhere at every time every image is ready on the spot: so great is the speed and availability of things. And because they are delicate the mind can only see sharply those of them which it strains to see. Hence the remainder all perish, beyond those for which the mind has prepared itself. The mind further prepares itself by hoping to see the sequel to each thing, with the result that this comes about. Don't you see how the eyes too, when they begin to see things which are delicate, strain and prepare themselves, and that there is no other way of seeing sharply? As a matter of fact, even with things plain to see you can discover that the result of failing to pay attention is that it becomes like something separated from you by the whole of time and far away. Why then is it surprising if the mind loses everything else beyond the matters to which it is devoting itself? (9) As for the other point, it is not surprising that the images move and rhythmically swing their arms and other limbs. The image seems to do this in dreams because when the first image perishes and a second then arises in a different stance it looks as if the first had changed its pose. You can take it that this happens fast, so great is the speed and availability of things. And so great is the availability of particles within a single period of time detectable by the senses that it is capable of keeping up the supply. We then on the basis of slender evidence add weighty opinions and plunge ourselves into the trickery of deception. Occasionally, too, an image of the same kind is not supplied, but what was previously a woman seems to have turned into a man in our arms, or one face or age is followed by another. The fact that this does not surprise us is the doing of sleep and oblivion.

E Diogenes of Oenoanda, new fragment 5.3.3–14

What is viewed by the eyesight is inherited by the soul, and after the impingements of the original images passages are opened up in us in such a way that, even when the objects which we originally saw are no longer present, our mind admits likenesses of the original objects.

F Diogenes Laertius 10.32 (=**16B 11**)

Also, all notions arise from the senses by means of confrontation, analogy, similarity and combination, with some contribution from reasoning too.

☐ Although each of the five senses has its own mechanism, vision is made the paradigm case and receives nearly all the attention (**A** 1–9). Analogously in the case of imagination, to which Epicurus attributes the same basic mechanism as sensation, visualization is used as the paradigm case (**A** 6–9, **D**, **E**). The explanandum (**A** 5) is our receipt of impressions of external objects which (a) graphically convey their properties, and (b) instantly undergo changes to match changes in the objects themselves (the probable meaning of 'co-affections'; cf. **A** 8, and also, for the case of hearing, **A** 16). The explanation (**A** 1–4 and 8–11) is in terms of 'images' – surface-layers one atom thick thrown off at tremendous speed and in rapid succession by solid bodies as a result of their internal atomic vibration (see **11A**), so fine-textured as usually to escape serious erosion or retardation through collisions during their travel, and thus almost instantly reaching the eye, or mind, as accurate 'delineations' of the object's surface shape and colour. The cumulative cinematographic effect of a uniform series of these amounts to an 'impression' of the object (**A 8–9**; in the case of imagination a single image may suffice, **D 4**). Without this mediation by images it would be impossible to explain the regular correspondence of our impressions to the actual surface features of external objects (**A 11, B**).

This last argument might be challenged by a sceptic as question-begging: how can we know that our sense-impressions do usually mirror the properties of external objects? Epicurus' method, however, is to assume a positivist attitude to sense-evidence throughout his physical treatise (cf. **17C**), reserving the formal refutation of its alternative, scepticism, as an independent exercise which need borrow no premise from physics – see **16A** with commentary. In support of his premise that sense-impressions usually correspond to their objects, Epicurus could point either to the pragmatic utility of assuming its truth (cf. **16A 10**), or to the tendency of diverse sense-impressions to support each other, e.g. of touch to confirm the eyes' reports of shape and texture. The latter line of argument seems to be legitimized at **B**, despite Epicurus' rejection of the converse possibility that one sense might confute another: see **16A 6–7, B 4–7**, and commentary.

Although images are the immediate cause of vision, in regular Epicurean usage what we actually 'see' is not normally the images but the external object itself, or at least its properties. This is the distinction underlying **C**, as **C 1** shows – and not, as might otherwise have seemed equally possible, the distinction that we see not individual images but only multiple series of images. **C**'s main object, however, is to defend the theory of images against the empirical objection that if there were such things we would perceive them. **C 3** can be interpreted as follows. It may be claimed in support of this objection that single layers of atoms *are* regularly discerned, by the sense of touch, so that if there were images they too would be perceived. The answer is that we can never feel by touch a single layer of atoms *in itself*. We only feel the cumulative hardness of the multiple layers supporting it: remove these and the surface layer would become imperceptible even to the touch.

Since the usual resemblance of impressions to external objects extends to the impressions of imagination too, even dream-impressions, they too must be caused by the impingement of images, extraordinarily fine ones capable of penetrating to the mind from outside our bodies (**A 11, D 2, 4–5; 14F 2**). Both memory (cf. **E**) and the peculiar features of dreams (**D 7 and 9**) can be explained by such a theory. But why did Epicurus choose so cumbersome an account? One explanation may be that, if he admitted that imagination can operate with no external cause, he would be unable to exclude the possibility that sensation might itself sometimes be an equally internal fantasy of the sense-organs. Hence the Epicurean Diogenes of Oenoanda attacks the Stoic view that dreams are 'empty shadow-drawings of the mind' (fr. 7 and new fr. 1, = **g** in vol 2; cf. **39B 5**), and Epicurus denies that sensation can ever be 'self-moved' (**16B 2**). Another factor is that 'the focusing of thought into an impression', the process of visualization described and explained at **D 7–8** (cf. **14E 2**), was one which

Epicurus gave quite a serious role in his epistemology, probably for its use in our memory and mental assessment of empirical data (see further on **17**); this too might have been harder to sustain without some assurance that such visualization genuinely puts us in touch with external reality. Underlying both motivations there may also be a lingering Platonist assumption, so common in Greek thought, that if I succeed in thinking of *x* then *x* must objectively exist for me to think of.

Bizarre fleeting pictures in imagination and dreaming arise from the impingement of isolated freak images, produced in mid-air either spontaneously or by chance cohesion of images, e.g. of those of man and horse into that of Centaur (**D 2–4**; cf. **A 4**). But the modes of notion-formation described in **F** are, as the fuller Stoic exposition at **39D** shows, *internal* mental processes in which we deliberately combine or otherwise modify our impressions. On this account we could deliberately create the mental notion of a Centaur by focusing on man and horse – that is, by apprehending streams of images of each – and internally synthesizing the resultant impressions. Whether the Epicureans adopted this full scheme from the Stoics or vice versa is unclear, but that Epicurus himself made important use of one part of it in his theology does seem probable: see **23F**.

Further mechanical questions about sensation, e.g. the role of light in vision, and how the image manages to get into the eye, must be passed over here. Naturally the theory must in any case prove crude and unsatisfactory in certain details. But the mediation of images in vision is sufficiently comparable to the mediation of light waves in the modern account to give the related epistemological thesis a live philosophical interest. This will be pursued in the next section. For **A 12**, see also **18** below.

EPISTEMOLOGY

16 The truth of all impressions

A Lucretius 4.469–521

(1) Now, if someone thinks that nothing is known, one thing he doesn't know is whether *that* can be known, since he admits to knowing nothing. I shall therefore not bother to argue my case against this man who has himself stood with his own head in his footprints. (2) And anyway, even allowing that he knows this, I'll still ask him: given that he has never before seen anything true in the world, from where does he get his knowledge of what knowing and not knowing are? What created his preconception of true and false? And what proved to him that doubtful differs from certain? (3) You will find that the preconception of true has its origin in the senses, and that the senses cannot be refuted. (4) For something of greater reliability must be found, something possessing the intrinsic power to convict falsehoods with truths. Well, what should be considered to have greater reliability than the senses? (5) Will reason have the power to contradict them, if it is itself the product of false sensation? For reason is in its entirety the product of the senses, so that if the senses

are not true all reason becomes false as well. (6) Or will the ears have the power to confute the eyes, and touch to confute the ears? Or again, will this sense of touch be denounced by the mouth's taste, confuted by the nose, or convicted by the eyes? That is not, in my view, the way things are. For each has its own separate capacity and its own power, thus making it necessary that sensing what is soft, cold or hot be a separate operation from sensing the various colours of things and seeing whatever properties regularly accompany colours. Likewise the mouth's taste has a separate power, the recognition of smells is separate, and separate again that of sounds. It necessarily follows that the senses cannot convict each other. (7) Nor, again, will they be able to confute themselves, since all will always have to be considered of equal reliability. (8) Hence whatever impression the senses get at any time is true. (9) Even if reason fails to explain why things which proved square when close up seem round at a distance, it is nevertheless better, when one's reason proves inadequate, to give wrong explanations of the respective shapes, than to let the self-evident slip from one's grasp and thus to violate the primary guarantee and shake the entire foundations on which life and survival rest. (10) For not only would all reason cave in, but life itself would instantly collapse, if you lost the confidence to trust your senses, and to avoid precipices and other such hazards while aiming towards things of the opposite kind. (11) Hence you will find that the entire battalion of words which has been marshalled and armed against the senses is futile. (12) Lastly, just as in a building, if the yardstick is defective at the outset, if the set square is misleading for lack of straight edges, and if the level has the slightest wobble anywhere in it, the inevitable result is that the whole house is made wrongly – crooked, distorted, bulging backwards and forwards, misproportioned – so much so that some parts seem already determined to cave in, and do cave in, all betrayed by false initial criteria, so too you will find that any account of the world must be distorted and false if it is based upon the falsity of the senses.

B Diogenes Laertius 10.31–2

(1) All sensation, he [Epicurus] says, is irrational and does not accommodate memory. (2) For neither is it moved by itself, nor when moved by something else is it able to add or subtract anything. (3) Nor does there exist that which can refute sensations: (4) neither can like sense refute like, because of their equal validity; (5) nor unlike unlike, since they are not discriminatory of the same things; (6) nor can reason, since all reason depends on the senses; (7) nor can one individual sensation refute another, since they all command our attention. (8) And also the fact of sensory recognitions confirms the truth of sensations. (9) And our seeing and hearing are facts, just as having a pain is. (10) Hence sign-inferences about the non-evident should be made from things evident.

(11) [= **15F**] (12) The figments of madmen and dreaming are true. For they cause movement, whereas the non-existent does not move anything.

C Anonymous Epicurean treatise on the senses (Herculaneum Papyrus 19/698), cols. 17, 18, 22, 23, 25, 26, fr. 21

(1) We hold that vision perceives visibles and touch tangibles, that the one is of colour, the other of body, and that the one never interferes in the other's sphere of discrimination. For if it were the case that vision perceived the size and shape of body, it would much sooner perceive body itself... (2) <To see shape is only to perceive the colour's> outline, and often not even that. If, then, visible shape is nothing but the external positioning of the colours, and visible size nothing but the positioning of the majority of the colours in relation to what lies outside, it is perhaps possible for that whose function is to register colours themselves to perceive the external positioning of the colours... (3) So it is by recourse to analogy that shape and size are spheres of discrimination common to these senses: as the shape and size of the colour are to the colour, so the shape and size of the body are to the body: and as the colour is to visual perception, so the body is to perception by touch... (4) Apart from the very broad and general respects discussed above we do not hold that there is, in the direct way, a common sphere of discrimination. In the indirect way, the one which exhibits such generality that it could easily be called analogy, we could say that shape is their common sphere of discrimination . . . (5) Let us then add a reminder of what peculiar characteristic each of the senses exhibits, apart from the sensory recognition of their objects of discrimination. Well, the most peculiar characteristic of vision as compared to the other senses, apart from the discrimination of colours and the things related to them, is the perception of shape at a distance, together with sensory recognition of the interval between itself and them. . . . (6) Touch, as far as its peculiar function is concerned, has [as its most peculiar characteristic] that of registering no quality at all. As far as concerns its common function of registering the qualitative states of the flesh – a concomitant property of the other senses too – it has as its most peculiar characteristic that of registering different kinds of qualities: for as well as discriminating hard and soft, it perceives both hot and cold, both within itself and adjacent to itself . . . (7) Although vision does not discriminate solidity, some people deceive themselves through thinking that it does. For they suppose that when we see rocks vision through its simple application conveys their solidity.

D Epicurus, *Key doctrines* 23

If you fight against all sensations, you will not have a standard against which to judge even those of them you say are mistaken.

E Sextus Empiricus, *Against the professors* 7.206–10 (Usener 247, part)

[Summarizing Epicurus] (1) Some people are deceived by the difference among impressions seeming to reach us from the same sense-object, for example a visible object, such that the object appears to be of a different colour or shape, or altered in some other way. For they have supposed that, when impressions differ and conflict in this way, one of them must be true and the opposing one false. This is simple-minded, and characteristic of those who are blind to the real nature of things. (2) For it is not the whole solid body that is seen – to take the example of visible things – but the colour of the solid body. And of colour, some is right on the solid body, as in the case of things seen from close up or from a moderate distance, but some is outside the solid body and is objectively located in the space adjacent to it, as in the case of things seen from a great distance. This colour is altered in the intervening space, and takes on a peculiar shape. But the impression which it imparts corresponds to what is its own true objective state. (3) Thus just as what we actually hear is not the sound inside the beaten gong, or inside the mouth of the man shouting, but the sound which is reaching our sense, and just as no one says that the man who hears a faint sound from a distance is mishearing just because on approaching he registers it as louder, (4) so too I would not say that the vision is deceived just because from a great distance it sees the tower as small and round but from near-to as larger and square. Rather I would say that it is telling the truth. Because when the sense-object appears to it small and of that shape it really is small and of that shape, the edges of the images getting eroded as a result of their travel through the air. And when it appears big and of another shape instead, it likewise is big and of another shape instead. But the two are already different from each other: for it is left for distorted opinion to suppose that the object of impression seen from near and the one seen from far off are one and the same. (5) The peculiar function of sensation is to apprehend only that which is present to it and moves it, such as colour, not to make the distinction that the object here is a different one from the object there. (6) Hence for this reason all impressions are true. Opinions, on the other hand, are not all true but admit of some difference. Some of them are true, some false, since they are judgements which we make on the basis of our impressions, and we judge some things correctly, but some incorrectly, either by adding and appending something to our impressions or by subtracting something from them, and in general falsifying irrational sensation.

F Sextus Empiricus, *Against the professors* 8.63 (Usener 253, part)

(1) Epicurus used to say that all sensibles are true, and that every impression is the product of something existent and like the thing which

moves the sense; (2) and that those who say that some impressions are true but others false are wrong, because they cannot distinguish opinion from self-evidence. (3) At any rate, in the case of Orestes, when he seemed to see the Furies, his sensation, being moved by the images, was true, in that the images objectively existed; but his mind, in thinking that the Furies were solid bodies, held a false opinion.

G Lucretius 4.353–63

(1) When we see from far off the square towers of a city, the reason why they often seem round is that any corner is seen as blunted from a distance, or rather is not seen at all, its impact fading away and failing to complete the passage to our eyes, because during the images' travel through a large expanse of air the corner is forced to become blunt by the air's repeated buffetings. Thus, when all the corners simultaneously escape our sensation, it becomes as if the stone structures are being smoothed on a lathe. (2) They are not, however, like things genuinely round seen close-to, but seem to resemble them a little in a shadowy sort of way.

H Lucretius 4.379–86

Nor in this [shadow illusions] do we admit that the eyes are in any way deceived. For their function is to see where light and shade are. But whether or not it is the same light, and whether the shadow that was here is the same one as is passing over there, or whether rather it happens in the way we said a moment ago, this falls to the mind's reason to discern. The eyes cannot discover the nature of things. So do not trump up this charge against the eyes, for a fault which belongs to the mind.

I Plutarch, *Against Colotes* 1109C–E (Usener 250, part)

As for the famous 'matching-sizes' and 'consonances' of the passages belonging to the sense organs, and 'multiple-mixtures' of the seeds which they [the Epicureans] say are distributed through all flavours, smells and colours and move different sensations of quality in different people, do these not drive things together right into the 'no more this than that' class, on their view? For to reassure those who think that sensation is deceived because they see its users affected in opposite ways by the same things, they teach the doctrine that since all things are jumbled and mixed up together, and some things are of a nature to fit into some things, others into others, it is not the same quality that is being brought into contact and apprehended, nor does the object move everyone in the same way with all its parts; rather, all individuals encounter only the things of a size to match their own sense, and therefore are wrong to dispute about whether the thing is good or bad or white or non-white in the belief that by confuting each other's sensations they are confirming their own. One should not resist a single sensation, for they all make contact with something, each of them taking from the multiple mixture, as from a well, whatever is fitting and appropriate to itself. And when we are making contact with parts we should make no assertions about the whole. Nor should we think that everyone is affected in the same way, since some are affected by one quality and power, some by another.

☐ Epicurus seems to envisage three possibilities: (a) all sensations are false; (b) some sensations are true and some are false; (c) all sensations are true. His dual task is to establish (c) by eliminating (a) and (b), and to explain precisely how (c) can be the case. For the latter purpose he makes use of his physical analysis of sensation (see **15**). For the former, with which we start, he could not use this analysis without circularity, since the physical analysis itself has to assume the accuracy of sense-perception among its premises. His method, therefore, is to show (a) to be inherently self-defeating, and (b) to be conceptually indefensible.

Thesis (a), that all sensations are false, is treated as tantamount to scepticism in **A**. Democritus' doubts about the validity of sense-perception had been developed into a full-scale scepticism by his fourth-century followers, such as Metrodorus of Chios and Anaxarchus (see **1D**), and the reversal of this trend in atomist philosophy is one of Epicurus' principal goals (see also **7**, **12**, and **20**; Pyrrhonian scepticism, which denies both truth and falsity to sensations, **1F 4**, is perhaps not directly addressed in the surviving arguments). Scepticism is self-refuting according to **A 1**, whose description of the sceptic's contortions is a picturesque rendering of Epicurus' technical term for self-refutation, *perikatōtropē*, literally 'turning around and down' (cf. **20C 5**). Scepticism is treated, not exactly as a self-contradictory thesis, but as one to which no one could consistently *commit* himself (cf. Aristotle, *Metaphysics* III.5). Secondly (**A 2**), even to assert his thesis coherently the sceptic inevitably employs a distinction between 'know' and 'not know', and hence between 'true' and 'false' and between 'certain' and 'doubtful', since 'true' and 'certain' must feature in any definition of 'know'. Yet the sceptic cannot admit to knowing these distinctions. Third (**A 4, D**), any outright dismissal of the senses must appeal to some superior criterion of truth; but there is no such criterion independent of the senses — not even reason, which is itself a product of the senses (**A 5, B 6**). This last claim is not explicitly defended, but probably reason was assumed to be constituted from universal conceptions, themselves the product of repeated sensory experience (see **17E** for these 'preconceptions', and compare the Stoic account, **39E**). Fourth – a standard anti-sceptic argument (cf. **40N**) – the sceptical life is unlivable in practice (**A 10–11**; **69A 6**).

This rejection of (a) still leaves intact the widely-held thesis (b) that *some* sensations are false. But that would only be a defensible position if some criterion were offered for distinguishing the true from the false impressions, and we have already seen that there is no such criterion other than the senses (**A 4, D**). Can sensation refute sensation?

First, if two impressions of a single sense (whether simultaneous impressions of two perceivers or successive impressions of one observer does not matter) disagree, they are both of 'equal validity' and we have no ground for choosing between them (**A 7, B 4**). As it stands, this is merely a formal pose adapted from the sceptic's regular weaponry (cf. **72E**). The sceptic expects the conclusion to be that neither should be accepted as true. But Epicurus, having refuted the sceptical thesis (a), secures instead the conclusion that both must be accepted as true. How this can be so we will not learn until later.

Second, it may be suggested that one sense provides the evidence to refute another (**A 6, B 5**; cf. **72D**), e.g. that the sense of touch reveals the falsity of a visual impression of an oar in water as bent. Here the answer is that strictly the five senses are incommensurable, since each reports a different type of object. Vision discriminates colour, smell odours, hearing sounds, taste flavours. The position for touch is more complex. Strictly its peculiar object is body *per se* as distinct from any of body's qualities (**C 1** and **6**; the need for this restriction can be deduced from **5B 5–7**, where the tangible-intangible antithesis is used to prove the exhaustiveness of the body–void dichotomy). It does, of course, discriminate qualities like hardness and heat in external objects, but this is more directly analysed (**C 6**) as the discrimination of changes in the qualitative state of the perceiver's own flesh. Now Hellenistic usage speaks of 'internal touch' as the 'common' sensory process by which the agent becomes aware of changes within himself, including those incidental to the operations of his individual senses, and the Epicurean view seems to be that it is only by exploiting this function that touch gains access to external qualities. Even though this technically subsumes the apprehension of qualities under a common, not a peculiar, function of touch, touch is unique in registering 'different kinds' of qualities – perhaps different from its own special object (body), or, more simply, different from each other. This is apparently held to make it legitimate, with qualification, to speak of texture and temperature as peculiar objects of touch (**A 6, C 6**).

The list of the senses' peculiar objects can be extended – cf. **C 5**. But are there *no* common objects, with regard to which one sense could refute another? Shape, for example? Even here the data of touch and vision are strictly incommensurable: **C 1–4**. Touch discriminates body, and hence, secondarily, the shape of body. Vision discriminates colour, and hence, secondarily, the shape of colour, or alternatively 'shape at a distance' (**C 5**). Thus the convention that shape is a common object of touch and vision amounts to no more than an analogy between two quite distinct sensory functions and their objects (**C 3–4**). So too in general, provided one does not expect any individual sense to exceed its actual cognitive capacity (cf. **C 7, E 2**), no conflict between sense-impressions will arise.

The five senses, then, cannot formally contradict each other. It follows that they cannot confirm each other's data either. Yet Epicurus is not wrong or inconsistent to allow some measure of mutual support between, say, touch and vision, as his arguments at **15A 11** and **15B** seemed to require (see commentary ad loc.). For a regular pattern of correlation between tangible shape and visible shape is certainly most *easily* explained by a theory which makes both derivative from the object's actual shape. (It is in that light that **15A 9** must be read.)

By the elimination of (a) and (b), then, (c) is established: all sensations are true.

An alternative formulation often reported is that all 'impressions' are true. This broader term differs in including non-sensory impressions, such as those of imagination and dreaming. Such impressions do indeed come out 'true', as we shall see, although this may sometimes be only trivially so from the point of view of knowledge of the external world. Hence the narrower formula, which alone of the two is capable of providing 'criteria' of truth (see **17**), is generally regarded as the more interesting one.

What does the slogan amount to? The Greek word for 'true' can also mean 'real'. But ideally the thesis should be interpreted in a stronger sense than 'all sensations are real events', if it is to provide any substantial alternative to scepticism: explanations of the type offered by **B 9** and **12** will at best give us one strand of the full theory. Nor, on the other hand, can the truth referred to exactly be that appropriate to propositions, for unlike the Stoics (see **39**) Epicurus is insistent that sensations are entirely irrational events, involving no interpretation at all (**B 1**, **E 5–6**, cf. **H**). The most promising lead is provided by **F 1**: the sense-impression is true because it always (1) is caused by something external, and (2) accurately depicts that external thing. The external thing will not, at least in the case of sight, be the perceived solid object itself, but the 'images' which arrive from it (see **15**), in whatever state they may be in at the moment of arrival at the eye. This need not, as may at first appear, jeopardize the Epicurean view that what we actually see is normally the external object, not the images from it (see on **15**). The point is best pursued by the analogy of a photograph. A photograph is properly regarded as a photograph of an external object, not of light waves, yet is 'true' not in so far as it accurately depicts the shape and colour of the object itself – it may well not do, e.g. because of perspective, and the use of a black and white film – but in so far as (to simplify somewhat) it accurately reports the pattern of light waves arriving at the lens, and thus provides *bona fide* evidence about the external object reflecting the light. Similarly a visual impression is properly regarded as an impression of an external object, not of the mediating images, yet is 'true' not because it accurately depicts the shape and colour of the object itself – it may well not do, e.g. because of the distortion undergone by the images in transit (**C 3–5**, **E 2–4**, **G**; **15A 4**), and the insensitivity of sense-organs to some grades of particle in them (**I**) – but because it accurately reports the state of the images entering the eye, and thus provides *bona fide* evidence about the external object emitting the images. Again, we do not feel any conflict between a photograph of Socrates looking small and indistinct and one of Socrates looking large and clear. We expect them to differ, because their objects are different, one being of Socrates distant, the other of Socrates near-by. So too, since vision's province is to report not actual bodily shape but 'shape at a distance' (**C 5**), we feel no conflict between the far-off and close-up views of the same square tower (**E 4**, **G**): naturally we expect a far-off tower to look different from a near-by tower, since they constitute different objects of sensation (**E 4**). We can legitimately maintain this expectation whether or not our chosen physical explanation of the optical difference is the correct one: what matters is that it has *some* physical basis (**A 9**). And in general, what makes the camera unable to lie, and likewise the eye's reports true, is precisely their purely mechanical character, their inability to embroider or interpret (**B** 1, **E** 5–6, **H**). We trust the camera so long as we believe it to be accurately reporting patterns of light waves reaching it from outside. We would distrust it if it were shown (a) to distort them, (b) to add to them, (c) to delete parts of them, or (d) to manufacture pictures by a purely internal process. Analogously, we should trust our vision so long as it is not shown (a) to distort the images while absorbing them, (b) to add to them, (c) to subtract from them, or (d) to be 'self-moved', without the mediation of images: see especially **B** 2. All error lies in the interpretation of these sense-impressions by opinion (**E** 6, **F**, **H**; **15A** 10–12, **D** 9), and it is emphasized that opinion, although causally dependent on the irrational and mechanical process of sensation, is itself a rational and non-mechanical process (**15A** 12: it is in the 'self', and has 'differentiation' – for these difficult but important notions see **20B** 5 with commentary).

The theory seems to provide a promising answer to the standard sceptical appeals to optical illusion (cf. **72E–F**). The visual impression of an oar in the water as bent is perfectly true – not as an impression of the oar's intrinsic bodily shape, on which vision is not qualified to pronounce, but, we might say, as an impression of the shape of its colour through a mixed medium of water and air. Apparently, though, the theory has to cope with cases of outright delusion too (**F**, cf. **B** 12). Can it assign truth to these without becoming entirely trivial? The example in **F** 3 is Orestes' delusion that he was seeing the Furies, fearsome women with snakes for hair. Presumably he encountered some freak images of this kind, produced by the chance cohesion of separate images from women and snakes (**15D** 2–3), and in his disturbed condition failed to recognize them as mere fleeting impressions without a solid body for their source (cf. **15D** 6 on similar failures of judgement in dreams). According to Epicurus, his sensation was true because the images existed, but his judgement that there were solid Furies was mistaken. In partial support of the analysis, we could compare our vision of a rainbow, which we are quite prepared to call 'true' – because it is an accurate report of the light waves reaching us. We would only call it deceptive if it were coupled with the mistaken judgement that the rainbow was a solid body. And then the fault would strictly lie in the judgement.

With the provinces of the senses as narrowly circumscribed as we have seen they are, how informative can they be about the nature of external objects? Clearly they are not an infallible guide. But, like photographs, sense-impressions do provide genuine evidence, which properly handled can lead to true judgements about external reality. We need never mistake the shape of a distant square tower, (a) because vision discriminates the distance of its objects (**C** 5) and thus warns us not to judge their shape prematurely; (b) because there is a difference between the apparent roundness of the distant square tower and the apparent roundness of the near-by round tower (**G** 2); and (c) because we can, and should, wait for a close-up view (cf. **18A** 2), in which distortion of the images is minimized and the data of vision show a regular and encouraging correlation to those of touch. Sound judgement in the assessment of sensory data is crucial. Epicurus' defence of the truth of sensations implies a vindication, against Democritus' denial, of the reality of sensible properties. For the theoretical consequences of this, see especially **7** and **20**.

17 The criteria of truth

A Diogenes Laertius 10.31

(1) Thus Epicurus, in the *Kanōn* ('Yardstick'), says that sensations, preconceptions and feelings are the criteria of truth. (2) The Epicureans add the 'focusings of thought into an impression'.

B Epicurus, *Key doctrines* 24

(1) If you are going to reject any sensation absolutely, and not distinguish opinions reliant on evidence yet awaited from what is already present through sensation, through feelings, and through every focusing of thought into an impression, you will confound all your other sensations with empty opinion and consequently reject the criterion in its entirety. (2) And if you are going to treat as established both all the evidence yet awaited in your conjectural conceptions, and that which has failed to <earn > attestation, you will not exclude falsehood, so that you will have removed all debate and all discrimination between correct and incorrect.

C Epicurus, *Letter to Herodotus* 37–8

(1) First, then, Herodotus, we must grasp the things which underlie words, so that we may have them as a reference point against which to judge matters of opinion, inquiry and puzzlement, and not have everything undiscriminated for ourselves as we attempt infinite chains of proofs, or have words which are empty. For the primary concept corresponding to each word must be seen and need no additional proof, if we are going to have a reference point for matters of inquiry, puzzlement and opinion. (2) Second, we should observe everything in the light of our sensations, and in general in the light of our present focusings whether of thought or of any of our discriminatory faculties, and likewise also in the light of the feelings which exist in us, in order to have a basis for sign-inferences about evidence yet awaited and about the non-evident.

D Epicurus, *Letter to Herodotus* 82

So we should pay heed to those feelings which are present in us, and to our sensations – universal sensations for universal matters, particular ones for particular matters – and to all self-evidence which is present by virtue of each of the discriminatory faculties.

E Diogenes Laertius 10.33

(1) Preconception, they [the Epicureans] say, is as it were a perception, or correct opinion, or conception, or universal 'stored notion' (i.e.

memory), of that which has frequently become evident externally: e.g. 'Such and such a kind of thing is a man.' (2) For as soon as the word 'man' is uttered, immediately its delineation also comes to mind by means of preconception, since the senses give the lead. (3) Thus what primarily underlies each name is something self-evident. (4) And what we inquire about we would not have inquired about if we had not had prior knowledge of it. For example: 'Is what's standing over there a horse or a cow?' For one must at some time have come to know the form of a horse and that of a cow by means of preconception. (5) Nor would we have named something if we had not previously learnt its delineation by means of preconception. (6) Thus preconceptions are self-evident. (7) And opinion depends on something prior and self-evident, which is our point of reference when we say, e.g., 'How do we know if this is a man?'

☐ Epicurus' term for epistemology is Canonic, and his handbook on the subject was called the *Kanōn* (**A** 1). A *kanōn* was a yardstick or ruler, used for determining straightness or for measurement, and the term throws light on another used almost interchangeably with it in Hellenistic epistemology, 'criterion' (**A** 1, **B** 1; **15A** 13, **16A**; the Greek word *kritērion* is also used by Epicurus at **C** 2, **D** and **15A** 11 for a cognitive 'discriminatory faculty', but this is a slightly different sense). In Epicurus' wake it becomes virtually obligatory for every doctrinaire Hellenistic philosopher to name one or more 'criteria of truth' (cf. **40**) – more literally 'means of discrimination', and hence yardsticks or ultimate arbiters, of truth, themselves not subject to any higher authority; cf. **16A** 4, 'something possessing the intrinsic power to convict falsehoods with truths'. Thus it is often said of such a criterion that it is 'self-evident' (cf. **D**, **E** 3, 7; **15A** 13). An opinion is judged true or false by measuring it up against one or more criteria.

Sensations are the first of Epicurus' three criteria (**A** 1, **B** 1, **D**; cf. **7B** 5; **14A** 1; **15A** 9). **D** divides them into 'universal' and 'particular'. Universal sensations will be, not universal judgements based on sensation, since opinion being fallible (see **16**) is ineligible as a criterion, but collections of similar sensations filed away in the memory as firm criteria for inductive judgements. Thus the 'universal sensation' which in **5B** 2 provides the evidence that bodies exist is identical with the sensation which in **5A** 2 bears witness 'universally', literally 'in all cases', to the existence of body. Precisely how empirical and scientific generalizations are tested against this criterion of universal sensation will be considered in **18**.

The testing of particular opinions against particular sensations is plausibly illustrated by the example used in **18A** 2. You provisionally judge a distant figure to be Plato. The judgement will include the expectation that seen close up he will be of such and such an appearance. When the figure is close enough, that expectation is tested against the features of the new impression and the judgement accepted or rejected accordingly. Error, if it occurs, will lie in the opinion which you form, not in the sense-impression.

'Preconception' (*prolēpsis*), a key term in Hellenistic epistemology (cf. **40**) whose introduction is reliably attributed to Epicurus, provides the second criterion. **E** is the principal evidence on it, but it is generally recognized to be the topic of **C 1** too (cf. especially **E 3**); the avoidance of the term itself in **C** will merely reflect Epicurus' concern in the opening moves of his physical exposition to appeal to the most general possible considerations, leaving the more heavily theory-laden terms to emerge in due course. A preconception is a generic notion of any type of object of experience, the concept naturally evoked by the name of that thing, as explained in **E 1–2**. Normally it will be synthesized out of repeated experiences of something external (**E 1**). Examples are body (**12E 2**); man (**13F 4**); utility (**13E 4, 19B4**, and cf. **22B 2**); truth (**16A 2–3**); and all properties of bodies (**7B 6**). It may, however, include data of introspection – our own responsibility, or agency (**20C 4, 8**), and the desirability of pleasure (**21A 4**) – and perhaps even, in a secondary way, empirically derived conceptions of the microscopic (**11B 7**).

The preconception of god is hard to allocate between these categories (see **23B–E**, and commentary). Theology nevertheless provides a useful illustration of the function of preconception as a criterion in Hellenistic debate. Theories about the gods are expected to measure up to our preconception of god. Stoics and others will claim that we preconceive god as provident (**54K**). But the Epicureans deny that this is a real preconception (**23B**) on the grounds (a) that it conflicts with a more secure or fundamental preconception, that of god as blessed (cf. **23C**); and (b) that the false quasi-preconception can be explained away as the product of faulty inference (**23A 3–6**).

While its empirical or natural origin must provide the ultimate justification for using preconception as a criterion of truth, the more general ground offered in **C 1** is its indispensability as a starting-point in philosophy. Unless something is taken as given, our inquiries will be drawn into a vicious regress of proofs. The danger of such a regress is an evident and familiar one (cf. Aristotle, *Posterior Analytics* 1.3), but why are preconceptions, in their guise of the meanings underlying words, singled out as the criterion capable of halting it? It is as a matter of fact, from Epicurus on, a philosophical commonplace that preconceptions are what make inquiry possible (cf. **40T**), and to see why we must compare **E 4** with Plato's conception of dialectic as developed in the *Meno* and *Phaedo*. Starting from Meno's celebrated paradox that you could not inquire about something unless you *already* knew what it was, Plato evolved the view that when we inquire into something we do in a way already know what it is, thanks to our soul's half-forgotten pre-natal experience – more specifically (in the *Phaedo*) thanks to its pre-natal acquaintance with the transcendent Form of the thing concerned. **E 4** strongly suggests that Epicurus saw his 'preconception' as an alternative response to Meno's paradox, providing the sort of prior acquaintance (hence 'pre-') required as a basis of inquiry, but without such unacceptable by-products as separated universals and pre-natal existence (for another way in which preconceptions serve to replace Platonic Forms, cf. **13F 4**). In consequence, its importance as a criterion lies especially in its guarantee that we know what the things we are discussing actually are. Our conjectures about them can be directly tested against that knowledge, and we avoid endless and inconclusive arguments about mere 'empty words' (cf. also **19I–J; 20C 8**).

Feelings are the third criterion of truth (**A 1, B 1, C 2, D**). The Greek word *pathos* varies between objective 'affection' – being acted upon or affected – and subjective 'feeling'. For example the compound *sympatheia*, translated 'co-affection' at **14A 1, 4** (cf. **14B 3**), and **15A 5, 8**, and 'interaction' in contexts like **45C**, tends to the former use but with some hint of the latter. In the present context 'feeling' seems the more appropriate translation. The primary 'feelings' are reported to be pleasure and pain (preamble to **16E** in vol. 2; cf. **7C 5**), which constitute the sole Epicurean *ethical* criterion, the standard for all choice and avoidance (**21B 2**; Diogenes Laertius 10.34; Cicero, *On ends* 1.22–3). But although later Scepticism makes a sharp distinction between criteria of truth, which it rejects, and criteria for action, which it in a sense accepts, it is doubtful whether Epicurus separated the two. He would, at least, take it that beliefs about the moral value of things can have as much objective truth as beliefs about their physical nature (cf. **7D; 16I**; p. 147), and that feelings are the arbiters of that truth. It is in any case clear that feelings play a critical role in physics too (**C 2** and **D** come from Epicurus' physical treatise), namely as our source of introspective data for ascertaining the nature of the soul (**14A 1–2**, cf. **14B**). It may well be that all such feelings would be subsumed under the headings 'pleasure' and 'pain' (cf. **7C 5**).

According to **A 2** Epicurus' followers added a fourth criterion to the list, the focusing of thought into an impression. Epicurus treats any deliberate mental act as 'focusing' (*epibolē*), but the species of focusing picked out here is that which involves a sense-like mental impression – that is, the process explained at **15D 7–8** of imagining something external by apprehending its 'image'. That Epicurus himself assigned cognitive importance to this process is clear from **B 1, C 2**, and **D** (where 'faculties' includes thought, cf. **15A 11**), and we know too that such impressions technically come out 'true' on his theory (see **16**). Indeed, the need to *think* accurately about empirical data is obvious enough, especially in 'universal sensation', but perhaps also in determining what is and what is not in principle imaginable, a standard to which Epicurus often appeals (cf. **5A 4; 7B 5; 10C 1; 14A 6–7, G**).

If the Epicureans thought that such 'focusing' was one of Epicurus' criteria of truth, they had some evidence in his writings to encourage the belief. But that Epicurus himself refrained from so calling it is not surprising: it would have been odd to suggest that we can test a theory about external objects *merely* by closing our eyes and imagining them. The imaginative process must be strictly ancillary to the criterion of direct sensory acquaintance. (For a possible exception in the special case of the gods, see **23**, especially pp. 145–7.)

18 Scientific methodology

A Sextus Empiricus, *Against the professors* 211–16 (Usener 247, part)

(1) Of opinions, then, according to Epicurus, some are true, some false.

True are those attested and those uncontested by self-evidence; false are those contested and those unattested by self-evidence. (2) Attestation is perception through a self-evident impression of the fact that the object of opinion is such as it was believed to be. For example, if Plato is approaching from far off, I form the conjectural opinion, owing to the distance, that it is Plato. But when he has come close, there is further testimony that he is Plato, now that the gap is reduced, and it is attested by the self-evidence itself. (3) Non-contestation is the following from that which is evident of the non-evident thing posited and believed. For example, Epicurus, in saying that there is void, which is non-evident, confirms this through the self-evident fact of motion. For if void does not exist, there ought not to be motion either, since the moving body would lack a place to pass into as a result of everything's being full and solid. Therefore the non-evident thing believed is uncontested by that which is evident, since there is motion. (4) Contestation, on the other hand, is something which conflicts with non-contestation. For it is the elimination of that which is evident by the positing of the non-evident thing. For example, the Stoic says that void does not exist, judging something non-evident; but once this is posited about it, that which is evident, namely motion, ought to be co-eliminated with it. For if void does not exist, necessarily motion does not occur either, according to the method already demonstrated. (5) Likewise, too, non-attestation is opposed to attestation, being confrontation through self-evidence of the fact that the object of opinion is not such as it was believed to be. For example, if someone is approaching from far off, we conjecture, owing to the distance, that he is Plato. But when the gap is reduced, we recognize through self-evidence that it is not Plato. That is what non-attestation is like: the thing believed was not attested by the evident. (6) Hence attestation and non-contestation are the criterion of something's being true, while non-attestation and contestation are the criterion of its being false. And self-evidence is the foundation and basis of everything.

B Diogenes Laertius 10.34

(1) Opinion they also call 'supposition', and they say that it is true and false. If it is attested or uncontested, it is true; if it is unattested or contested, it comes out false. (2) Hence their introduction of 'that which is awaited' — for example, waiting and getting near the tower and learning how it appears from near by.

C Epicurus, *Letter to Pythocles* 85–8

(1) First, we should not think that any other end is served by knowledge of celestial events, whether they be discussed in a context or in isolation, than freedom from disturbance and firm confidence, just as in the other

areas of discourse. (2) And neither should we force through what is impossible, nor should we in all areas keep our study similar either to discourses on the conduct of life or to those belonging to the solution of the other problems of physics, for example that the totality of things is body and intangible substance, or that there are atomic elements, and all the theses of this kind which are uniquely consistent with things evident. In the case of celestial events this is not the case: both the causes of their coming to be and the accounts of their essence are multiple. (3) For physics should not be studied by means of empty judgements and arbitrary fiat, but in the way that things evident require. What our life needs is not private theorizing and empty opinion, but an untroubled existence. (4) Now in respect of all things which have a multiplicity of explanations consistent with things evident, complete freedom from trepidation results when someone in the proper way lets stand whatever is plausibly suggested about them. But when someone allows one explanation while rejecting another equally consistent with what is evident, he is clearly abandoning natural philosophy altogether and descending into myth. (5) Signs relating to events in the celestial region are provided by certain of the things familiar and evident – things whose mode of existence is open to view – and not by things evident in the celestial region. For these latter are capable of coming to be in multiple ways. (6) We must, nevertheless, observe our impression of each one; and we must distinguish the events which are connected with it, events whose happening in multiple ways is uncontested by familiar events.

D Lucretius 5.509–33

(1) Let us now sing what are the causes of the heavenly bodies' motions. (2) First, if the great sphere of the sky rotates, we must say that the air exerts pressure on its pole at each end, and holds it imprisoned from both sides; and that then other air flows above and travels in the direction in which the shining stars of the fixed heavens rotate; (3) or else other air flows below, and pushes the sphere up in the opposite direction, just as we see rivers turn water-wheels and their scoops. (4) Another possibility is that the sky as a whole is stationary while the bright heavenly bodies move: (5) whether because fast aether currents, trapped within the world, go round seeking an outlet and spin fires all through the nocturnal zone of the sky; (6) or because air flowing from somewhere else, outside the world, drives the fires to rotate; (7) or because they themselves have the power to edge forward in the direction in which their food entices them as they travel, pasturing their fiery bodies all through the sky. (8) For it is hard to state with certainty which of these is the case in our world. But what I am expounding is what is possible, and happens in the various worlds variously formed throughout the universe, and my procedure is

to set out a plurality of causes which are able to be those of the motions of the heavenly bodies throughout the universe. Of them, one must also be the cause which gives the heavenly bodies their power of motion in our world. But it is not the job of one who proceeds with caution to lay down which of them it is.

E Lucretius 6.703–11

There are also a number of things of which it is not enough to name one cause, but rather many causes, one of which will however be the actual one – just as, if you were yourself to see at a distance the dead body of a man, it would be appropriate to list all the causes of death, so as to include the specific cause of his death. For you would not be able to establish that he had died by the sword, from cold, from disease, or by poison; yet we know that it was *something* of this kind that happened to him. And likewise in many other matters we are in a position to say the same.

F Philodemus, *On signs* 11.32–12.31

(1) For granted that 'If the first, then the second' is true whenever 'If not the second, not the first either' is true, it does not therefore follow that only the Elimination Method is cogent. (2) For 'If not the second, not the first either' comes out true *sometimes* in as much as, when the second is hypothetically eliminated, by its very elimination the first is eliminated too – (3) as in 'If there is motion, there is void', since, when void is hypothetically eliminated, by its mere elimination motion will be eliminated too, so that such a case fits the Elimination type – (4) but sometimes not in this way but because of the very inconceivability of the first being, or being of this kind, but the second not being, or not being of this kind: (5) for instance, 'If Plato is a man, Socrates is a man too.' For given that this is true, 'If Socrates is not a man, Plato is not a man either' comes out true as well, not because by the elimination of Socrates Plato is co-eliminated, but because it is impossible to conceive of Socrates not being a man but Plato being a man. And that belongs to the Similarity Method.

G Philodemus, *On signs* 34.29–36.17

(1) Those who attack sign-inference by similarity do not notice the difference between the aforementioned [senses of 'in so far as'], and how we establish the 'in so far as' premise, such as, for instance, that man in so far as he is man is mortal. . . . (2) For we establish the necessary connexion of this with that from the very fact that it has been an observed concomitant of all the instances which we have encountered, especially as we have met a variety of animals belonging to the same type which while differing from each other in all other respects all share such-and-such

common characteristics. (3) Thus we say that man, in so far as and in that he is man, is mortal, because we have encountered a wide variety of men without ever finding any variation in this kind of accidental attribute, or anything that draws us towards the opposite view. (4) So this is the method on which the establishment of the premise rests, both for this issue and for the others in which we apply the 'in so far as' and 'in that' construction – the peculiar connexion being indicated by the fact that the one thing is the inseparable and necessary concomitant of the other. (5) The same is not true in the case of what is established merely by the elimination of a sign. But even in these cases, it is the fact that all the instances which we have encountered have this as their concomitant that does the job of confirmation. For it is from the fact that all familiar moving objects, while having other differences, have it in common that their motion is through empty spaces, that we conclude the same to be without exception true also in things non-evident. And our reason for contending that if there is not, or has not been, fire, smoke should be eliminated, is that smoke has been seen in all cases without exception to be a secretion from fire. (6) Another error which they make is in not noticing our procedure of establishing that no obstacle arises through things evident. For the existence of chance and of that which depends on us is not sufficient ground for accepting the minimal swerves of atoms: it is necessary to show in addition that nothing else self-evident conflicts with the thesis.

☐ Sensory experience is a guaranteed, or 'self-evident', standard against which the truth or falsity of an opinion is to be judged (**A 1**; cf. **17**). More explicitly, opinions about facts which fall potentially within our direct experience are said to be verified if 'attested' by things evident, falsified if 'unattested'; correspondingly, scientific theories about the non-evident are verified if 'uncontested' by things evident, falsified if 'contested'. These distinctions are nowhere stated with full precision, but seem to underlie **A** (cf. **B**; **15A 12**), and correspond to actual Epicurean practice (cf. **12A 1**; **15A 1–5**; **22B 2**).

The example of attestation in **A 2** looks straightforward: see further **17**, commentary. In **A 5**, on the other hand, one may wonder why direct observation that an opinion is false would receive the weak characterization of 'non-attestation'. Why is the opposite of attestation not positive contestation? A probable answer is that attestation and non-attestation were conceived primarily as scientific methods, and hence as means of testing empirical generalizations, e.g., as in **22B**, that such and such a type of behaviour is socially beneficial. In such cases non-attestation – failure to discover confirmatory instances – will normally be a sufficient ground for rejecting the hypothesis, and perhaps the only possible ground.

A may consequently be accused of a certain superficiality in its choice of example. It is generally regarded as our prime text on Epicurean methodology, but its credentials are in fact rather suspect. Sextus' source for it was almost certainly a first-century B.C. history of epistemology by Antiochus of Ascalon, some of whose other reports of earlier philosophers were alarmingly unhistorical. Indeed, we will argue at the end of this section that his account of non-contestation and contestation in **A 3–4** rests on a gross error. In the mean time his evidence will be treated with caution.

A 3 takes it that an opinion about the non-evident is 'uncontested' by something evident only when it *follows* from it. In the example chosen the evident thing is the fact of motion, while the non-evident thing said to follow from it is its *explanans*, the existence of void. But while Epicurus certainly took the latter to follow from the former (**5A 3**; **6A**), there is little reason to think that he regarded this as an example of mere 'non-contestation' by phenomena. That expression (*ouk antimarturēsis*, literally 'no counter-evidence') plainly implies nothing stronger than *consistency* with phenomena, and when Epicurus appeals to the principle the phenomena invoked are not, as in **A 3**, the *explanandum* itself, but *analogous* phenomena within our direct experience. This is repeatedly emphasized in his *Letter to Pythocles* on celestial events (cf. **C 5–6**): an explanation of a celestial phenomenon is acceptable if and only if comparable causal processes are observed within our direct experience (cf. **D 3**). Similarly, the immense fineness attributed to the 'images' which account for vision and imagination is justified as 'uncontested by anything evident' at **15A 3**, and the fuller arguments supplied by Lucretius (4.110–28) are of just the kind that this phraseology leads us to expect: for example, the analogy of barely visible insects, whose individual organs must be far below the threshold of perception. Clearly what provision of such analogies establishes primarily is that the scientific theory in question is possible. Yet somehow this test of non-contestation is supposed to establish *truth* as well: **A 1**, **B 1**; **15A 12**.

This surprising claim is substantiated in three ways. Note, first, that the hypothesis to be tested is selected not at random but for its explanatory value in a specific scientific inquiry: e.g. **G 6** (comparing **11H 4**; **20**); **12E 2–3**; **15A 5**. It may often turn out in such a context that of several possible explanatory hypotheses only one survives the test of consistency with phenomena. And fortunately the basic tenets of Epicurean atomism are held to fall into this class: **C 2**. Such theories, then, should be unequivocally accepted as true.

It may, secondly, be the case that some thesis proves for theoretical reasons to be the only one capable of being entertained in the first place. Even so, to be accepted as true it still requires non-contestation in the form of an analogy which can show it to be possible and perhaps provide a model for our understanding of it. Probable examples can be found at **9A 9**; **11B 7**; **12D 4**, **E 4**.

In a third kind of case, notably the explanation of celestial phenomena (but not solely: cf. **15A 4–5**), several alternative theses may prove to be both equally useful and equally consistent with phenomena within our direct experience: **C**. When this happens, it is proper to accept them *all* – and not just as possible, but also, in a way, as true. For in an infinite universe nothing intrinsically possible could fail to be realized somewhere: **D 8**. Sometimes, indeed, more than one may be operating concurrently in our own world. More often only one will obtain here, others in other worlds; but even then the only proper scientific procedure is to adopt all the explanations, without attempting an arbitrary choice between them: **C 4**, **D 8**, **E**. Thus the power of non-contestation to establish 'truth' is technically salvaged even in cases such as these.

Non-contestation, then, emerges as a principle of verification best understood within the context of Epicurean science. It characteristically exploits the analogy of directly observed facts and processes to confirm hypotheses formed in the course of constructing a comprehensive scientific theory. But whether all of the many analogies employed in Epicurean physical argument belong under one or other of the three types of non-contestation is debatable.

Later Epicureans under the leadership of Zeno of Sidon (*c.* 100 B.C.) continued discussion of these issues in opposition to recent Stoic theories of 'signs' (cf. **42G–H**), and one of them, Philodemus, wrote a work *On signs* whose surviving fragments preserve some of the exchanges. While accurately reporting the essentially confirmatory role of non-contestation (see **G 6**), these Epicureans for their own part had shifted their interest to analysis of the precise ways in which a hidden entity or fact can 'follow', or be inferable, from its phenomenal 'sign'. The Stoics of their day held that the only valid connexion of this kind was one of strict logical entailment (the regular Stoic term is 'cohesion' – see **35B**). Such connexions are certified by the Elimination Method (cf. **F 2–3**): q follows from p if and only if when q is 'eliminated' p is *thereby* 'co-eliminated'. The Epicureans also accept this as a valid inferential principle, but add a second, the Similarity Method. The difference is as follows. The Similarity Method grounds inferences of the form 'If (or 'since') x is F, y is F', where y's similarity to x is held to make it 'inconceivable' that y should lack an essential predicate of x (cf. **F 4–5**). Such similarity may be direct, as in the inductive inference to the mortality of all men from that of men within our experience (cf. **G 3**); or analogical, as in certain basic Epicurean derivations of properties of atoms from those of sensible bodies. The Elimination Method is reserved by the Epicureans for cases where no such similarity obtains, notably for inferences from a phenomenal explanandum to its hidden explanans, such as the argument from motion to void (cf. **F 2–3**, **G 5**, where the parallel 'smoke' example illustrates their tendency to conflate logical with empirical connexion). But although the latter type of inference formally goes through by the Elimination Method, they insist that this does not constitute in itself a true 'sign-inference', probably because it is incapable by itself of revealing anything. All the hard work of 'confirmation' is done in a logically prior stage by the Similarity Method, which infers from the exceptionless dependence of motion within our experience on empty space that motion is altogether impossible without empty space (**G 5**); the Elimination Method is then called in merely to make the formal and relatively trivial step which this sanctions from atomic motion, at the non-evident level, to truly empty space, i.e. void, at the non-evident level. The Stoics overvalue the deductive Elimination Method, it is alleged, because they fail to appreciate its complete dependence on empirical premises inductively established by the Similarity Method.

We are now in a position to diagnose the error of Antiochus, the probable source of **A 3**'s exegesis of Epicurean 'non-contestation'. Seeking illustration of the method, he has dipped into a contemporary Epicurean handbook, probably the *On signs* itself. Not finding the precise term in such relevant passages as **G 6**, he has mistakenly associated it instead with a current Epicurean preoccupation, the Elimination Method. Read out of context, passages like **F 2–3** will yield just the illustration given in **A 3**, that the existence of void follows from that of motion, because (as **A 4** explains) if void is 'eliminated' motion is thereby 'co-eliminated'. But the assumed equivalence of this principle to non-contestation, the implication that it is itself sufficient to 'confirm' the existence of void, and the anachronistic attribution of its terminology to Epicurus himself, all reveal the inadequacy of his report.

19 Language

A Epicurus, *Letter to Herodotus* 75–6

(1) We must take it that even nature was educated and constrained in many different ways by actual states of affairs, and that its lessons were later made more accurate, and augmented with new discoveries by reason – faster among some people, slower among others, and in some ages and eras, owing to <individual needs, by greater leaps>, in others by smaller leaps. (2) Thus names too did not originally come into being by coining, but men's own natures underwent feelings and received impressions which varied peculiarly from tribe to tribe, and each of the individual feelings and impressions caused them to exhale breath peculiarly, according also to the racial differences from place to place. (3) Later, particular coinings were made by consensus within the individual races, so as to make the designations less ambiguous and more concisely expressed. (4) Also, the men who shared knowledge introduced certain unseen entities, and brought words for them into usage. (5) <Hence some> men gave utterance under compulsion, and others chose words rationally, and it is thus, as far as the principal cause is concerned, that they achieved self-expression.

B Lucretius 5.1028–90 (following **22K**)

(1) It was nature that compelled the utterance of the various noises of the tongue, and usefulness that forged them into the names of things. (2) It was rather in the way that children's inarticulacy itself seems to impel them to use gestures, when it causes them to point out with a finger what things are present. For everyone can feel the extent to which he can use his powers. The calf angrily butts and charges with his incipient horns before they have even protruded from his forehead. Panther and lion cubs already fight with claws, paws and biting at an age when their teeth and claws have barely appeared. Also, we see all birds putting trust in their wings and seeking the fluttering aid of their feathers. (3) So to think that someone in those days assigned names to things, and that that is how men learnt their first words, is crazy. Why should he have been able to

indicate all things with sounds, and to utter the various noises of the tongue, yet others be supposed not to have had that ability at the same time? (4) Besides, if others had not already used sounds to each other, how did he get the preconception of their usefulness implanted in him? How did he get the initial capacity to know and see with his mind what he wanted to do? (5) Again, one person could not subdue many and compel them to want to learn the names of things. Nor is it easy to find a way of teaching and persuading a deaf audience of what needs to be done: they would utterly refuse to tolerate any further his drumming into their ears the unfamiliar sounds of his voice. (6) Lastly, why is it so surprising that the human race, with its powers of voice and tongue, should have indicated each thing with a different sound to correspond to a different sensation? After all, dumb animals, tame and wild alike, regularly emit different sounds when afraid, when in pain, and when happiness comes over them. You can appreciate this from plain facts. When the great flabby jaws of Molossian hounds start to snarl in anger, baring their hard teeth, their threatening noise when drawn back in rage is far different from when they fill the place with their barking. When, on the other hand, they try coaxingly to lick their pups with their tongue, or when they toss them with their paws and, powerful biters though they are, hold back their teeth and make play of nibbling them gently, they fondle them with a yelping noise quite different from when they whimper, cowering from a blow . . . (7) If, then, different sensations compel animals, dumb though they are, to emit different sounds, how much more likely it is that mortal men at that time were able to indicate different things with different sounds.

C Diogenes of Oenoanda 10.2.11–5.15

As for the words, I mean the nouns and verbs, of which the men who sprang from the earth made the first utterance, let us not adopt Hermes as our teacher, as some say he was: that is manifest nonsense. Nor should we believe those philosophers who say that it was by coining and teaching that names were assigned to things, in order that men might have signs to facilitate their communication with each other. For it is absurd, indeed absurder than any absurdity, not to mention impossible, that someone should all on his own have assembled all those multitudes – there were no rulers at that time, and certainly no letters, seeing that there were no words, since it was about these <that they were meeting, so that it was not> by edict that their assembly was brought about – and having assembled them, instructed them like a schoolteacher, holding a rod, and touching each thing have said 'Let this be called "stone", this "stick", this "man", or "dog" . . .'

D Epicurus, *On nature* XXVIII, 31.10.2–12

Supposing that in those days we thought and said something equivalent, in the terminology which we then employed, to saying that all human error is exclusively of the form that arises in relation to preconceptions and appearances because of the multifarious conventions of language . . . [text breaks off]

E Epicurus, *On nature* XXVIII,31.13.23–14.12

But perhaps this is not the moment to prolong the discussion by citing these cases? Quite so, Metrodorus. For I expect you could cite many cases, from your own past observations, of certain people taking words in various ridiculous senses, and indeed in any sense rather than their actual linguistic meanings. Whereas our own usage does not flout linguistic convention, nor do we alter names with regard to things evident.

F Anonymous commentary on Plato's *Theaetetus*, 22.39–47

Epicurus says that names are clearer than definitions, and that indeed it would be absurd if instead of saying 'Hello Socrates' one were to say 'hello rational mortal animal'.

G Erotianus 34,10–20 (Usener 258)

For if we are going to explain the words known to everybody, we would have to expound either all or some. But to expound all is impossible, whereas to expound some is pointless. For we will explain them either through familiar locutions or through unfamiliar. But unfamiliar words seem unsuited to the task, the accepted principle being to explain less known things by means of better known things; and familiar words, by being on a par with them, will be uninformative for illuminating language, as Epicurus says. For the informativeness of language is characteristically ruined when it is bewitched by an account, as if by a homoeopathic drug.

H Cicero, *On ends* 1.22 (Usener 243, part)

In the other branch of philosophy, logic, which concerns inquiry and argument, your master [Epicurus] seems to me unarmed and naked. He abolishes definitions. He teaches nothing about division and partition. He gives no advice on framing a deductive argument. He does not show how to solve sophisms or to distinguish ambiguous terms.

Epicurean epistemology

I Diogenes Laertius 10.31 (Usener 257)

They [the Epicureans] reject dialectic as superfluous, saying that it is sufficient that natural philosophers should proceed in accordance with the words belonging to things.

J Diogenes Laertius 10.34 (Usener 265)

[The Epicureans say that] of inquiries, some are about things, others about mere utterance.

K Plutarch, *Against Colotes* 1119F (Usener 259, part)

Who is more in error than you [the Epicureans] about language? You completely abolish the class of sayables, to which discourse owes its existence, leaving only words and name-bearers, and denying the very existence of the intermediate states of affairs signified, by means of which learning, teaching, preconceptions, thoughts, impulses and assents come about.

☐ Epicurus' highly innovative theory of the natural origin of language (**A–C**) contrasts with the standard ancient assumption, ridiculed in **B 3–5** and **C**, that it was an artificial creation by one or more individuals, whether human or divine. Epicurus is here perhaps partly motivated by the aim of eliminating all divine intervention from his world-view. On this, see further **13**. But the theory also bears importantly on his view of the role of language in philosophy.

In the earlier of the two stages (**A 2, B**) primitive men instinctively uttered different sounds in reaction to different feelings and impressions, just as most animals do (**B 6–7**). Since they were also beginning to form social pacts, and thus using a rudimentary form of communication (**22K 2**), it became natural to them to employ these sounds as labels for the things prompting them. We may imagine at this stage a language consisting of uninflected nouns, adjectives and verbs, describing the immediate content of feelings ('pain', 'cold') and immediate objects of sense-impressions ('horse', 'blue', 'run'). This is indeed confirmed by **C**'s reference to the early words as 'nouns and verbs', since 'nouns' include adjectives in ancient grammar. In the later stage, described only in **A 3–4**, refinements were artificially introduced in the interests of clarity and succinctness: we may think of grammatical inflections, conjunctions and pronouns as contributing to the former, pronouns to the latter. Finally, according to **A 4** the vocabulary was artificially enlarged, or at any rate existing words were given additional meanings, by intellectuals turning their attention to abstruse or theoretical entities.

Before Epicurus, the doctrine that 'names are natural' had meant not that they arose without contrivance, but that they somehow mirror the nature of their nominata (the thesis examined in Plato's *Cratylus*). On Epicurus' theory both views are combined. Names arose not only uncontrivedly, but also in a way which ensured a certain one-to-one correspondence between words and types of thing. Nor is he embarrassed, as earlier 'naturalists' were or should have been, by the fact that languages differ from place to place. To judge from **A 2**, this was all part of the natural process: because environment and human physique differed from tribe to tribe, it was natural that both the feelings and impressions undergone and the resulting sounds should differ accordingly.

The upshot is a theory which leads us, within any one language or dialect, to expect simple nouns and verbs each to have a single 'natural' meaning, although this may have become overlaid, in the second stage, with metaphorical re-applications, the addition of prefixes, etc. Epicurus' advice to the philosopher in **17C 1** to start from 'the things which underlie words', or 'the primary concept corresponding to each word', may well refer to this single natural meaning. Here is a conjectural example. The physicist's term 'void' originally meant just 'empty', but has been extended by philosophers to designate absolute vacuum. In order to use it properly, then, philosophers should bear in mind the familiar notion of 'empty', which, for instance, treats emptiness as inseparably linked to the possibility of motion (cf. **5A 3**).

Another facet of the naturalist theory is that it justifies the occasional foray into etymology: cf. **5D**; **23D 3**. (For the Stoic attitude to etymology, see **32** commentary.)

'The things which underlie words' in **17C** are almost certainly what Epicurus also calls 'preconceptions' (cf. **17E 3**) – empirically formed universal conceptions of things. If, then, these can be taken to serve as the meanings of words in the Epicurean theory, Plutarch's criticism in **K** (which looks Stoic-inspired: for its terminology cf. **33**) will prove to be ill-founded. Cf. also **D**, a tantalizing fragment of a book written by Epicurus in mid-career, referring back to early work in which he had apparently already been associating preconception with word-meaning.

Epicurus seems to see the following attraction in his theory. According to the tradition founded by Plato and taken up by the Stoics (see **32**), each term used by a philosopher should be explicated by the dialectical process which results in definition. Epicurus is evidently worried that such an exercise will become an exclusively linguistic one, insulated from its real objects: **I–J**. Not only does dialectic present the threat of an infinite regress of proofs (**17C 1**), but, more important, the definition of a thing is relatively uninformative about it: **F–G**. It may seem that Epicurus does himself occasionally offer definitions, as at **13B** and **23B 1**, but these (the latter expressly) are rather 'outline accounts' – an Aristotelian notion, shared also by the Stoics (**32C 3**). An outline account (*hupographē*) is for Epicurus not the end-product of a dialectical investigation, as a definition should be, but an initial listing of the contents of the relevant preconception. For the dialectical technique of 'division', also not favoured by Epicurus (**H**), see **32**. Interestingly, later Epicureans like Demetrius of Laconia (cf. **7C**) seem to have reinstated it.

Epicurus' rejection of all such dialectical technique (**H**) is not a rejection of argument, but must be understood in relation to his insistence, as a linguistic 'naturalist', that there is no substitute for careful attention to the primary notion which naturally underlies every word.

The opposed 'conventionalist' view, according to which word meaning is a matter of mere convention and may be determined quite arbitrarily by the user, had been developed in Epicurus' day into an extreme form by Diodorus Cronus (**37N–O**). It is probably the Diodorean theory that is brusquely dismissed in **E**.

ETHICS

20 Free will

A Epicurus, *Letter to Menoeceus* 133–4

(1) Whom, after all, do you consider superior to the man who . . . would deride the <fate> which some introduce as overlord of everything, <but sees that some things are necessitated,> others are due to fortune, and others depend on us, since necessity is accountable to no one, and fortune is an unstable thing to watch, while that which depends on us, with which culpability and its opposite are naturally associated, is free of any overlord? (2) For it would be better to follow the mythology about gods than be a slave to the 'fate' of the natural philosophers: the former at least hints at the hope of begging the gods off by means of worship, whereas the latter involves an inexorable necessity.

B Epicurus, *On nature* 34.21–2

(1) But many naturally capable of achieving these and those results fail to achieve them, because of themselves, not because of one and the same responsibility of the atoms and of themselves. (2) And with these we especially do battle, and rebuke them, hating them for a disposition which follows their disordered congenital nature as we do with the whole range of animals. (3) For the nature of their atoms has contributed nothing to some of their behaviour, and degrees of behaviour and character, but it is their developments which themselves possess all or most of the responsibility for certain things. (4) It is as a result of that nature that some of their atoms move with disordered motions, but it is not on the atoms that all <the responsibility should be placed for their behaviour . . .> (5) Thus when a development occurs which takes on some distinctness from the atoms in a differential way – not in the way which is like viewing from a different distance – he acquires responsibility which proceeds from himself; (6) then he straightaway transmits this to his primary substances and makes the whole of it into a yardstick. (7) That is why those who cannot correctly make such distinctions confuse themselves about the adjudication of responsibilities.

C Epicurus, *On nature* 34.26–30

(1) From the very outset we always have seeds directing us some towards these, some towards those, some towards these *and* those, actions and thoughts and characters, in greater and smaller numbers. Consequently that which we develop – characteristics of this or that kind – is at first absolutely up to us; and the things which of necessity flow in through our passages from that which surrounds us are at one stage up to us and

dependent on beliefs of our own making . . . (2) <And we can invoke, against the argument that our eventual choice between these alternatives must be physically caused either by our initial make-up or by those environmental influences> by which we never cease to be affected, the fact that we rebuke, oppose and reform each other as if the responsibility lay also in ourselves, and not just in our congenital make-up and in the accidental necessity of that which surrounds and penetrates us. (3) For if someone were to attribute to the very processes of rebuking and being rebuked the accidental necessity of whatever happens to be present to oneself at the time, I'm afraid he can never in this way understand <his own behaviour in continuing the debate . . .> (4) <He may simply choose to maintain his thesis while in practice continuing to> blame or praise. But if he were to act in this way he would be leaving intact the very same behaviour which as far as our own selves are concerned creates the preconception of our responsibility. And in that he would at one point be altering his theory, at another <. . .> (5) <. . .> such error. For this sort of account is self-refuting, and can never prove that everything is of the kind called 'necessitated'; but he debates this very question on the assumption that his opponent is himself responsible for talking nonsense. (6) And even if he goes on to infinity saying that *this* action of his is in turn necessitated, always appealing to arguments, he is not reasoning it empirically so long as he goes on imputing to himself the responsibility for having reasoned correctly and to his opponent that for having reasoned incorrectly. (7) But unless he were to stop attributing his action to himself and to pin it on necessity instead, he would not even <be consistent . . .> (8) <On the other hand,> if in using the word 'necessity' of that which we call our own agency he is merely changing a name, and won't prove that we have a preconception of a kind which has faulty delineations when we call our own agency responsible, neither his own <behaviour nor that of others will be affected . . . > (9) <. . .> but even to call necessitation empty as a result of your claim. If someone won't explain this, and has no auxiliary element or impulse in us which he might dissuade from those actions which we perform calling the responsibility for them 'our own agency', but is giving the name of foolish necessity to all the things which we claim to do calling the responsibility for them 'our own agency', he will be merely changing a name; (10) he will not be modifying any of our actions in the way in which in some cases the man who sees what sort of actions are necessitated regularly dissuades those who desire to do something in the face of compulsion. (11) And the mind will be inquisitive to learn what sort of action it should then consider that one to be which we perform in some way through our own agency but without desiring to. For he has no alternative but to say what sort of action is necessitated <and what is

not . . .> (12) <. . .> supremely unthinkable. But unless someone perversely maintains this, or makes it clear what fact he is rebutting or introducing, it is merely a word that is being changed, as I keep repeating.

(13) The first men to give a satisfactory account of causes, men not only much greater than their predecessors but also, many times over, than their successors, turned a blind eye to themselves – although in many matters they had alleviated great ills – in order to hold necessity and accident responsible for everything. (14) Indeed, the actual account promoting this view came to grief when it left the great man blind to the fact that in his actions he was clashing with his doctrine; and that if it were not that a certain blindness to the doctrine took hold of him while acting he would be constantly perplexing himself; and that wherever the doctrine prevailed he would be falling into desperate calamities, while wherever it did not he would be filled with conflict because of the contradiction between his actions and his doctrine.

(15) It is because this is so that the need also arises to explain the matter which I was discussing when I first embarked on this digression, lest some similar evil <befall us.>

D Epicurus, *Vatican sayings* 40

The man who says that all events are necessitated has no ground for criticizing the man who says that not all events are necessitated. For according to him this is itself a necessitated event.

E Cicero, *On fate* 21–5 (following **38G**)

(1) At this initial stage, if I were disposed to agree with Epicurus and to deny that every proposition is either true or false, I would rather accept that blow than allow that all things happen through fate. For the former view is at least arguable, whereas the latter is truly intolerable. Chrysippus, then, strains every nerve to persuade us that every *axiōma* (proposition) is either true or false. For just as Epicurus is afraid that if he admits this he will have to admit that all events happen through fate – for if one of the two has been true from all eternity it is certain, and if certain then necessary too, which he considers enough to prove both necessity and fate – so too Chrysippus fears that if he fails to secure the result that every proposition is either true or false he cannot maintain that everything happens through fate and from eternal causes of future events. (2) But Epicurus thinks that the necessity of fate is avoided by the swerve of atoms. Thus a third type of motion arises in addition to weight and impact, when the atom swerves by a minimal interval, or *elachiston* as he terms it. That this swerve occurs without a cause he is forced to admit in practice, even if not in so many words. For it is not through the impact of another atom that an atom swerves. How, after all, can one be struck by another if atomic bodies travel perpendicularly in straight lines

through their own weight, as Epicurus holds? For it follows that one is never driven from its course by another, if one is not even touched by another. The consequence is that, even supposing that the atom does exist and that it swerves, it swerves without a cause. (3) Epicurus' reason for introducing this theory was his fear that, if the atom's motion was always the result of natural and necessary weight, we would have no freedom, since the mind would be moved in whatever way it was compelled by the motion of atoms. Democritus, the originator of atoms, preferred to accept this consequence that everything happens through necessity than to rob the atomic bodies of their natural motions.

(4) A more penetrating line was taken by Carneades, who showed that the Epicureans could defend their case without this fictitious swerve. For since they taught that a certain voluntary motion of the mind was possible, a defence of that doctrine was preferable to introducing the swerve, especially as they could not discover its cause. And by defending it they could easily stand up to Chrysippus. (5) For by conceding that there is no motion without a cause, they would not be conceding that all events were the result of antecedent causes. For our volition has no external antecedent causes. Hence when we say that someone wants or does not want something without a cause we are taking advantage of a common linguistic convention: by 'without a cause' we mean without an external antecedent cause, not without *some* kind of cause. Just as, when we call a jar 'empty', we are not speaking like natural philosophers who hold the empty (void) to be absolute nothing, but in such a way as to say that the jar is, for example, without water, without wine or without oil, so too when we say that the mind moves 'without a cause' we mean without an external antecedent cause, not entirely without a cause. (6) Of the atom itself it can be said that, when it moves through the void as a result of its heaviness and weight, it moves without a cause, in as much as there is no additional cause from outside. But here too, if we don't all want to incur the scorn of the natural philosophers for saying that something happens without a cause, we must make a distinction and say as follows: that it is the atom's own nature to move as a result of weight and heaviness, and that that nature is itself the cause of its moving in that way. (7) Similarly for voluntary motions of the mind there is no need to seek an external cause. For a voluntary motion itself has it as its own intrinsic nature that it should be in our power to obey us. And this fact is not without a cause: for the cause is that thing's own nature. [Followed by 70G]

F Lucretius 2.251–93 (continuing **11H**)

(1) Moreover, if all motion is always linked, and new motion arises out of old in a fixed order, and atoms do not by swerving make some beginning of motion to break the decrees of fate, so that cause should not follow

cause from infinity, from where does this free volition exist for animals throughout the world? From where, I ask, comes this volition wrested away from the fates, through which we proceed wherever each of us is led by his pleasure, and likewise swerve off our motions at no fixed time or fixed region of space, but wherever the mind itself carries us? (2) For without doubt it is volition that gives these things their beginning for each of us, and it is from volition that motions are spread through the limbs. Don't you see how also when at an instant the starting gates are opened the eager strength of horses can nevertheless not surge forward as suddenly as the mind itself wishes? For all the mass of matter has to be stirred up throughout the body, so that stirred up through all the limbs it may in a concerted effort follow the mind's desire. Thus you may see that the beginning of motion is created from the heart and proceeds initially from the mind's volition, and from there is spread further through the entire body and limbs. (3) Nor is it the same when we move forward impelled by a blow, through another person's great strength and great coercion. For then it is plain that all the matter of the whole body moves and is driven against our wish, until volition has reined it back throughout the limbs. So do you now see that, although external force propels many along and often obliges them to proceed against their wishes and to be driven headlong, nevertheless there is something in our chest capable of fighting and resisting, at whose decision the mass of matter is also forced at times to be turned throughout the limbs and frame, and, when hurled forward, is reined back and settles down? (4) Therefore in the seeds too you must admit the same thing, that there is another cause of motion besides impacts and weight, from which this power is born in us, since we see that nothing can come into being out of nothing. For weight prevents all things from coming about by impacts, by a sort of external force. But that the mind should not itself possess an internal necessity in all its behaviour, and be overcome and, as it were, forced to suffer and to be acted upon – that is brought about by a tiny swerve of atoms at no fixed region of space or fixed time.

G Diogenes of Oenoanda 32.1.14–3.14

Once prophecy is eliminated, how can there be any other evidence for fate? For if someone uses Democritus' account, saying that because of their collisions with each other atoms have no free movement, and that as a result it appears that all motions are necessitated, we will reply to him: 'Don't you know, whoever you are, that there is also a free movement in atoms, which Democritus failed to discover but Epicurus brought to light, a swerving movement, as he demonstrates from evident facts?' But the chief point is this: if fate is believed in, that is the end of all censure and admonition, and even the wicked <will not be open to blame.>

H Cicero, *On fate* 37

(1) Of any two contradictories – by contradictories here I mean a pair one of which asserts something while the other denies it – it is necessary, *pace* Epicurus, that one be true, the other false: for example, 'Philoctetes will be wounded' was true in all previous ages, and 'Philoctetes will not be wounded' false. (2) Unless perhaps we're inclined to follow the opinion of the Epicureans, who say that such propositions are neither true nor false, (3) or, when that shames them, say something still more shameless, namely that disjunctions of contradictories are true, but that of the original propositions contained in them neither is true.

I Cicero, *Academica* 2.97 (Usener 376)

For although Epicurus, who despises and ridicules the whole of dialectic, cannot be got to admit that a proposition of the form 'Either Hermarchus will be alive tomorrow, or he will not be alive' is true, despite the dialecticians' rule that all disjunctions of the form 'Either *p* or not-*p*' are not only true but also necessary, notice how circumspect is this man whom your Stoics consider dull-witted. 'For if', he says, 'I admit that one or the other is necessary, it will be necessary either for Hermarchus to be alive tomorrow, or for him not to be alive. But there is no such necessity in the nature of things.'

☐ Epicurus' problem is this: if it has been necessary all along that we should act as we do, it cannot be up to us, with the result that we would not be morally responsible for our actions at all (especially **A**, **E 3**, **F 1**, **G**). Thus posing the problem of determinism he becomes arguably the first philosopher to recognize the philosophical centrality of what we know as the Free Will Question. His strongly libertarian approach to it can be usefully contrasted with the Stoics' acceptance of determinism (see **62**).

Epicurus certainly saw the Democritean atomism which he had inherited as vulnerable to such a challenge, since it made all phenomena, including human behaviour, fully accountable in terms of rigid physical laws of atomic motion, and hence necessary: see **A 2**, **C 13–14**, **E 3**, **G**. It is perhaps the most widely known fact about Epicurus that he for this reason modified the deterministic Democritean system by introducing a slight element of indeterminacy to atomic motion, the 'swerve' (on which see also **11H** with commentary): **E 2–3**, **F**, **G**. But taken in isolation such a solution is notoriously unsatisfactory. It promises to liberate us from rigid necessity only to substitute an alternative human mechanism, perhaps more undependable and eccentric but hardly more autonomous. Epicurus' remarks in **A 1**, where 'that which depends on us' (or 'that which is up to us') is contrasted with *unstable* fortune as well as with necessity, suggest that he meant to avoid this trap. In order to see how, we must defer discussion of the swerve for now.

The swerve is not even mentioned in the surviving papyrus fragments of

[handwritten margin note: accountable for actions]

[handwritten margin note: unstable fortune]

*picurus' book on the issue of responsibility from which **B** and **C** are drawn. But the book still sheds abundant light on the question. In **C** he conducts a running debate with a Democritean determinist. Democritus himself, we are told, simply failed to see the implications of his determinism for human action (**C** 13–14). Epicurus' principal target in **C** 2–12, on the other hand, is someone who consciously applies mechanistic determinism to all human behaviour, including his own. He probably has in mind such fourth-century Democriteans as his own reviled teacher Nausiphanes – the heirs of Democritus derided in **C** 13, as perhaps also implicitly in **G**. (The early Stoics have sometimes been identified as his target, but cf. **62** with commentary; 'natural philosophers', **A** 2, would not normally be used of Stoics, in any case.)

In **C** 1 Epicurus is arguing that since we start with a wide range of potentials ('seeds') for character development our actual direction of development is not physically predetermined but 'up to us'. There are physical influences, but we can control them (cf. **15D** 7–8). If it were they that controlled us, our moral and critical attitudes to each other would make no sense (**C** 2). This leads him into his anti-determinist digression, which continues until its express conclusion at **C** 15. The determinist may simply regard these attitudes as themselves necessitated (**C** 3). But this does not save him from the charge of self-refutation (**C** 5, and perhaps already in the very fragmentary **C** 4): his own critical attitude in this very debate still implies what he wishes to deny, that the parties to the debate are responsible for their own views. The determinist will resort to the defence that he is *compelled* to behave in this way; when challenged once again for continuing to argue, will repeat the defence; and so on *ad infinitum*. Epicurus' objection to this infinite regress (**C** 6) is not that it is in itself vicious, but rather that it leaves the inconsistency untouched: at *every* stage of the regress the determinist's behaviour in continuing to argue his case as if with a responsible agent contradicts his thesis that everything, including our beliefs, is mechanically necessitated.

In the second stage of the digression, **C** 8–12, Epicurus suggests that determinism cannot amount to a substantive thesis about the world, and that its application of 'necessity' to human agency will turn out to be no more than a change of terminology. First (**C** 8) comes an appeal to 'preconception' (on which as a criterion, see **17** above). We all share a preconception of our own agency as that which is responsible for our behaviour: to defuse the evidential force of this, the determinist would have to show how the alleged preconception has come to embody a faulty 'delineation' (cf. **17E** 2, 5) of the facts. (Compare Epicurus' own grounds for dismissing the alleged preconception of the gods as provident, **23B–C** below.) If he cannot, the preconception remains valid and the determinist's contribution is merely a new name for it. Second (**C** 9), his thesis is pragmatically empty. Since he denies us an internal source of self-determination (an 'auxiliary element or impulse in us') he can never expect his arguments to dissuade us from any action. In this Epicurus contrasts him with someone who has a proper grasp (as recommended in **A** 1) of the difference between the necessitated and the unnecessitated, and who consequently can expect to dissuade us from actions which would involve resisting necessity (**C** 10) – perhaps, for example, dissuade us from a vain desire to evade the inevitability of death, because unlike the determinist he can appreciate that while death is necessary our wishes are up to us. Third (**C 11**), the determinist leaves himself no tools for analysing 'mixed' actions (as they are called by Aristotle, *Nicomachean ethics* III.1), those performed freely but reluctantly in avoidance of a greater evil, since he is unable to distinguish the voluntary from the necessitated elements in them.

The final stage of the argument, **C 13–14**, is pragmatic, appealing to the disastrous practical consequences that would have ensued had Democritus remembered to apply his thesis of universal necessitation to himself. No illustration is given, but one easy example would be the abandonment of decision-making (cf. **55S**).

It is remarkable how closely the internal structure of this anti-determinist argument matches that of **16A**'s anti-sceptic argument, with the sequence of a self-refutation challenge (**C 3–7**; cf. **16A 1**), an appeal to preconception and word-meaning (**C 8–12**; cf. **16A 2–3**), and a pragmatic argument (**C 13–14**; cf. **16A 9–10**). So too its function as a digression added late in the book to justify the preceding positive account of psychological causation matches the role of **16A** in relation to Lucretius' preceding positive account of sense-perception. None of this is likely to be mere coincidence. For scepticism and the kind of mechanistic determinism envisaged here were seen as joint consequences of Democritus' *reductionist* atomism. If phenomenal properties were reducible to mere configurations of atoms and void, it seemed to follow that the atoms and void alone were real while the sensible properties were arbitrary constructions placed upon them by our cognitive organs. The result was scepticism about the sensible world, which had become the characteristic stance of most fourth-century Democriteans (see further, **1** and **16**). Similarly, if the 'self' and its volitions were reducible to mere sequences of atomic motion in the soul, human action would easily appear to be mechanistic, fully explicable in terms of primary physical laws, with no additional explanatory or descriptive role left for such psychological entities as belief and volition. And that is just the kind of theory under attack in **C** (cf. especially **C 2, 9**).

Given the extent of this parallelism between scepticism and determinism, and between Epicurus' respective refutations of them, we might expect his own positive alternatives to them to be similarly comparable. And so they are. Just as his answer to scepticism is to affirm the reality of phenomenal properties and the truth of sense-impressions of them (see on **7** and **16**), so too his answer to mechanism is to affirm the reality and causal efficacy of the self and its volitions as something over and above the underlying patterns of atomic motion. This plainly emerges from **B**, despite the lack of context and certain difficulties of interpretation. Epicurus is speaking of self-determining animals. (Volitional autonomy is not restricted to human beings, cf. **F 1–2**; but elsewhere in the book, **j** in vol. 2, wild animals seem to be excluded, as lacking self-determination and hence as exempt from moral criticism, though not from hate.) Their misbehaviour is quite explicitly said (**B 1–4**) to be attributable not to their atoms but to their selves and their 'developments'. The latter term, which is crucial to the entire book's discussion, is explicated at **B 5**. The kind of 'development' which contributes psychological autonomy is one which is distinct from the underlying atoms in a 'differential' way ('transcendent' would be a tempting translation of the Greek word) – a way more radical than 'the way which is like viewing from a different distance'. The point is apparently that all bodies have certain properties, e.g. colour, over and above their constituent atoms, but that there the main difference is one of scale, one between macroscopic and microscopic analysis; whereas the 'developments' which supply autonomy differ from the atoms in a much more fundamental way. The fragmentary state of the text leaves us to guess at the nature of this difference, although it is hard to doubt that it includes the intentional properties associated with consciousness. How do these psychological entities relate metaphysically and causally to the mind's atoms? They can only be, technically speaking, 'accidental attributes' of those atoms (cf. **7**). But they are not mere epiphenomena, supervenient on atomic motions and causally determined by them. For Epicurus is quite explicit in attributing to them a causal efficacy distinct from that of the atoms. Hence, although atomic make-up may be responsible for disorderly motions of the mind-atoms (**B 4**), it does not follow that we cannot make decisions which override those motions, and according to **B 6** psychological causation actually operates *on* our component atoms. This throws immediate light on Lucretius' insistence at **14D 5** that although atomic composition of the soul determines our natural temperament, we can learn through reason to overcome that temperament. Perhaps, for instance, a natural coward can learn courage through rational reflection. His disorderly motions of soul atoms may then be stabilized, so that he ceases to suffer even the physical sensations of fear.

By now the familiar 'materialist' label is beginning to fit Epicurus less neatly. Although he holds *prima facie* an Identity Theory of mind (see **14**), he does not regard mental states as capable of straightforward physical analysis, for although properties of the corporeal mind they are not mere physical states of it. We have here, then, an interactionist dualism of the mental and the physical. But there is no hint of Cartesian dualism. A better comparison would be with the modern notion of Emergence. In Epicurus' view, matter in certain complex states can take on non-physical properties, which in turn bring entirely new causal laws into operation.

B 7 emphasizes that the distinction between physical and psychological causation is crucial to an understanding of responsibility. And certainly it does constitute at least the beginning of an answer to determinism. The 'self' which is responsible for our actions is, Epicurus will say, more than a mere bundle of atoms, and therefore is not reducible to a link in a physical causal chain. Indeed Carneades, in defending Epicurean libertarianism for his own dialectical purposes (see **70G** and commentary), suggested that this was already a sufficient answer to determinism: **E 4–7**. But how, it will be asked, *can* this emergent property of the corporeal mind so effectively take control of the soul, and through it of the body, as to move their atoms in ways in which according to the laws of physics alone they should not have moved? If the laws of physics are sufficient to determine the precise trajectory of every atom in us, how can the self be anything more than a helpless spectator of the body's actions?

Here at last a significant role for the swerve leaps to the eye. For it is to answer just this question, according to Cicero at **E 3**, that the swerve was introduced.

The evident power of the self and its volitions to intervene in the physical processes of soul and body would be inexplicable if physical laws alone were sufficient to determine the precise trajectory of every atom. Therefore physical laws are not sufficient to determine the precise trajectory of every atom. There is a minimal degree of physical indeterminism – the swerve. An unimpeded atom may at any given moment continue its present trajectory, but equally may 'swerve' into one of the adjacent parallel trajectories (see commentary on **11H**).

As far as physics is concerned there is simply no reason for its following one rather than another of these trajectories. Normally, then, the result will be, in this minimal degree, random. But in the special case of the mind there is also a non-physical cause, volition, which can affect the atoms of which it is a property. It does so, we may speculate, not by overriding the laws of physics, but by choosing between the alternative possibilities which the laws of physics leave open. In this way a large group of soul atoms might simultaneously be diverted into a new pattern of motion, and thus radically redirect the motion of the body. Such an event, requiring as it does the coincidence of numerous swerves, would be statistically most improbable according to the laws of physics alone. But it is still, on the swerve theory, an intrinsically possible one, which volition might therefore be held to bring about. For a very similar thesis relating free will to modern quantum indeterminism, see A. S. Eddington, *The nature of the physical world* (1928). (It may be objected that swerves are meant to be entirely uncaused; but, as **E 2** shows, that was only an inference by Epicurus' critics, made plausible by concentrating on the swerve's cosmogonic function, cf. **11H**, for there it must indeed occur at random and without the intervention of volition.)

Lucretius' evidence in **F** does not explicitly state the swerve's relation to volition, although numerous attempts have been made to discover it there. But if the above account of Epicurus' theory is justified by the other testimonia, it becomes clear that **F** is, at least, fully consistent with it. For the dominant theme of **F 1–3** is precisely the evident power of volition to redirect the bodily mass in defiance of its purely mechanical patterns of motion. This is said, in **F 1** and **4**, to be explicable only if there is an undetermined swerve of atoms, since if impact and weight were the only causes of atomic motion the mind's behaviour would be rigidly mechanistic. Some have also seen in **F 1** the further implication that the initiation of every new course of action directly involves the swerve. All this fits the above account comfortably enough. What is missing, of course, is an explanation of the non-physical character of psychological causation – not surprisingly, given that Lucretius' poem is about physics and that his sole object in the context is to complete his account of the laws of atomic motion (cf. **11**).

One further dimension to the debate emerges from **E 1, H** and **I**. Epicurus saw the threat of universal necessitation not only in unbreakable chains of physical causation, but also in the logical principle of bivalence according to which every proposition is either true or false, including those about the future. His solution of denying the principle as far as certain future-tensed propositions are concerned (the denial is slightly garbled in **I**'s version, where 'one or the other is necessary' ought to read 'one or the other is true'; but the example is clearly authentic – Hermarchus was Epicurus' pupil and successor) was essentially that of Aristotle, according to the traditional reading of his celebrated Sea Battle discussion at *De interpretatione* 9. But Epicurus, like the Stoic with whom he is contrasted in **E 1** (see further, **38G**), saw physical and logical determinism as two aspects of a single thesis. The two formulations of determinism tend to be treated as interchangeable, as do the two respective solutions, the swerve and the denial of bivalence (cf. Cicero, *On fate* 18–19, and perhaps **E 1–3**). This conflation seems to rest on the assumed equivalence of 'true in advance' with 'determined by pre-existing causes'; cf. also the telling comment at the end of **I**.

The interpretation of the swerve theory adopted above may help explain how it *could* be thought interchangeable with the denial of bivalence. Neither doctrine is involved in analysing the nature of volition itself (as many have thought the swerve to be). Their shared function is to guarantee the *efficacy* of volition, by keeping alternative possibilities genuinely open.

21 Pleasure

A Cicero, *On ends* 1.29–32, 37–9 (with omissions)

[The Epicurean spokesman, Torquatus] (1) We are investigating what is the final and ultimate good, which as all philosophers agree [cf. **63A**] must be of such a kind that it is the end to which everything is the means, but it is not itself the means to anything. Epicurus situates this in pleasure, which he wants to be the greatest good with pain as the greatest bad. His doctrine begins in this way: (2) as soon as every animal is born, it seeks after pleasure and rejoices in it as the greatest good, while it rejects pain as the greatest bad and, as far as possible, avoids it; and it does this when it is not yet corrupted, on the innocent and sound judgement of nature itself. Hence he says there is no need to prove or discuss why pleasure should be pursued and pain avoided. He thinks these matters are sensed just like the heat of fire, the whiteness of snow and the sweetness of honey, none of which needs confirmation by elaborate arguments; it is enough to point them out . . .(3) Since man has nothing left if sensations are removed from him, it must be the case that nature itself judges what is in accordance with or contrary to nature. What does it perceive or what does it judge except pleasure and pain as a basis for its pursuit or avoidance of anything? (4) Some of our school, however, want to transmit these doctrines in a subtler way: they deny the sufficiency of judging what is good or bad by sensation, saying that the intrinsic desirability of pleasure and the intrinsic undesirability of pain can be understood by the mind too and by reason. So they say that our sense that the one is desirable and the other undesirable is virtually a natural and innate preconception in our minds . . . To enable you to view the origin of the entire mistake of those who criticize pleasure and praise pain, I will disclose the whole matter and expound the actual words of the famous discoverer of the truth, the architect, as it were, of the happy life. (5) No one rejects or dislikes or avoids pleasure itself because it is pleasure, but because great pains result for those who do not know how to pursue pleasure rationally. Nor again is there anyone who loves, goes after or wants to get pain itself because it is pain, but because circumstances sometimes occur which enable him to gain some great pleasure by toil and pain . . . (6) The pleasure we pursue is not just that which moves our actual nature with some gratification and is perceived by the senses in company with a certain delight; we hold that to be the greatest pleasure which is perceived once all pain has been removed. For when we are freed from pain, we rejoice in the actual freedom and absence of all distress; but everything in which we rejoice is pleasure, just as everything that distresses us is pain; therefore the complete removal of pain has rightly been called pleasure. Thus when hunger and thirst have been removed by food and drink, the mere withdrawal of distress brings pleasure forth as its consequence. So quite generally the removal of pain causes pleasure to take its place. (7) Hence Epicurus did not accept the existence of anything in between pleasure and pain. What some people regarded as in between – the complete absence of pain – was not only pleasure but also the greatest pleasure. For anyone aware of his own condition must either have pleasure or pain. Epicurus, moreover, supposes that complete absence of pain marks the limit of the greatest pleasure, so that thereafter pleasure can be varied and differentiated but not increased and expanded. (8) But at Athens . . . there is a statue in the Ceramicus of Chrysippus seated with outstretched hand, which indicated his delight in the following little syllogism: 'Is there anything that your hand, in its present condition, wants?' 'Certainly not.' 'But if pleasure were the good, it would have a want.' 'I think so.' 'Therefore pleasure is not the good' . . . The argument is entirely valid against the Cyrenaics, but does not touch Epicurus.

B Epicurus, *Letter to Menoeceus* 127–32

(1) We must reckon that some desires are natural and others empty, and of the natural some are necessary, others natural only; and of the necessary some are necessary for happiness, others for the body's freedom from stress, and others for life itself. For the steady observation of these things makes it possible to refer every choice and avoidance to the health of the body and the soul's freedom from disturbance, since this is the end belonging to the blessed life. For this is what we aim at in all our actions – to be free from pain and anxiety. (2) Once we have got this, all the soul's tumult is released, since the creature cannot go as if in pursuit of something it needs and search for any second thing as the means of maximizing the good of the soul and the body. For the time when we need pleasure is when we are in pain from the absence of pleasure. < But

when we are not in pain > we no longer need pleasure. This is why we say that pleasure is the beginning and end of the blessed life. For we recognize pleasure as the good which is primary and congenital; from it we begin every choice and avoidance, and we come back to it, using the feeling as the yardstick for judging every good thing. (3) Since pleasure is the good which is primary and congenital, for this reason we do not choose every pleasure either, but we sometimes pass over many pleasures in cases when their outcome for us is a greater quantity of discomfort; and we regard many pains as better than pleasures in cases when our endurance of pains is followed by a greater and long-lasting pleasure. Every pleasure, then, because of its natural affinity, is something good, yet not every pleasure is choiceworthy. Correspondingly, every pain is something bad, but not every pain is by nature to be avoided. However, we have to make our judgement on all these points by a calculation and survey of advantages and disadvantages. For at certain times we treat the good as bad and conversely the bad as good. (4) We also regard self-sufficiency as a great good, not with the aim of always living off little, but to enable us to live off little if we do not have much, in the genuine conviction that they derive the greatest pleasure from luxury who need it least, and that everything natural is easy to procure, but what is empty is hard to procure. Plain flavours produce pleasure equal to an expensive diet whenever all the pain of need has been removed; and bread and water generate the highest pleasure whenever they are taken by one who needs them. Therefore the habit of simple and inexpensive diet maximizes health and makes a man energetic in facing the necessary business of daily life; it also strengthens our character when we encounter luxuries from time to time, and emboldens us in the face of fortune. (5) So when we say that pleasure is the end, we do not mean the pleasures of the dissipated and those that consist in having a good time, as some out of ignorance and disagreement or refusal to understand suppose we do, but freedom from pain in the body and from disturbance in the soul. For what produces the pleasant life is not continuous drinking and parties or pederasty or womanizing or the enjoyment of fish and the other dishes of an expensive table, but sober reasoning which tracks down the causes of every choice and avoidance, and which banishes the opinions that beset souls with the greatest confusion. (6) Of all this the beginning and the greatest good is prudence. Therefore prudence is even more precious than philosophy, and it is the natural source of all the remaining virtues: it teaches the impossibility of living pleasurably without living prudently, honourably and justly, < and the impossibility of living prudently, honourably and justly > without living pleasurably. For the virtues are naturally linked with living pleasurably, and living pleasurably is inseparable from them.

C Epicurus, *Key doctrines* 3–4

(1) [3] The removal of all pain is the limit of the magnitude of pleasures. Wherever pleasure is present, as long as it is there, pain or distress or their combination is absent. (2) [4] Pain does not last continuously in the flesh: when acute it is there for a very short time, while the pain which just exceeds the pleasure in the flesh does not persist for many days; and chronic illnesses contain an excess of pleasure in the flesh over pain.

D Epicurus, *Key doctrines* 8–10

(1) [8] No pleasure is something bad *per se*: but the causes of some pleasures produce stresses many times greater than the pleasures. (2) [9] If every pleasure were condensed in < location > and duration and distributed all over the structure or the dominant parts of our nature, pleasures would never differ from one another. (3) [10] If the causes of the pleasures of the dissipated released mental fears concerning celestial phenomena and death and distress, and in addition taught the limit of desires, we should never have any reason to reproach them [i.e. the dissipated], since they would be satisfying themselves with pleasures from all directions and would never have pain or distress, which constitutes the bad.

E Epicurus, *Key doctrines* 18, 25, 30

(1) [18] The pleasure in the flesh does not increase when once the pain of need has been removed, but it is only varied. And the limit of pleasure in the mind is produced by rationalizing those very things and their congeners which used to present the mind with its greatest fears. (2) [25] If you fail to refer each of your actions on every occasion to nature's end, and stop short at something else in choosing or avoiding, your actions will not be consequential upon your theories. (3) [30] Whenever intense passion is present in natural desires which do not lead to pain if they are unfulfilled, these have their origin in empty opinion; and the reason for their persistence is not their own nature but the empty opinion of the person.

F Epicurus, *Vatican sayings* 17, 21, 25

(1) [17] Blessed is not the young man but the old one who has lived honourably. For the young man keeps changing his mind and veers about under the influence of fortune. But the old one has lowered his anchor in old age as though in harbour, and with secure gratitude has clamped the good things he hardly hoped for previously. (2) [21] We must not compel nature but persuade her; and we shall persuade her by fulfilling the necessary desires, and the natural ones if they do no harm,

but harshly rebuking the harmful ones. (3) [25] Poverty, when measured by nature's end, is great wealth, but unlimited wealth is great poverty.

G Epicurus, *Vatican sayings* 33, 42, 51, 59

(1) [33] The flesh's cry is not to be hungry or thirsty or cold. For one who is in these states and expects to remain so could rival even Zeus in happiness. (2) [42] It takes just the same time for the greatest good to be created and for it to be enjoyed. (3) [51] [Letter from Metrodorus to Pythocles] You tell me that the movement of your flesh is too inclined towards sexual intercourse. So long as you do not break the laws or disturb proper and established conventions or distress any of your neighbours or ravage your body or squander the necessities of life, act upon your inclination in any way you like. Yet it is impossible not to be constrained by at least one of these. For sex is never advantageous, and one should be content if it does no harm. (4) [59] What is insatiable is not the stomach, as people say, but the false opinion concerning its unlimited filling.

H Epicurus, *Vatican sayings* 63, 71, 73, 81

(1) [63] There can be refinement even on slender means, and one who fails to take account of it is in a similar position to someone who goes astray through ignoring limits. (2) [71] This question should be applied to all desires: what will happen to me if the object of my desire is achieved and what if it is not? (3) [73] The occurrence of certain bodily pains is a help to protecting oneself against similar ones. (4) [81] What releases the soul's disturbance and produces worthwhile joy is neither possessing the greatest wealth, nor public recognition and respect, nor anything else which is dependent on indeterminate causes.

I Scholion on Epicurus, *Key doctrines* 29

Natural and necessary [desires], according to Epicurus, are ones which bring relief from pain, such as drinking when thirsty; natural but non-necessary are ones which merely vary pleasure but do not remove pain, such as expensive foods; neither natural nor necessary are ones for things like crowns and erection of statues.

J Porphyry, *On abstinence* 1.51.6–52.1 (Usener 464, part)

[Reporting Epicurean views] (1) As for eating meat, it relieves neither any of our nature's stress nor a desire whose non-satisfaction would give rise to pain. It involves a violent gratification which is swiftly combined with its opposite. What it contributes to is not life's maintenance but variation of pleasures, just like sex or the drinking of exotic wines, all of which our nature is quite capable of doing without . . . (2) Furthermore, meat is not conducive to health, but rather an impediment to it.

K Diogenes Laertius 10.121

Happiness is a twofold notion: the highest, such as god enjoys, which is incapable of increase; and the happiness which is capable of addition and subtraction of pleasures.

L Cicero, *Tusculan disputations* 3.41–2 (Usener 67, 69)

[Epicurus *On the end*] (1) 'For my part I cannot conceive of anything as the good if I remove the pleasures perceived by means of taste and sex and listening to music, and the pleasant motions felt by the eyes through beautiful sights, or any other pleasures which some sensation generates in a man as a whole. Certainly it is impossible to say that mental delight is the only good. For a delighted mind, as I understand it, consists in the expectation of all the things I just mentioned – to be of a nature able to acquire them without pain . . .' (2) A little later he adds: 'I have often asked men who were called wise what they could retain as the content of goods if they removed those things, unless they wanted to pour out empty words. I could learn nothing from them; and if they want to babble on about virtues and wisdoms, they will be speaking of nothing except the way in which those pleasures I mentioned are produced.'

M Athenaeus 546F (Usener 409, 70)

Epicurus says: 'The pleasure of the stomach is the beginning and root of all good, and it is to this that wisdom and over-refinement actually refer.' And in *On the end* he again says: 'We should honour rectitude and the virtues and suchlike things if they bring pleasure; but if not, we should say goodbye to them.'

N Plutarch, *Against Epicurean happiness* 1089D (Usener 68, part)

[According to the Epicureans] The comfortable state of the flesh, and the confident expectation of this, contain the highest and most secure joy for those who are capable of reasoning.

O Cicero, *On ends* 2.69

You [the Epicurean spokesman] will be embarrassed, I say, by that picture which Cleanthes made a habit of depicting in very apt words. He used to tell his listeners to imagine a painting of Pleasure most beautifully clad and seated on a throne with the trappings of a queen, and the virtues at her side as her handmaids: they made it their sole task and function to minister to Pleasure, and merely whispered in her ear the warning (if the picture could make this clear) to be careful not to do anything imprudently that might offend people's thoughts or from which any pain might arise. 'As for us virtues, we were born to be your slaves; we have no other business.'

P Diogenes of Oenoanda 26.1.2–3.8

Shortly I will speak about imprudence, but for the present about the virtues and pleasure. Now if, fellow men, the question at issue between these people [Stoics] and ourselves involved examining 'what is the means of happiness?', and they wanted to say the virtues, as is in fact true, there would be no need to do anything except to agree with them and abandon the matter. But since, as I was saying, the issue is not 'what is the means of happiness?', but what being happy is and what our nature ultimately desires, I affirm now and always, with a great shout, that for all Greeks and foreigners, pleasure is the end of the best lifestyle, while the virtues which are now being inappropriately fussed about by them (being transferred from the position of means to that of end) are in no way the end, but the means to the end.

Q Cicero, *On ends* 2.9–10

(1) Cicero: 'Does a thirsty man, may I ask, take pleasure in drinking?' Torquatus [the Epicurean spokesman]: 'Who could deny that?' Cicero: 'Is it the same as the pleasure of quenched thirst?' (2) Torquatus: 'No it is of a different kind. Quenched thirst involves static pleasure, but the pleasure of the actual quenching is kinetic.' (3) Cicero: 'Why, then, do you call such different things by the same name?' Torquatus: 'Don't you remember what I said just before, that when pain has been completely removed, pleasure is subject to variation but not to increase?' Cicero: '... I don't quite understand the nature of this variation, in your claim that when we are free from pain we then have the greatest pleasure, but that when we are enjoying those things which bring a pleasant motion to our senses, the pleasure is then a kinetic one, which causes a variation of pleasures without increasing that pleasure of freedom from pain.'

R Diogenes Laertius 10.136–7

(1) Epicurus disagrees with the Cyrenaics on pleasure: they do not admit static pleasure but only the kinetic type, whereas he accepts both types, for soul and for body, as he says in his book *On choice and avoidance* and in *On the end* and in book 1 of *On lives* ... In *On choices* he speaks as follows: 'Freedom from disturbance and absence of pain are static pleasures; but joy and delight are regarded as kinetic activities'. (2) He has a further disagreement with the Cyrenaics: they take bodily pains to be worse than mental ones ... but he takes the mental ones to be worse, since the flesh is storm-tossed only in the present, but the soul in past, present and future.

S Lucretius 4.622–32

When the bodies of the diffusing flavour are smooth, they give pleasure by touching and stimulating all the moist and oozing regions in the tongue's vicinity. But by contrast, the more each of the bodies is furnished with roughness, they prick the sense and tear it in their encounter. Next comes pleasure from the flavour at the boundary of the palate. But when it has plunged right down through the throat, there is no pleasure while it is all spreading into the limbs. And it makes no difference at all what diet nourishes the body, provided that you can digest what you take and spread it out in the limbs and keep a moist tenor in the stomach.

T Cicero, *Tusculan disputations* 5.95 (Usener 439, part)

[Report of Epicureanism] The body rejoices just so long as it perceives a present pleasure; but the mind perceives both the present pleasure, along with the body, and foresees the one that is coming without allowing the past one to flow away. Hence the wise man will always have a constant supply of tightly-knit pleasures, since the anticipation of pleasures hoped for is united with the recollection of those already experienced.

U Cicero, *On ends* 1.55

[The Epicurean spokesman, Torquatus] (1) No error arises in respect of the ultimate good and bad themselves, i.e. pleasure or pain, but people do make mistakes in these matters owing to their ignorance of the sources of pleasure and pain. (2) Furthermore, we admit that mental pleasures and pains have their source in bodily ones . . . but we do not suppose that this precludes mental pleasures and pains from being much greater than those of the body.

V Diogenes of Oenoanda 38.1.8–3.14

(1) It is difficult for people in general to calculate the superiority of these mental feelings [over bodily ones]. For it is impossible to suffer the extremes of both on a single occasion by way of a comparison . . . on account of the rarity of this occurrence and of the destruction of life when it does occur. (2) Therefore no criterion has been found for measuring the superiority of these over the others. Rather, when someone has bodily pains he says they are greater than mental ones, but when < he has mental pains he says they are the greater >. For < present things > are always more convincing than absent ones, and each person evidently either through necessity or through pleasure assigns the superiority to the feeling which has hold of him. (3) But by means of many other considerations a wise man reasons out this point that the majority find hard to calculate.

W Lucretius 2.1–61

(1) When winds are troubling the waters on a great sea, it is a pleasure to view from the land another man's great struggles; not because it is a joy or delight that anyone should be storm-tossed, but because it is a pleasure

to observe from what troubles you yourself are free. It is a pleasure too to gaze on great contests of war deployed over the plains when you yourself have no part in the danger. (2) But pleasantest of all is to be master of those tranquil regions well fortified on high by the teaching of the wise. From there you can look down on others and see them wandering this way and that and straying in their quest for a way of life – competing in talent, fighting over social class, striving night and day with utmost effort to rise to the heights of wealth and become owners of substance. (3) O miserable minds of men, O unseeing hearts! How great the darkness of life, how great the dangers too in which this portion of time, whatsoever it be, is spent. Do you not see that nature screams out for nothing but the removal of pain from the body and the mind's enjoyment of the joyous sensation when anxiety and fear have been taken away? (4) So we see that our bodily nature needs only the few things which remove pain, in such a way that they can also furnish many delights rather pleasurably from time to time. Nor does nature itself require it, if there are no golden statues of youths in the entrance halls grasping fiery torches in their right hands to provide evening banquets with light, or if the house does not gleam with silver and shine with gold and a carved and gilded ceiling does not resound to the lute, when, in spite of this, men lie together on the soft grass near a stream of water beneath the branches of a lofty tree refreshing their bodies with joy and at no great cost, especially when the weather smiles and the season of the year spreads flowers all over the green grass. Nor do hot fevers leave the body more swiftly if you toss on embroidered tapestries and shimmering purple than if you have to lie on common drapery. (5) Therefore, since riches are of no benefit in our body, nor social class nor a kingdom's glory, we should further suppose that they are of no benefit to the mind as well – unless it should happen, when you see your legions swarming over the area of the plain and stirring up mock war . . . that religion frightened by these things flees from your mind in terror, and the fears of death vacate your heart and leave it free from anxiety. (6) But if we see that this is absurd and ludicrous, and if in truth the fears of men and the anxieties that follow them are not afraid of the sound of arms and fierce weapons, but boldly consort with kings and owners of substance and show no respect for the glitter of gold nor the brilliant gleam of a purple robe, why do you doubt that all this power belongs to reason, especially when all life is struggling in darkness? For just as children are terrified and afraid of everything in blind darkness, so we in the light are at times afraid of things no more fearful than what children shudder at in darkness and imagine will happen. (7) This terror and darkness of the mind, then, must be dispelled not by the rays of the sun and the gleaming shafts of day, but by nature's appearance and rationale.

X Lucretius 6.1–28

(1) It was Athens of glorious name that first long ago bestowed on feeble mortals the produce of corn, and refurbished life, and established laws. It was Athens too that first bestowed soothing pleasures on life, when she gave birth to a man endowed with such insight, who long ago gave utterance to everything with truthful voice. Dead though he is, his godlike discoveries spread his fame of old and now it reaches to heaven. (2) When he saw that mortals were already supplied with almost everything that need demands for their livelihood, and that their life as far as possible was firm and secure, that men had abundance of power through wealth and social status and fame and took pride in the good name of their sons, yet that at home no one's heart was any less troubled, and that they were constantly wrecking their life, despite their intentions, under a compulsion to rage with aggressive complaints, he recognized that the flaw was *there*, caused by the utensil itself, and that by its flaw everything within was being befouled, whatever came in assembled from outside including beneficial things. (3) He saw that the cause was partly the leaks and holes, which made it impossible for the utensil ever to be filled up, and partly its virtually polluting everything it had taken in with a foul taste. And so he purged people's hearts with his truthful words, and established the limit of desire and fear, and laid out the nature of the highest good to which we all strive, and indicated the way by whose narrow path we may press on towards it on a straight course.

☐ By the time of Epicurus pleasure had become one of the most discussed topics in Greek philosophy. His own account of it indicates close familiarity with the arguments for and against hedonism that are marshalled in Plato and Aristotle; readers who are new to the subject are advised to study Plato *Protagoras* 351b–358d, *Gorgias* 492d–507e, *Republic* 9.581a–587e, *Philebus*, and Aristotle *Nicomachean ethics* VII.11–17, X.1–5, *Rhetoric* I.10–11. It can also be assumed that Epicurus knew and developed the blend of temperate enjoyment, quietude and self-sufficiency advocated by Democritus (see KRS 593–4), and reacted critically to the hedonism of Aristippus and the Cyrenaics. The sometimes defensive and attractively shocking style of a number of his pronouncements on pleasure shows that he anticipated opposition and misunderstanding from rival philosophers; and the Stoics readily accepted the bait (**A 8, O**). By the time of our secondary sources Stoic insistence on the indifference of pleasure and pain for happiness (cf. **58A 4**) had strongly coloured the moral tradition, which can give the mistaken impression that Epicurean hedonism must have seemed outlandish to the majority of his contemporaries. A reading of the Aristotelian material will give the proper historical perspective. Neither Plato nor Aristotle had any difficulty in regarding pleasure as a constituent of happiness, even though they would have firmly rejected Epicurus' restriction of intrinsic goodness to pleasure and his demotion of the virtues to purely instrumental goods (**L 2**, **M**, **O**, **P**). Furthermore, Epicurus himself insisted that the pleasurable life entails and is entailed by living prudently, honourably and justly (**B 6**). Much of the interest of his ethics resides in his attempt to retain a good many traditional moral values without compromising the consistency of his hedonism.

Contrary to what is often claimed, the details of Epicurus' atomic theory do not appear to be presupposed in his ethics. Pleasure and pain are never *identified* with movements of atoms, even though Lucretius explains the differences between pleasant and painful tastes by the shapes of the 'bodies' that affect our mouth and palate (**S**). As 'accidents' of perceivers (**7C 5**), pleasure and pain have no existence at the atomic level (**7A 3**), but only at that of consciousness. What must be borne in mind, in considering the grounds of his ethics, are Epicurus' rejection of teleology (cf. **13E**, **I**, **J**) and of divine administration of the world, and his rigorous empiricism. If he was to contest the Pyrrhonian thesis that 'nothing exists which is good or bad by nature' (**1I**), he had to do so on the basis of his own criteria of truth – sensations, preconceptions and feelings (**17A**). All three of these can be seen at work in **A 2–4**. Sense-perception, we may take it, confirms the truth of the commonplace claim (see Aristotle, *Nicomachean ethics* VII.13, 1153b25 and X.2, citing Eudoxus) that all living creatures pursue pleasure and avoid pain, thereby demonstrating the naturalness of judging pleasure to be good and pain bad. Secondly, each person's feelings indicate the self-evident desirability of pleasure and undesirability of pain. In a somewhat Cartesian manner Epicurus, as Cicero reports him (**A 3**), invites us to consider ourselves as nothing if not sentient beings, with pleasure and pain as the irreducible objectives of our pursuit and avoidance. The 'naturalness' of such awareness has no teleological import; Epicurus does not say, as the Stoics did (**57A**), that our primary impulses are *for the sake of* our self-preservation. His claim is just that we turn out to be so constituted that we naturally (i.e. unavoidably) pursue pleasure and seek to avoid pain. Teleology enters his ethics as philosophical instruction, as a plan of life which accords with our natural needs but is not, so to speak, programmed by them (cf. **B 1**, **F 2**). Finally, we may note that the intrinsic desirability of pleasure and undesirability of pain was also justified, by later Epicureans, as a 'preconception' (**A 4**): as such it is conceptually validated in a manner which, as with all preconceptions (see **17** commentary), is founded in immediate experience.

Every pleasure *qua* pleasure is good, and every pain *qua* pain is bad (**A 5**, **B 3**, **D 1**). But the 'natural affinity' of every pleasure and the converse for every pain are not reasons for pursuing the former and avoiding the latter irrespective of circumstances (**A 5**, **B 3**). I.e. not every pleasure is choiceworthy. The grounds of this proposition introduce us to the most distinctive feature of Epicurus' hedonism: 'the greatest pleasure is the removal of all pain' (**A 6–8**, cf. **B 1–2**, **C 1**, **E 1**). If complete absence of bodily and mental pain constitutes the greatest pleasure, then it is only reasonable to avoid any pleasures which will imperil this objective, or to accept any pains which will help to secure it. Epicurus develops his hedonistic calculus accordingly (**B 3**, cf. **D 1**, **3**, **H 3**), and recommends the avoidance of all pleasure sources which are likely to result in an excess of pain.

At first glance the denial of 'anything in between pleasure and pain' (**A 7**) seems counter-intuitive. Plato had made this point (*Republic* 9,583c–584a) arguing that it is just an illusion when in pain to think that the ending of the pain will actually be pleasure. However, his argument depends upon the assumption that both pleasure and pain are movements, with the absence of either constituting a state of rest. The Cyrenaics accepted his assumption, but Epicurus did not (**R 1**). In his theory it is essential to distinguish between 'kinetic' and 'static' pleasure. What the latter comprises is exemplified in **N** and **Q**, a bodily state which is 'comfortable' or suffering from no unsatisfied desire. That such a state can be called pleasurable is entirely plausible if we regard pain as a disruption of the condition we find naturally congenial – 'not being hungry or thirsty or cold' (**G 1**). Whether or not Epicurus knew Aristotle's *Nicomachean ethics*, he would have found general support for this concept of 'static' pleasure in Aristotle's claim that pleasure is 'the activity of the natural state' (*Nicomachean ethics* VII.12, 1153a14), and in his further observation that 'there is not only an activity of movement but an activity of immobility, and pleasure is found more in rest than in movement' (1154b28). Since Epicurus wants to establish a rational basis for a whole life in which pleasure will predominate over pain, we should not be surprised at his saying 'the time when we need pleasure is when we are in pain from the absence of pleasure' (**B 2**). Someone suffused with 'static' pleasure – free from all bodily and mental pain, and thus able to function fully in all his faculties – has all the pleasure he needs for happiness.

Epicurus appears to have used 'kinetic' pleasure to designate all experience which consists in the active stimulation of enjoyable bodily feelings or states of mind (cf. the Stoic goods 'in process' at **60J 1** where the Greek for 'in process' is the same expression which we translate 'kinetic' for Epicurus). As long as pain is absent we have static pleasure, but kinetic pleasure will last only as long as the activity giving rise to it. Hence, though necessarily good, it is incapable of challenging static pleasure as a long-term excellence which embraces the whole organism and removes all bodily and mental pain (cf. the interesting counterfactual propositions of **D 2–3**). In **Q** Cicero associates kinetic pleasure both with the process of removing pain (quenching a thirst) and with 'varying' a pre-existent pleasure consisting in no pain (presumably drinking when suffering from no thirst). Because such 'variations' supervene upon static pleasure without increasing it (**A 7**, **E 1**, cf. **I**, **J**), it is often supposed that Cicero was mistaken in also associating the process of removing pain with kinetic pleasure. But his evidence, if a bit misleadingly expressed, is almost certainly correct. Epicurus plainly recognized that we derive pleasure from the process of satisfying desires, i.e. removing pains. What he is anxious to combat is the Cyrenaic thesis that a truly pleasurable life consists solely in a constant succession of such enjoyments. Plato had satirized such a life as one of constantly seeking to replenish a leaking jar (*Gorgias* 493a), an image repeated by Lucretius (**X 2–3; 24F 5**). Hence Epicurus firmly subordinates kinetic to static pleasure, treating the former either as a stage on the way to the ultimate goal of absence of pain, or as a variation of that condition when achieved.

Such subordination does not imply that all desires which involve kinetic pleasure are to be eliminated or that some such pleasures are inessential to happiness. Certainly the Epicureans insist that many sources of kinetic pleasure, for instance sex (**B 5, G 3**) or luxurious food and drink (**B 5, J**), are likely to do us more harm than good in the long run; and that a frugal life, based upon an understanding of the cardinal difference between necessary, merely natural, and empty desires (**B 1–5, E 3, G 4, H**), is the best recipe for happiness. But the ideal Epicurean life, as described by Lucretius (**W 4**), includes sensual enjoyment as well as absence of pain; and the pleasures described as indispensable to the conception of anything good include ones which must be kinetic, 'those of taste . . . and listening to music and pleasant motions felt by the eyes' (**L**). Epicurus probably supposed that any condition in which we are free from bodily and mental pain normally includes some kinetic pleasures as well. And he explicitly acknowledged that the kinetic pleasure of joy (**R**) enabled him to counterbalance the most acute stomach pains (**24D**). The Epicurean expectation of a life of enduring pleasure is a more feasible objective if the variations produced by kinetic pleasures are an indispensable feature; they can help us to avoid pain, or counterbalance it at least, by prompting us to attend to sources of pleasure that happen to be available (e.g. listening to music if we cannot see our friends). Thus kinetic pleasures will not increase happiness beyond absence of pain, but they may prevent pain from interrupting static pleasure. Moreover, the principal Epicurean means of counteracting bodily pain is the recollection and anticipation of pleasures (**T**), and in order to provide sufficient variety for the purpose these would have to be kinetic. This, we suggest, adequately explains the undeniable emphasis on sensory stimulation in **L**, a passage which was (and continues to be) repeatedly quoted out of context by Epicurus' critics as evidence of crude sensualism on his part.

Despite the apparently exclusive concentration in such texts (cf. also **C 2, G 1, M, N**) on the pleasure or pain of the flesh, Epicurus nevertheless insists that 'the beginning and the greatest good' for living pleasurably is 'prudence' (**B 6**), which generates the other virtues, and provides the 'sober reasoning which tracks down the causes of every choice and avoidance, and which banishes the opinions that beset souls with the greatest confusion' (**B 5**). Allowing for differences of emphasis appropriate to different contexts, it seems correct to suppose that he did regard bodily pleasures in the static sense (cf. **G 1**) as primary, and also acknowledged, as primary to mental pleasure, awareness of and confidence in bodily well-being (cf. **E 1, N, T, U 2**). But the superiority of mental to bodily pleasure (**V**, cf. **U 2**) can hardly be restricted to the mind's ability to remember and anticipate the body's absence of pain. Such a restriction fails to account for the pleasures deriving from removal of fears of death and the gods, Epicurus' ability to overcome bodily pain with joyous remembrance of philosophical conversations (**24 D**), and, above all, the enormous emphasis placed upon the pleasures engendered by friendship (**22E 1, F 1, 7** etc.).

Although freedom from bodily pain and freedom from mental disturbance jointly constitute the Epicurean good (**B 1, 5, W**), the superiority of mental pleasure, noted above, makes freedom from mental disturbance (*ataraxia*), or tranquillity, the supreme hallmark of Epicurean happiness. It is perhaps no coincidence that tranquillity was represented as the good by Pyrrho (**1F 5 ; 2E**), whose personal example of lifestyle and temperament Epicurus had greatly admired (**1B 2**; cf. **2** commentary).

In assessing all this material it is essential to recognize Epicurus' insistence that hedonic happiness will emerge if people remove the impediments to it, which are largely due to false beliefs concerning inessential goods and avoidable pains (see **W**, **X**; **24C**). The sources of those pleasures that happiness requires are readily available (**X 2**), and pain need never outweigh such pleasures (**C 2**). Thus the Epicurean, equipped with true beliefs about the world and his own needs, and disposed to organize his actions in ways that conform to basic moral norms, will achieve not the invariable happiness symbolized by god (cf. **23**), but the incremental happiness (**K**) which in no way falls short of the divine kind (cf. **G 1**; **14D 5**; **23J–K**).

22 Society

A Epicurus, *Key doctrines* 31–5

(1) [31] Nature's justice is a guarantee of utility with a view to not harming one another and not being harmed. (2) [32] Nothing is just or unjust in relation to those creatures which were unable to make contracts over not harming one another and not being harmed; so too with all peoples which were unable or unwilling to make contracts over not harming and not being harmed. (3) [33] Justice was never anything *per se*, but a contract, regularly arising at some place or other in people's dealings with one another, over not harming or being harmed. (4) [34] Injustice is something bad not *per se* but in the fear that arises from the suspicion that one will not escape the notice of those who have the authority to punish such things. (5) [35] No one who secretly infringes any of the terms of a mutual contract made with a view to not harming and not being harmed can be confident that he will escape detection even if he does so countless times. For right up to his death it is unclear whether he will actually escape.

B Epicurus, *Key doctrines* 36–7, 17

(1) [36] Taken generally, justice is the same for all, since it is something useful in people's social relationships. But in the light of what is peculiar to a region and to the whole range of determinants, the same thing does not turn out to be just for all. (2) [37] What is legally deemed to be just has its existence in the domain of justice whenever it is attested to be useful in the requirements of social relationships, whether or not it turns out to be the same for all. But if someone makes a law and it does not happen to accord with the utility of social relationships, it no longer has the nature of justice. And even if what is useful in the sphere of justice changes but fits the preconception for some time, it was no less just throughout that time for those who do not confuse themselves with empty utterances but simply look at the facts. (3) [17] The just < life > is most free from disturbance, but the unjust life is full of the greatest disturbance.

C Epicurus, *Key doctrines* 7, 40

(1) [7] Certain people wanted to become famous and admired, thinking that they would thus acquire security from other men. Consequently, if such people's life was secure, they did obtain nature's good; but if it was not secure, they are not in possession of the objective which they originally sought after on the basis of nature's affinity. (2) [40] Those who had the power to eliminate all fear of their neighbours lived together accordingly in the most pleasurable way, through having the firmest pledge of security; and after enjoying the fullest intimacy, they did not grieve over someone's untimely death as if it called for commiseration.

D Epicurus, *Vatican sayings* 58, 70, 79

(1) [58] We must liberate ourselves from the prison of routine business and politics. (2) [70] Let nothing be done in your life which will bring you fear if it should be known to your neighbour. (3) [79] The undisturbed man causes no stress to himself or to anyone else.

E Epicurus, *Key doctrines* 27–8

(1) [27] Of the things wisdom acquires for the blessedness of life as a whole, far the greatest is the possession of friendship. (2) [28] Confidence that nothing terrible lasts for ever or even for a long time is produced by the same judgement that also achieves the insight that friendship's security within those very limitations is perfectly complete.

F Epicurus, *Vatican sayings* 23, 28, 34, 39, 52, 66, 78

(1) [23] All friendship is an intrinsic virtue, but it originates from benefiting. (2) [28] Neither those who are over-eager for friendship nor those who are hesitant should be approved, but it is also necessary to take risks for the sake of friendship. (3) [34] It is not our friends' help that we need so much as the confidence of their help. (4) [39] One who is always looking for help is not a friend, nor is one who never associates help with friendship. For the former trades sentiment for recompense, while the latter cuts off confident expectation in regard to the future. (5) [52] Friendship dances round the world announcing to us all that we should wake up and felicitate one another. (6) [66] Let us feel for our friends not by mourning but by thinking of them. (7) [78] The man of noble character is chiefly concerned with wisdom and friendship. Of these the former is a mortal good, but the latter is immortal.

G Plutarch, *Against Epicurean happiness* 1097A (Usener 544, part)

They themselves [Epicureans] in fact say that it is more pleasurable to confer a benefit than to receive one.

H Plutarch, *Against Colotes* 1111B (Usener 546)

Though choosing friendship for the sake of pleasure, he [Epicurus] says he takes on the greatest pains on behalf of his friends.

I Seneca, *Letters* 19.10 (Usener 542)

He [Epicurus] says you should be more concerned at inspecting whom you eat and drink with, than what you eat and drink. For feeding without a friend is the life of a lion and a wolf.

J Lucretius 5.925–38, 953–61

(1) But the human race at that time was much hardier on the land, as was fitting for creatures engendered by the hard earth. Supported from within on larger and more solid bones, they were fitted all over their flesh with powerful sinews, and were not easily capable of being harmed by heat or cold or unusual food or any damage to the body. (2) And for many of the sun's cycles through the sky they dragged out their life in the roving manner of wild beasts. There was no sturdy director of the rounded plough, no one who knew how to work the land with iron or to dig young shoots into the soil or to cut down the old branches of tall trees with pruning knives. What sun and rain had given, what earth had created of its own accord, was gift sufficient to satisfy their hearts . . . (3) As yet they did not know how to manipulate things with fire, nor how to use skins and clothe their bodies in the spoils of wild beasts. They dwelt in woods and mountain caves and forests, and used to hide their rough limbs amid shrubs when forced to take shelter from the lash of winds and rains. (4) Nor could they have the common good in view, nor did they know how to make mutual use of any customs or laws. Whatever prize fortune had provided to each man, he carried off, taught to apply his strength and live on his own account just for himself.

K Lucretius 5.1011–27

(1) Then after they obtained huts and skins and fire, and woman united with man withdrew into a single marriage, and they saw offspring engendered from themselves, then the human race first began to soften. For fire saw to it that their chilly bodies could not now bear cold so well under the covering of the sky; sex sapped their strength, and children by their charm easily broke their parents' stern demeanour. (2) Then too neighbours began to form friendships, eager not to harm one another and not to be harmed; and they gained protection for children and for the female sex, when with babyish noises and gestures they indicated that it is right for everyone to pity the weak. (3) Yet harmony could not entirely be created; but a good and substantial number preserved their contracts

honourably. Otherwise the human race would even then have been totally destroyed, and reproduction could not have maintained the generations down to the present day.

L Lucretius 5.1105–57

(1) Day by day those of outstanding intellect and strength of mind would give increasing demonstrations of how to change the earlier mode of life by innovations and by fire. Kings began to found cities and to establish citadels for their own protection and refuge. They distributed cattle and lands, giving them to each man on the basis of his looks and strength and intellect; for good looks counted for much and strength was at a premium. (2) Later came the invention of private property and the discovery of gold, which easily robbed the strong and handsome of their status; for in general people follow the wealthier man's party, however vigorous and handsome they may be by birth. But if someone should govern his life by true reasoning, a man's great wealth is to live sparingly with a tranquil mind; for there is never a shortage of little. (3) But men wished to be famous and powerful, to secure a stable foundation for their fortune and the means of living out a peaceful life with wealth. To no purpose – in struggling to climb up to the pinnacle of status, they made their journey perilous. Even from the summit, resentment in a while, like a thunderbolt, strikes and hurls them down with ignominy into a foul abyss. For resentment, like a thunderbolt, generally scorches the heights and everything that is much higher than the rest. It is far better, then, to be obedient and quiet than to want imperial rule and the occupation of kingdoms. (4) Let them accordingly toil in vain and sweat out their blood, as they fight along the narrow road of ambition. For the wisdom they savour is from another's mouth and they seek things from hearsay rather than from their own sensations. This was as much the case in the past as it is now and will be. (5) And so the kings were killed; the ancient majesty of thrones and proud sceptres lay overturned, and the illustrious badge of the sovereign head was stained with blood, mourning its great rank under the feet of the mob. For things are avidly stamped upon when they have previously roused extreme terror. Thus affairs were returning to the dregs of disorder, with each man seeking supreme power for himself. (6) Then some people taught how to institute magistrates and constitutional rights, with a view to the voluntary employment of laws. For the human race, worn out by its violent way of life, was enfeebled by feuds; all the more, then, of its own volition it submitted to laws and constraining rights. Each man had been ready out of passion to avenge himself more fiercely than is now permitted by equitable laws, and therefore people were nauseated by their violent way of life. (7) Since then, fear of punishment spoils the prizes of life. Violence and

wrongdoing entrap each person and generally recoil on their originator. It is not easy for one who infringes the common contracts of peace by his deeds to lead a calm and tranquil life. For even if he escapes notice by the race of gods and men, he must lack confidence that it will stay hidden for ever.

M Porphyry, *On abstinence* 1.7.1–9.4

[Reporting the Epicurean Hermarchus] (1) The Epicureans . . . say that the ancient legislators, after studying men's social life and their dealings with one another, pronounced murder a sacrilege and attached special penalties to it. Another factor may have been the existence of a certain natural affinity between man and man, deriving from their likeness in body and soul, which inhibited the destruction of this kind of creature as readily as that of others whom it is permitted to kill. But the principal reason for their refusal to tolerate murder and for pronouncing it sacrilegious was the belief that it is not useful to the general structure of human life. (2) Thereafter, those who understood the utility of the law had no need of any further reason to restrain them from this act; the others, who were unable to take sufficient cognizance of this, refrained from readily killing one another through fear of the magnitude of the punishment. It is evident that each of these inhibitions is still operative today . . . (3) Originally no law, whether written or unwritten, among those that persist today and are naturally transmitted, was established by force, but only by agreement of the users themselves. For what distinguished the men who popularized such practices from the masses was not their physical strength and totalitarian power but their prudence. They established a rational calculation of utility in those whose previous perception of this was irrational and often forgetful, while terrifying others by the magnitude of the penalties. For the only remedy against the ignorance of utility was fear of the punishment fixed by the law. Today too this is the only check and deterrent on ordinary people from acting against public or private interest. (4) But if everyone were equally able to observe and be mindful of utility, they would have no need of laws in addition; of their own volition, they would steer clear of what is forbidden and do what is prescribed. For the observation of what is useful and harmful is sufficient to secure avoidance of some things and choice of others. The threat of punishment is addressed to those who fail to take note of utility. For hanging over them, it compels them to master impulses which lead to inexpedient actions that are contrary to utility, and forcibly helps to constrain them to do what they should. (5) This explains too why the legislators did not exempt unintentional killing from all punishment; they wanted to avoid giving any pretext to people who might intentionally choose to imitate acts done unintentionally, and also to ensure that such matters should not be approached with a carelessness or casualness which would have many genuinely unintentional consequences. For unintentional killing was also incompatible with utility, and for the same reasons as people's intentional destruction of one another. (6) Consequently, since some unintentional acts arise from causes that are indeterminable and beyond man's nature to forestall, while others are due to our own negligence and inattention to what matters, they wished to restrain the carelessness which does harm to a man's neighbours. Hence they did not exempt unintentional action from all penalty, but through holding out the fear of punishments succeeded in removing most of this kind of offence. (7) In my own opinion, moreover, the reason why murders excused by the law are subject to the practice of expiation through purifications, as intended by those who initiated this excellent custom, was to deter people as far as possible from the intentional action. For ordinary people everywhere needed a check on their readiness to act contrary to utility. (8) Therefore those who were first aware of this not only drew up punishments but also held out the threat of a different and irrational fear, with the pronouncement that those guilty of any kind of homicide were impure until they had experienced purification. For the irrational part of the soul, by various forms of education, has arrived at the present condition of civility as a result of the civilizing devices applied to the irrational motion of desire by those who originally set the masses in order; and these include the prohibition of indiscriminately killing one another.

N Porphyry, *On abstinence* 1.10.1–12.7

[Reporting the Epicurean Hermarchus] (1) In determining what we should and should not do, the first legislators had good reason for not setting any ban on the destruction of other creatures. For in regard to these utility results from the opposite action: man would not have been able to survive without taking steps to defend himself against animals by living a social life. (2) Some of the most talented men of the time remembered that they themselves abstained from murder because that was useful for their preservation; and they reminded the rest of what they gained from their social life, that by keeping their hands off their own kind they might safeguard the community which contributed to the individual preservation of each person. Existing as a separate community and doing no harm to their fellow residents were useful for expelling creatures of other species; and also as a protection against men intent on doing harm. This is the reason why for a while people kept their hands off their own kind, in as much as the latter were entering into the same community of needs . . . (3) But as time passed, the population expanded;

creatures of other kinds were expelled . . . and some people acquired a rational calculation of what was useful in their social life, not just an irrational memory. (4) Accordingly they attempted to impose stronger restraints on those who were ready to kill one another and were weakening internal security by their forgetfulness of the past. In their efforts to do this, they introduced the legislation which still exists today among cities and peoples. The masses complied with their legislators voluntarily, as a result of now having a better grasp of what was useful in their social grouping. For their absence of fear was promoted equally by the merciless killing of everything harmful and the preservation of every means to its destruction. Hence, with good reason, one of the above mentioned [killings] was forbidden, the other permitted. (5) It is irrelevant to point out that the law permits us to kill certain animals that are not destructive to man or harmful to our lives in any other way. For practically none of the animals we are permitted by law to kill would fail to be harmful to us if it were allowed to proliferate to excess. Yet by being preserved in their present numbers they satisfy certain of our life's needs . . . Hence we completely destroy some animals [lions, wolves, etc.], but in the case of other animals [sheep, cattle etc.] we only get rid of the excess. (6) We must suppose that reasons similar to what has been mentioned influenced those who originally made laws concerning the regulation of eating living beings. In the case of the inedible, the reason was utility and its opposite. Hence it is a mark of gross stupidity for some people to say that everything excellent and just in the sphere of legislation is determined by individual judgements. This is not the case; rather it is just like other matters of utility, such as health and thousands of others. (7) In many cases, however, they miss what is universal as well as what is individual. For it is the case both that some people fail to see those laws which fit everyone alike, either ignoring them in the belief that they are indifferent or taking the opposite view about them, and that some people think things which are not universally useful to be useful everywhere. Accordingly, they attach themselves to measures which do not fit, even if in some cases they do discover what is profitable to themselves and what is universally beneficial. (8) Such laws include ones concerned with the eating and destruction of living things. Among most peoples these laws are formulated on account of the particular nature of the country, and *we* do not have to observe them since we do not live in the same place. (9) If, then, it were possible to make a kind of contract with the other animals, as with men, over their not killing us or being killed by us indiscriminately, it would have been good to push justice up to this point; for it would have extended our security. (10) But since it was impossible to associate creatures that lack reason with law, it was not possible to use such an instrument as the means of providing for utility in our security from other living beings any more than from lifeless things. All that can assure our security is the option, that we now have, of killing them.

O Cicero, *On ends* 1.66–70

[The Epicurean spokesman, Torquatus] (1) I notice that friendship has been discussed by our school in three ways. Some have said that the pleasures which belong to friends are not as desirable *per se* as those we desire as our own. This position is thought by certain people to make friendship unstable, though in my opinion its proponents are successful and easily defend themselves. (2) They say that friendship is no more separable from pleasure than are the virtues we discussed previously. A lonely life without friends is packed with risks and anxieties. Therefore reason itself advises the formation of friendships; their acquisition strengthens the mind and gives it the absolutely secure expectation of generating pleasures. (3) Moreover, just as enmities, resentments and disparagements are opposed to pleasures, so friendships are creators of pleasures, as well as being their most reliable protectors, for friends and for ourselves alike. The pleasures they enjoy are not only of the present, but they are also elated by the hope of the near and distant future. Without friendship we are quite unable to secure a joy in life which is steady and lasting, nor can we preserve friendship itself unless we love our friends as much as ourselves. Therefore friendship involves both this latter and the link with pleasure. For we rejoice in our friends' joy as much as in our own and are equally pained by their distress. The wise man, therefore, will have just the same feelings towards his friend that he has for himself, and he will work as much for his friend's pleasure as he would for his own ... (4) Some Epicureans, however, though intelligent enough, are a little more timid in facing the criticisms from you [Academics]: they are afraid that if we regard friendship as desirable just for our own pleasure, it will seem to be completely crippled, as it were. In their view, then, the first associations and unions and wishes to form relationships occur for the sake of pleasure; but when advancing familiarity has produced intimacy, affection blossoms to such an extent that friends come to be loved just for their own sake even if no advantage accrues from the friendship. If, at any rate, familiarity with places, temples, cities, gymnasia, playing-fields, dogs, horses, hunting and other sports, gets us in the habit of loving them, how much more easily and rightly could this happen in human relationships! (5) There are also some who say that wise men have a sort of contract to love their friends no less than themselves. We understand the possibility of this, and often observe it too. It is self-evident that no better means of living joyously can be found than such a relationship. (6) All of these points serve to settle not just the absence of any problem in accounting for friendship, if the highest good is located in pleasure, but the impossibility without this thesis of finding any basis at all for friendship.

P Diogenes of Oenoanda 25.2.3–11

In relation to each segment of the earth different people have different native lands. But in relation to the whole circuit of this world the entire earth is a single native land for everyone, and the world a single home.

Q Diogenes Laertius 10.117–20

[Epicurus' and his followers' opinions on the wise man] (1) The motives for one man harming another are enmity, resentment and disparagement, which the wise man masters by reason. (2) Once he has become wise, he no longer adopts the opposite character and does not intentionally feign it either; rather, he will be affected by feelings but without having his wisdom impeded. However, not every bodily condition nor every people makes the occurrence of a wise man possible. (3) Even if he is put on the rack, the wise man is happy . . . But when he is on the rack, he shrieks and groans. (4) He will have no sexual intercourse with a woman whom the laws forbid . . . Nor will he punish his slaves, but will rather pity them and forgive any who are of good character. (5) The Epicureans do not think that the wise man will fall in love, nor will he care about his funeral . . . or make fine public speeches . . . He will marry and have children . . . but he will not engage in politics . . . or rule as a tyrant or live as a Cynic . . . or a beggar. Even if he is robbed of his eyes, he will keep his share in life . . . He will feel grief . . . and bring lawsuits, and leave writings when he dies. But he will not make ceremonial speeches. He will be concerned about his property and the future, enjoy the countryside, be equipped against fortune, and never give up a friend. (6) He will be concerned about his reputation, up to the point of ensuring that he will not be disparaged. He will take more delight than other men in theatrical events. He will set up statues but be indifferent about having one. Only he could discourse correctly about music and poetry, but he would not actually write poems. One wise man is not wiser than another. He will make money, but only by his wisdom, if he is hard up. He will on occasion pay court to a king. He will take pleasure in someone's being put straight. He will set up a school, but not one which results in courting the mob. He will give public lectures, but not at his own wish. He will hold firm doctrines and not be aporetic. In sleep he will be just the same. And he will on occasion die for a friend.

R Plutarch, *Against Colotes* 1124D

Right at the end of the book he [Colotes] says that 'those who drew up laws and customs and established monarchical and other forms of government brought life into a state of much security and tranquillity and banished turmoil; and if anyone should remove these things, we would live a life of beasts, and one man on meeting another will all but devour him.'

S Diogenes of Oenoanda, new fr. 21.1.4–14, 2.10–14

Then truly the life of the gods will pass to men. For everything will be full of justice and mutual friendship, and there will come to be no need of city-walls or laws and all the things we manufacture on account of one another. As for the necessities derived from agriculture ... such activities will, to the extent that need requires, interrupt the continuity of philosophizing; for the farming operations <will provide us> with what our nature desires.

☐ As a moral philosopher, Epicurus is principally known for his hedonism. Coupled with his famous interdict on engagement in politics (cf. **D 1, Q 5**), to which the community of his Garden is often regarded as the model alternative, the Epicurean way of life has been criticized as narrowly self-interested, negative, and unresponsive to the needs of society in general. The material collected here, on justice, friendship, and social institutions, shows that such assessments fail to capture Epicurus' view of how human beings stand and should stand in relation to one another. If he anticipates Bentham's initial proposition, 'Nature has placed mankind under the governance of two sovereign masters, *pain* and *pleasure*' (opening of *An introduction to the principles of morals and legislation*), he also foreshadows Mill as well as Bentham in justifying courses of action and social practices by reference to their utility in promoting pleasure and diminishing pain, for communities as well as for the individuals that compose them (**A, B, M, N**). Our presentation of his teaching on pleasure and society in different sections is no more than a convenience of exposition. It does not imply that the two sets of texts can be adequately studied in isolation from one another, or that an Epicurean can achieve his goal of equanimity independently of the social prescriptions and theories assembled in this section.

Having totally dispensed with teleology in his cosmology (**13**), Epicurus opted for an evolutionist or experimental account of the origin and development of human institutions (**J–N**). Human nature has become drastically different physically and mentally from that of primitive man, in response to changes, partly man-made, to the external environment (**J, K, L**). Just as language evolved naturally, at a particular stage of human evolution (**19**), so the beginnings of co-operation are traced to the time when 'the human race began to soften' (**K 1**), under the influence of rudimentary technology and family life. Justice, then, is not something *per se* (**A 3, 4**), but a historically conditioned phenomenon, institutionalizing the recognition that members of a social group can best secure freedom from being harmed by a mutual agreement not to harm one another. The existence of justice is entirely dependent upon (1) the ability to make such contracts (**A 2**), and (2) their actually achieving the intended result –

'the utility of social relationships' (**B 2**). Hence a codified legal system will be just if and only if it satisfies this criterion (**B 2**). But 'the utility of social relationships' specifies invariant conditions for justice only in the most general way: it does not require every just society to make the particulars of its contract identical (**B 1**, cf. **N 8**), nor does it exclude conceptions of what the contract should include from being modified over time (**B 2**). Thus an Epicurean could hold both that apartheid, though legally sanctioned, is unjust, and also that no injustice was done to women before female suffrage was introduced, even though it would now be unjust to deprive them of the vote. It should be noted that condition (1) above does not strictly confine justice to human beings (cf. **A 2** on 'creatures'), and it is possible to interpret the mutually useful relationship between man and domesticated animals (**13I 2–3**) as an extension of the principle. But Hermarchus, Epicurus' successor, limits the making of the requisite contracts to rational beings (**N 9–10**).

Epicurus' approach to the origin and objective status of justice recalls fifth-century sophistic debates concerning the respective contributions of nature or convention to moral values. It is, however, original in essence, and significantly different from the 'social contract' outlined by Glaucon in Plato, *Republic* 2, to which it is often assimilated. According to Glaucon, the contract, 'not to do wrong or to suffer it', originated as a compromise. Those who agreed to it did so because they found the advantages of doing wrong more than counterbalanced by the disadvantages of being wronged without redress. On this view, justice inclines to the lesser of two evils; but no one, who had the power to do wrong with impunity, would be sane to enter into such a contract. The force of this point is then underlined by the story of Gyges, whose magic ring, by making him invisible, furnished immunity from detection. Glaucon infers that even the just man would commit Gyges' crimes if he could be sure of getting away with them.

As **A 5** (cf. **B 3**, **C 1**, **L 7**) shows, Epicurus insisted that no Gyges ever *could* have such confidence; he dismisses this threat to justice as utterly counterfactual. And his difference from Glaucon goes much deeper. On Epicurus' account, the social contract arises not as a compromise but as a 'natural guarantee' (**A 1**) that will help to secure the freedom from pain, and tranquillity, which are everyone's natural objective (**C 1**). The reasons for wrong-doing, like the misplaced ambitions for power and status with which they are frequently linked, stem from misunderstanding the means of obtaining security and tranquillity (**L**; cf. **21W**, **X**; **24C 3**).

Instead of treating nature or convention as exclusive alternatives between which the social anthropologist must choose, Epicurus allows explanatory force to both concepts, with utility as the causal factor that links them together. As language originated instinctively but became refined by artifice (**19A**, **B**), so uncontrived patterns of behaviour, which turned out to be collectively useful, were recognized to have this feature, thus stimulating rational and deliberate efforts to institutionalize what was 'useful to the general structure of human life' (**M 1**). This principle is rigorously and repeatedly deployed by Hermarchus in his account of the reasons for prohibiting and punishing intentional and accidental homicide, and the absence of these in relation to the killing of animals

(**M, N**). Like Epicurus (**19A 4**) and Lucretius (**L 1, 6**), Hermarchus traces the origin of decisive advances in human culture to the insight and prudence (**M 1–2, N 2**) of exceptionally intelligent individuals. The reader can follow for himself the stages which led to the formal institution of punishments and laws (**M 3–8, L 5–7**). Points deserving particular attention are Hermarchus' claim that rational calculation of utility, if universalized, would render laws redundant (**M 4–5**); his treatment of civilization as an educated restraint of irrational desire (**M 8**; cf. **14D5, 21F 2**); his distinction between irrational memory and rational calculation (**M 3, N 3–4**); his attack on moral subjectivism (**N 6**); and his and Lucretius' stress on the voluntary consent of the masses to the prescriptions of their legislators (**L 6, N 4**).

From Epicurus' own pen the origin of language (**19A**) is the only surviving item of cultural history. It chimes sufficiently well with the methods of Hermarchus and Lucretius to suggest that their evidence is generally valid for the founder himself. However, we should note the contrast between Hermarchus' dispassionate tone and the moral indignation or pessimism prevalent in Lucretius. The latter almost certainly was partly prompted by the experience of civic strife which had torn the Roman Republic apart throughout his life. Certain passages in Lucretius (e.g. 5.939–82, following **J 2**) have sometimes given rise to the view that Epicurus himself was a primitivist, who regarded all features of modern society as alien to man's natural needs. Such a reading (cf. **J 3, 21X 1–2**) does not suit Lucretius, in fact, and is wholly excluded for Epicurus and his contemporary followers. The neglected evidence of Colotes (**R**) on the benefits of law and constitutional government is wholly in line with Hermarchus, whose comment on the theoretical dispensability of laws (**M 4**) is not a recommendation for their removal from society at present. Only in a world where mankind in general has become Epicurean, 'full of justice and mutual friendship', will laws and other protective institutions cease to be necessary (**S**). Of a similar tenor, perhaps, is Diogenes of Oenoanda's further remark, distinguishing nationalist and internationalist conceptions of what constitutes someone's land (**P**). If particular states will have withered away at the Epicurean millennium, the world for which Epicurus devised his own social prescriptions continues to be that of the Greek *polis* (see the actions characteristic of the 'wise man', **Q**).

What Epicurus prohibits (as does Lucretius in his more balanced moments) is not all forms of conventional social life, but active and 'willing' (see Usener 554) involvement in competition for political office and popular renown. The grounds for disparaging these are not that they are intrinsically bad or harmful, but that they are highly unpromising means of obtaining the security that everyone naturally wants (**C 1, L 3–4; 21W 2–3**). Lucretius' stress on the 'resentment' inspired by fame and power, combined with Epicurus' insistence on the need to avoid courting this in one's neighbours (**C 2, D 2–3**, cf. **Q 1**), places the Epicurean policy within social realities that are illustrated time and again in Greek and Roman oratory or drama. To the charge that his attitude to politics is irresponsible and complacent, Epicurus could reply that his philosophy offers an alternative way of organizing society, which retains those institutions – justice, friendship, economic co-operation (see **S**) – that are truly useful to everyone's needs, but eliminates everything that promotes false conceptions of value and endangers people's happiness. When all the evidence is duly considered, Epicureanism would be better regarded as a radical but selective critique of contemporary politics, rather than the apolitical posture with which it is frequently identified.

This conclusion is reinforced by the Epicurean treatment of friendship. In reviewing this material (**E–I, O**), it is essential to remember that friendship, in its Graeco-Roman usage, has a political resonance absent from the modern concept. Covering familial and extra-familial relationships, *philia* in Greek (*amicitia* in Latin) was regularly conceived as the foundation of social cohesion – a political concept, in other words (cf. Aristotle, *Nicomachean ethics* VIII. I). In the absence of anything approximating to the welfare state, friends were expected to offer one another a mutual support system which implied a semi-institutionalized notion of reciprocal benefits; and this was of particular importance in public as well as private life. At the same time friendship was taken to include the mutual affection and sentiments characteristic of our modern concept. It is not surprising, then, that Lucretius links sentimental and prudential considerations in his account of the origin of friendships between neighbours, or that his account of its motivation is the social contract that defines justice (**K 2**). As Aristotle indicates (*loc. cit.*), friendship was naturally thought of as a relationship that included and transcended justice.

Epicurus' emphasis on the absolute necessity of friendship for happiness (**E 1, F 7, O 2–3**) is in line with popular Greek morality; but his conception of its nature is determined by the general principles of his ethics. Like justice, friendship is a means to absence of pain, or tranquillity, by the protection and confidence it provides (**F 3–4**, cf. **I**). Its utility in this regard is foundational (cf. **F 1, 4**). Unlike justice, however, friendship also produces joy (**O 3**, a 'kinetic' pleasure, see **21R 1**), and is describable as an 'immortal good' (**F 7**). That friendship outlasts death can be perceived in the recommendation that we should continue to think of (not mourn) our lost friends (**F 6**, cf. **C 2**). Epicurus had particular reason to stress the hedonic contribution of friendship in the light of his daring, if implausible, claim that severe pains are brief, and long pains mild (**21C 2**). Given his assumption that the means of satisfying necessary desires will normally be available (cf. **25J**), friendship offered itself as a secure and permanent source of pleasure which could counterbalance unavoidable pains. Its efficacy in this regard is attested by Epicurus for himself (**24D**), and seems to be the point of the obscure maxim **E 2** where confidence in the security of friendship is explicitly linked to the transitoriness of anything 'terrible'. Note also **O 2–3** on the connexion between friendship and 'secure expectation of generating pleasures' or hope of pleasures 'of the near and distant future'.

Thus far Epicurus can be seen to have combined two of the three motives for friendship that Aristotle recognizes, utility and pleasure (*Nicomachean ethics* VIII. 3). Aristotle himself regarded each of these as inadequate bases for true friendship, 'loving another for his own sake': such friendship, he argued, must be motivated by friends' excellence of character, and is possible only between good men (the Stoics similarly, **67P**). It is plausible to suppose that Aristotle's discussions of friendship incorporate viewpoints that were commonplace in philosophical circles. In any case, we have evidence that some Epicureans thought it possible to accommodate Aristotle's third motive.

Three strategies are summarized in **O**, which (it is argued) enable an Epicurean to claim that he loves his friend as much as himself. The second of these (**O 4**), which is explicitly revisionary and hence postdates Epicurus himself, concedes to the opposition that a friendship motivated by pleasure will not be one in which the friend is loved 'just for his own sake'; such a friendship, however, is achievable, starting from the hedonist motivation, as a result of the affection that friendly association generates. The first strategy (**O 2–3**) does not make this concession. All friendship, it maintains, is inseparable from pleasure; but in order to achieve friendships that are truly and lastingly pleasurable, we need to love our friends as much as ourselves, and be as pleased by their pleasures or as pained by their pains as our own. The second strategy appears to concede intrinsic value to something other than pleasure. None of Epicurus' own remarks, with the possible exception of **F 1** (see below), requires such a reading. On the basis of the first strategy, he can consistently claim that it is more pleasurable to confer a benefit than to receive one (**G**), and be willing to take risks (**F 2**) or endure great pains (**H**) for friends. The pleasures of friendship, we may take him to have thought, like pleasure in general, can always outweigh any pains that the relationship involves. Even giving up one's life for a friend (**Q 6**) could be intelligibly motivated by the Epicurean brand of hedonism.

It seems unlikely, then, that the altruism of the second strategy goes back to Epicurus himself. Should he also decline the authorship of **F 1**, which credits friendship with intrinsic as well as instrumental value? More precisely, friendship is described, in the one manuscript that transmits this fragment, as an 'intrinsic virtue'. (The word for virtue is generally emended to 'choiceworthy', but on insufficient grounds.) It seems credible that Epicurus could have described friendship in this way, even though he treats the standard moral virtues as purely instrumental goods (**21L, M, O, P**). Friendship, so integral to happiness (**E 1, F 5**), would thus be an inherently pleasurable state of mind, and not just a means to that end. On this interpretation, **F 1** does not imply anything as strongly altruistic as 'loving a friend just for his own sake'.

The *Letter to Menoeceus*, Epicurus' only surviving ethical treatise, omits any explicit mention of friendship. In the light of the material just discussed, it is tempting to think that the necessary connexion between living pleasurably and living honourably (**21B 6**) is best illustrated by the activities of friendship. **F 7**, together with the things an Epicurean will do for his friend, points in that direction. Living honourably (*kalōs*), in ordinary Greek, has a powerful political ring (cf. Aristotle, *Eudemian ethics* 1.5, 1216a25). In Epicureanism that resonance is rejected in reference to conventional public life, with the value of friendship correspondingly enhanced. Thus in microcosm the Epicurean Garden community anticipated the time when 'everything will be full of justice and mutual friendship' (**S**).

Like the Stoics, Epicureans listed characteristic actions of someone perfected in their philosophy. Some of those given in **Q** suggest deliberate attempts to rival or contradict the Stoics, e.g. 'being affected by feelings' (**Q 2**), 'groaning on the rack' (**Q 3**), 'pitying his slaves' (**Q 4**), 'not engaging in politics . . . or living as a Cynic' (**Q 5**), all negate Stoic precepts; 'being consistently wise' (**Q 2**), 'being happy on the rack' (**Q 3**), 'not being wiser than another wise man' (**Q 6**) accord with Stoicism.

23 God

A Lucretius 5.1161–1225

(1) An easier task now is to explain what cause spread the authority of the gods through the wide world, filled the cities with altars, and led to the institution of the holy rituals which now flourish in great states and places. These even now are the source of the awe which sits in mortal men's hearts, which raises new shrines to the gods all over the world, and which compels them to join the rites on holy days. (2) The reason is that already in those days the races of mortal men used to see with waking mind, and even more so in their dreams, figures of gods, of marvellous appearance and prodigious size. They attributed sensation to them, because they seemed to move their limbs, and to give utterance with voices of a dignity to match their splendid appearance and great strength. They endowed them with everlasting life, because their appearance was in perpetual supply and the form remained unchanged, and more generally because they supposed that beings with such strength could not easily be overcome by any force. And hence they supposed them to be supremely blessed, because none of them seemed oppressed by fear of death, and also because in their dreams they saw them perform many marvellous acts with no trouble to themselves. (3) Also, they saw how the patterns of heavenly motion and the various seasons of the year came round in a fixed order, and were unequal to discovering the causes which brought this about. They therefore took refuge in the practice of attributing it all to the gods and making everything be controlled by their authority. And they located the gods' abodes and precincts in the heavens, because it is through the heavens that night and moon are seen to rotate – moon, day, night and her stern beacons, the sky's night-wandering torches and flying flames, clouds, sun, rain, snow, winds, lightning, hail, sudden noises, and mighty menacing rumbles. (4) Unhappy human race, to attribute such behaviour, and bitter wrath too, to the gods! What lamentations did they lay up for themselves in those days, what wounds for us, what tears for our descendants! It is no piety to be seen with covered head bowing again and again to a stone and visiting every altar, nor to grovel on the ground and raise your hands before the shrines of the gods, nor to drench altars in the blood of animals, nor to utter strings of prayers; but rather, to be able to contemplate all things with a tranquil mind. (5) For when we gaze upwards at the heavenly

precincts of the great cosmos and at the aether studded with its shimmering stars, and when we turn our thought to the paths of sun and moon, then in our hearts, already beset with other troubles, a further anxiety is awakened and begins to raise its head, that what confronts us may be some unbounded power, belonging to the gods, which turns the gleaming stars on their various courses. For the lack of an explanation drives the mind to wonder whether the world had any beginning, and likewise whether there is any limit to the period for which its walls can bear the strain of this restless motion, or whether they are divinely endowed with everlasting immunity and can glide down the unending track of measureless time, defying its might. (6) Besides, whose mind does not shrink with fear of the gods, whose limbs do not crawl with terror, whenever the ground is scorched and shaken by the quivering impact of a thunderbolt and rumblings sweep across the great heavens? Do not whole nations tremble, and proud kings shrink, transfixed with fear of the gods, lest the grim hour of reckoning should have arrived for some wicked act or proud word?

B Epicurus, *Letter to Menoeceus* 123–4

(1) First, think of god as an imperishable and blessed creature, as the common idea of god is in outline, and attach to him nothing alien to imperishability or inappropriate to blessedness, but believe about him everything that can preserve his combination of blessedness and imperishability. (2) For there are gods – the knowledge of them is self-evident. (3) But they are not such as the many believe them to be. For by their beliefs as to their nature the many do *not* preserve them. The impious man is not he who denies the gods of the many, but he who attaches to gods the beliefs of the many about them. For they are not preconceptions but false suppositions, the assertions of the many about gods. It is through these that the greatest harms, the ones affecting bad men, stem from gods, and the greatest benefits too. (4) For having a total affinity for their own virtues, they are receptive to those who are like them, and consider alien all that is not of that kind.

C Epicurus, *Letter to Herodotus* 76–7

(1) Among celestial phenomena movement, turning, eclipse, rising, setting and the like should not be thought to come about through the ministry and present or future arrangements of some individual who at the same time possesses the combination of total blessedness and imperishability. For trouble, concern, anger and favour are incompatible with blessedness, but have their origin in weakness, fear and dependence on neighbours. (2) Nor should we think that beings which are at the same time conglomerations of fire possess blessedness and voluntarily take on

these movements. (3) But we must observe all the majesty associated with all the names which we apply to such conceptions, if they give rise to no belief conflicting with majesty. Otherwise the conflict itself will give rise to the greatest mental disquiet.

D Lucretius 6.68–79

Unless you expel these ideas from your mind and drive far away beliefs unworthy of the gods and alien to their tranquillity, the holy divinity of the gods, damaged by you, will frequently do you harm: not because of the possibility of violating the gods' supreme power, and of their consequent angry thirst for bitter vengeance, but because you yourself will imagine that those tranquil and peaceful beings are rolling mighty billows of wrath against you. You will be unable to visit the shrines of the gods with a calm heart, and incapable of receiving with tranquillity and peace the images from their holy bodies which travel into men's minds to reveal the gods' appearance. The direct effect on your life is obvious.

E Cicero, *On the nature of the gods* 1.43–9

[Speaker: the Epicurean Velleius] (1) Anyone who reflects how ungrounded and rash these [non-Epicurean theological] doctrines are ought to revere Epicurus and place him among the very beings whom this investigation concerns. (2) For he alone saw, first, that the gods existed, because nature herself had imprinted the conception of them in all men's minds. For what human nation or race does not have, without instruction, some preconception of the gods? Epicurus' word for this is *prolepsis*, that is what we may call a delineation of a thing, preconceived by the mind, without which understanding, inquiry and discussion are impossible. The power and value of this reasoning we have learnt from Epicurus' heaven-sent book on the yardstick and criterion. Thus you see the foundation of this inquiry admirably laid. For since the belief has not been established by any convention, custom or law, and retains unanimous consent, it must necessarily be understood that there are gods, given that we have ingrained, or rather innate, knowledge of them. But that on which all men's nature agrees must necessarily be true. Therefore it must be conceded that there are gods. (3) Since this is agreed among virtually all – the uneducated, as well as philosophers – let us also allow the following to be agreed: that what I called our preconception, or prenotion, of the gods (for new things require new names, just as Epicurus himself gave *prolepsis* its name, a name which no one had previously applied to it) is such that we think the gods blessed and immortal. For as well as giving us a delineation of the gods themselves, nature has also engraved on our minds the view of them as everlasting and blessed. (4) Therefore Epicurus' well-known maxim [= *Key doctrine*

1] puts it rightly: 'That which is blessed and imperishable neither suffers nor inflicts trouble, and therefore is affected neither by anger nor by favour. For all such things are marks of weakness.' (5) If our sole purpose were to worship the gods in piety and to be freed from superstition, what I have said would suffice. For the sublime nature of the gods, being everlasting and supremely blessed, would earn men's pious worship, since whatever ranks supreme deserves reverence. And all fear of the gods' power and anger would have been expelled. For it is understood that anger and favour are not part of a blessed and immortal nature, and that once these are removed no fears of those above menace us. But in order to confirm this belief the mind requires to know god's shape, way of life and mode of thought. (6) As regards their shape, we have the advice of nature, plus the proof of reasoning. For nature supplies us all, whatever our race, with no other view of the gods than as human in form: what other form does anyone ever think of, whether awake or in sleep? But lest we appeal exclusively to primary conceptions, we have the same conclusion on the authority of reason itself. For given that it seems fitting for that nature which is most sublime, whether because blessed or because everlasting, to be also the most beautiful, what configuration of limbs or features, what shape, what appearance can be more beautiful than the human kind? At any rate, your people [the Stoics], Lucilius, make it their habit (unlike my friend Cotta [the Academic], whose stance varies) when illustrating god's artistic creativity, to describe how all the features of the human figure are well-fashioned not only for utility but also for beauty. But if the human figure is superior to all other shapes of animate beings, and god is animate, he certainly possesses that figure which is most beautiful of all. And since the gods are agreed to be supremely blessed, and since no one can be blessed without virtue, and virtue is impossible without reason, and reason can exist only in the human form, it must be admitted that the gods are of human appearance. (7) However, that appearance is not body but quasi-body, and it does not have blood but quasi-blood. (Although these discoveries of Epicurus' are too acute, and his words too subtle, to be appreciated by just anyone, I am relying on your powers of understanding and expounding them more briefly than my case requires.) Epicurus, who not only sees hidden and profoundly obscure things with his mind but even handles them as if they were at his fingertips, teaches that the force and nature of the gods is of such a kind that it is, primarily, viewed not by sensation but by the mind, possessing neither the kind of solidity nor the numerical distinctness of those things which because of their concreteness he calls *steremnia*; but that we apprehend images by their similarity and by a process of transition, since an endless series of extremely similar images arises from the countless atoms and flows to the gods, and that our mind, by focusing intently on those images with the greatest feelings of pleasure, gains an understanding of what a blessed and everlasting nature is.

F Sextus Empiricus, *Against the professors* 9.43–7

(1) The same reply can be made to Epicurus' belief that the idea of gods arose from dream impressions of human-shaped images. For why should these have given rise to the idea of gods, rather than of outsized men? And in general it will be possible to reply to all the doctrines we have listed that men's idea of god is not based on mere largeness in a human-shaped animal, but includes his being blessed and imperishable and wielding the greatest power in the world. But from what origin, or how, these thoughts occurred among the first men to draw a conception of god, is not explained by those who attribute the cause to dream impressions and to the orderly motion of the heavenly bodies. (2) To this they reply that the idea of god's existence originated from appearances in dreams, or from the world's phenomena, but that the idea of god's being everlasting and imperishable and perfect in happiness arose through a process of transition from men. For just as we acquired the idea of a Cyclops . . . by enlarging the common man in our impression of him, so too we have started with the idea of a happy man, blessed with his full complement of goods, then intensified these features into the idea of god, their supreme fulfilment. And again, having formed an impression of a long-lived man, the men of old increased the time-span to infinity by combining the past and future with the present; and then, having thus arrived at the conception of the everlasting, they said that god was everlasting too. (3) Those who say this are championing a plausible doctrine. But they easily slip into that most puzzling trap, circularity. For in order first to get the idea of a happy man, and then that of god by transition, we must have an idea of what happiness is, since the idea of the happy man is of one who shares in happiness. But according to them happiness (*eudaimonia*) was a divine (*daimonia*) and godly nature, and the word 'happy' (*eudaimōn*) was applied to someone who had his deity (*daimōn*) disposed well (*eu*). Hence in order to grasp human happiness we must first have the idea of god and deity, but in order to have the idea of god we must first have a conception of a happy man. Therefore each, by presupposing the idea of the other, is unthinkable for us.

G Scholion on Epicurus, *Key doctrines* 1

In other works he [Epicurus] says that the gods are seen by reason, some numerically distinct, others with formal unity, resulting from a continuous influx of similar images to the same place, and human in form.

H Philodemus, *On piety* 112.5–12 (Usener 87)

Likewise in book XII [of Epicurus' *On nature*] he criticizes Prodicus, Diagoras, Critias and others, calling them crazy, and compares them to people in a Bacchic frenzy.

I Anonymous Epicurean treatise on theology (Oxyrhynchus Papyrus 215) 1.4–24

. . . nor, by Zeus, when someone or other speaks instead like this: 'I fear all the gods whom I revere, and wish to make all the burnt offerings and dedications to them.' For although such a person may sometimes be more sophisticated than other individuals, there is not yet, along these lines either, a firm basis for piety. My friend, consider it a matter of supreme blessedness to have discriminated properly the most excellent thing that we can think of among existing things. Marvel at your discrimination of it, and revere it without fear.

J Epicurus, *Letter to Menoeceus* 135

Practise these things [Epicurus' ethical teachings] and all that belongs with them, in relation to yourself by day, and by night in relation to your likeness, and you will never be disquieted, awake or in your dreams, but will live like a god among men. For quite unlike a mortal animal is a man who lives among immortal goods.

K Plutarch, *Against Epicurean happiness* 1091B–C (Usener 419, part)

What great pleasure these men [the Epicureans] have, what blessedness they enjoy, when they delight in suffering no evil, grief or pain! Does this not warrant their thinking and saying what they do say, in labelling themselves 'imperishable' and 'equal to gods', and in frenziedly bellowing under the influence of pleasure, because of their superabundance and maximization of goods, that they scorn all else, having alone discovered that great and divine good, the absence of evil!

L Lucretius 5.146–55

You cannot, likewise, believe that the holy abodes of the gods are in any region of our world. For the gods' nature is so tenuous and far-removed from our senses that it is scarcely viewed by the *mind*. Since it escapes the touch and impact of our hands, it cannot have contact with anything which we can touch. For what cannot itself be touched, cannot touch. Hence their abodes too must be unlike ours, in keeping with their tenuous bodies. This I will prove to you at length later on.

☐ The negative side of Epicurus' theology has been explored in **13**, and is relatively straightforward: any proper account of the universe must exclude all attempts at explanation by appeal to divine craftsmanship; gods do not intervene in our world. But the evidence for the positive side is difficult and controversial. The reader must be warned that the interpretation offered below is controversial. We ourselves, however, consider it to be the only philosophically satisfying interpretation, as well as the one best supported by the evidence.

An important preliminary to this section is to read 15 on images, the thin films of atoms which account for vision, imagination and dreaming. In the atomist system which Epicurus inherited from Democritus the gods simply were human-shaped images, but nevertheless alive. These entered men's minds and appeared to them in dreams, displaying prophetic powers and conferring benefit or harm. A recorded Epicurean criticism of this theory (Diogenes of Oenoanda, new fragment 1 = 15g in vol. 2) is that since images lack solidity they could not have any such vital powers. With this modification, however, Epicurus seems to have retained the basic identification of gods with images (cf. 54J 5). According to E 7, our most promising technical report of his theory, gods as primarily conceived are not numerically distinct solid bodies. They are simply the product of streams of images with human shape which enter our minds and form in us idealized impressions of a supremely blessed existence. The images are said to arise from the inexhaustible stock of atoms and to flow *to* the gods, not from them. That is, by converging on our minds they *become* our gods.

In order to make sense of this it is crucial to see that it is simply a standard Epicurean account of the mechanics of concept-formation. *Any* process of imagination is achieved by the mind's admitting from the surrounding air ('tuning in to', as it were) those of the countless available images which correspond to the required impression, either originating from solid bodies, such as men, or forming accidentally from the limitless stock of atoms (15A 1–4, D). The continuity of an impression is produced by the 'similarity' (E 7, G) of the selected images to each other. The impression can then be further adjusted by enlargement, combination, etc., as briefly explained at 15F (cf. the fuller Stoic account at 39D). Sextus Empiricus (*Against the professors* 3.40) tells us that the generic name for these processes of adjustment was 'transition' (*metabasis*), the term used at E 7, F 2–3. To take the example at F 2, we conceive of a giant by first focusing on a series of images of men, then enlarging the resultant mental impression.

Gods, like giants, are thought-constructs. Here too we proceed by 'transition' from an impression of extremely robust, long-lived and happy men, intensifying yet further their durability and happiness (F, cf. A 2). The resultant impression is of something very like the traditional anthropomorphic gods of Greek religion, whose essential features Epicurus takes to be blessedness and imperishability. But unlike the case of the giant we do not have to make any conscious effort to form this idea. The idea of such beings is 'innate', in the sense that it is part of our very nature to conceive it (E 2–3, 6), so that we do so even, indeed especially, in our dreams. It is a natural 'preconception' (see 17), common to all men.

Indirect inference from A 2 (which itself is primarily about the first stirrings of this instinct among primitive men), suggests two ways in which gods are 'imperishable'. First, as *concepts* they are everlasting. The physical explanation of this lies in the inexhaustible supply of similar images (a difficult doxographical report, **m** in vol. 2, adds 'gods' and 'similarities' to the Epicurean list of imperishable items given at **14H** I), its epistemological explanation in the fact that, rather like Platonic Forms, gods are eternal paradigmatic concepts (see below). Second, as imagined *living beings* the gods are imperishable, in so far as they seem invulnerable to the wear and tear which we cannot entirely eliminate from our own lives. It is up to *us* to endow them with this imperishability, to 'preserve' them, by the way in which we conceive them (**B** 1–3).

Why should this preconception of god come naturally to man? There are three clues. First, it is a well recognized fact that Epicurus' gods are paragons of the Epicurean good life. It is in their Epicurean tranquillity and detachment from worldly affairs that they are supremely blessed (**C**, **D**, **E** 4–5, **J**; cf. **21**–2). Their imperishability less obviously fits this account, since elsewhere Epicurus condemns men's vain desire to evade death (**24**); but, as **J**, **K** and a number of other texts show, Epicurus did think there was a sense in which an Epicurean sage possessed divine 'imperishability'. The analogy of the gods' imperishability, as explained above, suggests that he had in mind partly the Epicurean sage's ability to become, by the example he set, an eternal ethical model to future generations (see further below), and partly his invulnerability to fortune (**21B** 4, **F**). Second, the 'innateness' of our tendency to preconceive god in this way can be seen as echoing Epicurus' talk of our innate tendency to pursue pleasure as the good (**21A** 2). Third, the Epicureans suggested (**F** 3) on quite good etymological grounds that 'happiness' (*eudaimonia*, a scarcely translatable word which also shares some of the connotations of 'blessedness') was not only a 'divine and godly nature' but also the state of having one's own god properly sorted out.

These clues suggest that in Epicurus' view each person's gods are paradigms of his own ethical goal – the 'self-image' of which he dreams (cf. especially **J**) – or idealized models of what he aims to achieve in his own life. If our conceptions of god vary, that is because the preconception with which we are all naturally endowed (**E** 2–4), although itself 'true' in the sense of accurately representing our natural goal, is easily distorted with all sorts of false beliefs (**A–D**, **I**): that the gods exercise power, that they are affected by anger and favouritism, that they are malevolent. In this way a person's conception of the divine nature is both a measure and a cause of his own state of moral health. Good and bad alike choose their gods according to their own private views of moral excellence (**B** 4). The bad conceive the gods as power-seeking and meddling like themselves, and thus perpetuate in themselves a corresponding state of disquiet (**B** 3, **C** 3, **D**). The good retain the true preconception of god's blessedness as consisting in supreme tranquillity, and derive immense calm and moral uplift from it (**B** 4, **E** 7 *fin.*, **I**). This latter attitude finds its natural expression in worship, a practice wholeheartedly recommended by Epicurus to his followers, provided only that it is motivated by reverence, not by fear (**A** 4, **D**, **E** 5, **I**).

The idea of god as an object for man to emulate as well as revere was already well developed in the work of Plato and Aristotle, and Aristotle's successor Theophrastus had advanced beyond his master in querying even the last vestiges of god's causal influence in the world. But Epicurus' own distinctive achievement lies largely in his reconciling these features with ancient religion's plurality of anthropomorphic deities. Unwelcome aspects of traditional religion, such as divine interference in the world, are explained as false accretions to the basic conception, reflecting faulty moral outlooks – just as in another context (24F) the myths about the underworld were explained as projections of men's false moral values. But the hard core of popular theology is vindicated, and turned to philosophical advantage. His inspired suggestion that god is a projection of man's own ethical ideal can be ranked with the most impressive theological theories of antiquity.

We now come to a major stumbling-block. If the above interpretation of Epicurean gods as our own instinctive thought-constructs is correct, was Epicurus not an atheist? That inference was indeed frequently drawn by his critics (e.g. at 54J 5), but both Epicurus himself (B 2) and his followers (e.g. E 2) vehemently denied it, and in H Epicurus himself is reported to have been pointedly rude about three of his predecessors standardly listed as 'atheists'. Moreover, while some later Epicureans adhered to the interpretation advanced above (as F strongly suggests), many others represented his gods as real living beings. Most modern scholars have accepted this latter interpretation as correct.

In reply it can first be said that on Epicurus' own epistemological principles his assertions at B 2 that the gods exist and that we have self-evident knowledge of them are entirely consistent with their being objects of thought and not solid bodies. Our preconception of them will be a genuine piece of *moral* knowledge, an accurate intuition of man's natural good. As we have noted in 17, Epicurean 'truth' obtains as much in the moral as in the physical sphere, and true 'preconceptions' can have an introspective origin in our feelings as well as an empirical origin in our sensory experience of the external world. Thus our natural recognition of the existence of god is closely comparable to, perhaps identical with, our instinctive recognition that there exists for us a natural ethical goal.

If it was asked what kind of existence the gods had, in atomistic terms, then Epicurus' answer was that they existed not as solid bodies but as mere streams of images. This would not, on the normal principles of Epicurus' epistemology, weaken the claim that our impressions of them are true. According to 16F, even an impression of a mythical creature is 'true', in that it accurately reports objective images which our mind apprehends. Falsehood arises only when we add the mistaken belief that the object is a solid body or *steremnion*. Likewise, on the theory outlined in E 7, our impressions of gods are true, but their objects are not *steremnia*, just streams of images. (The assertion there that they have only 'quasi-body' is just what one might say of idealized thought constructs which lack solidity – cf. the similar locution at 30A – but would scarcely be intelligible if applied to an actually living organism.) Such a vindication of the gods' 'existence' must not be written off as a mere deception or sophistry. Rather, it is an instance of what we have described (15 commentary) as Epicurus' lingering Platonist assumption that any object of thought must somehow objectively exist in order to be thought of.

Moreover, if Epicurus chose to stress the way in which his gods did exist, rather than the way in which they did not, that was hardly surprising in a society notoriously intolerant of any hint of atheism, and even less surprising for someone who on sincere philosophical grounds recommended the worship of the gods recognized by that society. (Could Epicurus, in defiance of Zeno's celebrated syllogism at **54D**, have recommended the worship of the non-existent?) He can be compared to many nineteenth-century advocates of religion (e.g. Feuerbach, George Eliot, Matthew Arnold) whose professed theism proves on close inspection to be an essentially moral theory, which either evades or positively excludes any question of an objective superhuman deity. Even within Epicurus' own society it was normal practice for intellectuals to accept the teachings of traditional religion as symbolic rather than literal truths (cf. **54A** for the Stoics).

Furthermore, although the gods are *primarily* (**E 7**) concepts and not numerically distinct solid bodies, there are *also* numerically distinct gods (**G**). Epicurus may have meant by this that individual Epicurean sages can become 'gods' by taking on the divine role of perpetual ethical models for future generations. This would be, in effect, the deification which he offered his pupils (**J**, **K**; cf. **14D 5**, **21G 1**), and which his later followers bestowed on him (e.g. **E 1**; **21X**; the deification of great men was a common Hellenistic practice, and was not considered either exaggerated or sacrilegious; cf. **54B**).

Is that all? Or does Epicurus also mean in **G** to allow that somewhere in the universe there might exist living beings which are not only blessed but also biologically immortal? On the one hand, he says nothing that explicitly excludes such a possibility – even where he might most have been expected to do so, in his disproofs of divine intervention in the world (**13**). On the other hand, nothing in his theological theory in any way requires the existence of such beings, since even if they did exist they would play no causal part in our own mental apprehension of god (cf. especially **F**). He may have constructed his system in such a way that this peripheral question could be left open, to be settled, if at all, only within the school's inner circles. The inoffensive-looking theism of his public pronouncements (such as **B**) will have ensured freedom from persecution, while in no way conflicting with the philosophical system. If any of his pupils took it at its most superficial meaning, the resultant inclination to believe in the traditional gods as living beings was entirely consistent with their becoming good Epicureans. For such gods, if they existed, would indeed secure their blessedness by total non-involvement in the world. Hence the Epicurean arguments against divine intervention in the world (**C 1**, **D**; **13**) do not require explicitly atheistic premises, but are content to point out that no one could be both divine and meddling.

Even so, it does seem improbable that Epicurus himself would ultimately have pronounced in favour of these biologically immortal beings. It is extremely difficult to see how, in an Epicurean universe, any compound could be guaranteed to last for ever: cf. **14H 1**. But whatever his view on this question may have been – and it is likely that he said little or nothing in his published works to resolve the issue – it is crucial to see that it is of no more than marginal relevance to his central theological thesis, in which god's primary existence is as a moral concept, not as a specially privileged extraterrestrial life-form.

Despite all this, there is no doubt that Epicureans and others in the first century

B.C. were interpreting the 'god' of Epicurus' system as just such a life-form. Cicero in *On the nature of the gods* 1, from which **E** is drawn, seems to assume Epicurus' gods to be discrete spatial entities. His Epicurean spokesman Velleius clearly cannot understand how Epicurus' technical account of the gods as images is meant to fit in with this, virtually admitting his incomprehension in his parenthesis in **E 7**, and offers only quite inadequate reasons for these beings' literal imperishability (cf. the sequel to **E** in vol. 2). The most famous such reason is the idea that the gods live in the *intermundia*, the spaces between worlds, where they are less buffeted by other matter. This particular doctrine was probably not yet known to Cicero's sources (which may date from the second or early first century B.C.), since it is mentioned neither in Velleius' speech nor in the Academic Cotta's reply. But it was known to Cicero himself, who alludes to it in his introduction (1.18), and was accepted by his contemporaries Philodemus and Lucretius. The latter, while accurately transmitting part of the technical Epicurean account at **A 2**, nevertheless elsewhere assumes the gods to live in the *intermundia* (from where their images travel to us: **D**). His promise in **L** to explain how this can be is never fulfilled, and we may guess that this is because he found no help on the point in Epicurus' writings. Philodemus, in two fragmentarily surviving books, tries to establish the details of the gods' lifestyle (e.g.: do they speak Greek?). But it seems doubtful that he had anything more to go on than Epicurus' advice about how we are to *envisage* the gods as living (cf. **B 1, C**) – advice which *prima facie* may suggest that they are actual living organisms, but which is in fact no less consistent with their being mere thought-objects.

It is not hard to see how Epicurus' repudiations of atheism could have deceived some of his adherents into reading him this way. To find an interpretation consistent with their views as well as with Epicurus' own pronouncements seems impossible, and we have settled instead for the only one which seems to us to fit the items of evidence widely regarded as the most authentic; to account for the deviant items as influenced by a very understandable misreading of Epicurus' intentions; and to leave him with a theology which ranks in subtlety and originality with any of his central theories, and which could hope to compete on equal terms with the rival Stoic doctrine (54).

24 Death

A Epicurus, *Letter to Menoeceus* 124–7

(1) Accustom yourself to the belief that death is nothing to us. For all good and evil lie in sensation, whereas death is the absence of sensation. (2) Hence a correct understanding that death is nothing to us makes the mortality of life enjoyable, not by adding infinite time, but by ridding us of the desire for immortality. (3) For there is nothing fearful in living for one who genuinely grasps that there is nothing fearful in not living. (4) Therefore he speaks idly who says that he fears death not because it will

be painful when present but because it is painful in anticipation. For if something causes no distress when present, it is fruitless to be pained by the expectation of it. (5) Therefore that most frightful of evils, death, is nothing to us, seeing that when we exist death is not present, and when death is present we do not exist. Thus it is nothing to either the living or the dead, seeing that the former do not have it and the latter no longer exist. (6) The many sometimes shun death as the greatest of evils, but at other times choose it as a release from life's <evils. But the wise man neither deprecates living> nor fears not living. For he neither finds living irksome nor thinks not living an evil. But just as he chooses the pleasantest food, not simply the greater quantity, so too he enjoys the pleasantest time, not the longest. (7) He who advises the young man to live well but the old man to die well is naive, not only because life is something to be welcomed, but also because to practise living well and to practise dying well are one and the same. (8) Much worse, however, is he who says 'It's a fine thing never to be born. Or, once born, to pass through the gates of Hades with the utmost speed.' If he believes what he says, why does he not take his departure from life? He has every opportunity to do so, supposing that his resolve were serious. If he is joking, his words are idle and will be greeted with incredulity.

B Epicurus, *Vatican sayings* 31

Against other things it is possible to obtain security. But when it comes to death we human beings all live in an unwalled city.

C Epicurus, *Key doctrines* 19–21

(1) [19] Infinite time and finite time contain equal pleasure, if one measures the limits of pleasure by reasoning. (2) [20] The flesh places the limits of pleasure at infinity, and needs an infinite time to bring it about. But the intellect, by making a rational calculation of the end and the limit which govern the flesh, and by dispelling the fears about eternity, brings about the complete life, so that we no longer need the infinite time. But neither does it shun pleasure, nor even when circumstances bring about our departure from life does it suppose, as it perishes, that it has in any way fallen short of the best life. (3) [21] He who knows the limits of life knows how easy it is to obtain that which removes pain caused by want and that which makes the whole of life complete. He therefore has no need for competitive involvements.

D Diogenes Laertius 10.22 (Usener 138)

Here is the letter to Idomeneus which he [Epicurus] wrote on his death-bed: 'I wrote this to you on that blessed day of my life which was also the last. Strangury and dysentery had set in, with all the extreme intensity of which they are capable. But the joy in my soul at the memory of our past discussions was enough to counterbalance all this. I ask you, as befits your lifelong companionship with me and with philosophy: take care of the children of Metrodorus.'

E Lucretius 3.830–911

(1) Therefore death is nothing to us, of no concern whatsoever, once it is appreciated that the mind has a mortal nature. (2) Just as in the past we had no sensation of discomfort when the Carthaginians were converging to attack, . . . so too, when we will no longer exist following the severing of the soul and body, from whose conjunction we are constituted, you can take it that nothing at all will be able to affect us and to stir our sensation – not if the earth collapses into sea, and sea into sky. (3) Even if the nature of our mind and the power of our spirit do have sensation after they are torn from our bodies, that is still nothing to us, who are constituted by the conjunction of body and spirit. (4) Or supposing that after our death the passage of time will bring our matter back together and reconstitute it in its present arrangement, and the light of life will be restored to us, even that eventuality would be of no concern to us, once our self-recollection was interrupted. Nor do our selves which existed in the past concern us now: we feel no anguish about them. For when you look back at the entire past span of measureless time, and then reflect how various are the motions of matter, you could easily believe that the same primary particles of which we now consist have often in the past been arranged in the same order as now. Yet our minds cannot remember it. For in between there has been an interruption of life, and all the motions have been at random, without sensation. (5) For if there is going to be unhappiness and suffering, the person must also himself exist at that same time, for the evil to be able to befall him. Since death robs him of this, preventing the existence of the person for the evils to be heaped upon, you can tell that there is nothing for us to fear in death, that he who does not exist cannot be unhappy, and that when immortal death snatches away a mortal life it is no different from never having been born. (6) So when you see a man resent the prospect of his body's being buried and rotting after death, or being destroyed by fire or by the jaws of wild beasts, you may be sure that his words do not ring true, and that there lurks in his heart some hidden sting, however much he may deny the belief that he will have any sensation in death. For he does not, I think, grant either the substance or the ground of what he professes. Instead of completely stripping himself of life, he is unconsciously making some bit of himself survive. For when anybody in life imagines that in death the birds and beasts will rip up his body, he pities himself. For he does not distinguish himself from it or adequately detach himself from the

abandoned corpse: he identifies himself with it, and by remaining present he infects it with his own sensation. He thus comes to resent the fact that he was born mortal, and does not see that in the reality of death he will have no other self left alive, able to mourn his passing, and to stand by, suffering the agony of his fallen body being ripped or burnt . . . (7) 'No more for you the welcome of a joyful home and a good wife. No more will your children run to snatch the first kiss, and move your heart with unspoken delight. No more will you be able to protect the success of your affairs and your dependants. Unhappy man', they say, 'unhappily robbed by a single hateful day of all those rewards of life.' What they fail to add is: 'Nor does any yearning for those things remain in you.' If they properly saw this with their mind, and followed it up in their words, they would unshackle themselves of great mental anguish and fear. (8) 'You, at least, in death's sleep, will be evermore free of all pain and suffering. But we have stood viewing your ashes before us on the grim pyre, weeping inconsolably. Our grief will be everlasting. No day will come to purge our hearts of it.' Of the person who says this, we should ask what is so sad about a return to sleep and rest, that someone should be able to pine in everlasting grief.

F Lucretius 3.966–1023

(1) No one is sent down to the black pit of Tartarus. Their matter is needed so that future generations can grow. But these will all follow you too once their life is played out. No less than you, they have fallen and will fall. So ceaselessly does one thing arise from another. All have a lease on life, but none has the freehold . . . (2) Undoubtedly it is in our life that all those things exist which are fabled to be in the depths of hell. No unhappy Tantalus quakes at the huge rock hanging over him in mid-air, numbed by an empty terror. Rather, it is in life that an empty fear of the gods hounds mortals: each is afraid of the fall which his lot may bring him. (3) Nor is it true that Tityos lies in hell with birds tunnelling into him, or that they can really find an everlasting food supply to forage beneath his great chest. However huge were the spread of his body, even were his sprawling limbs to cover not just nine acres but the whole earth, he would still not be able to endure everlasting pain nor to go on for ever providing food from his own body. But we have our own Tityos here – the man who lies lovesick, torn apart by winged creatures and gnawed at by nervous agony, or rent by cares through some other passion. (4) Sisyphus too exists before our eyes in real life. He is the man who thirsts to run for the rods and cruel axes of public office, and who always returns beaten and dejected. For to pursue the empty and unattainable goal of power, and in its pursuit to endure unremittingly hard toil, that is the struggle of pushing uphill a stone which, in spite of all, at the very peak

rolls back and hurtles downward to the level ground below. (5) Then again, to be always indulging an ungrateful mind, and never to satisfy it with its fill of good things, as the seasons of the year do for us when they come round bringing their fruits and a variety of delights, despite which we are never satisfied with our fill of life's benefits – that, I believe, is the fable of the girls in the bloom of youth gathering water into a pitcher full of holes which it is impossible to fill. (6) As for Cerberus, the Furies, and the pitch black of Tartarus belching dreadful heat from its jaws, they do not, and indeed cannot, exist anywhere. What there is in real life is the fear of punishment for crimes – as prominent a fear as the crimes are prominent. And there is atonement for wrongdoing: prison, the dreadful hurling down from the rock, lashes, executioners, the rack, tar, metal plates, firebrands. Even when these are absent, still the mind, in the anxiety brought on by awareness of its deeds, goads itself and scorches itself with whips. And all the time it is failing to see what limit to evils there can be, and what the end to punishment is. It shudders at these things all the more for fear that in death they may get worse. Here on earth the life of the foolish becomes hell.

G Lucretius 3.1087–94

Nor do we, or can we, by prolonging life subtract anything from the time of death, so as perhaps to shorten our period of extinction! Hence you may live to see out as many centuries as you like: no less will that everlasting death await you. No shorter will be the period of non-existence for one who has ended his life from today than for one who perished many months or years ago.

☐ That death is complete extinction is the message forcefully driven home by the Epicurean analysis of the soul as a temporary amalgam of atomic particles: see the arguments excerpted at **14F–H**. The moral corollary, that you should not let the fear of death ruin your life, is a cardinal tenet of Epicurean ethics (cf. **25A 2, B 1, J**). Readers will want to form their own evaluations of the arguments presented in this section. Note the following salient features of them:

(a) Symmetry of past and future: **E 2, 5**. Being dead will be no worse than not yet having been born.

(b) Personal identity: **E 3–5**. Even supposing that there were some degree of survival, what would it take for it to count as *personal* survival?

(c) The irrationality of fearing or mourning death: **A 4, 6, E 6–8; 22C 2, F 6**.

(d) An allegory: **F**. The hell which people fear is really a projection of the moral terrors of this life.

(e) Life properly lived is practice for death: **A 7**. This is a twist on a theme of Plato's *Phaedo* (64a ff.). But Epicurus himself does not mean that the departure of the soul from the body is a positive moral or intellectual advance, just that dying well is the proper culmination of a good life (cf. **C 2**). His own last day was, he claimed, a truly happy one (**D**). Although the bodily pain was intense, its cessation was imminent; and he had all his philosophical pleasures to relive and treasure, perhaps more of them than on any previous day.

(f) A mathematical argument: **G**. No prolongation of your life can reduce the length of time spent dead.

(g) An infinite lifespan, for which those who shun death are implicitly yearning, would be no pleasanter than a finite one: **C**; cf. **A 2, 6; 21G 1–2** (compare also **63I**). Epicurus is not saying, as some have thought he was, that time has *no* bearing on the quantity of pleasure, but just that a finite time is as pleasant as an infinite time, provided one has lived a complete life. This Aristotelian-sounding notion of a 'complete' life is not fully explained in the texts, but **C 2** may suggest that anyone's life becomes complete as soon as he has achieved the philosophical understanding which puts him at peace with himself. Epicurus' point is presumably as follows. Despite our irrational drive to cling to life, once we have fulfilled our human nature the quality of our day-to-day living would in no way be further enhanced by the bestowal of immortality (as the Tithonus myth reminds us). The only apparent pleasure of immortality is that it would eliminate the fear of death. But that fear can also be eliminated by a proper rational understanding of the relevant philosophical issues. Once we have this, there is no hedonistic motive left for seeking an infinite lifespan.

A possible criticism of Epicurus' stance is that, having thus shown that *mortality* is not an evil, he wrongly supposes that he has shown that death is not an evil either. Since, however, untimely death prevents say thirty-five years of pleasure from being extended to seventy, why is the loss of the extra good not to be shunned? He would no doubt reply that the cessation of pleasure is normally a pain (see **21A 7**), and hence to be shunned as an evil, but that this cannot possibly apply to death, which (**A 1**) is the cessation of pleasure *and* pain, of good *and* evil. No doubt the prolongation of good is still preferable to its cessation: hence Epicurus advises us against positively courting death (**A 6–8; 22Q 5**). But equally its cessation is not an evil, so that death is not to be feared. If you believed otherwise, you might marginally improve your chances of completing seventy years instead of thirty-five, but the fear of death would make them far less pleasant. And we should judge a life more by quality than by quantity (**A 6**). Since avoidances are justified only if based on correct hedonistic calculation (**21B 2–3**), Epicurus is surely right that a fear becomes irrational when by its presence it diminishes our pleasure more than its object would if realized.

25 Philosophy

A Epicurus, *Letter to Menoeceus* 122

(1) Let no one either delay philosophizing when young, or weary of philosophizing when old. For no one is under-age or over-age for health of the soul. To say either that the time is not yet ripe for philosophizing, or that the time for philosophizing has gone by, is like saying that the time for happiness either has not arrived or is no more. (2) So both young

and old must philosophize – the young man so that as he ages he can be made young by his goods, through his thankfulness for things past, the old man so that he can be at once young and aged, through his fearlessness towards things future. (3) Therefore we must rehearse the things which produce happiness, seeing that when happiness is present we have everything, while when it is absent the one aim of our actions is to have it.

B Epicurus, *Key doctrines* 11–13

(1) [11] Were we not upset by the worries that celestial phenomena and death might matter to us, and also by failure to appreciate the limits of pains and desires, we would have no need for natural philosophy. (2) [12] There is no way to dispel the fear about matters of supreme importance, for someone who does not know what the nature of the universe is but retains some of the fears based on mythology. Hence without natural philosophy there is no way of securing the purity of our pleasures. (3) [13] There is no benefit in creating security with respect to men while retaining worries about things up above, things beneath the earth, and generally things in the infinite.

C Porphyry, *To Marcella* 31 (Usener 221)

[Quoting Epicurus] 'Empty are the words of that philosopher who offers therapy for no human suffering. For just as there is no use in medical expertise if it does not give therapy for bodily diseases, so too there is no use in philosophy if it does not expel the suffering of the soul.'

D Epicurus, *Vatican sayings* 29, 54

(1) [29] I would rather speak with the frankness of a natural philosopher, and reveal the things which are expedient to all mankind, even if no one is going to understand me, than assent to the received opinions and reap the adulation lavishly bestowed by the multitude. (2) [54] One should not pretend to philosophize, but actually philosophize. For what we need is not the semblance of health, but real health.

E Epicurus, *Vatican sayings* 45

Natural philosophy does not make people boastful and loud-mouthed, nor flaunters of culture, the thing so hotly competed for among the multitude, but modest and self-sufficient, and proud at their own goods, not at those of their circumstances.

F Athenaeus 588A (Usener 117)

[Quoting Epicurus] 'I congratulate you, Apelles, for embarking on philosophy while still untainted by any culture.'

G Diogenes Laertius 10.6

In his letter to Pythocles Epicurus writes: 'My fortunate friend, hoist your sail and steer clear of all culture.'

H Plutarch, *Against Epicurean happiness* 1095C (Usener 20)

Epicurus in his *Problems* declares that the wise man is a theatre-lover, who gets more joy than anyone else from festival concerts and shows. Yet he allows no place, even at table, for issues of musical theory or for literary-critical questions.

I Epicurus, *Vatican sayings* 27, 41

(1) [27] In other pursuits the reward comes at the end and is hard won. But in philosophy enjoyment keeps pace with knowledge. It is not learning followed by entertainment, but learning and entertainment at the same time. (2) [41] We should laugh, philosophize, and handle our household affairs and other personal matters, all at the same time, and never cease making the utterances which stem from correct philosophy.

J Philodemus, *Against the sophists* 4.9–14

... the fourfold remedy [*tetrapharmakos*]: 'God presents no fears, death no worries. And while good is readily attainable, evil is readily endurable.'

K Sextus Empiricus, *Against the professors* 11.169 (Usener 219)

Epicurus used to say that philosophy is an activity which by arguments and discussions brings about the happy life.

☐ The celebrated Epicurean 'fourfold remedy' (**J**) summarizes the ultimate lessons of Epicurean philosophy, corresponding to *Key doctrines* 1–4 (1 = **23E 4**; 2, not in our book, paraphrases **24A 1**; 3–4 = **21C**). The medical analogy underlying this expression is a favourite with Epicurus (cf. **A 1**, **C**, **D 2**), and in conjunction with texts like **B 1** it has sometimes fostered the impression that he assigned a purely negative, instrumental value to philosophy – the elimination of mental anguish. Such an interpretation cannot survive a reading of his words in **I 1**. Certainly he sees the attainment of tranquillity as the primary goal of philosophy (**B–C**), but he also considers the process of attaining it to be immensely pleasurable. In his letter written on his death-bed (**24D**) he claims that the joy of reliving past philosophical conversations outweighs the most intense bodily pains. Such philosophical pleasures will be of the 'kinetic' variety (for 'joy' as a kinetic mental pleasure, see **21R 1**), consisting not in freedom from mental pain but in the actual process of liberation from it. The medical analogy, then, should perhaps be read as making philosophical study comparable less to surgery or to drinking medicine than to lifelong healthy activity (cf. especially **A 1–2**, **K**).

Epicurus views true philosophy as the antithesis of 'culture' (*paideia*, **E–H**). This term represents the educational curriculum much prized in ancient Greece, including rhetoric, literary and musical theory, and mathematics. He apparently sees these as bogus sciences, more a matter of ostentation than of true enlightenment, and hence as positive obstacles to the pursuit of true philosophical values (**E**). **H** and **22Q 6** show that his attitude is far from being one of simple philistinism. On his reasons for rejecting geometry as a science, see commentary on **9**.

Stoicism

26 The philosophical curriculum

A Aetius 1, Preface 2 (*SVF* 2.35)

The Stoics said that wisdom is scientific knowledge of the divine and the human, and that philosophy is the practice of expertise in utility. Virtue singly and at its highest is utility, and virtues, at their most generic, are triple – the physical one, the ethical one, and the logical one. For this reason philosophy also has three parts – physics, ethics and logic. Physics is practised whenever we investigate the world and its contents, ethics is our engagement with human life, and logic our engagement with discourse, which they also call dialectic.

B Diogenes Laertius 7.39–41

(1) They [the Stoics] say that philosophical discourse has three parts, one of these being physical, another ethical, and another logical. This division was first made by Zeno of Citium in his book *On discourse*, and also by Chrysippus in his *On discourse* book 1 and in his *Physics* book 1 . . . and by Diogenes of Babylon and Posidonius. (2) Apollodorus calls these parts 'topics', Chrysippus and Eudromus 'species', and others 'genera'. (3) They compare philosophy to a living being, likening logic to bones and sinews, ethics to the fleshier parts, and physics to the soul. They make a further comparison to an egg: logic is the outside, ethics what comes next, and physics the innermost parts; or to a fertile field: the surrounding wall corresponds to logic, its fruit to ethics, and its land or trees to physics; or to a city which is well fortified and governed according to reason. (4) On the statements of some of them, no part is given preference over another but they are mixed together; and they [these Stoics] used to transmit them in mixed form. But others assign the first place to logic, the second to physics and the third to ethics; these include Zeno in his book *On discourse*, Chrysippus, Archedemus and Eudromus. Diogenes of Ptolemais starts with ethics, Apollodorus puts ethics second, while Panaetius and Posidonius start with physics . . . Cleanthes says there are six parts: dialectic, rhetoric, ethics, politics, physics, theology. But others, including Zeno of Tarsus, say these are not parts of [philosophical] discourse but of philosophy itself.

C Plutarch, *On Stoic self-contradictions* 1035A (*SVF* 2.42, part)

[Chrysippus from his *On lives* book 4] 'First of all, in my opinion, which corresponds to the correct statements by the ancients, there are three kinds of philosopher's theorems, logical, ethical and physical. Secondly, what should be ranked first of these are the logical, next the ethical, and third the physical; and what should come last in the physical theorems is theology. Hence the transmission of theology has been called "fulfilment".'

D Sextus Empiricus, *Against the professors* 7.19 (Posidonius fr. 88, part)

Since the parts of philosophy are inseparable from one another, whereas plants are observed to be different from fruits, and walls are separate from plants, Posidonius said he preferred to compare philosophy to a living being – physics to the blood and flesh, logic to the bones and sinews, and ethics to the soul.

[handwritten margin note: physics = blood, logic = bones, ethics = soul]

E Ammonius, *On Aristotle's Prior analytics* 8,20–2; and 9,1–2 (*SVF* 2.49, part)

The Stoics think that logic should not only not be called an instrument of philosophy; it should not be called an ordinary sub-part either, but a [primary] part . . . They say that philosophy itself gives birth to logic and that for this reason logic must be a part of it.

F Seneca, *Letters* 88.25–8 (Posidonius fr. 90, part)

(1) Many things are of assistance to us without thereby being parts of us. Indeed, if they were parts, they would not be of assistance. Food is the body's assistant, yet it is not a part of the body. Geometry is of some service to us; the philosopher needs it in the same way that geometry needs a technician. But the technician is not a part of geometry nor is geometry of philosophy. (2) Besides, each has its own goals. For the wise man both studies and knows the causes of the natural objects whose numbers and measures the geometer researches and computes. The wise man knows the rationale of the heavenly bodies, their power and their nature. The mathematician assembles their forward and backward movements and the phases through which they rise and set and sometimes give the appearance of being stationary . . . the wise man will know the explanation of mirror reflections; the geometer can tell you how far away a body must be and what shape of mirror produces what kind of reflections. (3) The philosopher will prove that the sun is large, the mathematician how large, advancing by experience and practice. But in order to advance, the mathematician must have certain principles granted to him; yet no expertise is autonomous whose foundation is a concession. Philosophy demands nothing from another. It erects its own

structure just by itself. Mathematics is superficiary, as it were, and builds on someone else's land. It accepts first principles by whose benefit it may make further advances.

G Seneca, *Letters* 89.4–5

First then, if you agree, I will state the difference between wisdom and philosophy. Wisdom is the human mind's good brought to perfection. Philosophy is the love and pursuit of wisdom; it strives for the goal which wisdom has achieved . . . Some have so defined wisdom that they call it scientific knowledge of the divine and the human. Others have defined it thus: wisdom is knowledge of the divine and the human and their causes.

H Stobaeus 2.67,5–12 (*SVF* 3.294)

'Pursuits', rather than 'sciences', is the name they [the Stoics] give to love of music, love of literature, love of horseriding, and love of hunting, both in general and with reference to 'curricular' expertises as they are called. The Stoics include these in virtuous tenors, and accordingly say that only the wise man is a lover of music and literature etc. This is their outline account of a pursuit: a method which by means of expertise or a part of expertise is conducive to the domain of virtue.

☐ Of all ancient philosophies, Stoicism makes the greatest claim to being utterly systematic. Arguably, the Stoics invented the notion of philosophy as 'system' (cf. the definitions of *epistēmē*, **41H**), though they may have been preceded in this by the post-Platonic Academy of Xenocrates, who probably first authorized the division of the subject into the three parts – logic, physics, ethics, as in **A–D**. These in turn were systematically divided by most Stoics into generic and specific topics, with careful attention being paid to the ordering of the topics (cf. logic **39A**, physics **43B**, ethics **56**, and Chrysippus' books of definitions and divisions, **32I**). The handbooks of Diogenes Laertius etc., on which we rely for so much of our evidence, stick more or less closely to this order of exposition; and we have largely followed suit in this book.

For the tripartite division of philosophy itself (rejected by the deviant Aristo, **31N**), we also follow the order, logic physics ethics, attributed to a number of leading Stoics (**B 4**). However, one of these, Chrysippus, put physics after ethics, according to his own words (**C**); and that order is elsewhere ascribed to the school in general (Sextus Empiricus, *Against the professors* 7.22). Two of the similes in **B 3**, the egg and the living being, correspond with this order, while the other, the fertile field, puts ethics (the fruit) after physics (the land or trees). Yet elsewhere ethics, not physics, is compared to the yolk of the egg (Sextus Empiricus, *Against the professors* 7.18). Such disagreements in our sources reflect their attempts to impose excessive unity on the contributions of individual Stoics. Taking **B**, **C** and **D** together, we get three different orders: logic, physics, ethics; logic, ethics, physics (Chrysippus); physics, logic, ethics (Posidonius). Whatever such divergences betoken, the distinction between Stoics who did or did not posit a preferred order (**B 4**) is certainly too sharp. We can well imagine that Chrysippus' lectures followed the order of **C**; but on his own testimony (**60A**) ethics has to be based upon theses from physics. Equally, logic is said to have a general bearing upon ethics (**31B–C**). Statements to this effect are borne out by the nature of Stoic philosophy as a whole. The ethical end, 'living in agreement with nature', requires a mind fully in tune both with god's causal role within the world and with the systematic understanding of the rules of reasoning that logic provides. Hence the 'mixture' of the parts of philosophy (**B 4**), or at least close attention to their implications for each other, can be assumed to have had the support of all heads of the school, especially Chrysippus, the principal contributor to logic.

At the same time, we should take it that individuals put their own trademark on the system. One indication of this is Chrysippus' conception of theological theorems as the ultimate ones (**C**). Another is Posidonius' preference for the living being simile over that of the garden, on the grounds that the latter fails to bring out the inseparable, organic relationship between the parts (**D**). Posidonius began with physics (**B 4**). One effect, or intention of this order, will have been the full integration of logic within the system. If this was the view of Stoics in general, as **E** maintains, Posidonius may have thought that an order of the parts which begins with logic still failed to differentiate Stoicism clearly enough from the Peripatetic conception of logic as an instrument (*organon*) of philosophy rather than an essential constituent. By comparing logic to the bones and sinews of a living being, he opted for a more vital image of that part than was provided by the shell of an egg or the wall of a garden, which stresses its defensive function.

Posidonius is probably the immediate authority for Seneca's distinction between the parts of philosophy and the purely instrumental status of the special sciences (**F**). The latter are not a part of the Stoic's philosophical curriculum, but he will make use of their findings. Underlying this distinction is the Platonic difference (*Republic* 6.510) between the mathematician's total dependence upon hypotheses, and the philosopher's quest for unhypothetical first principles. A Stoic sage, like the Platonic dialectician, is concerned with general principles of explanation rather than the accumulation of data or answers to specific questions of fact. Posidonius, who had particular interest in Plato, may be responsible for adding 'causes' to the definition of wisdom as 'knowledge of the divine and the human' (**G**). But there is no reason to think that the addition altered the substance of what was meant by 'scientific knowledge of the divine and the human', or that Chrysippus would have dissented from the doctrine of **F**.

Instead of distinguishing different kinds of philosophy, as Aristotle had done (theoretical, practical, productive), the Stoics stressed the practical utility of the subject in all its parts (see **A** and commentary to 42). Virtue pertains to each of these, with physics, which gives 'knowledge of the divine', a cardinal requirement for 'wisdom' (**A, G**), and logic no less so (see **31B–C** for logical virtue(s)). As to what the three parts are practically useful for, and constitutive of, the Stoic answer must be, 'living a well reasoned life'. For all three parts are parts of a particular kind of *logos* – philosophical discourse (**B 1**), where discourse includes the mind's dialogue with itself, or its rational character.

As an expertise (for the term see **42A**) or 'science', philosophy differs from expertise in (or dedication to) specific skills, such as the arts and sport, which are called 'pursuits' (**H**). These latter also include the special sciences of **F**, whose instrumental value is expressed in **H**'s account of a pursuit as 'conducive to the domain of virtue'. So far from detaching pursuits from the wise man, the Stoics treated them as 'goods' (**60J, L**) and thus had to defend the paradoxical claim that they are strictly confined to him (**H**). Even so, their difference from wisdom (philosophical virtue) is marked by giving them the status of 'tenors' and not 'characters' (**60L**; for these terms see **47S**). As an expert in a skill, or as a lover of the arts, one wise man may be superior to another. But all wise men are equally expert in that virtue which constitutes 'expertise concerned with the whole of life' (**61G 2**). Cf. also **42** commentary.

ONTOLOGY
27 Existence and subsistence

A Seneca, *Letters* 58.13–15 (*SVF* 2.332, part)

The Stoics want to place above this [the existent] yet another, more primary genus . . . Some Stoics consider 'something' the first genus, and I shall add the reason why they do. In nature, they say, some things exist, some do not exist. But nature includes even those which do not exist – things which enter the mind, such as Centaurs, giants, and whatever else falsely formed by thought takes on some image despite lacking substance.

B Alexander, *On Aristotle's Topics* 301,19–25 (*SVF* 2.329)

This is how you could show the impropriety of the Stoics' making 'something' the genus to which the existent belongs: if it is something it is obviously also existent, and if existent it would receive the definition of the existent. But they would escape the difficulty by legislating for themselves that 'existent' is said only of bodies; for on this ground they say that 'something' is more generic than it, being predicated not only of bodies but also of incorporeals.

C Sextus Empiricus, *Against the professors* 1.17 (*SVF* 2.330)

If something is taught, it will be taught either through not-somethings, or through somethings. But it cannot be taught through not-some-things, for these have no subsistence for the mind, according to the Stoics.

D Sextus Empiricus, *Against the professors* 10.218 (*SVF* 2.331, part)

They [the Stoics] say that of somethings some are bodies, others incorporeals, and they list four species of incorporeals – sayable (*lekton*), void, place, and time.

E Sextus Empiricus, *Against the professors* 8.409 (*SVF* 2.85, part)

(1) For they [the Stoics] say, just as the trainer or drill-sergeant sometimes takes hold of the boy's hands to drill him and to teach him to make certain motions, but sometimes stands at a distance and moves to a certain drill, to provide himself as a model for the boy – (2) so too some impressors touch, as it were, and make contact with the commanding-faculty to make their printing in it, as do white and black, and body in general; whereas others have a nature like that of the incorporeal sayables (*lekta*), and the commanding-faculty is impressed *in relation to them*, not *by* them.

F Simplicius, *On Aristotle's Categories* 66,32–67,2 (*SVF* 2.369, part)

The Stoics see fit to reduce the number of the primary genera, and others they take over with minor changes. For they make their division a fourfold one, into substrates, the qualified, the disposed, and the relatively disposed.

G Galen, *On medical method* 10.155,1–8 (*SVF* 2.322, part)

For the present I decline to speak of the over-refined linguistic quibbling of some philosophers . . . I mean the quibbling way in which they generically divide the existent and the subsistent.

☐ The following stemma represents the ontological distinctions explored in **27–9**.

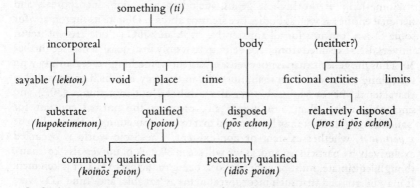

In Stoic usage, just as in Epicurean (cf. **5**), the ordinary Greek verb 'to be' (*einai*) can with relative safety be rendered 'exist', despite its vexed earlier history in Greek philosophy. This translation is further justified by some of the Stoic conceptual distinctions discussed below.

Plato and his successors had tended to assign ontological primacy to the intelligible over the sensible. In making corporeality the hallmark of existence (**B**; **45A–D**), the Stoics are in a way reverting to popular ontology. The philosophical grounds for this reversion, which will be explored in **45**, are extremely powerful. Alleged incorporeals, such as virtue and knowledge, exercise an obvious causal influence on bodies. Such interaction, the Stoics suggest, is simply unintelligible except as between bodies, and hence virtue, knowledge and their like must be analysed as corporeal (cf. also **60S**). We will see in **28–9** how this analysis is achieved.

However, as the above stemma indicates, it is not with the existent but with the prior notion of 'something' that the Stoic ontological scheme starts (**A, D**). The Stoics avoid the common Platonist assumption (invoked against them in **B**; compare e.g. Plato, *Parmenides* 132b–c) that to be something is already to exist. To be something is rather, it seems, to be a proper subject of thought and discourse. Most such things do also exist, in that they are bodies. But an incorporeal like a time, or a fictional object like a Centaur, does not. Since, however, expressions like 'Centaur' and 'today' are genuinely significant, they are taken to name *something*, even though that something has no actual or independent existence (independent, that is, of the world's motion in the case of time, or of someone's mental image, in the case of a Centaur). Although they deny themselves the term 'exist' for such cases, the Stoics have recourse to the broader term under which it falls, 'subsist' (*huphistasthai*: cf. **G**; **49C**; **50D–E**; **51F**). This latter term, in its Stoic usage, seems to capture the mode of being that Meinong called *bestehen* and Russell rendered by 'subsist' (in his 1904 articles on Meinong in *Mind* 13). For Meinong, similarity or Pegasus, for instance, subsist but do not exist. With existing things, however, they share the fact that they have a character (*Sosein*), just as in Stoicism both a real horse and a Centaur are 'something'. We could render the Stoic distinction between 'exist' and 'subsist' by saying 'There's such a thing as a rainbow, and such a character as Mickey Mouse, but they don't actually *exist*'.

'Something' is the highest genus, including as it does incorporeals and fictional entities as well as bodies (see stemma above). Despite its supremacy for some Stoics (but not for all apparently, cf. **A** and **30C 4**), one class of items, universals, is excluded from it, or belongs to it only in a 'quasi' sense: see further **30**. Thus the generic man is not even a subsistent 'something': there simply is no such thing as the universal man, not even in the way in which there is such a character as Mickey Mouse. Universals are dubbed 'not-somethings' (**30E**), and since this, rather than 'nothing at all', provides the normal contrast for 'somethings' (cf. **C**), it may be surmised that to be a 'something' is above all to be a *particular*, whether existent or non-existent. The Stoic world is occupied exclusively by particulars, and, as we will see in **30**, talk of universals like 'man', though legitimate, must be understood as being reducible to talk of token men. It may be guessed that such incorporeal items as 'sayable' and 'time' (**D**) were subjected to a similar analysis.

We now turn to the left-hand part of the stemma. The special significance of the four classes of incorporeal listed in **D**, for all their disparity, is perhaps that although not bodies they are felt to be an ineliminable part of the objective furniture of the world. Other leading contenders for incorporeality, such as virtue and knowledge, are ingeniously explained as bodies (**28–9**); but these four are not amenable to such analysis. On the incorporeality of 'sayables', see **33** and **55**. It was probably in the latter of these two contexts, that of causation, that their incorporeality was first proposed: a causal effect is an incorporeal predicate – not a body, but that which comes to be true of a body, or to belong to it as an attribute, when another body acts upon it. Hence although in a logical context sayables may be to some extent thought-dependent (**33**), in a causal context they subsist objectively. For void and place, see **49**; for time, **51**.

Since interaction is exclusively the property of bodies, the Stoics cannot allow these incorporeals to act upon bodies or be acted upon by them. How then do they play any part in the world? No satisfactory discussion of the problem has survived. But **E** is evidence that they attempted an answer in at least one connexion – how our corporeal souls can *think* about incorporeals. One answer, 'transition' (**39D** 7), is perhaps a process of abstraction from bodily entities.

This leaves the question, what status was assigned to items which, although 'somethings', are pure thought-constructs? Two prominent examples are the fictional creatures mentioned as 'somethings' in **A**, and mathematical limits such as lines and points (**50D–E**). These are often assumed to be incorporeals, but they are not listed as such in the sources (cf. **D**), and it may be more correct to classify them, as we have done tentatively in our stemma, as *neither* corporeal nor incorporeal. (Such trichotomies are characteristically Stoic: cf. 'true, false and neither', **31A** 5; 'equal, unequal, and neither', **50C** 5; 'good, bad, and neither', **58A**; 'the same, different, and neither', **60G** 3.) If something is a purely mental construct – an invention or idealization – the question of its corporeality or incorporeality might be held not to arise: it would be odd to say of Mickey Mouse either that he is corporeal or that he is incorporeal. (**30D** alone counts against this interpretation, and is probably too polemical to carry much weight.)

Finally, we move to the classification of body into four kinds. The list of four 'genera' of the existent given by Simplicius in **F** is confirmed by Plotinus (*SVF* 2.371). Plutarch (**28A** 6) also knows the figure four, and adds the crucial information that each individual entity belongs to all four genera. The ancient commentators (as in **F**) often compare them to the ten Aristotelian genera known as 'categories', and it has become conventional in modern scholarship to use the label 'categories' for the Stoic genera too. However, not only are they never so called in the ancient sources, but they are explicitly treated as cutting across the most basic categorial division favoured in antiquity, that between *per se* and relative (**29C**: 'relative' is split between the second and fourth Stoic genera). We will therefore stick to **F**'s less loaded term 'genera', although it is far from certain that this was the Stoics' own name for them either.

Following Stoic practice, the genera will here be treated as a classification of the metaphysical aspects under which a body can be viewed; it is possible that the scheme was meant to be applicable to incorporeals too (cf. **28L**), but we have too little to go on. Some interpreters link the scheme to Stoic grammar (cf. **33M**), for example by relating 'substrate' to the grammatical class which includes pronouns, 'qualified' to the two kinds of noun (roughly, common nouns and proper names), 'disposed' to intransitive verbs, and 'relatively disposed' to transitive verbs. But we have found too little evidence to support this, and all surviving examples of the four genera are designated by nouns and adjectives alone, e.g. 'matter', 'prudent', 'Dion', 'knowledge', 'father'.

In **28–9** the following suggestions will be developed: (a) the four-genera scheme originates with Chrysippus; (b) the first two genera are distinguished principally through the need, in response to Academic attacks, to give a coherent metaphysical account of change and identity; (c) the third and fourth genera have a variety of uses, especially in the analysis of allegedly abstract entities as bodies.

28 The first and second genera

A Plutarch, *On common conceptions* 1083A–1084A

(1) The argument about growth is an old one, for, as Chrysippus says, it is propounded by Epicharmus. Yet when the Academics hold that the puzzle is not altogether easy or straightforward, these people [sc. the Stoics] have laid many charges against them and denounced them as destroying our preconceptions and contravening our conceptions. Yet they themselves not only fail to save our conceptions but also pervert sense-perception. (2) For the argument is a simple one and these people grant its premises: *a* all particular substances are in flux and motion, releasing some things from themselves and receiving others which reach them from elsewhere; *b* the numbers or quantities which these are added to or subtracted from do not remain the same but become different as the aforementioned arrivals and departures cause the substance to be transformed; *c* the prevailing convention is wrong to call these processes of growth and decay: rather they should be called generation and destruction, since they transform the thing from what it is into something else, whereas growing and diminishing are affections of a body which serves as substrate and persists. (3) When it is stated and proposed in some such way, what is the judgement of these champions of the evident, these yardsticks of our conceptions? That each of us is a pair of twins, two-natured and double – not in the way the poets think of the Molionidae [legendary Siamese twins], joined in some parts but separated in others, but two bodies sharing the same colour, the same shape, the same weight, and the same place, <yet nevertheless double even though> no man previously has seen them. (4) But these men alone have seen this combination, this duplicity, this ambiguity, that each of us is two substrates, the one substance, the other <a peculiarly qualified individual>; and that the one is always in flux and motion, neither growing nor diminishing nor remaining as it is at all, while the other remains and grows and diminishes and undergoes all the opposite affections to the first one – although it is its natural partner, combined and fused with it, and nowhere providing sense-perception with a grasp of the difference. (5) . . . Yet this difference and distinction in us no one has marked off or discriminated, nor have we perceived that we are born double, always in flux with one part of ourselves, while remaining the

same people from birth to death with the other. (6) I am simplifying their account, since it is four substrates that they attribute to each of us; or rather, they make each of us four. But even the two are sufficient to expose the absurdity. (7) If when we hear Pentheus in the tragedy say that he sees two suns and a double Thebes we say he is not seeing but misseeing, going crazy in his arithmetic, then when these people propose that, not one city, but all men, animals, trees, furniture, implements and clothes are double and two-natured, shall we not reject them as forcing us to misthink rather than to think? (8) Here, actually, they can perhaps be excused for inventing different kinds of substrates, for there seems no other device available to people determined to save and protect the processes of growth.

B Anonymous commentary on Plato's *Theaetetus*, 70.5–26

The argument about what grows was first propounded by Pythagoras [the supposed master of Epicharmus, cf. **A** 1], and was propounded by Plato too, as we noted in our commentary on the *Symposium* [cf. *Symp.* 207d]. The Academics also defend it. They protest that they do believe in processes of growth; but since the Stoics establish by argument this fact which needs no proof, the Academics are teaching them that if someone is prepared to prove things which are self-evident someone else will have a plentiful supply of more convincing proofs to the contrary.

C Anonymous Academic treatise, Oxyrhynchus Papyrus 3008

... since the duality which they say belongs to each body is differentiated in a way unrecognizable by sense-perception. For if a peculiarly qualified thing like Plato is a body, and Plato's substance is a body, and there is no apparent difference between these in shape, colour, size and appearance, but both have equal weight and the same outline, by what definition and mark shall we distinguish them and say that now we are apprehending Plato himself, now the substance of Plato? For if there is some difference, let it be stated and demonstrated. But if <they can> not even say ...

D Stobaeus 1.177,21–179,17 (including Posidonius fr. 96)

(1) Posidonius says that there are four kinds of destruction and generation from the existent to the existent. (2) For they recognized that there was no such thing as generation from, or destruction into, the non-existent, as we said before. (3) But of change into the existent he says that one kind is by division, one by alteration, one by fusion, and one an out-and-out change which they call 'by resolution'. (4) Of these, that by alteration belongs to the substance, while the other three belong to the so-called 'qualified individuals' which come to occupy the substance. And it is along these lines that processes of generation come about. (5) The

substance neither grows nor diminishes through addition or subtraction, but simply alters, just as in the case of numbers and measures. (6) And it follows that it is in the case of peculiarly qualified individuals, such as Dion and Theon, that processes of both growth and diminution arise. (7) Therefore each individual's quality actually remains from its generation to its destruction, in the case of destructible animals, plants and the like. (8) In the case of peculiarly qualified individuals they say that there are two receptive parts, the one pertaining to the presence of the substance, the other to that of the qualified individual. For it is the latter, as we have said several times, that is receptive of growth and diminution.

(9) The peculiarly qualified thing is not the same as its constituent substance. Nor on the other hand is it different from it, but is all but the same, in that the substance both is a part of it and occupies the same place as it, whereas whatever is called different from something must be separated from it and not be thought of as even part of it. (10) That what concerns the peculiarly qualified is not the same as what concerns the substance, Mnesarchus says is clear. For things which are the same should have the same properties. (11) For if, for the sake of argument, someone were to mould a horse, squash it, then make a dog, it would be reasonable for us on seeing this to say that this previously did not exist but now does exist. So what is said when it comes to the qualified thing is different. (12) So too in general when it comes to substance, to hold that we are the same as our substances seems unconvincing. For it often comes about that the substance exists before something's generation, before Socrates' generation, say, when Socrates does not yet exist, and that after Socrates' destruction the substance remains although he no longer exists.

E Porphyry (Simplicius, *On Aristotle's Categories* 48,11–16)

(1) Substrate is twofold, not only according to the Stoics but also according to the earlier philosophers. (2) For unqualified matter, which Aristotle virtually names, is the primary meaning of substrate. (3) The secondary meaning is that which is commonly or peculiarly qualified. For the bronze, and Socrates, are substrate to whatever comes about in them or is predicated of them.

F Iamblichus, *On the soul* (Stobaeus 1.367,17–22; *SVF* 2.826)

But the philosophers who follow Chrysippus and Zeno, and all who consider the soul to be body, collect its faculties as qualities in the substrate. They posit soul as substance already underlying the faculties, and out of these two dissimilar components they bring together a composite nature.

G Syrianus, *On Aristotle's Metaphysics* 28,18–19 (*SVF* 2.398)

Even the Stoics place the commonly qualified individuals before the peculiarly qualified individuals.

H Simplicius, *On Aristotle's Categories* 222,30–3 (*SVF* 2.378, part)

The Stoics say that what is common to the quality which pertains to bodies is to be that which differentiates substance, not separable *per se*, but delimited by a concept and a peculiarity, and not specified by its duration or strength but by the intrinsic 'suchness' in accordance with which a qualified thing is generated.

I Simplicius, *On Aristotle's On soul* 217,36–218,2 (*SVF* 2.395)

... if in the case of compound entities there exists individual form – with reference to which the Stoics speak of something peculiarly qualified, which both is gained, and lost again, all together, and remains the same throughout the compound entity's life even though its constituent parts come to be and are destroyed at different times.

J Dexippus, *On Aristotle's Categories* 30,20–6

But if form is that which is predicated in the category of essence of a plurality of numerically different things, in what does single individual differ from single individual, seeing that each is numerically single? Those who solve this difficulty on the basis of the peculiarly qualified – that one individual is distinguished, say, by hookedness of the nose, by blondness, or by some other combination of qualities, another by snubness, baldness, or greyness of the eyes, and again another by other qualities – do not seem to me to solve it well.

K Simplicius, *On Aristotle's Categories* 271,20–2 (*SVF* 2.383)

Nor, on the other hand, does the doctrine of the Stoics agree with Aristotle's doctrine about shapes, when they say that shapes too, like other qualified things, are bodies.

L Simplicius, *On Aristotle's Categories* 217,32–218,1 (*SVF* 2.389, part)

(1) The Stoics say that the qualities of bodies are corporeal, those of incorporeals incorporeal. (2) Their mistake arises from the belief that causes are of the same essence as the things affected by them, plus their supposition of a common account of explanation for bodies and incorporeals alike. (3) But how will the substance of corporeal qualities manage to consist of breath, when breath itself is composite?

M Simplicius, *On Aristotle's Categories* 214,24–37 (*SVF* 2.391, part)

(1) The Stoics too, on their own assumptions, could raise the same difficulty against the principle under discussion that all qualified things are so called with reference to a quality. (2) For they call qualities 'havable', and allow what is havable to exist only in the case of unified things; (3) whereas in the case of things which exist by contact, like a ship, or by separation, like an army, they rule out there being anything havable, or there being found in their case any single thing consisting of breath or possessing a single principle, such as to achieve a realization of a single tenor. (4) The qualified, however, is seen even in things whose constituents are in contact or separated. For just as a single grammarian is enduringly differentiated as a result of a qualified study and education, likewise the chorus is enduringly differentiated as a result of a qualified training. So they are qualified on account of their organization and their co-operation towards the fulfilment of a single function. (5) But they are qualified things which lack a quality. For there is no tenor in them, since a quality or a tenor is never found in separated substances which have no inherent union with each other.

N Simplicius, *On Aristotle's Categories* 212,12–213,1 (*SVF* 2.390, part)

(1) Some Stoics give a threefold definition of 'qualified', and say that two of the meanings are broader than quality, but that one, or part of one, matches it. (2) For they say that on one meaning everything different-iated is qualified, whether its condition be a process or a state, and difficult or easy to destroy. In this sense not only the prudent individual and the individual sticking his fist out, but also the individual running, are qualified individuals. (3) There is a second sense, in which they no longer include processes, but only states, and which they also defined as 'in a differentiated state': for example, the prudent individual, and the individual with his guard up. (4) The third and most specific sense of qualified which they introduced is one in which they no longer included those in non-enduring states, and in which the individual sticking his fist out and the individual with his guard up did not count as qualified individuals. (5) Even of these, the ones 'in an enduring differentiated state', some are of this kind in a way which matches the expression and notion of them, others in a way which does not match; and the latter they excluded, but the former, those 'matching and in an enduring differentiated state', they set down as qualified individuals. (6) By 'matching the expression' they meant those commensurate with the corresponding quality, like the grammarian and the prudent individual; for each of these is neither broader nor narrower than the corresponding quality. Similarly the gourmet and the wine-lover; whereas those who

combine these properties with the corresponding activities, such as the glutton and the tippler, are so called if they have their bodily parts in a suitable condition for indulging themselves. So if someone is a glutton, he is necessarily a gourmet too. But if he is a gourmet, he is not necessarily a glutton too; for when the bodily parts through which he practises gluttony become defective, he is free of his gluttony, but has not lost the tenor of a gourmet. (7) Thus 'qualified' has three senses, and it is in the last sense of 'qualified' that the quality matches the qualified. Consequently, when they define 'quality' as 'the state of a qualified thing', we must understand the definition as if the third sense of 'qualified' were being adopted. For 'quality' has a single sense, according to the Stoics themselves, while 'qualified' has three.

O Plutarch, *On common conceptions* 1077C–E

(1) One can hear them [the Stoics], and find them in many works, disagreeing with the Academics and crying that they confuse everything by their 'indiscernibilities' and force a single qualified individual to occupy two substances. (2) And yet there is nobody who does not think this and consider that on the contrary it is extraordinary and paradoxical if one dove has not, in the whole of time, been indiscernible from another dove, and bee from bee, wheat-grain from wheat-grain, or fig from proverbial fig. (3) What really is contrary to our conception is these people's assertions and pretences to the effect that *two* peculiarly qualified individuals occupy *one* substance, and that the same substance which houses one peculiarly qualified individual, on the arrival of a second, receives and keeps both alike. For, if two, there will be three, four, five, and untold numbers, belonging to a single substance; and I do not mean in different parts, but all the infinite number of them belonging alike to the whole. (4) At least, Chrysippus says that Zeus and the world are like a man and providence like his soul, so that when the conflagration comes Zeus, being the only imperishable one among the gods, withdraws into providence, whereupon both, having come together, continue to occupy the single substance of aether.

P Philo, *On the indestructibility of the world* 48 (*SVF* 2.397)

(1) Chrysippus, the most distinguished member of their school, in his work *On the Growing* [*Argument*], creates a freak of the following kind. (2) Having first established that it is impossible for two peculiarly qualified individuals to occupy the same substance jointly, (3) he says: 'For the sake of argument, let one individual be thought of as whole-limbed, the other as minus one foot. Let the whole-limbed one be called Dion, the defective one Theon. Then let one of Dion's feet be amputated.' (4) The question arises which one of them has perished, and

his claim is that Theon is the stronger candidate. (5) These are the words of a paradox-monger rather than of a speaker of truth. For how can it be that Theon, who has had no part chopped off, has been snatched away, while Dion, whose foot has been amputated, has not perished? (6) 'Necessarily', says Chrysippus. 'For Dion, the one whose foot has been cut off, has collapsed into the defective substance of Theon. And two peculiarly qualified individuals cannot occupy the same substrate. Therefore it is necessary that Dion remains while Theon has perished.'

☐ We now turn to the first two of the four genera discussed at the end of **27** above.

To place a thing in the first genus, 'substrate', is to attribute existence to it without mentioning its qualities. Hence the occupant of this genus is most commonly described as 'substance' (*ousia*, literally 'being' or 'existence'). This in turn is generally equated with primary matter (cf. **q** in vol. 2), viewed in abstraction as 'unqualified' (see **44**). That is 'substrate' in its primary sense (**E 2**). In a secondary sense anything qualified may have the status of a substrate or matter (just as in Aristotle), in so far as it underlies further qualities and can survive the loss of those qualities (**E 3**; cf. **A 4, F**), like the clay in which a horse is modelled (**D 10–12**).

A quality is itself a second corporeal entity imbuing the matter, and able, thanks to its corporeality, to affect it causally (**K, L**). It is either the inseparable 'god' or 'reason' in the primary matter (see **44**; **46**), or, on the more typically Chrysippean analysis (see **47**), the breath which runs through a body and informs it (**L**). The second genus is not strictly 'quality', but the 'qualified', that is usually (for exceptions see **M, N 5–6**) a substance viewed as 'having' (containing as parts) certain qualities (**M**; cf. **33J**). Prudence is a quality, but the corresponding qualified thing is a prudent individual. Sometimes, however, this distinction seems to be neglected (**K, O, P**; **29E**; **33M**). Another common feature of Stoic usage, resulting from their preference for human examples, is the designation of the 'qualified' by the masculine instead of the expected neuter form of the adjective: in the translations of testimonies this is rendered as 'qualified individual'.

The cosmological theory of an active and a passive principle goes back to Zeno. But there is no evidence that Zeno or Cleanthes used it to make the metaphysical claim that an individual is in certain contexts properly treated as a 'substrate', in others as a 'qualified entity'. This distinction appears to have emerged only under the pressure of Academic attacks, with Chrysippus the key figure in the story. The Academics made great play of the Growing Argument, or 'argument about what grows' (**A 1–2, B**), traditionally traced back to the early fifth-century comic poet Epicharmus, who was quoted (Epicharmus fr. 2) as arguing that just as a number or measure when added to or subtracted from becomes a different number or measure, so too a person who grows or diminishes becomes a different person. This remains the core of the Academy's Growing Argument, although the problem was sometimes raised concerning any influx and efflux of material. Hence the Growing Argument was invoked in connexion with the Ship of Theseus, which was said to have been preserved for centuries at Athens, during which time every timber in it rotted and was replaced: was it still the same ship (Plutarch, *Life of Theseus* 23)? If ancient discussions tend to concentrate on cases which, unlike this, involve growth and diminution, it is partly because these latter constitute the plainest examples of the general problem under which both types fall, how a thing can retain its identity between times t_1 and t_2 if what it consists of at t_2 is different from what it consisted of at t_1; partly because they provide a better analogue for the parallel case of numbers and measures invoked by Epicharmus (cf. **A 2, D 5**); and partly because the official upshot of the argument is a rejection of the concepts of growth and diminution, on the ground that 'x grows' is only intelligible if x exists at the beginning and end of the process, and the denial of identity over time seems to exclude this.

That the Academics propounded the puzzle along these lines emerges from **A 1–2**, and it seems to be Chrysippus, presumably in his work *On the Growing [Argument]*' (**P 1**), who responded with the distinction between substance and the peculiarly qualified which is derided by the Academics at **A 3–8** and **C**. (Plutarch's *On common conceptions* seems to stem from the Carneadean Academy, and Chrysippus is his chief target throughout, cf. the explicit reference at **A 1**.)

The theory will be clearer if we start from the later exposition of it in **D** by Posidonius and Mnesarchus, two Stoics active in the early first century B.C., even if their agreement with Chrysippus may be less than total. In **D 1–4** Posidonius lists, not all kinds of change, but those by which a thing's identity can be lost or gained – 'destruction' and 'generation'. Normally (**D 3–4**) it is a qualified individual – say an egg – that is subject to such change, whether by division (into yolk and white), by fusion (into a cake), or by resolution (into its elements: cf. *SVF* 2.413). But for what the Stoics call a 'substance', i.e. a material substrate, any alteration can constitute a change of identity (**D 4**). Posidonius accepts Epicharmus' analogy with numbers and measures (**D 5**), and with some plausibility: for if you make any addition to or subtraction from an undefined lump of matter, it thereby strictly speaking ceases to be the same lump of matter. Hence – a further consequence – a substance cannot be said to grow (**D 5**), since it cannot retain an identity through the process. What does endure, however, and constitutes a proper subject of growth, is the 'peculiarly qualified' individual, Theon, whose uniquely identifying characteristics must for this purpose be lifelong (**D 6–7**), despite the constant flux of their material substrate. Crucial to this whole enterprise is the observation (**D 9–12**) that Theon, although *constituted* by his substance or matter, is not *identical* with it. Hence we cannot infer Theon's impermanence from the substance's impermanence.

Here **D 5–9** seems to match accurately the Chrysippean theory ridiculed by Plutarch at **A 4**; and at **A 6** Plutarch puts it beyond doubt that it is the metaphysical distinction between the first two of the four Stoic genera that is the proposed solution to the puzzle. We thus have a direct causal link between Academic deployment of the Growing Argument and Chrysippus' development of the theory of genera.

Strictly speaking 'peculiarly qualified' is only one half of the second genus 'qualified'. This divides up (for the grammatical basis, see **33M**) into the 'commonly qualified', i.e. anything as described by a common noun or adjective;

and the 'peculiarly qualified', i.e. qualitatively unique individuals, as designated by proper names like 'Socrates'. The former are prior to the latter (**G**), no doubt because to be a man, or white, is part of what it is to be Socrates, and not vice versa. What determines the quality of a given item is a 'concept' and a 'peculiarity' (**H**), and these may be taken to determine, respectively, its common quality and its peculiar quality. We will take these latter in turn.

In its loosest sense (**N 2**), the 'qualified' classifies anything possessing some inherent differentiating characteristic, however temporary, and this includes both absolute and relative properties, so long as the relative properties are inherent differentiations, like sweet and bitter, and not mere external relations like 'on the right' (**29C**). In the strictest sense (**N 4–6**), however, it is restricted to long-term dispositional properties, and one point of this may be to single out a type of quality which might in principle help to establish a thing's identity over time and thus circumvent the Growing Argument.

A common quality is, in physical terms, a portion of breath, for example the portion of breath in Socrates that makes him a man. If it is asked in virtue of what this breath is describable as the quality 'man', the answer (**H**) will be that it corresponds to the universal concept 'man'. That concept is not something present in Socrates; it is our own mental construct, a convenient fiction: see **30**. A common quality is often also called a 'tenor' (*hexis*) – a term which picks out any unifying property of a body (**M**; see further, **47**).

In turning now to the peculiar quality, we must observe that properly speaking it is this, and not the common quality, that constitutes a thing's identity over time (**D 6–7, I**). However, it may perhaps have been suggested that a thing's peculiar quality consists in a unique combination of enduring common qualities (**J**, e.g., for Socrates, 'man', 'Greek', 'prudent', 'snub-nosed', etc.). Many other useful differentiae, like 'son of Sophroniscus' and 'friend of Alcibiades', belong to the fourth genus, 'relatively disposed' (see **29C–F**), and therefore cannot be elements in the peculiar quality. The peculiar quality must be an inherent property, not an external relation. Only on this supposition, added to the doctrine that no two individuals are qualitatively identical, was Stoic epistemology able to maintain, as it always did, that every individual can in theory be infallibly recognized through sense-perception (see **40**).

It is in the light of this last thesis that the anti-Stoic invective in **O** must be interpreted. In attacking the theory, the Academics pointed to alleged cases of two things' being qualitatively indiscernible (see further, **40H–J**). The Stoic reply was that, if that were really so, one (peculiarly) qualified individual would, absurdly, occupy two substances (**O 1**). If, that is, Dion had a perfect double, there would be two materially separate Dions. (This would be particularly abhorrent to the Stoics, since they held that Dion's identity over time *depended* on his possessing a uniquely identifying quality.) Plutarch's Academic spokesman now tries to turn the tables with the suggestion that when the Stoics make Zeus and providence the joint occupants of aether during the conflagration (see **46**) they are absurdly implying that *two* peculiarly qualified individuals can occupy *one* substance (**O 3–4**). It is crucial to see that this is presented as the unwelcome *consequence* of the Stoic cosmological doctrine, not as an explicit claim of the school. For the Stoics were themselves fully committed to the principle that two peculiarly qualified individuals cannot occupy the same substance, as **P** amply confirms. Their reply to Plutarch's charge might be that, on the analogy cited in **O 4**, Zeus and providence no more have the status of distinct individuals than do a man and his own soul.

A further Academic attack on the Chrysippean theory, at **A** and **C**, presents as absurd the idea of two entities, Dion and his substance, occupying the same place. This one is answered by the later Stoics at **D 9** with the careful distinction that a part (which is how Dion's substance stands to Dion), while not identical with the whole, is not different from it either (cf. **60G 3**; and Plato, *Parmenides* 146b).

Finally we turn to **P**, whose context is a fuller version of the anti-Stoic argument in **O 3–4**. It cannot, as often supposed, concern two separate individuals who are made qualitatively identical by surgery, for it would then be about one peculiarly qualified individual coming to occupy two substances, as in **O 1**, whereas it in fact speaks of two peculiarly qualified individuals coming to occupy one substance, as in **O 3**. The key is to recognize this as the ancestor of a puzzle which has featured in recent discussions of place and identity. Take a cat, Tibbles, and assign the name Tib to that portion of her which excludes her tail. Tibbles is a cat with a tail, Tib is a cat without a tail. Then amputate the tail. The result is that Tibbles, now tailless, occupies precisely the same space as Tib. Yet they are two distinct cats, because their histories are different. The conclusion is unacceptable, and the philosophical interest lies in pin-pointing the false step.

That Chrysippus' puzzle works along similar lines is made clear by Philo's later comments, in which he takes Theon to be related to Dion as part to whole. Dion corresponds to Tibbles, Theon to Tib, and Dion's foot to Tibbles' tail. The differences are twofold. First, the problem is about occupying the same substance, not the same place. Second, Chrysippus assumes *both* the validity of the opening steps of the argument *and* the truth of the principle that two peculiarly qualified individuals cannot occupy the same substance at the same time. He therefore concludes that one of the two must have perished, and his problem is to see why it should be one rather than the other. Philo's elliptical summary leaves unclear his reason for selecting Theon for this honour (**P 6**), but it is probably that if we are asked *whose* foot has been amputated we can only answer 'Dion's'. Theon cannot have lost a foot which he never had.

The title of Chrysippus' work shows that this puzzle was developed in connexion with the Growing Argument. But to what purpose? The following is a guess. According to the Growing Argument, matter is the sole principle of individuation, so that a change of matter constitutes a change of identity. Hence Socrates is a different person from the same individual with one extra particle of matter added. Now these two individuals are related as part to whole – just as Theon and Dion in the amputation paradox are related. Thus the paradox's presupposition that Dion and Theon start out as distinct individuals is not one that Chrysippus need endorse; it is a premise attributed for dialectical purposes to the Academic opponents, who cannot deny it without giving up the Growing Argument. But once they have accepted it, the Growing Argument is doomed anyhow. For whereas the Growing Argument holds that any material diminution constitutes a loss of identity, Chrysippus has presented them with a case, based on their own premises, where material diminution is the *necessary condition* of enduring identity: it is the diminished Dion who survives, the undiminished Theon who perishes.

29 The third and fourth genera

A Alexander, *On soul* II.118,6–8 (*SVF* 2.823)

We must disprove the [Stoic?] thesis that there is a single power of the soul, such that the same thing when disposed in a certain way on individual occasions sometimes thinks, sometimes is angry, sometimes desires.

B Seneca, *Letters* 113.2 (*SVF* 3.307, part)

Virtue is nothing other than the mind disposed in a certain way.

C Simplicius, *On Aristotle's Categories* 166,15–29 (*SVF* 2.403, part)

(1) To put what I am saying more clearly, they [the Stoics] call 'relative' all things which are conditioned according to an intrinsic character but are directed towards something else; and 'relatively disposed' all those whose nature it is to become and cease to be a property of something without any internal change or qualitative alteration, as well as to look towards what lies outside. Thus when something in a differentiated condition is directed towards something else, it will only be relative: for example tenor, knowledge, sense-perception. But when it is thought of not according to its inherent differentiation but merely according to its disposition relative to something else, it will be relatively disposed. (2) For son, and the man on the right, in order to be there, need certain external things. Hence without any internal change a father could cease to be a father on the death of his son, and the man on the right could cease to be the man on the right if his neighbour changed position. But sweet and bitter could not alter qualitatively if their internal power did not change too. (3) If, then, despite being unaffected in themselves they change because of something else's disposition relative to them, it is clear that relatively disposed things have their existence in their disposition alone and not through any differentiation.

D Plutarch, *On Stoic self-contradictions* 1054E–F (*SVF* 2.550, part)

[In *On motion* book 2 Chrysippus says that] the world is a complete body, but the parts of the world are not complete because they are disposed in certain ways relative to the whole and are not *per se*.

E Galen, *On Hippocrates' and Plato's doctrines* 7.1.12–15 (*SVF* 3.259, part)

(1) As a matter of fact, most of it really is true, especially what comes in the book where he [Chrysippus] shows that the virtues are qualified

things. But one might find fault with him for the fact that what he says in this book is in conflict with someone who hypothesizes a single power of the soul, the so-called rational and critical one, and abolishes the appetitive and competitive powers, as Chrysippus does. (2) On the other hand, one would not find fault with him for the fact that Aristo's school of thought is correctly condemned by what he writes. For Aristo holds that virtue is a single thing called by many names because of relative disposition. (3) Chrysippus shows that it is not in relative disposition that the multiplicity of virtues and vices arises, but in the qualitative variation of the substances with which they belong – just as on the account of the ancients.

F Seneca, *Letters* 121.10 (*SVF* 3.184, part)

'Constitution', he says, 'is according to you [the Stoics] the commanding-faculty of the soul disposed in a certain way relative to the body.'

☐ **33P 2** gives a typical use of the third genus, 'disposed': the physicalist analysis of a supposedly abstract entity, scientific knowledge (*epistēmē*) as 'the commanding-faculty disposed in a certain way', where the commanding-faculty of the soul is itself corporeal 'breath' (see **53**). After all, mental conditions exert a causal influence on our bodies, and the Stoics find that explicable only if the mental conditions are themselves taken to be corporeal (**45C**). Instances of this genus can be hard to recognize in the sources, because when a definition is fully articulated 'disposed in a certain way' is replaced by a specific description – e.g. 'Winter is the air above the earth cooled because of the distancing of the sun' (*SVF* 2.693); for further examples, cf. **33H**; **53H, K, L**.

It is not obvious what marks this genus off from that of the 'qualified' (**28**). It is not that it covers accidental as opposed to essential properties, for many 'qualities' are accidental too (cf. **28N**). Nor that it is restricted to relatively temporary properties, for some qualities are short-lived (e.g. sticking a fist out, **28N**, cf. **28H**), and conversely some 'dispositions', such as understanding, are enduring once acquired. Part of the answer seems to be that whereas a quality is a differentiation of a substrate, a disposition must be a further differentiation of an already qualified thing. 'Fist', for example, could not be defined or understood except in terms of 'hand'. But it is clear that some things – e.g. 'understanding', 'virtue', 'walking' – are equally at home in either genus (compare **A, B** and **60G 2** with **E, 28F** and **28N**). In these cases, to use the second genus will be to view the thing directly in relation to the individual's substrate, while to use the third genus will be to analyse it as an aspect or part of his soul, which is itself already a qualified entity. There is no incompatibility, since in either case it is merely a portion of breath in him.

We turn now to the fourth genus, 'relatively disposed' (**C–F**). This genus does not include all relative terms. 'Sweet' is recognized as relative, in that to be sweet is to have such and such an effect *upon a perceiver*, but is also 'differentiated', in that sweetness is an intrinsic differentiation of a thing (**C**) – and that puts it in the genus 'qualified' (**28M 4, N 2**). The genus 'relatively disposed' covers things which are characterized by an *extrinsic* relation, such as 'the man on the right' (**C**), the test of this being that they could begin or cease to be thus described without undergoing any intrinsic change, if, say, the subject's neighbour moved (**C 2–3**; cf. Plato, *Theaetetus* 154b–155d). It must however be admitted that one or two sources seem to ignore this distinction and to treat 'relatively disposed' as synonymous with 'relative'. For probable examples, see **57C 3, G 1, H 6**.

We do not know how and why the Stoics came to distinguish the merely relative from the relatively disposed, but one guess would be that the original motive was epistemological. Greek sceptics standardly argued from the relativity of sweet and bitter to their unreality: if what is sweet for you may be bitter for me, why suppose it to be either in reality (cf. **7D**)? The Stoic classification of sweet and bitter (**C 2**) as relative but not relatively disposed asserts that external effects on each occasion are not enough to determine whether a thing is sweet or bitter: sugar remains in its own chemical nature sweet even when, due to illness, I find it bitter. Conversely, we find Carneades exploiting the fourth Stoic genus *in support of* a sceptical epistemology when he maintains (**69D 2**) that both the actual and the apparent truth value of a sense-impression are relative dispositions, being determined entirely by factors external to the impression itself.

In a Stoic world, where everything has some part to play in the grand design, a full account of anything would have to include a description in the fourth genus. This point seems to underlie Chrysippus' words in **D**. Normally an extrinsic relation is symmetrical – if I can cease to be the man on the right when my neighbour moves, my neighbour can cease to be the man on the left when I move. But this does not apply when it is a relation between part and whole. For while a part may change its description merely because of some external change elsewhere in the whole (e.g. my hand becomes an invalid's hand if I break my leg), the reverse cannot occur, because any intrinsic change in a part *is* at the same time an intrinsic change in the whole. By applying this insight to the world and its parts, Chrysippus can contrast the self-contained perfection of the world itself (cf. **54H**) with the imperfection of its parts, all of which are in some degree dependent for their characterization on extrinsic relations to the rest of the world.

But many occurrences of the fourth genus, as of the third, come in the context of definitional analysis: cf. **F**. The most celebrated of these is in the dispute between Aristo and Chrysippus over the proper genus of the virtues (**E; 61B–C**). Cleanthes and Aristo took Zeno to have represented the various virtues as a single state of mind in different relativities (cf. also **41I** for a similar Stoic treatment of vices), but Chrysippus interpreted him as making them all distinct although co-existent qualities. A full account of this will be found in the commentary to **61**.

This last example leads us back to the question of the origin of the four genera. Since Chrysippus' discussion explicitly employed the first, second and fourth genera (**E 3**), it would be unreasonable to doubt that the full scheme was operative in his day. But does the involvement of three first-generation Stoics in this debate push the scheme back to their time? No. First, the dispute between Chrysippus and Aristo could only have been made possible by Zeno's failure explicitly to assign a genus to the virtues (cf. **61B 5**; the mention of the fourth genus at **61C 2** will represent not Zeno's own words but later Academic attempts to uncover contradictions among the Stoics). Second, although Chrysippus not unreasonably understood Aristo's definitions as placing the virtues in the fourth genus, it may be doubted whether Aristo expressly authorized the classification. **61B 3** (Plutarch's less mischievous report) suggests that he merely used the common categorial term 'relative'. And Aristo's ingenious analogy between his conception of virtue as a single intellectual state in various relativities, and calling vision 'white-seeing', 'black-seeing', etc., according to the colour of its objects (**61B 3**), would constitute a poor example of the fourth genus, since extrinsic variations of colour are in fact regularly matched by intrinsic changes in the vision itself. This confirms the impression (see **27** commentary) that Chrysippus is himself the author of the four genera.

30 Universals

A Stobaeus 1.136,21–137,6 (*SVF* 1.65)

(1) (Zeno's doctrine) They say that concepts are neither somethings nor qualified, but figments of the soul which are quasi-somethings and quasi-qualified. (2) These, they say, are what the old philosophers called Ideas. For the Ideas are of the things which are classified under the concepts, such as men, horses, and in general all the animals and other things of which they say that there are Ideas. (3) The Stoic philosophers say that there are no Ideas, and that what we 'participate in' is the concepts, while what we 'bear' is those cases which they call 'appellatives'.

B Aetius 1.10.5 (*SVF* 1.65)

The Stoics of Zeno's school said that the Ideas were our own concepts.

C Diogenes Laertius 7.60–1

(1) A genus is a collection of a plurality of inseparable concepts, such as animal. For this embraces all the distinct animals. (2) A concept is a figment of the mind, which is neither something nor qualified, but a quasi-something and quasi-qualified, in the way that the pattern of horse arises even though none is present. (3) A species is that which is contained within a genus, as man is contained within animal. (4) Most generic is that which is a genus but has no genus – the existent. (5) Most specific is that which is a species but has no species, for example Socrates.

D Alexander, *On Aristotle's Topics* 359,12–16 (*SVF* 2.329)

In this way it will be shown that not even 'something' is the genus of everything. For there will also be a genus of 'one', which is either equal to it or broader than it – if, at any rate, 'one' is predicated of the concept, whereas 'something' is said only of bodies and incorporeals, and the concept is neither of these according to those who speak of these things.

E Simplicius, *On Aristotle's Categories* 105,8–16 *(SVF* 2.278, part)

(1) Indeed, Chrysippus too raises problems as to whether the Idea will be called a 'this something'. (2) One must also take into account the usage of the Stoics about generically qualified things – how according to them cases are expressed, how in their school universals are called 'not-somethings', and how their ignorance of the fact that not every substance signifies a 'this something' gives rise to the Not-someone [*Outis*] sophism, which relies on the form of expression. (3) Namely: 'If someone is in Athens, he is not in Megara; < but man is in Athens; therefore man is not in Megara.>' (4) For man is not someone, since the universal is not someone, but we took him as someone in the argument. And that is why the argument has this name, being called the 'Not-someone' argument.

F Sextus Empiricus, *Against the professors* 7.246 *(SVF* 2.65, part; continuing **39G**)

(1) Neither true nor false [impressions, according to the Stoics] are the generic ones. (2) For of things whose species are of this kind or that kind, the genera are neither of this nor of that kind. (3) For example, of men some are Greeks, others barbarians; but the generic man is neither Greek (since then all specific men would be Greek) nor barbarian (for the same reason).

G Syrianus, *On Aristotle's Metaphysics* 104,17–21 *(SVF* 2.361)

. . . of particulars, whether they were to be in total flux, . . . or whether one were also to call them existing things, as Aristotle used to, or whether one were even to say that only particulars exist, as the Stoics assert.

H Syrianus, *On Aristotle's Metaphysics* 105,21–5 *(SVF* 2.364)

. . . the Forms were introduced among these godlike men [Plato and his precursors] neither for the usage of linguistic convention, as Chrysippus and Archedemus and the majority of the Stoics later believed (for there are a great many differences between *per se* Forms and those uttered in linguistic convention), nor . . .

I Sextus Empiricus, *Against the professors* 11.8–11 *(SVF* 2.224, part)

(1) For the definition, according to the authors of technical handbooks, differs from the universalized proposition in nothing but syntax, and is identical in meaning. This is reasonable. For whoever says 'Man is a rational mortal animal' says the same thing in meaning as whoever says 'If something is a man, that thing is a rational mortal animal', although it

is verbally different. (2) That this is so is clear, because not only does the universalized proposition range over all particular cases, but the definition also extends to all the specific instances of the thing represented – that of man to all specific men, that of horse to all horses. And both the universalized proposition and the definition are vitiated by the subsumption of a single false instance. (3) Now just as these differ verbally but are identical in meaning, so too, they say, the complete division is universal in meaning but differs from the universalized proposition in syntax . . . The statement 'Of existing things some are good, some bad, some intermediate' is, according to Chrysippus, in meaning a universalized proposition of the form 'If some things are existents, they are either good or bad or indifferent.' Such a universalized proposition is, however, false if a single false instance is subsumed under it.

☐ The Stoic treatment of universals is a highly original one, which anticipates in most essentials the conceptualism of the British Empirical philosophers (compare for example J. Locke, *An essay concerning human understanding* 3.3). Universals are neither ontologically prior to their instantiations, as Forms are for Plato, nor immanent in them, but are 'concepts' (*ennoēmata*), mere figments of the rational mind.

By 'universal' here we do not mean that which is signified by any common noun or adjective, as in e.g. 'Socrates is a *man*', but the entity which apparently features as subject of such sentences as 'Man is a rational mortal animal' (cf. **I**) and perhaps also 'Man has been to the moon' (cf. **E**). Such universals had become a central focus of interest for Plato and Aristotle, because they appeared to be the proper object of all definition and scientific or dialectical analysis. Admittedly natural species like 'man' do not feature very prominently as Forms (or 'Ideas') in Plato's dialogues, but they do take centre stage in the entire subsequent debate about his theory of Forms (cf. **A**).

Plato was commonly charged with hypostatizing such items into individuals – 'somethings' in Stoic parlance (see **27**). That criticism can be seen to underlie the Stoics' own description of them as 'quasi-somethings' (**A** 1, **C** 2), and their very interesting attempt to show, by means of the 'Not-someone' argument, the impropriety of treating the universal man like an individual (**E**; cf. **37B** 5, and the similar considerations offered in **F**). In that argument, the Platonic universal man turns out to be a spurious individual who fails to conform even to the elementary laws of logic. An illuminating comparison might be with another spurious individual, the Average Man – who, if he existed, would have 2.4 children.

As 'not-somethings' (**A** 1, **C** 2, **D**, **E**; cf. **27C**), universals find themselves relegated to a metaphysical limbo, altogether outside the Stoic ontological scheme represented by our stemma in **27**. Stoic metaphysics simply has no place for non-individuals (cf. **G**). However, these strictures do not lead the Stoics to ban the universal man altogether from their philosophy. Like Plato and Aristotle, they recognize that he and his kind, as well as being a linguistic convenience (**H**), constitute the subjects of all definitions and all analysis by division, tools which are as basic to their dialectic as to that of their fourth-century forerunners (see **31–2**). What matters, they see, is to know *what* it is that you are defining or dividing: statements about man are not statements about a Platonic super-individual, but convenient paraphrases of conditionals with indefinite subject terms ranging over all individual men. This is the point made in **I** with regard to both definition and division. (For definition, see also **39C 3**; that the items mentioned in the specimen division analysed in **I 3** are universals, not particulars, is not unambiguous, but becomes clear when the division is followed through to its last line, as at **60J–M**: cf. also **32C**.)

With this important proviso, the Stoics are prepared to speak of universals in a fairly Platonic fashion, even echoing Plato's talk of individuals 'participating' (*metechein*) in them (**A 3**). Since they treat their universal concepts as virtually equivalent to species (**C**: the main terminological difference is that 'species' in their usage can include even individuals), we might take this 'participation' to be their way of signifying species membership.

Despite the nominalist ring of **H**, the Stoic theory is better described as conceptualist, since it formally analyses universals not as linguistic devices but as 'concepts' (**A, B, C 1–2**). Now one's generic thought of man is, in Stoic terminology, a 'conception' (*ennoia*). This, being a psychological state, is simply a body – the (corporeal) soul somehow disposed (see **29**). However, the universal man is not identical with this conception, he is its intentional object, that which I am thinking *about* when I entertain the conception 'man'. This distinction is represented by a change of grammatical termination. He is not the conception (*ennoia*) itself, but the corresponding 'concept' (*ennoēma*). However, he is the object of the conception not, as Platonism holds, because he pre-exists and somehow causes it. He is just the mental construct generated by the conception.

Since the concept corresponds to nothing in reality, it is labelled a 'figment' of thought, a term which is elsewhere exemplified by the imaginings of dreamers and madmen (**39A–B**). This may sound curiously harsh treatment of the items which, as the Stoics themselves accept, dialectic must be about. But it should be read above all as a warning to us not to follow the Platonist path of hypostatizing them. It is so tempting to believe, with Plato, that a conception would be vacuous if the concept which it represents did not objectively exist. The Stoic reply would no doubt be that, just as statements about the universal man are reducible to statements about token men (**I**), so too our conception of man is, at bottom, our understanding of the nature of *men*, and has its significance in virtue of the objective existence of individual men. For it is precisely its grounding in our natural and uncontrived experience of individual men that makes it a crucially informative criterion of truth (see **39E, 40**).

We have already distinguished Stoic 'concepts' from 'conceptions'. As a technical footnote, we must now add how they differ from two other items with which they might be confused. First, general terms like 'man'. These appear in **A 3** under the label 'appellatives', i.e. common nouns and adjectives (see **33M**; verbs rarely feature in ancient discussions of universals). Individuals, it is said there, do not 'participate' in these as they do in universals, they just 'bear' them, i.e. are called by them. (For the technical notion of 'bearing a case', used in **A 3**, see **33** commentary.) Appellatives raised no special metaphysical problem, since being words they are simply bodies (**33B, H**) – in the case of the spoken word, air vibrating in a certain way.

Secondly, there is that which an appellative signifies. This might be a common quality (**33M**), or a commonly qualified thing. On either account, it is simply another body: see **28**. If it is asked what makes someone's common quality count as 'man', not 'horse', the answer will no doubt be that it matches the universal concept called 'man' (cf. **28H**). But any resultant metaphysical problems are problems for concepts, not for common qualities themselves.

LOGIC AND SEMANTICS

31 Dialectic and rhetoric

A Diogenes Laertius 7.41–4

(1) Some [Stoic philosophers] say that the logical part [of philosophy] is divided into two sciences, rhetoric and dialectic. Certain of them also divide it into the branch concerned with definitions and that which deals with yardsticks and criteria; but some cut out the branch to do with definitions. (2) They adopt the one concerned with yardsticks and criteria as a means to the discovery of the truth, since they there establish the differences between impressions; (3) the one to do with definitions likewise for discovery of the truth, since things are grasped through conceptions; (4) rhetoric, since it is the science of speaking well in regard to continuous discourses; (5) and dialectic, since it is the science of correct discussion in regard to discourses conducted by question and answer, so that they also define it as the science of what is true and false and neither [of these]. (6) Rhetoric itself, they say, has three parts: one part of it is deliberative [i.e. political], another forensic, and another panegyric. Also it is divisible into invention, phraseology, arrangement, and delivery. A rhetorical discourse [is divisible into] introduction, narrative, replies to opponents, and peroration. (7) Dialectic, they say, is divided into the topics of significations and utterance; and that of significations into the topics of impressions and derivatively subsistent sayables – propositions, complete sayables, predicates and similar actives and passives, genera and species, along with also arguments, argument modes and syllogisms, and sophisms which depend on utterance and on states of affairs. (8) [= **37C**]. (9) Dialectic also includes the specific topic of actual utterance, mentioned above, which sets out written utterance and what the parts of language are, dealing also with solecisms and barbarisms, poetry, ambiguity, euphony, music, and, according to some Stoics, definitions, divisions and expressions.

B Diogenes Laertius 7.46—8 (*SVF* 2.130, part)

(1) They [the Stoics] take dialectic itself to be necessary, and a virtue which incorporates specific virtues. (2) Non-precipitancy is the science of when one should and should not assent. (3) Uncarelessness is a strong rational principle against the plausible, so as not to give in to it. (4) Irrefutability is strength in argument, so as not to be carried away by argument into the contradictory [of one's own thesis]. (5) Non-randomness is a tenor that refers impressions to the correct rational principle. (6) And scientific knowledge itself, they say, is either secure cognition or a tenor in the reception of impressions which is unchangeable by reason. (7) Without the study of dialectic the wise man will not be infallible in argument, since dialectic distinguishes the true from the false, and clarifies plausibilities and ambiguous statements. Without it too it is impossible to ask and answer questions methodically. (8) Precipitancy in assertions extends to what actually happens; so people who do not have their impressions trained veer into states of disorder and carelessness. Only in this way will the wise man show himself to be penetrating, sharp-witted and someone who, quite generally, is formidable in argument. For the person whose job it is to discuss and to argue correctly is the very person whose job it is to discuss debating topics and to respond to the questions put to him; and these are functions of the man experienced in dialectic.

C Diogenes Laertius 7.83 (*SVF* 2.130)

(1) The reason why the Stoics adopt these views in logic is to give the strongest possible confirmation to their claim that the wise man is always a dialectician. For all things are observed through study conducted in discourses, whether they belong to the domain of physics or equally that of ethics. As to logic, that goes without saying. (2) In regard to 'correctness of names', the topic of how customs have assigned names to things, the wise man would have nothing to say. (3) Of the two linguistic practices which do come within the province of his virtue, one studies what each existing thing is, and the other what it is called.

D Alexander, *On Aristotle's Topics* 1,8–14 (*SVF* 2.124)

It is well for us to realize in advance that the term 'dialectic' is not used by all philosophers with the same meaning: the Stoics, who define dialectic as the science of speaking well, taking speaking well to consist in saying what is true and what is fitting, and regarding this as a distinguishing characteristic of the philosopher, use it of philosophy at its highest. For this reason, only the wise man is a dialectician in their view.

E Sextus Empiricus, *Against the professors* 2.7 (*SVF* 1.75, part)

When Zeno of Citium was asked how dialectic differs from rhetoric, he clenched his fist and spread it out again, and said, 'like this' – characterizing compactness and brevity as the hallmark of dialectic by the clenching, and hinting at the breadth of rhetorical ability through the outspread and extension of his fingers.

F Cicero, *Topics* 6

(1) Since every thorough account of argument has two parts, one concerned with invention and the other with judgement, the founder of them both, in my opinion, was Aristotle. (2) The Stoics, however, have exerted themselves only in one of these. With that science that they call dialectic they have thoroughly pursued the methods of judgement, but they have completely neglected the art of invention called topics, although this is both more useful and certainly prior in the order of nature.

G Cicero, *On the orator* 2.157–8

Of those three illustrious philosophers, who you said came to Rome, do you realize that it was Diogenes [of Babylon] who said that he taught the expertise of speaking well and of deciding between true and false, which he called by the Greek term 'dialectic'?

H Plutarch, *On Stoic self-contradictions* 1047A–B (*SVF* 2.297–8)

(1) He [Chrysippus] defines rhetoric as an expertise concerned with the order of continuous speech and its arrangement. Furthermore, in book 1 he has even written the following: 'I think one should cultivate not just a frank and unaffected order but also, apart from the speech, the appropriate kinds of delivery in relation to the fitting tones of voice, facial expressions and gestures.' (2) Yet after being so ambitious about speech here, he says again in the same book, when discussing hiatus, that we should not only ignore hiatus and stick to what is better, but we should also ignore various kinds of unclarity, ellipses and – in heaven's name – solecisms, of which numerous others would be ashamed.

I Cicero, *On ends* 4.9 (*SVF* 1.47)

Dialectic was particularly developed by Chrysippus, but by Zeno much less than by previous philosophers.

J Epictetus, *Discourses* 4.8.12 (including *SVF* 1.51)

What, then, is a philosopher's matter? Not a ragged coat, surely? No it is reason. What is his end? Surely it is not wearing a ragged coat? No, it is keeping his reason right. What kind of theorems? Surely not ones to do with how to grow a large beard or long hair? No, but rather what Zeno says: to understand the elements of reason, what sort of thing each of them is, how they fit together and what their consequences are.

K Stobaeus 2.22,12–15 (*SVF* 1.49)

Zeno used to compare the expert skills of the dialecticians to right measures which do not measure wheat or anything else worthwhile but chaff and dung.

L Plutarch, *On Stoic self-contradictions* 1034E

(1) In response to him who said, 'Do not pass judgement until you have heard both sides', Zeno stated the contrary thesis, with this sort of argument. (2) 'The second speaker must not be heard, whether the first speaker proved his case (for the inquiry is then finished) or did not prove it (for that is just like his not having complied when summoned, or his having complied by talking nonsense). (3) But either he proved his case or he did not prove it. (4) Therefore the second speaker must not be heard' (5) After posing this argument, however, he continued to write against Plato's *Republic*, to solve sophisms, and to encourage his pupils to take up dialectic because of its power to do this.

M Diogenes Laertius 7.25 (*SVF* 1.279)

When a Dialectician showed him [Zeno] seven dialectical forms in the Mowing Argument, he asked how much he was selling them for. Being told a hundred drachmas, Zeno gave him two hundred. So great was his love of learning.

N Diogenes Laertius 7.160–1 (*SVF* 1.351, part)

He [Aristo] abolished the topics of physics and logic, saying that the former is beyond us and the latter none of our concern; ethics is the only topic which concerns us. He compared dialectical arguments to spider's webs: although they seem to display some expertise, they are completely useless.

O Diogenes Laertius 7.182–4 (with omissions; *SVF* 2.9, 2.1, part)

When a Dialectician was having an argument with Cleanthes and trying to propound sophisms to him, Chrysippus said: 'stop distracting your senior from more important matters, and propound such things to us youngsters' . . . Finally he joined Arcesilaus and Lacydes (according to what Sotion says in book 8), and studied philosophy with them in the Academy. This explains why he argued both for and against common sense.

P Plutarch, *On Stoic self-contradictions* 1035F–1037B (with omissions; *SVF* 2.127, 270, 129)

(1) He [Chrysippus] says he does not completely disapprove of arguing the opposite case, but he recommends that it be used cautiously, as in the court-room, not in a spirit of advocacy but in 'destroying their plausibility' [i.e. that of the opposite arguments; see below]. (2) He says: 'This practice is proper to those who suspend judgement about everything and it serves their purpose; those, on the contrary, who seek to engender scientific knowledge which will enable us to live in agreement should provide their pupils with basic principles and fixed positions from beginning to end, while destroying the plausibility of the opposite arguments, in cases when it is timely to refer to them too, just like the practice in the court-room' . . . (3) In *On lives* book 4 he writes as follows: 'The opposite arguments and the plausibilities of the opposite case must not be produced in a casual way but cautiously, lest people be diverted by them and give up their cognitions through not being able to understand the solutions adequately and through the instability of their cognitions; for those who base their cognitions on common sense and sense-objects and the other things that derive from the senses easily let these go when diverted by the puzzles of the Megarians and by a good many others which are more effective' . . . (4) In *On the use of reason*, after saying that the faculty of reason must not be used for inappropriate purposes, any more than weapons, he adds this: 'It must be used for the discovery of truths and for establishing their family relationships, not for the opposite ends, which is what many do.' By 'many' he perhaps means those who suspend judgement.

Q Diogenes Laertius 7.180 (*SVF* 2.1, part)

He [Chrysippus] became so renowned in dialectic that it was the general opinion that if the gods had dialectic, it would be no different from that of Chrysippus.

R Epictetus, *Discourses* 1.7.2–5, 10 (= **37J 2**)

(1) In every matter, we are investigating how the honourable and good man may find the procedure and behaviour which is proper in it. (2) Let them, then, say either that the virtuous man will not engage in question and answer, or that, having engaged, he will take no trouble to avoid behaving carelessly or casually in question and answer. Or if they accept neither of these, they must admit that some study should be made of the topics with which question and answer are chiefly concerned. (3) For what does reason profess? To establish truths, to remove falsehoods, to suspend judgement over what is unclear. Is it enough to learn just this? . . . It is not. [continued at **37J 3**]

Stoic logic and semantics

S Epictetus, *Discourses* 1.17.7–8

Unless we first apprehend what a measure is . . . or a scale, how shall we be able to take the further step of measuring or weighing anything? So, on the subject of logic, unless we have thoroughly learnt and mastered the criterion of other things, through which they are thoroughly known, shall we be able to gain thorough knowledge and mastery of anything else?

T Epictetus, *Discourses* 2.23.44–6

What prevents someone speaking like Demosthenes and being unhappy? And what prevents someone analysing syllogisms like Chrysippus and being miserable? . . . When I say these things to some people, they think I am disparaging the study of rhetoric or theorems. It is not this that I disparage, but the ceaseless concern with those things and resting one's hopes on them.

☐ The 'logical part' of Stoic philosophy (see **26**) covers a much wider spectrum of subjects than this term would embrace today. Logic in its modern sense is included among the topics of 'dialectic' (**A 7**), but dialectic is only one, though the most important, of the divisions of the logical part. Another is rhetoric (**A 1**), and some Stoics treated 'yardsticks and criteria' and 'definitions' as two further divisions of the part (**A 1–3**). Historically, however, there is nothing strange about the Stoics' procedure. In their usage logic is the study of everything to do with rational discourse (*logos*, cf. **C 1**); and this includes the phonetic and semantic aspects of language, phraseology and stylistics, analysis of sentences and arguments, and also epistemology ('yardsticks and criteria'), since thought and judgement are modes of rational discourse (internal speech, cf. **53T–U**). If so systematic a conception of the logical part was not a feature of the earliest Stoicism (cf. **26B 4** for Cleanthes' treatment of rhetoric and dialectic as distinct 'parts'), it can surely be credited to Chrysippus, the Stoa's principal logician; thereafter it became canonical.

Given their insistence on the rationality of nature, in general and particularly for man, with the divine *logos* immanent everywhere, the Stoics were disposed to treat logic as an integral part of their philosophy (**26E**), and not as a mere 'instrument' (the Peripatetic conception) or something with the limited scope of Epicurean 'Canonic' (see **17**; **19**). But their conception of the subject, and its development within the school, need to be related to the interests and methods of other philosophers in the early Hellenistic period.

One example is their handling of rhetoric. The philosophical status of this subject had been debated by Plato and Isocrates in the first half of the fourth century. Against Isocrates, and earlier Sophists, Plato had utterly rejected persuasion, based upon what is 'likely' or 'plausible', as a proper aim of philosophy. In his *Phaedrus*, however, he allows 'Socrates' to defend persuasive discourse, provided it is carried out by a 'dialectician' who 'knows' the truth about his subject-matter and how to relate it to the kind of audience he faces. The

Stoics seem to opt for a similarly restricted foundation for rhetoric. In Zeno's simile (E) rhetoric differs from dialectic in style and delivery; but both forms of discourse are 'sciences of speaking well' (A 4, D). As 'sciences', moreover (contrast Aristotle, *Rhetoric* I. I), they require the infallible and morally excellent wise man as their practitioner. A contrast with Aristotle's *Rhetoric* will show the Stoics' lack of concern with 'discovering the possible means of persuasion on every subject' (*Rhetoric* 1.2). The same impression is conveyed by Chrysippus' insistence on a 'frank and unaffected order', and by his disregard of stylistic refinement (H). (Later Stoics, especially Diogenes of Babylon, may have been more innovative in this area.) However, Cicero's complaint (F) about the Stoic neglect of 'invention' (i.e. techniques of rhetorical argument) is exaggerated; much of the material of his own book *On invention* draws on the kind of arguments and fallacies Chrysippus loved to explore. Cicero seems to be operating with an un-Stoic distinction between dialectic and invention.

Still, it is in the sphere of dialectic, not rhetoric, that the Stoics made their distinctive contribution. (Note the conservatism of their divisions of rhetoric, A 6). In Zeno's lifetime dialectic connoted at least four distinct, if overlapping, methods of argument. First, in its Platonic guise, it signified the testing of hypotheses and the quest for ultimate principles or true definitions, which are the essential procedures of every metaphysician. Secondly, as used by Aristotle, dialectic is the method of developing a convincing case, for or against a thesis (or commonly held 'opinion'), by logically valid reasoning; the conclusion of a dialectical argument does not count as a 'demonstrative' proof, but the procedure aids the sciences by scrutinizing theories, though it can also be used to furnish arguments on any subject, regardless of their truth. Thirdly, 'Dialectical' was the name given to the school associated with Diodorus Cronus (see Index of philosophers), which specialized in posing logical problems and fallacies. The work of such people was sometimes branded 'eristic' – contentious or mere logic-chopping – but it had decisive influence on Stoic dialectic. Fourthly, the sceptical Academy of Arcesilaus justified 'suspension of judgement about everything' by its profession to be able to answer every claim to knowledge or belief with argument of equal weight on the opposite side.

Common to all of these practices is the notion that arguments are questions put to an interlocutor and that their premises require his positive answer if they are to proceed (see commentary on 36). Hence all users of dialectic, whatever their particular aims and methods, could agree that it is argument by question and answer (cf. A 5, B 8, R 2). Beyond this, the Stoics can be seen to take account of all four conceptions of the procedure distinguished above.

That holds good for Chrysippus and his successors, but what of Zeno and his associates? Zeno's attachment to 'the elements of reason' (J) can be granted, and he invented some intriguing, if implausible, theological syllogisms (54D, F, G); but to later ages Stoic dialectic was virtually synonymous with Chrysippus' name (I, Q). On the evidence of L and M, Zeno was genuinely interested in dialectic in our third sense. He himself studied with the Dialecticians Diodorus and Philo, and recognized the need for his followers to 'solve sophisms' (L 5). Given K however, this looks like a defensive posture (cf. O on Cleanthes); and his idiosyncratic contemporary, Aristo, insisted on the ethical irrelevance of 'dialectical arguments' (**N**). Nothing suggests that these early Stoics credited dialectic with the constructive functions of our first sense of the term (Plato) or even the second (Aristotle). (For logic as in essence defensive, note the comparisons with eggshell and wall, **26B 3**.)

It was Chrysippus, we suggest, who propagated the definition of dialectic as 'the science of what is true and false and neither' (**A 5**, cf. **D**), presenting it as the expertise which specializes in distinguishing true from false impressions (cf. **B 7**, **G**; **37H**; **40I 2**), and thus fully integrating it with epistemology. This fits its canonical contents (**A 7–8**), and the claims made for the heuristic and moral importance of the subject (**B**, **C**). Thus, dialectic, in its concern with truth, knowledge, definitions etc. assumes a significance in Stoicism which is fully comparable to the Platonic conception. At the same time, by furnishing analysis and techniques of argument, it retains the original concern with logical puzzles and training against opponents, and also provides its expert with the ability to practise dialectic in the Aristotelian sense – arguing for and against a given thesis (cf. Chrysippus in **O** and **P**). In **P**, furthermore, we see Chrysippus' familiarity with and concern to distinguish himself from the dialectical methods of the sceptical Academy (our fourth sense). He will use 'argument on the opposite side', as an educational device, and not to induce suspension of judgement.

Officially, we may take it that Chrysippus regarded all dialectic as integral to the whole of Stoicism. In practice his enormous output in technical logic (cf. **37B**) must have seemed dubiously relevant to Stoicism as a way of life. Hence Epictetus defends the necessity of logic as an instrument of judgement (**S**), while warning against confusing logical expertise with the foundation of happiness (**T**).

32 Definition and division

A Diogenes Laertius 8.48

Favorinus says that Pythagoras used definitions throughout his mathematical material, and that they were used more widely by Socrates and his associates, and later by Aristotle and the Stoics.

B Scholia on Dionysius Thrax, 107,5–7 (*SVF* 2.226, part)

(1) Chrysippus says that a definition is a representation of a peculiar characteristic, i.e. that which expounds the peculiar characteristic. (2) Antipater the Stoic says: 'A definition is a statement expressed with necessary force', i.e. with reciprocal force. For the definition is meant to be reciprocal.

C Diogenes Laertius 7.60–2

(1) A definition is, as Antipater says in *On definitions* book 1, 'a statement of analysis matchingly expressed', (2) or, as Chrysippus says in his *On*

definitions, a representation of a peculiar characteristic. (3) An outline account is a statement introducing us to things by means of a sketch, or which conveys the force of the definition more simply than a definition does. (4) [= **30C**] (5) A division is the dissection of a genus into the proximate species: for example, 'Of animals, some are rational, some are non-rational.' (6) Contradivision is a dissection of a genus into a species in relation to its opposite, such as by negation: for example, 'Of existing things, some are good, some are not good.' (7) Subdivision is a division following a division: for example 'Of existing things, some are good, some are not good, and of the not good, some are bad, some indifferent.' (8) Partition is a classification of a genus into topics, as Crinis puts it: for example, 'Of goods, some belong to the soul, some to the body.' [continued at **37P**]

D Galen, *Medical definitions* 19.348,17–349,4

Some [i.e. the Stoics] have given these definitions: 'A definition is a statement of analysis matchingly expressed', or 'A definition is that which by a brief reminder brings us to a conception of the things underlying words.'

E Alexander, *On Aristotle's Topics* 42,27–43,2 (*SVF* 2.228, part)

Those [i.e. the Stoics] who say that a definition is a statement of analysis matchingly expressed (meaning by 'analysis' the filling out of the definiendum, and in succinct fashion, and by 'matchingly' that it is neither broader nor narrower) would say that the definition is no different from the representation of the peculiar characteristic.

F Augustine, *City of God* 8.7 (*SVF* 2.106, part)

[The Stoics say that from the senses] the mind forms conceptions – *ennoiai*, as they call them – of those things, that is, which they articulate by definition. The entire method of learning and teaching, they say, stems and spreads from here.

G Galen, *Against Lycus* 3.7 (*SVF* 2.230, part)

For it is in the recognition of the differentiae of each existing thing that the branches of expertise consist. The fullest account of this is Plato's, at the very beginning of the *Philebus*. But his view was maintained by Aristotle, Theophrastus and Chrysippus.

H Cicero, *Tusculan disputations* 4.53

(1) Are we then to say that madness is useful? Study the definitions of courage and you will understand that it has no need of bad temper. (2) Courage is 'a tenor of the soul obedient to the supreme law in matters

requiring endurance'. (3) Or 'the maintenance of stable judgement in undergoing and warding off those things which seem fearsome'. (4) Or 'scientific knowledge of things fearsome, the opposite of fearsome, or to be completely ignored, maintaining stable judgement of those things'. (5) Or, in Chrysippus' briefer formulation (for the preceding definitions were by Sphaerus, whom the Stoics rate as their best framer of definitions: the definitions are all pretty much alike, but some are more successful than others at conveying our common conceptions) – (6) how, then, does Chrysippus define it? 'Courage,' he says, 'is scientific knowledge of matters requiring persistence.' (7) Or 'a tenor of the soul fearlessly obedient to the supreme law in enduring and persisting'. (8) However much we may attack this school, as Carneades used to, I'm afraid that they may be the only real philosophers. For which of those definitions does not uncover the tangled conception of courage which lies buried within us all? And once this has been uncovered, who would require anything more for the warrior, the general, or the orator, and not think them capable of performing any courageous act without rage?

I Diogenes Laertius 7.199–200

[From the list of Chrysippus' works] (1) Ethical theory concerning the articulation of ethical conceptions, Group 1: (2) *Outline account of reason* to Theoporus, in one book; *Ethical theses*, in one book; *Convincing premises for doctrines*, to Philomathes, in three books; *Definitions of what belongs to the superior man*, to Metrodorus, in two books; *Definitions of what belongs to the inferior man*, to Metrodorus, in two books; *Definitions of the intermediates*, to Metrodorus, in two books; *Definitions addressed to Metrodorus, according to genus*, in seven books; *Definitions of things relating to the other branches of expertise*, to Metrodorus, in two books. (3) Group 2: *On similars*, to Aristocles, in three books; *On definitions*, to Metrodorus, in seven books. (4) Group 3: *On incorrect objections to definitions*, to Leodamas, in seven books; *Convincing material for definitions*, to Dioscurides, in two books; *On species and genera*, to Gorgippides, in two books; *On divisions*, in one book; *On opposites*, to Dionysius, in two books; *Convincing material against divisions and genera and species, and concerning opposites*, in one book. (5) Group 4: *On etymological matters*, to Diocles, in seven books; *Etymological matters*, to Diocles, in four books.

J Origen, *Against Celsus* 1.24 (*SVF* 2.146)

The foregoing matter is beset by the profound and mysterious issue of the nature of names. Are names, as Aristotle [*De interpretatione* 1] holds, the product of convention? Or, as the Stoics believe, of nature, the primary sounds being imitations of the things of which the names are said? This is the basis on which they introduce some elements of etymology.

☐ Definition and division are methods fundamental to Stoic dialectic, and are especially in evidence in ethical texts: cf. also the list of lost ethical works in **I**. First, a topic is marked out by 'partition' (**C 8**) of the generic subject matter into sub-headings. For example (**31A**; for further instances, cf. **43B**; **56**), one arrives at the topic of impressions by partitioning logic into rhetoric and dialectic, the latter into the topic of significations and that of utterance, and the topic of significations into several further sectors, one of which is 'impressions'. Importantly, impressions are not themselves a sub-species of significations in Stoic theory, but are classified here because of their direct *relevance* to the various species of significations (**31A 6**).

Thus partition is significantly different from the next stage, division (although there are inevitably some borderline cases, e.g. **26B 1–2**). This latter is the analysis of a genus into its constituent species (for the terminology see **30C**), and of these into subspecies. Sometimes each branch of the division is subjected to subdivision, the eventual objective being a complete classification of the original genus. The Stoic ethical division of existing things in terms of goodness exemplifies this: see **C 7** and **30I** for two versions of the initial division, and **60J–M** for lower lines. Sometimes, though, the object of the division is the precise demarcation of just one subspecies, and in such cases it is normal at each level to select just the one appropriate species for subdivision. This is exemplified by the series of divisions designed to mark off the 'cognitive' impression from other impressions. There are various available bases for the division of the genus of impressions (cf. **39A 4–7**), but the one relevant to the cognitive impression works through 'convincing' etc., then 'true' etc., to a last line consisting of 'cognitive' and 'incognitive' (**39G**; **40E**). In these one-sided divisions, a neglected species may even be left with no specific name and have to make do with the genus name: cf. **36A 5–6**; **39E 3**; **60J** with commentary.

This method of analysis by division is a legacy of Plato, developed in various ways by his pupils, notably Aristotle (cf. **G**). It originated both as a general technique of scientific and conceptual analysis, and, more precisely, as the proper method of establishing a definition, the definition being composed of the genus plus the differentiae used to mark off the definiendum from the other species. The Stoics may remain formally committed to the same definitional use of division. Thus for example their specimen definition, 'Man is a rational mortal animal' (**30I**), reflects the twin divisions of the genus animal into rational and irrational and into immortal and mortal. But in practice division seems to be used in Stoic texts almost exclusively as a method of conceptual or scientific analysis (e.g. **27**; **33F 3**; **36A**; **59E, M**; **65E–F**), and their ubiquitous definitions do not usually look like the end-products of divisions. (The only apparent case of definition by division in our excerpts is at **36B**, a text whose Stoic provenance is not beyond dispute.) Indeed, in the case of the cognitive impression (**39G**; **40E**), it is first elaborately demarcated by a series of divisions, but then defined in a way which reflects those divisions loosely or not at all. For further examples of definitions, cf. **H**; **26A, G**; **31A 4–5, B 2–6, D, H**; **33G, M**; **34A**; **35A, C**; **42A** (where Chrysippus corrects a definition by Cleanthes); **50E**; **51A, B, E**; **55A**; **59B 1**; **60G 1**; **61H**; **63A 2**; **65D**.

It must however be admitted that one or two apparent instances of definition which seem not to be the products of division could in fact be not definitions in the strict sense at all, but 'outline accounts'. 'Outline account' (*hupographē*) is an Aristotelian notion inherited by both Stoics (**C 3**; **26H**) and Epicureans (**19** commentary). It is a formula used for the preliminary marking off of a definiendum, prior to the construction of a true definition. It clarifies what it is that is under discussion, but may not yet reveal that thing's nature.

This contrasts with a genuine definition (**C 2**), which presents the (or 'a') 'peculiar characteristic' of a species. One critic of the Stoics, Alexander (in the sequel to **E**), argued that a peculiar characteristic might itself turn out to be something quite inessential to the nature of the definiendum, e.g. that man might on the Stoic view be defined as 'animal with a sense of humour'. But there seems no doubt (cf. **31D**; **58A 5**; **63D, M**) that 'peculiar characteristic' (*idion*) is an expression intended by the Stoics to apply only to features which are not just unique but also essential. Alexander is perhaps unduly influenced by the more flexible Aristotelian use of the term.

The charge may look more telling when levelled against Antipater's alternative definition in **C 1**, 'A definition is a statement of analysis matchingly expressed', since 'matchingly', as **E** helpfully explains, means merely that the definition must come out co-extensive with the definiendum. But we may guess that 'analysis', glossed in **E** as the 'filling out' of the definiendum (i.e. of its conception?) does much of the work, and is to be understood as articulation of its *essential* properties.

B 2 may appear to saddle Antipater with a second definition of definition, 'a statement expressed with necessary force, i.e. with reciprocal force'. But it is probably intended rather as an *extra* requirement for any account of definition, namely that a definition should be treated not as a predication but as an identity statement. The distinction between identity and predication is not a very sharp or familiar one in Greek philosophy, and Antipater is perhaps thinking of identifications simply as reciprocal, i.e. two-way, predications. Here we must recall from **30I** Chrysippus' logical diagnosis of definitions as standing for conditionals with indefinite subject terms: e.g. 'If something is a man, that thing is a rational mortal animal.' Thus expressed, the conditional does indeed misleadingly represent the definition as an ordinary predication. To convey the identity relation, Chrysippus really needed a biconditional formulation, 'If something is x it is y, and if something is y it is x' (or 'If and only if something is x it is y'). It is perhaps this that Antipater is trying to tell him. But it is unclear why he takes this to be equivalent to 'expressed with necessary force', which one might otherwise have interpreted as asserting that definitions express not contingent but *analytic* truths.

Epistemologically speaking, a definition is regarded as the linguistic articulation of a generic 'conception' (*ennoia*): cf. **D, F, H 8, I 1**; **31A 3**; **40G 2**; **60G 1**. Since conceptions are the very stuff of rationality (**39E 3–4**), and, when naturally embedded in us, a primary criterion of truth (**40**), it is clear why definition is regarded as a philosophically fundamental matter.

One recurrent feature of Stoic methodology, which brings them closer to Aristotle's than to Plato's practice, is the careful distinction between several senses of a word: see e.g. **28N**; **41H**; **44F**; **47A 6–9**; **58B, D 2–3**; **67L**. This can be connected with their un-Platonic sensitivity to ambiguity as a source of fallacy: **37B 2, N–S**.

One final topic on which the Stoics do self-consciously ally themselves to Plato is that of etymology. In his *Cratylus*, Plato examines a theory of 'correctness of names', to the effect that the names of things are coded descriptions from which their true nature can be extracted by the alleged science of etymology (literally, 'the true account'). His conclusion is that names are indeed to some extent descriptions, but too inaccurate to provide a route to knowledge, which implicitly must come rather from dialectical study of the essences of things themselves. This seems to be exactly the position adopted by the Stoics, especially at **31C 2–3**. On the one hand they do, like Plato, indulge themselves with the occasional excursion into etymology (cf. **J**; **34J**; **39B 3**; **54A**; **59C**; **63B 1** with commentary; and see the titles in **I 5**). On the other hand, they deny that etymological technique is part of real dialectic (**31C**).

It is sometimes claimed that the Stoics were major exponents of etymology, and took it to fantastic lengths. This seems exaggerated. Their uses of it are scarcely more frequent or more far-fetched than those of most other Greek intellectuals, philosophers included.

For Epicurus' strongly contrasting views on these same topics, cf. **19**, and for Pyrrhonist doubts, see Sextus Empiricus, *Outlines of Pyrrhonism* 2.205–27. For the metaphysical question, what are the entities which dialecticians define and divide, see **30**.

33 Sayables (*lekta*)

A Diogenes Laertius 7.57 (*SVF* 3 Diogenes 20, part)

Utterance and speech are different, because vocal sound is also an utterance but only articulated sound is speech. And speech is different from language, because language is always significant, but speech can lack significance, e.g. *blituri*, whereas language is not so at all. Furthermore, saying is different from voicing. For utterances are voiced but it is states of affairs which are said – they, after all, are actually sayables.

B Sextus Empiricus, *Against the professors* 8.11–12 (*SVF* 2.166, part)

(1) There was another disagreement among philosophers [concerning what is true]: some took the sphere of what is true and false to be 'the signification', others 'utterance', and others 'the process that constitutes thought'. (2) The Stoics defended the first opinion, saying that three things are linked together, 'the signification', 'the signifier', and 'the name-bearer'. The signifier is an utterance, for instance 'Dion'; the signification is the actual state of affairs revealed by an utterance, and

which we apprehend as it subsists in accordance with our thought, whereas it is not understood by those whose language is different although they hear the utterance; the name-bearer is the external object, for instance, Dion himself. (3) Of these, two are bodies – the utterance and the name-bearer; but one is incorporeal – the state of affairs signified and sayable, which is true or false.

C Sextus Empiricus, *Against the professors* 8.70 (*SVF* 2.187, part)

They [the Stoics] say that a 'sayable' is what subsists in accordance with a rational impression, and a rational impression is one in which the content of the impression can be exhibited in language.

D Diogenes Laertius 7.49 (*SVF* 2.52, part; = **39A 2**)

For the impression arises first, and then thought, which has the power of talking, expresses in language what it experiences by the agency of the impression.

E Seneca, *Letters* 117.13

(1) There are [the Stoic says] bodily substances: for instance, this is a man, and this a horse. These are accompanied by movements of thought which can make enunciations about bodies. (2) These movements have a property peculiar to themselves, which is separate from bodies. For example, I see Cato walking: sense-perception has revealed this, and my mind has believed it. What I see is a body, and it is to a body that I have directed my eyes and my mind. Then I say, 'Cato is walking.' What I now utter (he says) is not a body, but a certain enunciation about a body, which some call a proposition, others a thing enunciated, and others a thing said. (3) So when we say 'wisdom', we understand something corporeal; when we say, 'He is wise', we are speaking about a body. There's a very great difference between naming *it* and speaking *about* it.

F Diogenes Laertius 7.63

(1) The topic which deals with states of affairs and significations includes that of sayables, both those that are complete and propositions and syllogisms, and those which are incomplete, and active and passive predicates. (2) They say that a sayable is what subsists in accordance with a rational impression. (3) Sayables, the Stoics say, are divided into complete and incomplete, the latter being ones whose linguistic expression is unfinished, e.g. '[Someone] writes', for we ask, 'Who?' In complete sayables the linguistic expression is finished, e.g. 'Socrates writes.' So incomplete sayables include predicates, whereas ones that are complete include propositions, syllogisms, questions and enquiries.

G Diogenes Laertius 7.64 (*SVF* 2.183, part)

A predicate is what is asserted of something, or a state of affairs attachable to something or some things, as Apollodorus says, or an incomplete sayable attachable to a nominative case for generating a proposition.

H Diogenes Laertius 7.55–6

An animal's utterance is air that has been struck by an impulse, but that of a man is articulated and issues from thought, as Diogenes [of Babylon] says, and is perfected at the age of fourteen. Also, according to the Stoics, utterance is a body . . . for everything that acts is a body; and utterance acts when it travels from those who utter it to those who hear it.

I Stobaeus 2.88,2–6 (*SVF* 3.171)

(1) They [the Stoics] say that all impulses are acts of assent, and the practical impulses also contain motive power. (2) But acts of assent and impulses actually differ in their objects: propositions are the objects of acts of assent, but impulses are directed toward predicates, which are contained in a sense in the propositions.

J Stobaeus 2.97,15–98,6 (*SVF* 3.91)

(1) They [the Stoics] say that the difference between choiceworthy and what-should-be-chosen also applies to desirable and what-should-be-desired and wishworthy and what-should-be-wished, and acceptable and what-should-be-accepted. For goods are choiceworthy and wishworthy and desirable <and acceptable. But benefactions are what-should-be-chosen and what-should-be-wished and what-should-be-desired> and what-should-be-accepted since they are predicates and correlates of goods. (2) For we choose what-should-be-chosen and wish what-should-be-wished and desire what-should-be-desired. For choices and desires and wishes, just like impulses, are of predicates. (3) Yet we choose and wish and likewise desire to *have* goods, and so goods are choiceworthy and wishworthy and desirable. For we choose to *have* prudence and moderation, but not of course [to *have*] acting prudently and acting moderately, which are incorporeal and predicates.

K Ammonius, *On Aristotle's De interpretatione* 43,9–15

The Stoics reply that the nominative case itself has fallen from the thought which is in the soul. For when we wish to exhibit the thought of Socrates which we have within ourselves, we utter the name Socrates [i.e. Socrates in the nominative case]. Just as a pen is said both to have fallen and to have its fall upright if it is released from above and sticks upright, so we claim that the nominative case [literally 'the direct case'] falls from the thought, but is upright because it is the archetype of linguistic utterance.

L Scholia on Dionysius Thrax, 230,24–8

If the nominative is upright, why is it a case? Because it has fallen from what is incorporeal and generic into what is specific. But it is upright, because it has not yet been altered into an oblique [case], or because it is the foundation of what the Stoics call upright, that is active, verbs, e.g. 'Socrates strikes'.

M Diogenes Laertius 7.58 (*SVF* 3 Diogenes 22, part)

According to Diogenes [of Babylon] an appellative is a part of language which signifies a common quality, e.g. 'man', 'horse'; a name is a part of language which indicates a peculiar quality, e.g. 'Diogenes', 'Socrates'; a verb is a part of language which, according to Diogenes, signifies a non-compound predicate, or, as some say, a case-less constituent of a sentence which signifies something attachable to something or some things, e.g. 'I write', 'I speak'.

N Ammonius, *On Aristotle's De interpretatione* 17,24–8

Here Aristotle tells us what it is that they [nouns and verbs] primarily and immediately signify: his answer is 'thoughts', but through these as intermediates 'things', and it is not necessary to conceive of anything else additional to them, intermediate between the thought and the thing, which the Stoics postulated and decided to name a 'sayable'.

O Clement, *Miscellanies* 8.9.26.5

Case is agreed to be incorporeal; and hence the famous sophism is solved as follows: 'What you say passes through your mouth.' This is true. 'But you say: A house. Therefore a house passes through your mouth.' This is false. For what we say is not the house, which is a body, but the case, which is incorporeal and which a house bears.

P Sextus Empiricus, *Outlines of Pyrrhonism* 2.81–3

(1) True is said [by the Stoics] to differ from truth in three ways, substance, structure, and function. (2) In substance, since what is true is incorporeal, for it is a proposition and sayable; but truth is a body, for it is scientific knowledge capable of stating everything true; and scientific knowledge is the commanding-faculty disposed in a certain way, just as a fist is the hand disposed in a certain way; and the commanding-faculty is a body, being a breath in their view. (3) In structure, since what is true is something simple, e.g. 'I am conversing', but truth consists of the knowledge of many true things. (4) In function, since truth pertains to

scientific knowledge but what is true does not do so at all. Hence they say that truth is only in a virtuous man, but what is true is also in an inferior man; for the inferior man can say something true.

☐ The foundation of Stoic logic is a theory about the constituents of language in its phonetic and semantic aspects. Considered as 'utterances', words and sentences are distinguished from vocal sounds and speech quite generally in being 'significant' (**A**). However, significance or meaning is not reducible to the sound made when we utter words and sentences. Someone ignorant of English hears the same sound as an English speaker when 'Socrates writes' is uttered. Words and sentences are only meaningful to those who understand the language (**B 2**). Also, the meaning of 'Socrates writes' is something different from the particular moving body which could be describable in this way. Irrespective of whether Socrates is writing, the sentence 'Socrates writes' has a meaning, which will be true in the one case and false in the other.

Not all significant speech, however, is true or false. The truths and falsehoods, or propositions (see **34**), that we utter are only one, though the most important, species of what the Stoics called 'sayables' (*lekta*); these also include questions, oaths, imperatives etc. (Diogenes Laertius 7.66–7). *Lekta* are explained in various ways. Linguistically, they are the meanings of 'finished' sentences like 'Socrates writes' (**F 3**), or of verbs without a specified subject (and/or object, in the case of transitive verbs), e.g. 'writes' with no indication of who. The former type is called 'complete', the latter 'incomplete'. What completes a sayable is its being attached to 'a nominative case' (**G**) (or a dative of the person, with impersonal verbs) and, in the usage of transitive verbs, the further addition of an oblique case (cf. **q** in vol. 2). 'Case' (*ptōsis*) picks out the syntactical relation of a noun to the other constituents of a sentence. In the 'complete sayable' this syntactical relation seems to have been regarded as a component of the sentence's meaning.

Before clarifying the obscurities associated with 'case', the concept of 'sayable' needs further analysis. Ontologically, it is sharply distinguished from the 'signifier' (utterance) and the 'name-bearer' (the corporeal entity which the sayable is about) in being 'incorporeal' (**B 3**, **E**, **H**). The distinction is most clearly expounded in **E** (cf. **55B**). Cato, or wisdom, are bodies, instances of things which can be referred to by the subjects or objects of verbs – 'name-bearers' in **B**'s terminology. But the sayable expressed by 'Cato is walking' is not itself a body, but something which can be said *about* a body. In a similar vein, the Stoics held that an effect one body brings about in another, e.g. 'being cut' caused by a scalpel to flesh, is not another body, but an incorporeal 'predicate' which comes to be true of the persisting body, flesh (see **55B** and commentary). Given the Stoics' insistence that only bodies exist (see **27**; **44–5**), the incorporeal status of sayables and predicates has proved a difficult notion to accommodate. Why are they grouped together with place, void, and time (**27D**) whose incorporeality seems unproblematic?

No explicit answers to this question have survived, but at least two reasons can be given to justify the Stoics' thesis. First, as already observed, meaningful sentences can be false as well as true. If Cato is not walking, the false statement that he *is* walking cannot have a corporeal entity, the non-walking Cato, as its meaning. Secondly, statements distinguish subjects and predicates. But, it may be argued, there is nothing in the physical world which corresponds to this distinction. In physical terms, Cato's walking is the body Cato 'disposed in a certain way' (cf. **53L**). There is only one body – the man Cato. In saying 'is walking' of Cato, we abstract a feature of that body, and that abstraction or incorporeal predication is the only way in which the unitary body Cato can be meaningfully described in a sentence. Thus sayables can be regarded as abstractions from bodies – things which are 'body-less' (the literal meaning of *asōmaton*, the word for 'incorporeal'); and this may be the point of saying that they are conceived 'by transition' (**39D 7**).

Though not existent things, sayables 'subsist' within the class of 'somethings' (**27A**). What 'subsistence' means here has to be largely established from **C** (similarly **F 2**). A person's thought or 'rational impression' (see **39A 6**) is a particular psychological state of the 'commanding-faculty', which the Stoics regarded as corporeal. To say that 'sayables subsist in accordance with a rational impression' seems to be a way of making the point that the rationality of a thought (where thought means a particular psychological event) consists in its relationship (entertaining/assenting to etc.) to a sayable, which will normally be a proposition. This explains the insistence on the connexion between thought and language (**C, D**; cf. **31A 7** on the division of dialectic). If I think of Cato walking, my commanding-faculty will be disposed in a certain way: that is my thought or rational impression. The proposition that Cato is walking is the logical or linguistic correlate of my thought, my thought as expressed in a sentence. Only *I* can have *my* thoughts, but 'Cato is walking' is something which could fit the impression in any person's mind.

Taken on its own, a predicate is the main type of 'incomplete sayable' (**F 3, G**). It is, minimally, the signification of a verb. A 'complete sayable' is formed by attaching the predicate to a 'case' (**G**; **q** in vol. 2; **34K 5–6**). Since 'cases' function as the subjects of predicates, and serve to make sayables complete, we might expect that they would be defined or explained as the significations of nouns; but the best evidence does not support this expectation. Nouns are said to signify 'qualities' (**M**), and qualities of existing things are themselves bodies (**E 3; 28L, M**). A case is not this kind of quality, i.e. some characteristic of an external object's matter, but the specific, inflected form of a noun, a noun in its proper syntactical relation to the verb of a sentence. In the standard examples (cf. **G, L**; **34K 5–6**) this is a nominative, serving as subject to the verb.

That a complete sayable should have a (corporeal) word for subject, yet have a predicate which is the (incorporeal) signification of a verb, may occasion surprise. But cases and predicates are never treated as equal or co-ordinate constituents of complete sayables. 'Case' does not, for instance, appear to share the predicate's status of 'incomplete sayable'. Rather, the position is as follows. The class of 'significations' has predicates as its primary members: they are, for reasons outlined above, treated as abstracted, incorporeal entities. But predicates only play a part in *logic* when they are appropriately deployed by linguistic utterance (cf. **F 3**). They must have their subjects supplied, by nouns or pronouns in the appropriate case, and the simple propositions thus obtained must themselves be organized into more complex structures by the use of other parts of speech, such as conjunctions (**35A**). Thus sayables are not merely, as has often been observed, 'isomorphic' with language. They are parasitic on it, to the extent of being analysable largely into the words used to express them. Indeed, the nouns, conjunctions etc. are commonly treated as *parts* of the complete sayable. Yet although the complete sayable, like its incomplete counterpart, is itself an incorporeal 'signification' (**B 3, E**), it does not follow that every one of its constituent parts is, taken individually, an incorporeal signification. It would be hard to find any room in Stoic metaphysics (cf. **27**) for incorporeal significations of nouns or conjunctions.

It is attractive to guess that nouns, pronouns, conjunctions, etc., although themselves words, were thought to acquire as it were an incorporeal *function* when deployed in a proposition or other sayable. Unfortunately there is little evidence even for this. **O**, the only testimony on the point, does call a case incorporeal, and may reflect Stoic theory (cf. **37R**), but if so it contains at least one muddle, since the uttered case to which it refers undoubtedly *is* a body (see **H**).

A word of warning must be added about 'case'. Its most familiar modern meaning is the inflection of a noun or other substantival form, e.g. nominative, genitive. In its standard Stoic usage, however, it designates not the inflection itself but the inflected word. A 'nominative case' is a word inflected in the nominative. A consequence of this is that, when not specified as e.g. nominative, 'a case' simply means 'a word in some case', or 'a substantival form' – a generic term for those grammatical items, such as nouns (**O**; **30A 3**; **37Q 4**), pronouns, and even noun-clauses (**55C**), which in Greek decline through the cases. When subjects are called 'name-bearers' (**B**), the Greek word thus translated (*tunchanonta*) strictly stands for 'case-bearers', indicating that they are the items standardly designated by nouns and pronouns.

Aristotle had excluded the nominative from the 'cases' of nouns (*De interpretatione* 16a32 ff.). In his usage all the cases are 'oblique', inflections of the nominative form. The Stoics extended the term 'case' (literally 'falling') to the nominative, and fanciful explanations were given to justify this terminology (**K, L**). Behind them probably lies the notion that predication is most fundamentally exemplified by attributing an activity to a subject, e.g. 'Socrates writes'.

As to Aristotle more generally, the Stoics can be interpreted as filling a gap in his most celebrated doctrine of meaning (**N**). Identify 'meanings' with thoughts *simpliciter*, and you leave it unclear how your and my distinct acts of thinking can *be* the same meaning. By distinguishing rational impressions from sayables while at the same time connecting them together through the concept of subsistence, the Stoics have shown that the meaning of a thought is something which is transferable, through language, across minds. I cannot pass on to you the physical modification of my mind, but I can tell you what I am thinking about.

So far sayables look like items of a semantic theory which treats meaning as entirely dependent upon a person's thoughts. Some qualifications to this picture must now be considered. As true propositions (see **34**), one species of sayable is equivalent to facts, and the effects of causes are also sayables (**55B**). Neither facts nor effects can be plausibly understood as merely meanings, mind-dependent items. Properly articulated, sayables are our means of giving an objective account of the world. We can only apprehend them by thinking about something, and we can only express them by using language. But as facts or putative facts they are available to be thought and expressed whether anyone is thinking about them or not. This point would be met if 'subsists in accordance with a rational impression' can embrace the possibility as well as the actuality of such subsistence. Nor should it be assumed, as one reading of **C** and **D** might imply, that rational impressions are nothing more than the thoughts of their corresponding *lekta*. The same proposition can be thought in a variety of ways by the same person or by different persons. The rational impression that my cat is hungry will be a different thought if I see the cat or hear the cat or reflect that I failed to feed it this morning. What *lekta* correspond to will be the propositional content, not all the circumstances and individuality, of a rational impression.

Since predicates are incorporeal, they are not 'things' we can 'have' (cf. **28M**). The relationship of a predicate to a subject is parallel to but not reducible to something corporeal *having* something corporeal. This seems to be the point of **J**: it is perfectly proper to speak of choosing 'to have' something good, where something good refers to a body. But we cannot say 'I choose to *have* acting prudently', since 'acting prudently' is not a thing which can be had; it is a predicate, not a possible possession. Prudence, on the other hand, is a possible possession but not a predicate. The having of prudence, a corporeal quality (cf. **28**), justifies the attribution of the predicate 'is prudent' to the person who has prudence (cf. **55A 3**). Predicates are 'correlates' of things, another way, it seems, of describing their 'subsistence'. Thus language can accurately mirror the world by expressing the corporeal properties of things in the incorporeal form of sayables. So too 'impulses' are reasonably said to have 'predicates' as their objects (**I**). Impulse is the efficient cause of action (see **53A 4**, **P**), the psychological state which is triggered off by our assenting to a proposition of the form, 'It is right for me to walk'. 'To walk' is not a body I can get hold of but a predicate which I make true of myself by walking.

The incorporeal status of sayables extends to the particular truths or falsehoods found in those which are of propositional form (**P 2**). This seems an obvious point. But the Stoics did not conclude from this that 'truth' is simply the name for all particular truths. They used the noun 'truth' to refer not to the aggregate of true propositions but to the wise or good man's mental disposition, which is a body (**P 2**). Thus 'truth' is assimilated to scientific knowledge (see **41H**), and its relationship to the statement of particular truths becomes purely contingent. A wise man, who has 'truth', can say something false, for good moral reasons, and an ignorant man can say something true (**P 4**). The chief interests of this distinction between 'truth' and 'true' are epistemological and ethical. Stoic logic is principally concerned with the conditions for stating particular truths, and not with 'the truth' in the special sense outlined in **P**.

34 Simple propositions

A Diogenes Laertius 7.65 (*SVF* 2.193, part)

A proposition is that which is true or false, or a complete state of affairs which, so far as itself is concerned, can be asserted, as Chrysippus says in his *Dialectical definitions*.

B Sextus Empiricus, *Against the professors* 8.74 (*SVF* 2.187, part)

Given the considerable difference among sayables, the Stoics say that for something to be true or false, it must first of all be a sayable, secondly one which is complete, and not just any such sayable but a proposition; for, as I already said, it is only when we say a proposition that we speak truly or falsely.

C Cicero, *On fate* 38

How can that which is not true not be false? Or how can that which is not false not be true? We will hold fast to the position, defended by Chrysippus, that every proposition is either true or false.

D Sextus Empiricus, *Against the professors* 8.85–6

(1) They [the Stoics] say that a true proposition is that which is and is contradictory to something, and a falsehood is that which is not and is contradictory to something. (2) But when they are asked what 'that which is' is, they say that which activates a cognitive impression. (3) And then, when examined concerning the cognitive impression, they again retreat to 'that which is' (which is equally unknown), saying that a cognitive impression has its source in that which is, in conformity with the very thing that is.

E Diogenes Laertius 7.65 (*SVF* 2.193, part)

Someone who says 'It is day' seems to propose that it is day. If, then, it is day, the proposition advanced comes out true, but if not, it comes out false.

F Sextus Empiricus, *Against the professors* 8.103

Besides this, when they [the dialecticians] say that the proposition 'It is day' is at present true but 'It is night' false, and 'Not: it is day' is false but 'Not: it is night' true, one will wonder how a negative which is one and the same, by being joined to truths makes them false, and by being joined to falsehoods makes them true.

G Sextus Empiricus, *Against the professors* 8.88–90 (*SVF* 2.214, part)

(1) They [the Stoics] can certainly not establish 'the contradictory' for us; and so the true and the false will not be known, either. (2) For they say that contradictories are propositions one of which exceeds the other by a negative, for instance, 'It is day', 'Not: it is day'. For the proposition 'Not: it is day' exceeds the proposition 'It is day' by the negative 'not', and for this reason the former is the contradictory of the latter. (3) But if this is the contradictory, the following will also be contradictories: 'It is day <and it is light' and 'It is day> and not: it is light', since the

proposition ' <It is day and> not: it is light' exceeds the proposition 'It is day <and it is light> ' by a negative. (4) But in their opinion these are not contradictories; therefore contradictories are not [propositions] one of which exceeds the other by a negative. (5) 'Yes', they say, 'but they are contradictories provided that the negative is prefixed before one of the two; for only in that case does it control the whole proposition. But in the proposition "It is day and not: it is light", the negative is only a part of the whole and its control does not extend to make the whole negative.'

H Sextus Empiricus, *Against the professors* 8.93–8 (*SVF* 2.205)

(1) Virtually the first and chief difference among propositions, the dialecticians say, is that between simple and non-simple. (2) Those are simple which are not constructed out of a single proposition stated twice, nor out of different propositions by means of one or more conjunctions, e.g. 'It is day', 'It is night', 'Socrates is talking', and every proposition of similar form . . . (3) Of the simple propositions, some are definite, some indefinite, and others intermediate. (4) Those are definite which are expressed through demonstrative reference, e.g. 'This one is walking', 'This one is sitting'. For I am demonstratively referring to one particular man. (5) Those are indefinite, they claim, in which some indefinite constituent is primary, e.g. 'Someone is sitting'. (6) Intermediate propositions are of the form, 'A man is sitting' or 'Socrates is walking'. (7) 'Someone is walking' is indefinite, since it does not mark off any of the particular persons walking; for it can be expressed quite generally with reference to each of them. (8) But 'This one is sitting' is definite, since it marks off the person pointed out. (9) 'Socrates is sitting' is intermediate, since it is neither indefinite (for it does mark off the specific) nor definite (for it is not expressed by demonstrative reference), but seems to be between them both, the indefinite and the definite. (10) They say that the indefinite, 'Someone is walking' or 'Someone is sitting', comes out true, when the definite, 'This one is sitting' or 'This one is walking', is found to be true. For if no particular person is sitting, the indefinite, 'Someone is sitting', cannot be true.

I Sextus Empiricus, *Against the professors* 8.100 (*SVF* 2.205, part)

This definite proposition such as 'this one is sitting' or 'this one is walking' is said by them [the dialecticians] to be true whenever the predicate, such as 'sitting' or 'walking', belongs to the thing which falls under the demonstrative reference.

J Galen, *On Hippocrates' and Plato's doctrines* 2.2.9–11 (*SVF* 2.895, part)

(1) This is what Chrysippus wrote about the word *egō* ('I') in the first of his books *On the soul*, in a discussion of the commanding-faculty . . . (2)

'We say *egō* too in this way, pointing to ourselves at the place in which we declare thought to be, since the demonstrative reference is conveyed there naturally and appropriately. (3) And even without such demonstrative reference by the hand, we incline into ourselves when we say *egō*, since the word *egō* is just like this, and it is pronounced with the demonstrative reference next described. (4) For we utter the first syllable of *egō* by letting the lower lip move down into ourselves demonstratively; and the second syllable is connected accordingly with the chin's movement and inclination towards the chest and this kind of demonstrative reference; and it indicates nothing distant, as happens in the case of *ekeinos* ['that one'].'

K Diogenes Laertius 7.69–70 (*SVF* 2.204)

(1) The types of simple proposition are negative, negatively assertoric, privative, assertoric, demonstrative, and indefinite ... (2) < A negative proposition consists of a negative particle > and a proposition, e.g. 'Not: it is day'. One species of this is the double negative, which is the negation of a negative, e.g. < 'Not: > not: it is day'. (3) A negatively assertoric proposition consists of a negative particle and a predicate, e.g. 'No one is walking'. (4) A privative proposition consists of a privative particle and a potential proposition, e.g. 'This man is unkind'. (5) An assertoric proposition consists of a nominative case and a predicate, e.g. 'Dion is walking'. (6) A demonstrative proposition consists of a nominative demonstrative case and a predicate, e.g. 'This one is walking'. (7) An indefinite proposition consists of one or more indefinite particles < and a predicate >, e.g. 'Someone is walking', 'That one is moving'.

☐ As was evident in **33**, the basic material of Stoic logic is the 'complete sayable' of the type they called *axiōma*. Various Latin (cf. **33E 2**) and English translations of this term are possible, but 'proposition' is much the least misleading. Stoic *axiōmata* resemble propositions, as this term is most commonly used, in being (as sayables) the intentional object of certain mental acts and in being what expressions of the form 'S is P' mean. True propositions are standardly identified with facts, as is the case with true *axiōmata*, and both are abstract entities. But it needs to be recognized that *axiōmata* are not entirely independent, as propositions normally are nowadays, of the speaker's act in expressing them. An *axiōma* is a proposition as asserted at a particular time and place. Instead of being regarded as timelessly true or false, some *axiōmata* can change their truth value (see **37A 9, J, K**) without ceasing to be the same *axiōma*. This is apparent in **F**: 'It is day' is *at present* true. The Stoics[1] are not saying that the fact of its being day 'at time t' can change. They treat the *axiōma* which says that it is day as capable of changing its truth value (cf. **E**), because the *axiōma* can be expressed when it is no

---

[1] **F** like some of Sextus' other evidence (**H, I**) refers to the 'dialecticians'. It is uncertain whether he intends this to designate the Stoics or the Dialectical school of Diodorus. But, if the latter, it still constitutes good evidence for the Stoics, whose logic grew directly out of that of the Dialectical school.

longer day. Stoic *axiōmata*, in other words, have tenses and include token reflexive elements ('this', 'I', etc.) which a modern logician would characteristically regard as features of the linguistic act rather than features of the proposition itself. But with this proviso, no serious confusion need arise in attributing to the Stoics a doctrine of propositions.

The property of being true or false is what differentiates propositions from other types of complete sayable (**A**, **B**). Unlike Epicurus (**20H–I**) and Aristotle (as normally understood in *De interpretatione* 9), the Stoics strenuously defended the principle of bivalence (**C**; cf. **38G**), taking it to apply in just the same way to all propositions, whether they refer to the past, present or future. (See **38G** and commentary.)

A true proposition corresponds to the actual state of the item(s) in the world, to which it refers (**E**). Unmistakably correct evidence about existing things is conveyed to us through 'cognitive impressions', and a proposition which describes that evidence will be true (see **40**). The Stoics expressed this correspondence theory of truth by using the same verb, (*huparchei* / *ouch huparchei*) translated by 'is' and 'is not' in **D**, to differentiate true and false propositions, and existing and non-existing things. Far from involving circular reasoning, as Sextus Empiricus maintains in **D**, 'that which is' should be interpreted as indicating the necessary correspondence between a true proposition and the actual thing it describes. Both of these 'are', but how they 'are' is determined by the ontological difference between incorporeal propositions and actual things: the 'is' of a true proposition does not indicate its existence but its truth, its 'being the case'; but in reference to the sources of cognitive impressions, 'is' tells us that such a thing 'exists'.

Depending then on whether they are or are not (the case), propositions correspond or fail to correspond with existing features of the world. The definitions of true and false propositions (**D**), however, also include 'being contradictory to something', and being contradictory is not a feature of the world, but a purely formal characteristic of every proposition, indicated linguistically by the prefixing of a negative (**G**). Assertability, then, as a characteristic of every proposition (**A**), means having a truth value; and this, in its turn, can be analysed as 'saying something about the world', and saying it in such a form that it could, so far as being a proposition is concerned, be negated.

In order to be true or false, a Stoic proposition requires a referring expression as its subject. The Stoics would probably have agreed with those modern logicians who deny truth value to the meanings of such sentences as 'The present King of France is bald', sentences which fail to pick out anything to be true or false about. A Stoic proposition whose subject fails to identify its referent is said 'to be destroyed', which probably means that it ceases to satisfy the conditions which any complete sayable must meet, in order to be a proposition of any kind (**38F**): the Stoics assume that a dead person cannot be demonstratively indicated by the pronoun 'this one', where the pronoun is a substitute for, e.g., 'man'; so if Dion is dead, 'This one is dead' is impossible as a proposition referring to Dion. The example implies that all propositions need to be formulated by means of subjects which meet the conditions of reference currently obtaining in the world. Once Dion is dead, his death can be referred to through the use of his proper name, but not through the demonstrative pronoun, 'this one'.

The importance the Stoics attached to this point emerges in **H**, **I** and **J**. In the threefold classification of simple affirmative propositions (**H**), 'This one is walking', and 'Someone is walking', exemplify 'definiteness' and 'indefiniteness' of reference respectively, with propositions whose subject is an appellative or proper name treated as 'intermediate'. What gives demonstrative reference its special status is its directness or immediacy, fancifully illustrated by the supposedly 'inward' pointing of the two syllables of *egō*, the first person singular pronoun (**J**). Thus, for the Stoics, demonstrative (and probably first and second person) pronouns function like Bertrand Russell's 'logically proper names'. We say 'this one', when we are directly aware of an object; the demonstrative pronoun is the linguistic equivalent of a gesture of pointing to a 'definite' object that is 'here', so to speak, for a proposition to refer to. Truth is a concept which straddles logic and epistemology; and the Stoics, one may suppose, like Russell, had epistemic reasons for laying such weight upon demonstrative reference: it is the most direct way of indicating, without describing, something a speaker knows or believes to exist. Russell took ordinary proper names which fail to refer to be disguised descriptions. Since any proper names could fail to refer, he took them to refer in a manner different from that in which 'this' or 'that' do. It is interesting that the Stoics too rejected proper names as subjects of 'definite' propositions (though, unlike Russell, they regarded 'that one' as an 'indefinite' form of reference (**J** 4, **K** 7)). Appellatives and proper names signify 'qualities' common and peculiar respectively (**33M**; cf. **28G**). The 'Socraticity' of Socrates marks off a specific individual (**H** 9), but not something necessarily present now, as does 'this one'.

K 5–7 correspond, apart from minor differences of terminology, to the three forms of simple proposition set out in **H**. But **K** 2–4 supplement **H** by classifying three forms of negative as further types of simple proposition. The chief interest of these is the recognition that introducing a negative or privative particle does not, by itself, make a proposition complex, though negation can also apply to complex propositions, as is clear from **G**. In contradictories, the negative particle has to govern the whole proposition (**G** 5), and this is further exemplified in the 'negative' and 'double negative' propositions of **K** 2. (A proposition of the form, 'pleasure is not a good', was counted as affirmative, not negative: see on **G**, vol. 2.)

Neither in **H** nor in **K** is it stated that every proposition can be analysed under one or more of these 'simple' forms; but allowing for possible obscurities and deficiencies in the surviving evidence, this was probably the Stoic theory. They regarded generalizing sentences of the form, 'Man is a rational mortal animal' as identical in meaning to sentences of the form, 'If something is a man, that thing is a rational mortal animal' (**30I**). Thus propositions whose subject is 'all . . .' could be accommodated under 'indefinite' propositions and the same principle probably holds good for propositions whose subject is 'some . . .'. Such material (cf. **30I** commentary) strongly suggests that the classification of simple propositions was intended to embrace every form of subject which could be attached to a predicate and produce a statement with a truth value.

As for their truth conditions, those of the 'indefinite' are explicitly made contingent upon those of the 'definite' (**H 10**), and what these are is explained in **I**: 'This one is walking' is true whenever walking belongs to (i.e. is instantiated by) the thing identified by 'this one'. The priority for truth of the definite over the indefinite has to do with the specificity of the former, its reference to a particular individual. This, in turn, illustrates the basic importance the Stoics attached to particulars in their ontology and theory of knowledge. Sense-impressions, if they are cognitive, reveal to us exactly what is out there in the world (see **40**); true propositions, when they are 'definite', are our means of stating exactly what is out there (cf. **D**). A further purpose for the doctrine concerns argument validity: see **36B 9** and commentary.

35 Non-simple propositions

A Diogenes Laertius 7.71–4

(1) Of non-simple propositions, a conditional is, as Chrysippus says in his *Dialectical treatises* and Diogenes [of Babylon] in his *Dialectical handbook*, one linked by the conditional connective 'if'. This connective declares that the second follows from the first. For example, 'If it is day, it is light.' (2) A subconditional is, as Crinis says in his *Dialectical handbook*, a proposition joined subconditionally by the connective 'since', with an antecedent proposition and a consequent proposition. For example, 'Since it is day it is light.' This connective declares both that the second follows from the first, and that the first is the case. (3) A conjunctive proposition is one which is conjoined by certain conjunctive connectives. For example, 'Both it is day, and it is light.' (4) A disjunctive proposition is one which is disjoined by the disjunctive connective 'either'. For example, 'Either it is day, or it is night.' This connective declares that one or other of the propositions is false . . . (5) Further, propositions include ones contradictory to each other in terms of truth and falsehood, of which the one is the negation of the other. For example, 'It is day', and 'Not: it is day.' (6) Thus a true conditional is one the contradictory of whose consequent conflicts with its antecedent. For example, 'If it is day, it is light.' This is true, since 'Not: it is light', the contradictory of the consequent, conflicts with 'It is day.' A false conditional is one the contradictory of whose consequent does not conflict with its antecedent. For example, 'If it is day, Dion is walking.' For 'Not: Dion is walking' does not conflict with 'It is day.' (7) A true subconditional is one which has a true antecedent and a consequent which follows from it. For example, 'Since it is day, the sun is above the earth.' A false subconditional is one which has a false antecedent, or has a consequent which does not follow from the antecedent, such as 'Since it is night, Dion is walking' said in daytime.

B Sextus Empiricus, *Outlines of Pyrrhonism* 2.110–13

(1) But passing over this problem too, we will find that the sound conditional cannot be grasped. (2) For Philo says that a sound conditional is the one which does not have a true antecedent and a false consequent. For example, when it is day and I am talking, 'If it is day, I am talking.' (3) Diodorus, on the other hand, says it is the one which neither was nor is able to have a true antecedent and a false consequent. On his view the aforementioned conditional seems to be false, since when it is day but I have fallen silent it will have a true antecedent and a false consequent, but the following one is true: 'If there are not partless elements of things, there are partless elements of things.' For it will always have the false antecedent 'There are not partless elements of things' and the (in his view) true consequent 'There are partless elements of things.' (4) Those who introduce 'cohesion' say that a conditional is sound whenever the contradictory of its consequent conflicts with its antecedent. On their view the aforementioned conditionals will be unsound, but the following one true: 'If it is day, it is day.' (5) But those who make 'entailment' the criterion say that a true conditional is one whose consequent is potentially included in the antecedent. On their view 'If it is day, it is day', and every duplicated conditional proposition, will presumably be false. For it is impossible for something to be included in itself. (6) Well, to adjudicate on this disagreement will look likely to prove impossible.

C Sextus Empiricus, *Outlines of Pyrrhonism* 2.104–6

(1) For example, those who are thought to have made accurate distinctions about the sign, the Stoics, when they wish to establish the conception of the sign, say that a sign is a leading proposition in a sound conditional, revelatory of the consequent. (2) And the proposition, they say, is a complete sayable which, so far as it itself is concerned, can be asserted; (3) while a sound conditional is the one which does not have a true antecedent and a false consequent. For the conditional either has a true antecedent and a true consequent, e.g. 'If it is day, it is light'; or a false antecedent and a false consequent, e.g. 'If the earth flies, the earth has wings'; or a true antecedent and a false consequent, e.g. 'If the earth exists, the earth flies'; or a false antecedent and a true consequent, e.g. 'If the earth flies, the earth exists.' Of these, they say that only the one with a true antecedent and a false consequent is unsound, the others sound. (4) By 'leading' proposition they mean the antecedent in a conditional with true antecedent and true consequent. (5) It is 'revelatory' of the consequent, since in the conditional 'If this woman has milk, this woman has conceived', 'This woman has milk' seems to be indicative of 'This woman has conceived.'

D Gellius 16.8.10–11

Likewise what the Greeks [meaning the Stoics] call *sumpeplegmenon* and we call a 'conjunctive' or 'coupled' proposition. It is of this form: 'Publius Scipio, son of Paulus, both was twice consul, and had a triumph, and was censor, and was colleague of Lucius Mummius in the censorship.' But if in the whole conjunctive proposition there is one falsehood, even if the others are true, the whole is said to be false.

E Gellius 16.8.12–14 (continuing **D**)

(1) There is likewise another, which the Greeks call *diezeugmenon axiōma* and we call a 'disjunctive' proposition. It is of this form: 'Either pleasure is bad, or it is good, or it is neither good nor bad.' (2) But all the disjuncts must mutually conflict, and their contradictories (which the Greeks call *antikeimena*) must also be mutually opposed. (3) Of all the disjuncts, one must be true, the others false. (4) But if either none of them is true, or all or more than one of them are true, or the disjuncts do not conflict, or the contradictories of the disjuncts are not mutually incompatible, then that is false as a disjunctive proposition and is called *paradiezeugmenon* – subdisjunctive. (5) An example is the following, in which the contradictories of the disjuncts are not mutually opposed: 'Either you are running, or you are walking, or you are standing.' For in themselves they are mutually opposed, but their contradictories do not conflict. For 'not walk', 'not stand', and 'not run' are not mutually incompatible, since it is those things which cannot be simultaneously true that are called incompatible. For you could simultaneously neither walk nor stand nor run.

☐ Of non-simple propositions, whose definitions and truth-conditions are listed in **A**, three types are of special logical importance as providing the leading premises of syllogisms (see **36**). These are conditional, disjunctive and conjunctive propositions.

Diodorus and Philo, the Stoics' immediate forerunners in logic, had already established a controversy over the conditional: what is it for one proposition to 'follow' from another? (See **B**, whose source, the Sceptic Sextus, aims to set the leading doctrinaire positions against each other.) Philo's answer is essentially equivalent to the 'material implication' of the modern propositional calculus. For him the sole determinants are the respective truth values of the antecedent and the consequent at the time of utterance, regardless of their relevance or irrelevance to each other: **B 2**. Diodorus' modification, in **B 3**, apparently aims to convert the sound conditional into the kind of necessary truth which might ground scientific or dialectical inferences. Many Stoics, while sharing this objective, surprisingly continued to invoke the Philonian criterion. In **C**, which exemplifies this tendency (cf. also **37K**), both the context and the chosen examples show that they did nevertheless expect sound conditionals to exhibit an un-Philonian connectedness between antecedent and consequent. Presumably, then, while accepting Philo's analysis of the logical force of the connective 'if', they concentrated its use on cases where 'If p, q' (e.g. 'If the earth flies, the earth has wings') could be justified without prior knowledge of the respective truth-values of p and q – for example by appeal to an independent premise (e.g. 'It is impossible to fly without wings').

However, the eventual canonical Stoic criterion is 'cohesion': **B 4**. It probably had the approval of Chrysippus, and it features among the official rules at **A 6**. It obtains wherever the contradictory of the consequent 'conflicts' with the antecedent, and although no precise Stoic definition of 'conflict' survives, it is fairly clear from **E** and other evidence that a conceptual, rather than an empirical, incompatibility, is intended. Indeed, a Stoic account of 'following' slightly postdating Chrysippus (see **18F**; **42G, H, J**, with commentary) puts this point more clearly by requiring that when the consequent is hypothetically eliminated the antecedent should *thereby* be 'co-eliminated' – a formulation which appears to outlaw any considerations which cannot be extracted from our understanding of the antecedent and consequent themselves. (The last criterion of a conditional's soundness, listed at **B 5**, cannot be securely assigned to any specific school or philosopher, but it may not differ significantly from 'cohesion', and traces of it can be found in both Stoic (cf. **36G 4**) and medical sources.)

Although Chrysippus assigned this strong sense to 'if', he also retained a use for the Philonian conditional, to express a weaker form of connexion. But to avoid confusion he reformulated this as a negated conjunction, 'Not both: p and not-q': cf. **36A 11–14**, and see further **37D** and **38E 6**, with commentary.

One role of the conditional which may well have influenced this debate must be noted here. Hellenistic epistemology attaches special importance to 'signs', evident facts which serve to 'reveal' further, non-evident facts (see especially **51H**, and **42** commentary). And these facts are related as, respectively, the true antecedent and the consequent in a sound conditional: **C**. Such a true antecedent is also called the 'leading' proposition, with the connotation 'guiding'. A possible weakness of the conditional formulation is that it cannot in itself indicate the truth of the antecedent, and this may be why the post-Chrysippean Stoics mentioned above preferred to express signs with the 'subconditional', 'Since p, q', for the analysis of which see **A 2** and **7**.

The Stoics' eventual move away from Philo's truth-functional analysis of the conditional is matched by their regular treatment of disjunction: **A 4, E**; **36C 5**. Not only is disjunction understood as exclusive, so that one and only one disjunct is true, but a proper disjunction is one in which the individual disjuncts are so related in terms of incompatibility as to guarantee this result.

As for conjunctive propositions, however, the basic analysis of these is truth-functional (**D**; **36B 4**). So too for the *negated* conjunction 'Not both: p and not-q', the form in which the conjunctive proposition finds prominence in syllogistic (see **36A 14**). There is some tendency in the sources to treat this as requiring, once again, a relationship of incompatibility. Strictly, though, the position is that the truth-condition for a negated conjunction is nothing more than the falsity of at least one of its conjuncts; but that where the truth-values of the individual conjuncts must be left temporarily undetermined, as for instance in the leading premise of a syllogism like that at **36A 14**, the best ground on which the negated conjunction can be justified may indeed be the mutual incompatibility of its conjuncts. It is not, however, the only possible ground: cf. **36G 7**; **37D**; **38E 6**, with commentary; **42D 2**.

36 Arguments

A Diogenes Laertius 7.76–81

(1) An argument is, as Crinis says, that which consists of a premise or premises, an additional premise, and a conclusion. For example: 'If it is day, it is light. But it is day. Therefore it is light.' For 'If it is day, it is light' is the premise; 'But it is day' is the additional premise; and 'Therefore it is light' is the conclusion. (2) A mode is, as it were, the form of an argument. For example: 'If the first, the second. But the first. Therefore the second.' (3) A mode-argument is the combination of the two. For example: 'If Plato is alive, Plato is breathing. But the first. Therefore the second.' The mode-argument was introduced so as to avoid stating the long additional premise and the conclusion in extended trains of argument, but to reach the conclusion succinctly: 'But the first. Therefore the second.' (4) Of arguments, some are invalid, others valid. Invalid are those the contradictory of whose conclusion does not conflict with the conjunction of the premises. For example: 'If it is day, it is light. But it is day. Therefore Dion is walking.' (5) Of valid arguments, some are just called 'valid' (after the genus), others 'syllogistic'. Syllogistic are those which either are indemonstrable, or are reduced to the indemonstrables through one or more of the ground-rules. For example: 'If Dion is walking, <Dion is moving. But Dion is walking.> Therefore Dion is moving.' (6) 'Valid', in the specific sense, are those which are deductive but not syllogistically. For example: '"It is day and it is night" is false. But it is day. Therefore not: it is night.' (7) 'Non-syllogistic' are those which are plausibly comparable to syllogistic arguments but not deductive. For example: 'If Dion is a horse, Dion is an animal. But not: Dion is a horse. Therefore not: Dion is an animal.' (8) Further, some arguments are true, others false. True are those arguments which deduce through true premises. For example: 'If virtue benefits, vice harms. <But virtue benefits. Therefore vice harms.>' (9) False are those which have some falsity in their premises, or which are invalid, such as: 'If it is day, it is light. But it is day. Therefore Dion is alive.' (10) There are also possible, impossible, necessary and non-necessary arguments. (11) There are also certain 'indemonstrable' arguments, since they need no demonstration. The lists of them vary among the authorities, but Chrysippus gives five through which every argument is constructed.

They are invoked for valid arguments, syllogisms, and the argument modes. (12) The first indemonstrable is the one in which a complete argument is constructed out of a conditional and the antecedent of the conditional with its consequent for conclusion. For example: 'If the first, the second. But the first. Therefore the second.' (13) The second indemonstrable is the one formed with a conditional and the contradictory of the consequent, with the contradictory of the antecedent for conclusion. For example: 'If it is day, it is light. <But not: it is light. Therefore not: it is day.> ' For the additional premise is formed from the contradictory of the consequent, and the conclusion from the contradictory of the antecedent. (14) The third indemonstrable is the one which through a negated conjunction and one of the conjuncts has as conclusion the contradictory of the other conjunct. For example: 'Not Plato is dead and Plato is alive. But Plato is dead. Therefore not: Plato is alive.' (15) The fourth indemonstrable is the one which through a disjunctive proposition and one of the disjuncts has as conclusion the contradictory of the other disjunct. For example: 'Either the first or the second. But the first. Therefore not the second.' (16) The fifth indemonstrable is one in which every argument is constructed out of a disjunctive proposition and the contradictory of one of the disjuncts, with the other disjunct for conclusion. For example: 'Either it is day or it is night. But not: it is night. Therefore it is day.'

B Sextus Empiricus, *Outlines of Pyrrhonism* 2.135–43

(1) A demonstration, they say, is an argument which through agreed premises by means of deduction reveals a non-evident conclusion. What they mean will be clearer from what follows. (2) An argument is a complex of premises and a conclusion. What they call its premises are the propositions adopted by agreement for the establishment of a conclusion. A conclusion is the proposition established from the premises. For example, in 'If it is day, it is light. But it is day. Therefore it is light', 'Therefore it is light' is the conclusion, the rest are premises. (3) Of arguments, some are deductive, others non-deductive. They are deductive when the conditional which has as antecedent the conjunctive proposition formed from the premises of the argument, and as consequent its conclusion, is sound. For example, the argument quoted above is deductive because from the conjunction of its premises, namely 'It is day, and if it is day it is light', there follows 'It is light', in the following conditional: 'If: it is day, and if it is day it is light; then: it is light.' Non-deductive are those not of this kind. (4) Of deductive arguments, some are true, some not true. They are true when not only is the conditional consisting of the conjunction of the premises plus the conclusion sound, as explained above, but also the conclusion, and the

conjunctive proposition formed from the premises of the argument (i.e. the antecedent in this conditional), are true. And a true conjunctive proposition is the one which, like 'It is day, and if it is day it is light', has all its conjuncts true. (5) Not true are those not of this kind. For an argument like 'If it is night, it is dark. But it is night. Therefore it is dark' is deductive, because the conditional 'If: it is night, and if it is night it is dark; <then: it is dark>' is sound; but is not true, because the antecedent conjunctive proposition 'It is night, and if it is night it is dark' is false, containing as it does the falsehood 'It is night.' For the conjunctive proposition which contains a falsehood is false. (6) Hence they say that a true argument is one which by means of true premises deduces a true conclusion. (7) Again, of true arguments some are demonstrative, others non-demonstrative. Demonstrative are those which by means of things pre-evident deduce something non-evident. Non-demonstrative are those not of this kind. For example, an argument like 'If it is day, it is light. But it is day. Therefore it is light' is non-demonstrative. For its conclusion, that it is light, is pre-evident. But one like 'If sweat flows through the surface, there are ducts discoverable by thought. But sweat flows through the surface. Therefore there are ducts discoverable by thought' is demonstrative, having the non-evident conclusion 'Therefore there are ducts discoverable by thought.' (8) Of those which deduce something non-evident, some lead us by means of the premises to the conclusion in a merely progressive way, others in a both progressive and revelatory way. (9) Those which lead us in a merely progressive way are the ones which seem to depend on trust and memory, such as 'If some god has told you that this man will be rich, this man will be rich. But this god' (I refer demonstratively to, say, Zeus) 'has told you that this man will be rich. Therefore this man will be rich.' For we assent to the conclusion less because of the cogency of the premises than because we trust the god's statement. (10) Those which lead us to the conclusion in a not only progressive but also revelatory way are ones like this: 'If sweat flows through the surface, there are ducts discoverable by thought. But the first. Therefore the second.' For the proposition that sweat flows is revelatory of the proposition that there are ducts, thanks to our preconception that liquid cannot penetrate a solid body. (11) Thus a demonstration must be an argument, and deductive, and true, and with a conclusion which is non-evident and revealed by the force of the premises. That is why a demonstration is said to be an argument which through agreed premises by means of deduction reveals a non-evident conclusion.

C Sextus Empiricus, *Against the professors* 8.429–34, 440–3

(1) Invalid argument, they say, arises in four ways: by disconnexion, by redundancy, by being posed in an unsound form, or by deficiency. (2) It

arises by disconnexion when the premises have no unison and connexion with each other and with the conclusion, as in an argument like 'If it is day, it is light. But wheat is being sold in the market. Therefore it is light.' For we can see that in this example neither has 'If it is day' any harmony or link with 'Wheat is being sold in the market', nor has either of them with 'Therefore it is light', but each is disconnected from the others. (3) Argument is invalid through redundancy when something extraneous is superfluously added alongside the premises, as in 'If it is day, it is light. But it is day. But also virtue benefits. Therefore it is light'. For the premise that virtue benefits is superfluously added alongside the other premises, if on its removal it is possible through the remainder, 'If it is day, it is light' and 'But it is day', for the conclusion 'Therefore it is light' to be deduced. (4) An argument becomes invalid by being posed in an unsound form when it is posed in any of the forms envisaged beyond the sound forms. For example, given the soundness of the form 'If the first, the second. But the first. Therefore the second', and also of 'If the first, the second. But not the second. Therefore not the first', we say that an argument posed in the form 'If the first, the second. But not the first. Therefore not the second' is invalid, not because it is impossible for an argument to be posed in this form which through truths deduces a truth (it *is* possible: e.g. 'If $3 = 4, 6 = 8$. But not: $3 = 4$. Therefore not: $6 = 8$.'), but because some unsound arguments can be formulated in it, such as 'If it is day, it is light. But not: it is day. Therefore not: it is light.' (5) Argument becomes invalid by deficiency when something is missing from the deductive premises. For example: 'Either wealth is bad, or wealth is good. But not: wealth is bad. Therefore wealth is good.' For in the disjunction the proposition that wealth is indifferent is missing, so that the sound way of posing it is instead like this: 'Either wealth is good, or it is bad, or indifferent. But neither is wealth good, nor bad. Therefore it is indifferent.' . . . (6) In reply, then, the Sceptics will say that if that argument is invalid by redundancy in which on the removal of one premise the conclusion is deduced from the remainder, then the argument posed in the first mode, of the form 'If it is day, it is light. But it is day. Therefore it is light', must be called invalid. For in it the hypothetical premise 'If it is day, <it is light> ' is redundant with regard to the establishment of the conclusion, and 'Therefore it is light' can be deduced from 'It is day' alone. This fact is pre-evident even in itself, but it is also possible to support it from the relationship of following which so far as the Stoics are concerned obtains. For either they will say that its being light follows from its being day, or that it does not follow. And if it follows, once it is agreed that 'It is day' is true, 'It is light' is also directly deduced therefrom, since it necessarily follows from it; and that is the conclusion. Whereas if it does not follow, it will not follow in the conditional either, so that the conditional will be false since the consequent in it will not follow from the antecedent. Hence, to go by the classification stated above, one of two things must happen: either the argument posed in the first mode will be found to be invalid through the redundancy of the hypothetical premise in it, or totally false through the falsity of the hypothetical premise in it. (7) For to say that Chrysippus does not believe in one-premise arguments, as some will no doubt reply to such an objection, is utterly silly. First, we are not compelled to obey Chrysippus' pronouncements as if they were oracular decrees. And second, it is impossible to heed men's testimony for a self-imposed ban in the face of a witness who says the opposite. For Antipater, one of the most distinguished men in the Stoic sect, said that it was possible for even single-premise arguments to be constructed.

D Apuleius, *De interpretatione* 184,16–23

. . . no syllogism is constructed from a single premise, even though the Stoic Antipater holds, contrary to the universal consensus, that 'You are seeing. Therefore you are alive' is a complete deduction. In fact the complete form is 'If you are seeing, you are alive. But you are seeing. Therefore you are alive.'

E Sextus Empiricus, *Outlines of Pyrrhonism* 1.69

According to Chrysippus (that arch-enemy of irrational animals!) the dog even shares in their legendary 'dialectic'. At any rate, this man says that the dog applies himself to a multiple 'fifth indemonstrable' when he comes to a triple fork in the path, and, after sniffing the two paths which his quarry did not take, sets off at once down the third without even sniffing it. For, the ancient philosopher says, the dog is in effect reasoning: 'Either my quarry went this way, or this way, or this way. But neither this way, nor this way. Therefore this way.'

F Origen, *Against Celsus* 7.15

The Stoics also give this mode a concrete application, as follows: 'If you know that you are dead, <you are dead. If you know that you are dead,> it is not the case that you are dead. Therefore, it follows, it is not the case that you know that you are dead.'

G Sextus Empiricus, *Against the professors* 8.229–37

[According to Stoic logic] (1) Non-simple are those arguments formed by combination of the simple ones and still requiring analysis into them in order to be recognized as themselves deductive. (2) Of these non-simple arguments some are composed of arguments of a single type, others of arguments of diverse types. Examples of the former are those formed by combination of two first indemonstrables, or of two second indemonstrables; of the latter, those composed of a first <plus a third> indemonstrable, or of a second plus a third, and in general those of this kind. (3) An argument composed of arguments of a single type is: 'If it is day, < if it is day > it is light. But it is day. Therefore it is light.' For this is formed by combination of two first indemonstrables, as we will appreciate when we have analysed it. (4) We must recognize that there is a dialectical theorem transmitted for the analysis of syllogisms, as follows: when we have the premises from which some conclusion is deducible, we potentially have that conclusion too in these premises, even if it is not expressly stated. (5) Since, then, we have two premises – the conditional 'If it is day, <if it is day it is light>, which has the simple proposition 'It is day' for antecedent, and the conditional 'If it is day, it is light', which is non-simple, for consequent, and also its antecedent 'It is day' – from these we will deduce by a first indemonstrable that conditional's consequent, 'If it is day, it is light.' We have this, then, as a potential deduction in the argument, but not expressly supplied. By combining it with the additional premise of the argument as stated, 'It is day', we will have 'It is light' deduced by a first indemonstrable. And that was the conclusion of the argument as stated. Hence there are two first indemonstrables: 'If it is day, <if it is day> it is light. <But it is day. Therefore if it is day, it is light> '; and 'If it is day, it is light. But it is day. Therefore it is light.' (6) Such then is the character of arguments formed by combination from a single type. There remain those formed from diverse types, like the one posed in Aenesidemus' school about the sign, which goes as follows: 'If things evident appear alike to all those in like condition, and signs are things evident, signs appear alike to all those in like condition. But signs do not appear alike to all those in like condition. And things evident do appear alike to all those in like condition. Therefore signs are not things evident.' (7) For this kind of argument is composed out of a second and a third indemonstrable, as can be learnt from its analysis, which will be clearer if we use the mode for our exposition, as follows: 'If the first and the second, the third. But not the third. Moreover, the first. Therefore not the second.' For since we have a conditional with the conjunction of the first and second for antecedent and with the third for consequent, and we have the contradictory of the consequent, 'Not the third', we will also deduce the contradictory of the antecedent, 'Therefore not both: the first and the second', by a second indemonstrable. But in fact this very proposition is contained in the argument in potential form, since we have the premises from which it is deducible, although it is not expressly supplied. By combining it with the remaining premise, the first, we will have the conclusion, 'Therefore not the second', deduced by a third indemonstrable. Hence there are two indemonstrables: 'If the first and the second, the third. But not the third.

Therefore not both: the first and the second', which is a second indemonstrable; and a third indemonstrable, which goes 'Not both: the first and the second. But the first. Therefore not the second.' Such then, is the analysis if one uses the mode, and there is an analogous analysis for the argument too.

H Galen, *On Hippocrates' and Plato's doctrines* 2.3.18–19

(1) Now you can meet many people minutely skilled in the ways of analysing syllogisms constructed with two or three hypothetical premises, tautologically valid syllogisms, or certain others of this kind which use the first and second ground-rules, as also in connexion with others which they analyse by means of the third or fourth ground-rule. (2) Yet most of these can be analysed in another, more succinct way, as Antipater wrote. And anyway, all the construction of such syllogisms is no small overexpenditure of effort on something useless, as Chrysippus himself testifies in practice by never in his own works needing those syllogisms to demonstrate a doctrine.

I Apuleius, *De interpretatione* 191,5–10

There is a further test, which is also common to all the indemonstrable arguments. It is called the *per impossibile* test, and is entitled by the Stoics the first principle or ground-rule. They define it as follows: 'If from two propositions a third is deduced, then from either one of them together with the contradictory of the conclusion the contradictory of the other is deduced.'

J Alexander, *On Aristotle's Prior analytics* 278,11–14

The third so-called 'ground-rule' is itself like this in outline: 'When from two propositions a third is deduced , and extra propositions are found from which one of those two follows syllogistically, the same conclusion will be deduced from the other of the two plus the extra propositions from which that one follows syllogistically.'

☐ An argument is canonically defined (**B 2**, cf. **A 1**) as a complex of premises and a conclusion. The Stoic view of argument had a dialectical background in which each premise was posed as a question to an interlocutor and required his agreement (cf. **31A 5**, **B 8**). Despite the great formality imposed by the logical handbooks, this dialectical aspect was never lost sight of. Arguments are standardly 'asked', not just stated, and although the texts only rarely set out the premises in interrogative form (cf. **37L, S**) the reader is nevertheless (cf. **37A 5, 9, J**) expected to take them that way. (The Greek verb for 'ask' normally appears as 'pose' in our translations.)

Stoic logic concentrates on formally syllogistic arguments (**A 5–7**), and, among these, on syllogisms which relate whole propositions rather than, as in Aristotelian logic, terms. For argument validity see **A 4** ff., **B 3** (where 'deductive', slightly unusually, does duty for 'valid'), **C**. Validity is primarily established by the Principle of Conditionalization, as explained at **B 3** (the relevant criterion of a sound conditional being, as **A 4** shows, 'cohesion' – on which see **35B 4** and commentary). Other rules governing validity can, at best, be indirectly inferred. For example, the valid argument at **B 9** has the 'indefinite' antecedent in its leading premise verified by a corresponding 'definite' proposition in the additional premise. Here a comparison with **34H 10** will reveal the theoretical justification for the shift.

The interesting Pyrrhonist argument at **C 6** turns the Stoics' own 'redundancy' criterion of invalidity (**C 3**) against their own most basic syllogistic mode. It is tempting to guess that this argument had originated in the sceptical Academy, and was a cause of Antipater's heterodox introduction of one-premised arguments (**C 7, D**).

Beyond validity, and truth (**A 8–9, B 4–6**), further requirements govern the use of arguments as strict scientific demonstrations: **B 7–11**. These will be discussed in the commentary to **42**.

The analysis of arguments centres around five allegedly primary types of syllogism, the 'indemonstrable' arguments: **A 11–16**. These are marked by their use of three types of 'hypothetical' premise, more literally 'mode-premise' (*tropikon*) – the conditional, the disjunctive, and the conjunctive proposition – for whose truth-conditions see **35**. Note, however, that Stoic theory focuses on analysis of actual arguments, not their formalized 'modes' (on which see **A 2**), and that the latter are used only in explication of the former, as at **G 6–7**.

To demonstrate the validity of any more complex argument, it is necessary to reduce it to one or more indemonstrable arguments (**A 5, G 1**). The argument in **E**, which differs from a standard fifth indemonstrable only in that its major premise has three disjuncts instead of two, could be analysed for example into two fifth indemonstrables: 'Either *p* or (*q* or *r*); but not-*p*; therefore (*q* or *r*). Either *q* or *r*; but not-*q*; therefore *r*.' A complication of this, however, is that the bracketed pair '(*q* or *r*)' does not constitute a genuine disjunction, but only a 'subdisjunction' (see **35E** and cf. **C 5**). Other examples are expounded in **G**.

In aid of these analyses, Chrysippus listed at least four 'ground-rules' (*themata*): **A 5, H**. Recent work has done much to aid their rediscovery. For the first, see **I**, where it is equated with the Aristotelian *per impossibile* proof. The second, third and fourth are reported to have between them corresponded to the Peripatetic 'synthetic theorem', which derived chain-syllogisms from simple syllogisms. The third, quoted in **J**, clearly fits in with this report. The fourth, then, may have run roughly as follows: 'When from two propositions a third is deduced, and extra propositions are found from which one of those two follows syllogistically, and other extra propositions are found from which the other of those two follows syllogistically, the same conclusion will be deduced from all the extra propositions taken together.' Since the third and (presumably) fourth ground-rules deal with 'extra' premises, i.e. premises not identical with those of the initial syllogism, a further ground-rule seems to be required for cases where one and the same premise has to be used two or more times. For this and other reasons the second ground-rule may have run on the following lines: 'When from a set of propositions a conclusion is deduced, and from one of those same propositions, taken with that conclusion, a further conclusion is deduced, that further conclusion will be deduced from the original set of propositions.'

G, our fullest source on the analysis of complex syllogisms, does not use the individual Chrysippean ground-rules, but a single theorem (**G 4**) which appears to embrace the second, third and fourth ground-rules. It has been suggested that this theorem represents the subsequent work of simplification attributed to Antipater at **H 2**. If we invoke the Chrysippean ground-rules instead, it will be seen that the analysis of the complex argument at **G 3–5** requires the second ground-rule (as conjecturally identified above), while that at **G 6–7** requires the third.

Other complex syllogisms are said to be amenable to reduction by means of the ground-rules at **H 1** (the reader is invited to work out how). Of these, the one 'with two hypothetical premises' is the type quoted in **F**. That 'with three hypothetical premises' is less securely identified, but for a probable, if somewhat informal, example see **38 I**. And 'tautologically (lit. 'indifferently') valid' syllogisms are those with such forms as 'Either *p* or *q*; but *p*; therefore *p*', where the conclusion is identical with one of the premises.

37 Fallacy

A Sextus Empiricus, *Outlines of Pyrrhonism* 2.229–35

(1) It is perhaps not inappropriate to turn our attention briefly to the theory of sophisms, since those who glorify dialectic say that it is also for the solution of these that dialectic is necessary. For if, they say, it is capable of distinguishing true from false arguments, and sophisms are themselves false arguments, it must also be capable of discriminating these, which use their apparent plausibility to make a mockery of the truth. Hence the dialecticians [or 'Dialecticians'], claiming to be rescuing our tottering life, eagerly try to teach us both the conception of sophisms, and their differences, and their solutions. (2) A sophism, they say, is a plausible argument deceitfully framed to make us accept the false or false-seeming or non-evident or otherwise unacceptable conclusion. (3) An example of a false conclusion is that in the following sophism. 'No one makes you drink a predicate. But "drink absinth" is a predicate. Therefore no one makes you drink absinth.' (4) A false-seeming conclusion is like that in the following. 'What neither was nor is possible is not absurd. But "The doctor *qua* doctor murders" neither was nor is possible. < Therefore "The doctor *qua* doctor murders" is not absurd.' > (5) A non-evident conclusion is like this. 'Not both: I have asked you a previous question, and not: the number of the stars is even. But I have asked you a previous question. Therefore the number of the stars is even.' (6) An otherwise unacceptable conclusion is exemplified by the 'solecizing' arguments. E.g. 'What you look at, exists. But you look at your wits' end. Therefore your wits' end exists.' 'What you see, exists. But you see onto an inflamed place.

Therefore onto an inflamed place exists.' (7) But they then try to offer solutions to them, saying with regard to the first sophism that what has been agreed by means of the premises is different from the conclusion. For what has been agreed is that a predicate is not drunk, and that 'drink absinth' is a predicate: not that absinth is itself a predicate. So where the conclusion should be 'Therefore no one drinks "drink absinth"', which is true, that actually drawn is 'Therefore no one drinks absinth', which is false, and is not deduced from the agreed premises. (8) With regard to the second, they say that while it seems to lead to a false conclusion, so as to make the inattentive hesitate to assent to it, it in fact deduces a truth, 'Therefore "The doctor *qua* doctor murders" is not absurd.' For no proposition is absurd, and 'The doctor *qua* doctor murders' is a proposition. Hence it too is not absurd. (9) The one leading to the non-evident belongs, they say, to the class of 'changing' arguments. For when, *ex hypothesi*, no previous question has been asked, the negated conjunction comes out true, since the inclusion of the falsehood 'I have asked you a previous question' makes the conjunction false. But when the negated conjunction has been asked, the additional premise 'But I have asked you a previous question' becomes true, since the negated conjunction has been asked prior to the additional premise; and the premise consisting of the negated conjunction becomes false, the false conjunct having become true. Hence there is no time at which the conclusion can be deduced, if the negated conjunction does not obtain at the same time as the minor premise. (10) As for the last group, the solecizing arguments, these according to some are absurd inferences which flout linguistic usage.

B Diogenes Laertius 7.192–8 (with omissions)

[From the list of Chrysippus' logical works] (1) *On linguistic anomaly*, to Dion, in four books; *On Sorites Arguments relating to utterances*, in three books; *On solecisms*, in one book; *On solecizing arguments*, to Dionysius, in one book; *Arguments which depend on linguistic usages*, in one book; . . . (2) *Reply to those who reject division*, in two books; *On ambiguities*, to Apollas, in four books; *On mode ambiguities*, in one book; *On conditional mode ambiguity*, in two books; *Reply to Panthoides' 'On ambiguities'*, in two books; *On the introductory course on ambiguities*, in five books; *Epitome of the work 'Ambiguities' addressed to Epicrates*, in one book; *Conditionals for the introductory course on ambiguities*, in two books; (3) . . . *On the introductory course on the Lying Argument*, to Aristocreon, in one book; *Lying Arguments, an introduction*, in one book; *On the Lying Argument*, to Aristocreon, in six books; . . . *Reply to those who hold that there are propositions simultaneously false and true*, in one book; *Reply to those who solve the Lying Argument by cutting*, to Aristocreon, in two books;

Demonstrations that indefinite propositions should not be cut, in one book; *Reply to objections to what is said against the cutting of indefinite propositions*, to Pasylus, in three books; *Solution according to the ancients*, to Dioscurides, in one book; *On the solution of the Lying Argument*, to Aristocreon, in three books; *Solutions to Hedylus' hypothetical arguments*, to Aristocreon and Apollas, in one book; ... *Reply to those who say that the Lying Argument has its premises false*, in one book; (4) *On the Denying Argument*, to Aristocreon, in two books; *Denying Arguments: exercises*, in one book; *On the Little-by-little Argument*, to Stesagoras, in two books; *On arguments relating to suppositions, and Quiescent Arguments*, to Onetor, in two books; *On the Veiled Argument*, to Aristobulus, in two books; *On the Elusive Argument*, to Athenades, in one book; (5) . . . *On the Not-someone Argument*, to Menecrates, in eight books; *On arguments formed with an indefinite and a definite proposition*, to Pasylus, in two books; *On the Not-someone Argument*, to Epicrates, in one book; (6) . . . *On sophisms*, to Heraclides and Pollis, in two books; *On the puzzling arguments of the Dialecticians*, to Dioscurides, in five books; *Reply to the method of Arcesilaus*, to Sphaerus, in one book.

C Diogenes Laertius 7.44 (= **31A 7**)

These [sophisms which depend on utterance and states of affairs] include Lying Arguments, Truth-telling Arguments, Denying Arguments, Sorites Arguments, and those defective and insoluble and valid arguments which resemble these; and Veiled Arguments, Horned Arguments, Not-someone arguments, and Mowing Arguments.

D Diogenes Laertius 7.82

(1) There are also puzzling arguments – Veiled, Elusive, Sorites, Horned and Not-someone. . . . (2) <A Sorites is like this> : 'Not: 2 are few, but not 3 as well. Not: the latter but not 4 as well. And so on up to 10. But 2 are few. Therefore 10 are few as well.'

E Galen, *On medical experience* 16.1–17.3

(1) According to what is demanded by the analogy, there must not be such a thing in the world as a heap of grain, a mass or satiety, neither a mountain nor strong love, nor a row, nor strong wind, nor city, nor anything else which is known from its name and idea to have a measure of extent or multitude, such as the wave, the open sea, a flock of sheep and herd of cattle, the nation and the crowd. And the doubt and confusion introduced by the analogy leads to contradiction of fact in the transition of man from one stage of his life to another, and in the changes of time, and the changes of seasons. For in the case of the boy one is uncertain and doubtful as to when the actual moment arrives for his transition from boyhood to adolescence, and in the case of the youth when he enters the

period of manhood, also in the case of the man in his prime when he begins to be an old man. And so it is with the seasons of the year when winter begins to change and merges into spring, and spring into summer, and summer into autumn. By the same reasoning, doubt and confusion enter into many other things which relate to the doings of men in spite of the fact that knowledge of these things is obvious and plain. (2) There are some dogmatists and logicians who call the argument expressing this doubt 'Sorites' after the matter which first gave rise to this question, I mean the heap. Other people call it the Little-by-little Argument. They have only named it thus in accordance with its method which leads to doubt and confusion.... (3) Wherefore I say: tell me, do you think that a single grain of wheat is a heap? Thereupon you say No. Then I say: what do you say about 2 grains? For it is my purpose to ask you questions in succession, and if you do not admit that 2 grains are a heap then I shall ask you about 3 grains. Then I shall proceed to interrogate you further with respect to 4 grains, then 5 and 6 and 7 and 8; and I think you will say that none of these makes a heap. Also 9 and 10 and 11 are not a heap. For the conception of a heap which is formed in the soul and is conjured up in the imagination is that, besides being single particles in juxtaposition, it has quantity and mass of some considerable size.... I for my part shall not cease from continuing to add one to the number in like manner, nor desist from asking you without ceasing if you admit that the quantity of each single one of these numbers constitutes a heap. It is not possible for you to say with regard to any one of these numbers that it constitutes a heap. I shall proceed to explain the cause of this. If you do not say with respect to any of the numbers, as in the case of the 100 grains of wheat for example, that it now constitutes a heap, but afterwards when a grain is added to it, you say that a heap has now been formed, consequently this quantity of corn becomes a heap by the addition of the single grain of wheat, and if the grain is taken away the heap is eliminated. And I know of nothing worse and more absurd than that the being and not-being of a heap is determined by a grain of corn. And to prevent this absurdity from adhering to you, you will not cease from denying, and will never admit at any time that the sum of this is a heap, even if the number of grains reaches infinity by the constant and gradual addition of more. And by reason of this denial the heap is proved to be non-existent, because of this pretty sophism.

F Sextus Empiricus, *Against the professors* 7.416

For since in the Sorites the last cognitive impression is adjacent to the first non-cognitive impression and virtually indistiguishable from it, the school of Chrysippus say that in the case of impressions which differ so slightly the wise man will stop and become quiescent, while in the cases where a more substantial difference strikes him he will assent to one of the impressions as true.

G Chrysippus, *Logical questions* III, 9.7–12 (*SVF* 2.298, part)

Up to what point one should give the same answers will provide pause for thought in the matter of the Little-by-little Argument. And likewise in the question whether one should use cutting concerning one's answer.

H Cicero, *Academica* 2.92–6

[Speaker: Cicero on behalf of the New Academy] (1) But since you place so much weight on that science [dialectic], see that it does not in its entirety prove to be your natural foe. It starts out by cheerfully imparting the elements of discourse, an understanding of ambiguities, and the principles of deduction. But it then, by a few increments, gets to Sorites Arguments, a slippery and hazardous area, which you earlier described as a fallacious kind of questioning. What of that? Is the fallaciousness you speak of our fault? (2) Nature has permitted us no knowledge of limits such as would enable us to determine, in any case, how far to go. Nor is it so just with a heap of corn, from which the name (Sorites) is derived: there is no matter whatever concerning which, if questioned by gradual progression, we can tell how much must be added or subtracted before we can give a definite answer – rich or poor, famous or unknown, many or few, large or small, long or short, broad or narrow. (3) 'But Sorites Arguments are fallacious.' Well demolish them then, if you can, to stop them bothering you – for they will bother you if you don't take precautions. 'Precautions have been taken', comes the answer. 'For Chrysippus' policy when being asked by gradual progression whether, say, 3 is few or many, is to become quiescent (*hēsuchazein*, as they term it) some time before reaching many.' To which Carneades' reply is: 'For all I care you can snore, not just become quiescent. But what's the point? In time there'll be someone to wake you up and question you in the same fashion: "If I add one to the number at which you fell silent, will it be many?" And so on you will go, as far as you think fit.' Why say more? For what you're admitting is that you cannot answer which is the last of 'few' or the first of 'many'. Error of this kind spreads so easily that I do not see where it might not reach. 'That doesn't harm me', he says, 'for like a skilled driver I shall restrain my horses before I reach the edge, all the more so if what they're heading towards is a precipice. In like manner I restrain myself in advance and stop replying to sophistical questions.' If you have a clear answer but do not give it, that is arrogant behaviour. If you do not have one, then you too do not know. If it is because the matter is non-evident, I grant that. But in fact you say that you do not proceed as far as the non-evident cases, and hence you are stopping at cases which are clear-cut. If that is just a device for staying silent, you achieve nothing, for why should your pursuer care whether he traps you silent or speaking? If, on the other hand, you reply 'few' up to, say, 9, without hesitation, but stop on 10, you are actually withholding your assent from what is certain and clear-cut – the very move which you deny me in non-evident cases. (4) Hence this science of yours gives you no help against Sorites Arguments: it does not teach what is the lower or upper limit of increase or decrease. What of the fact that that same science, like Penelope unweaving her web, ends up by destroying what has come before? Is that your fault or ours? (5) It is presumably the foundation of dialectic that whatever is asserted (what they call *axiōma*, the equivalent of 'proposition') is either true or false. Well is this true or false? If you say that you are lying, and you say so truly, are you lying or telling the truth? Of course, you call this insoluble – that is, something more annoying than what our school calls 'unknown' and 'unperceived'. But, passing over that, my question is: if these puzzles of yours are insoluble, and no criterion is found for them, to enable you to answer whether they are true or false, what has become of that definition of the proposition as that which is either true or false? (6) To my premises I shall add this one, that of <inferences of the same type one of which is valid, the remainder> should be accepted, while others, of a contradictory type, should be rejected. Well then, what is your verdict on this inference? 'If you say that it is now light, and you say so truly, <it is now light. But you say that it is now light, and you say so truly.> Therefore it is now light.' You certainly endorse this type, and declare it an entirely valid inference, so that in your teaching you present it as the 'first mode' of inference. It follows that either you will endorse any inference in the same mode, or this science of yours amounts to nothing. So see whether you will endorse this inference: 'If you say that you are lying, and you say so truly, you are lying. But you say that you are lying, and you say so truly. Therefore you are lying.' How can you not endorse this one, when you endorsed the earlier one of the same type? This is Chrysippus' puzzle, but even he does not solve it.

I Plutarch, *On common conceptions* 1059D–E

This man [Chrysippus] seems to me to put all his efforts and ingenuity into overturning and wrecking common sense, as his own supporters to some extent testify when they disagree with him about the Lying Argument. For to deny that a conjunction formed from indefinite contradictories is unrestrictedly false, and again, to say that some arguments with true premises and sound inferences still have the contradictories of their conclusions true as well – what conception of demonstration or what preconception of confirmation does that not overturn? They say that the octopus gnaws off its own tentacles in winter. Well, Chrysippus' dialectic destroys by amputation its own vital parts and principles. So which of our other conceptions has it left free from suspicion?

J Epictetus, *Discourses* 1.7.1,10–21 ('On the use of changing arguments, etc.')

(1) Many people do not realize that the study of changing arguments, hypothetical arguments, arguments which become valid by being posed, and all arguments of this kind, has a bearing on proper function [see **42**]. (2) [= **31R**] (3) It is necessary to learn how one thing follows from others, and when one thing follows from one thing and when from many in combination. Presumably, then, this too must be mastered by whoever intends to conduct himself intelligently in argument, to demonstrate each thing himself in expounding it, to follow the demonstration of others, and not to be led astray by those who use sophistries in the guise of demonstrations. That is the reason for our study and exercise, which have proved themselves indispensable, concerning deductive arguments and modes. (4) But in some cases where we have granted the premises soundly such and such a conclusion follows from them, and follows none the less for being false. What is my proper course of action? To accept the falsehood? How can I? To say that I conceded the premises unsoundly? No, that is not open to me either. That the conclusion does not follow from the premises conceded? No, nor is that. What then should I do in these cases? Or perhaps, just as having borrowed is not a sufficient condition of still owing, but a further necessary condition is retaining the debt and not having discharged it, so too having granted the premises is not a sufficient condition of being obliged to concede the conclusion, but a necessary condition is retaining one's consent to them. Now if they remain to the end as they were when conceded, we are absolutely obliged to retain our consent to them and to accept what follows from them. <But if they change, we are not,> since for us and thanks to us the conclusion in question no longer follows, once we have abandoned our consent to the premises. Hence we need to investigate premises of this kind too, and this way they have of shifting and changing, in virtue of which in the very course of question–and–answer or syllogistic reasoning or some other such procedure they undergo their changes and lead the unintelligent into perplexity through failure to appreciate what follows from them. Why need we? So that we should not, in this area, conduct ourselves improperly or haphazardly or confusedly.

K Alexander, quoted by Simplicius, *On Aristotle's Physics* 1299, 36–1300,10

Starting from these arguments it is possible to show that the Stoic propositions sometimes called 'indeterminately changing' propositions are no such thing. An example is: 'If Dion is alive, Dion will be alive.' For although this is now true, having as it does the true antecedent 'Dion is alive' and the true consequent 'He will be alive', the time will come when the additional premise 'But Dion is alive' is true and yet the conditional will change to being false. This is because there will be a time when, although 'Dion is alive' is still true, 'He also will be alive' is not true. And when the latter is not true the whole conditional must change and become false. For 'He will be alive' is not true at all times at which 'He is alive' is true: that would make Dion immortal. On the other hand, it will not be possible to say definitely when it will be that he is alive but 'He will be alive' is not true. That is why they say that the change in propositions of this kind occurs at an indeterminate and indefinite time.

L Lucian, *Philosophers for sale* 22 (*SVF* 2.287, part)

Chrysippus: Next you're going to hear the quite fascinating Veiled Argument. Tell me, do you know your own father? *Customer:* Yes. *Chrysippus:* Well, if I place someone veiled in front of you and ask 'Do you know this person?', what will you say? *Customer:* Obviously that I don't know him. *Chrysippus:* But in fact this person is your very own father. So if you don't know this person, you clearly don't know your own father.

M Diogenes Laertius 7.75

A plausible [or 'convincing'] proposition is one which leads us to assent. For example: 'If someone bore something, she is that thing's mother.' This is false, because the hen is not mother of her egg.

N Gellius 11.12.1–3 (*SVF* 2.152; Diodorus fr. 7 Giannantoni, part)

(1) Chrysippus said that every word is ambiguous by nature, since two or more meanings can be understood from it. (2) But Diodorus Cronus said: 'No word is ambiguous. No one says or thinks anything ambiguous, and nothing should be held to be being said beyond what the speaker thinks he is saying. When you have understood something other than what I had in mind, I should be held to have spoken obscurely, rather than ambiguously. For the characteristic of an ambiguous word would have had to be that whoever said it was saying two or more things. But no one is saying two or more things if he thinks that he is saying one.'

O Ammonius, *On Aristotle's De interpretatione* 38,17–20 (Diodorus fr. 7 Giannantoni, part)

We will not accept the view of Diodorus the Dialectician that every utterance is capable of signifying – in support of which he named one of his own slaves 'However', and others with other connectives.

P Diogenes Laertius 7.62

An ambiguity is an expression which signifies two or even more things, properly expressed according to one and the same linguistic idiom. This expression consequently makes the plurality of meanings be understood simultaneously.

Q Galen, *On linguistic sophisms* 4 (*SVF* 2.153, part)

(1) We must take up their actual divisions of the so-called 'ambiguities'. The more refined (Stoics) list eight. (2) One they call 'common to the joined and the divided form'. For example, '*auletris pesousa*', which is common to the word *auletris*, 'flute-girl' [*auletris pesousa*: 'a flute-girl falling'] and the divided form [*aule tris pesousa*: 'a hall thrice falling']. (3) A second is due to equivocation in simple expressions, such as 'manly', which can describe a cloak ['man's'] and a person ['brave']. (4) A third kind is due to equivocation in complex expressions, such as 'Man exists'. For the sentence is ambiguous as to whether it signifies that the substance exists or that the case [i.e. the noun] exists. (5) A fourth is due to omission, such as 'Of which are you?' For the middle word is omitted, e.g. 'master', 'father'. (6) A fifth is due to pleonasm, for example 'He forbade him not sail', where the addition of 'not' renders the whole ambiguous as to whether what he forbade was sailing or not-sailing. (7) As sixth they list that which fails to clarify what non-signifying element is construed with what, as in '*kai nu ken e parelassen*' [Homer, *Iliad* 23.382]. For the letter e could < begin a word [. . . (*h*)*epar elasse*: 'and he would have driven a *liver*'], end a word [. . . *kene* . . .: 'and she would have driven past *empty*'], or > be the disjunctive particle ['and he would *either* have driven past, or . . .]. (8) Seventh is the one which fails to indicate what signifying element is construed with what, as in 'Fifty men having a hundred did Achilles leave.' (9) Eighth is the one which fails to indicate what refers to what, as you can find in 'Dion < is also > Theon.' For it is unclear whether it refers to the existence of both ['Dion is, also Theon'], or to something such as 'Dion is Theon' or vice versa.

R Diogenes Laertius 7.187

[Chrysippus asked this riddle:] 'If you say something, it goes through your mouth. But you say: A waggon. Therefore a waggon goes through your mouth.'

S Simplicius, *On Aristotle's Categories* 24,13–20

Hence in syllogisms which depend on equivocation the dialecticians advise us to 'become quiescent' until the questioner transfers the word to another sense. For example, if someone asks whether the cloak is 'manly' [see **Q 3**] we will agree (supposing that it is). And if he asks whether manly is brave, we will agree to this too, since it is true. But if he deduces that the cloak is therefore brave, at this point they advise us to distinguish the equivocation of 'manly' and to show that it has one sense in the case of the cloak, another in the case of someone who has manliness.

☐ As **B**'s excerpt from the list of Chrysippus' lost works exemplifies, the study of puzzles is even more central to Stoic logic than to other areas of Stoic thought (cf. **28A–B; 30E; 38A**). This interest was an inheritance from the Stoics' forerunner in logic, the Dialectical School, whose work may be represented in **A**, and it was further fostered by the Academics' insistent use of puzzles in their attacks on the Stoics (as in **H, I**). Cf. **B 6**. The title of a puzzle typically has the form 'The *x* Argument', where '*x*' both indicates the example used and characterizes the puzzle itself. Thus the Horned Argument ('Have you lost your horns?', to which 'Yes' and 'No' seem equally compromising answers; cf. **C**) is not just about a man alleged to have horns, but is itself a dilemma. The classic Academic weapons were the Lying Argument and the Sorites. For the celebrated Lying Argument, propounded by Eubulides in the fourth century, see **B 3, C, H 5–6, I**. The Academics, as represented by the latter two texts, used it to challenge Stoic faith in bivalence (**34C; 38G**), and Plutarch in **I** interprets Chrysippus' response as conceding some restriction on that principle: he gave no more than qualified approval to some negated conjunction of indefinite contradictories (for the logical form of which see **38E 6**), probably 'Not both: something is true, and it is false'. But the juxtaposition of titles in **B 3** suggests that he rejected at least one device for achieving this restriction on bivalence, namely the 'cutting' of indefinite propositions. We might guess this to have been the analysis of 'Something is true', when the something is 'I am lying', into component propositions, one true, another false – e.g. 'I regularly lie' is true, but 'I am lying now' is false. What was the alternative strategy by which Chrysippus incurred Plutarch's charge without, we must assume, actually abandoning the principle of bivalence? One conjecture would be that he took 'I am lying' to *change* its truth value from false to true during the course of utterance. For Stoic interest in 'changing' arguments, a consequence of the assumption of truth-at-a-time (see on **34F**), see **J, K**, and cf. **A 5, 9**.

For the Sorites, or 'Heaper Argument', see **C–H 4**. The title in effect covers all 'Little-by-little' arguments which exploit the absence of a sharp boundary between contrary predicates (cf. **51G; 70D–E**). Here too 'cutting' was apparently one of the proposed solutions not unhesitatingly accepted by Chrysippus (**G**). Perhaps in this case it involved the careful qualification of one's answers. E.g. Is 10 the highest numerical value of 'few'? Yes and no. Yes for a cricket team, no for a rugby team, or a quartet; etc.

Chrysippus himself seems to have made two recommendations. One was primarily procedural: stop answering ('become quiescent') *before* you get to the difficult cases (**H 3**; less carefully reported in **F**; for the terminology, cf. **S**). The other (exemplified at **D** and conjecturally attributable to Chrysippus himself via a comparison with **38E 6** and **51G**) is to formulate each step not as a conditional but as a negated conjunction, e.g. 'Not both: 4 are few, but 5 are not few.' While a conditional formulation would, on Chrysippus' view (see **35A 6** and commentary), have amounted to the evidently false claim that '4 are few but 5 are not few' is *self-contradictory*, the negated conjunction allows the more reasonable interpretation that thanks to the similarity of 4 to 5 this conjunction is so *hard to believe* as to merit denial. Even the Stoic sage assents to merely 'convincing' propositions in those cases where certainty is unobtainable (**42I–J**). The main advantage discernible is that now no universal conceptual principle is being assumed, which would have made 'n are few' entail 'n + 1 are few' for all values of n. Thus there may be a specific false step. Which one it is is perhaps irremediably obscure to man, as was said in another context of the answer to the question whether the number of stars is odd or even (cf. **A 5**; **68R 3**). Therefore the only proper procedure will be to play safe by the 'quiescence' tactic. But the faith that such a cut-off point exists, even undetectably, may have seemed enough to undo most of the damage done by the Sorites.

Other types of paradox can only be briefly noted here. The Veiled Argument (**B 4, L**) from a modern viewpoint raises questions about substitution in 'opaque' contexts, but its precise place in Stoic discussions is unknown. For the 'Not-someone Argument' (**B 5**), see **30E**. For the Mowing Argument (**C**), see **38I**, and cf. **31M**.

Ambiguity is not invoked in **A**'s analysis of sophisms, possibly representing the Dialectical school. This is perhaps because the school's leader, Diodorus, denied all ambiguity: **N**. Diodorus arrived at this denial by equating meaning with speaker's meaning (probably the basis of the story in **O**), and Chrysippus, in response (**N, P**), rescued ambiguity by insisting on the lexical character of meaning. He thus licensed the Stoic classification of ambiguities in **Q**, which provides plentiful material for the resolution of fallacies (cf. **S**). We are not told why Chrysippus claimed that *every* word is ambiguous (**N 1**), but **Q 4** would suggest an adequate ground, namely that every word, in addition to its regular signification(s), is also its own name. This point, frivolously illustrated by the sophism in **R** and **33O**, was in fact crucially important in a language which lacked the device of quotation marks.

The material in this section can be interestingly compared with Aristotle, *On sophistical refutations*.

38 Modality

A Epictetus, *Discourses* 2.19.1–5 (Diodorus fr. 24 Giannantoni, part)

(1) These seem to be the sort of starting-points from which the Master Argument is posed. (2) The following three propositions mutually conflict: 'Every past truth is necessary'; 'Something impossible does not follow from something possible'; and 'There is something possible which neither is nor will be true.' (3) Diodorus saw this conflict and exploited the convincingness of the first two to establish the conclusion that 'Nothing which neither is nor will be true is possible.' (4) Now some

will retain the pair 'There is something possible which neither is nor will be true' and 'Something impossible does not follow from something possible', but deny that 'Every past truth is necessary.' This seems to have been the line taken by Cleanthes and his circle, and was in general endorsed by Antipater. (5) Whereas others will retain the other pair, that 'There is something possible which neither is nor will be true', and that 'Every past truth is necessary, but hold that something impossible does follow from something possible. (6) To retain all three is impossible because of their mutual conflict. So if someone asks me, 'Which of them do you retain?' I shall answer 'I don't know; but my information is that Diodorus retained the first pair I mentioned, the circles of Panthoides (I think) and Cleanthes the second pair, and Chrysippus and his circle the third pair.'

B Alexander, *On Aristotle's Prior analytics* 183,34–184,10 (Diodorus fr. 27 Giannantoni, part)

(1) He [Aristotle, *Prior analytics* 1, 34a12] may possibly be talking also about the issue 'What things are possible?', and about the so-called 'Diodorean' answer, 'What either is or will be'. For Diodorus set down as possible only what either is or, in any event, will be. According to him, for me to be in Corinth was possible if I was in Corinth or if I was, in any event, going to be; if not, it was not even possible. And for the child to become literate was possible if he was, in any event, going to be. It is to establish this that Diodorus' Master Argument is posed. (2) And likewise about Philo's answer. This was: 'That which is predicated in accordance with the bare fitness of the subject, even if it is prevented from coming about by some necessary external factor.' On this basis he said that it was possible for chaff in atomic dissolution to be burnt, and likewise chaff at the bottom of the sea, while it was there, even though the circumstances necessarily prevented it.

C Boethius, *On Aristotle's De interpretatione* 234,22–6 (Diodorus fr. 28 Giannantoni, part)

Diodorus defines the possible as 'what is or will be', the impossible as 'what, being false, will not be true', the necessary as 'what, being true, will not be false', and the non-necessary as 'what either is now, or will be, false'.

D Diogenes Laertius 7.75

Further, some propositions are possible, some impossible, and some necessary, some non-necessary. Possible is that which admits of being true and which is not prevented by external factors from being true, such as 'Diocles is alive.' Impossible is that which does not admit of being true,

<or admits of being true but is prevented by external factors from being true>, such as 'The earth flies.' Necessary is that which is true and does not admit of being false, or admits of being false but is prevented by external factors from being false, such as 'Virtue is beneficial.' Non-necessary is that which both is true and is capable of being false, and is not prevented by external factors from being false, such as 'Dion is walking.'

E Cicero, *On fate* 12-15

(1) Be careful, Chrysippus, not to desert your cause, the one in which you battle mightily with the powerful dialectician Diodorus. For if this is a true conditional, 'If someone was born at the rising of the Dogstar, he will not die at sea', so is this one, 'If Fabius was born at the rising of the Dogstar, Fabius will not die at sea.' Therefore these propositions conflict with each other: that Fabius was born at the rising of the Dogstar, and that Fabius will die at sea. And since in Fabius' case the premise that he was born at the rising of the Dogstar is certain, there is also a conflict between the proposition that Fabius exists and the proposition that he will die at sea. Hence the conjunction 'Both: Fabius exists, and Fabius will die at sea' is one of incompatible conjuncts, because it is incapable of happening as stated. Hence 'Fabius will die at sea' belongs to the class of impossibilities. Therefore everything falsely stated about the future cannot happen. (2) But this conclusion is repugnant to you, Chrysippus, and it is on it that your main quarrel with Diodorus rests. For Diodorus says that only that is possible which either is true or will be true; that whatever will be is necessary; and that whatever will not be is impossible. (3) You say that even things which will not be are possible. For example, that this jewel be broken, even if that will never be the case. And you say that it had not been necessary that Cypselus should rule in Corinth, even though the oracle of Apollo had foretold it a thousand years earlier. (4) But if you are going to endorse these divine predictions you will also hold things falsely said about the future to be in such a class that they cannot happen, so that if it be said that Scipio will take Carthage, and if that is truly said about the future and it will be thus, you must say that it is necessary. And that is precisely Diodorus' anti-Stoic view. (5) For if 'If you were born at the rising of the Dogstar, you will not die at sea' is a true conditional, and the antecedent in it, 'You were born at the rising of the Dogstar', is necessary – for all past truths are necessary, as Chrysippus holds contrary to the view of his teacher Cleanthes, because past facts are immutable and cannot change from true to false – if, as I say, the antecedent is necessary, the consequent also comes out necessary. Chrysippus admittedly does not consider this rule universally valid. But the fact remains that if there is a natural cause for Fabius' not dying at sea, Fabius cannot die at sea. (6) At this point Chrysippus loses his cool. He

hopes that the Chaldaeans and other seers can be cheated, and that they will so use connectives as not to put their theorems in the form 'If someone was born at the rising of the Dogstar, he will not die at sea', but rather so as to say 'Not both: someone was born at the rising of the Dogstar, and he will die at sea.' What hilarious self-indulgence! To avoid collapsing into Diodorus' position, he teaches the Chaldaeans how they should express their theorems!

F Alexander, *On Aristotle's Prior analytics* 177,25–178,1 (*SVF* 2.202a, part)

Chrysippus, saying that nothing prevents something impossible following even from something possible, makes no reply to Aristotle's proof, but tries by means of some unsoundly constructed examples to prove that things are not so. He says that in the conditional 'If Dion is dead, this one is dead', which is true when Dion is being demonstratively referred to, the antecedent 'Dion is dead' is possible, since it can one day become true that Dion is dead; but 'This one is dead' is impossible. For when Dion has died the proposition 'This one is dead' is destroyed, the object of the demonstrative reference no longer existing. For demonstrative reference is appropriate to, and is said of, a living being. So if 'This one' is no longer possible once he is dead, nor does Dion come to be again, so that 'This one is dead' can be said of him, 'This one is dead' is impossible.

G Cicero, *On fate* 20–1

Chrysippus uses the following argument: 'If there is motion without a cause, not every proposition (what the dialecticians call *axiōma*) will be either true or false, since anything lacking efficient causes will be neither true nor false. But every proposition is either true or false. Therefore there is no motion without a cause. If this is so, everything that happens happens through antecedent causes – in which case, everything happens through fate. The result is that everything that happens happens through fate. [continued at **20E**]

H Alexander, *On fate* 176,14–24

To say that even if all things happen by fate the possible and the contingent are not eliminated, because that which nothing prevents from happening is possible even if it does not happen, and that the contradictories of things which happen by fate are not prevented, so that they are possible even if they do not happen; and to adduce as proof that they are not prevented from happening the fact that the things preventing them are unknown to us, although they exist in any case (since the causes which destine their contradictories to happen are also the causes of their not happening, if, as they say, it is impossible that identical circumstances should produce contradictory results: their claim that these things' not happening is not prevented is based on our unfamiliarity with what the causes are) – such talk betrays frivolity in arguments where frivolity does not belong.

I Ammonius, *On Aristotle's De interpretatione* 131,24–32

The more logical of the two arguments is propounded with regard to some such activity on our part as mowing, as follows. 'If', it goes, 'you will mow, it is not the case that perhaps you will mow and perhaps you will not mow, but you will at all events mow. And if you will not mow, it is likewise not the case that perhaps you will mow and perhaps you will not mow, but you will at all events not mow. But necessarily either you will mow or you will not mow. Hence "perhaps" is eliminated, if there is room for it neither on the antithesis of mowing and not-mowing, one or other of which must necessarily occur, nor on what follows from either hypothesis. But "perhaps" is the word which introduces the contingent. Therefore the contingent is eliminated.'

☐ For the Stoics' modal theory, we once again find Diodorus and Philo their most significant precursors. Diodorus' celebrated Master Argument, more literally 'Ruling Argument', has to be reconstructed mainly from the three propositions set out in **A 2**: Proposition 1, that every past truth, i.e. every true proposition about the past, is necessary; Proposition 2, that something impossible does not follow from something possible (a generally accepted law of modal logic); and Proposition 3, that there is something possible which neither is nor will be true. Many reconstructions have been attempted, and the following brief and informal outline represents only one of several possibilities. The title suggests (cf. **37** commentary) that the argument operated with the example of ruling (cf. **E 3**). Take someone who, *ex hypothesi*, is not, and never will be, ruling. From the false (i) '*x* is ruling' follows the false (ii) 'it has always been the case that *x* would rule'. But (iii), 'It has been false that *x* would rule', being true about the past, is by Proposition 1 necessary. Therefore (ii), which conflicts with (iii), is impossible. Therefore, by Proposition 2, (i), from which (ii) follows, is also impossible. By generalization from this example, Diodorus can eliminate Proposition 3, and establish his definition of the possible as 'what is or will be', together with the other three modal definitions derivable from it: **C** (cf. **B 1**).

Diodorus' position seems to have been read by the Stoics as unacceptably deterministic: **E** (and cf. **I** and **31M**, the Mowing Argument, a clearly deterministic argument, issuing from Diodorus' Dialectical school, which they apparently treated as a companion piece to the Master Argument). It is at first sight not obvious why, since his modal definitions (**C**) clearly separate the possible from the necessary and leave many possibilities beyond what actually happens. For example, if I accept a bribe, it was possible for me not to accept it, provided only that on some future occasion it will not be the case that I am accepting a bribe. Thus at **E 2** 'whatever will be is necessary' overstates Diodorus' position. But 'whatever will not be is impossible' gets it nearly right, needing only the addition 'Whatever *is not and* will not be . . .'

Hence Chrysippus' first example in **E 3** is appropriate to the case. One can envisage him reasoning as follows. Since I can only be held responsible for my behaviour in those cases in which I could have done otherwise, on Diodorus' view I cannot claim responsibility for not smashing this jewel, which I have chosen not to smash. For as a matter of fact, *ex hypothesi*, it will never be broken, and thus it is on Diodorus' view impossible for it to be broken. His second example looks less apposite: Diodorus would agree with Chrysippus that 'Cypselus is ruling' was not necessary, since it was going to be false at times. But Chrysippus could at least argue that the counter-factual possibility 'Cypselus is not ruling *in 640 B.C.*' is eliminated by Diodorus' definition of the possible, since it had never either been or been going to be true, and hence that *some* (non-Diodorean) kind of necessity seems to intrude here too.

Chrysippus therefore requires an interpretation of 'possible' more compatible with moral responsibility. Philo's suggestion of mere intrinsic 'fitness' at **B 2**, for all its merits, does not help in this respect. But the Stoic definition at **D**, which adds to this the requirement of favourable circumstances, gives just what is needed. For what it could easily be used to establish is, in effect, *opportunity*. If I want to claim credit for not smashing the jewel, I must in particular show that it was possible for me to smash it in the sense that I had the opportunity to do so. I must show (a) that it is breakable, and by someone with my strength (intrinsic fitness), and (b) that circumstances did not prevent me – it was not a thousand miles away, or locked up in a bank-vault. (In **H**, Alexander appears to attack a purely epistemic Stoic reading of 'not prevented'; but there is no evidence to connect this view with Chrysippus himself.)

If I had the opportunity to smash the jewel, that helps ground the inference that nothing but my own character is responsible for my not doing so. For the Stoics hold that in this context the possibility of doing otherwise does not *include* capacities of character: no one is capable of acting otherwise than he does if this is understood to mean acting against his own moral character (**61M; 62G, I**).

Stoic views on fate and responsibility will be further explored in **55** and **62**. For now it must just be noted that although some future counterfactuals are rendered 'possible', this is only in a very restricted sense. It is possible *for* them to come about, we might say, but there is no possibility *that* they will come about. For Chrysippus' faith in bivalence, even for future-tensed propositions (contrast Epicurus, **20E 1, H, I**), was enough to convince him that future events are already fully causally determined: **G**; cf. **34C**. What could there be to make it true *now* that such-and-such an event will occur tomorrow, if not its correspondence to a set of causes working now to bring that event about? His object was only to avoid the further move, via the elimination of counter-factual possibilities, to absolute *necessitation* of future events.

In defence of this fragile thesis, Chrysippus felt obliged to resist the Master Argument. Cleanthes had already joined Panthoides of the Dialectical School in denying Proposition 1: **A 4, 6**. They may have held that our inability to affect a past truth applies only to a genuine *fait accompli*, not to a past-tensed proposition whose truth-value still depends on future events. E.g. if A shot B yesterday, B may still, by dying today, bring it about that A fired a fatal shot yesterday. Likewise a politician, by refusing office, can *make* it have been false all along that he would rule. This simple solution was not available to Chrysippus, because his correspondence theory of truth (**G**; see previous paragraph) made *every* past-tensed truth dependent on a set of *bona fide* past facts. He therefore (**A 5–6**) shifted the attack to Proposition 2, with the ingenious counter-example recorded in **F** (see further, **34** commentary).

A different strategy is preserved in **E 4–6**. Directly derivable from Proposition 2 of the Master Argument is the rule that what follows from a necessary proposition is itself necessary. Chrysippus may have held his counter-example to Proposition 2 to invalidate this rule too (**E 5**, penultimate sentence), but on this occasion he assumed, at least for the sake of argument, that it was valid. Now Chrysippus was a firm believer in divination (see **42**; **55**), and hence in laws which derived truths about the future from truths about the past. But, the challenge runs, since the truths about the past are necessary (by Proposition 1 of the Master Argument), the truths about the future which follow from them will themselves be necessary, according to the above-mentioned rule. Chrysippus, in response, rightly notes that while a transitive property like necessity is indeed transmitted from one proposition to another in a *conditional*, which asserts a relation of logical dependence, it is not so transmitted in a negated conjunction, which asserts no direct logical connexion between the two conjoined propositions. For the distinction see **35A 6**, **B 4**, and commentary. And since laws of divination assert empirical rather than logical connexions between past and future truths, the negated conjunction is indeed the appropriate means of formulating them. Thus the necessity of future truths is not, at least, a consequence of divination.

EPISTEMOLOGY: STOICS AND ACADEMICS

39 Impressions

A Diogenes Laertius 7.49–51 (*SVF* 2.52, 55, 61)

[Diocles of Magnesia says] (1) 'It is the Stoics' policy to give primary position to the account which deals with impression [*phantasia*] and sense-perception, in as much as the criterion which decides the truth of things is generically an impression, and in as much as the account which deals with assent and cognition and thinking, while it precedes the rest, is not composed without impression. (2) For the impression arises first, and then thought, which has the power of utterance, expresses in language what it experiences by the agency of the impression. (3) An impression is different from a figment [*phantasma*]. A figment is the kind of fanciful thought which occurs in dreams, whereas an impression is a printing in the soul: i.e., an alteration, as Chrysippus suggests in his *On soul*; for the printing should not be taken to be like that of a signet-ring, since it is impossible for there to be many such prints at the same time affecting the same subject ... (4) They divide impressions into those which are sensory and those which are not. Sensory impressions are ones obtained through one or more sense-organs, non-sensory are ones obtained through thought such as those of the incorporeals and of the other things acquired by reason. (5) Some sensory impressions arise from what is, and are accompanied by yielding and assent. But impressions also include appearances which are quasi-products of what is. (6) Furthermore, some impressions are rational, and others non-rational. Those of rational animals are rational, while those of non-rational animals are non-rational. Rational impressions are thought processes; irrational ones are nameless. (7) Also, some impressions are expert and others not: a work of art is viewed in one way by an expert and differently by a non-expert.'

B Aetius 4.12.1–5 (*SVF* 2.54, part)

(1) Chrysippus says that these four [i.e., impression (*phantasia*), impressor (*phantaston*), imagination (*phantastikon*), figment (*phantasma*)] are all different. (2) An impression is an affection occurring in the soul, which reveals itself and its cause. Thus, when through sight we observe something white, the affection is what is engendered in the soul through vision; and it is this affection which enables us to say that there is a white object which activates us. Likewise when we perceive through touch and smell. (3) The word 'impression' [*phantasia*] is derived from 'light' [*phōs*]; just as light reveals itself and whatever else it includes in its range, so impression reveals itself and its cause. (4) The cause of an impression is an impressor: e.g., something white or cold or everything capable of activating the soul. (5) Imagination is an empty attraction, an affection in the soul which arises from no impressor, as when someone shadow-boxes or strikes his hands against thin air; for an impression has some impressor as its object, but imagination has none. (6) A figment is that to which we are attracted in the empty attraction of imagination; it occurs in people who are melancholic and mad.

C Cicero, *Academica* 2.21

[Speaker: the Antiochean Lucullus in defence of Stoic epistemology] (1) Those characteristics which belong to the things we describe as being cognized by the senses are equally characteristic of that further set of things said to be cognized not by the senses directly but by them in a certain respect, e.g., 'That is white, this is sweet, that is melodious, this is fragrant, this is bitter.' Our cognition of these is secured by the mind, not the senses. (2) Next, 'That is a horse, that is a dog.' (3) The rest of the series then follows, connecting bigger items which virtually include complete cognition of things, like 'If it is a human being, it is a mortal, rational animal.' (4) From this class [i.e. mental perceptions in general] conceptions of things are imprinted on us, without which there can be no understanding or investigation or discussion of anything.

D Diogenes Laertius 7.53 (*SVF* 2.87, part)

(1) It is by confrontation that we come to think of sense-objects. (2) By similarity, things based on thoughts of something related, like Socrates on the basis of a picture. (3) By analogy, sometimes by magnification, as in the case of Tityos and Cyclopes, sometimes by diminution, as in the case of the Pigmy; also the idea of the centre of the earth arose by analogy on the basis of smaller spheres. (4) By transposition, things like eyes on the chest. (5) By combination, Hippocentaur. (6) By opposition, death. (7) Some things are also conceived by transition, such as sayables and place. (8) The idea of something just and good is acquired naturally. (9) That of being without hands, for instance, by privation.

E Aetius 4.11.1–4 (*SVF* 2.83)

(1) When a man is born, the Stoics say, he has the commanding-part of his soul like a sheet of paper ready for writing upon. On this he inscribes each one of his conceptions. (2) The first method of inscription is through the senses. For by perceiving something, e.g. white, they have a memory of it when it has departed. And when many memories of a similar kind have occurred, we then say we have experience. For the plurality of similar impressions is experience. (3) Some conceptions arise naturally in the aforesaid ways and undesignedly, others through our own instruction and attention. The latter are called 'conceptions' only, the former are called 'preconceptions' as well. (4) Reason, for which we are called rational, is said to be completed from our preconceptions during our first seven years.

F Plutarch, *On common conceptions* 1084F–1085A (*SVF* 2.847, part)

Conception is a kind of impression, and impression is a printing in the soul . . . They [the Stoics] define conceptions as a kind of stored thoughts, and memories as permanent and static printings.

G Sextus Empiricus, *Against the professors* 7.242–6 (*SVF* 2.65, part)

[The Stoics say] (1) Of impressions, some are convincing, others unconvincing, others simultaneously convincing and unconvincing, and others neither convincing nor unconvincing. (2) Convincing are ones which produce an even movement in the soul, e.g., at this moment, that it is day and that I am talking, and everything which maintains a similar obviousness. (3) Unconvincing are ones which are not like this but make us decline to assent, e.g., 'If it is day, the sun is not above the earth', 'If it is dark, it is day.' (4) Convincing *and* unconvincing are ones which, according to their relative disposition, are sometimes of one kind and sometimes of another kind, such as the impressions of insoluble arguments. (5) Neither convincing nor unconvincing are ones which are impressions of such things as 'The number of the stars is odd', 'The number of the stars is even.' (6) Of the convincing (or unconvincing) [a misleading addition by Sextus or an interpolator], some are true, others false, others true and false, and others neither true nor false. (7) True are ones of which it is possible to make a true assertion, e.g., at the present 'It is day' or 'It is light.'(8) False are ones of which it is possible to make a false assertion, e.g., that the oar under the water is bent, or that the colonnade gets narrower. (9) True *and* false are ones like the impression Orestes had of Electra in his madness: in so far as he had an impression of an existing thing it was true – for Electra existed – but in so far as he had an impression of a Fury it was false – for there was no Fury. So too a dreamer's false and vacuous attraction when his impression of Dion, who is alive, is of Dion's actual presence. (10) Neither true nor false are the generic ones. [continued at **30F**]

☐ The texts of this section should be studied in conjunction with material in **53** where 'impression' is treated in relation to the other faculties of the soul. Here our focus is on the mental experiences which the Stoics considered to be founded on impressions, the cognitive value of those experiences, and the relation between impressions of the outside world received through the senses and the formation of concepts. The fundamental criterial role ascribed to 'cognitive' impressions specifically is treated in **40**.

Our translation of *phantasia* by 'impression' seeks to capture the Stoics' own elucidation of the term (**A 3**), while it also places this within the modern empirical tradition that they have influenced. The notion of an *imprint* in their usage gets its particular point from the assumption that any such 'affection' requires a corresponding 'impressor' as its cause (**B 4**). Through the mediation of the senses, external objects impress their sensory characteristics on the soul, and the resultant affection or impression 'reveals . . . its cause' (**B 2**), i.e. the object. This account, however, by itself does not explain awareness by the recipient of the revelation. That point seems to be covered by the statement (**B 2–3**) that the impression 'reveals itself', analogously to light. The comparison suggests that impressions are self-revealing in the sense that they make their recipient *aware* of their occurrence – i.e., aware of the objects that they reveal. The texts do not imply that impressions are internal pictures or images, so that what we perceive is images of objects. Rather, like light, impressions are the illumination of, or means of our observing, actual things. And just as light can vary in its illuminating effects, so sense-impressions can vary in the clarity and distinctness with which they represent their objective causes. The claim that every impression has a corresponding impressor does not imply that every impression will be an equally clear and distinct indication of its object. Impressions as a class, however, are distinguished from the 'imagination' of 'figments', which refers to purely illusory states, produced in the mentally abnormal without any 'impressor' (**A 3, B 5–6**).

An impression is not a belief (see **41**). To have an impression is simply to entertain an idea, without any implication of commitment to it. We may put this point by saying that a Stoic impression is not an impression *that* something is the case – which, in modern English, does imply some degree of belief – but just an impression *of* something's being the case. (In a cinema we get the impression of John Wayne's being on the screen in front of us, but not of course the impression *that* John Wayne is on the screen in front of us.) Belief consists in the mind's positive reaction to an impression, its 'assent' to it (see Zeno's celebrated hand simile, **41A 1–3**).

The general thrust of **A** and **B** is to affirm the *normal* reliability of impressions, treating sensory ones as paradigmatic (cf. **41B 3**), without raising questions about problem cases or the differences between certainly reliable impressions and all others. Notwithstanding the elaborate classifications of **G**, which does not even get to the 'cognitive impression' (see the continuation in **40E**) and includes examples of highly complex impressions, the Stoics probably took the majority of impressions to be cognitive (cf. **A 5**) and to comprise most basically impressions of simple sensory objects (cf. **B 2, 4**).

Such objects provide the foundations of all conceptions (**E 1–2**), which arise most primitively by 'confrontation' (**D 1**). In interpreting the 'priority' of impression to thought (**A 2**) and of sense-perception to other means of concept-formation, priority should be taken to include both temporal and logical priority. The first impressions of an infant, like those of other animals, are pre-conceptual or non-rational, providing as they do the basic materials for those conceptions which constitute the emergence of reason in the developing human (**E 2–4**). Apart from this chronological priority, sense-impressions seem to be envisaged as logically prior to the operations of reason (**A 1–2**, cf. **C**). This is intelligible in the sense that the mind's reacting to its sense-impressions presupposes their occurrence. Yet in the mature human being all impressions are 'rational' or 'thought processes' (**A 6**), and all conceptions are themselves 'a kind of impression' (**F**). This suggests that all impressions of mature human beings are envisaged to have a propositional content, and that we assent to impressions (e.g. **40B 1**) by assenting to their corresponding *lekta* or propositions, which are the proper objects of assent (see **33I**, and Arcesilaus' criticism in **41C 8**). Notice too that the truth and falsehood of impressions are defined in terms of the kinds of assertions that can be made of them (**G 7–8**). So understood, rational impressions of the external world will not imply a theory that the mind receives raw data which it subsequently interprets. Rather, we should take it that rational impressions themselves represent their objects in ways that presuppose language and concepts: minimally 'This is white' etc. (**C 1**). The rationality of all mature human impressions presumes that the mind's stock of conceptions is immediately activated when a sense-impression is received, with the result that the impression presents its object in a conceptualized form. There will of course be a richness and subjectivity to rational impressions – my manner of seeing, hearing etc. – which endows these mental events with characteristics that are not fully reproducible in their corresponding propositions (see **33** commentary). Just so, how an expert views an object will be different from the layman's impression (**A 7**).

Since all states of awareness involve impressions (see **53** commentary), their objects include, under the heading of 'non-sensory impressions' (**A 4**), both corporeal items, e.g. god (cf. **40P**), and incorporeals (see **27**). The former present no special problems for the Stoics, since they can be presumed to have a causal effect on the mind via their effect on the world; and the Stoics' anxiety, wherever possible, to employ a corporealist account of awareness is shown by their claim that even the virtues are bodies and perceptible (see **60R, S**). The incorporeals remained intractable to such an account. That the Stoics acknowledged this is clear from their attempt to find a relationship other than causal to fit the case (see **27E**). The claim there that the commanding-faculty 'is impressed in relation to sayables' and not physically 'by them' is too mysterious to explain the process. Perhaps, however, we should connect it with 'transition', a method by which incorporeals are said to be conceived (**D 7**); this refers, we suggest, to the mind's capacity to abstract, e.g. the idea of place from particular bodies. (For the philosophical contexts in which these incorporeals were isolated, see **27**; **33**; **49**; **51**; **55**.)

In any event, transition, along with the other mental processes listed in **D**, helps to provide the mind with all objects of thought which are not simply the particular memories ('permanent printings', **F**) of its sense-impressions. The natural accumulation of experience of perceptible objects, through 'many memories of a similar kind', results in generic impressions or 'conceptions' of man, horse, white etc. (**E**; cf. **C**, **40N**). As universal 'concepts', the objects of these impressions are 'figments' of thought (**30A I**), which lack any corresponding 'impressor' in the external world, since there is no generic man etc. to impress the senses. The conceptions themselves, however, differ from imagination and its figments (**B 5–6**), in being the way rational beings 'naturally . . . and undesignedly' (**E 3**) interpret their experience of the world; and so they retain the status of impressions through their foundation in sense-perception (cf. **40M, N; 41B3**). To indicate these characteristics of basic conceptualization, the Stoics called naturally acquired generic impressions 'preconceptions', using this term to distinguish them from conceptions that are culturally determined or deliberately acquired (cf. Epicureanism, **17**). As the stuff of reason itself (**E 4**), preconceptions have a fundamental role as criteria of truth (see **40**).

The priority accorded to impressions (**A 1–2**) suits their fundamental role in the philosophy quite generally. Sayables are defined by reference to rational impressions (**33C**), which also help to define scientific knowledge (**31B 6**) and the dialectical virtue of 'non-randomness' (**31B 5**). As one of the partitions of 'significations' (**31A 7**), impressions are acknowledged, along with language itself, to be a way of *interpreting* experience. Thus they are basic to the Stoics' analysis of impulse and action (cf. **40H 2–3**; **53A 4, P, Q, S**), and to their moral evaluation of these (cf. **56C 7**; **65X, Y**). The self-conscious use or scrutiny of impressions is Epictetus' favourite way of referring to moral intelligence at work (**62K**; **63E**).

40 The criteria of truth

A Diogenes Laertius 7.54 (including *SVF* 2.105, Posidonius fr. 42)

(1) They [the Stoics] say that the cognitive impression is the criterion of truth, i.e. the impression arising from what is. This is what Chrysippus says in the second book of his *Physics*, and also Antipater and

Apollodorus. (2) Boethus admits a number of criteria – intellect, sense-perception, desire and scientific knowledge. (3) And Chrysippus, at variance with himself, says in the first of his books *On reason* that sense-perception and preconception are the criteria; preconception is a natural conception of universals. (4) Some of the older Stoics admit right reason as a criterion, as Posidonius says in his book *On the criterion*.

B Cicero, *Academica* 1.40–1 (*SVF* 1.55, 61, 60, part)

[Speaker: the Antiochean Varro in defence of Stoic epistemology] (1) He [Zeno] made a great many changes in the third division of philosophy. First, he made some new statements about sense-perceptions themselves, regarding them as compounded out of a sort of blow provided from outside . . . but adding to these impressions received as it were by the senses the mind's assent, which he took to be located within us and voluntary. (2) He did not attach reliability to all impressions but only to those which have a peculiar power of revealing their objects. Since this impression is discerned just by itself, he called it 'cognitive' [*katalēpton*] . . . (3) But once it had been received and accepted, he called it a 'grasp' [cognition], resembling things grasped by the hand. [continued at **41B**]

C Diogenes Laertius 7.46 (*SVF* 2.53, part)

(1) Of impressions, one kind is cognitive, the other incognitive. (2) The cognitive, which they [the Stoics] say is the criterion of things, is that which arises from what is and is stamped and impressed exactly in accordance with what is. (3) The incognitive is either that which does not arise from what is, or from that which is but not exactly in accordance with what is: one which is not clear or distinct.

D Cicero, *Academica* 2.77–8 (following **68O**)

[Speaker: Cicero on behalf of the New Academy] (1) We may take him [Arcesilaus] to have asked Zeno what would happen if the wise man could not cognize anything and it was the mark of the wise man not to opine. (2) Zeno, I imagine, replied that the wise man would not opine since there was something cognitive. (3) What then was this? Zeno, I suppose, said: an impression. (4) What kind of impression? Zeno then defined it as an impression stamped and reproduced from something which is, exactly as it is. (5) Arcesilaus next asked whether this was still valid if a true impression was just like a false one. (6) At this point Zeno was sharp enough to see that if an impression from what is were such that an impression from what is not could be just like it, there was no cognitive impression. (7) Arcesilaus agreed that it was right to add this to the definition, since neither a false impression nor a true one would be cognitive if the latter were just such as even a false one could be. (8) But he applied all his force to this point of the argument, in order to show that no impression arising from something true is such that an impression arising from something false could not also be just like it. (9) This is the one controversial issue which has lasted up to the present. [continued at **69H**]

E Sextus Empiricus, *Against the professors* 7.247–52 (*SVF* 2.65, part)

(1) Of true impressions, some are cognitive, others not. (2) Non-cognitive are ones people experience when they are in abnormal states. For very large numbers of people who are deranged or melancholic take in an impression which is true but non-cognitive, and arises purely externally and fortuitously, so that they often do not respond to it positively and do not assent to it. (3) A cognitive impression is one which arises from what is and is stamped and impressed exactly in accordance with what is, of such a kind as could not arise from what is not. Since they [the Stoics] hold that this impression is capable of precisely grasping objects, and is stamped with all their peculiarities in a craftsmanlike way, they say that it has each one of these as an attribute. (4) First of all, its arising from what is; for many impressions have their origin in what is not, as happens with the insane, and these are not cognitive. (5) Secondly, its being both from what is and exactly in accordance with what is; for some impressions, though they are from what is, do not represent exactly what is, as for instance in the case of the insane Orestes . . . [see **39G 9**] (6) Furthermore, its being stamped and impressed, so that all the impressors' peculiarities are stamped on it in a craftsmanlike way . . . For, just as the seals on rings always stamp all their markings precisely on the wax, so those who have cognition of objects should notice all their peculiarities. (7) 'Of such a kind as could not arise from what is not' was added by the Stoics, since the Academics did not share their view of the impossibility of finding a totally indiscernible [but false] impression. For the Stoics say that one who has the cognitive impression fastens on the objective difference of things in a craftsmanlike way, since this kind of impression has a peculiarity which differentiates it from other impressions, just as horned snakes are different from others.

F Diogenes Laertius 7.177 (*SVF* 1.625) and Athenaeus 354E (*SVF* 1.624, part)

(1) Sphaerus . . . went to Ptolemy Philopator at Alexandria. One day a conversation took place on whether the wise man would opine, and Sphaerus said that he would not. Wishing to refute him, the king ordered wax pomegranates to be placed before him. (2) Sphaerus was deceived and the king cried out that he had given his assent to a false impression. Sphaerus gave him a shrewd answer, saying that his assent was not [to the impression] that they were pomegranates but [to the impression] that it

was reasonable that they were pomegranates. (3) He pointed out that the cognitive impression is different from the reasonable one . . . The former is incapable of deceiving, but the reasonable impression can turn out otherwise.

G Plutarch, *On common conceptions* 1059B–C (*SVF* 2.33)

(1) One Stoic said that in his opinion it was not by chance but by divine providence that Chrysippus came after Arcesilaus and before Carneades, the former of whom initiated the violence and offence against common sense, while the latter was the most productive of the Academics. (2) For by coming between them, Chrysippus with his rejoinders to Arcesilaus also fenced in the cleverness of Carneades; he left sense-perception many reinforcements, for it to stand siege as it were, and entirely removed the confusion regarding preconceptions and conceptions by articulating each one and assigning it to its appropriate place.

H Sextus Empiricus, *Against the professors* 7.402–10

(1) [With regard to the definition of the cognitive impression, **E 3**] Carneades says that he will concede the rest of it to the Stoics, but not the clause 'of such a kind as could not arise from what is not'. For impressions arise from what is not as well as from what is. (2) The fact that they are found to be equally self-evident and striking is an indication of their indiscernibility, and an indication of their being equally self-evident and striking is the fact that the consequential actions are linked to [both kinds of impression]. Just as in waking states a thirsty man gets pleasure from drinking and someone who flees from a wild beast or any other terror shouts and screams, so too in dreams people satisfy their thirst and think they are drinking from a spring, and it is just the same with the fear of those who have nightmares . . . Just as in normal states too we believe and assent to very clear appearances, behaving towards Dion, for instance, as Dion and towards Theon as Theon, so too in madness some people have the similar experience. When Heracles was deranged, he got an impression from his own children as though they were those of Eurystheus, and he attached the consequential action to this impression, which was to kill his enemy's children, as he did. (3) If then impressions are cognitive in so far as they induce us to assent and to attach to them the consequential action, since false impressions are plainly of this kind too, we must say that incognitive ones are indiscernible from the cognitive . . . (4) The Academics are no less effective in proving indiscernibility with respect to stamp and impression. They confront the Stoics with appearances. In the case of things which are similar in shape but different objectively it is impossible to distinguish the cognitive impression from that which is false and incognitive. E.g. if I give the Stoic first one and

then another of two exactly similar eggs to discriminate, will the wise man, by focusing on them, be able to say infallibly that the one egg he is being shown is this one rather than that one? The same argument applies in the case of twins. For the virtuous man will get a false impression, albeit one from what is and imprinted and stamped exactly in accordance with what is, if the impression he gets from Castor is one of Polydeuces.

I Cicero, *Academica* 2.57

[Speaker: the Antiochean Lucullus] (1) I will even concede that the wise man himself, who is the subject of this whole discussion, when he experiences similar things which he cannot keep distinct, will withhold his assent and will never assent to any impression unless it is of a kind which a false one could not be. (2) But just as he has a specific expertise which enables him to distinguish the true from the false in other matters, so he has to apply practice to those similarities you adduce. Just as a mother can distinguish between her twins by the habit of her eyes, so you will do if you practise.

J Cicero, *Academica* 2.83–5

[Speaker: Cicero on behalf of the New Academy] (1) There are four headings to prove there is nothing which can be known, cognized or grasped, which is the subject of this whole controversy. The first of these is that some false impression does exist. (2) The second, that it is not cognitive. (3) The third, that impressions between which there is no difference cannot be such that some are cognitive and others not. (4) The fourth, that no true impression arises from sensation which does not have alongside it another impression no different from it which is not cognitive. (5) Everyone accepts the second and third of these headings. Epicurus does not grant the first, but you [Stoics and sympathizers], with whom we are dealing, admit that one too. The entire battle is about the fourth. (6) If someone looking at Publius Servilius Geminus thought he was looking at Quintus, he was experiencing an impression of the incognitive kind because there was no mark distinguishing the true from the false. With that difference removed, what mark could he have of the kind which could not be false for recognizing Gaius Cotta who was twice consul with Geminus? (7) You say that such a degree of similarity does not exist in things . . . we will allow that for sure. Yet it can certainly appear to exist and therefore deceive the sense, and if a single likeness has done that, it will have made everything doubtful. With that criterion removed which is the proper instrument of recognition, even if the man you are looking at is just the man you think you are looking at, you will not make the judgement with the mark you say you ought to, viz. one of a kind of which a false mark could not be . . . (8) You say that everything is in a class of its own and that nothing is the same as something else. That is certainly a Stoic thesis and not a very plausible one – that no hair or grain of sand is in all respects of the same character as another hair or grain. (9) These claims can be refuted, but I don't want to fight. It makes no difference to the matter in hand whether a visual object is no different in every one of its parts, or even if it does differ, is incapable of being distinguished.

K Sextus Empiricus, *Against the professors* 7.253–60

(1) While the older Stoics say that this cognitive impression is the criterion of truth, the later ones added the words 'and one which has no impediment'. For there are times when a cognitive impression occurs, but it is incredible owing to the external circumstances. (2) Thus when Heracles stood before Admetus, having brought Alcestis back from the dead, Admetus then took in a cognitive impression of Alcestis, but did not believe it . . . for he reasoned that Alcestis was dead, and that one who is dead does not rise again though certain spirits do sometimes roam around . . . (3) Therefore the cognitive impression is not the criterion of truth unconditionally, but when it has no impediment. This impression, being self-evident and striking, all but seizes us by the hair, they say, and pulls us to assent, needing nothing else to achieve this effect or to establish its difference from other impressions. (4) So too, whenever someone is keen to grasp something precisely, he is seen to chase after such an impression of his own accord, as when, in the case of visible things, he gets a dim impression of the object. He strains his sight and goes close to the visible object so as not to go wrong at all; he rubs his eyes and does just everything until he takes in a clear and striking impression of what he is judging, as though he thought the reliability of the cognition rested on this. (5) Moreover it is quite impossible to state the contrary thesis; and one who holds back from the claim that an impression is the criterion, since he is in this state by virtue of a second impression's existence, inevitably confirms the fact that impression is the criterion. (6) For nature has given the sensory faculty and the impression which arises thereby as our light, as it were, for the recognition of truth. So it is absurd to abrogate so great a faculty and to rob ourselves of the light, so to speak. (7) Just as it is the height of absurdity to allow colours and the differences between them while removing sight as non-existent or unreliable, and to assert the existence of sounds while denying that of hearing – for without those organs through which we conceive colours or sounds we cannot experience colours or sounds – so too one who grants the facts while completely undermining the sense-impression through which he grasps them is thunderstruck and putting himself on a level with soulless things.

L Sextus Empiricus, *Against the professors* 7.424

For a [cognitive] sense-impression to occur, e.g. one of sight, five factors in their [the Stoics'] view must concur: the sense-organ, the sense-object, the place, the manner and the mind; since if all of these but one are present (e.g. if the mind is in an abnormal state), the perception, they say, will not be secured. For this reason some said that the cognitive impression is not a criterion universally, but when it has no such impediment.

M Cicero, *Academica* 2.22 (following **39C**)

[Speaker: the Antiochean Lucullus] (1) But if these conceptions were false or imprinted by the kind of impressions which were indiscernible from false ones, how on earth could we make use of them? (2) How too could we see what is consistent with each fact and what is inconsistent? (3) Quite certainly memory, which is the one chief foundation not only of philosophy but of all daily life and all expert skills, has no place at all left for itself. For how can there be a memory of what is false? Or what does anyone remember which he fails to grasp and hold in his mind?

N Cicero, *Academica* 2.30–1

[Speaker: the Antiochean Lucullus] (1) The mind itself, which is the source of the senses and is even identical with the senses, has a natural force which it applies to the things by which it is activated. So it seizes some impressions in order to make immediate use of them, others, which are the source of memory, it stores away so to speak, while all the rest it arranges by their likenesses, and thereby conceptions of things are produced, which the Greeks call sometimes *ennoiai* and at other times *prolepseis*. (2) With the addition of reason, logical proof and a multitude of innumerable facts, cognition of all those things manifests itself and reason, having been perfected by these stages, arrives at wisdom. (3) Since then the human mind is completely suited to the scientific knowledge of things and to consistency of life, it embraces cognition above all, and it loves that *katalepsis* of yours . . . both for its own sake and also for its utility. (4) Therefore it makes use of the senses and creates the expert skills as second senses, and strengthens philosophy itself up to the point where it produces virtue, the one thing on which the whole of life depends. (5) Those accordingly who say that nothing can be grasped tear out the very tools or equipment of life, or rather they actually ruin the foundations of the whole of life and rob the living being itself of the mind which gives it life, so that it is difficult to speak of their rashness as the case demands.

O Cicero, *Academica* 2.37–8

[Speaker: the Antiochean Lucullus] (1) When we were explaining the power which exists in the senses, it was simultaneously made clear that many things are grasped and cognized by the senses; and this cannot take place without assent. (2) Moreover, since the principal difference between the animal and the non-animal is that an animal is an active being (for a completely inactive animal is quite inconceivable), an animal must either have sense-perception removed from itself or it must be granted that kind of assent which lies in our power. (3) But those refused sense-perception and assent are virtually robbed of their minds. For just as a scale must sink when weights are placed in the balance, so the mind must give way to what is self-evident. It is no more possible for a living creature to refrain from assenting to something self-evident than for it to fail to pursue what appears appropriate to its nature.

P Diogenes Laertius 7.52

It is by sense-perception, they [the Stoics] hold, that we get cognition of white and black, rough and smooth, but it is by reason that we get cognition of conclusions reached through demonstration, such as the gods' existence and their providence.

Q Diogenes Laertius 7.52 (*SVF* 2.71)

Aisthēsis is the Stoics' name for the breath which extends from the commanding-faculty to the senses, and for the cognition of which they are the instruments, and for their surrounding structure in respect of which some people get injured. The activity [of sensing] is also called *aisthēsis*.

R Plutarch, *On common conceptions* 1060A

I want to enjoy the revenge of observing the men [the Stoics] being convicted of the same thing, doing philosophy contrary to the common conceptions and preconceptions, which they regard as the very seeds of their school and claim to be the source of its unique agreement with nature.

S Epictetus, *Discourses* 1.22.1–3, 9–10

(1) Preconceptions are common to all men, and one preconception does not conflict with another. For which of us does not assume that the good is expedient and choiceworthy and that in every circumstance we should go after and pursue it? . . . So when does the conflict arise? In fitting preconceptions to particular entities, as when someone says, 'He acted nobly, he is brave', and another says, 'No, he is crazy'. This is the source

of men's disagreement with one another . . . (2) What is education? Learning to fit the natural preconceptions to particular entities in agreement with nature, and further, making the distinction that some things are in our power and others are not.

T Sextus Empiricus, *Against the professors* 8.331a–332a

(1) It is agreed that a preconception and conception must precede every object of investigation. For how can anyone even investigate without some conception of the object of investigation? . . . (2) We grant this, then, and are so far from denying that we have a conception of the object of investigation that, on the contrary, we claim to have many conceptions and preconceptions of it, and that we come round to suspension of judgement and indecision owing to our inability to discriminate between these and to discover the most authoritative of them.

☐ Throughout their history the Stoics did not budge from the thesis, first adumbrated by Zeno (**B**; **41B**), that infallible knowledge of the world is possible, and that all normal human beings have a natural faculty to make secure discriminations between discoverable truths and falsehoods. During the first two centuries of the school's existence the sceptical Academy was equally resolute in resisting and criticizing these claims. When Antiochus of Ascalon, as an Academic, returned from scepticism to a positive interpretation of the Platonic tradition (see **68** commentary), he took over the main lines of the Stoics' epistemology, as may be seen from **I**, **M–O** (Lucullus' reports of his views, and cf. **K**). Sextus Empiricus, as a neo-Pyrrhonist, continued to attack the Stoics with arguments largely derived from the earlier Academic confrontation by Arcesilaus and Carneades. This epistemological debate, and the adjustments made by both sides over time (for the Academics, see **68T**, **U**; **69I**), is one of the high points of Hellenistic philosophy. The texts excerpted here should ideally be supplemented with reading the whole of Cicero's *Academica* 2, and much more from Sextus Empiricus, *Against the professors* 7 and 8, than it is possible to include here. (For some of this further material see **41**, and **68–70**.) Our present selection concentrates on evidence for the 'cognitive impression', which was the bastion of Stoic epistemology and the principal object of criticism. These texts also include some of the Academic objections, and rejoinders to them by later Stoics. It is essential to recognize the continuing dialectic between the schools, which fostered much that was best in their contributions to the theory of knowledge.

In explicitly nominating 'criteria of truth', the earliest Stoics followed the policy laid down by Epicurus (see **17**), and their own account of the subject should be studied against that background. Epicurus had defended the truth of all sense-impressions (**J 5**; cf. **16**), justifying this bold thesis by sharply distinguishing *impressions* as unfailingly accurate reports of atomic images from *judgements* (true or false) about objects that we make on their basis. In his philosophy, the senses' reports are taken to be entirely irrational events; their truth is purely a function of the mechanism that produces them, and imports no vestiges of judgement concerning the objects of which they are impressions. The Stoics, as was indicated in **39**, adopted the more (to us) familiar notion that impressions themselves can be false as well as true (cf. **J** 1, 5). This thesis suits their theory that any impression of a normal adult is a rational activity, which represents the object of the impression in the form of a putative judgement – 'This (which I see) is white' etc. Thus a Stoic could say, 'Purely on the basis of what I am now seeing, I would claim that the colonnade gets narrower as it recedes from my position (cf. **39G** 8); but I know, from my familiarity with optics and the colonnade's actual rectangularity, that this is a false impression.' In Stoicism impressions are entertained by the mind like competent or incompetent messengers (cf. Carneades' use of this simile in **70A** 7), and the faculty of assent has the function of judging the value of their reports (see **B**).

This task is supposedly made easy, and indeed causally necessary in most cases (see **K** 3, **O** 3), by the so-called 'cognitive impression', *phantasia katalēptikē*. A more literal translation would be 'impression capable of grasping (its object)', and Zeno exploited this tactile image in his simile of the hand (**41A**). Whereas Epicurus had argued that sensations cannot refute one another (**16A–B**), the Stoics, from Zeno onwards (**B**), maintained the converse thesis, holding that there is a type of impression which gives its recipient an absolute guarantee that it represents the object with complete accuracy and clarity. As the criterion of truth (**A** 1), the cognitive impression is nature's gift (**K** 6; **41B** 3) of a standard for securely determining what really is the case. Largely under Academic provocation, accounts of the cognitive impression and its criterial role were modified as the Stoa developed. From **B** to **O** our texts are arranged in their approximate chronological order, to exhibit this history.

In its earliest Zenonian form the cognitive impression has two attributes which jointly constitute its status as the criterion: (a) it has a real object as its cause; (b) it represents that object with complete accuracy and clarity (**C** 2, **D** 4; cf. **39B** 2–4 for (a) as characteristic of impressions generally). An impression which has (a) but not (b) fails to be cognitive (**C** 3; cf. the Orestes example, **39G** 9). The clarity and distinctness which are the mark of (b) are features which distinguish cognitive from all other kinds of impressions. In Zeno's terminology (**B** 2), cognitive impressions 'have a peculiar power of revealing their objects'; i.e. they make us perceive their objects in a way in which incognitive impressions do not. (Our word 'perception' derives from Cicero's translation of *katalepsis* by *perceptio*.) This peculiar power is an intrinsic feature of cognitive impressions, providing us, 'just by itself' (**B** 2), with the guarantee that we are perceiving real objects as they really are. The essence of Zeno's claim is probably captured by the notion (**K** 4) that it is sufficient to see things in a certain way (clearly and strikingly) to be sure that our perception is reliable (cf. Cicero, *Academica* 2.19).

Two assumptions underlie the self-certifiability of cognitive impressions. First, the Stoics take it to be basic to nature's plan that ensouled beings, and especially those endowed with reason, have the mental equipment to make the accurate discriminations which are necessary to living in accordance with nature (cf. **K** 6–7, **M–O**; **41B** 3). Secondly, they assume that the faculty of assent is naturally determined to give its approval to such impressions (**O**; cf. **K** 3). These form the foundations of the preconceptions (**N 1, S**; cf. **39E**) and other general notions which stock the mind, and enable it to conceptualize and recognize the objects presented by any fresh cognitive impression. The outcome of assent to a cognitive impression is 'cognition' (**B 3**), which will be discussed in **41**.

A cognitive impression, then, is supposedly peculiar in the accuracy and clarity with which it represents its real object. If, however, it is to serve as the final arbiter in all questions about what is really the case, the Stoics need to show that this peculiarity can and actually does mark off the cognitive from all other impressions. In response to Arcesilaus' challenge on this point (**D 5**), Zeno added a third attribute to the cognitive impression, 'of such a kind as could not arise from what is not' (**D 6–7**, cf. **E 7**), which then became canonical in definitions of the concept. The effect of this addition is to insist that only real things as they really are *can* produce the clarity and distinctness characteristic of cognitive impressions. Arcesilaus' rejoinder was 'no impression arising from something true is such that an impression arising from something false could not also be just like it' (**D 8**). The 'many different considerations' (**41C 8**) he adduced can be assumed to have included instances of deception over pairs of similar-looking objects (**H 4, J 6–7; 28O 1–2**), and use of the Sorites (see **37F, H**). Carneades continued to attack in the same vein. For the purpose of argument, he was quite prepared to accept the existence of impressions which arise from and accurately represent real objects (the first two attributes of **E 3–6**; cf. **H 1**). The fundamental issue, as Cicero observes (**D 9**), was the discernibility of the cognitive impression from what the Academics declared were its possibly false and deceptive congeners (cf. **70A, B**).

The debate seems to have focused upon various situations in which the requisite discriminations appear fallible. (a) Someone who behaves as Heracles did (**H 2**) shows by his actions that he took his impression to be like a cognitive one, but he was mistaken. His impression induced his assent, but it 'arose from what was false'. Thus *at the time when* he receives it, a person may find a false impression thoroughly 'self-evident and striking' (cf. Ptolemy's attempt to trick Sphaerus, **F**). (b) The cognitive impression supposedly fastens upon all the 'peculiarities' of its object (**E 6**). Yet there can be objects so similar that they prove to be indiscernible by the ways they stamp our impressions, and so fail to satisfy the second attribute of cognition (**H 4, J 6–7**) and therefore the third.

To (a) the Stoics reply that the impressions of a deranged Heracles say nothing about a normal mind's capacity to discriminate cognitive from incognitive impressions. They advance the cognitive impression as the way truth presents itself to normal minds (**E 2**), and point out that the kind of impressions which the Academics advance as problematic are the product of abnormal conditions (cf. **39G 8–9**). Nor did later Stoics at least deny that a normal person may mistake cognitive for incognitive impressions and vice versa, under unusual conditions such as those experienced by Admetus (**K 1–2**). The mental state of the percipient, and all the other perceptual conditions, are allowed to be factors which can prevent a cognitive impression from performing its criterial function (**L**). This restriction, as a defence against objection (a), prompted the revisionary thesis of **K 1**: the cognitive impression is the criterion of truth 'provided it has no impediment'.

As to objection (b), the Stoics rejected its premise. According to their metaphysics (**J 7–9**; cf. **28**), the identity of indiscernibles excludes the possibility of there being pairs of twins or eggs which are actually indiscernible. For if they exist as discrete objects, they must each exist as 'peculiarly qualified individuals' with distinguishable properties that impressions, in theory at least, can discriminate. This thesis does not imply that a normal person will have cognitive impressions to decide which of two eggs he is looking at. But the Stoics are not committed to the position (as implied in **H 4**) that people in general or even the wise man can expect cognitive impressions of every possible object. Suspension of judgement is the wise man's response to every case where his impressions fail to discriminate objects with the requisite clarity and distinctness (**I**). Yet, as was pertinently observed, familiarity and training enable experts to make extremely precise discriminations in many such cases (cf. **39A 7**), which implies that even here cognitive impressions are possible.

Contrary to what is often alleged, the Stoics have the better of the argument. In order to undermine the cognitive impression as a criterion of truth, the Academics need to prove that the true impressions we receive under normal conditions are always liable to be confused with similar but false impressions. Rather than addressing the problem cases which they chose to cite, they might have done better to challenge the feasibility of specifying normal conditions (cf. **72E**). Stoics acknowledge that human beings are frequently precipitate in giving assent to incognitive impressions; but they could explain this as due to mental weakness and lack of education (**41D, G**). Nor does the claim that there are cognitive impressions imply that their mere occurrence is sufficient to free their recipient from error; for he may be the kind of person who is incapable of recognizing the truth even when he sees it. What the Academics fail to refute is the thesis that certain true impressions are of a type to make a fully functioning rational being perceive things as they really are.

Along with their defence of the cognitive impression, later Stoics and Antiochus produced a battery of arguments directly attacking the sceptical Academics' refusal to grant the empirical foundations of knowledge (**K 5–7, M–O**). They charged their critics with logical incoherence (**K 5–7**), and flagrant disregard of psychology (**53S**) and ethics (**N 5, O**). (Much more of the same will be found in other sections of Cicero, *Academica* 2.17–39.) These Stoic strategies help to throw light on the status and interpretation of Chrysippus' other criteria of truth (**A 3**, cf. commentary on Epicureanism, **17**). There is evidence elsewhere (e.g. **48C 5**) for Chrysippus invoking 'common conceptions' (i.e. ones supposedly held by people in general) as well as 'preconceptions' as criteria, and his further mention of 'sense-perception' (**A 3**) is a clue to what they involve. By 'sense-perception' (*aisthēsis*) Chrysippus must mean our cognition of simple perceptible objects (cf. **P, Q**), which is brought about by the most basic cognitive impressions. Sense-perception, however, is also the foundation of all our conceptions and cognitions (**N 1**; cf. **39C–E**), and all our conceptions are impressions (**39F**). We need not, then, suppose that Chrysippus contradicted himself in specifying different criteria in different contexts, as **A 3** maintains. In their generality and complexity, preconceptions and common conceptions cover truths which cognitive impressions, or at least sensory ones, do not transmit directly; but Chrysippus can be assumed to have regarded these criteria as complementary to sense-perception, and grounded in the cognitive impressions of which it consists (cf. **G, M; 39C**).

The gods' existence and providence, cited as examples of cognition established by rational argument (**P**), are standard cases of items the Stoics referred to preconceptions and common conceptions (cf. **54K**). It appears, then, that these function as criteria to validate theories and to adjudicate truth in areas where simple cognitive sense-impressions will not serve. Thus Chrysippus claimed that his theory of mixture could be 'proved through the common conceptions' (**48C 5**) and that Epicurus' denial of divine providence was inconsistent with our conceptions of the gods as beneficent and philanthropic (see **54K**).

This of course is a deliberate dig at Epicurus' claim that his own non-providential theology is founded on 'preconceptions' which differ from the 'false suppositions' of the many (**23B 3**); and it shows up the frailty of both schools' attempts to extend empirically-based criteria beyond the domain of the uncontroversial and obvious. Critics found it all too easy to point out that Stoicism was full of doctrines, not to mention paradoxes, which were totally alien to the common conceptions of people (**R**) and therefore inappropriately heralded to be 'natural'. The Stoics, to be sure, will reply that their conceptions are properly (and so naturally) founded on experience (**N**); but the reply does nothing to weaken the force of Sextus Empiricus' admirable comments on the criterial impotence of conceptions and preconceptions (**T**). He can agree with the Stoics that conceptions are a prerequisite of all investigation (**39C 4**, so too Epicurus **17C, E**). Yet this totally fails to justify their claim (**M**) that the use we make of them is well grounded, especially since one philosopher's preconceptions may conflict with another's. Epictetus tries to retain community of preconceptions by referring disagreement to their application to particulars (**S**). For this quite promising move to work, the scope and content of preconceptions would need to be far more restricted than the Stoics were willing to admit. On this aspect of the debate over criteria of truth, the sceptics can be judged to have carried the day.

As for the other criteria mentioned in **A**, Posidonius' report concerning right reason (**A 4**) is a highly suspect piece of history (see vol. 2 note), while Boethus' extended list (**A 2**) is unique, and seems to rely on a broader notion of 'criterion' than was adopted by other Stoics.

41 Knowledge and opinion

A Cicero, *Academica* 2.145 (*SVF* 1.66)

[Speaker: Cicero on behalf of the New Academy] (1) Zeno used to clinch the wise man's sole possession of scientific knowledge with a gesture. (2) He would spread out the fingers of one hand and display its open palm, saying 'An impression is like this.' (3) Next he clenched his fingers a little and said, 'Assent is like this.' (4) Then, pressing his fingers quite together, he made a fist, and said that this was cognition (and from this illustration he gave that mental state the name of *katalēpsis*, which it had not had before). (5) Then he brought his left hand against his right fist and gripped it tightly and forcefully, and said that scientific knowledge was like this and possessed by none except the wise man.

B Cicero, *Academica* 1.41–2 (*SVF* 1.60, part; continuing **40B**)

[Speaker: the Antiochean Varro] (1) What was grasped by sense-perception Zeno called itself a sense-perception, and if it had been so grasped that it could not be disrupted by reason, he called it scientific knowledge; but if it were otherwise, he called it ignorance, taking this to be the source of opinion as well, which was something weak and related to what was false and incognitive. (2) That cognition I mentioned above [**40B 3**] he placed between scientific knowledge and ignorance, counting it neither as good nor as bad, but said that it was to be trusted on its own. (3) Accordingly, he also attached reliability to the senses, because, as I said above, he regarded cognition effected by them as both true and reliable; not because it grasped all of a thing's properties, but because it left out nothing capable of confronting it, and also because nature had given it as the standard of scientific knowledge and as the natural foundation for the subsequent impression of conceptions of things upon the mind, which give rise not just to the starting-points but to certain broader routes for discovering reason. (4) But from virtue and wisdom Zeno removed error, rashness, ignorance, opinion, conjecture, and in a word, everything foreign to firm and consistent assent.

C Sextus Empiricus, *Against the professors* 7.151–7

(1) The Stoics say there are three things which are linked together, scientific knowledge [*epistēme*], opinion [*doxa*] and cognition [*katalēpsis*] stationed between them. (2) Scientific knowledge is cognition which is secure and firm and unchangeable by reason. (3) Opinion is weak and false assent. (4) Cognition in between these is assent belonging to a cognitive impression; and a cognitive impression, so they claim, is one which is true and of such a kind that it could not turn out false. (5) Of these they say that scientific knowledge is found only in the wise, and opinion only in the inferior, but cognition is common to them both, and it is the criterion of truth. (6) Arcesilaus contradicted these statements of the Stoics by proving that cognition is no criterion in between scientific knowledge and opinion. (7) For what they call cognition and assent to a cognitive impression occurs in either a wise or an inferior man. But if it occurs in a wise man, it is scientific knowledge; and if in an inferior man, it is opinion; and there is no further variation except a purely verbal one. (8) And if cognition is assent belonging to a cognitive impression, it is

non-existent: first, because assent occurs not in relation to an impression but in relation to language (for assents belong to propositions). Secondly, because no true impression is found to be of a kind such that it could not turn out false, as is attested by many different considerations. (9) But if the cognitive impression does not exist, cognition will not occur either, for it was assent to a cognitive impression. And if cognition does not exist, everything will be incognitive. And if everything is incognitive, it will follow, according to the Stoics too, that the wise man suspends judgement. (10) We may consider it in this way: given that everything is incognitive, owing to the non-existence of the Stoic criterion, if the wise man should assent, the wise man will opine. For given that nothing is cognitive, if he assents to anything, he will assent to the incognitive, and assent to the incognitive is opinion. So if the wise man is one of those who assent, the wise man will be one of those who opine. But the wise man is certainly not one of those who opine (for they [the Stoics] claim this to be a mark of folly and a cause of wrongdoing). Therefore the wise man is not one of those who assent. And if this is so, he will have to withhold assent about everything. But to withhold assent is no different from suspending judgement. Therefore the wise man will suspend judgement about everything.

D Anonymous Stoic treatise (Herculaneum papyrus 1020) col. 4, col. 1 (*SVF* 2.131, part)

(1) < So it is > that we respect non-precipitancy and uncarelessness, but we are rightly criticized for their opposites. Non-precipitancy is a disposition not to assent in advance of cognition . . . strong in [dealing with] impressions and not yielding to those which are incognitive. For one who is non-precipitate should not be pulled by an incognitive impression . . . and keeps control over his assents . . . (2) We say that the wise man's absence of opinion is accompanied by such characteristics as, first of all, his supposing nothing; for supposal is an incognitive opinion . . . (3) A further consequence is that wise men are incapable of being deceived and of erring, and that they live worthily and do everything well. Therefore they also give greater attention to ensuring that their assents do not occur randomly, but only in company with cognition.

E Plutarch, *On Stoic self-contradictions* 1056E–F (*SVF* 2.993, part)

[Fate] . . . frequently produces impressions, in matters of very great importance, which are at variance with one another and pull the mind in opposite directions. On these occasions the Stoics say that those who assent to one of them and do not suspend judgement are guilty of error; that they are precipitate if they yield to unclear impressions, deceived if they yield to false ones, and opining if they yield to ones which are incognitive quite generally.

F Plutarch, *On Stoic self-contradictions* 1057A–B (*SVF* 3.177, part)

Furthermore, Chrysippus says that both god and the wise man implant false impressions, not asking us to assent or yield but merely to act and be impelled towards the appearance, but that we inferior persons out of weakness assent to such impressions.

G Stobaeus 2.111, 18–112,8 (*SVF* 3.548, part)

(1) They [the Stoics] say that the wise man never makes a false supposition, and that he does not assent at all to anything incognitive, owing to his not opining and his being ignorant of nothing. (2) For ignorance is changeable and weak assent. (3) But the wise man supposes nothing weakly, but rather, securely and firmly; and so he does not opine either. (4) For there are two kinds of opinion, assent to the incognitive, and weak supposition, and these are alien to the wise man's disposition. (5) So precipitancy and assent in advance of cognition are attributes of the precipitate inferior man, whereas they do not befall the man who is well-natured and perfect and virtuous.

H Stobaeus 2.73,16–74,3 (*SVF* 3.112, part)

[The Stoics say] (1) Scientific knowledge [*epistēmē*] is a cognition [*katalēpsis*] which is secure and unchangeable by reason. (2) It is secondly a system of such *epistēmai*, like the rational cognition of particulars which exists in the virtuous man. (3) It [scientific knowledge here = science] is thirdly a system of expert *epistēmai*, which has intrinsic stability, just as the virtues do. (4) Fourthly, it is a tenor for the reception of impressions which is unchangeable by reason, and consisting, they say, in tension and power.

I Stobaeus 2.68,18–23 (*SVF* 3.663)

They [the Stoics] also say that every inferior man is insane, since he has ignorance of himself and of his concerns, and this is insanity. Ignorance is the vice opposite to moderation, and this is insanity because in its relative dispositions it makes our impulses unstable and fluttering. Hence they give this outline of insanity – fluttering ignorance.

☐ The cognitive state that results from assent to a cognitive impression is 'cognition' (*katalēpsis*, **A** 4, **C** 4). Like the clenched fist, to which Zeno likened it (**A** 4), cognition (or 'perception', in Cicero's Latin translation) is the 'grasp' of its object – the state of affairs whose truth is guaranteed by the cognitive impression. Such impressions, by being assented to, give someone the certainty that he perceives some truth(s), and this cognition takes on the necessary reliability and criterial power (**B** 3, **C** 4–5) of the cognitive impression itself. It might seem accordingly that the Stoics should identify 'cognition' with knowledge, a hallmark of which is often regarded as certified true belief. Their doctrine in fact is more interesting and more complex. It would be possible to translate *katalēpsis* by 'knowledge' in many contexts, and *katalēpsis* is certainly the foundation of *epistēmē*, the highest cognitive state, which we render by 'science' or 'scientific knowledge' (cf. **A 4–5, B 3, H**). But cognition, though a necessary condition of this state, is not sufficient to constitute it. To become 'scientific knowledge', cognition must be made impregnable to any reasoning that might be adduced to persuade a change of mind (**B 1, H 1, 4**). We may approach elucidation of this further condition by noting a more striking indication of the insufficiency of cognition on its own to be the highest form of knowledge: it straddles the basic dichotomy between wise and inferior men (**C 5**, cf. **B 1–2**), and in the latter case coexists with 'ignorance'.

As 'changeable and weak assent' (**G 2**), 'ignorance' is defined as the contradictory of 'scientific knowledge' (cf. **H 1**). The ignorant 'fool', i.e. the vast majority of mankind, is not typified by the falsehood of his beliefs, nor even by his lack of knowledge in ordinary Greek senses of that term. 'Ignorance' accommodates all cognitive states, including 'cognitions' (certified true beliefs), which fall short of the impregnable stability and systematic consistency – hand over fist (**A 5**) – that belong to the wise man's scientific knowledge. The absolute disjunction between scientific knowledge and ignorance is an important instance of the Stoics' ruthless insistence on excluding any mental disposition intermediate between excellence and its opposite (virtue/vice, wisdom/folly, sanity/insanity, cf. **I**, and see 61I). Nor is this breached by the admission that 'cognition' is common to both classes of people (**C 5**) or 'between scientific knowledge and ignorance' (**B 2**). The same quasi-intermediate status belongs to 'proper functions' in ethics (**59B 4, F 1**). Inferior people will typically perform many of these – looking after their health, their parents etc. – and thus share the same moral domain as the wise man. Since, however, they lack his virtuous and perfectly consistent disposition, even their proper functions, though objectively right, are counted as 'wrong-doing' (**59F 3**). It is just the same with the evaluation of cognitions. Neutral though trustworthy in themselves (**B 2**), they acquire positive or negative epistemic status from the strength or weakness of the mind to which they belong. The wise man's grasp of truths is so secure and systematic that his commanding-faculty is identical to 'truth' (**33P 2, 4**). That of the inferior man, by contrast, is so insecure that even those truths of which he does have cognition do not save him from comprehensive ignorance.

In Sextus Empiricus' report of Arcesilaus' critique of Stoic epistemology, which should for chronological reasons refer to its Zenonian form (cf. **B**), the equivocal intermediacy of 'cognition' is exploited as part of an argument against its existence (**C 1–7**). As reported, Arcesilaus argued that the exclusive disjunction between the two classes of people and between their mental dispositions reduces cognition to either (a) scientific knowledge in the wise or (b) opinion in the inferior. Zeno's doctrine of **B 1** justifies (a), but (b) will only hold good if the Stoics counted the cognitions of inferior men as 'opinions'. That however would be a flagrant contradiction of **E** (cf. **D 2**), according to which the general characteristic of 'opining' is 'assent to the incognitive'. That claim too has Zeno's authority (**40D**, and cf. Cicero, *Academica* 2.60, 'opining is

257

assenting to a thing either false or incognitive'). But on the evidence of **B** 1, Zeno could have been taken not to have clearly distinguished 'ignorance', which includes the inferior man's true cognitions, from opining; and it should be noted that Arcesilaus says 'assent to the incognitive is opinion' (**C** 10) and not 'opinion is assent to the incognitive', which leaves it open that some opinions may involve assent to cognitive impressions. Such possible indecision by Zeno on the scope of 'opinion' could have allowed Arcesilaus to substitute 'opinion' for 'ignorance' in his argument, and thus imply that the inferior man's so-called cognition is really opinion in the wider sense, so negating the distinction within 'ignorance' between true cognitions and false or uncertified opinions. Arcesilaus' argument will still go through if 'ignorance' is substituted throughout **C** 1–7 for 'opinion', but this need not trouble later Stoics. They could accept the conclusion that cognition in the inferior man is ignorance, but deny that this robs cognition of its significance, since ignorance is made up of both cognitions and opinions, and only the latter are false or uncertified as true.

Unlike most previous philosophers (the clear exception is Parmenides), no Stoics officially recognize the existence of *true* 'opinions'. As they normally use the term *doxa*, it refers to beliefs that result from assent to the incognitive (**E**, **G** 1), where incognitive covers everything that cannot be grasped, both falsehoods and states of affairs whose truth is not clearly or distinctly certified (**40C**). (This pejorative assessment of 'opining' was a point on which Stoics and sceptics were in agreement: see **40D**; **69**.) The Stoic equivalent of true or correct opinion, as Plato uses that expression, would be the 'cognitions' of inferior men, which fall short of scientific knowledge (cf. Plato, *Meno* 98a, where correct opinions become knowledge when 'tethered by working out the reason'). A crucial difference between wise and inferior men is their disposition with respect to knowing when suspension of judgement is called for (cf. **40I**). The wise man has infallible control over his assent, giving it only to impressions of whose cognitive status he is quite certain (**D** 1); this is a characteristic of his scientific knowledge (**H** 4). In all other cases, he suspends judgement, which Arcesilaus exploits in the second part of his argument (**C** 9–10): he cleverly concludes that the Stoics' wise man, on their own admission, would have to suspend judgement about everything if the cognitive impression and cognition do not exist. (Suspension of judgement, which is the fundamental notion in Academic scepticism, was probably at home in the Stoa before Arcesilaus turned it against them in arguments, with Stoic premises, for scepticism). Inferior men, by contrast, are characterized by their 'precipitancy' (**E**, **G** 5), or disposition to assent to 'unclear impressions', their 'erroneous' assent where suspension of judgement is in order, and their 'self-deception in yielding to false impressions'. All of these are represented as types of 'assent to the incognitive', the general mark of 'opinion' (**E**).

From this and other evidence we have argued that the inferior man's true cognitions were not normally counted as cases of 'opining'. They must however share in the 'changeableness and weakness' which characterize his ignorance generally (**G** 2). 'Weakness' denotes the insecurity, instability and inconsistency of the inferior man's mental state, and seems to cover the following cases: (a) not assenting firmly to cognitive impressions, (b) not going through with right decisions, (c) assenting precipitately to incognitive impressions, (d) assenting to what is patently false. (For (a) cf. **B** 1, for (b) **65T**, for (c) **D** 1, **G 4–5**, for (d) **F** and **65C**.) Stobaeus' treatment of 'weak supposition' as a second type of 'opinion' (**G 4**) reads in its context like an alternative description of 'precipitancy'. But it is possible that he preserves traces of a (?) Zenonian doctrine in which the inferior man's weak assent to cognitive impressions was counted as an 'opinion' (cf. **B** 1, **C 3**), as well as his assent to what is false and incognitive.

By allowing all normal people to have some cognitions, albeit weakly held in most cases, the Stoics provided a basis for 'progress' (see **59I**) exactly analogous to their doctrine of 'proper functions'. What perfects these latter is not a change in their objective content, but the expert understanding, consistency and moral integrity of their agent. So too with the conversion of cognitions into scientific knowledge. The evidence does not suggest that the wise man must grasp more facts than other people. His scientific expertise is rather a function of what he knows and *how* he knows what he knows – systematically, completely securely, so rationally grounded that no reasons can be furnished which could possibly subvert it (cf. **H**). His ignorance of nothing (**G 1**) does not imply literal omniscience, but the absence of all doubt, uncertainty, falsehood and instability from his cognitive state.

At this point we should remember that the Stoics' principal philosophical motivation was ethical. What chiefly inhibits people from becoming wise, in their view, is proneness to emotional disorder, and this is reflected in the startling identification of ignorance with insanity (**I**). The 'unstable and fluttering impulses', which ignorance is said to exhibit, are the passions, which are false judgements of what is good and bad for men (see **65A**, **G**, and note the role of assent in the latter text). Scientific knowledge in Stoicism, it turns out, is an intensely practical disposition, and a far cry from Aristotelian 'contemplation' (*theōria*). In its prevailing emphasis on the avoidance of error and baseless opinion (cf. **B 4**, and see the 'dialectical virtues', **31B**), it is most convincingly interpreted as an attempt to provide foundations for the kind of knowledge that Socrates failed to find.

42 Scientific methodology

A Olympiodorus, *On Plato's Gorgias* 12.1

(1) Cleanthes says that expertise is a tenor which achieves everything methodically. (2) This definition is incomplete. After all, nature also is a tenor which does everything methodically. (3) That is why Chrysippus added 'with impressions', and said that expertise is a tenor which advances methodically with impressions . . . (4) Zeno says that an expertise is a systematic collection of cognitions unified by practice for some goal advantageous in life.

B Cicero, *Academica* 2.22

[Speaker: the Antiochean Lucullus, in defence of Stoic epistemology] (1) Indeed, what expertise can exist without being compounded out of, not just one or two, but many mental cognitions? Take away expertise, and how will you distinguish the expert from the ignoramus? For it is not by accident that we apply the name of expert to the one but withhold it from the other: it is because we see that the one retains a set of cognitions, while the other does not. (2) And given that there is one class of expertise whose function is to study a thing with the mind alone, another whose function is to achieve effects and products, how can a geometer study things which are either nothing or indistinguishable from falsehoods, or a harpist fill out rhythms and create lines in music?

C Cicero, *On divination* 1.34

[Speaker: Quintus Cicero, in defence of Stoic theory of divination] (1) Hence I follow those who have said that there are two kinds of divination, one involving expertise, the other not. The diviners who have expertise are those who pursue new data by conjecture, having learnt their old data by observation. (2) Those who lack expertise are the ones who foretell the future not by reason or conjecture through empirical observation of signs, but by either stimulating or relaxing the mind, as has often happened to dreamers, and sometimes to those who prophesy in a frenzy.

D Cicero, *On divination* 1.82–3 (*SVF* 2.1192)

[Speaker: Quintus Cicero, in defence of Stoic theory of divination] (1) That there really is divination is inferred with the following argument of the Stoics. (2) 'If there are gods but they do not indicate future events to men in advance, either they do not love men, or they are ignorant of what will happen, or they think it is not in men's interests to know the future, or they think it beneath their dignity to give signs of future events to men in advance, or even the gods are unable to give signs of them. But neither do the gods not love us (for they are beneficent and friendly to mankind); nor are they ignorant of what they themselves have set up and ordained; nor is it not in our interests to know future events (for we will be more careful if we know); nor do they think it foreign to their dignity (for nothing is more honourable than beneficence); nor are they unable to foreknow future events. Therefore it is not the case that there are gods but that they do not give signs of future events. But there are gods. Therefore they do give signs of future events. (3) And it is not the case that if they give signs they give us no routes to scientific knowledge of sign-inference (for in that case their giving signs would be pointless). And if they give us the routes, it is not the case that divination does not exist. Therefore divination exists.' (4) This argument is used by Chrysippus, Diogenes [of Babylon] and Antipater.

E Cicero, *On divination* 1.117–18 *(SVF* 2.1210)

[Speaker: Quintus Cicero, in defence of Stoic theory of divination] If we accept this [divine providence] – and I for one do not see how it can be confuted – it must indeed be the case that the gods give men signs of future events. But clearly we must specify how. For it is not a Stoic doctrine that the gods concern themselves with individual cracks in the liver or individual bird-songs. That is unbecoming, unworthy of the gods, and quite impossible. Their view is that the world was from its beginning set up in such a way that certain things should be preceded by certain signs, some in entrails, others in birds, others in lightning, others in portents, others in stars, others in dream impressions, others in frenzied utterances. Those who properly perceive these are rarely deceived. The falsehood of bad conjectures and bad interpretations is due, not to any fault in the world, but to the scientific ignorance of the interpreters.

F Cicero, *Academica* 2.36

[Speaker: the Antiochean Lucullus] But what could be more absurd than when they [the Academics] say 'This is a sign, or proof, of that, and I therefore follow it, but it could be that what it signifies is either false or nothing at all'?

G Philodemus, *On signs* 1.2–4.13

[Reporting Stoic arguments against the Epicureans] (1) It is a 'common' sign for no other reason than that this can exist whether or not the non-evident thing exists. When someone considers that such and such a man is good because he is rich, we say that he is using an unsound and common sign, since many dreadful rich men are found, as well as many good ones. Consequently the peculiar sign, if it is to be cogent, is incapable of existing except in conjunction with the thing which we say necessarily belongs to it, the non-apparent thing whose sign it is . . . And this is done through the Elimination Method of sign-inference. (2) Again, in relation to the unique instances which are seen in the regions familiar to us, the Similarity Method seems not to be cogent – if among the many different stones there is only one species which draws iron (the so-called 'magnetic' or 'Heraclean' stone), only amber attracts chaff, and four-by-four is the only square number to have its perimeter equal to its area. How then can we say that there is not a race of men which is unique in not dying when pierced through the heart? So there is no necessary inference, from the fact that men familiar to us die when pierced through the heart, that all men do. There are also some familiar rare cases, like the man in

Alexandria half a cubit high with a colossal head which could take hammer blows, whom the embalmers used to have on display; the person who was married as a girl in Epidaurus and then became a man; the man in Crete who was forty-eight cubits tall, according to sign-inference from the bones they discovered; and the pygmies whom they show in Acoris, who are indeed comparable to the ones Antony recently brought from Hyria . . . (3) When we judge that since men familiar to us are mortal so are all men, in choosing the Similarity Method we are using the hypothesis that men in non-evident places are in all respects similar to men familiar to us, and hence also in respect of being mortal, even independently of our argument. For if they are similar in all respects, our sign-inference that they are similar in this precise respect too will be perfectly correct, the argument mode presumably being as follows: 'Since the men familiar to us are mortal, so too if there are elsewhere men resembling the men familiar to us in other respects and especially in respect of being mortal, they would be mortal.' For you admitted this conclusion in the sign. How will this differ from the sign from which we ourselves make sign-inferences, if we hypothesize that both groups are mortal and say something like 'Since the men familiar to us are mortal, and if elsewhere there are mortal men, they are mortal'? But if we do not hypothesize that those men about whom we are making the sign-inference are similar also in respect of being mortal, but that they differ in this respect . . . the sign-inference clearly loses its cogency. Hence it will not be necessary that men in non-evident places are mortal, or that those other men who are similar in other respects but different in respect of being mortal should resemble the men familiar to us in this respect too. (4) In general, if one judges 'Since the men familiar to us are mortal, men everywhere are mortal too', if this is equivalent to 'Since the men familiar to us are mortal in that and in so far as they are men, men everywhere are mortal', the judgement will be correct; but if one judges 'Since the men familiar to us are mortal, men everywhere are mortal too', meaning that mortality belongs to the men familiar to us in some other, accidental way, the judgement will be empty. (After all, just because the men familiar to us are short-lived, we won't say that the Acrothoites are short-lived too!) Therefore we must show also that men are mortal in that and in so far as they are men, if we are going to establish the cogency of the proposed inference. But since we can show this by Elimination, we shall dispense with the Similarity Method.

H Philodemus, *On signs* 6.1–14

[Reporting Stoic arguments against the Epicureans] For sign-inference [by Similarity], shall we use that which is indiscernible? Or that which is similar? Or that which has *what* degree of resemblance? To say the indiscernible is ridiculous. For why will the apparent any more be a sign of the non-apparent than vice versa? Besides, if indiscernibility obtains we will no longer have one thing apparent and the other non-evident. But if they say similar, how will we be able to tell that it does not, in virtue of the difference it has, diverge from the apparent property from which we are making the sign-inference?

I Cicero, *Academica* 2.99–100

[Speaker: Cicero, in defence of the New Academy] Indeed, even the wise man whom your school [the stoicizing school of Antiochus] brings onto the scene follows many things which are convincing – not known, perceived or assented to, but likely. Were he not to accept them, all life would surely be abolished. After all, when the wise man boards a ship he surely doesn't know and perceive in his mind that the voyage will be successful – how can he? But if he were now setting out from here for Puteoli, a journey of thirty stades, with an honest crew and a good steersman in the present calm weather, it would seem convincing to him that he would get there safely.

J Philodemus, *On signs* 7.26–38

(1) Again, when our people [the Epicureans] say that according to them even freaks bear resemblances in some respects – unless we are going to abolish the existence of the familiar things which resemble them! – (2) he [the Stoic Dionysius] says, first, that the abolition will be by the Elimination Method; (3) but that anyway it is sufficient, concerning these things and concerning those which derive from experience, for us to be convinced in accordance with what is reasonable, just as when we sail in summer we are convinced that we will arrive safely.

☐ Four primary, and to the modern eye extraordinarily diverse, Stoic examples of an expertise (*technē*) or science (*epistēmē*) are medicine, divination, dialectic and virtue. These have in common their reliance on a system of cognitions, or more properly 'theorems'; their methodical way of proceeding; and the practical utility of their results. And these are the essential features embodied in the two definitions of 'expertise' given at **A 3–4**. Despite **A**'s apportionment of these definitions between individual Stoics, there is good reason to believe that both were canonical, and not meant as alternatives. That in **A 4** is the definition of *an* expertise, an objective body of knowledge, such as medicine. That in **A 3** is of expertise as such, i.e. of the mental disposition of an expert.

Officially 'science' differs from mere expertise, but here too we must distinguish two senses. *A* science (**41H 3**) differs from *an* expertise (**A 4**) by the absolute unshakeability of its results. But science as such (or 'scientific knowledge', as we also translate it, cf. **41A–C, H**) differs from expertise as such in that science is a 'character' (*diathesis*), which by definition (**47S**) does not admit of degrees, whereas expertise is a tenor (*hexis*), which does. One doctor can be more expert than another; but one virtuous man cannot be more virtuous than another, since virtue, being scientific knowledge, is a state of intellectual perfection (cf. **61H–I**).

The difference between science and mere expertise is important in some Stoic contexts, especially ethical, but will be disregarded in the following discussion, in which we will use 'science' non-technically for both. We will also be concentrating on cognitive aspects of science. However, the distinction between productive and cognitive sciences as such (**B 2**) need not be too rigidly observed: medicine, for example, in both its theory and its practice, was perceived largely as a cognitive science, despite its ultimately productive function of creating health. For the scientific features of dialectic and virtue, see **31** (especially **B**) and **61** respectively. There is no evidence there or elsewhere of any Stoic attempt to distinguish between pure sciences on the one hand and applied or empirical sciences on the other. Indeed, at **G 2** even mathematical truth is treated as directly comparable to empirical truth. The Stoics were not (with the exception of Posidonius) particularly familiar with current work in mathematics, and therefore do not, as Plato and Aristotle regularly do, invoke its various branches as paradigmatic sciences.

Most if not all sciences can be expected to employ empirical data. For example divination requires, in addition to a theoretical rationale for its existence and *modus operandi* (**D, E; 55O**), a set of detailed theorems from which to operate, and these theorems seem to be empirically derived rules. An example of a theorem is the law that people born at the rising of the Dogstar do not die at sea (**38E**). Since being born at the rising of the Dogstar is not conceptually related to not dying at sea, but is a divinely engineered concomitant 'sign' (**E**), there is no way of establishing their connexion short of inductive inference based on empirical observation of individual lives. And that is indeed how scientific divination proceeds: **C**. Even 'cognitions' (**A, B**), used as a standard Stoic equivalent for 'theorems', carries strong empirical implications (cf. **40**).

Portents are often, as in **C–E**, spoken of as 'signs' of future events, but in view of their inductive character there may be some uncertainty as to whether this was a technically accurate description. A sign, according to Stoic doctrine, is an evident truth by which some further, non-evident truth is revealed (**35C**). It is common ground for all Stoic discussions (cf. also **51H; 53T**) that the sign and what it signifies are related as, respectively, the true antecedent ('leading' proposition, with the connotation 'guiding') and consequent in a sound conditional (although the later Stoics in **G** prefer the 'subconditional' construction with 'since', on which see also **35A**). As we note in **35**, commentary, some Stoics, probably early, accepted the Philonian analysis of the conditional, which demanded no particular conceptual relation between antecedent and consequent. These Stoics were therefore, it seems, happy to accept sign-inferences whose basis was apparently inductive, e.g. 'If this man has been wounded in the heart, this man will die' (**51H**; see also **35C**). Later Stoics, on the other hand, accepted Chrysippus' 'cohesion' analysis of the sound conditional (see **35**), according to which the negation of the consequent comes out *incompatible* with the antecedent. Or, as the late second-century B.C. Stoics reported in **G–H** put it, by eliminating the consequent you *eo ipso* eliminate the antecedent (**18F**) – the so-called 'Elimination Method' (see commentary on **18**). The effect is a drastic narrowing of the range of possible sign-inferences. Indeed, the very example cited above from **51H** is treated as unsound by these later Stoics at **G 2**, along with the entire class of inductive inferences. Inductive inference was defended by their Epicurean opponents as one application of their 'Similarity Method' (**18F–G**), but according to the Stoics inductive signs threaten to be 'common' signs, i.e. not guaranteed to distinguish the true from the false (**G 1**, cf. **F**).

In defending this position, the Stoics raise powerful objections to induction: it is either invalid (**G 2, H**), or, at best, trivially true (**G 3**). They do, however, indicate a way in which induction might be replaced with a mode of inference combining validity with informativeness. This is by reliance on an essentialist principle. Provided that empirical study can establish the *essence* of a species, we can then construct true conditionals which will reveal truths about as yet unexamined members of the same species: **G 4**. (The Epicureans at **18G** accept this suggestion, but insist that induction is used in establishing essences.)

Where no essence is involved, these later Stoics will relegate an inductive inference to the status of the merely 'convincing' (as opposed to 'cognitive'): **I**, **J 3**. However favourable the weather conditions, you cannot *know* when you set sail that you will not die at sea. On the basis of past experience it is hard to disbelieve, but it does not strictly follow from the available data. Nor for that matter does this same conclusion that you will not die at sea strictly follow from the relevant astrological 'sign', e.g. your having been born at the rising of the Dogstar. Chrysippus apparently felt that, since there is no conceptual relation here between the sign and the truth signified, the theorem in question is not a proper conditional at all: **38E 6**. This did not diminish his faith in the accuracy of divination. But it does raise a doubt as to whether the term 'sign', in such divinatory contexts as **C–E** is being used in its full Stoic sense, which requires that the conditional relation obtain between sign and significatum.

The kind of sign which divinatory signs most closely resemble is the 'commemorative' sign. Sextus Empiricus (*Outlines of Pyrrhonism* 2.97 ff., *Against the professors* 8.141 ff.) reports the following set of distinctions, without explicit attribution. Some non-evident things are irremediably non-evident, e.g. whether the number of stars is odd or even; some are temporarily non-evident through inaccessibility; and yet others are 'naturally' non-evident, i.e. in their nature not directly available to inspection, but perhaps correctly inferable from evident signs. While these last are revealed by 'indicative' signs, whose definition corresponds almost exactly to the Stoic definition of 'sign' (**35C**), temporarily non-evident truths are revealed by 'commemorative' signs, which, having been previously observed in conjunction with certain other phenomena, e.g. a wound in the heart with death, *remind* us at every occurrence to expect the same conjoined phenomena. We might then do well to call divinatory signs 'commemorative'. Many scholars have indeed regarded the entire indicative/ commemorative theory as Stoic. But there is no clear evidence to confirm the attribution, and there are good reasons for regarding this distinction, like most of the debate on signs, as primarily medical. *If* the attribution to the Stoics is correct, it will be best to suppose that Stoics from Chrysippus on did not treat commemorative signs as signs in the strict sense, expressible by conditionals, but as 'convincing' grounds of inference, expressible by negated conjunctions (as at **38E 6**).

A scientific 'demonstration' (or 'proof') looks in many ways like the formal articulation of a sign, although there seems to be no requirement that it contain a specifically *conditional* premise. According to **36B 7–11**, an argument is demonstrative precisely if it is true and has pre-evident premises and a non-evident conclusion, e.g. 'If sweat flows through the surface of the skin, there are ducts discoverable by thought. But sweat does flow through the surface of the skin. Therefore there are ducts discoverable by thought.' Here the leading premise is claimed as some sort of conceptually evident truth, and the additional premise is of course empirically self-evident. But a formally 'demonstrative' argument may yet fail to be, what this one is, a genuine 'demonstration'. The reason for this fine distinction is apparently not logical but epistemological. In a true demonstration the conclusion must be 'revealed by the force of the premises'. Now in a case of conditioned or habituated belief, e.g. the belief that a prophecy will come true, an argument meeting the conditions for a demonstrative argument might be retrospectively constructed by way of justification, but no 'revelation' would be taking place. It is, then, a requirement of a real scientific demonstration that it be genuinely *enlightening*.

For sign-inference as intrinsic to human rationality, see **53T**; for signs in relation to tense, **51H**; for further evidence on expertise, **39A 7**; **64**; for demonstration, see also **40P**.

PHYSICS

43 The scope of physics

A Diogenes Laertius 7.148–9 (*SVF* 2.1022, 1132)

(1) Zeno says that the whole world and heaven are the substance of god, and likewise Chrysippus in *On gods* book 1 and Posidonius in *On gods* book 1 . . . (2) By 'nature' they sometimes mean what sustains the world, and sometimes what makes things on the earth grow: nature is a self-moving tenor, which completes and sustains its products in accordance with seminal principles at determinate times, and continues to perform the actions from which they came to light. Furthermore, it aims at utility and pleasure, as is evident from human craftsmanship.

B Diogenes Laertius 7.132

They [the Stoics] divide physics into the following topics: (i) bodies, (ii) principles, (iii) elements, (iv) gods, (v) limits, place, and void. This is a division into species. But they make a generic division into three topics: (i) the world, (ii) the elements, (iii) enquiry into causes.

☐ In approaching Stoic physics, we should recall its integral connexion with Stoic philosophy as a whole (**26B 4, D**). Whether regarded as philosophy's flesh and blood (**26D**) or its soul (**26B 2**), physics, which is literally the study of *nature*, offers systematic understanding of 'the world and its contents' (**26A**). The indispensability of such knowledge to the ethical end, 'living in agreement with nature' (**63A–C**), is based upon the principle that our individual human natures are parts of universal nature (**63C 2**).

Physics therefore provides us with the understanding of who we are and of how we fit into the general workings of the world. Since the world is the 'substance' of god, and god is the 'nature which sustains the world and makes things grow' (**A**), physics, in the final analysis, is theology (**26C**; cf. **63E**). To put it another way, physics is that part of Stoic philosophy which provides the terms and theories for understanding that the world functions according to laws of an omnipresent divine nature – a nature, moreover, which is through and through alive, generative, and designing all its products according to a rational plan. Most sections of this chapter, especially **44, 46, 52–5**, will underline these points repeatedly (and for further discussion of **A 2** see commentary on **46A**). Stoic physics contains many theories and strategies which are of great interest in their own right to the history of science. But in order to appreciate their conceptual significance, we should acknowledge the Stoics' lack of concern in general for quantitative analysis and the controlled observations characteristic of, say, Galen and Ptolemy. What fired the Stoics' imagination, in their observation of the world, was a total commitment to the rationalist theology just described.

Turning now to their detailed treatment, we find the topics of physics, just like those of logic (**31A**) and ethics (**56A**), systematically categorized (**B**). (For the technical niceties concerning division procedure, see **32C**.) This procedure will certainly have gone back to Chrysippus, although Diogenes Laertius' source for his summary was probably a handbook written shortly after the time of Posidonius. The general acceptability of the divisions Diogenes records is suggested by the fact that his own exposition sticks fairly closely to that order of topics. This can be seen by aligning his chapters and their subjects with the Topics of **B**:

1. *Specific division*
   D.L. 134 principles = (ii)
   D.L. 135 body and limits = (i) and (v)
   D.L. 136 god = (iv)
   D.L. 137 elements = (iii)

2. *Generic division*
   D.L. 137–51 world (including god, heavenly bodies, elements) = (i) and (ii)
   D.L. 152–9 meteorology, geography, psychology = (iii)

The two divisions appear to have as their basis a distinction between physics and metaphysics (as it would now be called), with the 'specific' division covering the kind of topics that Aristotle regarded as the business of 'first philosophy'. Diogenes' second division, the 'generic one', takes the present world-order as its starting-point. It offers an account of natural phenomena, with some reference to general principles but nothing comparable to the scope of the 'specific' division. In this latter the subject-matter is not restricted to the contents of the present world-order, which comes into being and ceases to exist (see **46**; **52**). The five topics of the 'specific' division seem to give an exhaustive account of the species of real things, whether they are everlasting and irreducible, or temporary, or 'subsistent' as non-bodily 'somethings' (see **27**). Thus we have a division into bodies (i)–(iv), and non-bodies (v) as exemplified by 'limits, place, and void'. The first four species seem to cover the bodily constituents of reality in ascending order of complexity. I.e., (i) the Stoics held that reality consists basically, permanently and irreducibly of 'bodies' (**27B**); (ii) the 'principles' themselves are 'bodies' (**44B**); (iii) the 'elements' are temporary dispositions of body caused by and reducible to the interaction of the 'principles' (see **47**); (iv) the 'gods' are bodies, which can be explained by reference either to the 'elements' or, in the case of Zeus, to the active 'principle'. Given (v), the non-bodies, there is nothing in the nature of things that this division omits.

Such an interpretation of Diogenes' 'specific' division can only be conjectural. Yet it coheres well with Stoic doctrines, especially their concept of the 'something' which embraces all particulars whether corporeal or not (see **27**). So understood, the 'specific' division details those items which are fundamental to any understanding of the world in general and its features. In one respect, however, the order of specific topics raises a problem. Diogenes presents 'bodies' as the first topic, but the one that he handles first is the second, 'principles'. Since the principles are bodies, this procedure, which we will also follow, may be taken to be an expository device that need not cast doubt on the ultimate priority of bodies in the Stoics' metaphysical scheme.

44 Principles

A Sextus Empiricus, *Against the professors* 9.332 (*SVF* 2.524, part)

The Stoic philosophers suppose that there is a difference between the 'whole' and the 'all'. For they say that the world is whole, but the external void together with the world is all. For this reason they say the 'whole' is finite, since the world is finite, but the 'all' is infinite, since the void outside the world is such.

B Diogenes Laertius 7.134 (*SVF* 2.300, part, 2.299)

(1) They [the Stoics] think that there are two principles of the universe, that which acts and that which is acted upon. (2) That which is acted upon is unqualified substance, i.e. matter; that which acts is the reason [*logos*] in it, i.e. god. For this, since it is everlasting, constructs every single thing throughout all matter . . . (3) They say there is a difference between principles and elements: the former are ungenerated and indestructible, whereas the elements pass away at the conflagration. The principles are

also bodies ['incorporeal', in the parallel text of the Suda] and without form, but the elements are endowed with form.

C Sextus Empiricus, *Against the professors* 9.75–6 (*SVF* 2.311)

(1) The substance of what exists, they [the Stoics] say, since it is without any motion from itself and shapeless, needs to be set in motion and shaped by some cause. (2) For this reason, as when we look at a very beautiful bronze we want to know the artist (since in itself the matter is in an immobile condition), so when we see the matter of the universe moving and possessing form and structure we might reasonably inquire into the cause which moves and shapes it into many forms. (3) It is not convincing that this is anything other than a power which pervades it, just as soul pervades us. (4) Now this power is either self-moving or moved by some other power. (5) But if it is moved by another power, this second power will not be capable of being moved unless it is moved by a third power, which is absurd. So there exists a power which in itself is self-moving, and this must be divine and everlasting. (6) For either it will be in motion from eternity or from a definite time. (7) But it will not be in motion from a definite time; for there will be no cause of its motion from a definite time. So, then, the power which moves matter and guides it in due order into generations and changes is everlasting. So this power would be god.

D Calcidius 292 (*SVF* 1.88, part)

(1) Zeno says that this very substance [*essentia*] is finite and that it is the one common substrate [*substantia*] of everything which exists. (2) It is also divisible and continuously subject to change. (3) Its parts are changed, but they do not perish so as to be destroyed from existing into nothing. But as is the case with the innumerable different shapes of wax as well, so he thinks there will be no form or shape or any quality at all intrinsic to the matter which is the basis of all things; yet it is always united and inseparably connected with some quality or other. (4) And since it is equally without origin or perishing, because it does not arise from something non-existent and will not perish into nothing, it does not lack breath and vitality from eternity, to set it in motion rationally, sometimes in its entirety, at other times in respect of its parts.

E Calcidius 293

(1) And so the universal body, according to the Stoics, is limited and one and whole and substance [*essentia*]. (2) It is whole, because it does not lack any parts; it is one, because its parts are inseparable and mutually coherent with themselves; it is substance, because it is the prime matter of all bodies, and through it, they say, complete and universal reason passes,

just like seed through the genital organs. (3) This reason they take to be an actual craftsman, while the cohering body they take to be without quality, i.e. matter or substance, completely passive and subject to change. (4) But while substance changes, it does not perish either as a whole or by the destruction of its parts, because it is a doctrine common to all philosophers that nothing either comes to be out of nothing or perishes into nothing. For even though all bodies disintegrate by some chance, matter still exists always and the craftsman god, that is, reason, by which it is established both at what time each thing will come to birth and when it will perish. (5) And therefore its birth arises out of existing things and passes away into what exists, because it is bounded by things which abide as immortals, i.e., that by which and that from which the generated thing comes into being.

F Diogenes Laertius 7.137 (*SVF* 2.526, part)

They [the Stoics] use 'world' [*kosmos*] in three ways: of god himself, the peculiarly qualified individual consisting of all substance, who is indestructible and ingenerable, since he is the manufacturer of the world-order, at set periods of time consuming all substance into himself and reproducing it again from himself; they also describe the world-order as 'world'; and thirdly, what is composed out of both [i.e. god and world-order].

☐ Stoic physical theory starts from the presupposition that a single world-order exists. Like their predecessors and contemporary rivals they then asked, what must the world possess as constituents and causal principles which will explain its state at all times? Their answer is given in **B–E**: an active principle, termed 'reason' (*logos*) or 'god' or 'cause' (cf. **55E**), and a passive principle, termed 'unqualified substance' or 'matter' or 'substrate'. God and matter are the foundations of the world, but this is not equivalent to the 'all' (**A**), i.e. literally everything. The world is a 'whole' but it is surrounded by infinite void (see **49A 2**). So the two principles are advanced not as an exhaustive account of everything but as comprising together the 'whole' of the world.

The capacity to act or to be acted upon (**B 1**) was no novelty as the defining characteristic of what exists. In so characterizing their principles, the Stoics could appeal to the Platonic and Aristotelian tradition (see **h** vol. 2); where they differed radically from this tradition was in their insistence that only bodies are capable of acting or of being acted upon (see **45**). The persistence of empirical entities through change (already heavily emphasized in Aristotle's account of primary substances) provides reasons for distinguishing between the matter of some object and its shape or structure (see **28D 10–12**). The Stoics, then, with startling economy, propose to explain all the formal or identifying characteristics of objects by reference to the presence, within their matter, of a divine principle that activates and shapes them.

According to this scheme any object, or the world as a whole, can be analysed as a composite of matter and god. But at this level of generality, neither matter nor god, just by itself, provides particular objects with any definite description; unlike the four elements (see **46–7**), whose form is earth, water etc., the principles, which constitute the elements, are themselves 'without form' (**B 3**). Matter is what you would get if (*per impossibile*) you could remove all the characteristics of an object which make it something particular. God accounts for those characteristics, but does not furnish the matter that must underlie anything with characteristics. Matter needs god in order to be a particular entity, and god needs matter in order that there shall be some entity for god to characterize.

It is important to notice that the two principles are so described that they do not depend upon specific theories about bodies, elements, or any of the detailed apparatus which underpins Stoic analysis of particular phenomena. We are asked, however, in **C–F** to accept the passive principle, matter, as the Stoics' answer to the question, 'What is substance?', and to acknowledge its possessing the properties stated in those passages: it is unqualified, incapable of initiating motion, finite, common to every body, plastic, everlasting, one, whole. Matter, as so described, underlies or provides the foundation for every particular object and thus for the differentiated world as a whole (**E 2**). Since it is uniform, finite, everlasting and unqualified, it makes for a world capable of persisting indefinitely and yet sustaining within itself constant and varied changes.

In **C 4–7** and **D 4** reasons are given for matter's being everlastingly pervaded, moved, and shaped by the active principle. And **C**, by steps which recall Plato's *Phaedrus* and Aristotle, *Physics* VIII, infers that the active principle, as universal efficient cause, is god. Because god or *logos* is always present *in* matter (**B 2**), matter always has 'some quality or other'. The effect of this constant combination of god and matter is to make the world in a sense equivalent to god (**D 3**). Hence the description (**F**) of god as 'the peculiarly qualified individual consisting of all substance' (cf. **28D–J**; **43A 1**). Under god's direction, this substance or matter alternates everlastingly between a state of pure fire (cf. **46G 1**) and a state which is the differentiated world.

The philosophical economy of the two principles is striking. They purport to answer at least three distinct questions about the world. (1) Matter and god together totally comprise the actual ingredients or constituents of the world. (2) Matter and god together provide the two concepts needed for causal explanations, since all particular beings are constructed by god out of matter (cf. **55E**). (3) Matter and god together give a metaphysical foundation for any statement about the world, since to predicate a property of a subject is to describe a quality or disposition of god in matter.

Their historical origin is complex. Reasoning that goes back to Parmenides helps to establish some of their properties (**D 4**, **E 4–5**; cf. **4A** with commentary for Epicurus' use of similar laws); but echoes of Plato and Aristotle are more significant. As the active principle, god is a 'craftsman' (**E 3–4**) recalling the cosmology of the *Timaeus*, with its 'receptacle' which is utterly plastic and functions as the recipient of qualities. Cosmogony apart, there is a general similarity to Aristotle's form and matter. But the principles are distinctively Stoic, not least because they introduce an all-pervasive divine causal agent *immanent* in matter. For details of their specific cosmological functions see **45–8, 52, 54–5**.

45 Body

A Cicero, *Academica* 1.39 (*SVF* 1.90)

[Speaker: the Antiochean Varro] Zeno also differed from the same philosophers [Platonists and Peripatetics] in thinking that it was totally impossible that something incorporeal (to which genus Xenocrates and his predecessors too had said the mind belonged) should be the agent of anything, and that only a body was capable of acting or of being acted upon.

B Sextus Empiricus, *Against the professors* 8.263 (*SVF* 2.363)

According to them [the Stoics] the incorporeal is not of a nature either to act or to be acted upon.

C Nemesius 78,7–79,2 (*SVF* 1.518, part)

(1) He [Cleanthes] also says: no incorporeal interacts with a body, and no body with an incorporeal, but one body interacts with another body. (2) Now the soul interacts with the body when it is sick and being cut, and the body with the soul; thus when the soul feels shame and fear the body turns red and pale respectively. (3) Therefore the soul is a body.

D Nemesius 81,6–10 (*SVF* 2.790, part)

(1) Chrysippus says that death is the separation of soul from body. (2) Now nothing incorporeal is separated from a body. (3) For an incorporeal does not even make contact with a body. (4) But the soul both makes contact with and is separated from the body. (5) Therefore the soul is a body.

E Diogenes Laertius 7.135 (*SVF* 3 Apollodorus 6, part)

According to Apollodorus in his *Physics*, body is what has threefold extension – length, breadth and depth; this is also called solid body.

F Galen, *On incorporeal qualities* 19.483,13–16 (*SVF* 2.381, part)

Why . . . do they [the Stoics] say that what has 'threefold extension together with resistance' is a definition of body alone, and do not also apply this definition to colour, flavour, taste and every remaining attribute?

G Aristocles (Eusebius, *Evangelical preparation* 15.14.1; *SVF* 1.98, part)

He [Zeno] says that fire is the element of what exists, like Heraclitus, and that fire has as its principles god and matter, like Plato. But Zeno says that they are both bodies, both that which acts and that which is acted upon, whereas Plato says that the first active cause is incorporeal. [continued at **46G**]

H Alexander, *On mixture* 225,1–2 (*SVF* 2.310, part)

They [the Stoics] say that god is mixed with matter, pervading all of it and so shaping it, structuring it, and making it into the world.

☐ From the thesis that the world is constituted by matter (passive principle) and god (active principle), it does not directly follow that either matter or god is itself corporeal. The corporeality of both principles, however, is asserted in **G** (cf. **44B 3**, and for matter **44E**), and follows by implication from **A–C**. If only bodies are capable of acting or of being acted upon, god and matter must each be corporeal since they are most basically what can act or be acted upon respectively. It is essential to see that the capacity to act or be acted upon, though peculiar to bodies, is not advanced as a defining characteristic of body *per se*. In confining this capacity to bodies, the Stoics were not redefining body but radically rejecting the thesis, accepted by Plato (cf. **A**, **G**) and Aristotle, that incorporeals can have any causal efficacy. Independent definitions of body were offered (**E**, **F**), thus allowing the Stoics to maintain that only entities which satisfy these definitions are capable of acting or of being acted upon. As for the confinement of existence to bodies (see **27B**), this thesis further requires the corporeality of the principles, since they constitute the complete foundations of the whole world's existence.

E was a standard 'mathematical' definition of body long before the Stoics (cf. Aristotle, *Physics* III.5, 204b20, Euclid, *Elements* 11, Def. 1, defining 'solid'). For their physics they needed to supplement it by adding 'resistance' (**F**) to 'threefold extension' in order to distinguish body from place or empty space (see **49**). The essence of this definition can be traced back at least as far as Plato (*Theaetetus* 155e, *Laws* 10.896d). The Stoic 'principles' plainly satisfy it since they are extended in three dimensions and in contact with one another (**44E 2**).

The notion of 'contact' is central to the Stoic conception of body and of substance (cf. Plato on the materialists, *Sophist* 246a–b). They had Aristotelian precedents for insisting that acting or being acted upon is impossible 'without contact' (*On generation and corruption* 322b22–4), and for holding that contact is necessary between all entities capable of being related to one another by mixing (322b26–29). 'Mixture' is the relationship between the two Stoic 'principles' (**H**; see **48**); but if they were influenced by Aristotelian accounts of acting and being acted upon, they saw no reason to follow Aristotle in exempting celestial physics from bodily mixture and contact. The result of contact between two bodies is 'interaction' (*sumpatheia*), as instanced in the relationship between body and soul

(**C**). (The illustration is a pointed rejection of the Platonic and Aristotelian tradition where soul is an incorporeal agent, cf. **A**.) Such interaction applies no less to the parts of the world as a whole, and is adduced in explanations of their global coherence (*SVF* 2.546, cf. **49**).

Evidence that the Stoic 'principles' are bodies is overwhelming, and reasoning to justify it can easily be reconstructed, as we have shown. However, the thesis is not without difficulty, and some scholars regard it as a misrepresentation of the true position. The chief difficulty might be developed as follows: any identifiable existing object is a body and is constituted as such by *both* the 'principles', god acting in matter. But the two principles are laid down to be inseparably connected with one another (**44D 3**), so they cannot exist separately as bodies. Moreover, since they constitute together something which is a body, they cannot themselves each be bodies. Hence we should say that the principles themselves are 'incorporeal', i.e. only conceptually distinguishable aspects of a single body.

The conclusion of this argument has dubious textual support in a variant reading at **44B 3**. But it cannot be correct. The incorporeality of the principles would render them incapable of satisfying their respective functions, acting and being acted upon (**A–C**). Thus the two distinct functions of god and matter, instead of being the foundation of everything, would turn out to be simply an analytical convenience. In fact either principle, taken on its own, satisfies the definition of body given in **F**. Unlike identifiable physical objects, god and matter are not severally capable *both* of acting *and* of being acted upon. They constitute respectively only one of these ontological functions. But **A** asserts that acting *or* being acted upon is restricted to bodies. There seems no difficulty in supposing that this disjunction holds exclusively for the 'principles' but inclusively for the particular bodies that they jointly constitute. From this it follows that particular bodies are of a dual nature – composites of matter (body under the description 'capable of being acted upon') and god (body under the description, 'capable of acting'), the composite being a 'qualified body' (see **28**). The corporeality of qualities is one of many Stoic theses implied by the corporeality of both 'principles'.

Thus the Stoic 'principles' skilfully combine the hard-line materialism of the Giants in Plato's *Sophist* with his alternative hallmark of existence, 'capacity to act or be acted upon', which was intended by Plato to undermine materialism (**44h** in vol. 2). In the world-order, as will be seen (**46–7**), god and matter are given definite descriptions which make their separate identification easier. But their corporeal existence as 'principles' is not made vacuous by their functioning correlatively and inseparably. It is also presupposed in the doctrine that two bodies can occupy the same place (**48F**).

46 God, fire, cosmic cycle

A Aetius 1.7.33 (*SVF* 2.1027, part)

(1) The Stoics made god out to be intelligent, a designing fire which methodically proceeds towards creation of the world, and encompasses

all the seminal principles according to which everything comes about according to fate, (2) and a breath pervading the whole world, which takes on different names owing to the alterations of the matter through which it passes.

B Diogenes Laertius 7.135–6 (*SVF* 1.102, part)

(1) God, intelligence, fate, and Zeus are all one, and many other names are applied to him. (2) In the beginning all by himself he turned the entire substance through air into water. Just as the sperm is enveloped in the seminal fluid, so god, who is the seminal principle of the world, stays behind as such in the moisture, making matter serviceable to himself for the successive stages of creation. (3) He then creates first of all the four elements, fire, water, air, earth.

C Diogenes Laertius 7.142 (*SVF* 1.102, part)

(1) The world is created when the substance is turned from fire through air into moisture; then the thicker parts of the moisture condense and end up as earth, but the finer parts are thoroughly rarefied, and when they have been thinned still further, they produce fire. (2) Thereafter by mixture plants and animals and the other natural kinds are produced out of these.

D Stobaeus 1.213,15–21 (*SVF* 1.120, part)

(1) Zeno says that the sun and the moon and each of the other stars are intelligent and prudent and have the fieriness of designing fire. (2) For there are two kinds of fire: one is undesigning and converts fuel into itself; the other is designing, causing growth and preservation, as is the case in plants and animals where it is physique and soul respectively. (3) Such is the fire which constitutes the substance of the stars.

E Plutarch, *On Stoic self-contradictions* 1052c–D (*SVF* 2.604, part)

(1) In *On providence* book 1 he [Chrysippus] says that Zeus continues to grow until he has used up everything on himself: 'For since death is the separation of soul from the body, and the soul of the world is not separated but grows continuously until it has completely used up its matter on itself, the world must not be said to die.' . . . (2) In the same book he has written clearly: 'The world alone is said to be self-sufficient because it alone has within itself everything it needs, and it gets its nourishment and growth from itself since its different parts change into one another.'

F Plutarch, *On Stoic self-contradictions* 1053B (*SVF* 2.605, part)

(1) He [Chrysippus] says that when conflagration has occurred through and through, <the world is through and through> alive and animal, but

as it goes out again and condenses, it turns into water and earth and bodily nature. (2) In his *On providence* book 1 he says: 'When the world is fiery through and through, it is directly both its own soul and commanding-faculty. But when, having changed into moisture and the soul which remains therein, it has in a way changed into body and soul so as to be compounded out of these, it has got a different principle.'

G Aristocles (Eusebius, *Evangelical preparation* 15.14.2; *SVF* 1.98, part; continuing **45G**)

[Reporting Stoic doctrine] (1) At certain fated times the entire world is subject to conflagration, and then is reconstituted afresh. (2) But the primary fire is as it were a sperm which possesses the principles [*logoi*] of all things and the causes of past, present, and future events. The nexus and succession of these is fate, knowledge, truth, and an inevitable and inescapable law of what exists. (3) In this way everything in the world is excellently organized as in a perfectly ordered society.

H Origen, *Against Celsus* 4.14 (*SVF* 2.1052, part)

The god of the Stoics, in as much as he is a body, sometimes has the whole substance as his commanding-faculty; this is whenever the conflagration is in being; at other times, when world-order exists, he comes to be in a part of substance.

I Alexander Lycopolis 19,2–4

The argument of Zeno of Citium, who states that the 'all' will be subject to conflagration: 'Everything which burns and has something to burn will burn it completely; now the sun is a fire and will it not burn what it has?' From this he concluded, as he supposed, that the 'all' will be subject to conflagration.

J Diogenes Laertius 7.141 (*SVF* 2.589, part)

They [the Stoics] also suppose that the world is perishable, since it is generated on the same principle as perceptible objects, and anything whose parts are perishable is perishable as a whole; but the parts of the world are perishable, since they change into one another; therefore the world is perishable.

K Eusebius, *Evangelical preparation* 15.18.2 (*SVF* 2.596, part)

On the world's periodic destruction into fire at very long intervals 'destruction' is not used in an unqualified sense by those who hold that the whole world is dissolved into fire, which they call the conflagration. They use the term destruction in place of natural change.

L Plutarch, *On common conceptions* 1075D (*SVF* 1.510)

Cleanthes, moreover, in defending the conflagration, says that the sun <as commanding-faculty> assimilates the moon and the rest of the stars to itself and changes them into itself.

M Philo, *On the indestructibility of the world* 90 (*SVF* 1.511, part)

At the conflagration the world . . . must either change into flame, as Cleanthes thought, or into light, as Chrysippus supposed.

N Plutarch, *On common conceptions* 1067A (*SVF* 2.606)

Whenever they [the Stoics] subject the world to conflagration, no evil at all remains, but the whole is then prudent and wise.

O Seneca, *Letters* 9.16 (*SVF* 2.1065)

What kind of life will a wise man have if he is abandoned by his friends and hurled into prison or isolated in some foreign country or detained on a long voyage or cast out onto a desert shore? It will be like the life of Zeus, at the time when the world is dissolved and the gods have been blended together into one, when nature comes to a stop for a while; he reposes in himself given over to his thoughts. The wise man's behaviour is just like this: he retires into himself, and is with himself.

P Philo, *On the indestructibility of the world* 76–7

Boethus of Sidon and Panaetius . . . gave up the conflagrations and regenerations, and deserted to the holier doctrine of the entire world's indestructibility. Diogenes [of Babylon] too is reported to have subscribed to the doctrine of the conflagration when he was a young man, but to have had doubts in his maturity and suspended judgement.

☐ In determining the properties of the world's active principle, the Stoics laid stress on its intelligence or craftsmanship and its self-directing vitality (**44B–F**). It is these considerations which primarily account for their claim that god is a 'designing fire' (**A 1**) which has as its complete plan for the world 'all the seminal principles'. As an actual constituent of the world, the Stoic god is not a detached Craftsman such as Plato had described, nor is there any metaphorical confusion in combining technology and biology to explain his activity. 'Seminal principles' describe the mode of god's activity in matter, a rational pattern of constructive growth which is both the life of god and the ordered development of all particular things (cf. **43A 2**). The idea is not that god 'seeds' the world, and then leaves its maturation to develop independently. He is in his own identity the causal chain of fate (**B 1**, **G 2**; see **55** and **62**). His own life-history is co-extensive with that of the world which he creates.

There are obvious and intentional links between Stoic physical theory and doctrines of Heraclitus. From him they drew support for the identity of god, *logos*, and fire; and his account of the 'transformations' of fire (KRS 218) has left a clear imprint on Stoic cosmogony. But the 'fieriness' of their active principle is no simple rehash of Heraclitus. Its strong biological and teleological aspects point to Platonic and Aristotelian preconceptions which may appear awkwardly linked to a fiery active principle. Fire, as a causal agent, naturally suggests a mechanistic method of explanation, and that seems to be attached uneasily, if not superfluously, to the providential intelligence and creativity the Stoics ascribe to god. Standard summaries of Stoic cosmogony (e.g. **C**) can give the impression that transformations of fire are sufficient by themselves to explain the origin and present order of things. If they are not sufficient, what reason do we have for thinking them even necessary?

Quite certainly the description of the Stoic god as fire is authentic. But the evidence for the two Stoic principles (see **44**) strongly implies that this description should be analysed strictly as a reference to the activity of god *in matter*. In abstraction from matter (an impossibility) god is not fire but an intelligent energizing power; this is a body but not one which corresponds to any empirical property. If this is correct, it becomes possible to associate the fieriness and providential intelligence of god without redundancy. 'Designing fire', which must be distinguished from the fire of ordinary experience (**D 2**), is the necessary consequence of god's constant conjunction with matter. He acts *in the form* of fire, but fire on its own is not sufficient to explain the nature of his activity. Hence the elaborate description of **A 1**. 'Breath pervading the whole world' (**A 2**) is Chrysippus' favoured specification of god's activity (see **47I 1**, **L 1**, and for further complex accounts of god, **54A–B**).

The 'designing fire' is the vital principle in living things (**D 2**), and its sustaining powers throughout all nature, with which it is regularly identified, were argued at length by Cleanthes (see **47C**). Since god and matter are everlasting and always conjoined, the universe never ceases to possess vital heat. But the early Stoics did not maintain that the *present* world-order (*kosmos*) is ungenerated and indestructible. Its existence, like that of its parts, is finite (**J**), and this thesis was vividly, if strangely, reinforced by reflection on the consequences of making fire the mode of god's activity. The present world-order will end in a total conflagration, activated by the sun (**I, L**), but will then be reconstituted again as the conflagration subsides (**G 1**). On this conception (which was questioned or rejected by some later Stoics, **P**), the universe is a cyclical process which alternates for ever between an ordered system, of which we ourselves are parts, and a state of pure fire, or 'light' in Chrysippus' interesting formulation (**M**).

Details concerning the world's everlasting recurrence will be studied later (see **52**). Two general points about it need to be noted now. First, it provides a subtle answer to the frequently stated objection that a providential deity (so strongly emphasized by Stoics, see **54**) would never destroy the excellent world he has created. Plato had insisted on this point in the *Timaeus* (41a–b); and Chrysippus' close reading and appropriation of that book is plain from **E 2** (cf. *Timaeus* 33c), which refers to the self-sufficiency of the world in the most extended sense of *kosmos*: i.e. the infinite sequence of finite world-orders and conflagrations (cf.

44F). Hence the end of the present world will not be a 'destruction' in an unqualified sense (**K**); it introduces no discontinuity in the life of the world at its most extended, but only a 'natural change'. The early Stoics adopt an option, considered and rejected by Aristotle (*On the heavens* 1.10), whereby there is not an everlasting single world-order but an everlasting succession of worlds which manifest exactly the same order. Secondly, the duration of any world-order and the conflagrations which precede and follow its existence are presented as phases in the life of god. The conflagration completely instantiates god's providence (**O**; cf. **28O 4**), and so what brings the present world-order to an end is that state of the universe which, in its total goodness and wisdom (**N**), will ensure the reconstitution of world-order in the best possible way. Thus the early Stoics sought to reconcile empirical evidence of the present world's long-term destructibility (see vol. 2 note on **J**) and a commitment to god's everlasting providence.

A world-order begins when the universal conflagration, a state of pure fire, subsides by changing to hot air and then condenses into moisture (**B 2, C 1**). This moist state of things in turn undergoes further changes which finally result in the production of the four distinct elements (see **47A**). Viewed outwardly the processes appear mechanical (as presented in **C**), but they are actually a self-transformation of god (**B 2–3, F 2, H**). The model we are offered for understanding this is biological, and specifically, anthropomorphic. The soul of a man is the rational 'commanding-faculty' which pervades and governs his body (see **53G–H**); god is the rational commanding-faculty of the universe. During the conflagration the universe and its divine soul or commanding-faculty are completely coextensive (**F 2, H**); in this state of pure fire the universe has nothing analogous to a human body. But at the onset of cosmogony the divine fire contracts to become a fiery 'sperm' or 'soul' (**B 2, F 2, G 2**) within a universe whose liquefaction, consequential on the subsidence of fire, is analogous to the growth of an animal's body. As the universe alternates between conflagration and world-order, so god alternates from being coextensive as fire with the whole universe to becoming a form of the fiery element of a world-order which is differentiated into three other elemental constituents (cf. **H**).[1] When the conflagration recurs, this differentiation comes to an end; the universe once again ceases to have a 'body', which is another way of saying that 'Zeus withdraws into providence' (cf. **O; 28O 4**). By withdrawing from the world-order, he brings it to an end, and occupies that state of forethought which will result in the germination of the next world-order.

In their transmitted form these theories seem stronger in imagination than in precision. But the imagination is powerful, and in a sense, compelling. On materialist foundations the Stoics offer a theory of events which seeks to unify the different explanatory forces of optimistic theology, goal-directed rational processes, a biological model of change, and a rigorous causal nexus.

---

[1] We say 'a form of the fiery element' because the nature of god seems to be fully instantiated only in the 'designing fire' (**A 1, D**). There is a problem (see e.g. **B 3**) about the relationship between designing fire and the element fire. This will be taken up in the next section.

47 Elements, breath, tenor, tension

A Stobaeus 1.129,2–130,13 (*SVF* 2.413, part)

(1) Chrysippus has the following views on the elements formed out of substance, following Zeno the leader of the school. (2) He says that there are four elements <fire, air, water, earth, out of which everything is composed – animals,> plants, the whole world and its contents – and that they are dissolved into these. (3) The element *par excellence* is so called because the remainder are composed out of it in the first place by alteration and into it lastly everything is diffused and dissolved, but it does not admit of diffusion or resolution into something else . . . (4) On the basis of this account fire is called an element *sui generis*, since it is not with another one; but according to the earlier account [i.e. (1) above], it is constitutive along with others, since the first change to occur is the one from fire into air by condensation, and the second ensuing from this into water, and the third, with water being still more compressed on the same principle, into earth. Reciprocally, from the dissolution and diffusion of earth, the first diffusion is into water, the second from water into air, the third and last into fire. (5) Everything of fiery form is called fire, the aeriform is called air, and similarly with the rest. (6) Element, then, according to Chrysippus has three meanings. (7) First, it means fire, because out of it the remaining elements are composed by alteration and into it they get their resolution. (8) Secondly, it means the four elements, fire, air, water, earth, since all other things are composed by means of a particular one of these or more than one of these or all of these – all four in the case of animals and all terrestrial compounds, two in the case of the moon, which is composed by means of fire and air, and just one, in the case of the sun, which is composed by means of fire; for the sun is pure fire. (9) On the third account, element is said to be that which is primarily so composed that it causes generation from itself methodically up to a terminus and from that receives resolution into itself by the like method.

B Diogenes Laertius 7.137 (*SVF* 2.580, part)

(1) Fire is the hot one [element], water the moist, air the cold and earth the dry . . . (2) Uppermost is the fire called 'aether' in which the sphere of the fixed stars is first created, and next the sphere of the planets. After this the air, and then the water, and as foundation of everything the earth, which is at the centre of all things.

C Cicero, *On the nature of the gods* 2.23–5, 28–30

[The Stoic spokesman Balbus] (1) It is a fact that all things which undergo nurture and growth contain within themselves a power of heat without which they could not be nurtured and grow. For everything which is hot and fiery is roused and activated by its own movement; but a thing which is nourished and grows has a definite and regular movement; as long as this remains in us, so long sensation and life remain, but when the heat has been chilled and extinguished, we ourselves die and are extinguished. (2) By the following evidence too Cleanthes shows how great is the power of heat within every body: he says there is no food so heavy that it is not digested in the course of a night and a day; and even in the remains of food which nature excretes heat is present. Moreover, the veins and arteries do not cease to pulsate by a flame-like movement, and it has often been observed that when a living thing's heart is torn out, it beats so rapidly that it resembles the swiftness of fire. Therefore every living thing, whether animal or vegetable, is alive on account of the heat enclosed within it. From this it must be understood that the element heat has within itself a vital power which pervades the whole world. (3) We shall recognize this more readily from a more detailed account of this all-penetrating fieriness in its entirety. All parts of the world (I shall speak only of the greatest) are supported and maintained by heat. This can be seen first in the element earth . . . (4) It follows from this that, since all parts of the world are maintained by heat, the world itself too has been preserved over so long a time by a comparable and like element – and all the more so because it must be understood that this hot and fiery entity is extended in every nature in such a way that it contains the power of reproduction and the cause of generation, since it is that by which all living things, including those whose roots are sustained by the earth, must be brought to birth and grow. (5) There is therefore an element which sustains the whole world and protects it, and it certainly does not lack sensation and reason. For every nature which is not isolated and simple but conjoined and composite must have within itself some commanding-faculty, such as intelligence in man, and something resembling intelligence in beasts, from which desires for things arise; trees too and plants are thought to have a commanding-faculty in their roots . . . So it must be the case that the element which contains the commanding-faculty of the whole of nature is the best of all things and the most worthy of having authority and power over everything. (6) Now we see that there is sensation and reason in the parts of the world (for there is nothing in all the world which is not a part of the whole world). Therefore they must be in that part which contains the world's commanding-faculty, and certainly they must be sharper and greater. So the world must be wise, and that element which holds all things together in its embrace must be perfectly and outstandingly rational. Therefore the world must be god, and all the power of the world must be sustained by a divine element.

D Nemesius 164,15–18 (*SVF* 2.418)

The Stoics say that some of the elements are active and others passive: air and fire are active, earth and water passive.

E Galen, *On natural faculties* 106,13–17 (*SVF* 2.406)

Since they [the Stoics] would explain the reciprocal change of even the elements themselves by certain expansions and contractions, it was reasonable for them to make the hot and the cold active principles.

F Galen, *On bodily mass* 7.525,9–14 (*SVF* 2.439, part)

The chief proponents of the sustaining power, such as the Stoics, make what sustains one thing, and what is sustained something different: the breathy substance is what sustains, and the material substance what is sustained. And so they say that air and fire sustain, and earth and water are sustained.

G Plutarch, *On common conceptions* 1085C–D (*SVF* 2.444, part)

They [the Stoics] say that earth and water sustain neither themselves nor other things, but preserve their unity by participation in a breathy and fiery power; but air and fire because of their tensility can sustain themselves, and by blending with the other two provide them with tension and also stability and substantiality.

H Galen, *On Hippocrates' and Plato's doctrines* 5.3.8 (*SVF* 2.841, part)

[Reporting and objecting to Chrysippus] This breath [i.e. the one which constitutes the soul's commanding-faculty] possesses two parts, elements or conditions, which are blended with one another through and through, the cold and hot, or if one wished to describe them by different names taken from their substances, air and fire; and it also acquires some moisture from the bodies in which it dwells.

I Alexander, *On mixture* 224,14–17, 23–6 (*SVF* 2.442, part)

[Arguing against the Stoics] (1) Moreover, if breath composed of fire and air passes through all bodies by being blended with them all, and each body has existence attached to it from breath, how could there still be any simple body? . . . (2) Also, what is the simultaneous movement of breath in opposite directions, by which it sustains everything in which it is present, since, in their own words, it is a breath which moves simultaneously out of itself and into itself. And by what form of movement does it take place?

J Nemesius 70,6–71,4

(1) Now if the soul is a body of any kind at all, even if it is of the rarest consistency, what is it that sustains it? (2) For it has been proved that every body needs something to sustain it, which is an endless regress until we reach something incorporeal. (3) If they should say, as the Stoics do, that there exists in bodies a kind of tensile movement which moves simultaneously inwards and outwards, the outward movement producing quantities and qualities and the inward one unity and substance, we must ask them (since every movement issues from some power), what this power is and in what substance it consists.

K Galen, *On muscular movement* 4.402,12–403,10 (*SVF* 2.450, part)

(1) Imagine a lofty bird which appears to be staying in the same place. Should one describe it as motionless, as though it happened to be suspended from above, or as moving upwards to the same extent as the weight of its body carries it downwards? I think the latter is more correct. If you killed the bird or destroyed its muscular tension, you would see it fall quickly to the ground. That makes it plain that the bird was evenly counterbalancing its innate downward inclination due to the weight of its body by the upward motion resulting from its soul's tension. (2) This is not the time to consider whether in all such cases the body moves now up and now down undergoing contrary movements in turn, while appearing to stay in the same place owing to the speed and suddenness of the changes and the minute distance of the movements, or whether it really occupies a single place during the whole time.

L Alexander, *On mixture* 223,25–36 (*SVF* 2.441, part)

[Arguing against the Stoics] (1) In this case [i.e. the impossibility of water being completely mixed with breath, as Alexander asserts], how could it still be true that the universe is unified and sustained by a breath which pervades the whole of it? (2) Furthermore, it would be reasonable for the sustainment generated by breath to be similar in all bodies. But this is not so. For some bodies are continuous, others discrete. It is more reasonable, therefore, to say that each of them is sustained and unified with itself by its own form, by virtue of each thing's essence, and that their mutual interaction is preserved both by their participation in matter and by the nature of the divine body which surrounds them, rather than by the bond of breath. (3) What too is the tension of breath which binds bodies together so that they both have continuity in relation to their own parts and are connected with the bodies adjacent to them?

M Plutarch, *On Stoic self-contradictions* 1053F–1054B (*SVF* 2.449)

(1) In his books *On tenors* he [Chrysippus] again says that tenors are nothing but currents of air: 'It is by these that bodies are sustained. The sustaining air is responsible for the quality of each of the bodies which are sustained by tenor; in iron this quality is called hardness, in stone density, and in silver whiteness.'... (2) Yet they maintain that matter, which is of itself inert and motionless, is everywhere the substrate for qualities, and that qualities are breaths and aeriform tensions which give form and shape to the parts of matter in which they come to be.

N Galen, *Medical introduction* 14.726,7–11 (*SVF* 2.716, part)

There are two kinds of innate breath, the physical kind and the psychic kind. Some people [i.e. the Stoics] also posit a third, the tenor kind. The breath which sustains stones is of the tenor kind, the one which nurtures animals and plants is physical, and the psychic breath is that which, in animate beings, makes animals capable of sensation and of moving in every way.

O Diogenes Laertius 7.138–9 (including *SVF* 2.634)

(1) The world is directed by intelligence and providence, . . . since intelligence pervades every part of it, just like the soul in us. (2) But it pervades some parts to a greater extent and others to a lesser degree. Through some parts it passes as tenor, as through bones and sinews. Through others as intelligence, as through the commanding-faculty. (3) So the whole world, which is an animal and animate and rational, has the aether as its commanding-faculty, as Antipater of Tyre says in his *On the world* book 8. (4) But Chrysippus in his *On providence* book 1 and Posidonius in his *On gods* say that the world's commanding-faculty is the heaven, and Cleanthes the sun. Yet Chrysippus in the same book has a rather different account – the purest part of the aether; this they say, as primary god, passes perceptibly as it were through the things in the air and through all animals and plants, and through the earth itself by way of tenor.

P Philo, *Allegories of the laws* 2.22–3 (*SVF* 2.458, part)

(1) Intelligence . . . has many powers, the tenor kind, the physical, the psychic, the rational, the calculative . . . (2) Tenor is also shared by lifeless things, stones and logs, and our bones, which resemble stones, also participate in it. (3) Physique also extends to plants, and in us there are things like plants – nails and hair. Physique is tenor in actual motion. (4) Soul is physique which has also acquired impression and impulse. This is also shared by irrational animals.

Q Philo, *God's immutability* 35–6 (*SVF* 2.458, part)

(1) He [God] bound some bodies by tenor, others by physique, others by soul, and others by rational soul. (2) In stones, and logs which have been severed from their physical connexion, he created tenor which is the strongest bond. This is breath which turns back towards itself. It begins to extend itself from the centre to the extremities, and having made contact with the outer surfaces it bends back again until it returns to the same place from which it first set out. (3) This continuous double course of tenor is indestructible.

R Philo, *Questions and answers on Genesis* 2.4 (*SVF* 2.802)

(1) Why does God command that the ark be tarred inside and outside?... (2) Everything that is sustained by glue is immediately forced into a natural union. (3) Now our body, which is composed of many parts, is united externally and internally, and it holds firm by its own tenor. And the higher tenor of these parts is the soul: being at the centre, it moves everywhere, right to the surface and from the surface it returns to the centre. The result is that a single animate nature is enveloped by a double bond, thus being fitted to a stronger tenor and union. (4) This ark, then, is smeared with tar inside and outside for the reason mentioned.

S Simplicius, *On Aristotle's Categories* 237,25–238,20 (*SVF* 2.393, part)

(1) It is worthwhile to understand the Stoics' usage in regard to these terms. In the opinion of some people, they reverse Aristotle by taking character [*diathesis*] to be more stable than tenor [*hexis*]. (2) What gives rise to such an opinion is not, however, a difference between these terms in virtue of differing stability, in Stoic doctrine, but a difference over characters. For they say that tenors can be intensified and relaxed, but characters are not susceptible to intensification or relaxation. So they call the straightness of a stick a character, even though it is easily alterable since it can be bent. For the straightness could not be relaxed or intensified, nor does it admit of more or less, and so it is a character. For the same reason the virtues are characters, not because of their stable feature but because they are not susceptible to intensification or increase. But expertises, although they are resistant to change, are not characters. (3) The Stoics also seem to think that tenor pertains to the general scope of the form, but character to the goal of the form and its fullest realization, whether it should be changed and modified, as with the straightness of the stick, or not. (4) There is the further question of whether perhaps state [*schesis*], in Stoic usage, is the same as the Aristotelian character [*diathesis*], differing from tenor [*hexis*] by reference to ease or difficulty of its destruction. But they do not agree on this either.

Aristotle says that unreliable health is a character; but the Stoics do not admit that health of any kind is a state. In their view it has the feature of a tenor. For they take states to be marked out by acquired conditions, tenors by their intrinsic activities. (5) So tenors, for them, are not specified by their duration or strength, but by a certain peculiarity and mark. Just as things with roots are rooted in different degrees but have the single common feature of holding to the earth, so tenor has the same meaning in things which change with difficulty and in those which change easily. It is a general truth that many things which are qualified generically are defective in the feature by which they are specified, such as sour wine, bitter almonds, Molossian and Maltese dogs. These all carry the mark of their genus, though to a slight and relaxed extent, and their tenor persists in a single condition so far as its actual defining terms are concerned; but frequently it is easy to change for some other reason.

T Plutarch, *On the principle of cold* 948D–E, 949B (*SVF* 2.430, part)

[Reporting Stoic doctrine] (1) Since fire is simultaneously hot and bright, the nature opposite to fire must be both cold and dark; for as dark is the opposite of bright, so is cold of hot, and as dark confuses sight, so cold has the same effect on touch. But heat diffuses the sense of the person touching, just as brightness does that of the person seeing. Therefore what is primarily dark in its nature is also primarily cold. Nor have poets failed to notice that what is primarily dark is air . . . (2) Moreover, freezing, which is the most extreme and violent effect of cold on bodies, is a case of water being acted upon and of air acting. For by itself water is fluid, and not stiff or solid; but when compressed by air under the agency of its cold it becomes tight and compact.

☐ Four distinct elements, as has already been seen (**46B 2, C**), are not, as they are in Aristotle's cosmology, permanent features of the Stoic universe, but the basic qualifications of matter throughout the duration of each temporally limited world-order (**A 8**). Within this quartet, however, fire occupies a special status (**A 3–4, 7, 9**). It is the element *par excellence* (**A 3**; cf. **45G**), and a permanent feature of the universe. Its own transformations, co-extensive with the designing activities of god or reason, bring about the alternating phases of the cosmic cycle, and they also control the beginning and the end of the other elements' reciprocal changes within the world (**A 4**). The Stoics acknowledged that any one of their four elements embraced a wide range of phenomena (**A 5**). The elements function as class names which denote generic properties, hot, cold etc. (**B 1**), admitting of continuous specific variation. This implies that we were correct to identify the full activity of god in the world-order with 'a form of the fiery element' (see **46** commentary). Both 'designing' and 'undesigning' fire (**46D 2**) are species of 'the hot', so there is no problem about finding god instantiated in the element fire, provided that element be also allowed to accommodate manifestations of heat which are not divine creative activity. Needing god to be active throughout the world-order, the Stoics did not follow Aristotle in nominating the aether as a fifth and peculiarly divine element. But they took over that term, with its Aristotelian connotations, for the celestial fire, and regarded it as the form of matter which quintessentially expresses god's activity (**B 2**, **O 4**; cf. **46D 3** and **28O 4**). Each element has a natural place assigned to it within the world (**B 2**, see **49J**), but transformations between them take place continually by condensation and rarefaction (**E**).

The special status of 'vital heat' or 'designing fire' is indicated in a long argument which goes back in essence to Cleanthes (**C**). This shows once again the powerful influence of biology on Stoic physics. Starting from the commonplace medical claim (**C 1**) that innate heat is the principle of all forms of life, Cleanthes took the much bolder step of citing evidence for the ubiquitous 'sustaining power' of heat throughout the whole of the world (**C 2–3**), and concluded from this that the world itself owes its coherence to that vital power. The next stage of his argument exploits an assumed connexion between the common vital principles of animate beings and the world itself (**C 5–6**). Men or animals have intelligence or quasi-intelligence as their 'commanding-faculty' (for accounts of this term see **53**). But they are *parts* of the world; and we should take it that the world itself possesses pre-eminent intelligence as its commanding-faculty. From this most dubious step, Cleanthes concludes that the world is a living being identical with god (or more strictly, having god as its commanding-faculty, cf. **44F**; **46H**).

The main fallacies in this argument from microcosm to macrocosm were probably inspired by Zeno (see **54G 9**). Its general effects for Stoic physics are more interesting. They recognized that the coherence of the world-order is a fact requiring explanation. The considerations of **C** persuaded them to seek the answer in a pervasive power which makes intelligent use of its own cohesive force to energize and sustain all parts of the world. This was a highly original extension of the biological conception of 'vital heat'.

In Cleanthes' argument no vitalizing or 'sustaining' power is attributed to any element besides fire. That view was modified in the more complex physics which we may attribute to Chrysippus. His predecessors had already identified the soul or vital principle of animals with *pneuma*, 'breath' which is hot air (cf. **53**). Following their analogical reasoning from microcosm to macrocosm, Chrysippus opted for 'breath' rather than heat on its own as the sustaining principle of the world. This prompted the distinction between 'active' and 'passive' elements (**D**; **55F**), which thus provided a neat description of the workings of god and matter, the 'active' and 'passive' principles (**44B**), within the world-order. Chrysippus had an Aristotelian precedent for the 'activity' of hot *and* cold, and the identification of dry and moist with 'matter' (*On generation and corruption* 329b24); but Stoic elements, unlike those of Aristotle, are characterized by only one basic property, hot for fire, cold for air etc. (**B**), though this does not exclude each element from having secondary, perceptible characteristics which also distinguish it from the others (cf. **T**).[1] Medical theory and Aristotelian biology had made much of the 'vital' powers of 'breath', but the

---

[1] Theophrastus differed from Aristotle, and anticipated the Stoics, in assigning cold to air (*On fire* 25–26), and he also treated the hot and cold as 'principles' (*ibid.* 8). In the physics of his successor, Strato, hot and cold are recorded as the 'elements' (Stobaeus 1.124,18).

extension of these to the world itself, as with the 'vital heat' of Cleanthes, was a Stoic innovation.

'Breath' consists of a 'through-and-through blending' of its two constitutive elements (**H**), which means that any portion of it, irrespective of size, is characterized by hot and cold. Chrysippus deduced from this that 'breath' is a dynamic continuum, in part expanding from its heat (fire) and in part contracting from its cold (air) (**E, T**). This complex motion was described as 'tension' or 'tensile movement' (**G, J, K, L 3**). It invokes the idea of elasticity expressed by the verb *teinein*, 'to stretch'. The special character of this motion is its *simultaneous* activity in opposite directions, outwards and inwards (**I 2, J**), whereby we should understand fire and air to be pulling, as it were, against each other in the blend which they constitute. Philo probably refers to the same conception, only more elaborately, when he speaks of the 'breath' within stones and logs as extending from the centre to the extremities and back again (**Q 2, R 3**). This need not imply alternating rather than simultaneous contrary movements, as his image of the double race-course (**Q 3**) may suggest. But 'tensile movement' could be interpreted as a very rapid alternation of contrary motions by those who put the Stoic theory to work for their own purposes (**K**).

In this evidence Galen may be modifying the Stoics' specification of simultaneity, but his use of 'tension' as a plausible explanation of muscular activity casts light on its most important function in Stoicism. Galen wants to explain how a hovering bird can *appear* to be at rest. He suggests that in fact the bird may be counterbalancing its downward movement, due to body weight, by an alternating succession of muscular movements which carry it upwards, so that it is imperceptibly moving up and down but giving the appearance of immobility. Thus the Stoics explained the apparent stability and properties of everyday objects by the 'tensile movement' of their constituent elements.[1] Though primarily an attribute of fire or air, and the compound 'breath' which they constitute, tensility is distributed to the passive elements, earth and water, through their being permeated by 'breath' (**G**). The Stoics expressed this causal relationship between the active 'breath' and the passive 'matter' (earth and water) by exploiting forms of the verb (*sun*)*echein*, 'to have' or 'to hold' (together), which we translate by 'sustain'. The coherence of earth and water, the elements which have absolute weight, is due to their being 'sustained' by the weightless elements, air and fire (**G, 49J**). Thus earth and water become the material base or substrate of objects. What something is, its duration, dimensions, and qualities, are all products of the 'sustaining' powers of 'breath' (**I 1, J, M 2; 55F, H**).

Within this scheme, it is to be noted that fire or heat retains its primacy as the activating and shaping principle. The quantities and qualities of a thing are due to the 'outward' tensile movement (**J**), and this should refer to the expansive character of fire, with cold or air responsible for the stabilizing movement inwards. If Chrysippus sometimes spoke of *air* currents (**M 1**) as the causes of a thing's qualities, he can hardly have meant anything different from 'breaths'

---

[1] Cleanthes made some use of 'tension', but its full development, like that of 'breath', was probably due to Chrysippus. They could invoke the authority of Heraclitus, who had explained the structure of a bow or a lyre as a result of 'back-turning' (or 'back-stretching') harmony (KRS 209).

(**M 2**), in which fire is an approximately equal constituent. But we should not suppose that the opposite motions of air and fire within 'breath' are always equal to one another. If that were so, the Stoics could not explain, as they did, all qualities and differentiated substances by reference to 'breath'. The Stoic conception of 'through-and-through blending' (see **48**) sets no limit to the relative quantities of its constituents; so we may reasonably conjecture that the proportions of air to fire in 'breath' vary in relation to the different qualifications they generate in matter; and matter itself, as constituted by earth and water, must be regarded as a further variable.

The 'sustaining' or, as it may equally well be called, the defining quality of a differentiated body was given the term 'tenor', which in Greek is the verbal noun *hexis* for the verb *echein*, 'to have' or 'to hold'. The 'tenor' of something is its constitutive 'breath', e.g. the hardness of iron or the whiteness of silver (**M 1**). 'Tenor' thus constitutes the defining characteristics of classes of things whose members admit of specific variations (**S 3, 5**): if two wines differ in their sweetness, or two dogs in their size or responsiveness to training, these are not differences of 'tenor'. The specific differences between such things, and indeed all their properties, are due to 'breath'; but 'tenor' refers to those essential features which make something a wine, a dog etc., and corresponds to the Stoic view of 'common qualities' (see **28**). 'Tenor' differs from 'character', e.g. straightness or the virtues, in accommodating things which may be imperfect specimens of their kind or possess its features to a varying degree (**S 2–3, 5**; see also **60J** and commentary), and also from 'state', which is strictly confined to (**54**), or at least includes (**60J 2**), acquired characteristics not intrinsic to the nature of the things which come to possess them.

There is clearly a measure of linguistic arbitrariness in these distinctions; the Stoics themselves use the term 'tenor' in the extended sense indicated above, and also more restrictively. On the one hand it is 'tenor' which differentiates all 'unified' things from those bodies which exist merely by contact (like a ship) or by separation (like an army, see **28M**). Thus 'tenor' refers to the pervading 'breath' which accounts for the unitary existence of natural substances. But 'tenor' is also used, within the class of 'unified' things, to mark off the 'sustaining' principle of inanimate substances (stones etc.) from that of plants and animate beings (**N, O 2, Q**). A passage from Philo (**P**) shows how the two uses of 'tenor' are really only differences of context. The 'breath' which forms the unifying principle of a plant is called 'physique' (*phusis*), but this is still a kind of 'tenor', differing from that of a stone, say, in giving the plant its inherent capacity to grow. Similarly, with animate things, 'soul' is their unifying principle. Their bodies have their own 'tenor', but in the final analysis the 'tenor' of every animal's bodily constituents is due to the all-penetrating soul (**R**).

'Breath', whatever the degree of its tension, is the vehicle of divine intelligence (**O 1, P 1**). But it only imparts intelligence to specific portions of matter where it is most pervasive (**O 2**). Within the world-order it has two related functions. It is the principle of internal coherence for individual bodies; and because it permeates everything without interruption, it makes the world as a whole a single coherent body (**L**; cf. **49J** on air and fire).

48 Mixture

A Diogenes Laertius 7.151 (*SVF* 2.479)

According to Chrysippus in his *Physics* book 3, blendings occur through and through, and not by surface contact and juxtaposition. For a little wine cast into the sea will coextend with it for a while, and will then be blended with it.

B Plutarch, *On common conceptions* 1078E (*SVF* 2.480, part)

Chrysippus says: 'Nothing stops a single drop of wine from tempering the sea'; and, to stop us being amazed at this, he says that in the blending the drop will extend through the whole world.

C Alexander, *On mixture* 216,14–218,6 (*SVF* 2.473)

(1) Chrysippus has the following theory of blending: he first assumes that the whole of substance is unified by a breath which pervades it all, and by which the universe is sustained and stabilized and made interactive with itself. (2) Then, as for the bodies mixed together in this substance, he argues that mixtures occur by juxtaposition of two or more substances put together in the same place, and juxtaposed with one another 'by joining', as he says, while they each preserve their own substance and quality at their surface contact in such a juxtaposition, as occurs, one may say, with beans and grains of wheat when they are placed side by side. (3) Other mixtures occur by through-and-through fusion of the substances themselves and their intrinsic qualities, which are destroyed together, as he says happens in the case of medical drugs when the things mixed together undergo mutual destruction and another body is generated out of them. (4) Other mixtures occur, he argues, when certain substances and their qualities are mutually coextended through and through, with the original substances and their qualities being preserved in such a mixture; this kind of mixture he calls specifically 'blending'; ... for the capacity to be separated again from one another is a peculiarity of blended substances, and this only occurs if they preserve their own natures in the mixture. (5) He tries to support the existence of these different mixtures through the common conceptions, and says that we take these from nature as excellent criteria of truth: (6) we certainly have one impression for the bodies composed by joining, and a different one for those that are fused and destroyed together, and another for those that are blended and mutually coextended through and through so that they each preserve their own nature; we would not have these different impressions if all things, however they were mixed, lay side by side one another by joining. (7) He believes that such a coextension of blended

bodies occurs when they pass through one another, so that no part among them fails to participate in everything contained in such a blended mixture; otherwise the result would no longer be blending but juxtaposition. (8) The supporters of this theory advance as grounds for their belief in its truth the fact that many bodies preserve their own qualities whether they are present in evidently larger or smaller masses (as can be seen in the case of frankincense: when burnt it becomes rarefied, but it preserves its own quality over a very large extent), and the further fact that many bodies which by themselves cannot advance to a certain size do so with the assistance of others. Gold certainly, through being mixed with certain drugs, can be spread and rarefied to an extent which is not possible when it is simply beaten . . . (9) Since all this is so, they say there is nothing remarkable in the fact that certain bodies, when assisted by one another, are so mutually unified through and through that while being preserved together with their own qualities they are mutually coextended as wholes through and through, even if some of them are small in bulk and incapable by themselves of spreading so far and preserving their own qualities. In this way too a measure of wine is blended with a large amount of water and assisted by it to attain an extension of that size. (10) As clear evidence of this being so they make use of the fact that the soul, which has its own individual existence, just like the body which receives it, pervades the whole of the body while preserving its own substance in the mixture with it. For none of the soul lacks a share in the body which possesses the soul. It is just the same too with the physique of plants, and also with the tenor of things which are sustained by tenor. (11) Moreover they say that fire as a whole passes through iron as a whole while each of them preserves its own substance. (12) Of the four elements they say that one pair, fire and air, which are rare, light, and tensile, pass as wholes through wholes through the other pair, earth and water, which are dense and heavy and lack tension, both pairs preserving their own nature and continuity.

D Stobaeus 1.155,5–11 (*SVF* 2.471, part)

[Reporting Stoic doctrine] That the qualities of blended constituents persist in such blendings is quite evident from the fact that they are frequently separated from one another artificially. If one dips an oiled sponge into the wine which has been blended with water, it will separate the water from the wine since the water runs up into the sponge.

E Plutarch, *On common conceptions* 1078B–D (including *SVF* 2.465, part)

(1) If blending occurs in the way they [the Stoics] insist, the constituents must come to be in one another, and the same thing must both be enveloped by being in the other and by accommodating it envelop it.

But on the other hand neither of these is possible, since the blending forces both things to pervade each other and no part to lack any part but every part to be filled with all. (2) This is the point presumably at which the leg made famous in Arcesilaus' lectures arrives stamping with derision on their absurdities. For if blendings are through and through, what prevents not only the armada of Antigonus, as Arcesilaus said, from sailing through the leg that has been severed, putrefied, thrown into the sea and dissolved, but the 1,200 triremes of Xerxes along with the 300 of the Greeks from having a battle within the leg?

F Themistius, *On Aristotle's Physics* 104,9–19 (including *SVF* 2.468)

(1) But watch out that we do not give place too glorious a status. You should also consider the arguments on the opposite side, which not only add nothing to it but destroy it altogether. For, they say, if you undertake ... to define place, you will be brought round to conceding that it does not exist. To begin with, what genus will you assign place to? Isn't it obvious, to body? For place has three dimensions. (2) But it will thus encounter what is completely out of place! For one body will pass through another body through and through, and two bodies will occupy the same place. For if both the place and what has come to be in it are bodies and both are of equal dimensions, one body will be in another equal body. This last belongs to the doctrines of Chrysippus and Zeno's followers, but the ancients reduced it to a self-evident impossibility.

☐ 'Blend' and 'pervade' were two terms connected with 'breath' in the preceding testimonies: 'breath' is constituted by the 'through-and-through' blending of air and fire (**47H**); 'breath' blends with the inert elements, earth and water (**47G, I 1**); 'breath' pervades the whole universe (**47L 1**, cf. **O**). 'Breath' is the vehicle of god, the active principle or *logos*, and since only bodies can act upon bodies (**45A–C**), its causal efficacy in the whole world was taken to require its presence throughout all substance or matter. Given such assumptions, the Stoics had to offer a physical theory which would explain the constant conjunction everywhere of 'breath' and matter. They found this in a species of mixture which they called 'blending'.

The theory appears to have been developed with deliberate reference and partial opposition to Aristotle (*On generation and corruption* 1.10). Like him the Stoics distinguished mechanical combinations, which they called 'juxtapositions' (**A, C 2**), from 'blending'. The constituents of a 'juxtaposition' are related to one another purely by surface contact. They undergo no essential change, and can be removed from the 'juxtaposition' with their essential qualities intact. In 'fusion' (**C 3**), which corresponds loosely to Aristotle's account of 'blending', the constituents lose their own properties and produce a compound which differs from each of them. According to Aristotle blending can only take place when the constituents are of roughly equal power. He explicitly denies that a drop of wine can be blended with a very large quantity of water (*On generation* *and corruption* 328a26–8). In such a case, he says, the wine loses its vinous property, perishes, and becomes part of the total volume of water. The Stoic distinction between 'fusion' and 'blending' attempts to locate an intermediate form of mixture which will provide a different explanation for the mixture of unequal constituents such as the wine and water in Aristotle's example.

As **C 4** makes plain, 'blending' resembles 'fusion' in that the constituents are related to one another 'through and through' and not merely at their surfaces. But it differs from 'fusion' and resembles 'juxtaposition' in that its constituents retain all their original properties in the mixture and can be separated out again. These two features of 'blending' were given empirical support by the case of the separability of wine from water (**D**).

It is regularly said of the constituents of 'blending' that they are 'mutually coextended through and through' (**C 4, 9**). Such coextension means that all the constituents of the blend are completely present in any part of it (**C 7**), no matter how small, a position which suits the Stoics' defence of the infinite divisibility of body (see **50A–C**). Examples which help to clarify coextension are the blending of soul and body, or iron and fire (**C 10, 11**). If fire be thought of as a material constituent of red-hot iron, it makes sense to think that iron and fire are mutually coextended through and through.

The Stoic conception of 'blending' has general application. But its chief function was certainly to explain how the light and tenuous elements of 'breath' could completely pervade portions of earth and water whose volume or density was very much greater. Such differences, the Stoics maintained, are irrelevant to the capacity of different kinds of bodies to be blended with one another. So Chrysippus asserted, unlike Aristotle, that a drop of wine can be blended with the sea, and indeed with the whole world (**A, B**). That the theory was particularly designed to accommodate the blending of unequal constituents is clearly suggested by the attention given to this point in **C 8–12**; and the statement of Chrysippus' views on blending starts with an account of 'breath' pervading the world (**C 1**). But there is no reason to suppose that 'blending' requires its initial constituents to differ in volume, and 'mutual coextension' will presumably be the outcome even if only one constituent is causally active. Earth and water are only the recipients of action when 'breath' extends itself through them. But when 'breath' is coextended through earth and water it seems to follow that they will be coextended through it (cf. **E 1**). Since the coextension results from the activity of 'breath', it is natural for the active constituent to be described as passing through the others (**C 10, 12**). The result, for the blend as a whole, is 'unification' or 'sustainment' (**C 1**, cf. **47G, L**).

As a Stoic doctrine, 'blending' probably precedes Chrysippus, since it was attacked by Arcesilaus (**E 2**). It could have been first stated by Zeno or Cleanthes to account for the presence of vital heat in every part of the world. But the very close integration of 'blending' with cosmic 'breath', in our sources, points to Chrysippus' formulations of the concept (cf. pp. 287–8).

Does 'blending' commit the Stoics, as some of their critics supposed, to the absurd-sounding claim that two bodies can occupy the same place? They certainly did not think, any more than Themistius in **F**, that place is a body. From Aristotle onwards it was acknowledged to be paradoxical that two bodies should occupy the same place (*Physics* IV.I). But its paradoxical character depends on the assumption that any two bodies are of a kind such that where one of them is, there can be no room for the other. That assumption obviously fits an atomic theory of body, but bodies in Stoicism are neither atomic (see **50A**) nor of a single kind. The active principle of the world is a different kind of body from the passive principle (see **44–5**). In the form of 'breath' the active principle constitutes the shape and structure of matter (the passive principle), and a body's shape and structure do occupy the same place as its bulk. Likewise an animal's life (or soul, as Stoics would say) occupies the same place as its body will occupy until the time when the body becomes a corpse. In order to do justice to Stoic intuitions, we should regard the two things that occupy the same place not as two determinate and independently existing bodies, but as the two bodily functions (breath and matter) which jointly constitute every determinate and independently existing body (see **45** commentary).

49 Place and void

A Stobaeus 1.161,8–26 (*SVF* 2.503, part)

(1) Chrysippus declared place to be what is occupied through and through by an existent, or what can be occupied by an existent and is through and through occupied whether by one thing or by several things ... (2) The void is said to be infinite. For what is outside the world is like this, but place is finite since no body is infinite. Just as anything corporeal is finite, so the incorporeal is infinite, for time and void are infinite. For as nothing is no limit, so there is no limit of nothing, as is the case with the void. In respect of its own subsistence it is infinite; it is made finite by being filled, but once that which fills it has been removed, a limit to it cannot be thought of.

B Sextus Empiricus, *Against the professors* 10.3–4 (*SVF* 2.505, part)

(1) The Stoics say that void is what can be occupied by an existent but is not occupied, or an interval empty of body, or an interval unoccupied by body. (2) Place is what is occupied by an existent and made equal to what occupies it (by 'existent' they now mean body, as is clear from the interchange of names). (3) And they say that room is an interval partly occupied by a body and partly unoccupied. Some have said that room is the place of the larger body.

C Cleomedes 8,10–14 (*SVF* 2.541)

[Endorsing Stoic doctrine] So void must have a kind of subsistence. The notion of it is very simple since it is incorporeal and without contact, neither has shape nor takes on shape, neither is acted upon in any respect nor acts, but is simply capable of receiving body.

D Galen, *On the differences in pulses* 8.674,13–14 (*SVF* 2.424, part)

They [the stoicizing Pneumatic doctors, cf. **55F 2**] think there is no such thing [as empty space] in the world, but that the whole substance is unified with itself.

E Galen, *On incorporeal qualities* 19.464,10–14 (*SVF* 2.502)

The Stoics are compelled to admit that extension in three dimensions is common to body and void and place, since they leave void in the nature of existing things even if they deny its presence within the world.

F Simplicius, *On Aristotle's On the heavens* 284,28–285,2 (*SVF* 2.535)

(1) The Stoics want there to be a void outside the world and prove it through the following assumption. (2) Let someone stand at the edge of the fixed sphere and stretch out his hand upwards. (3) If he does stretch it out, they take it that something exists outside the world into which he has stretched it, and if he cannot stretch it out, there will still be something outside which prevents him from doing so. (4) And if he should next stand at the limit of *this* and stretch out his hand, a similar question will arise. (5) For something which is also outside that point will have been indicated.

G Cleomedes 6,11–17 (*SVF* 2.537)

Even if the entire substance is resolved into fire, as the most refined of the natural philosophers [i.e. Stoics] think, it must occupy a vastly greater place, just like the vaporizations of solid bodies into smoke. Therefore the place occupied by substance flowing out during the conflagration is now void, since no body has filled it.

H Cleomedes 10,24–12,5 (*SVF* 2.540)

(1) They [the Peripatetics] also say that if void existed outside the world, substance would have flowed through it and been infinitely scattered and dissipated. (2) But we [endorsing Stoic doctrine] shall say that substance cannot experience this. For it has tenor which sustains and protects it. (3) On the one hand, the surrounding void causes nothing; and on the other hand, substance, making use of its superior power, protects itself altogether, contracting and again flowing out in the void by its natural changes, sometimes flowing out into fire, and at other times setting forth on cosmogony.

I Plutarch, *On Stoic self-contradictions* 1054E (*SVF* 2.550, part)

[Chrysippus says] In the void there exists no difference by which bodies are drawn in one direction rather than another, but the organization of the world is the reason for the motion of bodies inclining and moving from all directions towards its centre and mid-point.

J Stobaeus 1.166,4–22 (*SVF* 1.99)

[Zeno's doctrine] (1) Everything in the world which is constituted by its own tenor has parts which move towards the centre of the universe, and the same holds for the parts of the world itself. (2) It is therefore correct to say that all the parts of the world move towards its centre, and particularly those with weight. (3) There is an identical explanation both for the world's stable position in infinite void and similarly for the earth's being settled in the world with equipollence at its centre. (4) However, body does not have weight absolutely; air and fire are weightless. But they too extend in a way to the centre of the whole sphere of the world, and they create the coherence with its periphery. For they are naturally upward-moving owing to their having no share in weight. (5) Similarly they say that the world itself does not have weight since it is entirely composed of elements which do have weight and ones which do not. (6) The whole earth in their view does have weight intrinsically. From its position, by virtue of its central location (and the fact that such [i.e. heavy] bodies move towards the centre), it remains in this place.

☐ The Stoic definitions of place and void (**A–C**) show why these were classified as 'subsistent' and 'incorporeal' (see **27**). Both place and void presuppose the existence of body, place being that kind of incorporeal extension which a body can and does occupy, and void being that kind of incorporeal extension which a body can but does not occupy. In order to be the appropriate kind of incorporeal to fulfil these roles, place and void were probably regarded as 'three-dimensional' (**E**), differing from body in their intangibility (cf. **C**) and lack of resistance (cf. **45E, F**).

The Stoics, unlike Epicurus (see **5**), do not seem anxious to treat place and void as merely terms which pick out different aspects of the same concept. The void is not a place which is sometimes empty and sometimes filled (**A 2**). Strictly, the void is always external to the world and infinite. Place, being that which body actually occupies, is within the world and finite. When filled, the void ceases to exist as such, and becomes a place. But the Stoics acknowledged that a spatial continuum can be partly full and partly empty of a particular body. At the cosmic level this will hold good for the composite of world, which exhausts all place, and the external void. The Stoics probably used the term 'room' (**B 3**) to denote space which combines place and void (i.e. the 'all', **44A**); and they also acknowledged the less technical point that a spatial container within the world, for instance, a half-filled wine jar, can accommodate more of the body which partly fills it (see untranslated portion of **A**, vol. 2).

Aristotle had strenuously resisted giving any kind of existence to void within or outside the world (*Physics* IV.7–10). The Stoics saw no reason to differ from him concerning void within the world (cf. **D**). They did not agree with Epicurus

(6) on the need for void as a condition of locomotion, and their conception of the world as an organic unity was quite incompatible with the introduction of discrete spaces separating one body from another.[1] But in Stoicism the world is not, as Aristotle conceived it, invariant in volume. Before the 'conflagration' (see **46**) there has to be unoccupied space into which the world can expand as it burns and which it will leave unoccupied once again as it cools and contracts (**G**). Theoretical considerations, drawing upon the concept of an infinite regress, are also attested (**F**), but the cosmic cycle seems to have been the Stoics' main reason for needing an external void.

To Peripatetic objections (**H 1**, deriving from Aristotle *Physics* IV.8) that an external void must threaten the stability of the world, the Stoics have two excellent replies (**H 2–3**). First, the void as incorporeal has no causal efficacy (**C**, cf. **45B**), and therefore undifferentiated empty space cannot have any effect on the world whatsoever. Secondly, the world is so constituted that all its parts, including even the weightless elements air and fire, have a centripetal tendency (**J**). The weightlessness of these elements gives them a natural movement away from the world's centre, but this is counterbalanced by the unqualified centripetal movement of the heavy elements with which air and fire, as the sustaining 'breath' (see **47**), are blended. Thus air and fire unite the world's centre with its circumference, creating complete internal coherence (**J 4**; cf. **H 2**, which refers to the tenor or natural cohesiveness of substance). Hence there is no danger of the world's disintegrating into the external void, which in any case plays no part in accounting for locomotion. Aristotle (*Physics* IV.8, 215a8–9) had objected that an infinite void could have no centre, adducing a battery of arguments designed to cast doubt on the compatibility of such a void with a determinate and stable world. Chrysippus acknowledged that the infinite void excludes any reason for bodies to move in definite directions (**I**), but since the void is not part of the Stoic world, the only centre which need concern Chrysippus is that of the world itself: all bodies have a centripetal tendency, as we have seen, i.e. towards their own centre, the centre of the bodily continuum (**J**). The target of Aristotle's objections was an infinite void with a finite world at its (the void's) centre. But Chrysippus does not, as it were, place his world into an infinite void. Rather, he starts from a finite world which totally excludes void. The infinite void merely surrounds the world, providing the spatial condition ('room') for its changes of volume.

50 Continuum

A Stobaeus 1.142,2–6 (*SVF* 2.482, part)

Chrysippus said that bodies are divided to infinity, and likewise things comparable to bodies, such as surface, line, place, void and time. But although these are divided to infinity, a body does not consist of infinitely many bodies, and the same applies to surface, line and place.

---

[1] Cicero, *Academica* 2.125 may refer to a Stoic defence of motion by 'reciprocal replacement' (*antiperistasis*), cf. **6A 4**.

B Diogenes Laertius 7.150–1 (*SVF* 2.482, part)

(1) Division is to infinity, (2) or 'infinite' according to Chrysippus (for there is not some infinity which the division reaches, it is just unceasing). (3) And blendings, also, are through and through.

C Plutarch, *On common conceptions* 1078E–1080E (with omissions)

(1) It is also contrary to our conception that there should be in the nature of bodies neither an extremity nor a first or last part at which the magnitude of the body terminates, but that something always turns up beyond any magnitude taken, thus casting the object into infinity and indeterminacy. For it will be impossible to think of one magnitude as bigger or smaller than another, if an infinite progression of parts belongs to both alike ... (2) Yet how can it fail to be self-evident that man consists of more parts than man's finger, and the world than man? This is understood and appreciated by all, provided they have not become Stoics, but on becoming Stoics they say the opposite, and believe that man does not consist of more parts than his finger, nor the world than man. For division pulverizes bodies to infinity, and among infinities there is no more or less. ... (3) Chrysippus says that when asked if we have parts, and how many, and of what and how many parts *they* consist, we will operate a distinction. With regard to the inexact question we will reply that we consist of head, trunk and limbs – for that was all that the problem put to us amounted to. But if they extend their questioning to the *ultimate* parts, we must not, he says, in reply concede any such things, but must say neither of what parts we consist, nor, likewise, of how many, either infinite or finite. I have, I think, quoted his actual words, so that you may see how he conserved the common conceptions, urging us to think of each body as consisting neither of certain parts nor of some number of them, either infinite or finite. For if, just as 'indifferent' is intermediate between good and bad, so too there is an intermediate between finite and infinite, then he should have said what it is and resolved the difficulty. But if, just as we think of the not-equal as *eo ipso* unequal and the not-destructible as indestructible, so too we think of the not-finite as infinite, then for a body to consist neither of finitely nor of infinitely many parts is, I'd have thought, like an argument's consisting neither of true premises nor of false premises nor of < true premises and false premises >.

(4) On top of that, he has the puerility to say that, given that the pyramid is compounded out of triangles, their sides, where they are adjacent as they incline apart, are unequal, yet do not exceed in so far as they are larger. That's how he preserved our conceptions! For if

something is larger which does not exceed, there will be something smaller which does not fall short. Hence there will be something unequal which neither exceeds nor falls short. That is, the unequal will be equal, the larger not larger, and the smaller not smaller. (5) Again, look how he countered Democritus, who in the vivid manner of a natural philosopher raised the following puzzle. If a cone were cut along a plane parallel to its base, what should we hold the surfaces of the segments to be, equal or unequal? For if they are unequal they will make the cone uneven, with many step-like indentations and rough edges. But if they are equal, the segments will be equal and the cone will turn out to have the properties of a cylinder, through consisting of equal, not unequal, circles, which is quite absurd. Well here Chrysippus declares Democritus to be ignorant, and says that the surfaces are neither equal nor unequal, while the bodies, thanks to the surfaces' being neither equal nor unequal, are unequal. . . .

(6) Their favourite objection to the champions of partless magnitudes is that there is [i.e. on such a view] contact neither of wholes with wholes nor of parts with parts; for the former produces not contact but blending, while the latter is impossible because partless magnitudes do not have parts. (7) How then do they themselves avoid this trap, seeing that they allow no last or first part? Why, because they say that bodies touch each other by means of a limit, not by means of parts. (8) But the limit is not a body. So body will touch body with something incorporeal, and again will *not* touch, since something incorporeal is in between. But if it will touch, the body will both act and be acted upon by something incorporeal.

D Proclus, *On Euclid's Elements I* 89,15–18 (*SVF* 2.488, part)

. . . we should not hold that such limits, I mean those of bodies, subsist in mere thought, as the Stoics supposed . . .

E Diogenes Laertius 7.135

A surface is the limit of a body, or that which has only length and breadth without depth. This Posidonius in his *On celestial phenomena* book 5 retains both in thought and as subsistent. A line is the limit of a surface, or length without breadth, or that which has length alone. A point is the limit of a line – the smallest marker.

F Sextus Empiricus, *Against the professors* 10.121–6, 139–42

(1) Next, every motion involves three things, namely bodies, places and times – bodies to do the moving, places for the movement to happen in, and times for the movement to take. So it is either with these all being divided into infinitely many places, times and bodies that motion

happens, or with them all terminating at a partless and minimal magnitude, or with some of them divided to infinity while others terminate at a partless and minimal magnitude. But whether they are all divided to infinity, or all terminate at a partless magnitude, <or some are divided to infinity while others terminate at a partless magnitude>, the account of motion will be found problematic. (2) Taking them in order, let us start our argument with the first school of thought, according to which all are divided to infinity. Now its champions say that the moving body completes the whole of a divisible distance at one and the same time: it does not first cover the first part of the distance with its own first part and the second part second in sequence, but traverses the whole of the divisible distance in one single go. (3) This is absurd, and conflicts in a variety of ways with things which are evident. For if, to take the case of these sensible bodies, we think of someone running over a distance of one stade, it will certainly turn out that such a person must complete the first half-stade first, and the second second in sequence. To suppose that he completes the whole distance of one stade entirely in one go is absurd. And if we were to divide the second half-stade into two quarter-stades, he will certainly traverse the first quarter-stade first. So too if we were to divide it into more parts. And if he runs across the stadium when it is illuminated, evidently he will not cast his shadow over the stadium all in one go, but one part of it first, another second, another third. And if he were to run alongside the wall, touching it with a hand covered in red paint, he is not going to paint the whole stadium-wall red in one go, but in sequence, starting with the earlier part. What, then, our argument has shown in the case of sensible objects, we must accept also in the case of objects of thought . . . (4) That, then, is how problematic it is for these men to hold that motion happens over a distance all at once. But it is even more problematic than this to hold that it does not happen over a divisible distance all at once, but the earlier part first and the next part next. For if that is how motion happens, given that bodies, places and times are all divided to infinity, there will be no beginning of motion. For in order that something should move the distance of one cubit it must traverse the first half-cubit first and the second second in sequence. But in order that it should even complete the first half-cubit it must cross the first quarter of the one-cubit distance and then the second. But also, if it is divided into five, <the first fifth>, and if into six, the first sixth. Since, therefore, thanks to infinite divisibility, every first part has a further first part, there must necessarily be no beginning of motion, because the parts of the distance and those of the body are inexhaustible, and any one of these that you may take has further parts. (5) This, then, was the appropriate reply to those who say that bodies, places and times are divided to infinity, namely the Stoics.

G Proclus, *On Euclid's Elements I* 395,13–18 (*SVF* 2.365, part)

Such theorems [i.e. as the theorem that parallelograms on the same base and between the same parallels are equal in area], Geminus reports, were compared by Chrysippus to the Ideas [cf. **30**]. For just as the Ideas encompass the generation of infinite instances within defined limits, so too in these there is the encompassing of infinite instances within defined places.

☐ The Stoics' championship of the continuum places them in direct opposition to Epicurus' theory of indivisible magnitudes (on which see **9**). Their reply to Epicurus, and also perhaps to Diodorus Cronus, another proponent of minima, is reported in **C6**. In it they echo Aristotle's argument at *Physics* VI.1 (= **9d** in vol. 2) that since all contact is whole-to-whole, part-to-whole, or part-to-part, and since indivisibles do not have parts, there is no way short of total coincidence (i.e. whole-to-whole) that two indivisibles could be in contact. Epicurus' ingenious answer had been to offer a further way in which indivisibles might combine – see **9A 7–8** and commentary. The Stoic report here can be read, not as ignoring this solution and returning uncritically to Aristotle's original argument, but as pointing out that Epicurus' answer leaves indivisibles with no 'contact' in the strict sense.

At any rate, it is important to recognize the *ad hominem* nature of the argument at **C6**. That contact is by 'parts' was acceptable to Aristotle only because he considered *limits* to be parts, and the same belief could, dialectically, be demanded of Epicurus because he too considered limits to be parts, equating them as he did with minimal parts. The Stoics themselves, however, made the genuine advance of denying that limits are parts: **C7**.

While Plutarch, in the interests of polemic, takes Stoic 'limits' to be incorporeals (**C8**) the more reliable evidence of **A**, **D** and **E** avoids this description. The Stoics regarded limits as purely mental constructs (**D**, **E**), and as such they may well have seen them as falling altogether outside the corporeal–incorporeal dichotomy (see further, **27**; and cf. **C3** for this characteristically Stoic mode of exclusion). Readers familiar with Plato and Aristotle may be disappointed at the Stoics' evidently cursory treatment of such mathematical objects' ontological status. In the Hellenistic age philosophy and mathematics had become widely separated disciplines, and mathematics no longer greatly exercised the philosophers' interest or served them as the paradigm case of a science. (**G** represents a very rare Stoic excursion into philosophy of mathematics.)

It seems natural to read the Stoics' own account at **C7** as saying that two bodies touch when they share a limit. This limit might be, in different cases, a surface, a line, or just a point (**E**). This unfortunately compounds the difficulty of interpreting Chrysippus' solution to the cone puzzle in **C5**. Democritus' dilemma was, it seems, the following: of the two contiguous faces of a horizontally sliced conical body, either the lower face is larger, in which case, by constantly repeating the operation, we will find many indentations in the cone (this steplike irregularity arises because the lower, upward-facing surface cannot itself be envisaged as directly adjacent to a further surface below itself); or the two surfaces are equal, which, since we can repeat the experiment with the same result at any horizontal plane of the cone, will mean that it nowhere widens out, and is a cylinder. Democritus makes two important assumptions here: (a) the two contiguous surfaces of two bodies in contact are not coincident but directly *adjacent*; (b) a solid can be analysed as somehow *consisting of* a series of plane figures, the cylinder for example being describable as a stack of equal circles. (Some have seen a further, atomistic assumption at work, but there is no evidence for this, and it would have left the puzzle much less interesting to a non-atomist like Chrysippus.)

We might expect Chrysippus to reject both assumptions – the first by appeal to his own account of contact, as interpreted above, and the second because he appreciates that limits are not parts (**C 7**). If so, his solution in **C 5**, that the surfaces are 'neither equal nor unequal', should be read as an assertion that neither description is appropriate (for this mode of exclusion, cf. **C 3**), because we are dealing not with two surfaces but with only one. We will then have to read his final remark in **C 5**, that thanks to this fact the two bodies are unequal, as saying merely that Chrysippus' analysis *permits* us to reject the second horn of Democritus' dilemma.

This interpretation is not entirely satisfying. First, by setting up the puzzle in terms of a physical severance Democritus surely *has* provided us with two surfaces, those of the two respective bodies – in which case it is hard to see why Chrysippus did not simply say that they are equal. Second, it is difficult not to read Chrysippus' own 'pyramid' puzzle in **C 4** as essentially identical to the cone puzzle, and as assuming both (a) and (b) among its premises. Although this text has been translated and interpreted in other ways, we take it to analyse a pyramid as a stack of triangles parallel to the base, whose sides converge on zero magnitude at the apex, and to ask whether adjacent triangles in the stack have their sides equal or unequal.

On our preferred interpretation, Chrysippus is genuinely puzzled by the relationship of the two surfaces produced by slicing a cone or pyramid latitudinally. Pure mathematics may deny that two such limits can be contiguous, but the physical world seems nevertheless to provide evidence to the contrary. His two formulae, 'larger but not exceeding' (**C 4**) and 'neither equal nor unequal' (**C 5**) may then represent two alternative attempts to describe the difficult mathematical notion of convergence on a limit. The two adjacent faces cannot be perfectly equal, yet there is no finite quantity by which the one exceeds the other. (Similar agonies can result from an attempt in arithmetic to find a difference between ten and nine-point-nine-recurring.) The formula 'neither equal nor unequal', **C 5** ends, is enough to save the cone from being a cylinder.

If this is right, has Chrysippus here thrown away the advances concerning 'limits' which we observed above? There is no need to suppose so. Plutarch is a malicious reporter, who purposely omits any reference to the original context of the remarks. It was characteristic of Chrysippus to explore a question again and again from different angles and to experiment with alternative solutions. If in this case he adopted assumptions (a) and (b), he may have done so hypothetically, in order to explore their consequences. (Indeed, the grammatical construction translated 'given that . . .' which introduces assumption (b) in **C 4** can easily be understood as hypothetical.) Moreover, assumption (b), which is explicitly stated by both Democritus and Chrysippus, can be interpreted as mathematically quite innocuous. Both puzzles still work even if the description of a solid as *consisting of* plane figures of such and such a type is taken to mean, not that these figures are its constituent parts, but just that they are to be found in it at any chosen plane parallel to the base.

We now turn to the Stoic defence of infinite divisibility. Among familiar objections to this notion were Zeno of Elea's 'dichotomy' problem, echoed by Sextus at **F 4**, as to how motion could occur; and the Epicurean argument (**9C 3**), echoed by Plutarch at **C 1–2**, that infinite division would make differences of size unintelligible. The main Stoic gambit in replying to both the Zenonian and the Epicurean challenge is to deny, rather as Aristotle had done, that the infinitely divisible contains an actual infinity of parts: **A, B**. That is not to say that it contains finitely many parts either, but just that there is no non-arbitrary answer to the question how many parts it has: **C 2–3**.

This response deals effectively enough with the Epicurean objection, which relies on the assumption that size is a function of number of parts. It has a harder struggle against the Zenonian motion paradox. It is a fair guess that the Stoic strategy criticized by Sextus in **F 2–3** was originally evolved in answer to the Zenonian challenge which he sets out in **F 4**. This latter, by analysing the distance to be traversed into an infinite series of diminishing parts converging on the starting-point, asks how motion can begin: for *any* finite distance to be successfully traversed there is an infinite number of sub-distances to be traversed first. Hence there can be no first motion, and motion cannot begin. (An alternative version, in which the infinite series converges on the finishing line, is not importantly different.) Now we can envisage the Stoics' response, like Aristotle's in *Physics* VIII.8, as starting with an appeal to their principle (**A, B**) that there is no actual infinity of parts constituting the distance. In other words, although there may be a half-way point, a quarter-way point, etc. to be reached first, there are not infinitely many such intermediate points. Hence motion *can* begin. But, it will be objected, this only follows if there is some motion which is the first in the series. How are we to decide, except by arbitrary fiat, which one this is? This is surely the question which the Stoic thesis in **F 2** is intended to answer. There *are* such motions. Whatever these are, they cannot be meant to be atomic quanta of motion (as proposed by Diodorus and Epicurus, see **11**), since the Stoics are fully committed to the continuum. It has been suggested instead that they are 'divisible leaps' – a theory later invoked by Damascius, in which the moving body vanishes from one place and mysteriously reappears in another, without, however, the suggestion that the intervening space is indivisible. But the text lends inadequate support to so extravagant a thesis: nothing in it need imply either that the transition is instantaneous or that the object fails to pass through the intervening space. A less risky, and much more Stoic, reading is that these are portions of motion which are completed *legato* and not in stages. It is, after all, their view that limits subsist only as constructs of thought (**D**). Thus there are only as many dividing points on a runner's journey as anyone may choose to mark off in thought. At some point our mental power to mark further divisions will fail us, and we will be left with an undivided, although divisible, portion of distance, which can consequently be traversed with a single undivided motion. That this is how their solution is meant to work seems evident from Sextus' countermove in **F 3**. He first very pertinently argues the necessity *in physical fact* that any motion whatever possess constituent stages; he then questions our liberty to override this conclusion when constructing a mathematical analysis in terms of pure thought-objects.

For related Stoic theories, cf. **48** on 'mixture' and **51** on 'time'. The theory of total mixture presupposes infinite divisibility (note the juxtaposition of topics in **B**), and may perhaps be thought to be endangered by the thesis that an infinite division is never realized.

51 Time

A Simplicius, *On Aristotle's Categories* 350,15–16 (*SVF* 2.510, part)

Of the Stoics, Zeno said time is the dimension of all motion without qualification, but Chrysippus said it is the dimension of the world's motion.

B Stobaeus 1.106,5–23 (*SVF* 2.509)

(1) Chrysippus said time is the dimension of motion according to which the measure of speed and slowness is spoken of; or the dimension accompanying the world's motion. (2) And (he says) every single thing moves and exists in accordance with time ... Just as the void in its totality is infinite in every respect, so time in its totality is infinite on either side. For both the past and the future are infinite. (3) He says most clearly that no time is wholly present. For since continuous things are infinitely divisible, on the basis of this division every time too is infinitely divisible. Consequently no time is present exactly, but it is broadly said to be so. (4) He also says that only the present belongs; the past and the future subsist, but belong in no way, just as only predicates which are [actual] attributes are said to belong, for instance, walking around belongs to me when I am walking around, but it does not belong when I am lying down or sitting.

C Plutarch, *On common conceptions* 1081C–1082A

(1) It is contrary to the [common] conception to hold that future and past time exist while present time does not, but that recently and the other day subsist while now is nothing at all. (2) Yet this is the result for the Stoics, who do not admit a minimal time or wish the now to be partless but claim that whatever one thinks one has grasped and is considering as present is in part future and in part past. (3) Consequently no part of a present time corresponding to now remains or is left, if the time said to be

present is distributed into parts that are future and parts that are past . . .
(4) All other men assume and consider and suppose both recently and
soon to be different parts from now, and soon to be after now and
recently before now. But among Stoics Archedemus says that now is a
kind of joining and meeting of the past and future, forgetting, as it seems,
that he has destroyed the whole of time. For if now is not a time but a
limit of time, and every part of time is such as now is, the whole of time
clearly has no part but is completely dissolved into limits and meetings
and joinings. (5) But Chrysippus, wishing to be skilful in the division,
says in his book *On the void* and elsewhere that the part of time which is
past and the part which is future subsist but do not belong and only the
present belongs. But in *On parts* books 3, 4 and 5 he maintains that one
part of the present time is future and the other past. (6) So it turns out that
he divides the belonging constituent of time into non-belonging parts of
what belongs, or rather that he leaves nothing at all of time belonging, if
the present has no part which is not future or past.

D Stobaeus 1.105,8–16 (*SVF* 3 Apollodorus 8)

[Apollodorus' definition] Time is the interval of the world's motion; and
it is infinite in just the way that the whole of number is said to be infinite.
Some of it is past, some present, and some future. But the whole of time is
present, as we say that the year is present on a larger compass. Also, the
whole of time is said to belong, though none of its parts belongs exactly.

E Stobaeus 1.105,17–106,4 (Posidonius fr. 98)

[Posidonius' definition] (1) Some things are infinite in every respect like
the whole of time. Others in a particular respect like the past and the
future. For each of them is limited only by reference to the present. (2)
His definition of time is as follows: dimension of motion or measure of
speed and slowness. (3) And he holds that that time which is thought of in
terms of 'when' is partly past, partly future, and partly present. The last
consists of a part of the past and a part of the future, encompassing the
actual division. But the division is point-like. (4) Now and the like are
thought of broadly and not exactly. (5) But now is also spoken of with
reference to the least perceptible time encompassing the division of the
future and the past.

F Proclus, *On Plato's Timaeus* 271D (*SVF* 2.521)

(1) From what has been said one should also realize that Plato had a quite
different view of time from the Stoics or many of the Peripatetics. (2)
The Stoics make it a mere thought, insubstantial and very close to non-
existent. For in their view time was one of the incorporeals, which they
disparage as inactive and non-existent and subsisting merely in thoughts.
(3) The Peripatetics call time an accident of motion.

G Plutarch, *On common conceptions* 1084C–D (*SVF* 2.665)

Let them [the Stoics] not be angry at being brought to these things by the Little-by-little Argument [i.e. Sorites, see **37**), but remember Chrysippus' similar approach in his *Questions on physics* book 1: 'It is not the case that the night is a body and the evening and the dawn and midnight are not bodies; and it is not the case that the day is a body and the first day of the month is not also a body and the tenth and the fifteenth and the thirtieth and the month and the summer and the autumn and the year.'

H Sextus Empiricus, *Against the professors* 8.254–5 (*SVF* 2.221, part)

(1) In addition, they [the Stoics] say that the sign must be a present sign of a present thing. (2) For some people make a mistake and want a present thing to be also a sign of a past thing, as for instance, 'If this man has a scar, this man has had a wound.' For 'He has a scar' is something present, since it is evident, but his having had a wound is past, since there is no longer a wound. They also want a present thing to be a sign of a future thing, as is encompassed in a conditional like, 'If this man has been wounded in the heart, this man will die.' For they say that the wound in the heart is already present, but the death is in the future. (3) Those who make such statements do not realize in fact that, though the past and the future are different, the sign and its object, even in these cases, is a present thing of a present thing. (4) For in the earlier example . . . the wound has already happened and is past, but 'This man has had a wound', which is a proposition, is present, though it is said about something which has happened. And in the case of, 'If this man has been wounded in the heart, this man will die', the death is in the future, but the proposition, 'This man will die', is present, though it is said about what is future, because it is true even now.

☐ Stoic reflections on time are interesting but tantalizing. The evidence consists largely of summary theses, which lack defending arguments, and Plutarch's important testimony in **C** is deeply ingrained with his own polemic. The Stoics probably approached this subject from more than one point of view, which may explain the apparent inconsistencies in the doctrines attributed to Chrysippus.

Aristotle had discussed time at length in *Physics* IV.10–14. Whether directly, or through the mediation of later Peripatetics, his views seem to have been the starting-point for Stoic discussions. Both schools agreed that time has no existence in its own right, and the Stoics chose to classify it among the 'incorporeals' (**27D**). Aristotle had defined time as 'the number of motion by reference to before and after' (*Physics* IV.11,219b). Stoic definitions (**A**, **B 1**, **E 2**) establish a similar relation between time and motion, but they do not retain Aristotle's interest in counting. He had surmised that time, as a number, is dependent on a counter (the soul, *Physics* IV.14,223a25). The Stoics seem to take a less subjectivist view. As 'the dimension' of motion, time does not depend on being countable or counted but solely on the existence of motion, just as place, which is three-dimensional, depends solely on being occupied by body (**49A** 1, **B2**). The world or *kosmos* in its most extended sense (see **44F**; **46E**; **52A**) is everlasting and *always* in motion. Thus in linking time with the world's motion, Chrysippus (**A**) tied the duration of time to the one thing whose existence is not subject to intermittent starts and stops.

Proclus maintains that the Stoics regarded time as purely conceptual (**F**), but this is probably an incorrect inference from its incorporeality, which itself (as will be seen) requires qualification. If 'sayables' (*lekta*) depend on thought for their subsistence (cf. **33B–C**), there is no evidence that this is so for the other three incorporeals, place, void, and time. Unlike Aristotle, who denied that all things are 'in time' (*Physics* IV.12,221b3), Chrysippus located the movement and existence of everything in time (**B** 2). God, the world's active principle, is not a timeless being but a continuously self-moving agent.

Time is infinite in extension and infinitely divisible (**B 2, 3**). The second attribute is a basic Aristotelian doctrine, and he allowed that the circular movement of the heavens could be temporally infinite (*Physics* IV.10,241b18). In Stoicism the infinite extension of time is a function of the everlasting succession of cosmic cycles (cf. **52C**). Like Aristotle again, the Stoics treated past and future as 'parts' or 'constituents of time' (**B 2–3, C 5, D, E** 1; cf. Aristotle, *Physics* IV.10,217b33), and they had to take up a position on the paradoxes which such discourse generates. On the one hand they distinguished senses of infinity: time as a whole is infinite 'in every respect' (**B 2, E** 1). But as 'parts' of time, past and future cannot be infinite 'on either side' since they would then cease to be distinguishable as parts of all time. So they are infinite only on one side and 'limited' by the present (**E** 1).

This corresponds very closely to Aristotle's view of the present or 'the now'. He describes 'the now' as 'the link of time; for it holds together the past and the future, and is the limit of time' (*Physics* IV.13,222a10). By 'limit' Aristotle does not mean a fixed boundary, but an indivisible durationless point. The Stoic Archedemus took over his description of 'the now' wholesale (**C 4**), and it seems to be implied by other evidence: 'no time is exactly present' (**B 3**, cf. **C** 1–3, **E 4**). But we are allowed to speak of the present as if it had a duration or existence of its own. That is acceptable at the level of perception (**E 5**), but under strict analysis the present is specious since it 'consists of a part of the past and a part of the future' (**C 5, E 3**). Aristotle had already indicated that this is the unacceptable consequence of treating 'the now' as a time (*Physics* VI.3,234a9). In so describing the present, the Stoics were probably agreeing with Aristotle, or using this description to refer only to the broad use which conflicts with the exact view of time as a continuum.

We come now to the most original aspects of the Stoic theory, and these, as Plutarch readily noted (**C 5**), are superficially inconsistent with the doctrines just discussed. In **B 4** and **C 5**, contrary to what we have been led to expect, it is the present alone which is said to 'belong'. The past and the future do not belong but 'subsist'. This distinction is illustrated by an obscure passage (**B 4**) which seems to specify the temporal conditions for truly predicating an attribute of a subject. 'Walking' belongs to (can be truly predicated of) me just when I *am* (present) walking. When I *am* lying down or sitting I *am* not walking, and so walking does not then belong to me. At the time of my lying down or sitting, it may be true that I *have* walked or that I *shall* walk, but those walkings do not belong to me at that time, and so they only subsist.

Chrysippus' distinction between 'belongs' and 'subsists' is in fact quite consistent with his claim that no time is exactly present, or that the specious present, as a stretch of time, actually consists of parts of the past and the future. Any walking I do takes time, so if my walking can be 'present', Chrysippus must be using 'present' in the broad or inexact sense. It must be with reference to that usage, and the division of time into three extended 'parts' (cf. **D**), that the distinction between 'belongs' and 'subsists' holds good.

In that case, what does the distinction amount to? The subsistence of the past and the future indicates the status of those times which have been or will be present but do not belong to the world as it is right now. Thus a subsistent time dates all events which have occurred or will occur, as bounded by the present. The Stoics were careful to point out, however, that true propositions referring to such events 'are present', i.e. are true now (see **H**). What has occurred or what will occur subsists in relation to the present. But what is now the case can perfectly well be something that is past or future.

Given the notorious difficulties of the concept of time, the Stoics' flexibility on the subject is to their credit. They recognized that temporal discourse is unavoidably imprecise and may legitimately vary with the context: we may speak of a long extension of time, such as a year, as 'present' (**D**). Nor was their classification of time as incorporeal a denial of its reality as a feature of the world. If time as such is not a body, Chrysippus was prepared to treat day and night and longer durations of time as bodies (**G**). He seems to have reasoned that these are physical changes produced by the sun's movements (cf. *SVF* 2.693; **70E 3**).

52 Everlasting recurrence

A Philo, *On the indestructibility of the world* 52, 54

(1) People who are in the habit of defining things have correctly represented time as the dimension of the world's motion. Since this is sound, the world is of the same age as time, and its cause ... (2) Perhaps some quibbling Stoic will say that time is represented as the motion not only of the present world but also of the world imagined at the conflagration.

B Lactantius, *Divine institutes* 7.23 (*SVF* 2.623)

Chrysippus ... when speaking of the world's renewal, drew the following conclusion: 'Since this is so, it is evidently not impossible that we too after our death will return again to the shape we now are, after certain periods of time have elapsed.'

C Nemesius 309,5–311,2 (*SVF* 2.625)

(1) The Stoics say that when the planets return to the same celestial sign, in length and breadth, where each was originally when the world was first formed, at set periods of time they cause conflagration and destruction of existing things. (2) Once again the world returns anew to the same condition as before; and when the stars are moving again in the same way, each thing which occurred in the previous period will come to pass indiscernibly [from its previous occurrence]. For again there will be Socrates and Plato and each one of mankind with the same friends and fellow citizens; they will suffer the same things and they will encounter the same things, and put their hand to the same things, and every city and village and piece of land return in the same way. (3) The periodic return of everything occurs not once but many times; or rather, the same things return infinitely and without end. (4) The gods who are not subject to destruction, from their knowledge of this single period, know from it everything that is going to be in the next periods. For there will be nothing strange in comparison with what occurred previously, but everything will be just the same and indiscernible down to the smallest details.

D Eusebius, *Evangelical preparation* 15.19.1–2 (*SVF* 2.599, part)

[Reporting Stoic doctrine] (1) Universal reason having advanced thus far, or universal nature having grown and increased, it finally dries up everything and takes it up into itself, and comes to be in the whole substance. (2) It returns to the so-called primary reason and to that resur- rection which creates the greatest year, in which the reconstitution from itself alone [i.e. universal nature] into itself recurs. (3) Having returned because of the order from which it began to create the world in just such a way, it manufactures the same way of life again according to reason, since such periods occur everlastingly without ceasing.

E Simplicius, *On Aristotle's Physics* 886,12–16 (*SVF* 2.627, part)

In stating that the same I is born again in the recreation they [the Stoics] ask with good reason whether the I now and the I at another time are numerically one, because they are the same in substance, or whether I am fragmented by being assigned to a succession of cosmogonies.

F Alexander, *On Aristotle's Prior analytics* 180,33–6; 181,25–31 (*SVF* 2.624, part)

(1) They [the Stoics] hold that after the conflagration all the same things recur in the world numerically, so that even the same peculiarly qualified individual as before exists and comes to be again in that world, as Chrysippus says in his books *On the world* . . . (2) They say too that the

only discernibilities between later and earlier peculiarly qualified individuals are with respect to certain external accidents; these discernibilities, in the case of the same Dion persisting and living, do not change him. (3) For he does not become another man if he previously had moles on his face but no longer has them. Such discernibilities, they say, do occur between the peculiarly qualified individuals of one world and those of another.

G Origen, *Against Celsus* 4.68, 5.20 (*SVF* 2.626, part)

(1) Trying to soften the incongruities somewhat, the Stoics, I know not how, say that everyone in one period will be indiscernible from those in the previous periods: they don't want Socrates to recur but someone indiscernible from Socrates who is to marry someone indiscernible from Xanthippe and be accused by men indiscernible from Anytus and Meletus. I don't know how the world is always the 'same' and not 'indiscernible from' another world, while its contents are not the 'same' but 'indiscernible' . . . (2) Those of them who were embarrassed by the doctrine [of indiscernibility] said that there is a very slight discernibility between one period and the events of its predecessor.

H Marcus Aurelius 2.14

(1) Even if you were to live three thousand years or thirty thousand, nevertheless remember that no one loses another life than this which he is living, nor lives another life than this which he is losing. So the shortest comes to the same thing as the longest. For the present is equal for all, and so what is passing away is equal; and this shows that what is being lost is merely a moment. No one could lose what is past or what is future. For how could anyone deprive him of what he does not have? (2) Always remember, then, these two things: one, that everything everlastingly is of the same kind and cyclically recurrent, and it makes no difference whether one should see the same things for a hundred years or for two hundred or for an infinite time. Two, that the longest-lived and the quickest to die have an equal loss. For it is the present alone of which one will be deprived, since this is the only thing that he has, and no one loses what he does not have.

☐ The everlasting cycle of world-order and conflagration raises further questions concerning Stoic conceptions of time. As infinite *and* the dimension of the world's motion (**51B**), time could not be straightforwardly linked to a cosmic clock such as the succession of days and nights. During a conflagration nothing is going on in the universe except the fiery providential activity of god (**28O 4**, **46O**). Approaching time from the Platonic position of a single everlasting world, Philo (**A 1**) insists that time and the world are of equal duration. Any Stoic who accepted Chrysippus' definition of time (**51A**) and the conflagration doctrine will have had to extend time beyond the duration of the world as an ordered system in the Platonic or Aristotelian sense. In other words, since god is continuously active during all states of the Stoic universe, and especially during the conflagration, time must be presumed to continue even when no world-order in any sense measurable by us exists. This need not embarrass them. God's providential thoughts, as an ordered sequence of movements, may be taken to proceed in such a way that *B* occurs after *A* and before *C*, thus providing a temporal series for the activity of the conflagration.

What presses harder for clarification and philosophical assessment is everlasting recurrence itself. The doctrine which Chrysippus canvassed as a possibility, if not a firm thesis (**B**), was 'our return to the shape we are now' in a future world after our death; and in the most detailed summary this hardens into the claim that there is an everlasting sequence of worlds and conflagrations in which the individuals and actions of any one world are exactly the same as those of every other world 'down to the smallest details' (**C**). Such a cosmology is asserted rather than proved in our surviving evidence, but it appears to be an inevitable consequence of three basic Stoic theses: (1) the principles god and matter are everlasting and god is continuously active (**44B 2, E 4**); (2) the present world is a temporally finite set of events causally determined in its totality by the 'seminal principles' operative in cosmogony (**46A 1, G**, cf. **D**); (3) from the same causes the same effects invariably follow (**55N 3**). (1) and (2) entail that god's activity must continue beyond the end of our world, and the Stoics had independent reasons for identifying that continuing state with the conflagration (**46**). But the ensuing conflagration is also the state of the universe from which our world began, and therefore the world has returned to its starting-point. According to **C 2** the conflagration occurs at the completion of the 'great year' (cf. **D 2**), when the planets occupy the same position that they held when the world began. If that was 'the order from which it [universal reason] began to create the world in just such a way' (**D 3**), the conflagration itself appears to be a link in the causal nexus. At twelve o'clock, as it were (the planets in the same position), one world ends and another begins. But the clock of the great year stops for the duration of the conflagration, which is both the effect of the preceding world (cf. **46I**) and the cause of the next one.

It would be a mistake, however, to think of everlasting recurrence as a purely mechanical consequence of Stoic determinism. God is a supremely rational agent, and the most interesting fact about the conflagration is its omnipresent instantiation of his providence (**28O 4; 46O**, cf. **D**). In his own identity god is the causal nexus (cf. **54A–B; 55K–N**); hence the sequence of cause and effect is an enactment of divine rationality and providence. Since every previous world has been excellent (**46G 3**), god can have no reason to modify any succeeding world. The same point can be stated epistemologically (**C 4**, cf. **D 3**): god knows from acquaintance with any one world all that will happen in subsequent worlds. Moral significance was attached to his creativity, with the claim that all evil is purged from the universe by the conflagration, and thus each new world starts out from a condition of perfect wisdom (**46N**).

Everlasting recurrence, then, ensures that this world, the best possible, though finite in duration, will be for ever repeated. But does it ensure this in a manner that is logically coherent and ethically satisfying? In approaching these questions, we should notice that Stoics differed in their interpretations of 'the recurrence of the *same* things'. These range from the strongest claim (a) just the same down to the smallest details (**C 4**) = numerical identity (**F 1**, cf. **E**), to (b) indiscernible tokens of the same type (**G 1**), (c) numerical identity but inessential discernibility (**F2–3**), and (d) slightly discernible tokens of the same type (**G 2**). Since the Stoics defended the identity of indiscernibles (see **28O**), (b) looks like an unorthodox version of (a), with which it conflicts verbally at least (cf. **C 4**). (d) is explicitly revisionary, and its resemblance to (c) in **F 2–3** suggests that (c) was also a modification of (a). Since (b) (c) (d) all give up either indiscernibility and/or numerical identity, it is probable that (a), which states the strongest conditions for the recurrent identity, was the original thesis. The alternatives will then have been offered in response to difficulties encountered by (a).

On a linear conception of time, whereby every instant is absolutely before or after some other instant, (a) is undoubtedly problematic. For if t is the set of instants for the present world, and $t^\star$ is the set of instants for the next recurrence of that world, $t^\star$ must be a temporal dimension of movements all of which occur after t. But *ex hypothesi* the movements which occur at t are numerically identical to those which occur at $t^\star$. Hence a movement at t, which is before $t^\star$, is numerically identical to a movement at $t^\star$, which is after t. Now on linear time, this is incoherent; for it implies two quite separate temporal dimensions for one and the same movement. But there is a conception of time, called circular or closed, whereby every time is both before and after itself. In circular or closed time, forward movement will eventually reach a time (future) which is the same as the present, and backward movement will eventually reach a time (past) which is the same as the present. So what was problematic in linear time now becomes entirely coherent. The time at which Chrysippus is living now is also future to itself, and so he can be said to have a complete replication of his present life in a future which occupies the same temporal extension as he occupies here and now.

The tense-logic required by circular time includes such axioms as 'What will be so has been so', 'What has been so will be so', 'What is so has been so', 'What is so will be so.' All of these are stated or implied in **C–D**. Given Stoic determinism, and such images of time as 'the unwinding of a rope, bringing about nothing new' (**55O**), it is hardly too much to suggest that Chrysippus, if he defended (a), envisaged time as circular rather than linear. He would thus, like certain Pythagoreans, have treated the time of his next life, as well as all of his own future history, as exactly the same as that of his present life (cf. **i** in vol. 2).

The most interesting alternative to (a) is (c) in **F 2–3**. (c) allows numerically the same individual to recur, but with such differences as a mole on the face that do not change the essential identity of the individual. Such differences, if indifferent with respect to an individual's identity, imply a radically different cosmology from that of (a). Only one such difference is needed between any two worlds to render them distinct from one another. The occurrence of any difference between successive worlds also implies a difference in their antecedent causes, and thus an abandonment of the completely closed causality required by (a). Perhaps some Stoics supposed that the conflagration cleans out all vestiges of its antecedents, leaving indeterminate matter for god to start a new and independent causal sequence. His perfect rationality would then initiate essentially the same world, with numerically identical individual persons. The goodness of the next world would be unaffected by the presence or absence of such morally indifferent features as moles on the face. Such differences, however, would permit the next world to occur in a genuinely different temporal dimension, since Socrates with a mole could not occur at the same time as Socrates without this feature.

On balance, Chrysippus probably opted for (a). It seems the more challenging philosophical thesis, and the one that accords best with the Stoics' emphasis on complete coherence. Perhaps too it helps to indicate the moral significance or lack of significance for everlasting recurrence. If (a) is true, the life to come will not be different in the slightest feature from what one has now. The absolute sameness of everything and the indifference of cyclical recurrence are pointedly indicated by Marcus Aurelius (**H**), who insists that all a person *has* is the present moment. Marcus is writing too informally to cast light on the technical details of Chrysippus' theories. But we may conjecture that the moral perspectives of both men were broadly similar. Just as Nietzsche probably regarded everlasting recurrence as a way of saying that any other life one had would always be just the same – for how else could it be *your* life? – so in Stoicism the doctrine may have served to underline the necessity of accepting one's present situation. For that will be one's situation time and again in the everlasting nature of things.

53 Soul

A Origen, *On principles* 3.1.2–3 (*SVF* 2.988, part)

[Endorsing Stoic doctrine] (1) Of moving things, some have the cause of movement in themselves, while others are moved only from outside. (2) The latter comprise things which are transportable, like logs and stones and every material thing which is sustained by tenor alone ... (3) Animals and plants have the cause of movement in themselves, and so, quite simply, does everything sustained by physique or soul, which they say also includes metals ... (4) Some things of this kind, they say, are moved 'out of' themselves, and others 'by' themselves: the former comprise soulless things, the latter ones which are ensouled. Ensouled things are moved 'by' themselves when an impression occurs within them which calls forth an impulse ... (5) A rational animal, however, in addition to its impressionistic nature, has reason which passes judgement on impressions, rejecting some of these and accepting others, in order that the animal may be guided accordingly.

B Hierocles 1.5–33, 4.38–53

(1) If the seed falls into the womb at the right time and is gripped by the receptacle in good health, it no longer stays still as before but is energized

and begins its own activities. It draws matter from the pregnant body, and fashions the embryo in accordance with inescapable patterns, up to the point when it reaches its goal and makes its product ready to be born. (2) Yet throughout all this time – I mean the time from conception to birth – it remains [in the form of] physique, i.e. breath, having changed from seed and moving methodically from beginning to end. In the early stages, the physique is breath of a rather dense kind and considerably distant from soul; but later, when it is close to birth, it becomes finer . . . So when it passes outside, it is adequate for the environment, with the result that, having been hardened thereby, it is capable of changing into soul. (3) For just as the breath in stones is immediately kindled by a blow, on account of its readiness for this change, so the physique of a ripe embryo, once it is born, does not hesitate to change into soul on meeting the environment. So whatever issues forth from the womb is at once an animal . . . (4) At this point it should be borne in mind that every animal differs from the non-animal in two respects, sensation and impulse . . . (5) Since an animal is a composite of body and soul, and both of these are tangible and impressible and of course subject to resistance, and also blended through and through, and one of them is a sensory faculty which itself undergoes movement in the way we have indicated, it is evident that an animal perceives itself continuously. (6) For by stretching out and relaxing, the soul makes an impression on all the body's parts, since it is blended with them all, and in making an impression it receives an impression in response. (7) For the body, just like the soul, reacts to pressure; and the outcome is a state of their joint pressure upon, and resistance to, each other. (8) From the outermost parts inclining within, it travels . . . to the commanding-faculty, with the result that there is an awareness both of all the body's parts and of the soul's. (9) This is equivalent to the animal's perceiving itself.

C Plutarch, *On Stoic self-contradictions* 1053D (*SVF* 2.806, part)

As proof of the fact that the soul is engendered, and engendered after the body, Chrysippus chiefly uses the fact that children resemble their parents in temperament and character.

D Galen, *On the formation of the foetus* 4.698,2–9 (*SVF* 2.761, part)
(1) In the first place . . . they [Peripatetics and Stoics] assume that the heart is generated before everything else. (2) Secondly, that the heart generates the other parts, as if the agent of the heart's construction, whoever it is, were destroyed and not still existing. (3) Thirdly, as a consequence, they claim that even the deliberative part of our soul is situated in the heart.

E Galen, *On Hippocrates' Epidemics* VI 270,26–8 (*SVF* 2.782)

Everyone who supposes that the soul is breath says that it is preserved by exhalation both of the blood and of the < air > drawn into the body by inhalation through the windpipe.

F Sextus Empiricus, *Against the professors* 7.234

Some [of the Stoics] . . . say that soul has two meanings, that which sustains the whole compound, and in particular, the commanding-faculty. For when we say that man is a compound of soul and body, or that death is separation of soul and body, we are referring particularly to the commanding-faculty.

G Calcidius 220 (*SVF* 2.879, part)

(1) Chrysippus says: 'It is certain that we breathe and live with one and the same thing. (2) But we breathe with natural breath. (3) Therefore we live as well with the same breath. (4) But we live with the soul. (5) Therefore the soul is found to be natural breath . . . (6) The soul's parts flow from their seat in the heart, as if from the source of a spring, and spread through the whole body. They continually fill all the limbs with vital breath, and rule and control them with countless different powers – nutrition, growth, locomotion, sensation, impulse to action. (7) The soul as a whole despatches the senses (which are its proper functions) like branches from the trunk-like commanding-faculty to be reporters of what they sense, while itself like a monarch passes judgement on their reports. (8) The objects of sensation, as bodies, are composite, and the individual senses sense one definite thing, this one colours, another sounds . . . and in all cases of the present; no sense remembers what is past or foresees the future. (9) It is the function of internal reflection and reasoning to understand each sense's affection, and to infer from their reports what it [i.e. the object] is, and to accept it when present, remember it when absent, and foresee it when future.'

H Aetius 4.21.1–4 (*SVF* 2.836, part)

(1) The Stoics say that the commanding-faculty is the soul's highest part, which produces impressions, assents, perceptions and impulses. They also call it the reasoning faculty. (2) From the commanding-faculty there are seven parts of the soul which grow out and stretch out into the body like the tentacles of an octopus. (3) Five of these are the senses, sight, smell, hearing, taste and touch. Sight is breath which extends from the commanding-faculty to the eyes, hearing is breath which extends from the commanding-faculty to the ears . . . (4) Of the remainder, one is

called seed, and this is breath extending from the commanding-faculty to the genitals. (5) The other, . . . which they also call utterance, is breath extending from the commanding-faculty to the pharynx, tongue and appropriate organs.

I Nemesius 212,6–9 (Panaetius fr. 86)

The philosopher Panaetius takes the vocal faculty to be a part of the movement governed by impulse; and he is quite right to say so. He makes the reproductive faculty a part not of soul but of physique.

J Cicero, *On duties* 1.132 (Panaetius fr. 88)

Souls' movements are of two kinds: one belongs to thought, the other to impulse. The sphere of thought is principally the investigation of truth, while impulse is the stimulus to action. So we must take care to use thought for the best possible objects, and to make impulse obedient to reason.

K Iamblichus, *On the soul* (Stobaeus 1.368,12–20; *SVF* 2.826, part)

(1) How are the soul's faculties distinguished? Some of them, according to the Stoics, by a difference in the underlying bodies. For they say that a sequence of different breaths extends from the commanding-faculty, some to the eyes, others to the ears and others to other sense-organs. (2) Other faculties are differentiated by a peculiarity of quality in regard to the same substrate. Just as an apple possesses in the same body sweetness and fragrance, so too the commanding-faculty combines in the same body impression, assent, impulse, reason.

L Seneca, *Letters* 113.23 (*SVF* 2.836, part)

Cleanthes and his pupil Chrysippus did not agree on what walking is. Cleanthes said it was breath extending from the commanding-faculty to the feet, Chrysippus that it was the commanding-faculty itself.

M Aetius 4.23.1 (*SVF* 2.854)

The Stoics say that [bodily] affections occur in the affected regions, but sensations in the commanding-faculty.

N Diogenes Laertius 7.157 (*SVF* 2.867)

Seeing takes place when the light between the visual faculty and the object is stretched into the shape of a cone . . . The air adjacent to the pupil forms the tip of the cone with its base next to the visual object. What is seen is reported by means of the stretched air, as by a walking-stick.

O Nemesius 291,1–6 (*SVF* 2.991, part)

[According to Chrysippus and other Stoics] Every generated being has something given to it by fate: water has being cool as its gift, and each kind of plant has bearing a certain fruit; stones and fire have downward and upward movement respectively; so too animals, as their gift, have assent and impulse.

P Philo, *Allegories of the laws* 1.30 (*SVF* 2.844)

(1) The animal is superior to the non-animal in two respects, impression and impulse. (2) An impression is formed by the approach of an external object which strikes the mind through sensation. (3) Impulse, the close relation of impression, is formed by the tonic power of the mind. By stretching this out through sensation, the mind grasps the object and goes towards it, eager to seize and reach it.

Q Stobaeus, 2.86,17–87,6 (*SVF* 3.169, part)

(1) What activates impulse, they [the Stoics] say, is precisely an impression capable of directly impelling a proper function. (2) In genus impulse is a movement of soul towards something. (3) In species it is seen to include both the impulse which occurs in rational animals and the one found in the non-rational; but these species have not been given corresponding names. For desire is not rational impulse, but a species of this. (4) One would correctly define rational impulse by saying that it is a movement of thought towards something in the sphere of action. The contrary of this is repulsion.

R Plutarch, *On Stoic self-contradictions* 1037F (*SVF* 3.175, part)

According to Chrysippus, the impulse of man is reason prescribing action to him; he has written thus in his book *On law*. Repulsion then is prohibitive reason.

S Plutarch, *On Stoic self-contradictions* 1057A (*SVF* 3.177, part)

What is the subject most argued about by Chrysippus himself and Antipater in their disputes with the Academics? The doctrine that without assent there is neither action nor impulsion, and that they are talking nonsense and empty assumptions who claim that, when an appropriate impression occurs, impulsion ensues at once without people first having yielded or given their assent.

T Sextus Empiricus, *Against the professors* 8.275–6 (*SVF* 2.223, part)

(1) They [the doctrinaire philosophers] say that it is not uttered speech but internal speech by which man differs from non-rational animals; for

crows and parrots and jays utter articulate sounds. (2) Nor is it by the merely simple impression that he differs (for they too receive impressions), but by impressions produced by inference and combination. (3) This amounts to his possessing the conception of 'following' and directly grasping, on account of 'following', the idea of sign. For sign is itself of the kind 'If this, then that.' (4) Therefore the existence of signs follows from man's nature and constitution.

U Galen, *On Hippocrates' and Plato's doctrines* 2.5.9–13 (*SVF* 3 Diogenes 29, part)

[Diogenes of Babylon] (1) 'The source of articulate utterance is the same as the source of utterance, and therefore meaningful articulate utterance has that source too. (2) But this last is language. (3) Therefore language and utterance have the same source. (4) But the source of utterance is not the region of the head, but evidently somewhere lower down; for it is obvious that utterance passes out through the windpipe. (5) Therefore language too does not have its source in the head, but lower down. (6) But that too is certainly true, viz. that language has its source in thought; for some people actually define language as meaningful utterance sent out from thought. (7) It is also credible that language is sent out imprinted, and stamped as it were, by the conceptions present in thought, and that it is temporally coextensive with both the act of thinking and the activity of speaking. (8) Therefore thought too is not in the head but in the lower regions, principally no doubt around the heart.'

V Galen, *On Hippocrates' and Plato's doctrines* 5.2.49, 5.3.1 (*SVF* 2.841, part)

[Chrysippus] 'They are parts of the soul through which its reason and the character of its reason are constituted. A soul is noble or base according to the state of its commanding-part with respect to its appropriate divisions' . . . Perhaps you are reminding us of what you wrote in your books *On reason*: 'Reason is a collection of certain conceptions and preconceptions.'

W Eusebius, *Evangelical preparation* 15.20.6 (*SVF* 2.809)

(1) They [the Stoics] say that the soul is subject to generation and destruction. When separated from the body, however, it does not perish at once but survives on its own for certain times, the soul of the virtuous up to the dissolution of everything into fire, that of fools only for certain definite times. (2) By the survival of souls they mean that we ourselves survive as souls separated from bodies and changed into the lesser substance of the soul, while the souls of non-rational animals perish along with their bodies.

X Diogenes Laertius 7.143 (*SVF* 2.633, part)

That the world is ensouled is evident, they [the Stoics] say, from our own soul's being an offshoot of it.

Y Cicero, *On the nature of the gods* 2.58 (*SVF* 1.172, part)

[The Stoic spokesman Balbus] Just as other natural substances are each generated, made to grow and sustained by their own seeds, so the nature of the world has all the movements of volition, impulses and desires which the Greeks call *hormai*, and exhibits the actions in agreement with these in the way that we ourselves do who are moved by emotions and sensations.

☐ As in Greek usage generally (cf. **14** commentary), 'soul' has a wide range of applications in Stoicism. These comprise, at their narrowest, the vital functions of human beings quite specifically; then the vital functions of animals quite generally as distinct from plants; and finally, the functions of god, the 'active principle' of the world, which pervades 'matter', the 'passive principle', in a relation described as that of 'world-soul' to the 'body' of the world (**44C; 46E–F**). The Stoics had Platonic precedents for positing a 'world-soul' (cf. especially *Timaeus* 34 ff., *Laws* 10), an un-Aristotelian conception, as the immanent source of cosmic motion. They differed strongly from Plato, however, in treating the world-soul as identical to the divine Craftsman and in totally rejecting Plato's distinction between the physical world and the non-physical and everlasting Forms on which Plato's Craftsman models the world. As divine 'breath', the Stoics' world-soul is coextensive with the grosser matter which forms the world's body. Thus god and the world have the basic attributes of an 'animal' (**47C;54A, B, F**) in a literal sense that would have appalled Plato and Aristotle. Our texts refer to this macrocosmic dimension of soul in **X** and **Y**. As body-soul compounds, we humans are microcosmic beings; and attributes that we possess in virtue of having rational souls are features of the world. There is even a specific region of the world, the 'aether', which houses the world's 'commanding-faculty' (**47O**; cf. **54B**).

The world-soul is rational or intelligent through and through. This doctrine provides the physical foundation for the ethical injunction that human beings, as 'parts' of the whole, should conform themselves to universal nature by perfecting their rationality (cf. **63C**). As already noted however (see **47O–Q**), cosmic breath differentiates the contents of the world by the three structural principles, tenor/physique and soul (**A**). In this 'scale of nature' ensouled beings owe their highest place in the hierarchy to the fact that they are purposeful self-movers (**A 4**). In adopting this Aristotelian *differentia* of animals, the Stoics differed from Aristotle (and from Plato too) by removing soul from plants. A plant's life is explained by its 'physique' (*phusis*), its possession of a principle of movement which enables it to grow 'out of' itself (**A 3–4**).

So much of Stoic psychology recalls Aristotle that this difference over plants calls for explanation. Animal reproduction, moreover, which Aristotle had assigned to the nutritive soul, now gets a whole part of the soul to itself, on the orthodox Stoic account (**H** 4), though Panaetius relegated it to 'physique' (**I**). It looks as if the Stoics noticed an essential difference between the automatic processes of growth and the self-directing functions of an animal's life, a difference which would be crucially obscured by subsuming them all under soul. They also wanted to emphasize the evolution in modes of life from conception to maturity.

An embryo is like a plant up to the moment of birth (**B** 2, so too Aristotle, *Generation of animals* v.1,778b35). Once the heart has been formed, it becomes (as in Aristotle again) the agent for fashioning the rest of the embryo (**D**). Only at the moment of birth is this 'physique' transformed into soul, which suggests the sufficiency of vegetative processes to account for the life and growth of an embryo. Are we to suppose that the newly emergent soul takes over the functions of the physique which was its previous state? This may seem to be implied in **G** 6 where the soul's parts include provision of nutrition and growth to the limbs (and cf. **47P** 4). Yet no other texts which give standard accounts of the soul's eight parts make any references to nutrition and growth. If moreover we take it that the commanding-faculty directly controls these vital functions, it is hard to see how it does so in virtue of its basic powers, impression and impulse (**P** 1). The upshot of all the evidence strongly suggests that an animal's 'physique', its plant-like principle, continues to direct its growth automatically after the soul has been formed. If pressed, the Stoics would probably have been willing to attribute all features of an animal's life to its soul. In practice, their account of its powers suits only the restricted conception, whereby it refers to the 'commanding-faculty' (**F**) and its seven subordinate parts. This has the effect of sharply focusing on soul as the distinguishing characteristic of an agent (self-mover) who can (in the case of humans, with their additional powers, **A** 5, **R**, **T** etc.) be held to account for what he does (**62K**). (Cf. *SVF* 1.538, where Cleanthes calls man 'soul alone'.)

The texts reporting the soul's nature as breath (**G** 1–5; cf. **47H**), and the proofs of its corporeality (**45C–D**), generation and destruction (**C,W**) speak for themselves. As breath, the soul is characterized by its tensile motion (**47Q–R**), a physical property with important bearing on a person's moral condition (cf. **65T**). The 'commanding-faculty' (a new term for the centre of consciousness, which is sometimes called mind (*nous*)) and its seven subordinate parts can be compared respectively to the brain and the nervous system, as with Epicurus' 'mind' and 'spirit' (**14B**). As the seat of all mental states, including emotion (cf. **65G**), the commanding-faculty is located in the region of the heart rather than the head. This traditional belief was strenuously defended by the Stoics against the new findings of contemporary physiologists. Apart from the kind of considerations adduced in **U** (and cf. **34J**; **65H**; also **14B** 1 for the Epicureans), they had vested interests in retaining the priority of the heart (**D**) for their account of growth and nutrition. Heart and soul are in physical contact with one another. Taken together, they constitute the union of an animal's vegetative and mental powers. Furthermore, as **E** shows, blood has a vital role to play in maintaining the soul's pneumatic nature.

Just as animals start their life as plant-like beings, without any cognitive faculties, so humans are like the other animals to begin with. Rationality, which distinguishes humans from beasts, develops only gradually (**39E 4**). Their common vital characteristics are indicated by the same eight 'parts' of the soul (**H**), though an animal's commanding-faculty lacks reason. The term 'part' primarily denotes a spatial division of the soul, starting from the commanding-faculty or 'highest part'. Hence the image of the octopus (**H 2**), which helps us to visualize the soul's structure as expansible and contractible currents of breath. The seven subordinate parts – senses, utterance and reproduction – are purely instrumental executives of the commanding-faculty (cf. **G 7–9**). It is there that all awareness takes place (**M**).

More interesting and more problematical are the soul's faculties, in the sense of that word in **K 2**. These are not physically distinguishable, by reference to different bodily organs, any more than is an apple's fragrance from its sweetness. Though sometimes misleadingly called parts (cf. **V**), the faculties, as we shall call them here, pick out 'qualities' (see **28F**) of the commanding-faculty itself. They designate its different modes of operation, and in such a way that the soul or self is not fragmented into a plurality of psychic entities, as in the Platonic model. The subject of impression, impulse etc. is one and the same commanding-faculty. This unitary view of the soul was Chrysippus' doctrine. Though firmly rejected by Posidonius, who reverted to Platonic tripartition (cf. **65K, M, P**), and possibly by Panaetius, in whom some find Aristotelian bipartition (cf. **J**), Chrysippus' unitary model is of great philosophical interest (see further **65**). How far it had already been adumbrated by his Stoic predecessors it is impossible to say.

Logically, and within a creature's experience, impression is the primary faculty. In the same context as **B**, at **57C**, Hierocles insists that an animal immediately on birth 'perceives itself', and that self-perception is prior to any perception of externals. Self-perception (**B 5–9**), or recognition of the kind of animal one is (cf. **57B**), seems to be the outcome of the fact that body and soul are constantly conjoined and interacting (cf. **45C**; **48C 10**). **B** does not use the standard word for impression, *phantasia*, but the terms for describing the body–soul interaction can be so translated (most literally, 'striking against' and 'being struck in return'): from this interaction an awareness or 'impression' in the mental sense results. Most basically then, impression is that in virtue of which an animal is aware of how *it* is affected (cf. **P–Q**; **39A–B**). While this will frequently refer to sense-perception (**P 2**), we may take the faculty itself to cover all states of awareness, including pleasures and pains, which were explained as objects of 'internal touch' (Cicero, *Academica* 2.20, cf. **16** commentary).

The meagre evidence on the mechanics of sensing (**N** is a representative instance) suggests that the Stoics were largely content to take over Peripatetic doctrines, adapting these to suit their dynamic materialism; note the contribution of 'tension' (the 'stretched' medium) to seeing. The legacy of Aristotle seems no less strong in the general account of animal motion as the product of impression and 'impulse', the second basic faculty of soul (**P,Q**). This recalls e.g. *Movement of animals* 701a6: 'an animal moves and goes forward by desire or choice when some change has occurrred in accordance with sensation or *phantasia*'. The common ground becomes all the more evident in the light of Aristotle's recourse to 'ingrown breath' (*sumphuton pneuma*, *Movement of animals* 10) as the 'expansible and contractible body' which transmits the soul's desires into the body's movements. (Cf. **47R** and Cleanthes' account of walking in **L**.) These similarities however do not make the Stoics mere transmitters of Peripatetic thinking. Arguably they avoided some of the latter's difficulties by treating the soul itself as *pneuma*. This removed the problem of showing how a body could be moved by an incorporeal soul. Furthermore, by unifying all states of awareness in the faculty of *phantasia* (impression), they seem to have intuited a notion of the unity of consciousness, which is scarcely pellucid in the intricate Aristotelian relationships between sensation, *phantasia* and intellect. A final and very important innovation is the explicit causal connexion between an animal's appetition and its awareness of an objective suited to its natural constitution (a 'proper function' **Q 1**; **57B–C**).

Non-rational animals experience only 'simple' impressions (**T**). Presumably the impulses of such creatures are immediately stimulated by moment-by-moment sense-impressions of things appropriate or inappropriate to the kind of animals they are. In humans, however, at least when rationality has developed, a third faculty of soul, 'assent', mediates between impressions and impulses (**S**). This too is a Stoic innovation, and one of cardinal importance to their epistemology and ethics (cf. **40B**; **62C**; **69A** with commentary). What it implies, in a nutshell, is 'going along with' or 'committing oneself to' the truth, desirability etc. of the state of affairs which forms the content of an impression, and the capacity to refrain from doing so; Epictetus calls assent 'the power to use impressions' (**62K 3**). In humans all impulses are acts of assent (**33I**; cf. **S**), a thesis which entails that we are responsible for all our desires. Assent, then, looks like a distinguishing mark of rationality, and this is no doubt correct. It should be noted, none the less, that some texts (e.g. **O**; **62G 6**) credit animals quite generally with assent as well as impulse. If this is a mistake, the seemingly authoritative **K 2** points in the same way; for if assent is simply a function of reason, we need to explain how it can be specified here as a faculty alongside impression, impulse *and* reason. Possibly, then, even non-rational animals should be credited with a primitive form of assent – 'yielding' (cf. **S**) to the appropriate impression. What animals decisively lack is reason (**A 5**). This human endowment fundamentally qualifies the entire human soul, making its impressions (**39A 6**) and impulses (**R**) rational, and so too its powers of giving or withholding assent. If the animal soul has all three faculties in rudimentary, non-rational form, this would help us to understand how the Stoics could regard reason as the mode of the whole adult human soul's operation, a new disposition which totally alters all the pre-rational endowment. In any event, a soul's commanding-faculty, whether animal or human, is to be regarded as a unitary agent. (Cf. Chrysippus' account of walking in **L**.)

A final point of general interest is a pronounced focus on specifying the character of reason itself. Four principal features are to be noted here: (a) the analysis of reason by reference to the disposition of the three faculties just discussed (the probable sense of Chrysippus in the first part of **V**); (b) its conceptual generality (second part of **V**); (c) its logical power, derived from the nature of a rational animal's impressions (**T**); (d) its manifestation in language (**U**), perhaps derived from the nature of a rational animal's impulses (cf. **I**). Even if some of this takes up issues from earlier philosophy (cf. Plato, *Theaetetus* 189e, *Sophist* 263e for thought as internalized discourse), it has a systematic character and clarity which appears thoroughly original.

For other aspects of Stoic psychology, see **39–41**; **57**; **59**; **61–2**; **65**.

54 Theology

A Diogenes Laertius 7.147 (*SVF* 2.1021, part)

They [the Stoics] say that god is an animal which is immortal and rational or intelligent, perfect in happiness, not admitting of any evil, provident towards the world and its occupants, but not anthropomorphic. He is the creator of the whole and, as it were, the father of all, both generally and, in particular, that part of him which pervades all things, which is called by many descriptions according to his powers. For they call him Zeus [*Dia*] as the cause [*di' hon*] of all things; Zēn in so far as he is responsible for, or pervades, life [*zēn*]; Athena because his commanding-faculty stretches into the aether; Hera because it stretches into the air; . . . [etc.]

B Cicero, *On the nature of the gods* 1.39 (*SVF* 2.1077, part)

For he [Chrysippus] says that divine power resides in reason and in the mind and intellect of universal nature. He says that god is the world itself, and the universal pervasiveness of its mind; also that he is the world's own commanding-faculty, since he is located in intellect and reason; that he is the common nature of things, universal and all-embracing; also the force of fate and the necessity of future events. In addition he is fire; and the aether of which I spoke earlier; also things in a natural state of flux and mobility, like water, earth, air, sun, moon and stars; and the all-embracing whole; and even those men who have attained immortality.

C Cicero, *On the nature of the gods* 2.12–15

[The Stoic spokesman Balbus] (1) Therefore the main point is agreed among all men of all races. For all have it inborn and virtually engraved in their minds that there are gods. Opinions vary as to what they are like, but that they exist no one denies. (2) Cleanthes, of our school, said that conceptions of the gods have been formed in men's minds for four reasons. (3) The first conception which he mentioned was the one of which I spoke just now, the one which had arisen from precognition of future events. (4) Second was the one which we received from the magnitude of the benefits which we get from temperateness of climate, the earth's fertility, and the vast array of other advantages. (5) Third was the one which had men's minds terrified by lightning, storms, [etc.] . . . Through their terror of these, men have suspected the existence of some divine celestial force. (6) The fourth and chief cause was the regularity of the motion, the revolution of the heavens, and the individuality, usefulness, beauty and order of the sun, the moon, and all the stars. The mere sight of these things, he said, was proof enough that they are not products of accident. Just as, if someone enters a house, a gymnasium or a forum, when he sees the controlled methodical pattern of all that goes on he cannot think that these things happen without cause, but understands that there is someone in charge who is obeyed, much more must he, in the case of these great motions and phases and of the orderings of things so numerous and immense, none of which has ever been reported otherwise by a tradition of measureless antiquity, conclude that it is by some mind that these great motions of nature are controlled.

D Sextus Empiricus, *Against the professors* 9.133–6

(1) Zeno also argued like this. One might reasonably honour the gods. \<One might not reasonably honour those who do not exist.\> Therefore gods exist. (2) Some, in parody of this argument, say: 'One might reasonably honour the wise. One might not reasonably honour those who do not exist. Therefore wise men exist.' This was contrary to Stoic doctrine, since to this day no one fitting their account of the wise man has turned up. (3) Diogenes of Babylon countered this parody with the claim that the second premise of Zeno's argument had the force 'One might not reasonably honour those whose nature it is not to exist'. For when it is taken in this sense, it is evident that it is the gods' nature to exist, in which case they do *eo ipso* exist. For if they once existed they exist now too, just as if atoms ever existed they exist now too (for such bodies are indestructible and ungenerated according to their conception). Hence the argument will also, by means of a conclusion which follows from the premises, secure the deduction. Of the wise, on the other hand, it is not the case that since it is their nature to exist they do *eo ipso* exist. (4) Others say that Zeno's first premise, 'One might reasonably honour the gods', is ambiguous. For one meaning is 'One might reasonably *honour* the gods', the other '. . . *hold in honour* . . .' It is the former which is used as the premise, and that is false when applied to the wise.

E Cicero, *On the nature of the gods* 2.16 (*SVF* 2.1012, part)

(1) For if, says Chrysippus, there is something in nature which man's mind, reason, strength and power cannot make, that which makes it must be better than man. But the things in the heavens and all those whose regularity is everlasting cannot be created by man. Therefore that

by which these are created is better than man. But what more suitable name for this is there than 'god'? (2) Indeed, if the gods do not exist, what can there be in nature better than man, seeing that he alone possesses that highest possible mark of distinction, reason? But that there should be a man who believes there to be nothing in the whole world better than himself is crazy arrogance. Therefore there is something better. Therefore god really does exist.

F Sextus Empiricus, *Against the professors* 9.104, 108–10

(1) Again, Zeno says: 'The rational is superior to the non-rational. But nothing is superior to the world. Therefore the world is rational. And similarly with "intelligent" and "participating in animation". For the intelligent is superior to the non-intelligent, and the animate to the non-animate. But nothing is superior to the world. Therefore the world is intelligent and animate.' . . . (2) But Alexinus parodied Zeno as follows. The poetical is superior to the non-poetical, the grammatical to the non-grammatical, and the skilled to the non-skilled in the other crafts. But nothing is superior to the world. Therefore the world is poetical and grammatical. (3) The Stoics counter this parody by saying that Zeno's premise refers to the absolutely superior, i.e. the rational to the non-rational, the intelligent to the non-intelligent, and the animate to the non-animate, whereas Alexinus' does not: for the superiority of the poetical to the non-poetical and the grammatical to the non-grammatical is not absolute. Hence a great difference can be seen in the arguments. Take Archilochus, who is poetical but not superior to the non-poetical Socrates, and Aristarchus, who is grammatical but not superior to the non-grammatical Plato.

G Cicero, *On the nature of the gods* 2.22

(1) Zeno also argued as follows: 'Nothing lacking sensation can have a sentient part. But the world has sentient parts. Therefore the world does not lack sensation.' (2) He then proceeds to a tighter argument: 'Nothing without a share in mind and reason can give birth to one who is animate and rational. But the world gives birth to those who are animate and rational. Therefore the world is animate and rational.' (3) He also, as often, argued by analogy, as follows: 'If from an olive tree there grew flutes playing in tune, you would surely not doubt that there was in the tree some knowledge of flute-playing. Or if plane trees bore lyres sounding in rhythm, no doubt you would also suppose that there was some musicianship in the plane trees. Why then should the world not be judged animate and wise, when it engenders the animate and the wise from itself?'

H Cicero, *On the nature of the gods* 2.37–9

(1) For nor is there anything else besides the world which has nothing missing, and which is equipped from every point of view, perfect, and complete in all its measures and parts. As Chrysippus cleverly put it, just as the shield-cover was made for the sake of the shield and the sheath for the sake of the sword, so too with the exception of the world everything else was made for the sake of other things: for example, the crops and fruits which the earth brings forth were made for the sake of animals, and the animals which it brings forth were made for the sake of men (the horse for transport, the ox for ploughing, the dog for hunting and guarding). Man himself has come to be in order to contemplate and imitate the world, being by no means perfect, but a tiny constituent of that which is perfect. But the world, since it embraces everything and there is nothing which is not included in it, is perfect from every point of view. (2) How then can it lack that which is best? But nothing is better than intellect and reason. Therefore the world cannot lack these. (3) Therefore Chrysippus did well to prove by appeal to analogies that all things are better in perfect and mature specimens – for instance, in horse than in foal, in dog than in pup, in man than in child. Likewise, he argued, that which is the best thing in the whole world should be found in something which is perfect and complete. But nothing is more perfect than the world, and nothing better than virtue. Therefore virtue is intrinsic to the world. (4) Indeed, man's nature is not perfect, yet virtue is achieved in man. Then how much more easily in the world! Therefore there is virtue in the world. Therefore the world is wise, and hence is god.

I Cleanthes, *Hymn to Zeus* (*SVF* 1.537)

(1) Most majestic of immortals, many-titled, ever omnipotent Zeus, prime mover of nature, who with your law steer all things, hail to you. For it is proper for any mortal to address you: we are your offspring, and alone of all mortal creatures which are alive and tread the earth we bear a likeness to god. Therefore I shall hymn you and sing for ever of your might. (2) All this cosmos, as it spins around the earth, obeys you, whichever way you lead, and willingly submits to your sway. Such is the double-edged fiery ever-living thunderbolt which you hold at the ready in your unvanquished hands. For under its strokes all the works of nature are accomplished. With it you direct the universal reason which runs through all things and intermingles with the lights of heaven both great and small. ... (3) No deed is done on earth, god, without your offices, nor in the divine ethereal vault of heaven, nor at sea, save what bad men do in their folly. But you know how to make things crooked straight and to

order things disorderly. You love things unloved. For you have so welded into one all things good and bad that they all share in a single everlasting reason. It is shunned and neglected by the bad among mortal men, the wretched, who ever yearn for the possession of goods yet neither see nor hear god's universal law, by obeying which they could lead a good life in partnership with intelligence. Instead, devoid of intelligence, they rush into this evil or that, some in their belligerent quest for fame, others with an unbridled bent for acquisition, others for leisure and the pleasurable acts of the body . . . <But all that they achieve is evils,> despite travelling hither and thither in burning quest of the opposite. (4) Bountiful Zeus of the dark clouds and gleaming thunderbolt, protect mankind from its pitiful incompetence. Scatter this from our soul, Father. Let us achieve the power of judgement by trusting in which you steer all things with justice, so that by winning honour we may repay you with honour, for ever singing of your works, as it befits mortals to do. For neither men nor gods have any greater privilege than this: to sing for ever in righteousness of the universal law.

J Cicero, *On the nature of the gods* 2.75–6

[The Stoic spokesman Balbus] (1) I therefore assert that it is by the providence of the gods that the world and all its parts were first compounded and have been governed for all time. The defence of that thesis is usually divided into three parts by our school. (2) The first part derives from the reasoning which proves that the gods exist: once this is granted, it has to be conceded that the world is governed by their counsels. (3) Second is the part which proves that all things are under the control of a sentient nature, and that nature's works are all of the utmost beauty: once this is established, it follows that they are generated from animate origins. (4) Third comes the topic which derives from our awe at things in the heaven and on earth.

(5) First, therefore, either it must be denied that the gods exist, as Democritus in effect does by introducing his 'likenesses' and Epicurus his 'images', or, if it is granted that the gods exist, it must be admitted that they do something, indeed something distinguished. But there is nothing more distinguished than governing the world. Therefore the world is governed by the gods' counsels.

K Plutarch, *On common conceptions* 1075E (*SVF* 2.1126)

Moreover they themselves [the Stoics] are unceasingly busy crying woe against Epicurus for ruining the preconception of the gods by abolishing providence. For, they say, god is preconceived and thought of not only as immortal and blessed but also as benevolent, caring and beneficent.

L Cicero, *On the nature of the gods* 2.88

[The Stoic spokesman Balbus] Suppose someone were to bring to Scythia or Britain the armillary sphere recently built by our friend Posidonius, which revolution by revolution brings about in the sun, the moon and the five planets effects identical to those brought about day by day and night by night in the heavens. Who in those foreign lands would doubt that that sphere was a product of reason? And yet these people hesitate as to whether the world, from which all things come into being, is itself the product of some kind of accident or necessity or of a divine mind's reason. And they rate Archimedes' achievement in imitating the revolutions of the heavenly sphere higher than nature's in creating them – and that when the original is a vastly more brilliant creation than the copy.

M Cicero, *On the nature of the gods* 2.93

[The Stoic spokesman Balbus] Does it not deserve amazement on my part that there should be anyone who can persuade himself that certain solid and indivisible bodies travel through the force of their own weight and that by an accidental combination of those bodies a world of the utmost splendour and beauty is created? I do not see why the person who supposes this can happen does not also believe it possible that if countless exemplars of the twenty-one letters, in gold or any other material you like, were thrown into a container then shaken out onto the ground, they might form a readable copy of the *Annals* of Ennius. I'm not sure that luck could manage this even to the extent of a single line!

N Cicero, *On the nature of the gods* 2.133

[The Stoic spokesman Balbus] Suppose someone asks for whose sake this vast edifice has been constructed. For the trees and plants, which although not sentient are sustained by nature? No, that is absurd. For the animals? No, it is no more plausible that the gods should have done all this work for the sake of dumb ignorant animals. Then for whose sake will anyone say that the world was created? Presumably for those animate creatures which use reason: that is, for gods and men. Nothing is better than them, for reason is the supreme gift. Thus it becomes credible that it was for the sake of gods and men that the world and everything in it was made.

O Plutarch, *On Stoic self-contradictions* 1044D (*SVF* 2.1163)

In *On nature* book 5 he [Chrysippus] says that bed-bugs are useful for waking us, that mice encourage us not to be untidy, and that it is only to be expected that nature should love beauty and delight in variety. He then adds, in these very words, 'The best evidence of this would be supplied by the peacock's tail. For it shows that in this case the animal has been created for the sake of the tail, and not vice versa. That is how the peacock came to be created, with the peahen as concomitant.'

P Porphyry, *On abstinence* 3.20.1, 3 (including *SVF* 2.1152, part)

(1) It was certainly a persuasive idea of Chrysippus' that the gods made us for our own and each other's sakes, and animals for our sake: horses to help us in war, dogs in hunting, and leopards, bears and lions to give us practice in courage. As for the pig, that most appetizing of delicacies, it was created for no other purpose than slaughter, and god, in furnishing our cuisine, mixed soul in with its flesh like salt. . . . (2) Now let anyone who finds this at all persuasive, and fitting for god, consider how he is going to reply to the following argument of Carneades. 'Every product of nature, when it achieves the natural end for which it was born, is benefited. ('Benefit' here is to be understood in its broader sense, which these people call 'advantage' [for the narrower sense, see **60G 1**]). But the pig has been born for the natural end of being slaughtered and eaten. When this happens to it, it achieves its natural end, and is benefited.'

Q Gellius 7.1.1–13 (*SVF* 2.1169–70)

(1) Those who disbelieve that the world was created for the sake of god and man, and that human affairs are governed by providence, think that they are using a weighty argument when they say that if there were providence, there would be no evils. For nothing, they say, is less compatible with providence than that in the world which it is alleged to have made for men there should be such a host of troubles and evils. Chrysippus' reply to this, when arguing the point in his *On providence* book 4, is as follows: 'There is absolutely nothing more foolish than those who think that there could have been goods without the coexistence of evils. For since goods are opposite to evils, the two must necessarily exist in opposition to each other and supported by a kind of opposed interdependence. And there is no such opposite without its matching opposite. For how could there be perception of justice if there were no injustices? What else *is* justice, if not the removal of injustice? Likewise, what appreciation of courage could there be except through the contrast with cowardice? Of moderation, if not from immoderation? How, again, could there be prudence if there were not imprudence opposed to it? Why do the fools not similarly wish that there were truth without there being falsity? For goods and evils, fortune and misfortune, pain and pleasure, exist in just the same way: they are tied to each other in polar opposition, as Plato said. Remove one, and you remove the other. (2) Chrysippus also, in the same book, takes seriously and tackles the

question 'whether human illnesses come about in accordance with nature' – that is, whether nature herself or providence, who created the structure of our world and the human race, also created the illnesses, infirmities and diseases of the body which men suffer from. In his judgement it was not nature's principal intention to make men liable to disease: that would never have been fitting for nature, the creator and mother of all good things. But, he adds, while she was bringing about many great works and perfecting their fitness and utility, many disadvantageous things accrued as inseparable from her actual products. These, he says, were created in accordance with nature, but through certain necessary 'concomitances' (which he calls *kata parakolouthēsin*). Just as, he says, when nature was creating men's bodies, it was required for the enhancement of our rationality and for the very utility of the product that she should construct the head of very thin and tiny portions of bone, but this utility in the principal enterprise had as a further, extraneous consequence the inconvenience that the head became thinly protected and fragile to small blows and knocks – so too, illnesses and diseases were created while health was being created. (3) Likewise, he says, while through nature's plan virtue was being created for men, at the same time vices were born, thanks to their relationship of oppositeness.

R Lactantius, *On the anger of God* 13.9–10 (*SVF* 2.1172)

But the Academics, when arguing against the Stoics, often ask why, if god made everything for the sake of man, many things are also found in the sea and on land which oppose, attack and plague us. The Stoics, failing to discern the truth, reply most clumsily that among plants and animals there are many whose usefulness has up to now gone unnoticed; but that this will be discovered in the course of time, just as numerous things unknown in earlier centuries have been discovered by necessity and use.

S Plutarch, *On Stoic self-contradictions* 1051B–C (*SVF* 2.1178, part)

(1) Despite having often written on the theme that the world is altogether blameless and above reproach because everything is accomplished in accordance with the best possible nature, (2) elsewhere he [Chrysippus] does concede certain blameworthy cases of negligence, in matters which are by no means minor or unimportant. For in *On substance* book 3 he mentions that such things do befall good and honourable men, and asks 'Is it because some things are neglected, just as in larger houses the odd husk and a little wheat go astray even though the overall housekeeping is good? Or is it because the sort of matters in which real blameworthy cases of negligence occur have evil spirits in attendance?' (3) He says that there is also a considerable involvement of necessity.

T Plutarch, *On Stoic self-contradictions* 1050C–D (*SVF* 2.937, part)

Chrysippus grants an unrestricted licence for vice when he treats it as not only the product of necessity or in accordance with fate, but also as in accordance with god's reason and with the best nature. This is also evident in his actual words: 'For since universal nature reaches everywhere, it must be the case that however anything happens in the whole and in any of its parts it happens in accordance with universal nature and its reasons in unhindered sequence, because neither is there anything which could interfere with its government from outside, nor is there any way for any of the parts to enter any process or state except in accordance with universal nature.' What are these states and processes of the parts? Clearly the states are vices, diseases, lusts for money, pleasure and fame, and cases of cowardice and injustice, while the processes are acts of adultery, theft, betrayal, murder and parricide. In Chrysippus' view no instance of these, small or great, is contrary to the reason, law, justice and providence of Zeus.

U Calcidius 144 (*SVF* 2.933)

(1) Thus some believe it to be an assumption that there is a difference between providence and fate, the reality being that they are one. For providence will be god's will, and furthermore his will is the series of causes. In virtue of being his will it is providence. In virtue of also being the series of causes it gets the additional name 'fate'. Consequently everything in accordance with fate is also the product of providence, and likewise everything in accordance with providence is the product of fate. That is Chrysippus' view. (2) But others, like Cleanthes, while holding the dictates of providence to come about also by fate, allow things which come about by fate not to be the product of providence.

☐ The place of god in Stoic cosmology, psychology and ethics is treated in **44**, **46**, **52–3**, **57**, and **63**. The topic of the present section is the arguments for the existence and providence of god.

The Stoics' god is, first, an immanent, providential, rational, active principle imbuing all matter (see **44**; **46**), sometimes identified with nature or with fate (**B**; cf. **55**); second, the whole world, or its constituent elemental masses (**B**; cf. **F–H**); and third, the traditional gods of the Greek pantheon, interpreted allegorically as symbolizing the Stoic immanent deity in these various aspects (**A**). This is the theology which texts **C–U** defend. Their vacillation between singular 'god' and plural 'the gods' may to some extent reflect the deity's multiplicity of guises, but is probably to a larger extent indiscriminate, as often in Greek usage.

Some distinctive contributions of individual Stoics can be noted. Zeno's theological syllogisms in **D**, **F** and **G** show more flair than philosophical discipline. Some were parodied (*parabolē* is the technical term) by opponents like the contemporary dialectician Alexinus, and it was left to loyal later Stoics like

Diogenes of Babylon to salvage their respectability. That in **D** has reminded some of St Anselm's Ontological Argument.

Cleanthes has the reputation of being the most religious of the Stoics. While **C** and **47C** reflect his contribution to rational theology, his celebrated *Hymn to Zeus* (**I**) conveys the depth and power of his religious sentiments, presenting in the traditional clothing of the Greek hymn a god who is at once the Zeus of popular religion, the ordering fire-god of Heraclitus, and the Stoic providential deity. For example, Zeus' traditional weapon the thunderbolt, popularly a symbol of divine wrath, stands instead for the creative and beneficent force of fire in the world (**I 2**; cf. **46**).

Finally, Chrysippus emerges in **B, E, H** and **O–U** as the most ambitious defender of Stoic theology, particularly its doctrine of providence, which had probably come under Academic attack (cf. **R**), and continued to do so (**P 2**).

The arguments themselves can be read in the following sequence. First, defence of the existence of god (**C–H**; **47C**; **53X**). This is regularly equated with proving the world to be a rational animal (for the related notion of the world's perfection in **H**, cf. **29D**).

Second, arguments for god's providence, by appeal to preconception (**K**; cf. **C** and **40** commentary, and contrast Epicurus at **23B, C, E 2–6**) and, more especially, to the extremely seductive evidence of teleology: **J–P**. These arguments are not kept altogether distinct from the first group (cf. **J 2**), because the much-repeated Argument from Design serves both ends. The universal, hierarchical teleology is more reminiscent of Plato than of Aristotle, who as a rule restricts the end served to that of the individual plant or animal. But the Stoic premise borrowed by Carneades at **P 2** (standard Academic methodology, see **68** commentary) shows that they did try to incorporate an element of Aristotelian teleology as well. Carneades neatly exposes the contradiction into which this appears to lead them.

Third, theodicy: **Q–U**. Six types of explanation of cosmic evil are contemplated.

(a) The somewhat Heraclitean principle of opposition outlined in **Q 1** and **3**; cf. also **I 3** and **61R**. It seems to combine an epistemological thesis, that opposites are only intelligible in relation to each other, with the ontological thesis, borrowed with acknowledgement from Plato, *Phaedo* 60, that opposites necessarily come into being out of each other. (Chrysippus may imply at **Q 2–3** that this type of explanation is a special case of type (d), on which see below.)

(b) Blessings in disguise: **R**. Cf. the bed-bugs, mice, leopards etc. of **O** and **P 1**.

(c) Individual wickedness, or undeserved suffering, for the overall good: **I 3**, **T**; **58J**.

(d) Necessary 'concomitants' of purposive working: **Q 2, S 3**; cf. **O** on the peahen. This is a direct legacy of Plato's *Timaeus*: cf. *Tim.* 75 for the original of **Q 2**'s example, the necessary fragility of the human head.

(e) Oversights: **S 2**.

(f) Evil spirits: **S 2**. But both (e) and (f) appear to be casual suggestions, probably never wholeheartedly incorporated into Stoic theology, with which they are scarcely compatible.

With regard to (c), and perhaps (d), Cleanthes' view, rejected by Chrysippus (cf. **Q 2, T, U 1**), is that god and providence can be absolved from direct responsibility, perhaps on the ground that they do not actually *want* the defects to occur, even though their plans make them inevitable: **I 3, U 2**.

For the development by later Stoics of the providence doctrine into a central feature of their ethics, cf. Seneca, *On providence*; Epictetus, *Discourses* 1.6 (including **63E**).

The material in this section should be compared with Epicurus' arguments against teleology (**13**) and against a providential deity (**23**), and with Carneades' anti-theological arguments (**70C–E**; cf. **P2**).

55 Causation and fate

A Stobaeus 1.138,14–139,4 (*SVF* 1.89 and 2.336)

(1) Zeno says that a cause is 'that because of which', while that of which it is the cause is an attribute; and that the cause is a body, while that of which it is a cause is a predicate. (2) He says that it is impossible that the cause be present yet that of which it is the cause not belong. (3) This thesis has the following force. A cause is that because of which something occurs, as, for example, it is because of prudence that being prudent occurs, because of soul that being alive occurs, and because of temperance that being temperate occurs. For it is impossible, when someone possesses temperance, for him not to be temperate, or, when he possesses soul, for him not to be alive, or, when he possesses prudence, for him not to be prudent. (4) Chrysippus says that a cause is 'that because of which'; and that the cause is an existent and a body, <while that of which it is the cause is neither an existent nor a body> ; and that the cause is 'because', while that of which it is the cause is 'why?' (5) He says that an explanation [*aitia*] is the statement of a cause [*aition*], or statement concerning the cause *qua* cause.

B Sextus Empiricus, *Against the professors* 9.211 (*SVF* 2.341)

The Stoics say that every cause is a body which becomes the cause to a body of something incorporeal. For instance the scalpel, a body, becomes the cause to the flesh, a body, of the incorporeal predicate 'being cut'. And again, the fire, a body, becomes the cause to the wood, a body, of the incorporeal predicate 'being burnt'.

C Clement, *Miscellanies* 8.9.26.3–4

Hence becoming, and being cut – that of which the cause is a cause – since they are activities, are incorporeal. It can be said, to make the same point, that causes are causes of predicates, or, as some say, of sayables [*lekta*] – for Cleanthes and Archedemus call predicates 'sayables'. Or else, and preferably, that some are causes of predicates, for example of 'is cut', whose case [i.e. substantival form] is 'being cut', but others of propositions, for example of 'a ship is built', whose case this time is 'a ship's being built'.

D Clement, *Miscellanies* 8.9.30.1–3 (*SVF* 2.349)

(1) Causes are not *of* each other, but there are causes *to* each other. For the pre-existing condition of the spleen is the cause, not of fever, but of the fever's coming about; and the pre-existing fever is the cause, not of the spleen, but of its condition's being intensified. (2) In the same way, the virtues are causes to each other of not being separated, owing to their inter-entailment, and the stones in the vault are causes to each other of the predicate 'remaining', but they are not causes of each other. And the teacher and the pupil are causes to each other of the predicate 'making progress'. (3) Things are said to be causes to each other sometimes of the same effects, as the merchant and the retailer are causes to each other of making a profit; but sometimes of different effects, as in the case of the knife and the flesh; for the knife is the cause to the flesh of being cut, while the flesh is the cause to the knife of cutting.

E Seneca, *Letters* 65.2

Our Stoic philosophers, as you know, say that there are two things in nature from which everything is produced – cause and matter. Matter lies inert, an entity ready for anything but destined to lie idle if no one moves it. Cause, on the other hand, being the same as reason, shapes matter and directs it wherever it wants, and from matter produces its manifold creations. Hence a thing must be made *from* something, and *by* something. The latter is its cause, the former its matter.

F Galen, *On sustaining causes* 1.1–2.4

(1) The first philosophers of my acquaintance to speak of a sustaining cause were the Stoics. Their view is that from the four elements are produced those bodies that Aristotle calls homogeneous and that are described by Plato as 'the first to be generated', while all other bodies are simply compounds of these. Of the elements themselves, some they call material and some active and dynamic. They maintain that the material elements are held together by those that are dynamic, fire and air being dynamic and active in their view, while earth and water are material. They say that in compounds the dynamic elements pervade the material through and through, that is to say, air and fire penetrate water and earth. Air is cold and fire is hot. The natural effect of air is to consolidate and thicken a substance, whereas fire naturally causes expansion, loosening and widening. The two active elements have fine parts and the other two thick parts. All the substance with fine parts the Stoics call breath, and

they think that the function of this breath is to sustain natural and animal bodies. By natural bodies I mean those that are produced by nature and not by human skill, like copper, stones, gold, wood and those parts of the animal body that are called the primary and homogeneous parts, that is, nerves, arteries, veins, cartilages, bones and everything else of the same sort. Men join bits of wood together with glue, nails, pegs, clay, gypsum and lime. Similarly nature is found connecting all the parts of the body so as to form a united whole by means of cartilages, ligaments and tendons. If you like, you can call the parts of the body that produce this union in the simple members sustaining causes of the compounds, and the same term can be applied to clay, gypsum, lime and the other things that serve the same purpose in externals which are connected by the skill of man and not by nature. It is not these, however, but rather the material substance with fine parts, that the Stoics call the containing cause of existing things. (2) As for Athenaeus of Attaleia, he founded the medical school known as the Pneumatists [from *pneuma* = 'breath']. It suits his doctrine to speak of a sustaining cause in illness, since he bases himself upon the Stoics, and he was a pupil and disciple of Posidonius. But it does not suit the theories of those other doctors who hold different doctrines to look for a sustaining cause in every illness, nor to try to find it in the natural homogeneous bodies. And they cannot say, as Athenaeus did, that there are three primary and most universal types of cause. (3) Athenaeus' three types are as follows: first that of the sustaining causes, then that of the antecedent causes, while the third type is comprised of the matter of the preliminary causes. This last term is applied to externals whose function is to produce some change in the body, whatever this change may be. If what is thus produced in the body belongs to the class of what causes disease, then, while it has not yet actually given rise to the disease, it is known as an antecedent cause. Alterations are produced in the natural breath by these causes and also by those which are external, leading to moisture, dryness, heat or cold, and these are what he calls the sustaining causes of diseases. For the breath pervades the homogeneous bodies and changes them along with itself. Often, he says, the sustaining cause is produced directly from the preliminary cause without an intermediary, though sometimes it comes through the medium of the antecedent cause.

G Aetius 1.11.5 (*SVF* 2.340)

The Stoics call all causes corporeal, because they are portions of breath.

H Galen, *Synopsis of the books on pulses* 9.458,8–14 (*SVF* 2.356)

However, it is above all necessary to remember how we said we were speaking of the 'sustaining cause' – not in its strict sense, but using the appellative loosely. For no one before the Stoics either spoke of or admitted the existence of the 'sustaining cause' in the strict sense. And what have even before our time been spoken of as 'sustaining' have been causes of something's coming about, not of existence.

I Clement 8.9.33.1–9 (*SVF* 2.351)

(1) When 'preliminary' [*prokatarktika*] causes are removed the effect remains, (2) whereas a 'sustaining' [*sunektikon*] cause is one during whose presence the effect remains and on whose removal the effect is removed. The sustaining cause is called synonymously the 'complete' [*autoteles*] cause, since it is self-sufficiently productive of the effect. (3) If this cause is indicative of a complete activity, the 'auxiliary' [*sunergon*] cause signifies assistance, and service alongside another. Hence if no result is produced it will not even be called auxiliary, but if one is produced it does become a cause of what is actually being produced, that is, of what is coming about through it. So an auxiliary cause is one which was present while its effect was coming about. When it is pre-evidently present its effect is pre-evident, whereas when it is non-evidently present its effect is non-evident. (4) The 'joint-cause' [*sunaition*] is another member of the genus of causes (in the way that the joint-soldier is a soldier and the joint-trainee a trainee). Whereas the auxiliary cause aids the sustaining cause, so as to intensify what comes about through the latter, the joint-cause does not correspond to the same conception, since a joint-cause can exist even if there is no sustaining cause. For the joint-cause is conceived jointly with another which is itself likewise incapable of independently producing the effect, since it is jointly that they are causes. (5) The difference between the joint-cause and the auxiliary cause lies in the fact that the joint-cause produces the effect along with another cause which is not independently producing it, whereas the auxiliary cause, in creating the effect not independently but by accruing to another, is acting as auxiliary to the very cause which *is* independently creating the effect, so that the effect is intensified. It is above all an auxiliary cause's having grown out of a preliminary cause that establishes that it is intensifying the force of the cause.

J Aetius 1.28.4 (*SVF* 2.917)

The Stoics [describe fate as] a sequence of causes, that is, an inescapable ordering and interconnexion.

K Gellius 7.2.3 (*SVF* 2.1000, part)

In *On providence* book 4, Chrysippus says that fate is a certain natural everlasting ordering of the whole: one set of things follows on and succeeds another, and the interconnexion is inviolable.

L Cicero, *On divination* 1.125–6 (*SVF* 2.921)

[Speaker: Quintus Cicero in defence of Stoic theory of divination] (1) By 'fate', I mean what the Greeks call *heimarmenē* – an ordering and sequence of causes, since it is the connexion of cause to cause which out of itself produces anything. (2) It is everlasting truth, flowing from all eternity. Consequently nothing has happened which was not going to be, and likewise nothing is going to be of which nature does not contain causes working to bring that very thing about. (3) This makes it intelligible that fate should be, not the 'fate' of superstition, but that of physics, an everlasting cause of things – why past things happened, why present things are now happening, and why future things will be.

M Stobaeus 1.79,1–12 (*SVF* 2.913, part)

(1) Chrysippus calls the substance of fate a power of breath, carrying out the orderly government of the all. That is in *On the world* book 2. (2) But in *On seasons* book 2, in *On fate*, and here and there in other works, he expresses a variety of views: 'Fate is the rationale of the world', or 'the rationale of providence's acts of government in the world', or 'the rationale in accordance with which past events have happened, present events are happening, and future events will happen'. (3) And as substitute for 'rationale' he uses 'truth', 'explanation', 'nature', 'necessity', and further terms, taking these to apply to the same substance from different points of view.

N Alexander, *On fate* 191,30–192,28 (*SVF* 2.945)

(1) They [the Stoics] say that since the world is a unity which includes all existing things in itself and is governed by a living, rational, intelligent nature, the government of existing things which it possesses is an everlasting one proceeding in a sequence and ordering. The things which happen first become causes to those which happen after them. In this way all things are bound together, and neither does anything happen in the world such that something else does not unconditionally follow from it and become causally attached to it, nor can any of the later events be severed from the preceding events so as not to follow from one of them as if bound fast to it; but from everything that happens something else follows, with a necessary causal dependence on it, and everything that happens has something prior to it with which it causally coheres. (2) For nothing in the world exists or happens causelessly, because none of the things in it is independent of, and insulated from, everything that has happened before. For the world would be wrenched apart and divided, and no longer remain a unity, for ever governed in accordance with a

single ordering and management, if an uncaused motion were introduced. And an uncaused motion would be introduced, were everything that exists or happens not to have some preceding causes from which it necessarily follows. For something to happen causelessly is, they say, both similar to and as impossible as something's coming to be out of what is not. Being of this kind, the government of the all goes on from infinity to infinity self-evidently and unceasingly. (3) In setting out the difference which exists among causes they list a swarm of causes – preliminary causes, joint-causes, . . . sustaining causes, and others (we need not prolong our account by including all the ones they name, we need only indicate the intention underlying their fate doctrine); but, given this plurality of causes, they say that it is equally true with regard to all of them that it is impossible, where all the same circumstances obtain with respect to the cause and that to which it is cause, that a result which does not ensue on one occasion should ensue on another. For if this happened, there would be an uncaused motion. (4) They say that the very fate, nature and rationale in accordance with which the all is governed is god. It is present in all things which exist and happen, and in this way uses the proper nature of all existing things for the government of the all.

O Cicero, *On divination* 1.127 (*SVF* 2.944)

[Speaker: Quintus Cicero in defence of Stoic theory of divination] Besides, since all things happen by fate, as will be shown elsewhere, if there were some human being who could see with his mind the connexion of all causes, he would certainly never be deceived. For whoever grasps the causes of future things must necessarily grasp all that will be. But since no one but god can do this, man must be left to gain his foreknowledge from various signs which announce what is to come. For things which will be do not spring up spontaneously. The passage of time is like the unwinding of a rope, bringing about nothing new and unrolling each stage in its turn.

P Diogenianus (Eusebius, *Evangelical preparation* 4.3.1; *SVF* 2.939, part)

In the aforementioned book [i.e. Chrysippus, *On fate*] he offers a further demonstration, along the following lines. The predictions of the soothsayers could not be true, he says, if all things were not embraced by fate.

Q Cicero, *On fate* 7–8

(1) Let us return to Chrysippus' snares, and reply to him first about the influence of environment, then pursue the rest later. We see how great the differences are between the natures of places. Some are healthy, some disease-ridden. In some the people are phlegmatic to the point of

overflowing, in others they are utterly dried out. And there are many other immense differences between places. At Athens the atmosphere is rarefied, resulting in the Attics' reputedly sharp wits; while at Thebes it is heavy, so that the Thebans are stout and tough. (2) Yet neither will that rarefied atmosphere bring it about whether someone attends Zeno's lectures or those of Arcesilaus or of Theophrastus, nor will the heavy atmosphere bring it about that someone competes at the Nemean rather than the Isthmian games. . . . (3) But [Chrysippus will reply] given that men's natures differ, so that some love sweets while others love savouries, some are passionate while others are irascible or cruel or arrogant, and others shrink from such vices – given, he says, such gulfs between different natures, why should it occasion surprise that these dissimilarities are the products of different causes?

R Plutarch, *On Stoic self-contradictions* 1056B–C (*SVF* 2.997, part)

(1) Anyone who says that Chrysippus did not make fate the complete cause of these things [right and wrong actions], but only their preliminary cause, will reveal him once again as in conflict with himself, where he extravagantly praises Homer for saying of Zeus 'Therefore accept whatever evil or good he may send to each of you', . . . and himself writes many things in agreement with this, and ends up saying that no state or process is to the slightest degree other than in accordance with the rationale of Zeus, which he says is identical to fate. (2) What is more, the preliminary cause is weaker than the complete cause, and is insufficient when dominated by other, countervailing causes; yet he himself declares fate an invincible, unblockable and inflexible cause . . .

S Cicero, *On fate* 28–30 (= **70G 9**)

(1) Nor will we be blocked by the so called 'Lazy Argument' (the *argos logos*, as the philosophers entitle it). If we gave in to it, we would do nothing whatever in life. They pose it as follows: 'If it is your fate to recover from this illness, you will recover, regardless of whether or not you call the doctor. Likewise, if it is your fate not to recover from this illness, you will not recover, regardless of whether or not you call the doctor. And one or the other *is* your fate. Therefore it is pointless to call the doctor.' . . . (2) This argument is criticized by Chrysippus. Some events in the world are simple, he says, others are complex. 'Socrates will die on such and such a day' is simple: his day of dying is fixed, regardless of what he may do or not do. But if a fate is of the form 'Oedipus will be born to Laius', it will not be possible to add 'regardless of whether or not Laius has intercourse with a woman'. For the event is complex and 'co-fated'. He uses this term because what is fated is *both* that Laius will have intercourse with his wife *and* that by her he will beget Oedipus. Likewise,

suppose it has been said 'Milo will wrestle at the Olympic Games.' If someone replied 'Will he then wrestle regardless of whether or not he has an opponent?' he would be mistaken. For 'He will wrestle' is complex, because there is no wrestling without an opponent. (3) All fallacies of this kind, then, are refuted in the same way. 'You will recover, regardless of whether or not you call the doctor' is fallacious. For it is just as much fated for you to call the doctor as for you to recover. His term for these cases is, as I said, 'co-fated'.

☐ In the fourth century B.C. cause had been closely linked to *explanation*. Hence, for example, both Plato and Aristotle had, as teleologists, felt that one of the best ways to state a thing's cause was to say what it was for. The Stoics, on the other hand, although equally teleological in outlook (see **54**), never speak of final *causes*. The word translated 'cause', *aition*, literally means the 'thing responsible', and for the Stoics a cause is a thing which, by its activity, brings about an effect. Under Stoic influence this view of cause became widespread, especially in ancient science, although it seems that the Stoics themselves were in general most interested in bringing out the implications for moral responsibility: see **62**.

More precisely (**A–D, G**), a cause is a body, e.g. a scalpel. It is a fundamental Stoic tenet that only bodies can act or be acted upon (**45**, cf. **60S**). The scalpel, by acting upon another body, flesh, generates an effect, being cut. This effect is not another body, but an incorporeal predicate, or 'sayable' (on which see **33**). Why so? The alternative was presumably to say that thanks to the scalpel one body, uncut flesh, ceases to exist and is replaced by a new body, cut flesh. But that would imply that *no* body persists through the process, so that there is no body in which we can say that the change has been brought about. Since the object changed, must, normally speaking, persist through the change (as the Stoics recognized in another context, see **28D, I**), it proved more palatable for them to say that the effect is not a new body but the incorporeal predicate 'is cut' (or 'being cut'), which comes to be true of the persisting flesh. The predicate should perhaps be thought of less as an extra entity that appears on the scene than as an aspect of the cut flesh which we abstract in order to present a proper causal analysis.

How, then, are we to analyse causal processes which do result in the creation of new corporeal entities, e.g. shipbuilding? This is presumably the problem which led to the suggestion at the end of **C** that in such cases the effect is not just a predicate but an entire proposition, 'a ship is built' (or 'a ship's being built'), which comes to be true as a result of the shipbuilder's activity. It would follow that the causal process involves no bodily interaction between shipbuilder and ship, and this seems acceptable if we take it that the ship does not even exist to be acted upon until the shipbuilding is complete. (There is of course interaction between the shipbuilder and the timber, but that is a different causal relation from the one in question.)

Now although the interaction of spatially discrete bodies provides the easiest introduction to Stoic causal theory, a far more fundamental causal relation operates within any single body between its active and passive aspects or components (for a sceptical critique of this, cf. **72N**). At the most basic level, this is the causal operation of the active principle god, on the passive principle matter: **E**; cf. **44C**. At the level of analysis favoured by Stoics from Chrysippus on, it is the causal operation of the active 'breath', consisting of the elements air and fire, on the two inert elements earth and water: **F–G**; cf. **47**. The breath in any body is what shapes and characterizes it. As 'tenor' breath makes it a unified object, as 'physique' it makes it an organism, as 'soul' it makes it an animate organism (**47M–R**, with commentary). And soul itself embodies a range of separate qualities, such as prudence, which are themselves portions of breath (**28L–M**). In these various guises, breath is the dominant active cause both of things' existence and of their behaviour. The technical term is 'sustaining' cause (**F, H, I**).

The doctrine of the sustaining cause seems to be applied in two ways. Primarily (according to **H**) the sustaining cause is the cause of existence, since an object's persistence as a single entity depends entirely on the qualifying activity of breath (**F 1**; **47F–G, I**; cf. **28M**; the 'soul' example in **A 3** may also come under this heading).

Secondarily, a thing's component breath, viewed as its various qualities, is the sustaining cause of the changes which it undergoes. Officially (**I 2**) the sustaining cause is a sufficient condition of the effect: hence its alternative name, 'complete' cause. In some cases this can be taken at face value. Indeed, in Zeno's examples at **A 3**, the necessitating relation looks so strong that the cause might almost be thought to entail its effect. So long as, say, prudence is present in you, you cannot fail to 'be prudent' (perhaps meaning 'behave prudently'). In a medical context like the Stoic-influenced work of the doctor Athenaeus (first century B.C.; see **F 2–3**), the sustaining cause of a disease is the disordered state of the patient's 'breath', and we may take it that the disease lasts precisely for the duration of this disordered state, even though this time the causal relation may be further from one of simple entailment.

In other cases the 'sufficient condition' gloss on the sustaining cause is, at best, imprecise. In **62C** (cf. **62D 4**) Chrysippus offers the analogy of a rolling cylinder. The essential cause of its rolling is its cylindrical shape. But this is so not because being cylindrical is a sufficient condition of rolling, but because given an external cause, namely a push, the cylindrical shape is sufficient to *keep* it rolling. It is ultimately the object's shape which bears the responsibility for its rolling, and in virtue of which it rolls 'through its own force and nature'. In very much the same way, Chrysippus maintains, the 'complete' (= 'sustaining', see **I 2**) causes of our actions are our moral qualities, and the externally prompted impressions, e.g. of a stealable purse or of a damsel in distress, are no more than the initiating, 'proximate' causes. For the all-important ethical implications, see **62**.

A true complete/sustaining cause will, given only the initiating assistance of proximate causes, sustain its effect as long as it itself lasts (**I 2**). Of course, the thief will not be stealing *this* purse for the entire time that he is thievish. But so long as he remains thievish he will certainly always steal, whenever affected by the 'proximate' cause of seeing a stealable item. Likewise, if the cylinder is to provide an *example* of a complete cause, and not just (as may be intended) a partial analogy, its shape should be thought of as the complete cause, not of its rolling on *this* occasion, an event which its cylindrical shape will outlast, but of its rolling-when-pushed throughout its existence.

62C contrasts complete (and 'primary': perhaps not a separate class) causes with 'auxiliary' and 'proximate' causes. 'Proximate' here is probably Cicero's rendition, or equivalent, of the Greek word we translate 'preliminary' in **F 3**, **I**, and **R** (since 'complete' and 'preliminary' in **R** appear to refer precisely to the distinction made by Chrysippus in **62C** between 'complete' and 'proximate'). 'Preliminary' causes are not defined in our texts, but **I 1**'s description of them matches **62C** well. As for 'auxiliary' causes, the reason for their being bracketed with these preliminary causes in **62C** will be not just that they too are somehow secondary, but that they and the auxiliary cause will often coincide or overlap. **I 3–5** explains that they are intensifiers of effects which would occur anyway (e.g. fanning a fire?). In that case, a preliminary cause might frequently survive *as* an auxiliary cause. The sight of a stealable purse may be the preliminary cause of the thief's pursuit of it, but the continued sight of it can intensify the pursuit. A single push starts the cylinder rolling, but prolonged pushing will make it roll faster. Indeed, as **I 5** observes, the easiest cases of auxiliary causation to recognize are those of just this kind.

What has been emerging is a classification of causes designed to permit a correct apportionment of responsibility among the contributory factors to any event. Very evidently, the sustaining cause is where the responsibility chiefly rests. Another cause, the 'joint-cause', is explained at **I 4–5**, and caters for cases where *no* sustaining cause exists. To adapt an example from **28M**, when a choir is the cause of our hearing a harmony, there is no sustaining cause in the form of a single 'breath' characterizing the choir as a unitary entity, only the several qualities of the individual choristers. Each one's talent is therefore a joint-cause, but none a sustaining cause. No one of them is sufficient to produce the sound heard, and no one of them can take the credit for it.

Finally, 'antecedent' (*proēgoumenon*, Latin *antecedens*) cause. This is an expression used in a bewildering variety of ways by ancient writers, but in Stoicism it is perhaps no more than a generic term for causes, of whatever variety, which pre-exist their effects – including sustaining causes, which, pending the triggering preliminary causes, can precede their individual effects. (Athenaeus' narrower usage of the term in **F 3** need not be standard Stoicism.) That, at any rate, is all that **62C** requires. There antecedent causes are picked out as those by which 'fate' must operate. Since fate is viewed as a causal nexus, it is bound to lead at times to a focusing of interest on the temporal sequence of causes, even where this may threaten to blur the other careful distinctions between varieties of cause: cf. **N 3**. It is to the Stoic doctrine of fate that we now turn.

We will suggest in the commentary on **62** that Zeno and Cleanthes may have entertained no more than a fairly traditional Greek picture of fate, as the preordainment of certain landmarks in individual lives and in human history; a victory, a hero's return home, an illness, someone's murdering his father, the date of his own death. These things will happen whether or not we try to avert them. Far from threatening our independence, they provide precisely the proper context for autonomous moral choice.

At first sight this view of fate, in which outcomes are predetermined but not necessarily the routes to them, still plays a part in Chrysippus' outlook. He seems to make the point explicitly as regards the date of someone's death (**S 2**), and is said (**62A**) to have repeated Zeno's simile of man as a dog tied to a cart who must follow whether reluctant or willing, which also implies such a view.

Somehow, nevertheless, Chrysippus is also committed to a much stronger view, which amounts to determinism. At the beginning of each world cycle a causal nexus is providentially planned and initiated, in virtue of which *every* detail of the entire subsequent world process is predetermined: **J–Q**; cf. **46G**; **52**. This is presented largely as a physical thesis (cf. **Q**, despite the criticisms at **65M**), superseding the old religious idea of fate (**L 3**). Presumably, then, we must reinterpret his acceptance of Zeno's doctrine of fate, according to which certain outcomes will ensue regardless of how we act. For Chrysippus this will mean, not that alternative actions are genuinely open to us, but that the outcomes in question are determined by causal chains which do not operate through our actions at all. When, by contrast, they are determined *via* our actions, they are said to be 'co-fated' with our actions: **S**; **62F**. In either case, our actions are themselves as predetermined as the outcomes.

The theoretical details of the causal nexus seem to receive little attention in our sources. Since it is the entire conjunction of causes that guarantees subsequent effects, the distinctions between kinds of cause which we examined above generally get little emphasis in this context (cf. **N 3**). Nor are we told the metaphysical nature of a causal chain. For example how, if causes are bodies but effects are incorporeal, can there ever be a chain of cause and effect? We will have to take it that it is not a simple chain *A–B–C*, where *B* is the effect of *A* and the cause of *C*, but that the cause of *C* is the body of which the effect *B* has come to be predicable, acting as cause because of the corresponding quality which it now possesses. For example, if I strike a match, which in turn sets my house on fire, I am the cause to the match of the predicate 'burning', and the burning match, a body, is then the cause to the house of the same predicate.

Only in **R** and **62C** are the distinctions between types of cause invoked with regard to fate. Chrysippus suggested that fate should be seen not as the entire causal nexus but merely as the set of triggering or 'preliminary' causes. The merit, as he saw it, was that fate would then be absolved from *compelling* our actions. This *prima facie* conflicts with the other reports (especially **N**), which strongly suggest that fate is the entire conjunction of causes. But the two views may differ more in emphasis than in substance: see further, **62** commentary.

The arguments for the existence of fate are three in kind.

(a) Metaphysical. Any gap in the causal nexus – something's occurring without cause, or the failure of an identical conjunction of causes to produce an identical effect each time – would breach some fundamental law, perhaps approximating to the Principle of Sufficient Reason: **N 2**; **62H**.

(b) Empirical. Both the world's evident organic unity (**N 2**), and the alleged success of divination (**P**, cf. **O**; **38E**; **42C–E**), confirm the existence of fate.

(c) Logical. The causal predetermination of all future events follows from the principle of bivalence: **38G**, with commentary.

On fate in relation to providence, see **54**, especially **U**.

ETHICS

56 The division of ethical topics

A Diogenes Laertius 7.84 (*SVF* 3.1)

They [the Stoics] divide the ethical part of philosophy into (i) the topic of impulse, (ii) that of good and bad things, (iii) that of passions, (iv) of virtue, (v) of the end, (vi) of primary value and actions, (vii) of proper functions and (viii) encouragements and discouragements. This is how Chrysippus divides it, along with Archedemus, Zeno of Tarsus, Apollodorus, Diogenes [of Babylon], Antipater and Posidonius. Zeno of Citium and Cleanthes treated the subjects less elaborately, as an earlier generation would do. But they also made divisions of logic and physics.

B Seneca, *Letters* 89.14

Since, then, philosophy has three parts, let us begin to arrange its moral part first of all. For this again a threefold division has been settled on ... The first deals with your assessment of the value of each thing, the second with your adopting a controlled and balanced impulse towards them, and the third with the achievement of an agreement between your impulse and your action so that you are consistent with yourself in all these matters.

C Epictetus, *Discourses* 3.2.1–5

(1) There are three topics in which the would-be honourable and good man needs to have been trained. (2) That of desires and aversions, to ensure that he succeeds in getting what he desires and does not encounter what he seeks to avoid. (3) That of impulses and repulsions, or proper function quite generally, to ensure that he acts in ways that are orderly, well reasoned and not thoughtless. (4) The third has to do with infallibility and uncarelessness, or acts of assent quite generally. (5) Of these [three] the most important and urgent is the one concerned with the passions. For a passion only occurs if a desire is unsuccessful or an aversion encounters [what it seeks to avoid]. This is the topic which brings up disturbances, confusions, misfortunes, disasters, sorrows, lamentations, envies ... through which we are unable even to listen to reason. (6) The second has to do with proper function; for I ought not to be impassive like a statue, but maintain my natural and acquired relationships, as a religious man, as a son, a brother, a father and a citizen. (7) The third topic applies to those who are already making progress, and concerns security in just these matters mentioned, to ensure that even in dreams or intoxication or depression a mental impression should not slip by which has not been tested.

☐ Imagine a would-be Stoic man, with a profession and a family. In return for rigorous study in all three parts of philosophy (26), combined with intense practice and self-examination, Stoicism offers him a moral character (virtue, 61) that guarantees his happiness (the end, 63) in all times and circumstances. This character – a systematically rational outlook – consists in utterly secure knowledge of how he should act, in order to base his life on the recognition that moral value is the sole *differentia* of good and bad things (60), and that though it is naturally appropriate for him to prefer health, wealth etc. to sickness and poverty, such conventional desirables/undesirables make no difference to his happiness (58). He will realize that he is by nature constituted to act in ways that, generally speaking, aim to promote his material well-being and that of his family, friends and country; his rationality and the rational structure of the world at large underwrite such 'proper functions' (59), which take account of the particular circumstances of his life. But his 'natural impulse' (57) to perform such actions is consistently shaped by his moral outlook, which has taught him that he has a pre-ordained role to play in the world, and that his value system gives him the means of adapting himself freely and harmoniously to everything that external contingencies impose (62). The impulses which launch his behaviour are determined by the moral propositions to which he assents. Because he has securely grasped the fact that goodness is confined to moral excellence and badness to the opposite of this, he never assents to the goodness or badness of anything else; consequently he is quite immune to the passionate impulses characteristic of the unenlightened majority, which derive from misdescribing and falsely assessing the value of things (65). To help him progress towards this end, he receives training in moral rules based upon the doctrines of the system (66). It does not require him to give up his family or career or political allegiances, since its principal purpose is not to change his circumstances but his outlook. It does require him to view the world at large as a quasi-political community (67), governed by natural laws whose morality, rationality and divinity are evident in the subordination of all parts of the world, including himself, to the good of the whole.

Turning now to the formal division of these topics, we can note that it reflects with particular emphasis the Stoic interest in systematic presentation of philosophy (see 26). Chrysippus was the key figure here, as his list of ethical works concerned with definitions, divisions etc. indicates (32I); the 'division' of topics in **A** is there said to have been authorized by him and followed by his successors. Actually it appears to be a 'partition' – a classification of topics – rather than a division in the technical sense (32C). The topics it includes do not readily lend themselves to an analysis into genus and species. Most of them – (i)– (v) and (vii) – corrrespond, though not in just this order, to sections in the surviving summaries of Stoic ethics in Cicero, *On ends* 3, Diogenes Laertius 7, and Stobaeus 2. All three of these sources, however, treat 'indifferents' (cf. our 58) as a topic in its own right. Since indifferents are naturally connected with the concept of value, we suspect that **A**'s sixth topic, 'of primary value and actions', should include them; but nowhere else are 'actions' singled out as a topic. It is also curious that 'passions' feature so early in **A**'s list. Conceivably, they, and some of

345

the other topics, were originally represented as subdivisions of others: for instance, passions could be properly located as a subdivision of 'impulses' (cf. **65A** 1) and 'proper functions' as a subdivision of 'primary value and actions'. The eighth topic, 'encouragements and discouragements', naturally comes last, as the educational precepts based upon the previous doctrines (cf. **66J**).

In organizing the ethical material ourselves, we have accepted these topics as section headings but have adapted the order of **A** as follows: **57** = (i), **58** = ?(vi), **59** = (vii), **60** = (ii), **61** = (iv), **63** = (v), **65** = (iii), **66** = (viii).

Seneca and Epictetus (**B, C**) specify a threefold division. Though differing over details, their accounts are sufficiently similar to indicate an agreed logical and educational progression. The first heading, in this system, is concerned with the assessment of what it is worthwhile to pursue or avoid; the second with the impulses and resulting actions appropriate to this assessment; the third with the achievement of consistency and full understanding. Epictetus helpfully observes that the third 'applies to those who are already making progress' (**C 7**). This threefold arrangement, if articulated in **A**'s terms, would broadly incorporate under the first heading, 'good and bad things', 'passions' (cf. **C 5**), 'primary value and actions'; under the second, 'impulse', and 'proper functions'; under the third, 'virtue', and 'the end'.

57 Impulse and appropriateness

A Diogenes Laertius 7.85–6 (*SVF* 3.178)

(1) They [the Stoics] say that an animal has self-preservation as the object of its first impulse, since nature from the beginning appropriates it, as Chrysippus says in his *On ends* book 1. (2) The first thing appropriate to every animal, he says, is its own constitution and the consciousness of this. For nature was not likely either to alienate the animal itself, or to make it and then neither alienate it nor appropriate it. So it remains to say that in constituting the animal, nature appropriated it to itself. This is why the animal rejects what is harmful and accepts what is appropriate. (3) They hold it false to say, as some people do, that pleasure is the object of animals' first impulse. For pleasure, they say, if it does occur, is a by-product which arises only when nature all by itself has searched out and adopted the proper requirements for a creature's constitution, just as animals [then] frolic and plants bloom. (4) Nature, they say, is no different in regard to plants and animals at the time when it directs animals as well as plants without impulse and sensation, and in us certain processes of a vegetative kind take place. But since animals have the additional faculty of impulse, through the use of which they go in search of what is appropriate to them, what is natural for them is to be administered in accordance with their impulse. (5) And since reason, by way of a more perfect management, has been bestowed on rational beings, to live correctly in accordance with reason comes to be natural for them. For reason supervenes as the craftsman of impulse [continued at **63C**]

B Seneca, *Letters* 121.6–15 (with omissions)

(1) No one sets his limbs in motion with difficulty, no one is hesitant in the activation of himself. Animals do this as soon as they are born. They begin life with this knowledge . . . (2) So little does fear of pain compel them to [move their parts appropriately] that they strive for their natural motion even against the pressure of pain. A baby who is set on standing up and is getting used to supporting himself, as soon as he begins to try his strength, falls down and with tears keeps getting up again until he has trained himself through pain to do what nature demands . . . A tortoise on its back feels no pain, but desire for its natural state makes it restless, and it does not stop struggling and shaking itself until it stands on its feet. So all animals are conscious of their own constitution, and this explains such easy handling of their limbs . . . (3) Each period of life has its own constitution, one for the baby, and another for the boy, < another for the youth, > and another for the old man. They are all related appropriately to that constitution in which they exist.

C Hierocles 1.34–9, 51–7, 2.1–9

(1) It seems right to say a few words about sensation. For this contributes to knowledge of the first thing which is appropriate, the subject which we said would be the best starting-point for the elements of ethics. (2) We should realize that as soon as an animal is born it perceives itself . . . The first thing that animals perceive is their own parts . . . both that they have them and for what purpose they have them, and we ourselves perceive our eyes and our ears and the rest. So whenever we want to see something, we strain our eyes, but not our ears, towards the visible object . . . Therefore the first proof of every animal's perceiving itself is its consciousness of its parts and the functions for which they were given. (3) The second proof is the fact that animals are not unaware of their equipment for self-defence. When bulls do battle with other bulls or animals of different species, they stick out their horns, as if these were their congenital weapons for the encounter. Every other creature has the same disposition relative to its appropriate and, so to speak, congenital weapons.

D Hierocles 9.3–10, 11.14–18

(1) The appropriate disposition relative to oneself is benevolence, while that to one's kindred is affection . . . Just as our appropriate disposition relative to our children is affection, and, to external property, choice, so an animal's appropriate disposition relative to itself is < self-preservation > and, to things which contribute to the needs of its constitution, selection . . . (2) We are an animal, but a gregarious one which needs someone else as well. For this reason too we inhabit cities; for there is no human

being who is not a part of a city. Secondly, we make friendships easily. By eating together or sitting together in the theatre . . . [text breaks off]

E Plutarch, *On Stoic self-contradictions* 1038B (*SVF* 3.179, 2.724)

(1) Why then again for heaven's sake in every book on physics and ethics does he [Chrysippus] weary us to death in writing that we have an appropriate disposition relative to ourselves as soon as we are born and to our parts and our offspring? (2) In his *On justice* book 1 he says that even the beasts have an appropriate disposition relative to their offspring in harmony with their needs, except for fish, since their spawn is nurtured through itself.

F Cicero, *On ends* 3.62–8 (with omissions)

[Speaker: the Stoic Cato] (1) They think it is important to understand that nature engenders parents' love for their children. That is the starting-point of the universal community of the human race which we seek to attain. This must be clear first of all from bodies' shape and limbs, which make it plain by themselves that reproduction is a principle possessed by nature. But it could not be consistent for nature both to desire the production of offspring and not to be concerned that offspring should be loved. Even among animals nature's power can be observed; when we see the effort they spend on giving birth and on rearing, we seem to be listening to the actual voice of nature. As it is evident therefore that we naturally shrink from pain, so it is clear that nature itself drives us to love those we have engendered. (2) Hence it follows that mutual attraction between men is also something natural. Consequently, the mere fact that someone is a man makes it incumbent on another man not to regard him as alien. Just as some parts of the body, like the eyes and ears, are created as it were for their own sake while others, such as the legs and the hands, serve the needs of the other parts; so, some large animals are created only for themselves, whereas . . . ants, bees, and storks do certain things for the sake of others as well. Human behaviour in this respect is much more closely bonded. We are therefore by nature suited to form unions, societies, and states. (3) The Stoics hold that the world is governed by divine will: it is as it were a city and state shared by men and gods, and each one of us is a part of this world. From this it is a natural consequence that we prefer the common advantage to our own . . . This explains the fact that someone who dies for the state is praiseworthy, because our country should be dearer to us than ourselves . . . (4) Furthermore we are driven by nature to desire to benefit as many people as possible, and especially by giving instruction and handing on the principles of prudence. Hence it is difficult to find anyone who would not pass on to another what he himself knows; such is our inclination not only to learn but also to teach . . . (5) Just as they think that rights bind men together, so they deny that any rights exist between men and animals. For Chrysippus excellently remarked that everything else was created for the sake of men and gods, but these for the sake of community and society; consequently men can make beasts serve their own needs without contravening rights. (6) Since, moreover, man's nature is such that a kind of civil right mediates between himself and the human race, one who maintains this will be just, and whoever departs from it, unjust. (7) But just as the communal nature of a theatre is compatible with the correctness of saying that the place each person occupies is *his*, so in the city or world which they share no right is infringed by each man's possessing what belongs to him. (8) Furthermore, since we see that man is created with a view to protecting and preserving his fellows, it is in agreement with this nature that the wise man should want to play a part in governing the state and, in order to live the natural way, take a wife and want children by her.

G Hierocles (Stobaeus 4.671,7–673,11)

(1) Each one of us is as it were entirely encompassed by many circles, some smaller, others larger, the latter enclosing the former on the basis of their different and unequal dispositions relative to each other. (2) The first and closest circle is the one which a person has drawn as though around a centre, his own mind. This circle encloses the body and anything taken for the sake of the body. For it is virtually the smallest circle, and almost touches the centre itself. (3) Next, the second one further removed from the centre but enclosing the first circle; this contains parents, siblings, wife, and children. The third one has in it uncles and aunts, grandparents, nephews, nieces, and cousins. The next circle includes the other relatives, and this is followed by the circle of local residents, then the circle of fellow-tribesmen, next that of fellow-citizens, and then in the same way the circle of people from neighbouring towns, and the circle of fellow-countrymen. (4) The outermost and largest circle, which encompasses all the rest, is that of the whole human race. (5) Once these have all been surveyed, it is the task of a well tempered man, in his proper treatment of each group, to draw the circles together somehow towards the centre, and to keep zealously transferring those from the enclosing circles into the enclosed ones . . . (6) It is incumbent on us to respect people from the third circle as if they were those from the second, and again to respect our other relatives as if they were those from the third circle. For although the greater distance in blood will remove some affection, we must still try hard to assimilate them. The right point will be reached if, through our own initiative, we reduce the distance of the relationship with each person. The main procedure for this has been stated. (7) But we should do more, in the terms of address we use, calling cousins brothers, and uncles and aunts,

fathers and mothers . . . For this mode of address would be no slight mark of our affection for them all, and it would also stimulate and intensify the indicated contraction of the circles.

H Anonymous commentary on Plato's *Theaetetus*, 5.18–6.31

(1) We have an appropriate relationship to members of the same species. (2) But a man's relationship to his own citizens is more appropriate. For appropriation varies in its intensification. (3) So those people [the Stoics] who derive justice from appropriation, if on the one hand they are saying that a man's appropriation in relation to himself is equal to his appropriation in relation to the most distant Mysian, their assumption preserves justice; on the other hand no one agrees with them that the appropriation is equal. That is contrary to plain fact and one's self-awareness. (4) For appropriation in relation to oneself is natural and irrational, whereas appropriation in relation to one's neighbours, while also natural, is not independent of reason. (5) If, at any rate, we charge people with misbehaviour, we not only criticize them but we are also alienated from them, whereas they themselves, having done wrong, although they do not welcome the < criticisms >, cannot hate themselves. (6) So appropriation in relation to oneself is not equal to appropriation to anyone else, given that our relationship to our own parts is not one of equal appropriation. For we are not disposed in just the same way relative to our eyes and our fingers, let alone to our nails and hair, seeing that we are not alienated from their loss equally either, but to a greater or lesser extent. (7) If on the other hand they themselves should say that appropriation can be intensified, we may grant the existence of philanthropy, but the situations of shipwrecked sailors will refute them, where it is inevitable that only one of two survive. (8) Even apart from situations, they themselves are in a position to be refuted. Hence the members of the Academy pose the following argument as well . . .

☐ The Stoics made 'impulse' (see **56A**) the first topic of their ethical theory. Impulse, together with sensation, distinguishes animals quite generally (including man) from plants (**A 4**; cf. **53A 4**), and gives them the innate capacity to activate themselves in an animal's way of life. This way of life is programmed, as it were, by the fact that animals are born with self-preservation as the object of their first impulse (**A 1**). Against the Epicureans, who held that living creatures are impelled to pursue pleasure and avoid pain from the moment of birth (**A 3**, **B 2**; cf. **21A 2**), the Stoics argued that an animal's first motivation is determined by its innate awareness of its physical constituents and their functions (**B 1–2**, **C 2–3**). These passages from Seneca and Hierocles base their claims for this thesis on empirical data. In **A 1–2** Chrysippus proceeds more theoretically. The argument reported there derives its force from implicit teleological assumptions about nature in general, which is equivalent to both the sum of all particular 'natures' and their creative or organizing principle. In this sense nature is identical to god or cosmic reason (60H 3–4), and this is doubtless the unexpressed ground for rejecting 'alienation' as a likely action by nature with regard to animals. The logic of A 2 is: not-*p*; but either *p* or *q*; therefore *q* (where *p* = alienation and *q* = appropriation). Like the craftsman which nature is, it has good reason to take an interest in its products.

'Alienation' and 'appropriation' are literal translations of the Greek terms *allotriōsis* and *oikeiōsis*. Their English associations with property ownership capture the main force of the Stoic concepts here, though any translation will miss something of the original. The advantage of 'appropriation' is its providing a means, through the verb or adjective 'appropriate', of rendering grammatically related forms of the Greek root *oik-*. This connotes ownership, what belongs to something, but in Stoic usage that notion is also conceived as an affective disposition relative to the thing which is owned or belongs. Hence the English associations of 'appropriation' with forcible possession are to be discounted in our translations. Correspondingly, the notion of claiming or desiring ownership needs to be read in our translation of the adjective *oikeion* by 'appropriate'. So, in A 2, the 'first thing appropriate to every animal', means the first thing 'fitting' or 'suitable', but the relevant suitability is like that of a house to its owner, a recognition of ownership, or like that of a kinsman to a blood relation, a recognition of affinity coupled with affection.

In A 1–2 Chrysippus uses the concept of 'appropriation' to establish causal links between the creative organization of nature, the first impulses of animals, and the empirical fact that animals have an innate capacity to behave discriminatingly towards their external environment. In the letter excerpted in B Seneca stresses the fact that the earliest animal behaviour is instinctive (B 1). 'Appropriation' ensures that animals are born with dispositions of affectionate ownership towards themselves, and this is the consequence of nature's disposition towards them. Our text in A 1–2 is probably correct in moving from 'nature appropriates the animal' to 'nature appropriates the animal to itself' (i.e. to the animal). This will mean that nature manifests her affectionate ownership of animals by giving them this disposition relative to themselves.

The 'appropriate' object of an animal's first impulse can thus be described as 'self-preservation'. In A 2 this is expanded into 'its own constitution and the consciousness of this'. The stress on consciousness or awareness is a feature of B and C (cf. 53B 5–9). Stoics may have defined 'appropriation' as 'perception of what is appropriate' (see note on E in vol. 2). Why this should be thought to require *self*-consciousness, however rudimentary (see Seneca, *Letters* 121.11–13), may seem inadequately explained in their reasoning. But not too much weight need or should be attached to the term 'consciousness'. It is an attempt, and an interesting one, to do justice to data which would now be explained by reference to natural selection and genetic coding. The Stoics were probably little interested in animal behaviour for its own sake. But they did suppose, very unusually, that its principles could provide them with the foundations for their ethical theory.

What links animals, and even plants (**A 4**) to men, so far as ethics is concerned, is nature. Any ethical theory must make provision for the proper rearing of children. The Stoics were impressed by the fact that animals, as well as humans, take pains over the rearing of their young (**F 1**), and some animals also have forms of social organization (**F 2**). Nature, then, even in its more rudimentary products, provides a programme of 'impulsive activity' which is both immediately self-sustaining, and also other-related. The principle of 'appropriation', even at the level of animal behaviour, extends beyond the self to affectionate ownership of offspring (**E**).

The entry of strictly ethical norms and values is a topic for later sections. What the present material indicates is a basic common ground in nature between animal and human behaviour in preserving oneself and looking after one's young. The Stoics are not saying *we* should do these things because animals do them. They are claiming that animals and humans alike are so structured that such behaviour is natural and appropriate to them both. It is pertinent to ask what the introduction of animals contributes to the ethical theory. As already noted, it serves as a basis from which to reject the Epicurean thesis of pleasure as all creatures' natural objective, and that is of great importance to the foundations of Stoic ethics. Related to this point is the insistence that nature, as a providential power, establishes values or norms of appropriateness along with the physical structures it creates. Against sceptical challenges which sought to undermine any objective criteria of values the Stoics could point to the discriminating faculties natural to men and animals (see **53B, O, P**). If there is continuity as well as difference between human and animal 'appropriation', that fact can draw attention to the significance of the difference. The nature of man as a rational being (cf. **A 5**) requires understanding of the impulses he shares, or seems to share, with the animals.

Moral virtue is the perfection of man's specific nature, his rationality in harmony with universal nature or divine reason (**60H 4**). Texts in this section show how this ethical ideal is based upon a conception of human nature which is as general in its scope as the philosophy of animal behaviour. In **D** Hierocles outlines a series of 'appropriate relationships' which purport to explain normal characteristics of human behaviour with regard to one's self, one's children, property, other human beings. The procedure in **F** is similar: it is natural for human beings to be friendly and philanthropic, to live in organized communities, to possess private property, to marry and have children. Community life is represented as a natural consequence of a man's instinctive love of his children. It is important to observe that Hierocles and Cicero are not concerned here with the *distinctive* activities and attitudes of the Stoic wise man; rather the wise man is mentioned in **F 8** as conforming to the general pattern of human nature. Strictly no one but the wise man can be just in Stoicism, but the justice and injustice of **F 6** are hardly to be given so exclusive an interpretation. The whole thrust of this passage is to endorse the normal customs and institutions of human society as natural.

This point will be reinforced in the doctrine of 'proper functions' (see **59E 2**; and cf. **53Q 1**). On these foundations the Stoics will seek to erect a moral theory which takes account of the fact (**A 5**) that human reason must be the ultimate arbiter of what is appropriate to human nature; as the 'craftsman' of impulse, reason can be presumed to establish 'assent' as a necessary precondition of all mature human action (cf. **33I**; **53A 5, S**). 'Appropriation' as something innate and animal-like is only a foundation, a beginning. But our 'appropriate' attitudes of self-love, affection towards kindred, choice towards external property (**D**), are not forgotten in the fully developed doctrine of the virtues. We are born with 'tendencies' towards the virtues (**61L**), and an example of how this should work out is presented, for the case of justice, in **G** and criticized in **H**.

According to **G** a man instinctively, without training, experiences himself as the closest object of his concern, while his concern for other people progressively diminishes as their blood relationship to him declines from that of his closest relatives to 'the whole human race'. Hierocles implies that this arrangement of 'concentric circles', though natural to the untutored mind, is incompatible with a proper understanding of our 'appropriation' of our fellow human beings (cf. **67A**). We should (and here the moral 'ought' has its full force) make every effort to 'reduce the distance of the relationship with each person' (**G6**). The unexpressed assumption of this passage seems to be this: we have an instinctive disposition to show affection to our relatives as well as ourselves, but without training we remain self-centred and treat others as increasingly alien. Hierocles proposes that we 'appropriate' other people to our self, and so extend to them the same kind of concern we show to ourselves. In **H** an attack (probably Academic) is launched against the practicality of 'appropriation' as the foundation of justice. The Stoics probably did not commit themselves to the claim (**H 3**) that appropriation in relation to others is *equal* to that in relation to oneself (cf. however **67A**), but **H**'s polemic presents a dilemma according to which problems for justice arise whether the appropriation is equal or variant; equal appropriation is false to experience (**H 3**), and variant appropriation (**H 7**) will not fit problem cases where self-interest conflicts with the equal rights of a second person. There is independent evidence (*SVF* 1.197) for the claim that the Stoics made 'appropriation' the origin of justice (**H 3**), and the thought appears to be similar to the doctrine of **G** (cf. **F 2–7**). Self-preservation will promote justice if it is recognized that concern for other people is a natural development of concern for one's self.

As much of this material makes plain (**B 3, D, F–H**), the Stoics did not confine the scope of 'appropriation' to the evaluative discriminations of our 'first impulse'. That receives emphasis in the texts because of its priority, but the paramount desirability of moral virtue was also represented as a function of 'appropriation' (see **65M 2** where the claim that 'we have an appropriate relation only with rectitude' has to be understood in reference to people at the higher stages of moral progress). It is thus a mistake to complain, as Alexander of Aphrodisias did (*SVF* 3.165), that the Stoics limited the scope of 'appropriation' to 'self-preservation' as distinct from 'the good itself'. The grounds of his misunderstanding probably relate to a more fundamental difficulty frequently seized upon by opponents of Stoicism: how can it be consistent to derive 'the good', a term exclusively limited to moral value, from natural impulses which justify the appropriateness of other values? The gist of the Stoics' answer is given

353

by Seneca in **B** 3: 'constitution' and therewith 'appropriateness' evolve over a lifetime. He uses this point to dismiss the objection (*Letters* 121.14) that a young child, 'not yet rational', could not have an 'appropriate' relation to a rational constitution.

58 Value and indifference

A Diogenes Laertius 7.101–3

(1) They [the Stoics] say that some existing things are good, others are bad, and others are neither of these. (2) The virtues – prudence, justice, courage, moderation and the rest – are good. (3) The opposites of these – foolishness, injustice and the rest – are bad. (4) Everything which neither does benefit nor harms is neither of these: for instance, life, health, pleasure, beauty, strength, wealth, reputation, noble birth, and their opposites, death, disease, pain, ugliness, weakness, poverty, low repute, ignoble birth and the like . . . For these things are not good but indifferents of the species 'preferred'. (5) For just as heating, not chilling, is the peculiar characteristic of what is hot, so too benefiting, not harming, is the peculiar characteristic of what is good. But wealth and health no more do benefit than they harm. Therefore wealth and health are not something good. (6) Furthermore they say: that which can be used well and badly is not something good. But wealth and health can be used well and badly. Therefore wealth and health are not something good.

B Diogenes Laertius 7.104–5 (*SVF* 3.119)

(1) 'Indifferent' is used in two senses: unconditionally, of things which contribute neither to happiness nor unhappiness, as is the case with wealth, reputation, health, strength, and the like. For it is possible to be happy even without these, though the manner of using them is constitutive of happiness or unhappiness. (2) In another sense those things are called indifferent which activate neither impulse nor repulsion, as in the case of having an odd or even number of hairs on one's head, or stretching or contracting a finger. (3) But the previous indifferents are not spoken of in this sense. For they are capable of activating impulse and repulsion. Hence some of them are selected and others disselected, but the second type is entirely equal with respect to choice and avoidance.

C Stobaeus 2.79,18–80,13; 82,20–1

(1) Some [indifferent things] are in accordance with nature, others are contrary to nature, and others are neither of these. (2) The following are in accordance with nature: health, strength, well functioning sense organs, and the like . . . (3) They [the Stoics] hold that the theory on these starts from the primary things in accordance with nature and contrary to

nature. For difference and indifference belong to things which are said relatively. Because, they say, even if we call bodily and external things indifferent, we are saying they are indifferent relative to a well-shaped life (in which living happily consists) but not of course relative to being in accordance with nature or to impulse and repulsion . . . (4) All things in accordance with nature are to-be-taken, and all things contrary to nature are not-to-be-taken.

D Stobaeus 2.83,10–84,2 (*SVF* 3.124)

(1) All things in accordance with nature have value and all things contrary to nature have disvalue. (2) Value has three senses: a thing's contribution and merit *per se*, the expert's appraisal, and thirdly, what Antipater calls 'selective': according to this, when circumstances permit, we choose these particular things instead of those, for instance health instead of disease, life instead of death, wealth instead of poverty. (3) Disvalue, they say, also has three senses analogous to these.

E Stobaeus 2.84,18–85,11 (*SVF* 3.128)

(1) Some valuable things have much value and others little. So too some disvaluable things have much disvalue and others little. (2) Those which have much value are called 'preferred' and those which have much disvalue 'dispreferred'. Zeno was the first to apply these terms to the things. (3) That is preferred, they say, which, though indifferent, we select on the basis of a preferential reason. The like principle applies to being dispreferred, and the examples are analogous. (4) No good thing is preferred since they possess the greatest value. But the preferred, since it has the second place and value, is in some way adjacent to the nature of goods. For in the court the King is not in the rank of the preferred, but they are preferred who rank after him.

F Sextus Empiricus, *Against the professors* 11.64–7 (*SVF* 1.361)

(1) Aristo of Chios denied that health and everything similar to it is a preferred indifferent. (2) For to call it a preferred indifferent is equivalent to judging it a good, and different practically in name alone. (3) For without exception things indifferent as between virtue and vice have no difference at all, nor are some of them preferred by nature while others are dispreferred, but in the face of the different circumstances of the occasions neither those which are said to be preferred prove to be unconditionally preferred, nor are those said to be dispreferred of necessity dispreferred. (4) For if healthy men had to serve a tyrant and be destroyed for this reason, while the sick had to be released from the service and, therewith also, from destruction, the wise man would rather choose sickness in this circumstance than health. (5) Thus neither is health

unconditionally preferred nor sickness dispreferred. Just as in writing people's names we put different letters first at different times, adapting them to the different circumstances . . . not because some letters are given priority over others by nature but because the circumstances compel us to do this, so too in the things which are between virtue and vice no natural priority for some over others arises but a priority which is based rather on circumstances.

G Diogenes Laertius 7.160 (*SVF* 1.351, part)

Aristo of Chios . . . said that the end is to live with a disposition of indifference towards what is intermediate between vice and virtue, not retaining any difference at all within that class of things, but being equally disposed towards them all. For the wise man is like the good actor who, whether he puts on the mask of Thersites or Agamemnon, plays either part in the proper way.

H Plutarch, *On Stoic self-contradictions* 1048A (*SVF* 3.137)

In his *On good things* book 1 he [Chrysippus] concedes in a sense and gives way to those who wish to call the preferred things good and their opposites bad, in the following words: 'If someone in accordance with such differences [i.e. between the preferred and dispreferred] wishes to call the one class of them good and the other bad, and he is referring to these things [i.e. the preferred or the dispreferred] and not committing an idle aberration, his usage must be accepted on the grounds that he is not wrong in the matter of meanings and in other respects is aiming at the normal use of terms.'

I Cicero, *On ends* 3.50 (*SVF* 1.365)

[Speaker: the Stoic Cato] Next comes an explanation of the difference between things, by the denial of which all life would be made completely undiscriminated, as it is by Aristo, and no function or task for wisdom could be found, since there would be no difference at all between the things that concern the living of life, and no choice between them would have to be made.

J Epictetus, *Discourses* 2.6.9 (*SVF* 3.191)

Therefore Chrysippus was right to say: 'As long as the future is uncertain to me I always hold to those things which are better adapted to obtaining the things in accordance with nature; for god himself has made me disposed to select these. But if I actually knew that I was fated now to be ill, I would even have an impulse to be ill. For my foot too, if it had intelligence, would have an impulse to get muddy.'

K Stobaeus 2.76,9–15

(1) Diogenes [of Babylon represented the end as]: reasoning well in the selection and disselection of things in accordance with nature . . . (2) and Antipater: to live continuously selecting things in accordance with nature and disselecting things contrary to nature. He also frequently rendered it thus: to do everything in one's power continuously and undeviatingly with a view to obtaining the predominating things which accord with nature.

☐ The bastion of Stoic ethics is the thesis that virtue and vice respectively are the sole constituents of happiness and unhappiness. These states do not in the least depend, they insisted, on the possession or absence of things conventionally regarded as good or bad – health, reputation, wealth etc: 'It is possible to be happy even without these' (**B** 1). They expressed this thesis by restricting 'good' to what is morally excellent and 'bad' to the opposite of this, and termed everything which makes no difference to happiness or unhappiness 'indifferent' (**B** 1, cf. **A**; and **1F 3** for Pyrrhonian use of the term). In relation to happiness health is no more of a contributor than an odd rather than an even number of hairs on one's head. Yet, as we saw in the last section, living beings are naturally impelled to preserve themselves, and to do so by discriminating between things which are appropriate to their constitution, and their opposites (**57A 2**). Such behaviour, moreover, has the providence and rationality of cosmic nature as its foundation. In relation to a creature's nature and what it is impelled to pursue or avoid, health and its opposite are not indifferent, by contrast with the absolute indifference of an odd or even number of hairs.

Thus the class of items indifferent to happiness includes things that have value or disvalue 'relative to being in accordance with nature, or to impulse and repulsion' (**C 3**). At the most elementary level these are instantiated in the objects specified in **C 2** – health, strength etc. and their opposites, which are called 'primary things in accordance with nature' (*PAN* things) and 'primary things contrary to nature' (*PCN* things). Founded as they are upon the primary needs of a creature's nature, these primary valuables must be construed as objective; 'accordance with nature' is laid down as the criterion of value (**D 1; 59D 2**). The same naturalness or objectivity pertains to the value of the things specified as 'indifferent', i.e. to happiness, in **A 4**, **B 1**; some of these, such as wealth or noble birth, can be interpreted as 'secondary' things in accordance with nature. Their activation of impulse will be subsequent in a human life to that of *PAN* things. A human being is represented as developing awareness of a larger range of *AN* (in accordance with nature) and *CN* (contrary to nature) things as it matures (cf. **57B 3**). (For apparent discrepancies in the sources concerning the strict scope of 'accordance with nature' as the criterion of indifferent things' value, see note on **m** in vol. 2.)

Valuable though they are, *AN* things lack goodness, for reasons set out in **A 5–6**. Here we are invited to regard 'good' as a property analogous to the heat of anything which is hot. A hot thing necessarily heats and never chills anything with which it is in contact. By analogy we are to take it that a good thing necessarily benefits and never harms that with which it is associated (cf. **60G**). But *AN* things lack this necessary relation to benefiting, and they can also be possessed by someone who puts them to bad use. Similarly, it is implied, something *CN* like poverty does not necessarily harm a person nor is it bound to be misused. These arguments, which are Platonic in origin (see vol. 2 note on **A**), identify the virtues and vices as the only things which exhibit the requisite connexion between benefit and good use, or harm and misuse.

For orthodox Stoics, none the less, the value attaching to *AN* things and the disvalue of their *CN* counterparts provide prima facie grounds for 'selecting' the former and 'disselecting' the latter (**B 3**). These discriminations conform in general to nature's provisions for human life, since *AN* things naturally activate our impulses and *CN* things our repulsions. This 'selective value' (**D 2**), though conditional upon circumstances (contrast the absolute value of virtue), resides in the natural preferability of health to sickness etc. That is to say, the value of health is not based upon an individual's judgement but is a feature of the world. The role of moral judgement is to decide whether, given the objective preferability of health to sickness, it is right to make that difference the paramount consideration in determining what one should do in the light of all the circumstances (see **J**). In the case of those indifferents of 'preferred' status (**A 4**, **E 2**), there will be 'preferential' reason (**E 3**) for selecting these 'when circumstances permit' (**D 2**). It is up to the moral agent to decide, from knowledge of his situation, whether to choose actions that may put his health at risk rather than preserve it, but the correctness of sometimes deciding in favour of the former does not negate the normal preferability of the latter. Only an unusually prescient or unfortunate person will have the foreknowledge to adapt his impulses to unavoidable *CN* states of affairs, as in **J**, where Chrysippus indicates that consistent selection of *AN* things is the right policy 'as long as the future is uncertain'.

'To-be-taken' is another standard way of describing the value of such things (**C 4**). This attribute, like that of 'selection', indicates the attitude a Stoic should adopt towards *AN* things which happen to be available (cf. **D 2**), and which he can take or select without compromising his moral principles. He should not go out of his way to 'choose' or 'desire' such things, since such unreservedly positive attitudes are appropriate only in relation to the good (**59D 5**). Provided, however, that he realizes the indifference of *AN* things to his happiness, it is rational and appropriate to discriminate in favour of anything which accords with other features of human nature.

The relative value of 'indifferent' things, which admit of their own ranking (e.g. 'preferred' things are more valuable than other *AN* things), goes back to Zeno himself (**E 2**). But not every early Stoic was happy with the concept. Aristo (**F**) rejected all distinctions within the class of the 'indifferents'. The nub of his argument is **F 4–5**: in some circumstances the wise man would select sickness rather than health (cf. Chrysippus in **J**); therefore health is not unconditionally preferable to sickness. Zeno could accept this conclusion, but reply that the intrinsic preferability of health over sickness is not overturned. Aristo's objection does not show that there are no *natural* preferences, but only that circumstances can alter preferences.

The interest of Aristo's heresy is its attempt to exclude all factors except virtue and reason in moral judgement (see **2F–H**). His formula for the 'end' was 'indifference towards what is intermediate between vice and virtue' (**G**), supposing such a disposition to be undermined if non-good or non-bad things were deemed to activate impulse or repulsion by their intrinsic nature. An orthodox reply to his position is given in **I**: unless there are intrinsic differences of value between *AN* and *CN* things, life becomes completely undiscriminated and the wise man will have no objective criteria for grounding his preferences.

The controversial character of Zeno's teaching on 'indifferents' is evident from the fact that Herillus, another of his immediate followers (see **1J**), also rejected the difference between *AN* and *CN* things as far as the wise man's end is concerned. According to Diogenes Laertius 7.165 (= **1** in vol. 2) Herillus distinguished a 'subordinate end', aimed at by non-wise men, and probably having supposedly *AN* things as its content. (Another source relates 'subordinate end' to objects of the first impulse, see note on **1** in vol. 2.)

Orthodox Stoics were adamant that the 'preferred' values did not introduce any equivocation over the absolute and incomparable goodness of virtue, though Chrysippus conceded that 'preferred' and 'dispreferred' coincided with ordinary-language use of 'good' and 'bad' (**H**, cf. **66B**). Both sets of values are natural to man, and the distinction between *AN* and *CN* things is the starting-point for understanding what 'accordance with nature' should mean to a mature rational being (see **59D**). No more than Aristo did Zeno and Chrysippus make *AN* things a constituent of happiness. Unlike him they held that the required attitude towards them is not unqualified indifference but knowledge of how they should be used (cf. **B** 1). (Epictetus' constant insistence on 'making correct use of impressions', cf. **62K**, may be viewed as a later, and perhaps expanded, version of this doctrine.)

In later sections we shall see how orthodox Stoics attempted to integrate *AN* and *CN* things into their other ethical doctrines, while retaining the differences of moral and non-moral value. For convenience we give one example here: Diogenes of Babylon and Antipater (**K**), in striking contrast with Aristo and Herillus, incorporated 'selection of' or 'efforts to obtain' *AN* things into their accounts of the end. The interpretation of these proposals, together with the Academic criticism they generated or responded to, will be studied in **64**.

59 Proper functions

A Plutarch, *On common conceptions* 1069E (*SVF* 3.491)

He [Chrysippus] says: 'What am I to begin from, and what am I to take as the foundation of proper function and the material of virtue if I pass over nature and what accords with nature?'

B Stobaeus 2.85,13–86,4 (*SVF* 3.494)

(1) Proper function is so defined: 'consequentiality in life, something which, once it has been done, has a reasonable justification'. The contrary

to proper function is defined as the opposite of this. (2) Proper function also extends to the non-rational animals, for these too display a kind of activity which is consequential upon their own nature. (3) In the case of rational animals it is specified in the words: consequentiality in one's way of life. (4) They [the Stoics] say that some proper functions are perfect, and that these are also called right actions. The activities which accord with virtue are right actions, such as acting prudently, and justly. Those which are not like this are not right actions, and they do not call them perfectly proper functions, but intermediate functions, such as marrying, serving on embassies, conversing, and the like.

C Diogenes Laertius 7.107 (*SVF* 3.493, part)

(1) It [proper function] also extends to plants and animals. For proper functions can be seen in them as well. (2) Zeno was the first to use this term *kathēkon*, the name being derived from *kata tinas hēkein*, 'to have arrived in accordance with certain persons'. (3) Proper function is an activity appropriate to constitutions that accord with nature.

D Cicero, *On ends* 3.17,20–2

[Speaker: the Stoic Cato] (1) As to why we love the first objects which are appropriated by nature, it seems sufficient proof that no one, given the choice, would not prefer to have all the parts of his body sound and whole rather than defective or twisted though no less functional . . . (2) Let us proceed therefore, since we digressed from these starting-points of nature, and what follows must be consistent with them. One consequence is this primary classification: the Stoics say that that is 'valuable' (for we may use this term, I think) which is either itself in accordance with nature or such as to bring about that state of affairs; accordingly it is worthy of being selected because it possesses something of sufficient weight to be valued (they call this *axia*), whereas the opposite of this is disvaluable. (3) With the principles thus established that those things which are in accordance with nature are to be taken for their own sake, and that their opposites similarly are to be rejected, the first 'proper function' (this is my term for *kathēkon*) is to preserve oneself in one's natural constitution; the second is to seize hold of the things that accord with nature and to banish their opposites. Once this procedure of selection and rejection has been discovered, the next consequence is selection exercised with proper functioning; then, such selection performed continuously; finally, selection which is absolutely consistent and in full accordance with nature. (4) At this point, for the first time, that which can be truly called good begins to be present in a man and understood. For a man's first affiliation is towards those things which are in accordance with nature. But as soon as he has acquired understanding, or rather, the conception which the Stoics call *ennoia*, and has seen the regularity and, so to speak, the harmony of conduct, he comes to value this far higher than all those objects of his initial affection; and he draws the rational conclusion that this constitutes the highest human good which is worthy of praise and desirable for its own sake. (5) Since that good is situated in what the Stoics call *homologia* ('agreement' will be our term for this, if you don't mind) – since it is in this, then, that that good consists to which everything is the means, that good which is the standard of all things, right actions and rectitude itself, which is reckoned the only good, though later in origin, is the only thing desirable through its intrinsic nature and value, whereas none of the first objects of nature is desirable for its own sake. (6) But since those things which I called proper functions originate in nature's starting-points, it must be the case that the former are the means to the latter; so it could be correctly said that the end of all proper functions is to obtain nature's primary requirements, but not that this is the ultimate good, since right action is not present in the first affiliations of nature. It is an outcome of these, and arises later, as I have said. Yet it is in accordance with nature, and stimulates us to desire it far more strongly than we are stimulated by all the earlier objects. [continued at **64F**]

E Diogenes Laertius 7.108–9 (*SVF* 3.495, 496)

(1) Of activities in accordance with impulse, some are proper functions, others are contrary to proper function, and others belong to neither type. (2) Proper functions are ones which reason dictates our doing, such as honouring parents, brothers and country, spending time with friends; contrary to proper function are ones which reason does not dictate our doing, such as neglecting parents, not caring about brothers, not treating friends sympathetically, not acting patriotically etc. Activities which are neither proper functions nor contrary to proper function are ones which reason neither dictates our doing nor forbids, such as picking up a twig, holding a pen or a scraper, and such like. (3) Some proper functions do not depend on circumstances, but others do. The following do not depend on circumstances, looking after one's health, and one's sense organs, and such like. Proper functions which do depend on circumstances are mutilating oneself and disposing of one's property. And so analogously with actions which are contrary to proper function. (4) Furthermore, some proper functions are always proper while others are not. It is always a proper function to live virtuously, but not always a proper function to engage in question and answer, to walk about, and such like. The same principle applies to actions which are contrary to proper function.

F Cicero, *On ends* 3.58–9

[Speaker: the Stoic Cato] (1) But although we declare rectitude to be the only good, it is nevertheless consistent to perform a proper function, even though we count this neither in good things nor in bad . . . (2) It is self-evident too that some of the wise man's actions are in this intermediate region. So he judges when he acts that his action is a proper function, and since he never errs in making a judgement, proper function will exist in the intermediate region. (3) This is also established by the following argument: we see that something exists which we call a right action; but this is a perfectly proper function; so there will also be such a thing as an imperfect one. (4) For instance, if it is a right action to return a deposit in the just manner, to return a deposit should be counted as a proper function. It becomes a right action by the addition, 'in the just manner', but the act of return just by itself is counted a proper function. (5) Since it is certain as well that the region we call intermediate includes things which are to-be-taken, and others which are to-be-rejected, everything so done or described is embraced by proper function. (6) This proves that since love of self is natural to everyone, a fool just as much as a wise man will take what accords with nature and reject the opposite. (7) So the wise man and the fool possess some proper functions in common, and this leads to the result that proper functions belong among the things we call intermediate.

G Sextus Empiricus, *Against the professors* 11.200–1 (*SVF* 3.516, part)

[The Stoics say] (1) The virtuous man's function is not to look after his parents and honour them in other respects but to do this on the basis of prudence. (2) For just as the care of health is common to the doctor and the layman, but caring for health in the medical way is peculiar to the expert, so too the honouring of parents is common to the virtuous and the not virtuous man, but to do this on the basis of prudence is peculiar to the wise man. (3) Consequently he also has expertise in his way of life, the peculiar function of which is to do everything on the basis of the best character.

H Philo, *On the cherubim* 14–15 (*SVF* 3.513, part)

(1) There are times when what ought to be done is not enacted as it should be, and sometimes something which is not a proper function is done in a proper way. (2) In the case, for instance, of returning a deposit, when this does not take place on the basis of a sound judgement, but with a view to the injury of the recipient . . . an action which is a proper function is performed as it should not be. (3) But if a doctor does not tell the truth to

a sick person, when he has decided to evacuate him or use surgery on him or cauterize him, for his own benefit . . . an action which is not a proper function is performed as it ought to be.

I Stobaeus 5.906,18–907,5 (*SVF* 3.510)

Chrysippus says: 'The man who progresses to the furthest point performs all proper functions without exception and omits none. Yet his life', he says, 'is not yet happy, but happiness supervenes on it when these intermediate actions acquire the additional properties of firmness and tenor and their own particular fixity.'

J Diogenes Laertius 7.88 (*SVF* 3 Archedemus 20, part)

Archedemus [says the end is] to perfect all proper functions in one's life.

K Stobaeus 2.93,14–18 (*SVF* 3.500)

They [the Stoics] say that a right action is a proper function which possesses all the measures . . . while a wrong action is one which is done contrary to right reason, or one in which some proper function has been omitted by a rational animal.

L Cicero, *On ends* 3.32 (*SVF* 3.504)

[Speaker: the Stoic Cato] (1) Whatever takes its start from wisdom must be immediately perfect in all its parts. For in it is situated what we call 'desirable'. (2) Just as it is wrong to betray one's country, to show violence to one's parents, to steal from temples, actions which consist in bringing about certain results, so even without any result it is wrong to fear, to show grief, or to be in a state of concupiscence. (3) As the latter are wrong not in their after-effects and consequences but immediately in their first steps, so those things which take their start from virtue are to be judged right from their first undertaking and not by their accomplishment.

M Stobaeus 2.96,18–97,5 (*SVF* 3.501)

(1) Furthermore, they [the Stoics] say that actions are divided into ones which are right, wrong, and neither of these. (2) The following are right actions: behaving prudently, moderately, justly, gladly, kindly, and cheerfully, and walking about prudently, and everything which is done in accordance with right reason. (3) The following are wrong actions: behaving foolishly, immoderately, unjustly, grieving, fearing, and stealing, and quite generally acting contrary to right reason. (4) The following are neither right nor wrong actions: talking, asking and answering questions, walking about, leaving town, and the like.

N Stobaeus 2.99,3–8

Zeno and the Stoic philosophers of his persuasion hold that there are two kinds of men, the excellent and the inferior. The excellent kind employs the virtues throughout all its life, but the inferior kind employs the vices. Hence the former always acts rightly in everything which it undertakes, but the latter wrongly.

O Stobaeus 2.113,18–23 (*SVF* 3.529, part)

(1) All wrong actions are equal, and likewise all right actions; and all fools are equally foolish since they have one and the same character. (2) But although wrong actions are equal, they contain certain differences depending on the fact that some of them arise from a hardened and incurable character but others not.

P Cicero, *On duties* 1.15,152

[Probably representing Panaetius] While these four [i.e. cardinal] virtues are mutually connected and interwoven, yet it is from them taken individually that determinate types of proper functions have their origin ... I think I have adequately explained how proper functions are derived from those divisions [i.e. the four above] of rectitude.

Q Epictetus, *Discourses* 2.10.1–12

(1) How is it possible to discover proper functions from titles? (2) Consider who you are: in the first place a human being, that is, someone who has nothing more authoritative than moral purpose, but subordinates everything else to this and keeps it free from slavery and subordination ... (3) Furthermore you are a citizen of the world and a part of it, not one of the underlings but one of the foremost constituents. For you are capable of attending to the divine government and of calculating its consequences. What then is a citizen's profession? To regard nothing as of private interest, to deliberate about nothing as though one were cut off [i.e. from the whole] ... (4) Next keep in mind that you are a son ... next know that you are also a brother ... next if you are a town councillor, remember that you are a councillor; if young, that you are young, if old, that you are old; if a father, that you are a father. For each of these titles, when rationally considered, always suggests the actions appropriate to it.

☐ The unity or intended unity of Stoic ethics is seen in the connexions between much of this material and the two previous sections. 'Accordance with nature' was there presented as the foundation of an animal's or person's primary behaviour ('appropriation' or *oikeiōsis*) and as the basis of evaluative discriminations within the class of 'indifferent' things. Just as 'nature' and 'value' in

Stoicism extend from animal life quite generally to the specifically rational and moral, so it is with the central concept of *kathēkon* (**C 2**), translated 'proper function'. The breadth of reference of this term is indicated by the fact that it includes, at one extreme, activities of animals (**B 2**) or even plants as well (**C 1**), and that utterly rare class of 'right actions' which are the peculiar province of the completely and unfailingly wise or virtuous man (**B 4**).

'Proper functions' denote all those activities which are 'appropriate' or 'natural' to a living being's constitution (**A, C 3, D 3**). As such they comprise, most basically, activities prompted by a creature's impulse to self-preservation, followed, in the case of humans, by the much fuller range of actions which is natural to man as he matures and his social awareness increases (see **57A 5, D 2, F**). The standard definition of *kathēkon* employs the term *akolouthia*, translated 'consequentiality' (**B 1–3**), which indicates conformity or accordance with a creature's natural way of life. 'Living in agreement with nature' is the standard Stoic definition of the ethical end (**63A–C**), and there is no confusion in also drawing upon this concept in the definition of 'proper function'. A 'proper function', whatever its agent, is an activity, or in the case of mature persons, an action which accords with the nature, construed normatively, of its doer. But it does not refer, as does the definition of the ethical end, to the doer's disposition or whole plan of life. It picks out a particular action or activity (**E 2**), the ethical grounding of which, in the case of humans, is 'reason' (**E 2**, cf. **B 1**), but not necessarily 'right' reason, the foundation of 'right actions' (**M 2**). For this fallible sense of 'reasonable', cf. **40F**.

Focusing now exclusively on humans, we should observe again that 'proper functions' include but are not confined to 'right actions'. These latter are a special class of 'proper functions', picked out by the term 'perfect' (**B 4**) and standardly illustrated by reference to the virtues (**M 2**). The virtues do not describe the particular or type of thing done in a 'perfect proper function'. They describe and evaluate the moral character of the agent, which is transferred adverbially to the action itself: thus 'walking about prudently' (**M 2**) is a 'right action' and therefore a 'perfect proper function', its 'perfection' resulting from the virtue of prudence. This point is brought out clearly in Sextus Empiricus' account (**G**) of the virtuous man's function.

It is a very important point, because the concept of 'proper function' has frequently been misunderstood in modern times, partly because of sloppy reporting by some of our sources. The material selected here shows that there is not the least justification for supposing, as some scholars have done, that the orthodox Stoics had two moral systems, clumsily related together: an ideal theory of right actions performed only by wise men, and a second-best, practical morality of 'proper functions' available to the imperfect. Everything which a wise man does *is* a 'proper function'. This follows by definition from **B 4**. Right actions are 'perfect proper functions', and everything done by the wise man is a right action. Not only the addition of the virtues but also the classifications of 'proper functions' probably accommodate anything a virtuous or wise man might do. Philo (**H**) entertains the notion of a non-proper function, e.g. lying, being done 'in a proper way', and if this were orthodox Stoicism, some of the wise man's actions would not be 'proper functions'. But it seems likely that the Stoics themselves would have taken account of Philo's example by the category of 'proper functions which depend on circumstances' (**E 3**). If these can include mutilating oneself or disposing of one's property, 'proper functions' will include both actions admitting of no exceptions, such as honouring one's parents, and actions which are justified by a rational assessment of the circumstances even though these conflict with what would be proper in most cases. The theory of 'proper functions' does not require an exhaustive listing of all qualifying actions. 'Consequentiality in life', or what admits of 'reasonable justification' (**B 1–3**), should be interpreted generously enough to accommodate anything a wise man would choose to do as well as conventional morality. But to be effective as a concept, 'proper function' must not be left vacuous or purely formal. It avoids these characteristics by being founded on a conception of what man's nature, as a rational being (**E 2**), demands.

Further support for the claim that 'proper functions' comprehend the descriptive content of all moral actions, those of the wise and inferior alike, is provided by **I–K**. What the man who has made maximum progress lacks (**I**) is not an understanding of how he should act. He will continue to perform all 'proper functions' when he has become a wise man, but he will then do so on the basis of an absolutely firm disposition currently lacking. Archedemus' definition of the end (**J**), *'perfecting* all proper functions', would thus be completely orthodox and not deviant, as it has sometimes been taken to be.

What has caused great difficulty in the interpretation of 'proper functions' is that set of them which is regularly called 'intermediate' (**B 4**, **F**, **I**). These are exemplified by verbs unmodified by an adverbial reference to a virtue, e.g. marrying, conversing, walking about. The last example, however, is also cited as a 'right action' when performed 'prudently' (**M 2**), and so 'walking about' can be 'intermediate' *or* 'perfect'. The meaning of 'intermediate' can be elicited from Cicero's confusing account in **F**. He speaks of 'proper functions' being 'neither good nor bad' (**F 1**), and of some of them being common to the wise man and the fool (**F 7**). From this it might seem to follow that there is a whole class of actions which are morally indifferent, intermediate between good and bad, and this is actually asserted in **M 4**. But how is this to be squared with the fundamental Stoic thesis that everything done by the wise man is a right action, and everything done by the fool is wrong (**N**)? The Stoics' exclusive division between these two classes of men appears to leave no room for intermediate actions any more than for intermediate human beings.

The solution to this difficulty has already been adumbrated. The 'rightness' of a wise man's actions or the 'perfection' of his 'proper functions' is specifically indicated not by what he does but by the virtuous disposition which his action exhibits. Wise men and fools alike get married, serve on embassies, etc. These actions, taken by themselves, provide no means of distinguishing two moral classes of men. Hence the moral distinctions which mark out those two classes cannot be revealed if all we know about someone is that he or she performed a 'proper function'. 'Intermediate proper functions' are analogous to and characteristically constituted by *AN* things (**A**), which are themselves, as 'indifferents', also called 'intermediate'. As health or wealth is neither good nor bad, but capable of *being used* well or badly (**58A 6, B 1**), so 'intermediate proper functions' are neither good nor bad, when considered in abstraction from their agents, but in reference to these they are either 'perfect' or 'imperfect' (**F 3**), right actions or wrong ones.

The 'imperfection' of a 'proper function' seems to denote a quality of the agent's moral disposition, and not a failing in what was done, considered extensionally, nor even a failing of moral intention, ordinarily speaking. The key text is again **I**. It would be absurd to suppose that 'the man who progresses to the furthest point' must, in order to 'perform all proper functions', always succeed in achieving the result of his action (e.g. actually returning the deposit), or again, that his intentions are irrelevant to his performance. Any 'proper function' must require that its agent act on the promptings of 'reason' (**E 2**), that is, be rationally motivated to do what is appropriate. The crucial difference between 'perfect' and 'imperfect' proper functions is the moral character of their agent. A perfect proper function, as a right action, 'possesses all the measures' (**K**; cf. **64H**). This attribute signifies the completeness and harmony of the moral principles exhibited in anything that a virtuous agent does. Whatever he does is consistent with *all* the virtues (**61F 1**), whereas imperfect people may act appropriately in the sphere of one virtue but not in that of all (**60E**). As actions determined by right reason, perfect proper functions conform to 'the laws of life as a whole' (Seneca, *Letters* 95.57; cf. **63C 3–4**).

It follows from this that the wise man's performance of proper functions (in the intermediate sense) reveals important facts about him and the kinds of things that he does, but not facts which differentiate him as a type; it also follows that regular performance of proper functions, though it will not guarantee perfection, is a crucially important feature of moral progress. Having determined that the demands of morality are so stringent that there are no degrees of virtue (see **61I**), the Stoics nonetheless distinguished, among wrong actions, between those that are wrong by the formal criterion of the agent's disposition, and those which *additionally* involve the omission of a proper function (**K**; cf. **O 2**). The latter (exemplified by the contraries of **E 2**) are wrong both in terms of the agent's disposition and in terms of what he did. This is probably the point of **L 2**. 'Showing violence to one's parents' is the contrary of a proper function, but such an action will also betoken a morally and emotionally bad disposition, irrespective of what was done. Correspondingly, anything that virtue initiates is *ipso facto* right, a 'perfect proper function' that will qualify as such independently of its external success (cf. **L**).

The exclusive disjunction between right and wrong actions has sometimes been interpreted to imply that 'picking up a twig' and similarly trivial doings are either right or wrong. This would be a silly claim on the Stoics' part, and it seems to be negated in **E 2**. If 'picking up a twig' etc. is neither a proper function nor contrary to this, the Stoics are most plausibly interpreted as holding that some 'activities' are too trivial to qualify as 'actions' and thus as amenable to moral appraisal in any sense. At least it is hard to see how they could regard anything that 'reason neither dictates our doing nor forbids' (loc. cit.) as an action of any ethical significance.

One of the most helpful texts in this set is **D**. Cicero is here sketching moral development from its origins in the instinctive pursuit and avoidance of *AN* and *CN* things (**D** 3) to understanding of the 'only good'. **D** 3 envisages five progressive stages, each one of which is represented as performance of 'proper functions' as these should evolve for a human being. At the fifth stage, 'selection [of things in accordance with nature] which is absolutely consistent and in full accordance with nature', 'agreement' (with nature) is discovered to be the supreme value, totally different in its worth from the *AN* things that 'proper functions' aim at securing. This fifth stage fits the interpretation of 'perfect proper functions' that has been offered above. Such actions always aim at bringing about certain results in the external world, results normally defined by reference to *AN* things; but getting those results is not the ultimate good nor the 'perfect' feature of a 'proper function' (**D** 5–6; cf. **64F**). 'Perfection' is constituted by virtue, here presented as agreement or harmony of conduct. The concept of virtue will be studied in **61**. What should be noted here is its origin in and formal connexion with a sphere of 'accordance with nature' (**A**) that continues to play a secondary part even in 'perfect proper functions', while it features primarily in proper functions when they are considered as the 'intermediate' actions of people generally.

The material excerpted here may be taken as representative of what is known concerning Chrysippus' position on 'proper functions'. Later Stoics no doubt extended his work, but there is no good reason for supposing that they altered its substance. Cicero's *On duties* is explicitly based upon Panaetius' writings *On proper function*. A notable feature of that study (**P**) appears to have been the grounding of 'proper functions' in the sphere of activity peculiar to each of the cardinal virtues. This does not signify a weakening of the distinction between 'perfect' and 'intermediate' (cf. *On duties* 1.8, 2.14–15). Performance of 'proper functions' on a reasoned, systematic foundation is an essential precondition of acquiring a virtuous disposition (**I**); the virtues are dispositions to perform these 'perfectly' (**G**, **J**, **L**). So it is legitimate to analyse 'proper functions' both ascendingly, by reference to the individual's evolving rationality (as in **D**), and descendingly, by reference to the virtues which are their ultimate fulfilment and justification (cf. **66J** 1). The latter was Panaetius' procedure.

A further variant, of considerable interest, is **Q**, where Epictetus illuminates the functionalism of Stoic ethics in terms of action appropriate to a person's 'title' (cf. **66F**). Thus proper functions can be seen to be rooted not only in a person's human nature, considered quite generally, but also in the specific relationships and jobs which define the person one is. This conception recalls Panaetius' division of persons into a series of different *personae* (see **66E**).

60 Good and bad

A Plutarch, *On Stoic self-contradictions* 1035C–D (*SVF* 3.68)

(1) Again in his *Physical postulates* he [Chrysippus] says, 'There is no other or more appropriate way of approaching the theory of good and bad

things or the virtues or happiness than from universal nature and from the administration of the world.' (2) And later: 'For the theory of good and bad things must be attached to these, since there is no other starting-point or reference for them that is better, and physical speculation is to be adopted for no other purpose than for the differentiation of good and bad things.'

B Plutarch, *On Stoic self-contradictions* 1041E (*SVF* 3.69)

He [Chrysippus] says that the theory of good and bad things introduced and approved by himself is most in harmony with life and connects best with the innate preconceptions.

C Diogenes Laertius 7.53 (= **39D 8**)

The idea of something just and good is acquired naturally.

D Cicero, *On ends* 3.33–4 (*SVF* 3.72)

[Speaker: the Stoic Cato] (1) Since the conceptions of things arise in minds if something has become known, either by experience or combination or similarity or analogy, it is by the fourth and last of these that a conception of the good has arisen. (2) For when the mind by means of analogy has climbed up from those things which are in accordance with nature it then arrives at the conception of the good. (3) But we perceive this actual good and name it good not as a result of addition or magnification or comparison with other things but from its own specific power. (4) For just as honey, though it is very sweet, is yet perceived to be sweet by its own specific kind of flavour and not by comparison with other things, so this good, which is our subject-matter, is what is supremely valuable, but the significance of that value is one of kind and not of magnitude. (5) For since value (which is called *axia*) is counted neither among good things nor yet among bad, however much you add to it, it will remain in its own kind. Therefore the specific value of virtue is a different value, and this is a significance of kind and not of magnification.

E Seneca, *Letters* 120.3–5, 8–11

(1) Now I return to the question you want discussed, how we arrive at the first conception of the good and of rectitude. (2) Nature could not have taught us this; it has not given us knowledge but seeds of knowledge. Some people claim that we light upon the conception by chance. But it is beyond belief that anyone has encountered the form of virtue in this way. (3) Our school takes the view that it is observation and mutual comparison of repeated actions which has assembled this conception. In the judgement of our philosophers rectitude and the good are perceived

through analogy . . . We were familiar with bodily health. From this we have worked out that there also exists a health of the mind. We were familiar with bodily strength. From this we have worked out that there also exists a strength of the mind. (4) Certain acts of generosity or humanity or courage had amazed us. We began to admire them as though they were perfect. But they had many faults under the surface, which were hidden by the brilliant appearance of some splendid deed. We overlooked these. Nature tells us to magnify praiseworthy actions, and everyone has elevated glory beyond truth. From such deeds therefore we have derived the idea of a good of great magnitude . . . (5) Badness sometimes takes the appearance of rectitude, and excellence shines forth from its opposite. Virtues and vices, as you know, border on one another, and a likeness of what is right pertains to those who are also depraved and base. An extravagant man gives a false appearance of someone generous, although there is the greatest difference between one who knows how to give and one who does not know how to save . . . (6) The similarity between these forces us to take thought and to distinguish things which are related in appearance but are immensely different in fact. In observing men who have become famous through doing an outstanding deed, we began to notice the sort of man who has done something with magnanimity and great zeal, but once only. This man we saw brave in war, frightened in the forum, enduring poverty with spirit while abject in his endurance of disgrace. We praised the deed, but despised the man. (7) We saw someone else who was kindly to his friends, forbearing to his enemies, dutiful and pious in his public and private behaviour . . . Moreover he was always the same and consistent with himself in every action, good not through policy but under the direction of a character such that he could not only act rightly but could not act without acting rightly. We perceived that in him virtue was perfected. (8) We divided virtue into parts: the obligation of curbing desires, checking fears, foreseeing what has to be done, dispensing what has to be given. We grasped moderation, courage, prudence, justice, and gave to each its due. From whom then did we perceive virtue? That man's orderliness revealed it to us, his seemliness, consistency, the mutual harmony of all his actions, and his great capacity to surmount everything. From this we perceived that happy life which flows on smoothly, complete in its own self-mastery.

F Epictetus, *Discourses* 3.3.2–4

(1) Just as it is every soul's nature to assent to the true, dissent from the false, and suspend judgement in reference to the non-evident, so it is its nature to be moved appetitively towards the good, with aversion towards the bad, and in neither of these ways towards what is neither

good nor bad . . . (2) Once the good appears it immediately moves the soul towards itself, while the bad repels the soul from itself. A soul will never refuse a clear impression of good any more than it will refuse the Emperor's coinage. This is the source of every movement both of men and of god.

G Sextus Empiricus, *Against the professors* 11.22–6 (*SVF* 3.75, part)

(1) The Stoics, sticking fast to the common conceptions so to speak, define the good as follows: 'Good is benefit or not other than benefit', meaning by 'benefit' virtue and virtuous action, and by 'not other than benefit' the virtuous man and his friend. (2) For virtue, which is a disposition of the commanding-faculty, and virtuous action, which is an activity in accordance with virtue, are benefit directly. But the virtuous man and his friend, while also themselves belonging to goods, could neither be said to be benefit nor other than benefit, for the following reason. (3) Parts, the sons of the Stoics say, are neither the same as wholes nor are they different from wholes; for instance, the hand is not the same as a whole man, since the hand is not a whole man, but nor is it other than the whole since the whole man is conceived as man together with his hand. (4) Since, then, virtue is a part of the virtuous man and of his friend, and parts are neither the same as wholes nor other than wholes, the good man and his friend have been called 'not other than benefit'. (5) So every good is taken in by the definition, whether it is benefit or not other than benefit.

H Seneca, *Letters* 124.13–14

(1) The truly good does not exist in trees or in dumb animals. That which is good in these is called good by indulgence. 'What is it?' you say. It is what accords with the nature of each of them. (2) But the good can in no way fall to a dumb animal. It belongs to a happier and superior nature. There is no good except where there is a place for reason. (3) Of these four natures, tree, animal, man, and god, the last two, which are rational, have the same nature; they differ by the fact that one is immortal, the other mortal. The good of one of them, god's of course, is perfect by nature, the other's, man's, by practice. (4) The remainder, which lack reason, are perfect only in their own nature, not truly perfect. For that is finally perfect which is perfect in accordance with universal nature, and universal nature is rational. Other things can be perfect in their own kind.

I Clement, *The teacher* 1.8.63.1–2 (*SVF* 2.1116, part)

(1) One who loves something wishes to benefit it; and that which benefits must be completely superior to that which does not benefit; but nothing is superior to the good; therefore the good benefits. (2) God is agreed to

be good; therefore god benefits. (3) But the good in so far as it is good does nothing but benefit; therefore god benefits everything. (4) And of course he does not benefit man in one respect but not take care of him, nor does he take care of him but not also attend to him; for that which benefits in accordance with rational judgement is superior to that which does not benefit in this way; but nothing is superior to god; and benefiting in accordance with rational judgement is nothing but attending to man; therefore god cares for and attends to man.

J Stobaeus 2.73,1–13 (*SVF* 3.111)

(1) Of goods, some are 'in process', others 'in state'. Of the former types are joy, delight, modest socializing; of the latter type are well-organized leisure, undisturbed stability, manly concentration. (2) And of those that are 'in state', some are also 'in tenor', e.g. the virtues; but others, like those mentioned above, are 'in state' only. (3) 'In tenor' are not only the virtues but also the other expertises in the virtuous man which are modified by his virtue and become unchangeable, since they become like virtues. (4) They [the Stoics] also say that goods 'in tenor' include the so-called 'pursuits' as well, like love of music, love of literature, love of geometry and the like [see **26H**].

K Stobaeus 2.58,5–15 (*SVF* 3.95, part)

(1) Of goods, some are virtues but others are not. Prudence, moderation, < justice > and courage are virtues; but joy, cheerfulness, confidence, well-wishing and the like are not virtues. (2) Of virtues, some are sciences and expertises of certain things, but others are not. Prudence and moderation and courage and justice are sciences and expertises of certain things, but magnanimity and vigour and strength of soul are not. (3) And analogously, of bad things some are vices but others are not.

L Stobaeus 2.70,21–71,4 (*SVF* 3.104, part)

Of goods pertaining to the soul, some are characters, others are tenors but not characters, and others are neither of these. All the virtues are characters, but pursuits such as prophecy and the like are tenors only and not characters. Activities in accordance with virtues are neither of these.

M Stobaeus 2.71,15–72,6 (*SVF* 3.106, part)

Of goods, some are final, others instrumental, and others are good in both respects. The prudent man and the friend are only instrumental goods. Joy, cheerfulness, confidence and prudent walking about are only final goods. But all the virtues are both instrumental and final goods. For they both generate happiness and they complete it, since they are its parts. And analogously with bad things . . .

N Cicero, *On ends* 3.27

[Speaker: the Stoic Cato] (1) 'Everything which is good is praiseworthy. But everything which is praiseworthy is honourable. Therefore that which is good is honourable. Does this argument appear valid? Certainly. You observe that the conclusion is situated in the proposition which is brought about by the two premises. (2) Now it is customary to deny the major premise and say that not everything good is praiseworthy. For it is granted that what is praiseworthy is honourable. (3) But it is the height of absurdity to claim that something is good which is not desirable, or desirable that is not pleasing, or if pleasing, not also valuable, and therefore also approvable; and so also praiseworthy. But the praiseworthy is honourable. So it follows that what is good is also honourable.

O Diogenes Laertius 7.101 (*SVF* 3.92)

They [the Stoics] hold that all goods are equal, and that every good is choiceworthy in the highest degree and does not admit of relaxation or intensification.

P Stobaeus 2.101,21–102,3 (*SVF* 3.626, part)

All goods are common to the virtuous, and all that is bad to the inferior. Therefore a man who benefits someone also benefits himself, and one who does harm also harms himself. All virtuous men benefit one another . . . but the foolish are in the opposite situation.

Q Cleanthes (Clement, *Protrepticus* 6.72.2; *SVF* 1.557)

You ask me what the good is like? Listen then. Well-ordered, just, holy, pious, self-controlled, useful, honourable, due, austere, candid, always useful, fearless, undistressed, profitable, unpained, beneficial, contented, secure, friendly, precious < . . . > consistent, fair-famed, unpretentious, caring, gentle, keen, patient, faultless, permanent.

R Plutarch, *On Stoic self-contradictions* 1042E–F (*SVF* 3.85)

(1) Chrysippus admits that good and bad things are entirely different from one another. This must be so if the latter, by their presence, immediately make men utterly unhappy while the former make them happy to the highest degree. (2) He says that good things and bad are perceptible, writing as follows in *On the end* book 1: '. . . Not only are the passions, grief and fear and the like, perceptible along with [people's] appearances, but also it is possible to perceive theft and adultery and similar things, and in general, folly and cowardice and many other vices, and not only joy and benefactions and many other right actions but also prudence and courage and the remaining virtues.'

S Seneca, *Letters* 117.2

(1) Our school holds that what is good is a body because what is good acts, and whatever acts is a body. What is good benefits; but in order to benefit, something must act; if it acts, it is a body. (2) They say that wisdom is a good. It follows that they must be speaking of it too as corporeal.

☐ The most distinctive characteristic of Stoic ethics is its restriction of the ordinary Greek terms for 'good' and 'bad' to what we would call the *moral* sense of these words. In the case of 'good' this is expressed most generally by claiming that the only good thing is 'rectitude' (**59D 5**) or 'the honourable' (*to kalon*, literally 'the beautiful', cf. **65M 2**). A comprehensive set of moral attributes exemplifying the nature of 'the good' is provided in Cleanthes' little epigram (**Q**). Some of the reasons for limiting the scope of 'good' and 'bad' in this way have already been treated in **58A**. Any Greek would have accepted the first part of the Stoic definition of 'good' – 'benefit' (**G 1**); what was controversial was the Stoics' direct equation of benefit with virtue and virtuous action (ibid.).

This is plainly not a statement of synonymy but a claim about what things in the world are truly beneficial. We have seen (**58A 5**) why ordinary 'goods' such as health and wealth fail to be beneficial in the required sense. The Stoics had formal arguments for the identity of 'good' and 'honourable' (morally good, cf. **N**), which look contrived and question-begging. Their best line of defence was the thesis that only the morally good is beneficial to man in his specific nature as a rational being. Seneca (**H**) provides the main lines of Stoic thought on the relationship between the good and the rational, and what he says here can be supplemented by many other texts (e.g. **63C–E**). Human beings are taken to have 'the same nature' as god. God's activity is one of perfect rationality ('universal nature' in this text is equivalent to god). Therefore what is good for a person is the perfection of his own reason (cf. Diogenes Laertius 7.94).

Rationality, then, and the good coincide in god, and can coincide in man if he perfects his reason. Since the good is beneficial, and god is agreed to be good, god's sum of activities is beneficial and helpful to man (**I 4**, part of an argument whose form has the style of Zeno and Chrysippus). Such theological and physical underpinning to Stoic ethics provides one of the answers to the obvious question, why should perfect rationality coincide with moral goodness? That just is the nature of god, is the Stoic reply, and as 'parts' of god or universal nature human beings are designed to find their fulfilment in this kind of good (cf. **54H**; **63C 2–4**, **E**, **F 3**).

When Chrysippus maintains (**A**) that 'universal nature' and 'the administration of the world' are the foundation for Stoic theory on good and bad things, he is appealing to the rational and providential activities of god, conformity with which constitutes the good for man and lack of conformity what is bad for man (**63C 3–4**). Like Plato (see especially *Laws* 10) and unlike Aristotle, the Stoics regarded ethics as an exact science founded on the nature of the world.

A weakness in what has been said so far may seem to be dogmatic assertions which have no obvious connexion with the moral discriminations which people naturally make; and that difficulty can appear all the greater since Stoic thinking on the good is supposedly founded on what really is man's nature. Another approach is found in **B–F**. These texts purport to show that Stoic theory of the good is based on the nature of man and his evolving experience of the world. If the bald statement in **C** is compatible with **E 2**, the Stoics drew a distinction between the naturalness of any person's having an idea of 'something just and good' (i.e. taking some particular to be so; cf. **27** for 'something' = particular) and the fully developed Stoic theory of *the* truly good to which nature contributes only 'seeds of knowledge'. Emphasis is placed upon the learning and experience required for perception of the truly good (**D 2**, cf. **E 3**, **39D**). Yet though it is different in kind from all other values, the truly good is something we perceive by analogical reasoning from the value of such *AN* (see **58**) things as bodily strength (**E 3**). Now the value of *AN* things is uncontested, and the Stoic theory of 'appropriation' offers an explanation of why it is natural for living beings to behave in ways which accord with their innate constitutions. This may be implicit in Chrysippus' claim (**B**) that Stoic theory on good and bad things 'connects best with the innate preconceptions'. These preconceptions are not of course endowed with definite content at birth but are assumed to develop naturally in the course of the earliest human experience (cf. **39E**). Chrysippus, on the evidence of **D**, will hardly be saying that the fully-fledged Stoic theory of good and bad things is an 'innate preconception'. The content of these preconceptions is likely to be the rudimentary awareness, founded on 'appropriation', that certain things are natural and useful to one's human constitution and others are not. (It is not difficult to connect the *natural* acquisition of primitive moral awareness (**C**) with these values.) As has already been seen, human constitution and thereby 'appropriation' evolve with the development of rationality (**57A**, **B**; **63E 6**), so that finally the perfection of reason becomes the one thing 'appropriate' and natural to the mature man (cf. **65M 2**). Yet though this, the morally good, is a different kind of value from the objects of our primary impulse, the Stoics probably reasoned that its relation to a fully rational constitution is analogous to that 'appropriation' of things in accordance with nature, which all or most men would accept as the basis of evaluative distinctions.

Exactly how the analogical reasoning (cf. **39D 3**) is supposed to work is made clearer in **E** than in **D**. Taken together with **59D 4–6**, **D** seems to envisage the good as a general principle of order or harmony connected with but transcending the natural values of which we were previously aware. **E** shows that the requisite reasoning is not effortless, and fills out the content of the good: observation enables us to distinguish morally consistent from inconsistent behaviour, and to identify the former as the foundation of human perfection replete with all the virtues.

We may still ask, why should we be attracted to moral perfection? Epictetus in **F** blandly replies that this is the soul's nature. Since the Stoics regarded all or most men as imperfect, they could only accept the doctrine of **F** by supposing that external circumstances prevent the good from manifesting itself to us in such a way that we fully apprehend its nature (see **65M 7**). Thus, as in Socratic ethics, moral weakness is treated as a failure to see the good as it really is.

According to Sextus' careful analysis in **G**, good is a concept of wider extension than virtue, but every good thing other than virtue or virtuous action has virtue as one of its parts. These other goods satisfy the second disjunct of the definition of good, 'benefit or not other than benefit'. Whereas virtue and virtuous action are *wholly* defined by 'benefit', benefit is intrinsic to but not exhaustive of such good things as virtuous man and friend. ('Friendship exists only among the virtuous', **67P**.) The more complex classifications of goods reported by Stobaeus (**J–M**) may appear to open the door to a much more diverse set of items, and to drop the essential connexion between benefit = virtue/virtuous action and good. But the point of Stobaeus' divisions, we can assume, is not to give up this principle but to exhibit differences between goods in ways that are fully compatible with it. Thus friends (one of the examples in **G**) are classified as purely 'instrumental' goods: i.e. they share with the virtues the property of generating happiness, but are not, in addition, its actual constituents, as is the case with the virtues. Joy, cheerfulness etc. are 'final' goods only (**M**), and not virtues (**K 1**). But since we know that joy, cheerfulness etc. are 'good feelings' (**65F**) which are peculiar to the virtuous man, they evidently arise only in such a disposition. Similarly with the 'pursuits' of **J 4** and **L**, which are said to be included in 'virtuous tenors' (**26H**).

The relation of goods to 'tenor' must be handled with caution. **J**, where virtues are tenors, may appear to conflict with **L**, where they are said not to be tenors. But the appearance is misleading. Tenor is one kind of 'state', an enduring state, while 'character' is an enduring state which additionally does not admit of degrees (**47S**). Consequently 'tenor' (like 'state' itself in **J 2**; cf. a parallel case at **39E 3**) seems to be used in two senses: sometimes of the genus of which 'character' is one species (e.g. at *SVF* 3.525), sometimes for *mere* tenor, as a species of tenor alongside character, marking off those enduring states which *do* admit of degrees. Thus we can construct a tree (see diagram).

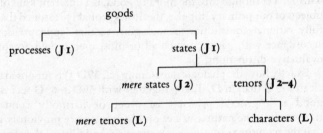

We can now eliminate the apparent conflict between **J** and **L**, by observing that the former uses 'tenor' in its generic sense, the latter in its specific sense. The Stoic doctrine is consistent. Virtues, as states of moral perfection, do not admit of degrees. But the wise man's other talents, e.g. at music, do admit of degrees, while still counting as 'goods' because he uses them wisely.

There are no degrees of virtue or vice, of happiness or unhappiness; the absence of variation within these mutually exclusive classes tallies with the thesis that all men are either completely virtuous or completely vicious (**61I**), perfectly happy or utterly unhappy (**R 1**). **P**, if all too briefly, makes a claim that bears crucially on the relation between moral goodness and happiness. If I am benefited by benefiting you, and vice versa, the distinction between altruism and egoism collapses into a single beneficial relation of mutual betterment. The coincidence of happiness and moral virtue, so adamantly endorsed by Plato, acquires its distinctive Stoic colouring in the 'community' of goods belonging to all the wise, whose life is characterized by a common set of principles (*homonoia*, see note on **P** in vol. 2).

As a character of the commanding-faculty (see **61B 8**), which itself consists of breath (**53**), virtue, and thus the prime instance of the good, is corporeal. Independent reasons for the corporeality of the good are advanced in **S**, and **R 2** develops one consequence of this in its interesting claim that good and bad things are perceptible. Passions, virtues, and vices are states of persons, and there is every reason to agree with the Stoics that we do perceive such things. Obvious cognitive problems arise about the foundations of objective moral judgement if **R 2** is denied.

The conception of good and bad as moral benefit and moral harm respectively gave rise to some of the most famous Stoic paradoxes: no harm can affect the good man, since he cannot be injured by vice, and nothing except vice is harmful in the strict sense. By parity of reasoning, no inferior man can do anything beneficial or be the recipient of such an act (cf. *SVF* 3.567–81).

61 Virtue and vice

A Diogenes Laertius 7.89 (*SVF* 3.39)

(1) Virtue is a consistent character, choiceworthy for its own sake and not from fear or hope or anything external. (2) Happiness consists in virtue since virtue is a soul which has been fashioned to achieve consistency in the whole of life.

B Plutarch, *On moral virtue* 440E–441D

(1) Menedemus of Eretria eliminated the plurality and the differentiations of the virtues, holding that there is a single one, called by many names; for it is the same thing that is called moderation and courage and justice, like 'mortal' and 'man'. (2) Aristo of Chios also made virtue essentially one thing, which he called 'health'. (3) It was by relativity that he made the virtues in a way different and plural, just as if someone wanted to call our vision 'white-seeing' when it apprehended white things, 'black-seeing' when it apprehended black things, and so on . . . (4) as the knife, while being one thing, cuts different things on different occasions, and fire acts on different materials although its nature is one and the same. (5) Zeno of Citium also in a way seems to be drifting in this direction when he defines prudence in matters requiring distribution as justice, in matters requiring choice as moderation, and in matters

requiring endurance as courage. (6) In defence of this they take it to be science that Zeno is here calling prudence. (7) But Chrysippus, invoking the 'qualified' and holding a virtue to be constituted by its own quality, unwittingly stirred up, in Plato's words, a 'swarm of virtues', both unwonted and unfamiliar. For corresponding to courage in the courageous man . . . and justice in the just man, he has posited graceliness in the graceful man . . . and greatliness in the great man . . . and filled philosophy with many absurd names which it does not need. (8) All these men agree in taking virtue to be a certain character and power of the soul's commanding-faculty, engendered by reason, or rather, a character which is itself consistent, firm, and unchangeable reason. (9) They suppose that the passionate and irrational part is not distinguished from the rational by any distinction within the soul's nature, but the same part of the soul (which they call thought and commanding-faculty) becomes virtue and vice as it wholly turns around and changes in passions and alterations of tenor or character, and contains nothing irrational within itself. (10) It is called irrational whenever an excessive impulse which has become strong and dominant carries it off towards something wrong and contrary to the dictates of reason. (11) For passion is vicious and uncontrolled reason which acquires vehemence and strength from bad and erroneous judgement.

C Plutarch, *On Stoic self-contradictions* 1034C–E

(1) Zeno admits several different virtues, as Plato does, namely prudence, courage, moderation and justice, on the grounds that although insepar-able they are distinct and different from each other. (2) Yet in defining each of them he says that courage is prudence <in matters requiring endurance, moderation is prudence in matters requiring choice, pru-dence in the special sense is prudence> in matters requiring action, and justice is prudence in matters requiring distribution – on the grounds that it is one single virtue, which seems to differ in actions according to its dispositions relative to things. (3) And not only does Zeno seem to contradict himself over this, but so does Chrysippus, who criticizes Aristo because he said that the other virtues were dispositions of a single virtue, (4) yet supports Zeno for defining each of the virtues in this way. (5) And Cleanthes in his *Physical treatises*, having said that tension is a stroke of fire, and that if it becomes adequate in the soul to achieve what is fitting it is called strength and might, adds the following words: 'This strength and might, when it arises in what seem to be matters requiring persistence, is self-control; when in matters requiring endurance, courage; concerning deserts, justice; concerning choices and avoidances, moderation.'

D Stobaeus 2.63,6–24 (*SVF* 3.280, part)

(1) All the virtues which are sciences and expertises share their theorems and, as already mentioned, the same end. Hence they are also inseparable. For whoever has one has all, and whoever acts in accordance with one acts in accordance with all. They differ from one another by their own perspectives. (2) For the perspectives of prudence are, primarily, the theory and practice of what should be done; and secondarily the theory also of what should be distributed, <what chosen, and what endured,> for the sake of infallibly doing what should be done. (3) Of moderation the special perspective is, primarily, to keep the impulses healthy and to grasp the theory of them; but secondarily, the theory of what falls under the other virtues, for the purpose of conducting oneself infallibly in one's impulses. (4) Likewise courage primarily grasps the theory of everything that should be endured; and secondarily, that of what falls under the other virtues. (5) And justice primarily studies individual deserts; but secondarily, the rest too. (6) For all the virtues focus upon the range of objects that belongs to all of them and upon each other's subject-matter.

E Seneca, *Letters* 113.24

One could say, 'The virtues are not a plurality of living beings, and yet they are living beings. For just as someone is both a poet and an orator but still one person, so the virtues are living beings but not a plurality of these. The same mind is both moderate and just and prudent and brave, being disposed in a certain way with respect to the individual virtues.'

F Plutarch, *On Stoic self-contradictions* 1046E–F (*SVF* 3.299, 243)

(1) They [the Stoics] say that the virtues are inter-entailing, not only because he who has one has them all but also because he who does any action in accordance with one does so in accordance with them all. For they say that a man is not perfect unless he possesses all the virtues nor an action either, unless it is performed in accordance with all the virtues. (2) But in his *Moral questions* book 6 Chrysippus says that the cultivated man is not always being courageous or the inferior man cowardly, since it is when certain things arise in their impressions that the former must remain steadfast in his decisions and the latter back away; and it is plausible, he says, that the inferior man is not always being immoderate either.

G Stobaeus 2.66,14–67,4 (*SVF* 3.560)

(1) They [the Stoics] also say that the wise man does everything well – that is to say, everything that he does: for as we say that the flute-player or

the lyre-player does everything well, with the implications 'everything to do with flute-playing', and 'everything to do with lyre-playing', so the prudent man does everything well, so far as concerns what he does, and not of course also what he does not do. (2) In their opinion the doctrine that the wise man does everything well is a consequence of his accomplishing everything in accordance with right reason and in accordance with virtue, which is expertise concerned with the whole of life. (3) By analogy, the inferior man does everything that he does badly and in accordance with all the vices.

H Stobaeus 2.59,4–60,2; 60,9–24 (*SVF* 3.262, 264, part)

(1) Prudence is the science of what should and should not be done and of neutral actions, or the science of things that are good and bad and neutral as applied to a creature whose nature is social . . . (2) Moderation is the science of what should be chosen and avoided and of neutral situations. (3) Justice is the science concerned with distributing individual deserts. (4) Courage is the science of things that are fearful and not fearful and neither of these. (5) Imprudence is <ignorance> of things that are good and bad and neutral, or ignorance of what should and should not be done and of neutral actions . . . (6) Some virtues are primary, but others are subordinate to these. The primary virtues are four: prudence, moderation, courage, justice . . . (7) To prudence are subordinated good sense, good calculation, quick-wittedness, discretion, resourcefulness; (8) to moderation, good discipline, seemliness, modesty, self-control; (9) to courage, endurance, confidence, high-mindedness, cheerfulness, industriousness; (10) to justice, piety, honesty, equity, fair dealing.

I Diogenes Laertius 7.127

(1) It is their [the Stoics'] doctrine that nothing is in between virtue and vice, though the Peripatetics say that progress is in between these. For as, they say, a stick must be either straight or crooked, so a man must be either just or unjust, but not either more just or more unjust, and likewise with the other virtues. (2) Chrysippus holds that virtue can be lost, on account of intoxication or depression, but Cleanthes takes it to be irremovable owing to secure cognitions. (3) They regard virtue as choiceworthy for its own sake. For we are ashamed at our bad behaviour as if we knew that rectitude is the only good. And virtue is sufficient for happiness.

J Plutarch, *On common conceptions* 1076A (*SVF* 3.246)

[According to Chrysippus:] 'Zeus does not exceed Dion in virtue, and Zeus and Dion, given that they are wise, are benefited alike by each other whenever one encounters a movement of the other.'

K Diogenes Laertius 7.91 (*SVF* 3.223)

Virtue is teachable ... as is evident from the fact that inferior men become good.

L Stobaeus 2.65,8 (*SVF* 1.566, part)

[Cleanthes says] All men have natural tendencies to virtue.

M Alexander, *On fate* 196,24–197,3 (*SVF* 2.984, part)

(1) 'If', they [the Stoics] say, 'those things are in our power of which we are also capable of the opposites, and it is to such cases that praise and blame and encouragements and discouragements and punishments and rewards are given, being prudent and having the virtues will not be in the power of those who have them, since they are no longer capable of receiving the vices which are opposite to the virtues. And in like manner vices will not be in the power of those who are bad. For it is not in their power to be bad no longer. (2) But it is ridiculous to deny that the virtues and vices are in our power and that praise and blame are given with respect to these. (3) Therefore, what is in our power is not like this.'

N Alexander, *On fate* 199.14–22 (*SVF* 3.658, part)

(1) If virtue and vice alone, in their [the Stoics'] opinion, are good and bad respectively, and no other creatures are capable of receiving either of them; (2) and if the majority of men are bad, or rather, if there have been just one or two good men, as their fables maintain, like some absurd and unnatural creature rarer than the Ethiopians' phoenix; (3) and if all bad men are as bad as each other, without any differentiation, and all who are not wise are all alike mad, (4) how could man not be the most miserable of all creatures in having vice and madness ingrown in him and allotted?

O Cicero, *Tusculan disputations* 4.29, 34–5

(1) Viciousness is a tenor or character which is inconsistent in the whole of life and out of harmony with itself ... (2) It is the source of disturbances which ... are disorderly and agitated movements of the mind, at variance with reason and utterly hostile to peace of mind and of life. (3) For they cause troubling and severe ailments, oppressing the mind and weakening it with fear. They also inflame the mind with excessive longing ... a mental powerlessness completely in conflict with temperance and moderation ... (4) So the only cure for those vices is situated in virtue alone.

P Marcus Aurelius 8.14

Whoever you meet, say to yourself at once: 'What are his doctrines concerning good and bad things?' For if he has doctrines of a certain sort concerning pleasure and pain and their sources, and fame and its absence, and death and life, I shall not think it remarkable or strange if he acts as he does. I shall remember that he is compelled to act in this way.

Q Plutarch, *On Stoic self-contradictions* 1039E (*SVF* 3.761, part)

Later he [Chrysippus] says that it is appropriate even for inferior men to continue to live . . . 'For, to begin with, virtue quite on its own has no relevance to our living, and similarly neither is vice of any relevance to our needing to depart.'

R Plutarch, *On Stoic self-contradictions* 1050F, 1051A–B (*SVF* 2.1181, part; 1182)

(1) In his *On nature* book 2 he [Chrysippus] writes as follows: 'Vice, by comparison with terrible accidents, has its own peculiar explanation. (2) For in a way it does occur in accordance with the rationale (*logos*) of nature, and its occurrence is not, so to speak, useless in relation to the whole world. (3) For otherwise the good would not exist either.' . . . (4) Again, in *On justice* book 2, having described the gods as resistant to certain acts of wrong-doing, he says: (5) 'Vice cannot be removed completely, nor is it right that it should be removed.'

S Plutarch, *On moral progress* 75C (*SVF* 3.539, part)

(1) So in philosophy we should assume neither progress nor any perception of progress, if the soul discards and purges itself of none of its stupidity, but deals in absolute badness right up to its acquisition of the absolute and perfect good. (2) In that case, the wise man has changed in a moment from the greatest possible worthlessness to an unsurpassable virtuous character, and has suddenly shed all the vice of which he failed to remove even a part over a considerable time.

T Plutarch, *On common conceptions* 1063A–B (*SVF* 3.539, part)

'Yes', they [the Stoics] say, 'but just as in the sea the man an arm's length from the surface is drowning no less than the one who has sunk five hundred fathoms, so even those who are getting close to virtue are no less in a state of vice than those who are far from it. And just as the blind are blind even if they are going to recover their sight a little later, so those progressing remain foolish and vicious right up to their attainment of virtue.'

U Plutarch, *On common conceptions* 1062B

What you would find most extraordinary . . . is their [the Stoics'] belief that, having got virtue and happiness, a man often does not even perceive them, but it eludes him that he has now become both prudent and supremely happy when a moment earlier he was utterly wretched and foolish.

☐ As the primary species of good, virtue is supremely beneficial or useful to its possessor (**60G**; cf. **26A**). It can be summed up as 'the natural perfection of a rational being as a rational being' (Diogenes Laertius 7.94), a perfection brought about by the person himself on the foundation of his innate mental equipment (cf. **57A 5**; **60H 3**). The unlikelihood of anyone's achieving this utterly secure and faultless character was admitted by Stoic philosophers (**N 2**). Yet they insisted on its possibility (**K**; **54H 4**), its relation to all men's natural tendencies (**L**; cf. **59A**), and its coincidence with happiness (**A 2**, **U**). Because happiness is wholly constituted by virtue, virtue is 'choiceworthy for its own sake' (**A 1**), and not as a means to achieving anything, including happiness, other than itself (contrast Epicurus, **21O–P**). That was the essence of Socratic ethics, and the Stoics showed their indebtedness to Socrates and Plato in treating virtue as an 'expertise concerned with the whole of life' and analogous to the ability to 'do well' in professional pursuits (**G 1–2**; for the concepts of expertise, science, and pursuit, see **41H**; **42**; **26H**). Central to Stoic ethics is the claim that virtue is an utterly self-sufficient art of living. At its most general, it embraces the whole of philosophy (**26A**), and includes the virtue(s) of dialectic (**31B–C**), as well as the more familiar moral excellences.

The good itself was characterized as agreement or consistency (**59D 5**), and this notion, filling out what is beneficial about goodness, is incorporated in the standard account of virtue as a 'consistent character' (**A 1**, **B 8**). *Homologia*, the term translated 'consistency', was ideally suited to capture the essence of Stoic virtue, since its linguistic form (*homo-logia*) is interpretable as 'harmony of (or with) reason'. Virtue, then, is rational consistency, a character of the soul's commanding-faculty (**B8**; cf. **60G**). The distinctively Stoic conception of rationality emerges in their claim that the soul's powers cannot be divided, as other Greek philosophers proposed, into rational *and* irrational. (For Posidonius' return to this alternative model, see **65K**.) The commanding-faculty (see **53G–H**) is rational through and through. The 'irrationality' which constitutes vice is an aberrant state of the unitary reason (**B 9–11**). This 'monistic psychology', as it is sometimes called, helps to explain such doctrines as the absence of degrees of virtue or vice, or of any intermediate state (**I 1**, **T**). A person's reasoning faculty is conceived as being either consistent or inconsistent; this consistency, or the virtues it promotes, is analogous to the straightness of a perfectly straight line (**I**). It is their inability to admit degrees that earns virtues their technical designation 'character' (*diathesis*: **A 1**, **B 8**; **47S 2**; **60L**).

The four 'primary' virtues (**H 6**) had been canonical since the time of Plato. The thesis that they are inseparable had won widespread acceptance, and its originator Socrates, as represented for example in Plato's *Protagoras*, may well have meant by it that they are essentially identical – alternative characterizations of a single state of mind, knowledge of good and bad. At any rate, that extreme version of the unity thesis was standard in the fourth-century Socratic schools, represented at **B 1** by Menedemus.

The Stoic Aristo's thesis (**B 2–4**; see also **29E**) is itself self-consciously Socratic, identifying the unitary virtuous state of soul as 'health', or, in another source, 'knowledge of good and bad', and regarding the individual virtues as merely accidental differentiations of this state due to circumstances – courage when it is applied to matters requiring endurance, justice when applied to matters requiring distribution, etc. Zeno may have seemed to legitimize this thesis by his own definition of each virtue as 'prudence in matters requiring . . .' (**B 5, C 2**). Aristo's contemporary Cleanthes (**C 5**) reasonably enough took 'prudence' to designate an identical state of soul in each of its occurrences in Zeno's definitions; and Aristo's position is essentially the same. For a parallel Stoic treatment of vices, cf. **41I**.

But Zeno is also reported (**C 1**) to have believed in a plurality of different virtues. Chrysippus was therefore probably right, from the point of view of orthodoxy, to criticize Aristo's position and defend Zeno's definitions (**C 4**) by the suggestion that his 'prudence' (*phronēsis*) was equivalent to 'science' (*epistēmē*, **B 6**; a standard Socratic equivalence). This enabled him to interpret each of the primary virtues in Zeno's definitions as constituting a *different* science – a view reflected in the canonical definitions in **H** (cf. also **60K 2**). Chrysippus put this point technically by locating the virtues in the genus of the 'qualified', making each of them a distinct quality of the soul (**B 7**, cf. **E**; see further **28–9**).

A notable merit of the Chrysippean version is that it is better equipped than Aristo's account to explain why we should continue to describe a man as courageous even when he is not employing his courage. Its corresponding disadvantage, from the Stoic point of view, is that it now becomes much less obvious why the virtues should be inseparable.

Chrysippus' defence of the inseparability thesis emerges from **D**. A primary virtue, being a science (cf. **60K 2**), is characterized by its constituent theorems (see **26C**; **42**), which we can take to be principles of conduct. All the virtues have their theorems in common, but from differing perspectives. Each takes as its primary perspective the theorems governing its own special area of conduct: this is sufficient to differentiate it as a distinct virtue. But each takes as a secondary perspective the theorems governing other areas of conduct; and this is sufficient to guarantee that they have all their theorems in common, and hence are inseparable. This doctrine of 'secondary perspective' (cf. **63G**) could be defended with the following example. A moderate act may not itself be properly described as a brave act. Even so, it is a necessary condition of the act's being moderate that it should not be performed with cowardice, injustice or folly. And this can only be guaranteed if the moderate man has mastered the principles of conduct, or 'theorems', proper to courage, justice and prudence. To this extent, but to this extent only, to act in accordance with moderation is to act 'in accordance with all the virtues' (**D 1, F 1**). (Thus the contradiction alleged by Plutarch in **F** is illusory: when Chrysippus says that the virtuous man need not always manifest his courage in action, he is naturally thinking of courage as normally understood, and as defined by its *primary* perspective.)

We follow convention in translating *kakia*, the contradictory of *aretē* (virtue), by 'vice'; but the modern associations of 'vice' should be discounted here. *Kakia* is the noun answering to the commonest Greek adjective for 'bad'. In Stoic usage the relevant badness is exclusively moral defectiveness/absence of perfection, which covers the whole range of moral dispositions, including those of men 'making progress', which are not virtue. This indiscriminate treatment of all who fall short of moral perfection (**N** 3) was an inevitable consequence of **I** 1: the denial of any intermediate state or of degrees of virtue or vice (**T, U**). The decisive characteristic of virtue is the absolute firmness of the wise man's rationality (**B8**), the certitude of his knowledge which guarantees his 'doing everything well' (**G**). This is what the person who has made maximum progress still lacks (**59I**), and it helps to explain the bold claim that a wise man is as virtuous as Zeus (**J**), and also Chrysippus' disagreement with Cleanthes concerning the possible loss of virtue (**I** 2). Cleanthes took it that the wise man's understanding of true values is so secure that nothing could ever change his moral disposition. Chrysippus seems to have supposed that even the wise man could be knocked off balance by (presumably uncontrollable) factors such as depression and intoxication, and would then (temporarily?) lose the perfect consistency of his soul's 'tension'. This was perhaps no more than an *ad hominem* response to the objection that even a wise man could be the victim of circumstances outside his control (cf. **66G**).

Vice is the negation of virtue, and its principal characteristics were established by parity of reasoning (**F** 2, **G** 3, **H** 5, **O** 1): note the emphasis on ignorance and inconsistency. The injuries which bad men do are injurious to themselves, just as virtuous acts redound to the benefit of their agents as well as those affected by them (**60P**). This point fits the Stoics' practice of interpreting virtue and vice in terms of mental health, a conception which is cardinal to the identity of virtue with happiness and vice with unhappiness. Medical analogies had been characteristic of Greek philosophical ethics since Socrates and Plato (for Epicurus, see **25C**); but the Stoics elaborated the point in distinctive detail, as is evident from their 'pathology' of the emotions (**65**). That subject must be treated later in its own right. What should be noticed here is the conception of vice as mental sickness, manifesting itself in emotional disturbances which are contrary to virtuous dispositions (**O**). The foundation of such 'sickness' is ignorance, or errors of value judgement (**B** 11, **P**). (For their causes and cure, see **65**.) Passages such as **P** (which abound in Marcus Aurelius and Epictetus) indicate that committed Stoics tempered the harshness of their absolute moral categories by a charitable attitude towards those whose values are mistaken. Virtue is what human life is ultimately for; but living involves having the wherewithal to live, which requires an adequate provision of the 'preferred indifferents'; suicide is not required of the man who lacks virtue (**Q**, cf. **66G**)!

As determinists (see **38**; **55**; **62**) the Stoics were faced with problems concerning the propriety of taking virtue and vice to be 'in our power'. Apart from determinism, however, their conception of virtue and vice as absolute and mutually exclusive characters rendered any transition from one to the other problematical. Yet they insisted that 'inferior men become good' (**K**; cf. **54H** 4). This is technically in conflict with **M**, where moral responsibility ('being in our power') is asserted, but detached from the possibility of receiving the opposite character: we can be praised or blamed for our moral character, even though, once having acquired it, we are incapable of acquiring its opposite. But some oversimplification may be suspected here, since the central point, that our responsibility for our moral character cannot *depend* on its being open to us to acquire the opposite character (cf. **62G 1**), requires only the weaker, and more orthodox, premise that such transitions are *normally* not possible. The rare exceptions noted in **N 2** may be exempted from the generalization. Nor does anything in **M** conflict with the thesis that one vicious person may be much closer than another to attaining virtue (**T**). In line with this, the Stoics defended what their critics found paradoxical: the change from vice to virtue is instantaneous (**S**), and may even elude the notice of the person undergoing it (**U**). Since virtue and vice are related as contradictories, no intermediate, transitional state is possible.

A further problem was how to reconcile the existence of vice with a world providentially organized to be the best possible (see **54**). The Stoics faced difficulties similar to those of Christian theologians, but they rejected any conception of original sin (see **65M 3–8**). Among their various defences, that found in **R** and **54Q** is the most prominent: vice is compatible with cosmic order, since without it its opposite could not exist. Moreover, from the cosmic perspective harmony prevails in the whole, even if it is not perceptible from the human position (see **54I**).

62 Moral responsibility

A Hippolytus, *Refutation of all heresies* 1.21 (*SVF* 2.975)

They too [Zeno and Chrysippus] affirmed that everything is fated, with the following model. When a dog is tied to a cart, if it wants to follow it is pulled and follows, making its spontaneous act coincide with necessity, but if it does not want to follow it will be compelled in any case. So it is with men too: even if they do not want to, they will be compelled in any case to follow what is destined.

B Cleanthes, quoted by Epictetus, *Manual* 53 (*SVF* 1.527)

Lead me, Zeus and Destiny, wherever you have ordained for me. For I shall follow unflinching. But if I become bad and am unwilling, I shall follow none the less.

C Cicero, *On fate* 39–43 (*SVF* 2.974)

(1) The ancient philosophers had taken two views. There had been those who thought that all things came about by fate, in such a way that that fate applied the force of necessity. That was the view taken by Democritus, Heraclitus, Empedocles and Aristotle. (2) The holders of the other view believed that there are voluntary motions of our minds, free from all fate. (3) My own impression is that Chrysippus wanted to act as

unofficial umpire between these views, and to strike a happy medium. But while his leanings are more towards those who want the motions of our minds to be freed from necessity, in developing his own personal account he slides into difficulties which lead him unintentionally to assert the necessity of fate. (4) Let us see how this works out in the context of assent, which I treated in my first disquisition. Those ancient thinkers who held that all things come about through fate said that acts of assent were the result of force and necessity. Their opponents, on the other hand, freed acts of assent from fate, denying that they could, if made subject to fate, be dissociated from necessity. They argued as follows: 'If all things come about through fate, all things come about through an antecedent cause. And if impulses do this, so do the things which are consequent upon impulse; therefore so do acts of assent. But if the cause of impulse is not located in us, neither is impulse itself in our power. If that is so, not even the results of impulse are in our power. Therefore neither acts of assent nor actions are in our power. The result is that neither commendations nor reproofs nor honours nor punishments are just.' Since this argument is unsound, they think it a plausible inference that not all events come about through fate. (5) But Chrysippus, disapproving of necessity and at the same time wanting nothing to happen without antecedent causes, distinguishes between kinds of cause, in order to escape necessity while retaining fate. 'Of causes', he explains, 'some are complete and primary, others auxiliary and proximate. Hence when we say that all things come about through fate by antecedent causes, we do not mean this to be understood as 'by complete and primary causes', but 'by auxiliary and proximate causes'. (6) He thus counters the argument which I expounded a moment ago in the following way: 'If all things come about through fate, it does follow that all things come about by prior causes – not however by primary and complete causes, but by auxiliary and proximate causes. If these latter are not in our power, it does not follow that not even impulse is in our power. If, on the other hand, we said that all things come about by complete and primary causes, it *would* follow that, since these causes were not in our power, impulse would not be in our power either.' (7) Therefore against those who introduce fate in such a way as to import necessity, the earlier argument will be valid. But it will have no validity against those who will not speak of the antecedent causes as complete or primary. (8) He thinks that he can easily explain the statement that acts of assent come about by prior causes. For although assent cannot occur unless it is prompted by an impression, nevertheless, since it has that impression as its proximate, not its primary, cause, Chrysippus wants it to have the rationale which I mentioned just now. He does not want assent, at least, to be able to occur without the stimulus of some external force (for assent must be prompted by an impression). But he resorts to his cylinder and spinning-top: these cannot begin to move without a push; but once that has happened, he holds that it is thereafter through their own nature that the cylinder rolls and the top spins. (9) 'Hence,' he says, 'just as the person who pushed the cylinder gave it its beginning of motion but not its capacity for rolling, likewise, although the impression encountered will print and, as it were, emblazon its appearance on the mind, assent will be in our power. And assent, just as we said in the case of the cylinder, although prompted from outside, will thereafter move through its own force and nature. (10) If something were brought about without an antecedent cause, it would be untrue that all things come about through fate. But if it is plausible that all events have an antecedent cause, what ground can be offered for not conceding that all things come about through fate? It is enough to understand what distinction and difference obtains between causes.'

D Gellius 7.2.6–13 (*SVF* 2.1000, part)

(1) Against this [the objection that Stoic 'fate' is inconsistent with the condemnation of wrongdoing] Chrysippus has many subtle and acute arguments, but virtually all his writings on the issue make the following point. 'Although it is true', he says, 'that all things are enforced and linked through fate by a certain necessary and primary rationale, nevertheless our minds' own degree of regulation by fate depends on their peculiar quality. (2) For if our minds' initial natural make-up is a healthy and beneficial one, all that external force exerted upon them as a result of fate slides over them fairly smoothly and without obstruction. But if they are coarse, ignorant, inept, and unsupported by education, then even if they are under little or no pressure from fated disadvantages, they still, through their own ineptitude and voluntary impulse, plunge themselves into continual wrongdoings and transgressions. (3) And the very fact that it turns out this way is the product of that natural and necessary sequence of things called "fate". For it is in itself a virtually fated and sequential rule that bad minds should not be without wrongs and transgressions.' (4) He then uses an illustration of this fact which is fairly appropriate and appealing. 'Just as', he says, 'if you push a stone cylinder on steeply sloping ground, you have produced the cause and beginning of its forward motion, but soon it rolls forward not because you are still making it do so, but because such are its form and smooth-rolling shape – so too the order, rationale and necessity of fate sets in motion the actual types of causes and their beginnings, but the deliberative impulses of our minds and our actual actions are controlled by our own individual will and intellect.' (5) In accordance with this he then says (and these are his actual words): 'Hence the Pythagoreans are right to say "You will learn that men have chosen their own troubles", meaning that the harm they suffer lies in each individual's own hands, and that it is in accordance with their impulse and their own mentality and character that they go wrong

and are harmed.' (6) For these reasons he denies that those who, whether through laziness or through wickedness, are harmful and reckless, should be tolerated and given a hearing, if when caught red-handed they take refuge in the necessity of fate, as if it were the shrine of a temple, and say that their worst misdeeds are attributable to fate, and not to their own recklessness.

E Diogenes Laertius 7.23

The story goes that Zeno was flogging a slave for stealing. 'I was fated to steal', said the slave. 'And to be flogged', was Zeno's reply.

F Diogenianus (Eusebius, *Evangelical preparation* 6.8.25–9; *SVF* 2.998)

(1) In book 1 of *On fate* he [Chrysippus] uses proofs of this [etymological] kind; and in book 2 he tries to resolve the absurd apparent consequences of the thesis that everything is necessitated, which we set out at the start – for example, that it is instrumental in destroying our own self-motivated determination concerning censures, commendations and encouragements, and everything that seems to come about as a result of our own causation. (2) Hence he says in book 2 that it is obvious that many things originate from us, but that these too are none the less co-fated along with the government of the world. (3) And he uses certain examples, like the following. That the cloak should not perish, he says, was fated not absolutely but together with its being looked after. Someone's escaping from the enemy was fated together with his running away from the enemy. And having children was fated together with wanting to have intercourse with a woman. (4) For just as, he says, if someone said that Hegesarchus the boxer would come out of the fight without sustaining a single punch, it would be ridiculous to expect Hegesarchus to fight with his hands by his sides on the ground that he was fated to come out without sustaining a punch, since the person making the denial said it because of the man's superior guard against being punched, so too it is in other matters. (5) For many things cannot come about without our wanting them and applying the most intense determination and efforts over them, since it is together with this, he says, that they are fated to come about.

G Alexander, *On fate* 181,13–182,20 (*SVF* 2.979)

(1) For they [the Stoics] deny that man has the freedom to choose between opposite actions, and say that it is what comes about *through* us that is in our power. (2) For, they say, of the things which exist and come to be, different ones have different natures. Animate things have different natures from inanimate, and not even all the animate have the same nature; for existing things' differences in species indicate the differences between their natures. And what each does is in accordance

with its proper nature: what a stone does is in accordance with a stone's nature, what a fire does is in accordance with a fire's nature, and what an animal does is in accordance with an animal's nature. Hence, they say, none of the things each of them does in accordance with its proper nature can be otherwise: everything they do is done of necessity. (3) By 'necessity' here they mean not that due to compulsion, but that due to the incapacity of something of such a nature, given such circumstances, circumstances which are at the time incapable of not obtaining, to move in a different way from that in which it does. (4) For the stone, if released from a height, and not prevented, cannot fail to travel downwards. Since it has weight in itself and weight is the natural cause of this kind of motion, whenever the external causes which encourage the stone's natural motion are also present, the stone of necessity moves with its natural motion. And these causes of its moving are, at the time, unconditionally and necessarily present. Not only is it incapable of not moving when they are present, but it also moves of necessity at that time, and such a movement is brought about by fate *through* the stone. (5) The same account applies to the other things: they say that what applies to inanimate objects applies to animals too. For animals too have a certain natural motion, namely motion in accordance with impulse. Every animal *qua* animal moves, when it moves, in accordance with impulse – a motion which is brought about *by* fate *through* the animal. (6) . . . They say that the motions brought about by fate through animals are 'in the power of' the animals. In terms of necessity their motions are like everything else, since for them too the external causes must, at the time, be present of necessity, with the result that in some such way it is of necessity that they enact their self-propelled motion in accordance with impulse. But because these motions come about through impulse and assent, whereas the motions of those other things come about because of weight, heat or some other cause, they call this motion 'in the power of' the animals, but do not call each of those others 'in the power of' the stone, or the fire. (7) Such, in brief, is their doctrine concerning that which is in our power.

H Alexander, *On fate* 185,7–11 (*SVF* 2.982)

Their [the Stoics'] reliance on the argument 'If in identical circumstances someone will act differently on different occasions, an uncaused motion is introduced', with their consequent assertion that it is not possible for someone to perform the opposite action to the one he will perform, suggests an oversight on their part . . .

I Alexander, *On fate* 205,24–206,2 (*SVF* 2.1002)

(1) For they [the Stoics] take it that everything naturally constituted is such as it is in accordance with fate, 'natural' being the same thing as 'in

accordance with fate', (2) and they add 'Therefore it will be in accordance with fate that animals have perceptions and impulses. And some animals will merely be active, while others will perform rational actions. And some will do wrong, while others will perform right actions. For these are natural to them. (3) But so long as wrong and right actions remain, and their natures and qualities are not removed, there also remain commendations and censures, punishments and honours. For such are the sequence and order to which they are subject.'

J Alexander, *On fate* 207,5–21 (*SVF* 2.1003)

(1) They [the Stoics] say: 'For it is not the case that while fate is of this kind, destiny does not exist; nor that while destiny exists, apportionment does not; nor that while apportionment exists, retribution does not; nor that while retribution exists, law does not; nor that while law exists, there does not exist right reason enjoining what must be done and prohibiting what must not be done. (2) But it is wrong actions that are prohibited, and right actions that are enjoined. Therefore it is not the case that while fate is of this kind wrong and right actions do not exist. (3) But if wrong and right actions exist, so do virtue and vice. If these exist, so do rectitude and turpitude. But rectitude is commendable and turpitude is reprehensible. Therefore it is not the case that while fate is of such a kind, commendable and reprehensible do not exist. (4) But commendable things deserve honour, and reprehensible things deserve punishment. Therefore it is not the case that while fate is of this kind, honour and punishment do not exist. (5) But honour is the bestowal of privilege, and punishment is correction. Therefore it is not the case that while fate is of this kind, the bestowal of privilege and correction do not exist. (6) But if this is so, all the things mentioned remain, even if all things come about in accordance with fate – right and wrong actions, honours, punishments, bestowals of privilege, commendations and censures.

K Epictetus, *Discourses* 1.1.7–12

(1) Fittingly enough, the one thing which the gods have placed in our power is the one of supreme importance, the correct use of impressions. (2) The other things they have not placed in our power. Is this because they didn't want to? My belief is that they would have entrusted them to us too, had they been able to, but that they simply weren't able. For we are on the earth and bound by an earthly body and earthly partners. How then could we have failed to be hampered by externals with regard to these things? (3) What does Zeus say? 'Epictetus, if it had been possible, I would have made your wretched body and trappings free and unhindered. But as it is, please note, this body is not your own, but a subtle mixture of clay. Since, however, I was not able to do this, I gave you a portion of myself, this power of impulse and repulsion, desire and

aversion – in a word, the power to use impressions. If you take care of it and place in it everything you have, you will never be blocked, never hindered. You will never complain, never blame, never flatter anyone.'

☐ The Stoic world is governed by a fate which predetermines every detail of every world cycle. This determinism has its basis in both logic (**38**) and physics (**55**). Is ethics the loser? So any Epicurean would maintain, on the ground that moral responsibility is flatly incompatible with determinism (see **20**). Since the Stoics themselves certainly hold otherwise, they are often called 'compatibilists' by scholars (cf. **C 3**). This, however, may understate the position. On the Stoic view determinism and moral responsibility are not merely compatible, they actually presuppose each other (**I, J; 53O**).

There is no evidence that the first generation of Stoics felt any tension between fate and morality. This is because, to judge from **A** and **B**, 'fate' for them corresponded to a fairly traditional Greek picture of human destiny. Certain salient features of your life are laid down from the outset: your principal achievements and failures, your progeny, your illnesses, the day of your death. Any attempt to circumvent these landmarks in your life will inevitably be frustrated, such is the power of fate. What early Stoicism adds, or at least states with a new emphasis, is that fate's plan for you is thoroughly providential. This world is the best possible, and you are in it to perform a very specific role. Recognizing your own apparent setbacks are part of the great design is thus held out as a source of comfort and optimism. The main point made by **A** and **B** is that moral goodness largely *consists* in living willingly and to the best of your ability the life assigned to you by fate (cf. **63C**). If instead you resent your ill fortune, you remain powerless to avert it, and by standing against the plans of providence you become morally bad.

Whatever the precise scope of 'fate' here (see also **E** for an extra refinement), there is no suggestion yet (cf. especially **B**) that our own attitudes are also fully predetermined. That further tightening of the screw is what eventually produces Stoic determinism, a doctrine which the sources overwhelmingly link with the name of Chrysippus. On what became through him the canonical Stoic position, there is no detail, however minute, that escapes the causal nexus of fate: **55J–Q**; cf. **52**.

The problems of determinism now become inescapable. How can our individual impulses and actions be 'in our power', if they were necessary all along? How, in other words, can we be held responsible for them if it is not the case that we could have done otherwise (**C 4, D 6**)? And why need we deliberate and make decisions at all, if our actions will ensue regardless (the 'Lazy Argument': see **55S 1**)?

This last question is relatively easily answered. We deliberate and make decisions because that is the means by which many of our actions are fated to come about (**F; 55S 2–3**). But such a solution is bought at the price of exposing even more starkly the apparent unavailability to us of alternative decisions. It is to this, therefore, that we must turn.

It may be tempting to suppose that an agent is responsible only when he 'could have done otherwise' in the strong sense that *nothing*, internal or external to him, had predetermined the action which in the event he chose. To the Stoics this is unintelligible. Not only does it contravene the fundamental logical and metaphysical laws on which the fate doctrine is founded (**H**; **38G**; **55N 2**), it also requires that people be capable of acting contrary to their moral character (**G**; cf. **61M**). Yet it would be absurd to suggest that what makes a bad man responsible for his misdeed is that he was at that moment capable of performing a good deed, or, even more repugnant, that a good man is responsible for his good deeds because he is capable of morally bad acts.

Even so, Chrysippus is reluctant to abandon altogether the 'could have done otherwise' criterion. For if there is no sense in which alternative actions (or abstentions from acting) are possible for us, our actual actions become necessary. And although he seems at times to have accepted that fate in some sense necessitates (**D, F, G**; **55M 3**), his more interesting tactic, emphasized in Cicero's *On fate*, was that of trying to separate causal determination from necessitation. His method was to retain a notion of counterfactual possibility: **38E 3**. We suggest in the commentary on **38** that this amounted to *opportunity*: when someone has committed a crime, given his criminal character and the temptation that confronted him there was no possibility *that* he would not commit it, but he may be held responsible provided that it was possible *for* him not to commit it, i.e. that he had the *opportunity* to do otherwise.

A further way in which fate is separated from necessitation is in terms of causes: **C**. We have attempted in **55** commentary to distinguish the types of cause invoked by Chrysippus in **C**. Here, for the sake of simplicity, we will just speak of them as 'primary' and 'triggering' causes. A man's moral character is the primary cause of his performing good or bad acts. Each act additionally requires a triggering cause, normally in the form of a sense-impression, since all acts are somehow responses to external circumstances. But because the major share of responsibility belongs to the primary cause, the triggering cause cannot itself be said to necessitate the assent which initiates his action. (It would, for instance, be strange to suggest that a dangled carrot *compels* a donkey to move, however inevitable that result may be: the principal cause is the donkey's own stupidity.) Now what kind of causation is exerted by fate? From a cosmic perspective, fate is the entire conjunction of causes: especially **55N**. But from the point of view of the human individual, there is a sharp divide between himself, comprising his beliefs, moral qualities, etc., and the external world with which he interacts. It would seem absurd to him to become a mere spectator of a single undifferentiated causal nexus in which his own beliefs and attitudes were swallowed up. He must, especially when the apportionment of responsibility is at issue, distinguish himself from the chain of external influences. Thus fate, from his point of view, is the set of external causes which, by acting upon him, work to bring about their destined effects. But since these external causes are no more than triggering causes, he cannot hold them in any strong sense *responsible* for his actions, let alone sufficient to necessitate them. The primary cause is himself.

That, then, is the solution to the responsibility issue sketched by Chrysippus in **C**, and alluded to at **55R**. A variant version, exemplified in **D** and **F** and made explicit at **G 3**, was to concede that fate necessitates but to distinguish the kind of necessity involved from compulsion. On either version, answerability for our actions in no way requires an open future and might even be seriously jeopardized by one. What it requires is a proper system for apportioning responsibility between the relevant causal factors. For actions to be 'in our power' is simply for us to be their principal causes: **G**. Fate can be said to bring them about *through* us.

This is perhaps promising as an explanation of how we actually allocate moral credit and discredit from day to day. What may seem less clear is why, in such an inflexibly structured world, the notion of individual morality should have any place at all. Now if the dominating causal nexus were purely mechanical, as in an atomistic universe, Chrysippus might accept that his theory did not vindicate morality, but merely accounted for the illusion of it. On the Stoic view, however, morality belongs first and foremost to the entire cosmic plan. It is from there that it filters down to individual human lives – a thesis supported in **J** by a Sorites, or Little-by-little Argument (for the logical form of which, see **37D** and commentary), sliding from the notion of fate, through increasingly moral concepts, to individual responsibility. Far from conflicting with morality, fate *is* the moral structure of the world (cf. also **D 3, I**; **53O**). Our minds are fragments of the divine mind, and by lining up our own impulses with the pre-ordained good we can achieve individual goodness, and the only true freedom (**K**; cf. **D 1–2**; **67M–O**).

63 The end and happiness

A Stobaeus 2.77,16–27 (*SVF* 3.16)

(1) They [the Stoics] say that being happy is the end, for the sake of which everything is done, but which is not itself done for the sake of anything. This consists in living in accordance with virtue, in living in agreement, or, what is the same, in living in accordance with nature. (2) Zeno defined happiness in this way: 'Happiness is a good flow of life.' Cleanthes too has made use of this definition in his writings, as have Chrysippus and all their successors, saying that happiness is no different from the happy life. (3) Yet they say that while happiness is set up as a target, the end is *to obtain* happiness, which is the same as being happy.

B Stobaeus 2.75,11–76,8

(1) Zeno represented the end as: 'living in agreement'. This is living in accordance with one concordant reason, since those who live in conflict are unhappy. (2) His successors expressed this in a more expanded form, 'living in agreement with nature', since they took Zeno's statement to be an incomplete predicate. (3) Cleanthes, his first successor, added 'with nature', and represented it as follows: 'the end is living in agreement with nature'. (4) Chrysippus wanted to make this clearer and expressed it thus: 'living in accordance with experience of what happens by nature'.

C Diogenes Laertius 7.87–9 (continuing **57A**)

(1) Therefore Zeno in his book *On the nature of man* was the first to say that living in agreement with nature is the end, which is living in accordance with virtue. For nature leads us towards virtue. So too Cleanthes in his book *On pleasure*, and Posidonius and Hecato in their books *On ends*. (2) Further, living in accordance with virtue is equivalent to living in accordance with experience of what happens by nature, as Chrysippus says in *On ends* book 1: for our own natures are parts of the nature of the whole. (3) Therefore, living in agreement with nature comes to be the end, which is in accordance with the nature of oneself and that of the whole, engaging in no activity wont to be forbidden by the universal law, which is the right reason pervading everything and identical to Zeus, who is this director of the administration of existing things. (4) And the virtue of the happy man and his good flow of life are just this: always doing everything on the basis of the concordance of each man's guardian spirit with the will of the administrator of the whole . . . (5) The nature consequential upon which one ought to live is taken by Chrysippus to be both the common and, particularly, the human. But Cleanthes admits only the common nature, as that which one ought to follow, and no longer also the particular.

D Seneca, *Letters* 76.9–10 (*SVF* 3.200a)

(1) What is best in man? Reason: with this he precedes the animals and follows the gods. Therefore perfect reason is man's peculiar good, the rest he shares with animals and plants . . . (2) What is the peculiar characteristic of a man? Reason – which when right and perfect makes the full sum of human happiness. Therefore if every thing, when it has perfected its own good, is praiseworthy and has reached the end of its own nature, and man's own good is reason, if he has perfected reason, he is praiseworthy and has attained the end of his nature. (3) This perfect reason is called virtue and it is identical to rectitude.

E Epictetus, *Discourses* 1.6.12–22

(1) You will find many things in us alone, of which the rational animal had particular need, but many things which we share with the non-rational animals. (2) Do they too attend to what happens? By no means. Using and attending to are different from one another. God had need of the animals' making use of impressions, but of our attending to their use. (3) For this reason it is sufficient for them to eat and drink and rest and procreate and do everything else which each kind of animal does; for us, on the other hand, to whom he has also given the power of attending to things, these animal activities are no longer sufficient, but unless we act

appropriately and regularly and in agreement with our individual nature and constitution, we shall no longer attain our own end. (4) Beings which have different constitutions also have different functions and ends ... (5) God introduced man as a student of himself and his works, and not merely as a student but also as an interpreter of these things. (6) Therefore it is wrong for man to begin and end where the non-rational animals do; he should rather begin where they do and end where nature has ended in our case. Nature ended at studying and attending to things and a way of life in harmony with nature. See to it then that you do not die without having studied these.

F Seneca, *Letters* 92.3

(1) What is a happy life? Peacefulness and constant tranquillity. Loftiness of mind will bestow this, and consistency which holds fast to good judgement. (2) How are these things reached? If all of truth has been seen, if orderliness, moderation, and seemliness are preserved in actions, and a will which is guiltless and kindly, focused upon reason and never departing from it, as lovable as it is admirable. (3) To put it in a nutshell for you, the wise man's mind should be such as befits god.

G Stobaeus 2.63,25–64,12 (Panaetius fr. 109, part)

(1) Panaetius said what happens in respect of the virtues is similar to a single target set up for many archers, which contains within itself lines of different colours. (2) In that case each archer would aim to hit the target, but one would do so, if he were successful, through striking into the white line, and another through striking into the black line, and another through doing so into a line of different colour. (3) For just as these people make hitting the target their highest end, but propose to achieve it in different ways, so all the virtues make being happy their end, which consists in living in agreement with nature, but they achieve this in different ways.

H Plutarch, *On Stoic self-contradictions* 1042A (*SVF* 3.55)

He [Chrysippus] maintains that vice is the essence of unhappiness, insisting in every book that he writes on ethics and physics that living viciously is identical to living unhappily.

I Plutarch, *On common conceptions* 1061F (*SVF* 3.54, part)

[The Stoics say] A good is not increased by the addition of time, but even if someone becomes prudent only for a moment, in respect of happiness he will in no way fall short of someone who employs virtue for ever and lives his life blissfully in virtue.

J Clement, *Miscellanies* 2.21.129.4–5 (Panaetius fr. 96; Posidonius fr. 186, part)

(1) In addition to these [earlier Stoics] Panaetius declared the end to be 'living in accordance with the tendencies bestowed on us by nature'. (2) After all of them, Posidonius proposed: 'living as a student of the truth and order of the whole, and helping to promote this as far as possible, completely uninfluenced by the irrational part of the soul'. (3) Some of the later Stoics represented it as follows: 'The end is living in agreement with the constitution of man.'

K Marcus Aurelius 5.16

(1) Each thing <is made with a view to that> for whose sake it is constituted; (2) and each thing is moved towards that with a view to which it is constituted; (3) and its end consists in that towards which it is moved; (4) and where its end is, there too exists its interest and its good. (5) Therefore the good of a rational being is community; (6) for it has long been proved that we are born with a view to community. (7) Or was it not evident that inferior beings are for the sake of the superior, and the superior for the sake of one another? (8) But animate beings are superior to inanimate, and rational to merely animate.

L Cicero, *Tusculan disputations* 5.40–1

[In defence of Stoic ethics] (1) In my opinion, virtuous men are also supremely happy. For if a man is confident of the goods that he has, what does he lack for living happily? Or how can someone who lacks confidence be happy? Yet a man who adopts the threefold division of goods inevitably lacks confidence. For how will he be able to be confident of bodily strength or secure fortune? Yet no one can be happy without a good which is secure, stable and lasting . . . (2) The man who would fear losing any of these things cannot be happy. We want the happy man to be safe, impregnable, fenced and fortified, so that he is not just largely unafraid, but completely.

M Cicero, *Tusculan disputations* 5.81–2

[In defence of Stoic ethics] (1) It is a peculiar characteristic of the wise man that he does nothing which he could regret, nothing against his will, but does everything honourably, consistently, seriously, and rightly; that he anticipates nothing as if it were bound to happen, is shocked by nothing when it does happen under the impression that its happening is unexpected and strange, refers everything to his own judgement, stands by his own decisions. (2) I can conceive nothing which is happier than this. (3) It is an easy conclusion for the Stoics, since they have perceived the final good to be agreement with nature and living consistently with nature, which is not only the wise man's proper function, but also in his power. (4) It necessarily follows that the happy life is in the power of the man who has the final good in his power. (5) So the wise man's life is always happy.

☐ Stoic thought about the 'end' of human life has already been foreshadowed in our sections on 'good and bad' and 'virtue and vice'. All three of these, however, in spite of their common ground, were treated as separate topics of ethics (56A), and the Stoics could easily defend this procedure. In Hellenistic philosophy the different schools were regularly characterized by their different specifications of the end (64G), a concept on whose formal definition they could all agree: 'that for the sake of which everything is done,[1] but which is not itself done for the sake of anything' (A 1), or 'the ultimate object of all desires'. Such agreement, which may seem curious within the non-teleological context of modern ethics, was made possible by the scarcely questioned assumption (cf. even Epicurus 21A–B) that human life must be purposive by nature, and by the identification of the end with 'happiness' (*eudaimonia*) or 'living well' (*eu zēn*). Hence investigation of the end is a functionalist inquiry, a specification of the kind of life which will enable a person to fulfil his or her nature, to act in the way that human nature requires. Agreement on these points imposes important constraints on Greek ethics, which may seem to cause particular difficulty for the Stoics. They accepted the then traditional conception of the end as 'living well', 'being happy', 'the fulfilment of all desires'. Yet they made moral goodness the sole constituent of 'being happy', going as far as to claim that the sufferings of Priam will not disturb the virtuous man's happiness (*SVF* 3.585). Thus they rejected the Aristotelian doctrine that happiness requires some good fortune in addition to virtue. If the Stoics had conceded this point (a fundamental objection to their ethics), they would have had to drop their grand claims concerning the wise man's supreme and impregnable happiness (L), and their insistence that happiness is always in his power (M).

The paradox would be toned down if we took the Stoics to be redefining 'happiness', severing its connexions with any accepted sense of 'self-fulfilment' or satisfaction of desires. Their ethics is often represented along these lines – a move away from teleology towards the conception of doing what is right because it is right, with 'self-satisfaction' totally excluded from all consideration. Yet this Kantian reading of Stoicism is a serious misrepresentation. The Stoics preferred being charged with paradox (cf. 66A) to dropping their teleology and eudaemonism. The material here (A, B 1, C 4, F, H, I) shows that virtue and vice respectively are taken to constitute happiness and unhappiness as these latter terms were understood within the mainstream tradition. What 'happiness' means, in this regard, is summed up in a definition falsely attributed to Plato

---

[1] Or 'should be done' in the Stoic formulations of Stobaeus 2.46,5–10. Certainly the end is what *should* be pursued; but, as 'happiness', it could also be described as what is actually pursued, cf. Aristotle, *Nicomachean ethics* 1.4, 1095a14–20.

(*Definitions* 412d): 'the sum of all goods; a potency sufficient for living well; fulfilment in accordance with virtue; a living being's sufficient benefit'. The Stoics claim that a virtuous man does possess all that he needs to fulfil himself, to live well, to have his desires satisfied (cf. **L, M**). They challenge us to suppose that a life so constituted (not of course the intermittent satisfaction of momentary wants) is what we all naturally desire, or would desire, if we were capable of fully grasping its benefits to ourselves as well as to those who benefit from being the recipients of virtuous actions.

Detailed arguments for the Stoic conception of happiness, if there were any, have not survived. But plainly happiness is neither synonymous with virtue nor arbitrarily constituted by virtue. Zeno defined happiness as 'a good flow of life' (**A 2**), and this is expressed by Seneca (**F 1**) as 'peacefulness and constant tranquillity'. The benefits of such a state, which recalls Epicurean 'freedom from disturbance' (see **21**), may have been regarded as intuitively obvious. Zeno at any rate appealed to the unhappiness of 'those who live in conflict' (i.e. with themselves) as the ground for his account of the end: 'living in agreement', amplified in keeping with the etymology of *homologoumenos* by 'living in accordance with one concordant reason' (*logos*, **B 1**). If, as the Stoics argued independently (**61B 8**), rational consistency defines virtue, the benefits of happiness must be constituted by virtue (cf. Seneca's procedure in **F**). Like virtue, happiness is an all-or-nothing affair, and it is complete at any moment (**I**), a striking difference from Aristotle's insistence on a whole lifetime. Since happiness has no requirements except moral goodness, the Stoics could disregard the ordinary vicissitudes of life in defending its momentary completeness.

Does the Stoics' eudaemonism sully the purity of their morals? Only for the purest of Kantians. Panaetius was prepared to say that the virtues have our own good or happiness as their objective (**G**), and that each virtue is targeted at a different 'colour' of this single objective – an image which explains the 'different perspectives' of the inseparable virtues (**61D 1**). But the virtues are 'final' as well as 'instrumental' goods (**60M**): they are both the means of attaining happiness *and* the excellences of which it consists. Therefore someone who desires happiness, in the Stoics' sense, must desire virtue *for its own sake* since the former consists in the latter. Like Plato and Aristotle, the Stoics held that the intrinsic desirability of the moral life is identical to a person's self-fulfilment. There is thus a continuity between the primary impulse to self-preservation, directed at physical well-being, and the self-satisfaction of the moral life. But 'self', in the case of the latter, is extended to something analogous to Kant's universalized imperative – the good of all rational beings: harmony of one's own nature and that of the whole (**C 2–4**) or 'community' (**K**).

Since the part a person is assigned in the whole (cf. **62B**) may involve little or no self-satisfaction in terms of conventional goods ('indifferent' for happiness), one understands why our sources lay far more stress on virtue than on happiness, a tendency more pronounced in Roman Stoicism. Yet much of the interest of Stoic ethics resides in the fact that happiness and virtue, while remaining semantically or conceptually distinct, are both instantiated in rational consistency. One and the same state of mind is the objective which will satisfy all

399

people's natural desire for happiness *and* constitute the moral life they all ought to pursue.

Happiness is an objectively specifiable state of affairs, the same for all, but our end as individuals is 'to be happy' by getting happiness for ourselves. This seems to be the point of the rather strained distinction between happiness as 'target' and being happy as 'end' (**A 3**). 'Being happy' will be the incorporeal predicate which signifies someone's possession of happiness (the corporeal disposition, cf. **60S**): we aim at happiness in order that 'being happy' can be truly predicated of ourselves (see **33E, J**).

Every leading Stoic is credited with his own account of the end. This alerts us to the fact that heads of the school were free to impose their own trademark on the system, but most of the accounts appear to differ in emphasis rather than in doctrine. There was general agreement to the formula 'living in agreement with nature' (**C 1–3**). Even if Zeno himself did not include the words 'with nature' (**B 2**), he will hardly have disagreed with the gist of **C 2–4** which is probably a summary of Chrysippus' *On ends* book 1. Nor is it likely that Chrysippus differed seriously from Cleanthes, as **C5** (cf. **B 3–4**) seems to imply. The nature with which one is to live in agreement is both one's own rational constitution as a person, and the rationality of universal nature or god. These are related as 'part' to 'whole' (**C 2**). If Cleanthes emphasized 'agreement with universal nature', this would fit his insistence on assenting willingly to all one's circumstances (**62B**). But Chrysippus makes the same point (**C 4**; cf. **60A**). For a Stoic there should be complete accord between particular and universal nature (**C 3–4**; and cf. **67R–S** for universal nature = natural law). It will sometimes be rational to prefer a course of action which, in the event, turns out contrary to one's preference (cf. **58J**). This potential conflict between particular and universal nature (what actually happens) will be avoided by the virtuous man. He accepts that his own preference, though rationally justified, should now be discarded in favour of the 'right reason' of what actually happens (see **62** commentary). It was perhaps in order to drive this point home that Chrysippus used the formula, 'living in accordance with experience of what happens by nature' (**B 4, C 2**).[1] Such experience could be taken to comprise awareness of, say, the normal preferability of health to sickness, and the recognition that everyone can expect to be ill some of the time.

Stoic teleology, as in Aristotle's psychology and ethics, draws its essential content from the sharp distinction between rationality, which unites man and god, and the other attributes of human life which are shared with the animals (**D, E**). We have already encountered this point in connexion with the analysis of 'good' (**60H**). Aristotle's ethics was founded on the assumption that human life has a 'function', which can be specified by reference to the distinctively human attribute of 'living rationally' (*Nicomachean ethics* 1.6). It is just the same in Stoicism. Virtue is the perfection of reason, and thus the end of human nature (**D**). Epictetus develops this thought with reflections which complement Chrysippus' 'experience of natural events' (**E**): our rational nature demands that

---

[1] Criticized, however, by Posidonius, **64I 4**, on which see vol. 2 note.

we study and seek to understand the world, and adapt ourselves to it. Epictetus calls this 'attending to things', where 'attending to' covers both mentally following and living accordingly. This notion is present in Posidonius' formula for the end (J 2), in which he added the need to subjugate 'the irrational part of the soul', in line with his unorthodox Platonic psychology (see 64I; 65).

Cleanthes had already said that 'all men have natural tendencies to virtue' (61L), and those tendencies are what Seneca calls 'the seeds of knowledge' (60E 2). When Panaetius described the end by reference to natural tendencies (J 1), he presumably intended to signal the fact that 'living in agreement with nature' is the end for which we are innately programmed or internally motivated. Cicero (On duties 1.11–18) shows how Panaetius regarded the cardinal virtues as perfections of a person's natural endowments. If there is innovation here, it lay not so much in the wording of Panaetius' formula, as in his interpretation of agreement with nature. He seems to have prescribed agreement between individual human capacities and the general nature of man (see 66E), rather than the Chrysippean relationship between god (= universal nature) and human nature (C 2–4). With Posidonius, on the other hand, the theological dimension is again stressed (J 2).

More difficulty arises over the accounts of the end attributed to Chrysippus' successors, Diogenes of Babylon and Antipater. These have already been cited (58K) because they introduce AN things (indifferent but in accordance with nature) within a formulation of the end. No other accounts do this, and that prompts the question whether Diogenes and Antipater differed radically from other Stoics; see 64.

64 The end: Academic criticism and Stoic defence

A Cicero, On ends 3.31 (SVF 3.15)

[Speaker: the Stoic Cato] We are left with the conclusion that the final good is a life in which one applies knowledge of those things that happen by nature, selecting those in accordance with nature and rejecting those contrary to nature, that is – a life in agreement and consistent with nature.

B Alexander, On soul II 164,3–9

(1) No other expertise selects something merely for the sake of selecting it, but it is with reference to the end that everything is selected. For the end consists in the use of the things selected and not in the selection of the materials. (2) To put it generally, it is surely absurd [for the Stoics] to say that virtue applies only to selecting. For if getting the things selected is indifferent and does not contribute to the end, the selection would be utterly pointless.

C Plutarch, On common conceptions 1070F–1071E

(1) It is contrary to the common conception that life should have two ends or targets set before it and that all our actions should not be referred

to just one thing. (2) But it is still further contrary to the common conception that the end should be one thing and the point of reference for every action something else. (3) Yet they [the Stoics] must stick to one of these alternatives. (4) For if what is good is not the primary things in accordance with nature but the rational selection and taking of them and doing everything in one's power for the sake of getting these things, all actions must have this as their reference, viz., getting the primary things in accordance with nature. (5) But if they think that people are in possession of the end without aiming at getting or desiring to get these things, something other than getting these must be the purpose to which the selection of them is referred. (6) For selecting and taking those things with prudence *is* the end; but they themselves and getting them are not the end but the underlying matter, as it were, which has selective value . . . (7) If someone were to say that an archer does everything in his power not for the sake of hitting the target but for the sake of doing everything in his power, one would suppose him to be speaking in a riddling and fantastic way. (8) So it is with the idiots who insist that the end of aiming at things in accordance with nature is not the getting but the taking and selecting of them, and that being healthy is not each man's end in his desire and pursuit of health, but on the contrary being healthy has reference to the desire and pursuit of being healthy . . . (9) For what is the difference between someone's saying that health has come into being for the sake of drugs, not drugs for the sake of health, and one who makes the selection of drugs and their composition and use more choiceworthy than health, or rather regards health as not choiceworthy at all, but locates the end in activity concerning the drugs, and declares desire to be the end of the getting, not the getting the end of the desire? (10) 'Yes, by Zeus, for reasoning well and prudence are attributes of the desire.' (11) That is fine, we shall say, if it views the getting and possession of what it desires as related to its end. But if not, its reasoning well is destroyed, since it does everything for the sake of getting what is not important or a source of happiness to get.

D Plutarch, *On common conceptions* 1072E–F (*SVF* 3 Antipater 59, part)

(1) Now that you have revealed it, observe their [the Stoics'] situation: the end is reasoning well in selections of things which have value in relation to reasoning well. For the men deny that they have or conceive any substance of the good or happiness other than this priceless reasoning well about the selections of the things with value. (2) But some think that this is an argument against Antipater and not the school. For it was he, they say, who resorted to these verbal strategies under pressure from Carneades.

E Cicero, *On ends* 5.16

[Speaker: the Antiochean Piso] (1) Since there is great disagreement on what this [the ultimate end] consists in, we should draw on Carneades' division, which our Antiochus enjoys habitually using. Carneades, then, inspected not just all opinions on the final good which philosophers have held up to now, but all the possible opinions. (2) He therefore said that no expertise can originate simply from itself. Its sphere of activity is always something extraneous. There is no need to develop this point with examples; for it is evident that no expertise is concerned just with itself, but the expertise and its object are distinct. (3) Since, then, corresponding to medicine as the expertise in health and navigation as the expertise in sailing, prudence is the expertise in living, it must be the case that prudence derives its constitution and origin from something else. [continued at **G**]

F Cicero, *On ends* 3.22 (*SVF* 3.18; continuing **59D**)

[Speaker: the Stoic Cato] (1) But from this doctrine [that rectitude is much more desirable than all the prior things in accordance with nature], one must at the outset remove the mistake of supposing that there are two final goods. (2) For if a man's object were to aim a spear or an arrow straight at something, his doing everything in his power to aim it straight would correspond to our doctrine of the final good. (3) On that kind of analogy, this man must do everything to aim straight. (4) And yet his doing everything to attain his object would be his end, so to speak, analogous to what we are calling the final good in life, whereas his striking the target would be something 'to-be-selected', as it were, not 'to-be-desired'.

G Cicero, *On ends* 5.17–20 (continuing **E**)

[Speaker: the Antiochean Piso] (1) Practically everyone has agreed that the sphere of prudence and what it desires to obtain must be suited and appropriate to our nature, and of a kind just by itself to attract and stimulate mental impulse, which the Greeks call *hormē* . . . (2) Some suppose that the primary impulse is for pleasure and the primary repulsion is from pain; others consider that freedom from pain is the first thing appropriated and pain the first thing avoided; others set out from what they call the primary things in accordance with nature, among which they count the sound condition and preservation of all one's parts, health, satisfactory senses, freedom from pain, strength, beauty and the like, comparable to which are the primary mental qualities, the sparks and seeds, as it were, of the virtues. (3) Since it is by one of these three things that our nature is first activated, whether to impulse or repulsion, and there can be nothing at all in addition to these three, every proper function of avoidance or pursuit must have its reference to one of these; consequently the prudence which we called the expertise in living is occupied with one of these three things, and derives from it the starting-point of the whole of life. (4) Now out of that which prudence has resolved to be the source of nature's first activation there will arise a theory of right and of rectitude, which can be consistent with one of those three things. So rectitude is either doing everything for the sake of pleasure even if you do not obtain it, or for the sake of absence of pain even if you cannot achieve it, or for the sake of obtaining the things in accordance with nature even if you obtain none of them ... Others again, on the basis of the same starting-points, will refer every proper function either to obtaining pleasure or absence of pain or the primary things in accordance with nature. (5) Six opinions on the final good have now been outlined. The chief proponents of the latter three are, of pleasure, Aristippus; of absence of pain, Hieronymus; of enjoying what we called the primary things in accordance with nature, Carneades, though he did not champion the position but defended it for dialectical reasons. (6) The three earlier views were possible, but only one of them has been supported, and with vigour. For no one has said that the principle of doing everything for the sake of pleasure, even if we do not obtain pleasure, is intrinsically desirable and right and the only good. Nor has anyone supposed that the activity of avoiding pain is intrinsically desirable if one cannot actually avoid it. But doing everything in order to obtain the things in accordance with nature, even if we do not obtain them, is rectitude and the only thing of intrinsic desirability and the only good, according to the Stoics.

H Cicero, *On ends* 3.24–5 (*SVF* 3.11, part)

[Speaker: the Stoic Cato] (1) We do not regard wisdom as comparable to navigation or medicine, but rather to acting ... and dancing, so that its end is within itself and not to be sought outside, i.e., the practice of the expertise. (2) Yet there is also a dissimilarity between wisdom and these expertises, because in the latter case right performances do not contain all the parts which constitute the expertise. (3) But what we may call 'right' or 'rightly performed actions', if you are agreeable, (which they call *katorthōmata*) contain all the measures of virtue. For wisdom alone is occupied entirely with itself, which does not happen in the other expertises.

I Galen, *On Hippocrates' and Plato's doctrines* 5.6.10–14 (Posidonius fr. 187, part)

(1) Not content with this, Posidonius upbraids Chrysippus and his followers more vividly and keenly for their incorrect interpretations of

the end. (2) This is what he says: 'Neglecting these points, some people contract "living in agreement" into "doing everything possible for the sake of the primary things in accordance with nature", making it similar to actually positing pleasure or freedom from pain or some such things as the target. But the very formulation involves a manifest inconsistency, and nothing honourable or productive of happiness. For it denotes an activity which is a necessary accompaniment of the end, but is not the end. (3) Yet, when this formulation has been analysed correctly, it can be used for cutting through the difficulties raised by the sophists. (4) But one cannot so use the formula, "living according to experience of what happens in accordance with the whole of nature", which is equivalent to saying, "living in agreement when this is not mean-spiritedly aimed at obtaining the indifferents". (5) This may perhaps suffice to show the absurdity of what Chrysippus said in his interpretation of how someone might succeed in living in agreement with nature. But I think it is better to set down what Posidonius wrote immediately after this passage: (6) 'Once the cause of the emotions was seen, it resolved this absurdity. It revealed the origins of the maladjustment in what should be sought and avoided, defined the procedures of training, and solved the difficulties regarding the impulse that arises from emotion.'

J Seneca, *Letters* 92.11–13

(1) The point might be made, 'If good health, rest, and freedom from pain are not going to thwart virtue, will you not pursue them?' (2) Of course I will. Not because they are good, but because they are in accordance with nature, and because they will be taken on the basis of my good judgement. (3) 'What then will be good in them?' Just this – being well selected. For when I put on the right sort of clothes, or walk as I should, or dine as I should, neither the dining nor the walking nor the clothes are good, but the intention I display in them by preserving a measure, in each thing, which conforms to reason . . . (4) So it is not elegant clothes which are a good in themselves, but the selection of elegant clothes, since the good is not in the thing but in the quality of the selection. It is our actions that are right, not their results . . . (5) I shall take good health and strength, if the selection is granted me, but the good will be my judgement regarding them, and not the things themselves.

K Cicero, *On ends* 4.26–7, 29–30, 32, 39

[Speaker: Cicero on behalf of Antiochus] (1) My question is how these weighty recommendations issued by nature have been suddenly abandoned by wisdom. Even if we were investigating the final good of some creature other than man, consisting of nothing but mind . . . that mind would not accept this end of yours. (2) For it would want health and freedom from pain, and would also desire their security and its own preservation; it would establish living in agreement with nature as its end, meaning (as I have said) the possession of all or most and the most important of the things in accordance with nature . . . (3) But if he [Chrysippus] says that some things are overshadowed and disappear, because they are quite tiny, we too grant the point . . . yet the bodily advantages, which are so great and durable and numerous, are not in that category . . . They add something worth working for. So I think the Stoics must sometimes be joking on this point, when they say that the virtuous life which has an oil-bottle or toilet-brush added to it will be taken in preference by the wise man, but will not make him any the happier . . . (4) Yet if, as we should agree, there does exist a natural impulse to pursue the things in accordance with nature, a total should be made of them all . . . (5) Reason does not abdicate its attendance to the primary gifts of nature. Having been set in authority over them, it has to direct the whole course of life. So I cannot wonder too much at the Stoics' inconsistency. They take natural impulse . . . proper function and virtue itself to belong to the things in accordance with nature. Yet when they want to reach the final good, they jump over them all, and leave us two tasks instead of one – to take some things and to desire others, instead of including them both in a single end.

L Cicero, *On ends* 4.78

[Speaker: Cicero on behalf of Antiochus] Can there be a greater inconsistency than for the same person to say both that rectitude is the only good, and that we have an impulse issued by nature to pursue the things appropriate for life? In wanting to keep points consistent with the former doctrine, they [the Stoics] collapse into Aristo's position. In escaping from this, they endorse the same doctrines in fact as the Peripatetics, while clinging tooth and nail to their own terminology.

☐ The foundation and materials of living in agreement with nature are provided by the *AN* 'indifferents' (**58A**) – the natural preferability of health, for instance, to sickness. As between health and sickness, agreement with nature requires a consistent preference of the former to the latter, in a person's plan of life. The wise man of course understands that his natural allotment may include sickness, that health is not desirable *per se*, and that reason may dictate his doing things which put his health at risk. But it could never be the case that he should deliberately, given the choice, neglect his health (**59E 3**). The natural differences of value between *AN* and *CN* things are a clear and authoritative indication of the external objectives which a Stoic will have good reason for pursuing or seeking to avoid.

This appears to have been Chrysippus' position (cf. **58J**) and the orthodox doctrine of the school. His distinctive formula for the end of life (**63B 4**) is found in **A**, amplified with the words, 'selecting those [things] in accordance with nature and rejecting those contrary to nature'; and the expanded statement is summed up in the standard formula, 'a life in agreement and consistent with nature'. The amplification, 'selecting . . . and rejecting . . .', constitutes the basis of accounts of the end attributed to Chrysippus' immediate successors, **58K**: 'Diogenes [of Babylon] represented the end as: reasoning well in the selection and disselection of things in accordance with nature . . . and Antipater: to live continuously selecting things in accordance with nature and disselecting things contrary to nature.' The explicit identification of such a life with 'agreement with nature' (**A**) is endorsed in **59D 3–4**, where 'selection which is absolutely consistent' coincides with a man's possession and understanding of the final good.

Possibly these Ciceronian passages were derived from the writings of Diogenes. But, however that may be, his formulation of the end was certainly offered as a supplement to Chrysippus' and not as a deviation from it. We may take Diogenes to have asserted that the standard formulae, together with Chrysippus' 'living in accordance with experience of what happens by nature' **63B 4**, were implicit in and elucidated by his own reference to 'reasoning well in the selection . . .' Antipater's formula, with its mention of 'continuously', reads like an attempt to incorporate 'consistency' within Diogenes' account. Both statements, it seems, could have been approved by Chrysippus. They amount to saying that the rational life, in agreement with nature, manifests itself in the right attitude and activity with respect to *AN* and *CN* things. These provide the external content, criteria, and positive or negative objectives of understanding nature and living accordingly.

The merit of Diogenes' formulation of the end is the guidance it offers on the practice of living in agreement with nature. But once *AN* and *CN* things had been included in a specification of the final good, the Stoics were faced with tough challenges concerning the relationship between happiness and things supposedly irrelevant to happiness. If our end is specified in terms of our selecting certain items, must not the selecting itself be carried out for the sake of an end – getting and using the things selected (a challenge reflected in **B**'s later polemic)? What point could there be in positing selection *per se*, and selection of things indifferent to happiness, as the end of every action? This criticism, which almost certainly began with the Academic Carneades, Diogenes' younger contemporary, took the form of a two-pronged attack. On the one hand, it was argued (**D 1**), the selection formula was vitiated by circularity: if well-reasoned selection is that for the sake of which everything is to be done, then the items worthy of selection must be valuable just in so far as they are the objects of well-reasoned selection: we are to reason well in selecting the objects of well-reasoned selection. Diogenes and Antipater could reject this charge by pointing out that the value of *AN* things was their being 'in accordance with nature', quite independent of the agent's reasoning and selection. But this rejoinder invited a further and more disturbing challenge: if the objects of rational selection are valuable in themselves, then the Stoics' selection of these should be undertaken for the sake of 'getting' them; it was mere equivocation to deny this. In effect, the Stoics were setting up two ends (**C 1**, **K 5**), contrary to their conception of a unitary goal of life – selecting or 'taking' *AN* things on the one hand, and getting them, the true purpose of such selection in the critics' eyes, on the other (**C 5, 7–9**). This seems to be the gist of Plutarch's criticism of the selection formula in **C** (cf. **C 6**, reporting the Stoic position), constituting the first horn of a dilemma (**C 1**). The second horn (**C 2**), probably concerned with Antipater's further formulation of the end, may be postponed for the present. (But the reader should be warned that in **C** Plutarch appears to conflate both of Antipater's formulae (**58K 2**), which makes interpretation of that text extremely difficult.)

Before turning to Antipater's response to Carneades, note should be taken of **J**, which shows how the Stoics sought to defend Diogenes' selection formula. The key-word is 'reasoning well' (cf. **C 10**). That is the end, what is good in itself, as manifested in the selection of *AN* things. Their naturalness is a reason for selecting them, but what is (morally) good about them is exclusively a property of the agent, his well-reasoned decision concerning them.

This position, however, reveals the difficulty of accommodating two orders of value – moral good and the *AN* things – under the common heading of 'accordance with nature' while taking moral excellence to be the only good and the only constituent of happiness. If we are constitutionally designed, as the Stoics admitted, to pursue those things which accord with our nature, should the end not include our getting all, or at least the majority, of these (**K**)? The Stoics do not want this 'Peripatetic' doctrine, but nor do they want, either, to agree with Aristo that complete indifference covers everything except virtue and vice (**L**). Their Academic critics accused them of trying to have it both ways – defining the end, with Diogenes, in intentionalist terms, while importing consequentialism in their reference to external objectives. This criticism was developed by Carneades, and answered by Antipater in his second formulation of the end.

The historical evidence for their dispute is found by combining **E, F, G,** and **I**. It seems probable that Carneades' criticism of the 'selection' formula included the insistence that an 'expertise in living', like any expertise, is a goal-directed activity undertaken to achieve something other than its own exercise (**E**). Hence the criticism of the selection formula for being circular or introducing two ends. In **G** we have evidence of Carneades' approval of representing the end in terms of an expertise ('prudence') which does everything for the sake of the objective that can be described as primarily appropriate to our nature. On this basis he outlines six possible views of the end (**G 4**), dividing them into two categories depending on whether they do or do not make 'obtaining' the natural objective essential to the end. The Stoics are cited (**G 6**) as the only school to opt for a view of the second type. Carneades himself defended one which nominated the same natural objective as the Stoics, but differed from them in requiring actual possession of 'the things in accordance with nature'.

What is here attributed to the Stoics closely resembles Antipater's second formula: 'to do everything in one's power continuously and undeviatingly with a view to obtaining the predominating things which accord with nature' (**58K 2**). A version of this is reported by Posidonius in **I 2**, where it is described as similar to the goal-directed activities supported by Carneades as models for formulations of the end (**E, G**). Though disapproving of it as an account of the end, Posidonius seems to allow its value as 'a necessary accompaniment of the end', which 'can be used for cutting through the difficulties raised by the sophists' (I 3). Given the implicit reference to Antipater, 'sophists' most plausibly refers to Carneades, a point which gains support from D 2, since Plutarch's criticism has been directed against Antipater's second formula as well as the 'selection' formula.

Assuming, then, that Antipater advanced his second formula as a rejoinder to Carneades' criticism of the 'selection formula', how may we best reconstruct the debate and its issues? The decisive passage is F. Antipater's second formula, 'doing everything in one's power . . .', is invoked here to defend the Stoics against the objection that their doctrines concerning virtue and AN things import 'two final goods'. There are unfortunate obscurities in the text of F, but the main thrust of the passage is clear: an archer's objective is to aim straight (i.e. actually hit the target). His function, as an archer, is to do everything in his power to aim straight. Similarly, obtaining AN things is the external 'objective' of all actions, according to Antipater's formula, but someone's function as a moral agent is to do everything in his power to obtain them. The archer analogy fits Carneades' conception of a craft which needs an objective outside itself (E). Possibly he used it himself against the 'selection formula'. In any case, Antipater seems to have argued that the Stoics could accept Carneades' conception of virtue as a goal-directed expertise, without abandoning their indifference to the actual getting of AN things.

Plutarch takes Antipater's formula to be absurd, interpreting it as saying that the archer does everything in his power for the sake of doing everything in his power (C 7). But Antipater's end is 'doing everything in one's power *to get AN* things'. It is not in the least absurd to say that the end of exercise is doing everything in one's power to become healthy. Generalized to cover all actions, the formula maintains that everything should be done for the sake of consistently striving at the getting of AN things. The end is not the getting (the external objective) but the consistent striving at getting. This latter is always in one's power, not liable to the contingencies which may prevent attainment of the objective.

Antipater, then, apparently accepted Carneades' formal requirement that expertise in living requires an objective outside itself. This objective becomes an element in his specification of the end, thus avoiding the charge of positing two ends, but as something to be striven for, irrespective of its attainment. Thus the end itself lies firmly where Diogenes had left it – the consistently rational disposition of the agent. If G 6 gives Carneades' reaction, he regarded Antipater's formula as a distortion of any practical conception of a goal-directed expertise (cf. C 2, 4). Having got a Stoic to admit the desirability of trying to obtain AN things, Carneades wanted the further admission of the desirability of actually obtaining them. If Stoic virtue was analogous to branches of expertise such as medicine, as Antipater was accepting, it seemed perverse to hold that virtue could treat the actual attainment of its objective as something 'to be selected' (F 4) and indifferent for happiness. Against Carneades, however, it could be argued that the proper moral evaluation of a goal-directed activity should be in terms of the agent's efforts and intentions, if praise and blame are to have any reasonable foundation, and happiness to be consistently within our power. If this was Antipater's main point, his formula may have been intended as a purely dialectical manoeuvre, to show that the Stoics could hit back at Carneades. The formulation still fails, of course, to show how it can be rational to make happiness depend upon aiming at objectives whose attainment is irrelevant to happiness.

Such an interpretation gains support from Stoic reactions to Antipater's formula. His recourse to the goal-directed conception of an expertise was explicitly rejected in Stoic analogies of wisdom with acting or dancing (**H**), and Posidonius' comments (**I 2**) are equally hostile to the inclusion of *AN* things as a 'target'. But those were the terms which Carneades had chosen for attacking the 'selection' formula; Antipater could disclaim responsibility for them, and retreat to more orthodox accounts of the end in his dealings with fellow Stoics. Why his definition should merit Posidonius' charge of 'inconsistency' (**I 2**), is not entirely clear. Perhaps the inconsistency is the presence in the end of an objective (getting *AN* things) which is not the end (cf. **C 2**). But while Posidonius dismisses Antipater's formula as a valid interpretation of 'living in agreement', he concedes its value as a dialectical device, once it is granted that 'doing everything possible for the sake of the first things in accordance with nature' is a 'necessary accompaniment of the end', rather than the end itself. Coupled with **D 2**, this strongly suggests that Antipater's second formula was designed to give the Stoics an answer to Carneades in the Academic's own terms.

If any leading Stoic had actually abandoned the sufficiency of virtue for complete happiness, we should expect to find mention of this in Cicero. But in **K**, which reports Antiochus' criticisms, objection continues to be made to the Stoics' refusal to accept possession of *AN* things as a constituent of the end. Antipater is said by Seneca to have attributed to 'externals' a tiny importance for the final good (*Letters* 92.5 = **m** in vol. 2). This may be little more than a reflection of **K 3**, in which case his concession may have been an *ad hominem* point, not intended to compromise the standard doctrine, which is still presupposed in his own formulations. Given **I 2**, Posidonius can hardly have regarded health and wealth as 'goods' (as claimed at Diogenes Laertius 7.103 = **n** in vol. 2), and his and Panaetius' alleged denial of virtue's sufficiency (Diogenes Laertius 7.128 = **o** in vol. 2) is not borne out by any other evidence. The upshot seems to be as Cicero says (*On ends* 3.33): 'there are slight differences between Stoic definitions of good, but they all point in the same direction.'

65 The passions

A Stobaeus 2.88,8–90,6 (*SVF* 3.378, 389, part)

(1) They [the Stoics] say that passion is impulse which is excessive and disobedient to the dictates of reason, or a movement of soul which is irrational and contrary to nature; and that all passions belong to the soul's commanding-faculty. (2) Therefore every fluttering is also a passion, and likewise, every passion is a fluttering. (3) Since passion is of this kind, one

must suppose that some passions are primary and dominant, while others have these as their reference. The generically primary ones are these four: appetite, fear, distress, pleasure. (4) Appetite and fear come first, the former in relation to what appears good, and the latter in relation to what appears bad. Pleasure and distress result from these: pleasure, whenever we get the objects of our appetite or avoid the objects of our fear; distress, whenever we fail to get the objects of our appetite or experience the objects of our fear. (5) [= C] (6) 'Irrational' and 'contrary to nature' are not used in their ordinary senses: 'irrational' is equivalent to 'disobedient to reason'. For every passion is overpowering, since people in states of passion frequently see that it is not suitable to do this but are carried away by the intensity, as though by a disobedient horse, and are induced to do it . . . (7) The sense of 'contrary to nature', in the outline account of passion, is of something that happens contrary to the right and natural reason. Everyone in states of passion turns aside from reason, but not like those who have been deceived in something or other, but in a special way. (8) For when people have been deceived, for instance over atoms being first principles, they give up the judgement, once they have been taught that it is not true. But when people are in states of passion, even if they realize or are taught to realize that one should not feel distress or fear or have their soul, quite generally, in states of passion, they still do not give these up, but are brought by them to a position of being controlled by their tyranny.

B Andronicus, *On passions* 1 (*SVF* 3.391, part)

[Reporting Stoic definitions:] (1) Distress is an irrational contraction, or a fresh opinion that something bad is present, at which people think it right to be contracted [i.e. depressed]. (2) Fear is an irrational shrinking [aversion], or avoidance of an expected danger. (3) Appetite is an irrational stretching [desire], or pursuit of an expected good. (4) Pleasure is an irrational swelling, or a fresh opinion that something good is present, at which people think it right to be swollen [i.e. elated].

C Stobaeus 2.88,22–89,3 (= **A 5**; *SVF* 3.378, part)

In the case of all the soul's passions, when they [the Stoics] call them 'opinions', 'opinion' is used instead of 'weak supposition', and 'fresh' instead of 'the stimulus of an irrational contraction or swelling'.

D Galen, *On Hippocrates' and Plato's doctrines* 4.2.1–6 (*SVF* 3.463, part)

(1) In his first definitions of the generic passions, he [Chrysippus] completely departs from the doctrine of the ancients, defining distress as 'a fresh opinion that something bad is present . . .' (2) In these definitions he obviously mentions only the rational part of the soul, omitting the

appetitive and competitive . . . (3) But in some of his next definitions he writes things more consistent with Epicurus and Zeno than with his own doctrines. (4) For in defining distress, he says that it is 'a shrinking at what is thought to be something to avoid', and he says pleasure is 'a swelling up at what is thought to be something to pursue'. (5) 'Shrinkings and swellings', of course, and 'expansions and contractions', which he sometimes mentions as well, are affections of the irrational faculty that result from opinions.

E Stobaeus 2.90,19–91,9 (*SVF* 3.394, part)

(1) The following are classified under appetite: anger and its species . . . intense sexual desires, cravings and yearnings, love of pleasures and riches and honours, and the like. (2) Under pleasure: rejoicing at another's misfortunes, self-gratification, trickery, and the like. (3) Under fear: hesitancy, anguish, astonishment, shame, confusion, superstition, dread, and terror. (4) Under distress: malice, envy, jealousy, pity, grief, worry, sorrow, annoyance, mental pain, vexation.

F Diogenes Laertius 7.116 (*SVF* 3.431)

(1) They [the Stoics] say that there are three good feelings: joy, watchfulness, wishing. (2) Joy, they say, is the opposite of pleasure, consisting in well-reasoned swelling [elation]; and watchfulness is the opposite of fear, consisting in well-reasoned shrinking. For the wise man will not be afraid at all, but he will be watchful. (3) They say that wishing is the opposite of appetite, consisting in well-reasoned stretching [desire]. (4) Just as certain passions fall under the primary ones, so too with the primary good feelings. Under wishing: kindness, generosity, warmth, affection. Under watchfulness: respect, cleanliness. Under joy: delight, sociability, cheerfulness.

G Plutarch, *On moral virtue* 446F–447A (*SVF* 3.459, part)

(1) Some people [meaning the Stoics] say that passion is no different from reason, and that there is no dissension and conflict between the two, but a turning of the single reason in both directions, which we do not notice owing to the sharpness and speed of the change. (2) We do not perceive that the natural instrument of appetite and regret, or anger and fear, is the same part of the soul, which is moved by pleasure towards wrong, and while moving recovers itself again. (3) For appetite and anger and fear and all such things are corrupt opinions and judgements, which do not arise about just one part of the soul but are the whole commanding-faculty's inclinations, yieldings, assents and impulses, and, quite generally, activities which change rapidly, just like children's fights, whose fury and intensity are volatile and transient owing to their weakness.

H Galen, *On Hippocrates' and Plato's doctrines* 3.1.25 (*SVF* 2.886, part)

[Chrysippus:] 'I think that people in general come to the view that our commanding-faculty is in the heart through their awareness, as it were, of the passions that affect the mind happening to them in the chest and especially in the region where the heart is placed. This is so particularly in the case of distress, fear, anger and above all, excitement.'

I Galen, *On Hippocrates' and Plato's doctrines* 5.6.34–7 (Posidonius frr. 33, 166, part)

(1) Posidonius also shows in what follows that [Chrysippus] is not only at variance with the facts, but also with Zeno and Cleanthes. (2) He says that Cleanthes' doctrine concerning the passionate part of the soul is revealed in these verses:

> 'What is it, Passion, that you want? Tell me this.'
> 'I want, Reason? To do everything I want.'
> 'A royal wish; but tell me it again.'
> 'Whatever I desire I want to happen.'

(3) Posidonius says that these alternating verses by Cleanthes give clear indications of his doctrine concerning the soul's passionate part, since he has represented reason and passion in conversation, as two different things. (4) Chrysippus, however, does not believe that the soul's passionate part is different from the rational; and he takes passions away from the non-rational animals, although they are plainly governed by appetite and competition, as Posidonius also explains in a fuller treatment of them.

J Galen, *On Hippocrates' and Plato's doctrines* 4.2.10–18 (*SVF* 3.462, part)

[Chrysippus in *On passions* book 1] (1) 'First of all we should bear in mind that a rational animal follows reason naturally, and acts in accordance with reason as if that were its guide. (2) Often, however, it moves towards and away from certain things in a different way, pushed to excess in disobedience to reason. (3) Both definitions [i.e. the definitions of passions both as 'irrational' and as 'excessive impulses', cf. **A 1**] refer to this movement: the movement contrary to nature which occurs irrationally in this way, and the excess in impulses. (4) For this irrationality must be taken to mean "disobedient to reason" and "reason turned aside"; with reference to this movement we even speak in ordinary language of people "being pushed" and "moved irrationally, without reason and judgement". What we mean by these expressions is not as though a person moves in error and overlooking something that accords with reason, but we refer chiefly to the movement of which the expressions provide an outline account, since it is not a rational animal's nature to move in his soul in *this* way, but in accordance with reason . . . (5) This also explains the expression "the excess of impulse", since people overstep the proper and natural proportion of their impulses. (6) My meaning can be made more intelligible in this way. When someone walks in accordance with his impulse, the movement of his legs is not excessive but commensurate with the impulse, so that he can stop or change whenever he wants to. (7) But when people run in accordance with their impulse, this sort of thing no longer happens. The movement of their legs exceeds their impulse, so that they are carried away and unable to change obediently, as soon as they have started to do so. (8) Something similar, I think, takes place with impulses, owing to their going beyond the rational proportion. The result is that when someone has the impulse he is not obedient to reason. (9) The excess in running is called "contrary to the impulse", but the excess in the impulse is called "contrary to reason". For the proportion of a natural impulse is what accords with reason and goes only so far as reason itself thinks right.'

K Galen, *On Hippocrates' and Plato's doctrines* 4.3.2–5 (Posidonius fr. 34, part)

(1) On this point [i.e. his holding the passions to be judgements], he [Chrysippus] is in conflict with Zeno and himself and many other Stoics, who do not take the soul's judgements themselves to be its passions, but identify these with results of the judgements – the irrational contractions, cowerings, tearings, swellings and expansions. (2) But Posidonius completely dissented from both opinions. He does not regard the passions as either judgements or as results of judgements, but as effects of the competitive and appetitive faculty, in full accordance with the ancient doctrine. (3) In his study *On passions* he frequently asks Chrysippus and his followers: 'What is the cause of the excessive impulse? For reason could not exceed its own occupations and limits. So it is evident that some other irrational faculty causes impulse to exceed the limits of reason, just as the cause of running's exceeding the limits of choice is irrational, the weight of the body.'

L Galen, *On Hippocrates' and Plato's doctrines* 4.5.21–5 (*SVF* 3.480, part)

(1) [Chrysippus from his book *Emotional therapy*:] 'The passions are called ailments not just in virtue of their judging each of these things to be good, but also with regard to their running towards them in excess of what is natural' . . . (2) One might take him [Chrysippus] to say . . . that the opinion that possessions are a good is not yet an ailment, but becomes so when someone takes them to be the greatest good and supposes that life deprived of property is not worth living: for this is what the ailments love of property and money consist in.

M Galen, *On Hippocrates' and Plato's doctrines* 5.5.8–26 (Posidonius fr. 169, part)

(1) We have by nature these three appropriate relationships, corresponding to each form of the soul's parts – to pleasure because of the appetitive part, to success because of the competitive part, and to rectitude because of the rational part. (2) Epicurus only took notice of the appropriate relationship belonging to the soul's worst part; Chrysippus only that which belongs to the best, saying that we have an appropriate relationship only with rectitude, which he takes to be evidently good as well. (3) In neglecting two of them, Chrysippus was understandably puzzled about the origin of vice . . . He was unable to discover how it is that children do wrong. These were all matters on which Posidonius, quite rightly in my opinion, criticized and refuted him. (4) For if children had an appropriate relationship to rectitude, right from the start, vice would have had to be engendered in them not internally nor from themselves but solely from outside. Yet even if they are brought up in good habits and properly educated, they are always seen to do something wrong, and Chrysippus too admits this. (5) He could of course have overlooked the obvious facts and accepted only what agreed with his own assumptions, claiming that children will invariably become wise in the course of time if they are well brought up. (6) But he did not have the nerve to falsify the facts on this point at least; he accepted that even if children were reared by no one but a philosopher and never saw or heard any example of vice, they would still not necessarily become philosophers . . . (7) When he says that the persuasiveness of impressions, and conversation, are responsible for the maladjustments which occur in inferior men concerning good and bad things, we should ask him why pleasure projects the persuasive appearance that it is good, and pain that it is bad. Similarly, why are we readily persuaded, when we hear victory at Olympia and erection of statues being praised and blessed as good things by people in general, and defeat and disgrace regarded as bad? (8) Posidonius criticizes Chrysippus on this as well . . . holding that impulse is sometimes generated as a result of the judgement of the rational part, but often as a result of the movement of the passionate part. (9) Posidonius was quite right to connect these theories with the findings of the physiognomist. Animals and men that are broader-chested and hotter are all more competitive by nature, but those that are wide-hipped and colder are more cowardly. (10) He also says that their habitat makes no small difference to men's characters in respect to cowardice and daring, or attitudes to pleasure and pain, on the grounds that the soul's passionate movements always follow the body's disposition, which is altered to no small extent by the mixture [of elements] in the environment. For even the blood in animals, he says, differs in temperature and density and in

many other ways, which Aristotle expounded at length . . . (11) At present my argument is against Chrysippus and his followers, who understand nothing about the passions, including the fact that the body's mixtures produce the 'passionate movements' (as Posidonius normally calls them) that are appropriate to them.

N Galen, *On Hippocrates' and Plato's doctrines* 5.6.18–19 (Posidonius fr. 161, part)

[Summarising Posidonius:] Some people in error have the opinion that what is appropriate to the soul's irrational faculties is appropriate without qualification. They do not know that having pleasure and dominating one's neighbours are the objects desired by the brutish part of the soul, but wisdom and everything good and honourable are the objects desired by the part which is rational and divine.

O Galen, *On Hippocrates' and Plato's doctrines* 4.7.12–17 (*SVF* 3.466, part)

[Chrysippus in *On passions* book 2] (1) 'On the lessening of distress, the question might be asked as to how it occurs, whether because a particular opinion is altered, or with them all persisting, and for what reason this will be so . . . (2) I think that this kind of opinion does persist – that what is actually present is something bad – but as it grows older the contraction and, as I take it, the impulse towards the contraction, lessen. (3) Perhaps also the impulse persists, but the consequences will not correspond because a differently qualified disposition supervenes, which does not reason from those events. (4) So it is that people cease weeping and people weep who do not want to, when different impressions are created by external objects, and something or nothing stands in the way. For the way grief and weeping stop is probably what happens in those other cases as well: at their onset things cause greater movement, as I said happens with what activates laughter, and the like.'

P Galen, *On Hippocrates' and Plato's doctrines* 4.7.24–41 (Posidonius fr. 165, part)

(1) He [Posidonius] himself shows that passions are caused by competition and appetite, and why they subside in time even if the opinions and judgements of something bad belonging to or having happened to the affected persons persist . . . (2) For as the passionate part of the soul pursues objects of desire appropriate to it, so having got them, it has its fill, and thereupon puts a stop to its own movement, which was controlling the animal's impulse and leading it by itself towards its own misguided end. (3) Therefore the causes of the passions' ceasing are not beyond reason, as Chrysippus used to say . . . (4) Habits and time in general evidently are of

the greatest effectiveness for the passionate movements. For the soul's irrational faculty slowly appropriates itself to the habits in which it has been reared.

Q Galen, *On Hippocrates' and Plato's doctrines* 5.6.22–6 (including Posidonius fr. 162)

(1) It is through irrational activities that the irrational faculty is helped and harmed, whereas knowledge and ignorance have these effects on the rational faculty. (2) These then are the benefits that Posidonius says we derive from understanding the cause of the passions [see **64I**], and in addition, 'it explained the problems concerning the impulse that arises from passion . . . (3) For I think you are quite familiar with the way people are without fear and distress when they have been rationally persuaded that something bad for them is present or approaching, but they have these passions when they get an impression of those things themselves. (4) How could anyone activate the irrational by means of reason, unless he set before it a picture like a perceptual impression? Thus some people have their appetite roused by a description, and when someone vividly tells them to flee the approaching lion, they are frightened without having seen it.'

R Galen, *On Hippocrates' and Plato's doctrines* 5.2.3–7 (Posidonius fr. 163, part)

(1) Chrysippus says that it [the soul of inferior men] is comparable to bodies which are liable to contract fevers or diarrhoea or something else like this, on a slight and chance cause. (2) Posidonius criticizes his comparison: the soul of inferior men, he says, should not be compared to them but to bodies that are healthy without qualification. (3) For whether one contracts a fever from large causes or little, it makes no difference to one's being affected by it and being brought into any affected state at all. Bodies differ from one another by the fact that some are prone to fall sick while others are not. (4) So Chrysippus, he says, was incorrect in comparing the soul's health with that of the body, while comparing the soul's sickness to the condition of the body that falls easily into sickness; for the mind of the wise man is immune to affection, obviously, whereas no body is immune. (5) It was more correct to compare the souls of inferior men 'either to bodily health with a proneness to sickness' (this was Posidonius' expression), 'or to sickness itself', since they are either a kind of sickly tenor or one that is already sick. (6) But he himself agrees with Chrysippus to the extent of saying that all inferior men are sick in soul and that their sickness is like the stated conditions of the body. (7) His actual words are: 'Therefore the soul's sickness is not, as Chrysippus supposed, like the sickly disorder of the

body whereby the body is driven to fall into irregular, non-periodic fevers; the soul's sickness, rather, is like either bodily health with proneness to sickness, or sickness itself. For bodily sickness is a tenor already sick, but the sickness Chrysippus speaks of is more like proneness to fevers.'

S Stobaeus 2.93.1–13 (*SVF* 3.421)

(1) Proneness to sickness is a tendency towards passion, towards one of the functions contrary to nature, such as depression, irascibility, malevolence, quick temper, and the like. Proneness to sickness also occurs in reference to other functions which are contrary to nature, such as theft, adultery, and violence; hence people are called thieves, violators and adulterers. (2) Sickness is an appetitive opinion which has flowed into a tenor and hardened, signifying a belief that what should not be pursued is intensely worth pursuing, such as the passion for women, wine and money. By antipathy the opposites of these sicknesses occur, such as loathing for women or wine, and misanthropy. (3) Sicknesses which occur in conjunction with weakness are called ailments.

T Galen, *On Hippocrates' and Plato's doctrines* 4.6.2–3 (*SVF* 3.473, part)

Some of men's wrong actions are referred by Chrysippus to faulty judgement, others to the soul's lack of tension and its weakness, just as their right actions are guided by right judgement together with the soul's good tension . . . He says there are times when we give up right decisions because the soul's tension gives in, and does not persist till the end or fully execute the commands of reason.

U Epictetus, *Manual* 5

It is not things themselves that disturb men, but their judgements about things. For example, death is nothing terrible, otherwise Socrates would have thought so; what is terrible is the judgement that death is terrible. So whenever we are impeded or disturbed or distressed, let us blame no one but ourselves, that is, our own judgements.

V Epictetus, *Discourses* 1.12.20–1

(1) You are impatient and discontented, and if you are alone, you call it isolation, but if you are with people, you call them plotters and bandits, and you even criticize your own parents and children and brothers and neighbours. (2) But when staying alone, you ought to call it peace and freedom and regard yourself as like the gods; and when you are with a number of people, you should not call it a crowd or a mob or an unpleasantness, but a feast and a festival, and so accept everything contentedly.

W Stobaeus 2.155,5–17 (*SVF* 3.564, 632)

(1) They [the Stoics] say that the good man experiences nothing contrary to his desire or impulse or purpose on account of the fact that in all such cases he acts with reserve and encounters no obstacles which are unanticipated. (2) He is also gentle, his gentleness being a tenor by which he is gently disposed in acting always appropriately and in not being moved to anger against anyone. (3) He is also calm and orderly, his orderliness being knowledge of fitting activities, and his calm the proper regulation of his soul and body's natural activities and rests. (4) The opposites of these occur in all inferior men.

X Seneca, *On anger* 2.3.1–2.4

(1) None of those things which rouse the mind fortuitously should be called passions; the mind suffers them, so to speak, rather than causes them. Therefore, passions consist not in being moved as a result of impressions of things, but in surrendering oneself to them and following up this fortuitous movement. For if anyone thinks that pallor, floods of tears, sexual arousal, heavy breathing or a sudden brightening of the eyes and the like, are evidence of passion and a mark of the mind, he is mistaken and fails to realize that these are bodily drives . . . (2) Anger not only has to be moved but has to rush out. This is because it is an impulse, and impulse never exists without the mind's assent. For it is impossible that any action concerning revenge and punishment should take place without the mind's awareness.

Y Gellius 19.1.17–18 (Epictetus fr. 9)

(1) When some terrifying sound . . . or anything else of that kind occurs, even a [Stoic] wise man's mind must be slightly moved and contracted and frightened – not by a preconceived opinion of anything bad but by certain rapid and involuntary movements which forestall the proper function of mind and reason. (2) Soon, however, the wise man does not . . . assent to such impressions nor does he add an opinion to them, but he rejects and belittles them and finds nothing in them that should be feared.

☐ Although control of the passions was a basic principle in all Greek ethics, popular as well as philosophical, its importance in Stoicism was and has remained notorious. Here the word 'stoical' retains a direct connexion with the ancient school. Socratic doctrines, as mediated by the Cynics, help to explain the Stoics' conception of the wise man as free from all disturbing passion. But the Stoics treated passion in several novel ways which are among the best guides to their view of the good and happy life. Passion is the source of unhappiness, wrong-doing and the flaws of character which issue in wrong-doing (**A 6–7**, **R**). The term *pathos* includes not only the obviously turbulent emotions of sexual desire, ambition, jealousy etc., but also such states of mind as hesitancy, malice and pity, all classified under one of the four primary passions, appetite, pleasure, fear and distress (**E**). The classification needs to be read in conjunction with that of the 'three good feelings' in **F**. (There is no good feeling corresponding to 'distress'.) Passion is thereby revealed as an unhealthy state of mind, not synonymous with emotion in ordinary language. The 'good feelings' include a wide spectrum of attractive human characteristics which temper the 'austerity' of the wise man, so strongly emphasized in the more hostile ancient sources. In acknowledging, as one must, the apparent harshness of including pity as a passion (**E** 4), it should also be noted that the wise man could be sociable, generous, affectionate, cheerful and gentle (**W** 2).

Chrysippus seems to have approached the elucidation of passion from the assumption that a person in such a state, by assenting to a certain kind of false value-judgement, has issued himself with an 'excessive impulse' to pursue or avoid something (for the relation between assent and impulse, cf. **33I**). The meaning of 'excessive' is explained in **J** 5–9: given that someone can seek to achieve what he wants by walking, such a person could be said to 'exceed' his wants by running, an action which prevents immediate control of his body's movements. By analogy, Chrysippus argued, an impulse or want is 'excessive' if it goes beyond the natural control of reason. The idea might be more clearly conveyed by a speedometer which marks all speeds beyond 70 mph in red – someone who drives beyond that speed is driving excessively, with speeds below that figure corresponding to impulses commensurate with reason. The important and original insight expressed by the analogy is the continuity and difference between normal, healthy impulses and passions. According to Chrysippus' psychology (cf. **53Q**), any impulse is an efficient cause of action. Impulses are that activity of the soul's commanding-faculty which converts its judgements of what it should pursue or avoid into purposive bodily movements. Since reason characterizes the whole commanding-faculty (**61B** 9), there is nothing irrational about an impulse as such: volition is a natural and necessary function of reason. In the case of passion, however, Chrysippus used 'irrational', as explained in **J** 1–4 (cf. **61B** 10–11), to describe impulses which exceed the natural limits of reason. Their unnaturalness or irrationality, he stresses, consists in the immoderation of their movement (**J** 4). They are not like ordinary errors of fact (cf. **A** 7–8), a point which probably means that the pro or contra judgement underlying a passion may be perfectly natural in itself (cf. **L**): the wise man will naturally select or seek to avoid many of the things that form the objects of passions; but he will do so at a walking pace, as it were, on the basis of a properly rational judgement of such things' moral indifference. He always gets what he desires, since he 'acts with reserve'; and thus his impulses are rationally regulated so as to accord with everything that occurs in his environment, impervious to disappointment or any passion (**W**). Passions are characterized by their 'excess', which is revealed both in the nature of the judgement – taking what is not good or bad in the strict sense to be such (cf. **B**) – and in the concomitant psychosomatic movements, the 'shrinkings' and 'stretchings', 'swellings' and 'contractions' (**B**, **D** 4–5), which form their coordinate definitions. A passion is a *weak* opinion (**C**; see **41**), whereby 'weakness' describes the state of a 'perverted' reason, assenting to impressions that trigger off impulses inconsistent with a well-reasoned understanding of what their objects are worth.

The precedence of appetite and fear to pleasure and distress (**A** 4) can be explained by the fact that the former motivate actions which result in one of the latter. Appetite and fear are defined by reference to the agent's 'expectations', pleasure and distress by his 'fresh' beliefs about the good or bad things he is presently experiencing (**B**). Thus the objects of appetite and fear will typically be external states of affairs towards which we literally 'stretch forth' or from which we 'shrink back'. (The Stoics, as our translations seek to bring out, liked to exploit the etymological sense of ordinary words, in this case 'desire' and 'aversion'.) The two 'resultant' passions, pleasure and distress, have internal objects which are (or manifest themselves in) the soul's 'swelling' and 'contraction'. **B** taken together with **O** shows that the 'freshness' of the false judgements which constitute pleasure and distress reveals itself in the opinion that one ought to be elated or depressed. Hence Chrysippus was prepared to explain the lessening of distress (**O**) not as an alteration of the false opinion that something bad is present, but as a weakening of the impulse to the 'contraction', that is, the *further* false opinion that one ought to be depressed. To suppose that property is something good is a basic error, but not a sufficient condition of having a passion for wealth – judging it to be the greatest good (**L**).

As the name of a primary passion, 'pleasure' needs to be distinguished from the synonymous state described as a 'by-product' (**57A** 3) and variously classified as 'indifferent but preferred', 'natural but without value', 'neither natural nor valuable' (see note on **A** 4 in vol. 2). What this neutral pleasure signifies is established by the fact that its opposite is one of the standard words for physical pain (**58A** 4). The pleasure which is indifferent should be taken to cover pleasurable sensations which are entirely involuntary or unavoidable by-products of natural human behaviour. Pleasure only becomes a passion when a person assents to false judgements concerning the desirability and goodness of pleasurable experiences. So too with the undesirability and badness of pain when this refers to the passion 'distress'. More generally, the Stoics are not committed to the utterly implausible claim that every state of a person's mind is immediately under the control of reason. They acknowledged that even a wise man is so constituted that he may be *involuntarily* subject to weeping, sexual arousal, shock at sudden noises etc. (**X, Y**). Such responses to circumstances will only be signs of passions if they belong to someone who has misjudged his situation, and thereby given himself an excessive impulse manifested in appetite, fear etc.

Because we are responsible for the state of our reason, we are responsible for our passions, a fundamental Stoic doctrine which explains their emphasis on strength of will and character (cf. **T**). The passions' dependence on faulty judgements, and thus on the perversion of reason, is exemplified in **U** and **V**. We *as a whole* are to blame for our passions, Epictetus maintains, which follow directly upon mistaken interpretation of our mental impressions, or misdescription of experience. Thus passion, as reason gone astray, is not a feature of the non-rational animals (**I** 4).

At the basis of this theory is Chrysippus' important denial that the human soul consists of rational *and* irrational faculties. He rejected the Platonic model of a simultaneously divided self, whereby emotional conflict is explained in terms of reason and passion pulling a person in opposite ways at the same time (**G**). For Chrysippus, emotional conflict is a fluctuation of the unitary commanding-faculty, which is capable of changing so swiftly that it gives the misleading appearance of being divided into two distinct powers (cf. **61B 9–11**). Zeno had already described passion as a 'fluttering' (*SVF* 1.206, cf. **A 1-2**), the ornithological metaphor being chosen to convey its volatility; and that thought is developed in **G**. Thus the dominant Stoic conception of those subject to passion is their instability and lack of consistent direction; note the references to 'weakness' and 'lack of tension' (**C**, **T**). Galen, our principal source for Chrysippus' psychology, was tediously critical of Chrysippus' abandonment of Plato's tripartite division of the soul into rational, appetitive and competitive faculties, and of his locating reason as well as passion in the heart (**H**). He attacked him by means of Posidonius, who had returned to the Platonic model of the soul (**K 2**), using this as his explanation of the *naturalness* of the passions to the latter two irrational faculties (**M 1-2**, **P 1**, cf. **N**). Posidonius had also represented Chrysippus as being out of line with Zeno and Cleanthes (**I 1-2**), but the surviving evidence is insufficient to corroborate his opinion. Most of Chrysippus' terminology for the passions goes back to Zeno (cf. *SVF* 1.205–15), and Cleanthes' verses, quoted in **I 1**, do not prove that he distinguished reason and passion in the way Posidonius alleged. Against Posidonius is **61B**, which attributes monistic psychology to Zeno and Aristo as well as Chrysippus.

Some innovations and developments, however, were doubtless made by Chrysippus himself, probably with a view to clarifying the difficulty (cf. **K 3**) of positing an 'irrational' state of a rational faculty. Where Zeno had spoken, somewhat loosely perhaps, of judgements *resulting* in 'irrational movements', Chrysippus insisted that the passion itself is a judgement (**K 1**). This suggests that he identified the cognitive activity and the 'irrational movement', a thesis which would be reflected in the co-ordinate definitions of **B** (cf. **D**).

Posidonius' principal objections to Chrysippus' doctrine of passion are recorded in **K**, **M**, **P**, and **Q**. One of these is conceptual, the impossibility of reason exceeding itself (**K 3**). Taking up Chrysippus' analogy with running (**J 7**), Posidonius argued that running's 'excess' over rational choice is due to an irrational factor, the body's weight. But this is a hopeless rejoinder. Chrysippus' point is that the runner's impulse to run is an aberrant activity of reason itself – a volition which makes a person lose control of himself. That indicates perception of the fact that passions are both voluntary or intentional *and* sometimes recognized by their subjects to be excessive (cf. **A 6-8**). Posidonius' more interesting objections are empirical. Chrysippus had explained the origin of vice by reference to the corrupting effect of the external environment (**M 7**; but cf. **62D** and commentary, which show that Chrysippus' position was much more complex than Posidonius allows). Posidonius challenged the implicit optimism concerning human nature in an ideal environment. On his view the 'persuasive-ness' of the environment is only intelligible on the assumption that the passions are predisposed by internal features of the soul and of the bodily constitution. Posidonius found support for his doctrines in the effectiveness of habits (**P 4**) and 'irrational activities' (**Q I**) in stimulating and assuaging the passions. As **Q 3** shows, he interpreted reason more restrictively than Chrysippus, counting a perceptual impression on its own as something 'irrational'. The difference between the two Stoics emerges particularly clearly in **M 8** and **64I 6**: for Posidonius, impulse is a mental function which has *either* reason *or* passion as its source. For Chrysippus, passion itself is a rational impulse which has deviated from nature's norm. Posidonius' definition of the end (**63J 2**) indicates the centrality to his ethics of accepting the irrational as an independent and corrupting power in human nature.

On his tripartite view of the soul, pleasure and power *are* 'appropriate' to its irrational faculties, appetite and competition, and these facts of human nature explain people's 'proneness to sickness' (**S I**), when they mistake what is naturally desirable to the soul's 'brutish' part as desirable without qualification (**N**). By thus internalizing the causes of the passions, Posidonius thought he had done more than Chrysippus to explain their origin and cure (cf. **M 3, P, Q**). Even so, it is not an obvious truth that a life devoted to philosophy is any more rational than one committed to wine-tasting or political ambition. As moral therapy, Posidonius' doctrines have some interest, but they do far less than Chrysippus' to promote understanding of what passion is and its relation to reason.

In Chrysippus' use of the analogy with bodily health (**R I**), the unpredictability of the passions and slightness of their external causes are emphasized. Posidonius, in line with his conception of internal disorder, preferred to stress the dispositional tendencies, 'proneness to sickness' (**R 5**), a doctrine which has left its mark in the terminology of **S**.

66 Ethics in action

A Plutarch, *On Stoic self-contradictions* 1041F (*SVF* 3.545)

In his *On Justice* book 3 he [Chrysippus] said: 'For this reason then, owing to the extreme magnitude and beauty [of justice], we seem to be talking fiction and not on the level of man and human nature.'

B Plutarch, *On Stoic self-contradictions* 1034B (*SVF* 3.698)

Chrysippus, again, by writing in his *On rhetoric* that the wise man will make public speeches and engage in politics as if he regarded wealth and reputation and health as good, agrees that the Stoics' theories are not for public consumption and of no social relevance.

C Seneca, *Letters* 116.5 (Panaetius fr. 114, part)

I think Panaetius gave a charming answer to the youth who asked whether the wise man would fall in love: 'As to the wise man, we shall see. What concerns you and me, who are still a great distance from the wise man, is to ensure that we do not fall into a state of affairs which is disturbed, powerless, subservient to another and worthless to oneself.'

D Cicero, *On duties* 1.46

[Probably drawing on Panaetius] Since life is passed not in the company of men who are perfect and truly wise, but those who do very well if they show likenesses of virtue, I think it must be understood that no one should be entirely neglected in whom any mark of virtue is evident.

E Cicero, *On duties* 1.107, 110–11, 114–17 (including Panaetius fr. 97)

(1) It should also be understood that nature has endowed us with two roles, as it were. One of these is universal, from the fact that we all share in reason and that status which raises us above the beasts; this is the source of all rectitude and propriety, and the basis of the rational discovery of our proper functions. (2) The second role is the one which has been specifically assigned to individuals. Just as there are great bodily differences between people . . . so too there are still greater mental divergences . . . (3) To secure that propriety more easily which we are seeking, each person should firmly hold on to those characteristics of his which are not vicious but peculiar to himself. For we must so act that we do nothing in opposition to human nature in general, and yet, while keeping that secure, follow our own nature. Thus, even if a different course would be more dignified and superior, we should still regulate our own pursuits by the rule of our own nature. For it is pointless to resist one's own nature and to pursue something which one cannot attain . . . (4) The whole essence of propriety is quite certainly consistency, both in life as a whole and in individual actions, and you cannot secure this if you imitate other people's nature and overlook your own . . . (5) Each person therefore should get to know his own temperament and show himself an acute judge of his own merits and weaknesses . . . (6) We shall work most effectively, then, at those things to which we are best suited. But if we are sometimes shoved by circumstances into roles which are not germane to our temperament, we should give all our thought, effort and attention to performing them, if not with propriety, at least with as little impropriety as possible . . . (7) To the above-mentioned two roles, a third is appended, which some chance or circumstance imposes: and a fourth as well, which we take upon ourselves by our own decision. Headships of state, military commands, noble birth, public office, wealth, resources and their opposites depend on chance and are ruled by circumstances. But what role we ourselves are willing to take on depends on our own free choice. Hence some take up philosophy, others civil law, others oratory, and people differ as to which virtues they prefer to excel in . . . (8) Above all we must decide who and what sort of people we want to be, and what kind of life we want to lead; and this is the most difficult question of all.

F Epictetus, *Discourses* 4.12.15–19

(1) First then, we must keep these principles ready to hand and do nothing apart from them but have our soul intent on this target: pursuing none of the externals, none of the things which are not ours, but as the almighty has determined – pursuing what we should choose to the utmost, and taking the rest in whatever way they are given to us. (2) Next we must remember who we are and what is our title, and try to regulate our proper functions to suit the possibilities of our social relationships: what is the right time for singing, for playing, and in whose presence; what will be out of place . . . ; when to poke fun and who to laugh at; under what conditions and with whom to keep company; and finally how to preserve one's own self in company . . . (3) Very well, is it possible to remain quite faultless? That is beyond our power, but it is possible to be continually intent on not doing wrong. We must be content if we avoid at least a few faults by never relaxing this attention.

G Cicero, *On ends* 3.60–1 (*SVF* 3.763)

[Speaker: the Stoic Cato] (1) When a man has a preponderance of the things in accordance with nature, it is his proper function to remain alive; when he has or foresees a preponderance of their opposites, it is his proper function to depart from life. (2) This clearly shows that it is sometimes a proper function both for the wise man to depart from life, although he is happy, and for a fool to remain alive, although he is wretched. (3) For the real good and bad, as has been frequently said already [see **59D 6**], arise later. But the primary natural things, whether favourable or adverse, fall under the wise man's decision and choice, forming as it were the material of wisdom. (4) Therefore, the reason for remaining in and departing from life is to be measured by those things. For it is not virtue which retains < the wise man > in life, nor are those without virtue obliged to seek death. (5) And it is sometimes a wise man's proper function to abandon life even though he is supremely happy if he can do so at the right time . . . (6) Since, then, vices do not have the power of providing a reason for suicide, even fools, who are wretched, plainly have the proper function of remaining alive if they have a preponderance of the things we call in accordance with nature.

H Diogenes Laertius 7.130 (*SVF* 3.757)

They [the Stoics] say that the wise man will commit a well-reasoned suicide both on behalf of his country and on behalf of his friends, and if he falls victim to unduly severe pain or mutilation or incurable illness.

Stoic ethics

I Seneca, *Letters* 94.2, 31, 50–1

(1) The Stoic Aristo regards this part [i.e. the part of philosophy which gives specific precepts to each person] as trivial . . . what is most effective, he says, are the actual doctrines of philosophy and the constitution of the highest good: 'One who has understood and learned this well prescribes to himself what he should do in every matter' . . . 'If someone does not have the right doctrines,' he says, 'how will injunctions help him when he is chained down by vicious ones?' (2) By liberating him from them, of course; for his natural character has not lost its spark irrevocably, but is concealed and weighed down. Thus it also attempts to revive and struggle against corruption, but having got assistance and been helped by precepts it regains strength, provided that it has not been infected and destroyed by persistent disease. For the latter will not be made good even by philosophical training which exerts itself to the utmost. What is the difference between the doctrines of philosophy and precepts other than the fact that the former are general precepts, the latter specific? Each of them prescribes things – the former quite generally, the latter in particular . . . (3) Weaker characters need someone to lead the way: 'This you will avoid, this you will do.' If, moreover, someone waits for the time when he will know through himself what it is best to do, he will go astray in the interim and thus be prevented from reaching the point when he can be content with himself; therefore, he needs to be ruled while he is beginning to be able to rule himself.

J Seneca, *Letters* 95.10–12, 61, 63–4

(1) Philosophy is both theoretical and practical; it observes and acts at the same time . . . Consequently, since it is theoretical, it has its own doctrines. Note that no one also will properly perform what he should do unless he has acquired the system of being able to execute all the measures of proper functions in every matter. These will not be secured by someone who has received precepts for the matter in hand but not for everything . . . It is doctrines which fortify, which protect our safety and tranquillity, which embrace the whole of life and, at the same time, the whole nature of things. The difference between the doctrines of philosophy and its precepts is the same as the difference between elements and limbs; limbs depend on elements, whereas elements exist for their sake and for everything . . . (2) In philosophy certain things need an injunction, and certain others need proof . . . If proofs <are necessary>, so too are the doctrines which give reasoned arguments for the truth . . . Finally, when we advise someone to treat a friend just like himself, or to think that an enemy can become a friend, or to stimulate this man's affection and to moderate that man's hatred, we add the words, 'it is just and honourable'. But what is just and honourable is comprised by the system of our

doctrines. This system, therefore, is the necessary condition of those precepts. But let us unite precepts and doctrines. Without a root, in fact, branches are useless, and the roots themselves are aided by what they generate.

☐ With this section we reach the last acknowledged topic of Stoic ethics, 'encouragements and discouragements' (**56A**), and related material. The division of all mankind into two absolute categories, the wise and the foolish, or the virtuous and the inferior (**61I, N, T; 67M, P**), combined with the extreme rarity of the former category throughout history, exposed the Stoics to the charge of being completely unpractical in their ethics. Given their conditions for wisdom or virtue – infallibility, absolute consistency, rational perfection, doing everything well – the Stoics could not dismiss the charge as a misrepresentation (cf. **A**). They did, however, admit the possibility of becoming good (**54H 4; 61K**), the natural tendencies to virtue of all people (**61L**), and the existence of 'a likeness of what is right' in bad men (**60E 5**). Their favoured term for the immoral majority was *phauloi*, which means inferior or ordinary, rather than vicious or wicked. And this category includes 'progressives', people who, though still absolutely distinct from the wise, are making progress towards this end (**59I, 61T**).

Starting with Chrysippus himself, we can observe an increasing readiness to acknowledge the idealization of their ethical standard (**A**), and to admit the qualified propriety of a more extended use of 'good' and 'bad' than Zeno, or certainly Aristo, would have accepted (**B**; cf. **58H**). The accommodation of the ethical system to something like moral education for a general audience was the special concern of Panaetius. In his books *On proper function*, the basis of Cicero *On duties*, he insisted that the philosophy's emphasis on wisdom and moral perfection did not preclude its relevance and adaptation as a guide to the training of anyone 'in whom any mark of virtue is evident' (**D**, cf. **C**). His interest in educating 'progressives', if a different emphasis from his predecessors' focus on the wise man (**C**), did not involve any alteration of the basic moral theory. That much is clear from Cicero: although the 'proper functions' Panaetius discussed were *derived* from analysis of the virtues (**59P**), it was entirely orthodox to regard them as performable by the inferior as well as the strictly virtuous. But Panaetius probably gave Stoicism a more humane tone than it had known before. Such sensitivity to human fallibility, prompted perhaps by the success Stoicism was now enjoying in its diffusion beyond the Greek world, is a notable feature of Stoics writing under the Roman Empire (cf. **C, F 3**).

Earlier Stoics, like other Greek philosophers, had been interested in analysing different lifestyles and careers (cf. **67X, Y**). That interest may have helped to stimulate Panaetius' almost certainly original doctrine that proper functions are specifiable by reference to 'four roles' which each person has (**E**). The word translated 'role' is *persona* (the Latin for an actor's mask), and Panaetius' theory intriguingly anticipates modern conceptions of personality and role play. Roles one and two (**E 1–6**) refer respectively to the shared rationality of all human beings ('universal nature') and the physical, mental and temperamental nature of the individual. In proposing the latter, in agreement with the former, as a guideline of how persons should act and shape their lives, Panaetius gave Stoicism an insight that has some resemblance to the Aristotelian 'mean that is relative to us': Aristotle had stipulated personal idiosyncrasies as factors each person should consider in developing a moral disposition that avoids excess or deficiency in feelings and actions (*Nicomachean ethics* 2.9). But Panaetius' insistence on the moral relevance of 'personality' is an idea without clear parallel in ancient ethics. Equally impressive is the clarity with which he distinguishes the entirely accidental determinants of personal identity (role three) from the career and specializations people choose for themselves (role four, **E 7**). Collectively the four roles offer an account of the general considerations people should review in deciding on their proper functions – what I ought to do as a member of the human race, as the person with my natural strengths and weaknesses, as unavoidably involved in these external circumstances, and with the lifestyle and bent I have chosen for myself.

As presented by Cicero, Panaetius' doctrine is too bland in its assumptions that people can distribute their moral identity so neatly, and that what is done under the guidance of roles two to four (think of an Islamic fundamentalist) will conform to supposedly universal moral norms (role one). But personal responsibility is stressed (**E 8**), and all the more acutely in the absence of any underpinning by 'the wise man' or fate. The 'universal nature' of Panaetius' first role is that of man in general, not the cosmic nature whose normative force for man is stressed in early Stoic accounts of the 'end' (see **63**). What little we know of Panaetius' physics (cf. **46P**) suggests a reticence on the cosmo-biology or pantheism of his predecessors, and reinforces the impression of his interest in the widespread *practice* of Stoic ethics. The same, with some qualifications, is true of Epictetus. His analysis of proper functions by reference to 'titles' (**F 2**; cf. **59Q**) makes use of a functionalism – what is my job under this description? – very similar to Panaetius' delineation of roles. More distinctive of Epictetus' concern with ethics in action is his prescription to cultivate moral purpose, 'what is ours', to the exclusion of all concern with the active pursuit of externals, 'which are not ours' (**F 1**).

Even the wise man, however, needs the wherewithal to live. Faced with a preponderance of *CN* things (see **58**) – chronic ill-health, persistent pain, poverty, loss of family and friends – he cannot live in accordance with the nature of man in general; he also lacks the material conditions necessary to virtuous action, which requires him to select things in accordance with nature and reject their opposites (cf. **59A**; **64A**). In such adverse circumstances, it was argued, suicide becomes the wise man's proper function (**G**). This thesis underlines once again the Stoics' precarious position between Aristo's complete indifference to all non-moral values and the Aristotelian stipulation that the external goods virtue needs for its exercise are constituents of happiness (cf. **64L**; also **58F–I**). For Chrysippus and his successors, any allocation of *AN* and *CN* things is indifferent with respect to happiness, and yet sufficiently powerful to provide reasons for living or ceasing to live (**G 4–6**; cf. **61Q**).

The rationality of suicide 'at the right time' was a notorious Stoic doctrine (contrast the Epicurean wise man, **22Q 5**; **24A 6–8**), and liable, like early

Christian martyrdom, to be misused as the test of ultimate commitment to the creed. Biographical fabrication may account for the reputed suicides of Zeno, Cleanthes and Antipater. But under the Roman Empire especially, a number of prominent Romans who were Stoics and opposed to the regime ended their lives in this way (cf. **H** for the rationality of patriotic suicide). Though not wise men in the technical sense, they exemplify the 'power of autonomous action' (= freedom, **67M** 1) of which suicide, appropriately chosen, was the school's most potent expression.

Is the position adopted on suicide a doctrine or a precept? The point of this question brings us to **I** and **J**, where these terms are clarified. A precept is a specific recommendation to an individual or type of individual to do this or avoid that (**I** 2–3). Doctrines are generic, or 'elements' of the system, which justify precepts by giving the reasons for their suitability. The precept, 'do all you can to moderate X's hatred', is grounded in the doctrine that such a course of action is what the nature of justice requires (**J** 2). Aristo argued that the whole topic of 'encouragements and discouragements' (**56A**) was pointless, in keeping with his focus upon the wise man's ability, without any external guidelines, to adapt appropriately to all circumstances (**I** 1, cf. **58G**). In **I** 2–3 Seneca defends the educational value of precepts against Aristo. Later (**J** 1) he stresses their limitations, and the indispensability of the right doctrines (cf. **61P**). Finally (**J** 2) he recommends their joint utility.

Space prevents us from excerpting more material from these interesting *Letters*. They indicate the Stoics' recognition of a standing problem for moral rules. The more theoretically a rule is formulated, the less it offers as a directly practical prescription. Highly specific precepts, on the other hand, may do nothing to show why they should be complied with, and, if generalized, they may be too sweeping to fit particular cases. Underlying Seneca's discussions is the concept of proper functions (**J** 1; cf. **59**). In their perfect form, as a wise man's right actions, these issue from his knowledge of doctrines and his correct assessment of his circumstances. As the actions of ordinary people, they may comply with a precept, but fall short in their agent's lack of consistency and understanding of their rationale. Progressives can be viewed as people who regularly follow rationally based precepts, and are beginning to understand the doctrines which underlie them.

67 Political theory

A Plutarch, *On the fortune of Alexander* 329A–B (*SVF* 1.262, part)

(1) The much admired *Republic* of Zeno . . . is aimed at this one main point, that our household arrangements should not be based on cities or parishes, each one marked out by its own legal system, but we should regard all men as our fellow-citizens and local residents, and there should be one way of life and order, like that of a herd grazing together and nurtured by a common law. (2) Zeno wrote this, picturing as it were a dream or image of a philosopher's well-regulated society.

B Diogenes Laertius 7.32–3

(1) Some people, including the circle of Cassius the Sceptic, criticize Zeno extensively: (2) first, for declaring at the beginning of his *Republic* that the educational curriculum is useless; (3) and secondly, for his statement that all who are not virtuous are foes, enemies, slaves and estranged from one another, including parents and children, brothers and brothers, relations and relations. (4) They criticize him again for presenting only virtuous people in the *Republic* as citizens, friends, relations and free . . . and for his doctrine set out there concerning community of wives, and his prohibition at line 200 against the building of temples, lawcourts and gymnasia in cities. (5) They also take exception to his statement on currency: 'The provision of currency should not be thought necessary either for exchange or for travel', and for his instruction that men and women should wear the same clothes and keep no part of the body completely covered.

C Plutarch, *On Stoic self-contradictions* 1034B (*SVF* 1.264, part)

It is a doctrine of Zeno's not to build temples of the gods; for a temple not worth much is also not sacred, and nothing made by builders or workmen is worth much.

D Athenaeus 561C (*SVF* 1.263, part)

Pontianus said that Zeno of Citium regarded Eros as god of friendship and freedom, and the provider in addition of concord, but of nothing else. Hence in the *Republic* Zeno said: 'Eros is a god which contributes to the city's security.'

E Clement, *Miscellanies* 5.9.58.2 (*SVF* 1.43)

The Stoics say that the first Zeno wrote certain things which they are reluctant to give to their pupils to read unless they have first proved themselves to be genuine philosophers.

F Plutarch, *On Stoic self-contradictions* 1044F–1045A (*SVF* 3.753, part)

In one of his books of *Exhortations*, he [Chrysippus] says that sexual intercourse with mothers or daughters or sisters, eating certain food, and proceeding straight from childbed or deathbed to a temple have been discredited without reason. He also says that we should look to the beasts and infer from their behaviour that nothing of this kind is out of place or unnatural.

G Sextus Empiricus, *Outlines of Pyrrhonism* 3.247–8

[Chrysippus from his *Republic*:] (1) 'If from the living person a part should be cut off which is edible, we should not bury it or dispose of it in some other way, but consume it, so that from our parts a new one may be generated.' (2) In his books *On proper function*, he says explicitly concerning the burial of parents: 'When parents die, we should use the simplest methods of burial, as though the body, like the nails or teeth or hair, were nothing to us, and we need give no care or attention to anything like that. So too, if the flesh is edible, people should use it, as they should use one of their own parts such as a severed foot and the like.'

H Plutarch, *On exile* 600E (*SVF* 1.371, part)

By nature, as Aristo said, there is no native land, just as there is no house or cultivated field, smithy or doctor's surgery; each one of these comes to be so, or rather is so named and called, always in relation to the occupant and user.

I Stobaeus 2.103,14–17 (*SVF* 1.587, part)

[Cleanthes:] 'If a city is a habitable structure, in which people who take refuge have access to the dispensation of justice, a city is surely something civilized; but a city is this sort of habitation; therefore a city is something civilized.'

J Dio Chrysostom 36.20 (*SVF* 3.329)

They [the Stoics] say that a city is a group of people living in the same place and administered by law.

K Seneca, *On leisure* 4.1

Let us take hold of the fact that there are two communities – the one, which is great and truly common, embracing gods and men, in which we look neither to this corner nor to that, but measure the boundaries of our state by the sun; the other, the one to which we have been assigned by the accident of our birth.

L Arius Didymus (Eusebius, *Evangelical preparation* 15.15.3–5; *SVF* 2.528, part)

(1) The world is also called the habitation of gods and men, < and the structure consisting of gods and men, > and the things created for their sake. (2) For just as there are two meanings of city, one as habitation and two as the structure of its inhabitants along with its citizens, so the world is like a city consisting of gods and men, with the gods serving as rulers and men as their subjects. (3) They are members of a community because of their participation in reason, which is natural law; and everything else is created for their sake.

M Diogenes Laertius 7.121–2

[The Stoics say:] (1) Only he [the wise man] is free, but the inferior are slaves. For freedom is the power of autonomous action, but slavery is the lack of autonomous action. There is also a different slavery which consists in subordination, and a third consisting in possession as well as subordination; this last is contrasted with despotism, which is also a morally inferior state. (2) Besides being free the wise are also kings, since kingship is rule that is answerable to no one; and this can occur only among the wise, as Chrysippus says in his work *On Zeno's proper use of terminology.* For he says that a ruler must have knowledge of what is good and bad, and that no inferior man has this. (3) Likewise only the wise are holders of public offices, judges and orators, whereas no inferior man is.

N Philo, *On every virtuous man's being free* 97 (*SVF* 1.218)

Surely it is worth mentioning Zeno's statement that: 'Someone could sooner immerse a bladder filled with air than compel any virtuous man against his will to do anything he does not want.' For the soul which right reason has braced with firm doctrines is unyielding and invincible.

O Plutarch, *On listening to poetry* 33D (*SVF* 1.219)

Zeno corrected Sophocles' passage: 'Whoever does business with a tyrant is the latter's slave, even if he goes as a free man', rewriting it as, 'is not a slave, if he goes as a free man'.

P Diogenes Laertius 7.124 (*SVF* 3.631)

They [the Stoics] say that friendship exists only among the virtuous, on account of their similarity. They describe friendship as a certain sharing of life's wherewithal, since we treat our friends as we treat ourselves. They declare too that a friend is choiceworthy for his own sake and that it is good to have a number of friends. But no friendship exists among the inferior, and no inferior man has a friend.

Q Athenaeus 267B (*SVF* 3.353)

Writing in his *On concord* book 2, Chrysippus says that there is a difference between a slave and a servant: freedmen are still slaves, but those who have not been released from ownership are servants. 'A servant', he says, 'is a slave designated by ownership.'

R Marcian 1 (*SVF* 3.314)

[The opening of Chrysippus, *On law*] 'Law is king of all things human and divine. Law must preside over what is honourable and base, as ruler and as guide, and thus be the standard of right and wrong, prescribing to animals whose nature is political what they should do, and prohibiting them from what they should not do.'

S Cicero, *Republic* 3.33 (*SVF* 3.325)

[Speaker: the Stoic Laelius] (1) True law is right reason, in agreement with nature, diffused over everyone, consistent, everlasting, whose nature is to advocate duty by prescription and to deter wrongdoing by prohibition. (2) Its prescriptions and prohibitions are heeded by good men though they have no effect on the bad. (3) It is wrong to alter this law, nor is it permissible to repeal any part of it, and it is impossible to abolish it entirely. We cannot be absolved from this law by senate or people, nor need we look for any outside interpreter of it, or commentator. (4) There will not be a different law at Rome and at Athens, or a different law now and in the future, but one law, everlasting and immutable, will hold good for all peoples and at all times. (5) And there will be one master and ruler for us all in common, god who is the founder of this law, its promulgator and its judge. (6) Whoever does not obey it is fleeing from himself and treating his human nature with contempt; by this very fact he will pay the heaviest penalties, even if he escapes all conventional punishments.

T Cicero, *Republic* 1.34 (Panaetius fr. 119)

I [Laelius] remembered that you [Scipio] were in the habit of discussing politics very frequently with Panaetius when Polybius was present, the two Greeks perhaps most accomplished in the subject, and that you produced many arguments to show that by far the best form of government is the one bequeathed by our ancestors.

U Diogenes Laertius 7.131 (*SVF* 3.700)

They [the Stoics] say that the best constitution is a combination of democracy, kingship and aristocracy.

V Cicero, *On duties* 2.73 (Panaetius fr. 118)

Communities and governments were founded above all for the preservation of private property. For although men banded together under nature's guidance, it was in the hope of safeguarding their possessions that they sought the protection of cities.

W Stobaeus 2.109,10–110,4 (*SVF* 3.686, part)

(1) They [the Stoics] say that there are three preferable lives, the kingly, the political and thirdly, the scholarly. (2) Likewise there are three preferable ways of earning money, first from a kingdom either by being king oneself or being provided for from the king's property. (3) Secondly, from the community, since the wise man will take part in politics on the basis of the preferential reason; and he will marry and produce children, since these are in accordance with the <nature> of an animal which is rational, sociable and gregarious. He will make his income from those of his friends who occupy prominent positions as well as from the community. (4) As to practising as a sophist [i.e. giving public lectures] and earning one's living thereby, the members of the school had

a semantic disagreement. They agreed that they would earn a living from education and that they would sometimes take fees from those wanting to learn. But they had a disagreement over the meaning of the term, some taking 'practice as a sophist' to mean giving access to philosophical doctrines for a fee, while others sensed something pejorative in the term, like trading in arguments.

X Plutarch, *On Stoic self-contradictions* 1033C–D (*SVF* 3.702)

[Chrysippus from his *On lives* book 4:] 'All who suppose that philosophers should particularly follow the scholarly life seem to me to be initially mistaken in presuming that one should do this for the sake of some pastime or something else similar, and protract one's entire life in this sort of way which, if clearly studied, means "pleasurably". We should not mistake their meaning, since many say this openly, and a good number more obscurely.'

Y Seneca, *Letters* 90.5–7 (Posidonius fr. 284, part)

(1) In that age which is called golden, Posidonius maintains that rule was in the hands of the wise. They restrained aggression, protected the weaker from the stronger, advised and dissuaded, and indicated what was advantageous and what was not. Their prudence saw to it that their people lacked for nothing, their courage averted dangers, and their generosity enabled their subjects to progress and flourish . . . (2) But with the subsequent infiltration of vices and the alteration of kingdoms into tyrannies, the need for laws arose, which were themselves, to begin with, introduced by the wise . . . (3) Up to this point I agree with Posidonius; but that philosophy invented the techniques which daily life uses, I refuse to allow, nor will I claim technology's fame for philosophy. He says: 'Philosophy taught men how to construct buildings at a time when they were scattered and living in huts or caves or hollowed-out tree trunks.'

☐ Although only Cleanthes is known to have made politics a distinct part of philosophy (**26B 4**), Stoic interest in the subject was by no means fleeting. Zeno's *Republic* (**A–E**) was much the most renowned book written by any Stoic, and Chrysippus also composed a work with the same title (cf. **G 1**). The absence of political theory from the latter's canonical division of ethical topics (**56A**) probably indicates that he perceived it as a dimension of ethics in general, and indeed of the whole system. In Stoicism the world-order itself was regularly represented as a 'political' structure (cf. **K, M; 46G 3; 57F 3**) whose divine administration and natural laws are the grounds of moral values and the basis of a human life in agreement with nature (cf. **59Q 3; 63C 3–4**).

The integration in ethics of much that could be called political is evident from our earlier sections (see especially **57F–H; 59B 4, E 2, L 2**). Here we have assembled material that shows the Stoics' more specialized contributions.

Pride of place must be given to Zeno's *Republic*. The little that survives from this fascinating work is enough to show how and why he rapidly established credentials as a prominent critic and would-be reformer of contemporary values and institutions. His wholesale rejection of the educational curriculum, public buildings including temples, and currency, and his recommendations concerning community of wives and unisex clothing (**B, C**), embarrassed later Stoics (cf. **E**) when the school had acquired bourgeois respectability; and he probably included the still more shocking justifications of incest and cannibalism attributed to Chrysippus' *Republic* (**F, G**). In assessing the overall purpose of Zeno's work (probably a single papyrus roll, cf. the reference to line 200 at **B 4**), the following points, in addition to those mentioned, should be noted: 'one way of life and order' as the system of economy and law, in contrast with local and civic demarcations (**A**); virtue, not kinship or any other bond, as the criterion of friendship, and also as the criterion of freedom (**B 3–4**; cf. **M, P**); restriction of citizenship to the virtuous, who appear to have included women, contrary to normal Greek practice (**B 4–5**); sublimation of the sex drive into a source of friendship, freedom and social solidarity (**D**).

Radical though these views will have seemed to Zeno's contemporaries, he was indebted for many of them, if not for their detailed organization, to the Cynics. As noted in our Introduction (p. 3), the Cynic Crates gave Zeno his first training in philosophy, and the *Republic* probably reflects Crates' influence. This in turn will have been inspired by the Cynic Diogenes, reputedly the author of a *Republic*, and certainly a fierce critic of Plato. That Zeno continued this tradition is clear both from Plutarch (**31L 5**) and from some of the points outlined above. Unlike the Platonic *Republic*, with its three classes, Zeno's state was completely uniform (**A 1**) with no minority ruling class. Its economic and social prescriptions, and its exclusively moral interpretation of enmity, freedom etc., must have implied that Plato's ideal state failed to incorporate some features necessary to 'a philosopher's well-regulated society' (**A 2**). On the other hand, Zeno's ideas on sexual arrangements, control by the wise, and sublimated Eros have a strong affinity to Plato. It is best to regard Zeno's *Republic* not as narrowly anti-Platonic, but as a programmatic essay setting out his view of the extreme discrepancy between existing societies as they are and society as it ought to be. Study of his proposals will show that they are systematically calculated to exclude everything divisive or inessential to moral excellence, and to prescribe a completely unitary social order.

Was Zeno's vision internationalist? It used to be thought so, on the strength of the Stoics' penchant for the expression 'citizen of the world' (**59Q 3**) and from the general import of **A**. But Zeno's *Republic* itself hardly envisaged a world state. **A** is Plutarch's reading of Zeno as a theoretical exponent of the unification which Alexander the Great 'realized in practice' by empire-building, and 'citizen of the world' has less to do with the United Nations than with the rationality all humans share with their divine ruler (cf. the probably Stoic-influenced **L**). What the Stoics did undoubtedly promote was a very powerful conception of law as the basis of civic life (cf. **A, I, J, R**). Their main contribution to internationalism was their treatment of moral principles as laws of human nature, transcending all accidents of birth and local identities (cf. **H, S**).

When Stoicism infiltrated the Roman Empire, these ideas found an environment larger than any that Zeno can have foreseen. His interest in removing all boundaries between people is particularly well exemplified several centuries later in Hierocles' elaborate proposals (**57G**). For the presence of related ideas in Epicureanism under the Roman Empire, cf. **22P, S**.

As we have noted, Chrysippus followed Zeno in endorsing Cynic attacks on the irrationality of some social conventions; and he too criticized some features of Plato's *Republic* in his work *On justice* (*SVF* 3.313). But his apparent support for incest and cannibalism (**F, G**) was scarcely a recommendation to universalize these practices. We can take the propriety of eating one's dead parents to be a 'proper function' (note the book title of **G 2**) like mutilating oneself, which depends on circumstances (**59E 3**). Chrysippus accepted the naturalness of many standard practices and evaluations (see **58–9**), but always with the proviso that reason must have complete autonomy over the action appropriate to the particulars of each situation (cf. **58J**). His appeal to animal behaviour as a criterion of naturalness (**F**), though a Cynic strategy, invited the objection that men, as the Stoics constantly emphasized, are unique among animals in their rationality. But Chrysippus could reply that his critics must accept, as the Stoics did, a considerable number of characteristics shared by both kinds of animal (cf. **36E**; **57A**; **63D 1, E 1**). The question he raises is the rationality of deeming behaviour like incest and cannibalism to be natural to beasts but not to humans.

Although Chrysippus' challenging approach to social thought is evident, he also prepared the way for the much more conservative political theory of Panaetius, which strongly appealed to Cicero (cf. **T–V; 57F 5–8**). Nothing better exemplifies Zeno's radicalism than his claim that conventional conceptions of freedom (**M 1, O**), kingship and political office (**M 2**), friendship etc. (**B 3, P**) are completely misguided: these terms, he argued, apply only to the virtuous and wise, and therefore, ordinary language is quite incorrect. Chrysippus defended Zeno's reforms, endorsing his conception of wisdom as the only ground for freedom and authority (**M 2**), but he (or his followers) allowed the existence of different kinds of slavery (**M 1**; cf. **Q**), which include slavery in its conventional sense. Such concessions to ordinary language (cf. **58H; 66B**) lost Stoicism some of its cutting edge, but facilitated its later employment as an authoritative framework for general moral education (cf. **66C–F**). Adaptability to political realities was, in any case, an almost inevitable outcome for Stoicism. It was encouraged by the diffusion of Hellenistic culture, and theoretically justified by the divine providence of all that happens, the indifference of all non-moral values, and the emphasis on man's political nature (**R**; cf. **57D 2, F; 63K**).

As the 'practice of expertise in utility' (**26A**), philosophy demands a useful life of its practitioner. Chrysippus' warning against restricting philosophers to professors (**X**) implies that what makes a philosopher is not devotion to asceticism or scholarship but a life consistently shaped by the right doctrines (cf. **31J, O, T**). In contrast with the Epicureans (cf. **22Q 5–6**), a Stoic wise man will prefer a career that involves him in public life (**W**). Here again we see a tendency to bring Zeno's ethics into line with the practicalities of life. If Zeno's *Republic* was a blueprint for man's ideal future, Posidonius contrasted modern corruption with a past Golden Age ruled by the wise (**Y 1–2**). His claiming philosophy responsible for technological progress as well as for enlightened rule (cf. the Epicurean culture heroes, **22L 1, M, N**) is a bizarre application of the wise man's omnicompetence.

The Academics

68 Methodology

A Cicero, *Academica* 1.43–6

(1) Then Varro said: 'It is now up to you, as one who deviates from the philosophy of the ancients and approves the innovations of Arcesilaus, to explain what the schism was and why it took place, so that we can see whether your desertion is adequately justified.' (2) I [Cicero] then said: 'It was with Zeno, so we have heard, that Arcesilaus began his entire struggle, not out of obstinacy or desire for victory – in my opinion at least – but because of the obscurity of the things which had brought Socrates to an admission of ignorance; and before him already, Democritus, Anaxagoras, Empedocles, and almost all the ancients, who said that nothing could be grasped or cognized or known, saying that the senses are restricted, the mind weak, the course of life short, and that (to quote Democritus) truth has been submerged in an abyss, with everything in the grip of opinions and conventions, nothing left for truth and everything in turn wrapped in darkness. (3) So Arcesilaus was in the practice of denying that anything could be known, not even the one thing Socrates had left for himself – the knowledge that he knew nothing: such was the extent of the obscurity in which everything lurked, on his assessment, and there was nothing which could be discerned or understood. (4) For these reasons, he said, no one should maintain or assert anything or give it the acceptance of assent, but he should always curb his rashness and restrain it from every slip; for it would be extraordinary rashness to accept something either false or incognitive, and nothing was more dishonourable than for assent and acceptance to run ahead of cognition and grasp. (5) He used to act consistently with this philosophy, and by arguing against everyone's opinions he drew most people away from their own, so that when reasons of equal weight were found on opposite sides on the same subject, the easier course was to withhold assent from either side. (6) They call this Academy new, though I think it is old if we count Plato as one of the old Academy. In his books nothing is asserted and there is much argument pro and contra, everything is investigated and nothing is stated as certain. But, none the

less, let the one you [Varro] expounded be called the Old, and this one the New: it stuck firmly to Arcesilaus' philosophy right down to Carneades, who was its fourth head after Arcesilaus.

B Cicero, *Academica* 1.13

Varro: 'I hear that you have abandoned the Old Academy and are treating with the New.' *Cicero:* 'What of it? . . . Will our friend Antiochus have more freedom to shift from a new home to an old than we have to go from an old into a new? The latest things are all, to be sure, the most correct and improved; although Philo (the teacher of Antiochus and a great man as you yourself consider him) says in his books – and we used to hear this from him in person as well – that there are not two Academies, and he demonstrates the mistake of those who thought so.' *Varro:* 'Quite so; but I think you are not unfamiliar with what Antiochus wrote against Philo's statements.'

C Cicero, *Academica* 2.16

[Speaker: the Antiochean Lucullus] (1) Arcesilaus, so it is thought, criticized Zeno for discovering nothing new but merely correcting his predecessors by altering words; in wanting to undermine Zeno's definitions he tried to draw a veil of darkness over matters of the utmost clarity. (2) His philosophy was not much accepted at first, although he excelled both in sharpness of intellect and a certain admirable charm of discourse. Lacydes alone was the next to keep it going, but subsequently it was perfected by Carneades.

D Diogenes Laertius 4.28

He [Arcesilaus] was the originator of the Middle Academy, being the first to suspend his assertions owing to the contrarieties of arguments. He was also the first to argue pro and contra, and the first to change traditional Platonic discourse and, by question and answer, to make it more of a debating contest.

E Diogenes Laertius 4.32–3

(1) When Crates died, Arcesilaus took charge of the Academy, a man called Socratides having given way to him. Some say he did not write a single book because of suspending judgement about everything. Others maintain that he was caught out revising some books, which he published, according to one view, but which others say that he burnt. He certainly seems to have admired Plato, and he had acquired his books. (2) Some say that he emulated Pyrrho as well. He was very keen on dialectic, and made use of the arguments of the Eretrians. For this reason Aristo gave this description of him: 'Plato in front, Pyrrho behind, Diodorus in

the middle'. And Timon refers to him thus: 'Having Menedemus as lead in his heart, he will hurry either to the all-flesh Pyrrho or to Diodorus.' And after an interlude Timon makes him say: 'I will swim to Pyrrho and to crooked Diodorus.'

F Numenius (Eusebius, *Evangelical preparation* 14.6.4–6)

(1) On the strength of this varied training [i.e. association with Theophrastus, Crantor, Diodorus and Pyrrho], Arcesilaus stayed faithful to Pyrrho, except for the name, by the denial of everything. At any rate Mnaseas, Philomelus and Timon, the Sceptics, call him a Sceptic, as they were themselves, since he too denied the true, the false and the convincing. (2) Though he might have been called a Pyrrhonist by reason of his Pyrrhonian features, he allowed himself to go on being called an Academic, out of respect for his lover [i.e. Crantor]. Hence in all but the name he was a Pyrrhonist; he was not an Academic, except for being so called. For I do not believe Dicaeocles of Cnidos in his books called *Diatribes*, where he claims that Arcesilaus for fear of Theodorus and his like and Bion the sophist, who launched attacks on philosophers and shrank from nothing to refute them by every means, protected himself against trouble by advancing no manifest doctrine but projected suspension of judgement in front of himself, like the ink of the cuttlefish. This I do not believe.

G Numenius (Eusebius, *Evangelical preparation* 14.6.12–13)

When Arcesilaus saw that Zeno was a professional rival and a challenger, he launched an all-out attack on the arguments that streamed from him . . . And observing the fame at Athens of that doctrine and its name, which Zeno first discovered – the cognitive impression – he used every resource against it.

H Plutarch, *Against Colotes* 1120C, 1121E–1122A

(1) Having done with the ancients, Colotes turns to his contemporary philosophers, without naming any of them . . . He intends, I suspect, to refute the Cyrenaics first, and secondly the Academy of Arcesilaus. These were the people who suspended judgement about everything . . . (2) Our Epicurean [i.e. Colotes] seems to have been unduly offended by the standing of Arcesilaus, who was more highly regarded at the time than any other philosopher. He says that Arcesilaus had nothing of his own to say but made uneducated people think and believe that he did . . . (3) Yet Arcesilaus was so far from loving any reputation for novelty or arrogating to himself anything belonging to the ancients, that the sophists of his time accused him of rubbing off his doctrines about suspension of judgement and non-cognition on Socrates, Plato, Parmenides and Heraclitus, who did not need them; whereas he

attributed them as it were, by way of confirmation, to famous men. On his behalf, then, we thank Colotes and everyone who asserts that the Academic system reached Arcesilaus from the past. [continued at **69A**]

I Sextus Empiricus, *Outlines of Pyrrhonism* 1.232–4

(1) Arcesilaus, the head and leader of the Middle Academy as we were saying, seems to me to have very much in common with the Pyrrhonian discourses, so that his school is practically the same as ours. (2) For he is not found asserting the existence or non-existence of anything, nor does he prefer one thing to another by way of credibility or incredibility, but suspends judgement about everything. (3) He also says that suspension of judgement is the [ethical] end, along with which we were saying that freedom from disturbance comes in. He also says that particular suspensions of judgement are good and particular assents bad. (4) Except for the point that *we* say all this on the basis of what appears to us, and not affirmatively, whereas he does so in reference to nature, and consequently says that suspension of judgement itself is good and assent bad. (5) And if one should also believe what is said about him, the story is that he gave the outward appearance of being a Pyrrhonist, but was in truth doctrinaire; and that since he used to test his associates by means of aporetic, to see if they were naturally suited to receive Platonic doctrines, he was thought to be aporetical, but that to those of his associates who were naturally suited he transmitted Plato's philosophy.

J Cicero, *On ends* 2.2

[Speaker: Cicero, advocating the Socratic method] By thorough inquiry and questioning, he [Socrates] was in the habit of drawing forth the opinions of those with whom he was arguing, in order to state his own view as a response to their answers. This practice was not kept up by his successors; but Arcesilaus revived it and prescribed that those who wanted to listen to him should not ask him questions but state their own opinions. When they had done so, he argued against them. But his listeners, so far as they could, would defend their own opinion.

K Cicero, *On ends* 5.10

[Speaker: the pro-Antiochean Piso] Aristotle introduced the practice of arguing pro and contra on particular subjects, not, like Arcesilaus, with the object of always arguing against everything, but in order that he might none the less set out all the possible arguments on either side in every subject.

L Cicero, *On the orator* 3.80

If there should ever be anyone who could argue pro and contra on all subjects, in the Aristotelian manner, and with knowledge of Aristotle's rules deliver two opposing speeches in every case, or should argue, in the manner of Arcesilaus and Carneades, against every thesis, anyone who combined that methodology and training with this rhetorical experience and practice of speaking [which I mentioned before] would be the true, the perfect, indeed the only orator.

M Lactantius, *Divine institutes* 5.14.3–5 and *Epitome* 50.8

When he [Carneades] was sent by Athens as an ambassador to Rome, he discoursed at length on justice in the hearing of Galba and Cato the Censor, the foremost orators of the time. On the next day he overturned his own discourse with a discourse on the opposite side, and subverted justice, which he had praised on the previous day, not with the seriousness of a philosopher, whose opinion should be firm and stable, but in the manner of a rhetorical exercise in which argument is given pro and contra . . . With the object of refuting Aristotle and Plato, supporters of justice, Carneades in his first discourse assembled all the arguments in favour of justice in order that he might overturn them, as he did . . . not because he thought justice ought to be disparaged, but to show that its defenders had no certain or firm arguments about it.

N Cicero, *Academica* 2.28–9

[Speaker: the Antiochean Lucullus] (1) When he [Antipater] used to say that it was consistent for someone who asserted that nothing was cognitive to say that this one thing, none the less, was cognitive, viz. that everything else was not, Carneades was sharper in his rejoinder: he used to say that so far from being consistent, it was actually the greatest of inconsistencies. For someone who said nothing was cognitive made no exception; necessarily, then, not even this statement, which had not been excepted, could be grasped and cognized in any way. (2) Antiochus seemed to get a tighter hold on this topic: he argued that since the Academics held it as a 'doctrine' (you notice this is now my term for the Greek word *dogma*) that nothing was cognitive, they should not waver in their own doctrine as they did in everything else, especially since it constituted their main point – for they took the settlement of true and false or cognitive and incognitive to be the yardstick belonging to philosophy as a whole; and that since this was the philosophy they engaged in, and wanted to show what impressions should be accepted and what rejected, they certainly ought to have cognized this very doctrine, which was the foundation of every judgement of truth and falsehood.

O Cicero, *Academica* 2.76–7

[Speaker: Cicero on behalf of the New Academy] Arcesilaus fought with Zeno not for the sake of criticizing him, but from a wish to discover the truth, as what follows makes plain: no one previously had clearly expounded, or even stated, the thesis that a human being can refrain from opining and that a wise man not only can but must do so. To Arcesilaus this idea seemed both true and honourable and worthy of a wise man. [continued at **40D**]

P Augustine, *Against the Academics* 2.11

It was the doctrine of the Academics that man cannot attain knowledge so far as those things are concerned which pertain to philosophy – for Carneades used to say he did not care about other things – and yet that man can be wise, and that a wise man's whole function . . . is exhibited in the quest for truth.

Q Cicero, *Academica* 2.60

[Speaker: the Antiochean Lucullus] Finally, there is their statement that it is obligatory to argue pro and contra everything for the sake of discovering the truth. I want, then, to see what they have discovered. 'It is not our practice', he [the sceptical Academic] says, 'to give revelations.' 'What are these holy secrets of yours then, or why do you conceal your own opinions as though they were something dishonourable?' 'In order', he says, 'that our listeners may be guided by reason rather than authority.'

R Cicero, *Academica* 2.32

[Speaker: the Antiochean Lucullus] (1) Nor in fact can I adequately decide what their [the Academics'] policy is or their intentions. For sometimes when we apply this kind of discourse to them, 'If your arguments are true, then everything will be non-evident', they answer: 'What, then, has that to do with us? It is not our fault, is it? Blame nature for having utterly buried truth in an abyss, as Democritus says.' (2) But others give a more subtle response, and even complain at our accusing them of saying that everything is non-evident; and they try to explain the extent of the difference between what is non-evident and what is not cognitive, and to distinguish between them. (3) Let us, therefore, deal with those who make this distinction, abandoning as hopeless the others who say that everything is as non-evident as whether the number of the stars is odd or even. For they want . . . there to be something convincing or resembling the truth, and to use it as a yardstick both in the conduct of life and in investigation and discussion.

S Cicero, *Academica* 2.7–8

[Speaker: Cicero on behalf of the New Academy] (1) Our arguments have no other objective than, by speaking pro and contra, to draw out and fashion something which is either true or comes as close to truth as possible. (2) Nor is there any difference between ourselves and those who think that they know something except that they have no doubt that their positions are true, whereas we hold many things to be convincing which we can easily follow but scarcely assert. In this respect, moreover, we are more free and unconstrained, because our power of judgement is unimpaired, and we are not compelled by any necessity to endorse all the rules and virtual commands of certain people.

T Sextus Empiricus, *Outlines of Pyrrhonism* 1.235

Philo says that, so far as the Stoic criterion is concerned (i.e. the cognitive impression), things are incognitive, but, so far as the nature of things themselves is concerned, cognitive. Moreover, Antiochus transplanted the Stoa into the Academy, so that it was even said of him that he practised Stoic philosophy within the Academy; for he used to show that the Stoics' doctrines are present in Plato.

U Cicero, *Academica* 2.17–18

[Speaker: the Antiochean Lucullus] (1) Your Philo was a student of Clitomachus for many years, and while he was alive the Academy did not lack advocacy. (2) But our present project of arguing against the Academics was completely excluded by some philosophers of high distinction. They thought there was no reason to argue with those who accepted nothing, and they criticized the Stoic Antipater for being much involved in this. They also said it was not necessary to define the nature of knowledge or cognition or 'grasp' (if we want a word-for-word translation of the Stoic term *katalēpsis*), and that those who wanted to urge that there is something that can be grasped and cognized were acting unscientifically, because there was nothing clearer than self-evidence . . . and they held that things with this degree of clarity did not require definition . . . (3) Philo, however, in setting some new ideas in motion, because he could scarcely withstand the arguments against the Academics' obstinacy, is a manifest liar . . . and, as Antiochus showed, he fell into the very position he was afraid of. For when he thus denied that there was anything that could be grasped [i.e. by the Stoics' cognitive impression] . . . he removed the criterion of the cognitive and the incognitive. From this the outcome was that nothing could be grasped, with Philo incautiously reversed into the position he least wanted.

V Galen, *On the best teaching* 1

(1) Favorinus says that argument pro and contra is the best teaching. This is the name the Academics give to argument in which they speak in favour of opposite sides. Now the older Academics think that it ends in suspension of judgement, using 'suspension of judgement' for what one

might call lack of determination, i.e. making no determination or firm assertion about anything. (2) But the younger ones – not just Favorinus – sometimes carry suspension of judgement as far as not even granting that the sun is an object of cognition, but at other times they carry judgement so far that they even entrust it to their pupils without first giving them instruction in a scientific criterion . . . Yet in his . . . *Alcibiades* he praises the Academics for, on the one hand, speaking in favour of both sides in opposing arguments, and, on the other hand, trusting their pupils to choose the truer ones. (3) Here he has said that it seems convincing to him that nothing is cognitive; but in his *Plutarch* he seems to concede that there is something firmly cognitive.

☐ We have already, in our Introduction (p. 5), described in outline the nature of Arcesilaus' revolution in the Academy. The complexities of evaluating the sources for his 'New Academy' in its various phases will be handled later. What must be emphasized at the outset is his official position as the leading Platonist of his time. As a youth he studied with a variety of philosophers (cf. **F 1** where the reference to Pyrrho is probably unhistorical), but he soon settled for the Academy. He was on excellent terms with the older establishment there – Polemo, Crates, Crantor (**F 2**) – and it is unthinkable that he would have been elected to succeed Crates (**E 1**) if his relationship to Plato had seemed quite deviant or traitorous. In fact there had been no consensus interpretation of Plato's philosophy at any time since his death, some seventy-five years before Arcesilaus' election. If, as seems likely, Polemo and his contemporaries had already begun to react against the efforts of their predecessors, Speusippus and Xenocrates, to create a hard-and-fast system out of Plato's dialogues, this will have encouraged Arcesilaus to challenge the whole enterprise of reading Plato as a doctrinaire philosopher. He probably possessed Plato's own manuscripts (**E 1**) and lectured on them, which could explain the fanciful suggestion that he transmitted Platonic doctrines to suitable pupils (**I 5**). His alleged changes of 'traditional Platonic discourse' (**D**) are best explained, we suggest, as a recommendation to do philosophy as Socrates does it in Plato's early dialogues, and not to codify supposed doctrines in the manner of a Xenocrates: note the references to argument pro and contra and question and answer in **D** (cf. **A 6**), and to his revival of Socratic dialectic in **J**.

Such a scenario will account for Arcesilaus' methodology as a Platonist quite independently of external influences. But he also had powerful reasons for assuming the role of a latter-day Socrates in response to the upstart philosophy of his older contemporary, the Stoic Zeno. Our sources emphasize Arcesilaus' unremitting opposition to Stoicism, and especially to Zeno's empiricist theory of knowledge (**A 2, C, G, O**; cf. also Diogenes Laertius 7.162 on Aristo's arguments with Arcesilaus). Zeno as well as Arcesilaus had studied with the Academic Polemo. To Arcesilaus Zeno and his followers probably seemed to be misappropriating much of the Platonic tradition (compare Antiochus' later approval of this appropriation), and at the same time advancing new doctrines that any Platonist must strenuously resist. Arcesilaus could maintain that Plato never put forward any position as more than a hypothesis; that he had shot down his own 'theory of Forms' in the *Parmenides*; and that he had undermined the cognitive claims of sense-perception in the *Theaetetus*, while failing to arrive there at any other defensible account of knowledge. If a consistently aporetic Plato seems a distortion now, is it any more so than the Neoplatonic focus upon a few selected passages as the heart of supposedly Platonic doctrine?

In the light of Arcesilaus' acknowledgement of his Platonic pedigree, it is neither necessary nor plausible to add his older contemporaries Diodorus and Pyrrho as comparably significant influences (**E 2**, **F**, **I**). As a master of dialectic himself, Arcesilaus certainly appreciated the Dialectician Diodorus and absorbed some of his techniques, and he must have known about Pyrrho. But the Academics themselves never acknowledged Pyrrho, and for good reason. His scepticism, as we interpret it, was a dogmatic position; and the tranquillity it yielded gave Pyrrho no reason to engage in philosophical argument (see **1** and **2**). Nor do we hear of tranquillity and suspension of judgement being connected by the Academics (note Sextus' addition in **I 3**). If Pyrrho was of any interest to Arcesilaus, it was probably as the actual example of a life lived without opinion.

'Sceptic', as in **F 1**, is an anachronistic designation of Arcesilaus, retrojected from later Pyrrhonism. The standard characterization of him and his school was as 'those who suspend judgement about everything' (**H 1** and **31P 2**, a quotation from Chrysippus). This characterization fits one of the two cardinal conclusions for which he is said to have argued: that all things are incognitive (henceforth *I*), and that we should suspend judgement about them (henceforth *S*). *I* is the proposition most distinctive of the whole New Academy. Although Arcesilaus drew support for it from illustrious predecessors (cf. **A 2**, **H 3**), the justification he gave it was original to him, namely the 'indiscernibility' principle according to which, for every true impression an identical but false one could arise (**40D**; cf. **40E 6**, **H**, **J**; **70A 8**, **B 4**). *I* remained the characteristic thesis of the New Academy throughout its history, whereas *S* was modified or abandoned by many later adherents (see e.g. **69H**). We can no longer postpone the difficult question whether *I* and *S* were in any sense Arcesilaus' own philosophical positions, and, if so, how he could maintain them without *eo ipso* compromising them. Do they not fall within their own and each other's scope?

At least four types of answer are available.

(1) *I* is in some sense Arcesilaus' own conclusion, and *S* is the only proper response to it (**A 3–5**, **H 3**, **I 3–4**, **O**).

(2) *S* is a purely defensive strategy conveying nothing about Arcesilaus' real aims (**F 2**; cf. **I 5**).

(3) *I* is a strictly *ad hominem* refutation of the Stoic criterion of truth, the cognitive impression (see **40**), and *S* is the embarrassing consequence which, on the Stoics' own premises, must follow for the Stoic wise man (**G**; **41C**).

(4) For every thesis Arcesilaus has been offered he finds it possible to advance a counter-argument of equal weight. *S* is his response to this (**A 5**, **D**, cf. **J–L**).

Of these, (2) with its imputation of crypto-dogmatism can be quickly dismissed. There is no evidence from any unbiased source that Arcesilaus was a doctrinaire Platonist, and plenty that he was not. Answer (3) certainly succeeds in conveying one important aspect of Arcesilaus' dialectic (cf. **69G** with commentary); and it reminds us that suspension of judgement was the Stoics' required response to anything incognitive (cf. **41E–G**). But answer (3), taken on its own, fails to explain why both *I* and *S* were consistently attached to Arcesilaus and his immediate circle (**A**, **E**, **F** 1, **H**, **I** 2–4, **O**, **V** 1; **31P** 2; **69G** 1). Answer (4) is plainly the strategy underlying Arcesilaus' many critiques of individual philosophical theses, which will be found listed in the commentary to **70**. By itself, however, it is inadequate to explain the frequently emphasized link between *I* and *S*. Hence answer (1) cannot be excluded either.

If, as the texts do suggest, *I* was in some sense Arcesilaus' own position, no immediate self-contradiction is involved. That would arise only if he claimed to have *cognition* that all things are incognitive. But on this point at least, the evidence for the entire New Academy is consistent: *I* was their 'doctrine' (**H** 3, **N** 2, **P**), their own philosophical position (**A** 3; **40D**; **69K**; **71C** 9, 11), but they steadfastly disavowed cognition of it (**A** 3, **N**).

The real difficulty arises only for those Academics, such as Arcesilaus himself, who also insisted on *S*. A later revisionary like Philo (cf. **69K**), who interpreted Academic orthodoxy as permitting qualified assent, could present *I* as his own fallible, albeit convincing, belief (cf. **V** 3). The difficulty is to see how Arcesilaus could intend either *I* or *S* as in any sense his own view without at least assenting to them and thus contravening *S*. One possible answer might be sought in our next section, where Arcesilaus will be seen suggesting that there are ways of being motivated by an impression *without* assenting to it, i.e. without taking it to be true. *I* and *S*, he might say, are his own views in so far as they are the ones which he finds motivating him.

These considerations, even if accepted, should not be allowed to disguise the supremely dialectical character of early Academic scepticism. This is the feature which above all ties it to its Platonic heritage and severs it from Pyrrhonism. Where Pyrrhonism warns us to steer clear of all theoretical entanglements in the interests of our own tranquillity, early Academic scepticism thrives on theoretical controversies; it teaches us to retain an open mind on them, for the sake not of tranquillity but of intellectual integrity (cf. **A** 4, **O**). Its frequent reliance on its opponents' premises (for examples see **41C** and **69**) is integral to its dialectical project of exploring the implications of every theoretical stance. Hence interpretation (3) noted above, according to which Arcesilaus' defence of *I* and *S* is a strictly anti-Stoic move, must not be ignored. Perhaps the best overall view of Arcesilaus' strategy combines (1), (3) and (4) as follows. If, on the one hand, you adopt a policy of Academic open-mindedness, giving due weight to the pros and cons of every thesis, you will *ipso facto* suspend judgement. If, on the other hand, you adopt a doctrinal stance like Stoicism, it will follow from premises to which this stance commits you, in conjunction with its inability to resist *I*, that you should suspend judgement. Hence whatever philosophical positions you adopt or avoid adopting, you will, if wise, suspend judgement. See for example Arcesilaus' argument at **41C** 9: 'And if everything is incognitive, it will follow, according to the Stoics *too*, that the wise man suspends judgement.'

Arcesilaus, if he did adopt such a strategy, may have operated it largely or exclusively with reference to Stoicism; he seems to have regarded this philosophy as specifying the conditions which cognition, if it were possible, would have to meet. For completeness, however, the same conclusions needed to be wrung not just out of Stoicism but out of every other doctrinaire position. It was apparently left for Arcesilaus' celebrated successor Carneades, in the second century B.C., to carry out this enterprise (**70A**). In at least one area of debate, ethics, he extended his critique to all possible as well as all actual positions (**64E 1**).

Carneades is featured extensively in our next two sections, but a few further points about his general stance as an Academic must be noted here. He maintained the school's sceptical lines, as initiated by Arcesilaus (**A 6, C 2**). Both philosophers made it their trademark 'to argue against every thesis' (**L**). In the case of Arcesilaus, however, we have the impression that he required an interlocutor to state *his own* opinion (cf. **J**) and used that opinion as the basis for an elenchus, just like the Socrates of Plato's early dialogues. But Carneades was prepared to take opposite sides on the same subject himself, as in his virtuoso lectures pro and contra justice (**M**). Although the same procedure is attested in summary accounts of Arcesilaus (cf. **D** and **31O**), Chrysippus, too early to be influenced by the methods of Carneades, only specifies arguing the opposite case as the sceptical Academy's practice (**31P**). If Carneades' pro and contra argumentation represents a genuine difference from Arcesilaus, one reason may have been that he took his cue from Platonic dialogues like the *Meno* and *Theaetetus*, in which Socrates is portrayed as first developing, then attacking, the same thesis. Also, by speaking equally persuasively on *both* sides himself, he could hope to induce suspension of judgement without giving his listeners any grounds for thinking he favoured either the view he had defended or the view on the opposite side (cf. **69H**).

The history of the Academy after Carneades is complicated. Without some understanding of the rival factions, however, it is impossible to assess the source material, especially that in Cicero; so a sketch of the developments must be given.

So great was Carneades' stature and authority that after his death it was his philosophy more directly than that of Socrates and Plato that Academics felt required to interpret and defend. (This is perhaps why some sources treat his headship as the inauguration of the 'New Academy' with the school under Arcesilaus forming the 'Middle Academy', i.e. a transitional phase, cf. **C 2, D, I 1**; we ourselves prefer Cicero's use of 'New' for the whole Hellenistic Academy from Arcesilaus to Philo.) His eventual successor, and most conservative reporter, was Clitomachus, who catalogued Carneades' immense battery of arguments without any claim that the great man had accepted any of them (**69L**). But these arguments could be interpreted *either* as purely dialectical in purpose, *or* as leading to some opinions which he himself endorsed (cf. **69H, L**). The latter option was taken up by Carneades' associate Metrodorus of Stratonicia, and passed on by him to Philo of Larissa (**69H**). Philo, who headed the school in its final phase (early first century B.C.), strongly influenced Cicero's own philosophical outlook. He abandoned the strict Academic commitment to S (**69H, K**), invoking Carneades' apparent approval of opinion (**69F, G 2**) and of following the 'convincing' (**R 3; 69D–E**), which we ourselves, like Clitomachus, prefer to read as primarily dialectical moves (see **69** commentary).

On this basis he replaced scepticism with a modest fallibilism, which permitted the philosopher a wide range of opinions, subject only to the recognition that any one of them might be mistaken, and authorized 'truth or approximation to truth' (**S**; cf. **Q**, **V** 2) as the Academic's objective – the foundation of Cicero's own methodology. Such Philonian doctrines helped to give the Academy the ambiguous posture (cf. **V** 2–3) which prompted Aenesidemus to leave the school, which he witheringly described as 'Stoics fighting with Stoics', and to refurbish scepticism under the name of Pyrrho (**71C** 9–11).

All this constitutes the weakened Academic philosophy in which Philo's own leading pupil Antiochus had been trained, and which is represented in Cicero's *Academica* by such texts as **Q**, **R** 2–3, **S**; **69K**. But in 89 B.C. Antiochus completely broke with the Philonian Academy, and established his own unofficial 'Old' Academy (**B**). Each of them made new moves in defending his own position as the true custodian of the Platonic tradition. Antiochus represented Plato as a fully dogmatic philosopher whose stance on knowledge was truly captured by the Stoic doctrine of cognitive certainty. (Hence our use in **39–41** of Cicero's Antiochean spokesmen, Lucullus and Varro, as sources for Stoic epistemology.) Indeed, he regarded the Stoic Zeno, and the Peripatetics, as the only true heirs of Platonism among his Hellenistic predecessors, though he reserved the right to criticize Stoicism for deviations from that tradition in ethics (see **64K**; **L**).

Meanwhile, Philo tried to represent the whole Academy from Plato to himself as concurring in a carefully qualified version of *I*, the principle that all things are incognitive: *I* holds not because of the intrinsic nature of things (e.g. their being in too rapid flux to permit secure knowledge ?), but because there simply is no such thing as the Stoic criterion, i.e. any criterion which establishes cognition with the certainty required for the Stoic 'cognitive impression' (**T**; cf. **U** 3). In defending this dubious piece of philosophical history, Philo could at least refer to Plato's apparent endorsement in the *Meno* of true opinion which falls short of knowledge, and his willingness in the *Timaeus* to resort to a 'plausible' cosmology; to Arcesilaus' and Carneades' almost exclusive concentration on the Stoic version of the criterion of truth; and to the contemporary Academic practice, noted above, of taking 'convincing impressions' as provisional truths, a practice which presupposed the existence of objective truths to be guessed at.

Antiochus retorted with an outright denial both of Philo's historical veracity, and of the internal coherence of this new version of *I* (**U** 3; cf. **B**): Philo's position became self-contradictory once it was recognized that the Stoic criterion of truth was the only basis on which sense could be given to the notion of things being intrinsically cognitive.

Since the spokesmen in Cicero's *Academica* are looking back on the earlier Academic tradition largely from these two partisan viewpoints, the evaluation of them as sources is a delicate matter. The difficulty is compounded by the fact that both Arcesilaus and Carneades, like the historical Socrates, published no written version of their arguments, leaving it to their successors to quarrel over their actual philosophical intentions. This problem must continue to be borne in mind when studying the texts in **69**.

69 Living without opinions

A Plutarch, *Against Colotes* 1122A–F (continuing **68H**)

[Speaker: Plutarch on behalf of the New Academy] (1) Nor was suspension of judgement about everything disturbed by those who toiled away and wrote lengthy arguments against it. But having finally confronted it from the Stoa with 'inactivity' like a Gorgon, they faded away, since for all their twisting and turning, impulse refused to become assent, and did not accept sensation as tipping the balance, but was seen to lead to action on its own initiative without needing assent . . . For those who attend and listen, the argument runs thus. (2) The soul has three movements – impression, impulse and assent. The movement of impression we could not remove, even if we wanted to; rather, as soon as we encounter things, we get an impression and are affected by them. (3) The movement of impulse, when aroused by that of impression, moves a person actively towards appropriate objects, since a kind of turn of the scale and inclination occur in the commanding-faculty. So those who suspend judgement about everything do not remove this movement either, but make use of the impulse which leads them naturally towards what appears appropriate. (4) What, then, is the only thing they avoid? That only in which falsehood and deception are engendered – opining and precipitately assenting, which is yielding to the appearance out of weakness and involves nothing useful. (5) For action requires two things: an impression of something appropriate, and an impulse towards the appropriate object that has appeared; neither of these is in conflict with suspension of judgement. For the argument keeps us away from opinion, not from impulse or impression. So whenever something appropriate has appeared, no opinion is needed to get us moving and proceeding towards it; the impulse arrives immediately, since it is the soul's process and movement . . . (6) 'But how is it that someone who suspends judgement does not rush away to a mountain instead of to the bath, or stands up and walks to the door rather than the wall when he wants to go out to the market-place?' Do you [the Epicurean Colotes] ask this, when you claim that the sense-organs are accurate and impressions true? Because, of course, it is not the mountain but the bath that appears a bath to him, not the wall but the door that appears a door, and likewise with everything else. (7) For the rationale of suspending judgement does not deflect sensation or implant a change in the irrational affections and movements themselves, which disturbs the occurrence of impressions; it merely removes our opinions, but makes natural use of all the rest.

B Sextus Empiricus, *Against the professors* 7.158 (continuing **41C**)

(1) But since after this it was necessary to investigate the conduct of life too, which is not of a nature to be explained without a criterion, on

which happiness too, i.e. the end of life, has its trust dependent, Arcesilaus says that one who suspends judgement about everything will regulate choice and avoidance and actions in general by 'the reasonable'; and that by proceeding in accordance with this criterion he will act rightly; (2) for happiness is acquired through prudence, and prudence resides in right actions, and right action is whatever, once it has been done, has a reasonable justification; (3) therefore one who attends to the reasonable will act rightly and be happy.

C Diogenes Laertius 7.171

When someone said that Arcesilaus did not do what he should, he [Cleanthes] said, 'Stop, don't criticize him; for even if in argument he destroys proper function, he holds to it by his actions at least.' Arcesilaus said: 'I am not flattered.' Cleanthes answered him: 'True. My flattery is to say that you argue one thing and do something else.'

D Sextus Empiricus, *Against the professors* 7.166–75 (continuing **70A**)

(1) These [see **70A**] were the arguments which Carneades set out in full as a strategy against the other philosophers, to prove the non-existence of the criterion. But since he himself too has some criterion demanded of him for the conduct of life and the attainment of happiness, he is virtually compelled, as far as he himself is concerned, to adopt a position on this by taking as his criterion both the 'convincing' impression and the one which is simultaneously convincing, undiverted and thoroughly explored. (2) What the difference is between these must be briefly indicated. The impression is an impression of something, i.e., both of that from which it arises and of that in which it arises: the former is, for instance, the external object of sensation, and the latter, say, a man. Being of this kind, it would have two dispositions, one relative to the impressor, the other relative to the person experiencing the impression. Now in regard to its disposition relative to the impressor, it is either true or false – true when it is in agreement with the impressor, and false when it is not in agreement. But in regard to its disposition relative to the person experiencing the impression, one impression is apparently true and the other not apparently true; of these, the apparently true is called 'manifestation' by the Academics, and 'convincingness' and 'convincing impression', while the not apparently true is called 'non-manifestation' and 'unconvincing impression'. For neither what appears immediately false, nor what is true but does not appear so to us, is of a nature to convince us. (3) Of these impressions, the one which is apparently false and not apparently true is to be ruled out and is not the criterion. (4) Of the apparently true impressions, one kind is dim, e.g. in the case of those whose apprehension of something is confused and not distinct, owing to the smallness of the thing observed or the length of the distance or even

the weakness of their vision; the other kind, along with appearing true, is additionally characterized by the intensity of its appearing true. Of these again, the dim and feeble impression could not be a criterion; for since it does not clearly indicate either itself or its cause, it is not of a nature to convince us or to pull us to assent. But the impression which appears true and fully manifests itself is the criterion of truth according to Carneades and his followers. (5) As the criterion, it has a considerable breadth; and by admitting of degrees, it includes some impressions which are more convincing and striking in their form than others. Convincingness, for our present purpose, has three senses: first, what both is and appears true; secondly, what is actually false but appears true; and thirdly, <what appears> true, <which is> common to them both. Hence the criterion will be the impression which appears true – also called 'convincing' by the Academics – but there are times when it actually turns out false, so that it is necessary actually to use the impression which is common on occasion to truth and falsehood. Yet the rare occurrence of this one, I mean the impression which counterfeits the truth [i.e. the second], is not a reason for distrusting the impression [i.e. the third] which tells the truth for the most part. For both judgements and actions, as it turns out, are regulated by what holds for the most part.

E Sextus Empiricus, *Against the professors* 7.176–84

(1) Such then [i.e. **D**] is the first and general criterion of Carneades and his followers. But since an impression never stands in isolation but one depends on another like links in a chain, a second criterion will be added which is simultaneously convincing and undiverted. E.g. someone who takes in an impression of a man necessarily also gets an impression of things to do with the man and with the extraneous circumstances – things to do with him like his colour, size, shape, motion, conversation, dress, foot-wear; and external circumstances like atmosphere, light, day, sky, earth, friends and everything else. So whenever none of these impressions diverts us by appearing false, but all with one accord appear true, our belief is all the greater. For we believe that this is Socrates from his having all his usual features – colour, size, shape, conversation, cloak, and his being in a place where there is no one indiscernible from him . . . (2) When Menelaus left the image of Helen (which he brought from Troy as Helen) on his ship, and disembarked on the island of Pharos, he saw the true Helen; but though he took in a true impression from her, he still did not believe an impression of that kind since he was diverted by another one, in virtue of which he *knew* he had left Helen on the ship. That is what the undiverted impression is like; and it too seems to have breadth, since one such impression is found to be more undiverted than another. (3) Still more credible than the undiverted impression, and the one which

makes judgement most perfect, is the impression which combines being undiverted with also being thoroughly explored. Its features must next be explained. In the case of the undiverted impression, it is merely required that none of the impressions in the concurrence should divert us by appearing false but all should be ones which appear true and are not unconvincing. But in the case of the concurrence which involves the thoroughly explored impression, we meticulously examine each impression in the concurrence, in the way that happens at government assemblies, when the people cross-examine every candidate for political office or the judiciary, to see whether he is worthy to be entrusted with the office or the position of judge. (4) Thus . . . we make judgements about the properties of each of the items pertaining to the place of the judgement: the subject judging, in case his vision is faint . . .; the object judged, in case it is too small; the medium of the judgement, in case the atmosphere is murky; the distance, in case it is too far . . .; the place, in case it is too vast; the time, in case it is too short; the character, in case it is observed to be insane; and the activity, in case it is unacceptable. (5) For all of these in turn become the criterion – the convincing impression, and the one which is simultaneously convincing and undiverted, and in addition the one which is simultaneously convincing and undiverted and thoroughly explored. For this reason, as in everyday life when we are investigating a small matter we question a single witness, but in the case of a larger one several, and in a still more crucial matter we cross-question each of the witnesses from the mutual corroboration provided by the others – so, say Carneades and his followers, in matters of no importance we make use of the merely convincing impression, but in weightier matters the undiverted impression as a criterion, and in matters which contribute to happiness the thoroughly explored impression.

F Cicero, *Academica* 2.59

[Speaker: the Antiochean Lucullus] (1) It is utterly absurd of you [Academics] to say that you follow what is convincing, if you are diverted by nothing. First, how can you not be diverted when [as you claim] there is no difference between true and false impressions? Secondly, what criterion of a true impression is there, when [as you claim] the criterion is common to what is false? (2) These claims necessarily engendered that suspension of judgement . . . in which Arcesilaus was the more consistent with himself, if some people's assessments of Carneades are true. For if nothing is cognitive, which was the view of them both, assent must be abolished; for what is as futile as accepting anything not cognized? (3) But even yesterday we kept being told that Carneades was also in the habit of lapsing from time to time into saying that the wise man will opine, that is, do wrong.

G Cicero, *Academica* 2.66–7

[Speaker: Cicero on behalf of the New Academy] (1) I am not a wise man, and so I yield to impressions and cannot resist them. But Arcesilaus, agreeing with Zeno [see **40D**], judged it to be the wise man's greatest power that he avoids being taken in, and sees to it that he is not deceived . . . [see **68O**]. (2) Consider first the validity of this argument: 'If the wise man ever assents to anything, he will sometimes also opine; but he will never opine; therefore he will never assent to anything.' Arcesilaus used to accept this argument, for he endorsed both the leading and the additional premise. Carneades sometimes used to grant, as the additional premise, 'The wise man on occasion assents'; thus it followed that the wise man also opines, which you, Lucullus, reject, and rightly as I think.

H Cicero, *Academica* 2.78 (continuing **40D**)

[Speaker: Cicero on behalf of the New Academy] This [i.e. the indiscernibility of true from false impressions] is the one controversial issue which has lasted up to the present time. For the thesis that 'The wise man will assent to nothing' [cf. **G 2**] had nothing to do with this dispute; for he might 'grasp nothing and yet opine' – a thesis Carneades is said to have accepted, although for my part, trusting Clitomachus more than Philo or Metrodorus, I think that this was put forward in debate by him rather than accepted.

I Cicero, *Academica* 2.103–4

[Cicero, reporting Clitomachus] (1) 'The Academics hold that there are differences between things of such a kind that some things seem convincing and others the opposite. But this is not a sufficient reason for saying that some things are cognitive and others not, because many false things are convincing but nothing false is cognitive. Hence Clitomachus says that they are wildly wrong who say that the senses are torn away by the Academy, for its members never said that colour or taste or sound did not exist; their argument was that these do not contain a peculiar mark of truth and certainty which exists nowhere else. (2) Having developed these points, he adds that 'The wise man withholds assent' has two senses: one, when it means that he assents to nothing at all; the other, when he checks himself from responding in such a way as to accept or reject something, with the result that he neither denies nor asserts something. This being so, he adopts the former, so that he never assents, but retains the latter [kind of assent], with the result that by following convincingness he can respond 'yes' wherever it is present or 'no' wherever it is missing. (3) Since it is our view in fact that he who restrains himself from assent about all things nevertheless does move and does act, he does not remove those impressions which impel us to act, or, likewise, answers pro or contra, that we can give to questions merely by following our impression, provided that we do so without assent. It is not our view, however, that all such impressions are accepted, but those which are not diverted by anything.

J Cicero, *Academica* 2.108

[Speaker: Cicero on behalf of the New Academy] While I think that the highest of activities fights against impressions, withstands opinions, checks assents from slipping, and while I agree with Clitomachus when he writes of a Herculean labour that Carneades endured in expelling from our minds that wild and savage monster, assent – i.e. opinion and rashness – yet . . . what will divert the action of the man who follows what is convincing when nothing diverts this?

K Cicero, *Academica* 2.148

[Speaker: the Philonian Academic, Catulus] I am coming round to my father's view, which he used to say was Carneades' in fact, that I do think nothing is cognitive; yet I also think that the wise man will assent to what is incognitive, i.e. will opine, but in such a way that he realizes he is opining and knows that there is nothing which can be grasped and cognized.

L Cicero, *Academica* 2.139

[Speaker: Cicero on behalf of the New Academy] Carneades used to defend Callipho's opinion so zealously [i.e. the highest good is virtue plus pleasure] that he even seemed to accept it; yet Clitomachus used to assert that he had never been able to understand what Carneades did accept.

☐ The Academic sceptic is concerned with opinions at two or possibly three different levels. First, in his arguments against the Stoics' epistemology, where he confronts them with uncongenial conclusions concerning the wise man's cognitive state. Secondly, in rebutting Stoic criticism that suspension of judgement about everything excludes purposive activity. Thirdly (which may also be seen as an extension of the second concern), in proposing that the sceptic, consistently with his scepticism, can regulate his activities in the way that ordinary people, as distinct from doctrinaire philosophers, do or think they should do. Since the debates on these issues lasted from Arcesilaus and Zeno down to Philo and Antiochus, our commentary is organized accordingly.

As the ideal human condition, wisdom had been a ubiquitous concept in earlier Greek philosophy. But it was the Hellenistic philosophers, Stoics especially, who made 'the wise man' the subject of all desirable attributes and the paradigm of virtuous action. A wise man, uncontroversially, was extraordinary in his consistent rationality and freedom from error. Within these broad limits his characteristics varied according to the standpoint of each school. Early

Pyrrhonists, Epicureans and Stoics disagreed on what the wise man knows and what he does. But they were unanimous in regarding him as totally exempt from the unfounded opinions which characterize ordinary people.

This is the background for understanding the two arguments in **G 1–2**, which should be studied in conjunction with **40D** and **41C**. The wise man in question is the Stoics'. Stoic doctrine maintains that (1) the wise man assents (to cognitive and only to cognitive impressions), and (2) that he never opines. Arcesilaus' argument concludes by negating (1), and Carneades' conclusion negates (2). Each argument starts from the same leading premise (which presupposes the non-existence of cognitive impressions for the wise man to assent to). As his additional premise Arcesilaus advances (2) in order to infer the negation of (1), while Carneades advances (1) in order to infer the negation of (2). Once these procedures are exposed, we can see that both arguments are closely analogous in their dialectical strategy. It is the Stoics, not the Academics, who are committed to the truth of (1) and (2). Hence Cicero's fuss in **G** (cf. **F 2–3**, **H**, **K**) about Carneades' conception of the wise man's opining is out of order. These arguments are not designed to show any substantive views held by Arcesilaus or Carneades. Their purpose is to embarrass the Stoics by drawing on their own form of syllogistic inference in order to establish anti-Stoic conclusions with the help of Stoic premises.

Nevertheless, these arguments would be useless if they could not be defended against Stoic counter-attack. From a comparison between **A** and **53S** we can infer that Arcesilaus was the first Academic to defend suspension of judgement about everything against the frequently repeated Stoic objection (cf. **40M**, **N**, **O 3**) that it would make action impossible. From Plutarch's further comments in **A 6–7** it also emerges that Arcesilaus was attacked for this posture by contemporary Epicureans. Arcesilaus, however, couches his reply (**A 2–5**) to the Stoic Gorgon of 'inactivity' in exclusively Stoic terms.

From the Stoic theory of action he takes over the three key concepts, impression, impulse and assent (see **53A**, **O–S**). He then argues that assent can be dispensed with. The elimination of assent excludes knowledge or opinion as a causal component of action, and so makes action compatible with suspension of judgement about everything. Study of **A** will reveal Arcesilaus' skill in exploiting Stoic concepts: note the beguiling attractions of avoiding precipitancy (cf. **41D**, **G**) and his ingenious use of 'impulse towards the appropriate object', which should be compared with **53Q**. In effect, Arcesilaus applies to human action the Stoics' account of non-rational animal behaviour; and this is an obvious weakness of his argument. Still, by focusing upon Stoicism for his rejoinder, Arcesilaus achieves two things: he shows that Stoic theory of action is adaptable to his conclusion about their wise man, and that it is they who have given the wise man, or Arcesilaus himself, the mechanism for conducting his life without assent.

If Arcesilaus' argument in **A** fails to address the issue of rationality and moral responsibility, his strategy in **B** takes account of these, again in the Stoics' own terms. Immediately prior to **B** he had argued that the Stoic wise man, given his freedom from all opinion and the unavailability of cognitive impressions, will suspend judgement about everything (**41C**). The criterion of 'the reasonable',

credited to Arcesilaus in **B**, is presented there as if it were a *doctrine* forced on him
by the need to accommodate his scepticism to daily life. But this imputation is
tendentious, and probably imported by Sextus' likely source, the hostile
Antiochus (see **68** commentary). Arcesilaus' recourse to 'the reasonable' should
be seen as a strategy which enables him to use what is again a Stoic concept in
defence of his conclusion concerning the wise man's suspension of judgement.[1]

The subtlety of his argument consists in the fact that it allows the Stoics to
retain their doctrines on the connexion between happiness, prudence and right
action, while denying that all three of these depend upon knowledge. According
to the Stoics themselves, 'right actions' are 'proper functions', which are in turn
defined in terms of the 'reasonable justification' that can be given of them
(**59B** 1). The Stoics, to be sure, treat right actions as a subdivision of proper
functions in general, ones which are perfect (**59B** 4; cf. **59G, K**). But Arcesilaus
has already eliminated the knowledge constitutive of virtue (see **61**), which
perfects proper functions as the Stoics conceive of them. Hence, he now argues,
the rightness of the wise man's actions must consist simply in their 'reasonable
justification'. The Stoics should allow this criterion to be compatible with
suspension of judgement since they acknowledge that even fools, whose assents
and opinions are useless because never securely based (see **41**), can nevertheless
perform proper functions (cf. **59F** 7), presumably in reliance on nothing more
than their reasonableness. Thus the wise man can guide his actions by reason, and
be prudent and happy thereby, even though he assents to nothing. Moreover,
since he does not assent, he will not be misled on occasions when 'the reasonable
impression' might deceive ordinary people (cf. **40F**; **42J** 3).

This interpretation of Arcesilaus' dialectical strategy in **B** accords very well
with the anecdote in **C**. If **B** were his own position, he would be committed to
the existence of proper functions, as specified by 'the reasonable'. But Cleanthes
tells us, on the contrary, that Arcesilaus destroyed them in argument. On how to
live one's life, as on everything else with the possible exception of the need to
suspend judgement itself (see p. 447), we suggest that Arcesilaus disavowed all
doctrines.

Is it the same with Carneades? This question turns on the interpretation of his
'criterion . . . for the conduct of life and the attainment of happiness' (**D** 1).
Notice that Sextus, as with his account of Arcesilaus (**B**), treats this as something
Carneades was 'virtually compelled' to give; again we may suspect an innuendo
stemming from the polemical Antiochus. Carneades establishes his candidate for
this criterion – the 'convincing' impression, and its increasingly refined forms,
'undiverted' and 'thoroughly explored' – by a division of impressions. As our
diagram makes plain, Carneades' criterion is entirely subjective. An apparently
true impression may be false, and an apparently false one may be true. What is
convincing, and 'pulls us to assent', is an impression which appears true with
'intensity' (**D** 4). Since apparent truth, even with intensity, is compatible with
objective falsehood, this criterion is fallible; it is incompetent to distinguish 'the

---

[1] Apparently a version of Arcesilaus' strategy which combines it with assent, but only to
propositions of the form, 'it is reasonable that *p*', even gained a foothold in the Stoa itself (see
40F).

apparently true, and true' from 'the apparently true, and false'. Hence the 'third sense' of convincing impression (**D 5**), in addition to these two, is simply equivalent to the generic sense of 'convincing', i.e. 'what appears true (with intensity)', which spans the other two. This is Carneades' way of saying that he uses 'convincing' in a way which leaves the question of truth or falsehood entirely open. The top left-hand portion of the diagram now comes into play, since 'what appears true' does 'tell the truth for the most part' (**D 5**). However, Carneades does not imply that its doing so is the reason why it convinces 'us', i.e. people in general. Rather, he says that the occasional falsehood of an apparently true impression is not a reason for distrusting such impressions.

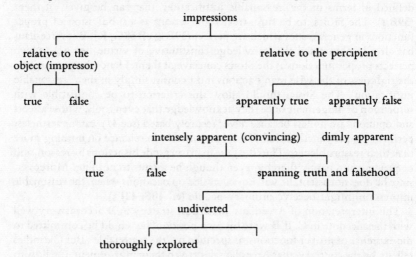

Next (**E**) two higher levels of convincingness are specified. The first of these is 'undivertedness'. In any situation, we receive a multiplicity of interconnected impressions. If all of these together appear true (e.g. if an impression that Socrates is present is not simultaneously diverted by any impression that appears to falsify this state of affairs), 'our belief is all the greater' (**E 1**). Undivertedness, then, indicates the contribution of coherence and mutual corroboration to the strength of the judgements people make. In the third and most convincing type of impression, the condition of 'being thoroughly explored' is added to undivertedness. All that was required of the undiverted impression was that none of its associated impressions should appear to conflict with the apparent truth of all the rest. In the case of the thoroughly explored impression, each associated impression is subjected to a meticulous examination, comparable to the scrutiny of candidates for public office. Thus the apparently true and coherent set of impressions is tested against standards of reliability derived from experience which is independent of the present situation.

Carneades concludes (**E 5**) that an impression which meets all these conditions is the one 'we' use in forming judgements about everything that is supremely important to us.

What is the purpose of his discussion? He has not specified a criterion of truth in the Stoics' sense. That was a standard of judgement which assured absolute certainty. Carneades' criterion, even in its most refined form, deals only with the subjective appearance of truth. Traditionally it has been regarded as a doctrine of probabilism. But is it a doctrine, and has it anything to do with probability? *Probabile* is Cicero's translation in the *Academica* of the Greek *pithanon*, which we translate by 'convincing'. In everyday language the word 'probable' is used to indicate what is likely as distinct from what is certain or necessary, and more exactly, as a measure of the relative frequency of some occurrence. Carneades, however, seems quite reticent about drawing any firm connexion between the features of an impression that make it convincing and the actual likelihood of its being true. He does say that such impressions turn out to be true 'for the most part' (**D 5**), but he does not say that this is the reason why they appear true.

Yet when he comes to the two higher levels of convincingness, Carneades does claim that coherence and meticulous scrutiny of impressions increasingly strengthen people's convictions. It is hard to see why he should say this unless he intends to indicate that rationality and verification procedures make a salient contribution to the kinds of judgements that people are inclined to hold strongly. Thus probability does seem to have a great deal to do with the criterion which Carneades attributes to 'us', as the basis of impressions which are actually found to be highly convincing.

Now, the philosophical status of his account. We interpreted 'the reasonable' of Arcesilaus (and his argument in **A**) as a rejoinder to the Stoics, showing that Stoicism gave him the concepts for meeting their objection that scepticism ruled out action. If Carneades' 'convincing' impression is a similar strategy, it ought to be designed to show that he can sustain his *generalized* attack on 'the other philosophers' criterion' (**D 1**) without succumbing to the criticism that he leaves people with nothing to regulate their lives.

The best clue to his intentions is the striking use of Stoic concepts, both in his earlier destructive arguments and in his account of the 'convincing' impression. (For the former, cf. **70A 4–10** with **39B, 40B–D**.) For the latter, note particularly the Stoic division of impressions, which starts from 'convincing, unconvincing . . .' (**39G**); the relation between convincingness and assent (**39G 2–3**); and Chrysippus' use of 'diverted' in reference to the effect of opposing arguments on cognition (**31P 3**). Two further parallels may be still more revealing: 'later' Stoics added to the necessary attributes of a cognitive impression a requirement strongly reminiscent of Carneades' 'undivertedness' (**40K**), and they also specified five 'concurrent' factors (**40L**), which closely resemble his account of what must be 'thoroughly explored' in the third level of convincing impression. These later Stoic additions read like actual importations from Carneades, gratefully accepted as improvements to the original Stoic doctrine in response to his criticisms.

We suggest, then, that Carneades, though aiming his attack on the criterion (**70A**) against all doctrinaire philosophers, regarded the Stoics' cognitive impression as his primary target. If this could be undermined, he supposed, no other criterion of truth would be left standing (cf. Arcesilaus' agreement to Zeno's characterization of what a cognitive impression would have to be like, **40D 7**). Once this Stoic context is exposed, the temptation to interpret

Carneades' 'convincing' impression as his substantive doctrine can be dispelled. Just like Arcesilaus' 'reasonable', Carneades' 'convincing' impression is a Stoic concept. He hands it back to them, with his own refinements, as a way of indicating that 'convincingness' will serve them just as well as the non-attainable certainty they insist upon.

One intriguing question remains. Carneades' convincing impression implicitly 'pulls us to assent' (**D 4**). Yet, according to his closest associate Clitomachus, Carneades performed a Herculean labour in expelling assent, and thereby all opinion (**J**). Can he, then, invoke his convincing impression in answer to the charge that the Academics' complete suspension of judgement makes life impossible? There is, happily, firm evidence that Carneades and his colleagues admitted the question and resolved it. They distinguished two kinds of assent, and the context in which they did so is explicitly that of Carneades' criterion (**I**). In all circumstances the Academic suspends judgement about everything: he never commits himself to anything's being true or false. While maintaining this strong suspension of judgement, he does allow himself a weak form of assent, in the sense that he says 'yes' to convincing impressions and 'no' to unconvincing ones. But he takes himself in such cases to be merely responding to what appears to him true or false. Such impressions are sufficient to motivate his actions, but they do not saddle him with opinions (cf. Arcesilaus in **A 3**).

Compared with Arcesilaus', Carneades' approach to living without opinions seems more sophisticated. In part, this must reflect the great development of Stoicism after Zeno and Cleanthes. Once this difference is admitted, there is no reason to credit Carneades with any concessions to dogmatism or alteration from the dialectical aims of Arcesilaus. But Carneades' 'convincing impression' was so brilliantly constructed that it gave Philo the foundation for a philosophy of fallibilism and Antiochus the motivation to press hard for certainty (see **68** commentary).

The most familiar modern strategy of simply not allowing philosophical scepticism to intrude upon daily life (e.g. Hume) is barely even contemplated in ancient scepticism, with the isolated exception of **68P**.

70 Contributions to philosophical debates

A Sextus Empiricus, *Against the professors* 7.159–65

(1) On the subject of the criterion, Carneades marshalled arguments not only against the Stoics but also against all previous philosophers. (2) His first argument, aimed against all of them jointly, is one on the basis of which he establishes that there is not, in an unqualified sense, any criterion of truth – not reason, not sensation, not impression, not any other existing thing. For all of these alike deceive us. (3) His second argument is one on the basis of which he shows that even if this criterion does exist, it is not independent of the way we are affected by what is self-evident. (4) For since the animal differs from inanimate things by its

sensory capacity, it will be entirely through this capacity that it registers both itself and external things. Sensation which is unmoved, unaffected and unaltered is not sensation at all, and is incapable of registering anything: it is when it is altered, and affected in some way in accordance with the impingement of things which are self-evident, that it reveals objects. (5) Therefore it is in the way that the soul is affected as a result of self-evidence that the criterion must be sought. This affection must be capable of revealing itself and the object which produced it in us. Such an affection is nothing other than the impression. Hence we should say that an impression is a sort of affection belonging to the animal, capable of presenting both itself and that which is distinct from itself. (6) For example, when (as Antiochus puts it) we look at something, we have our vision in a certain condition, and not in the same condition as we had it in before the act of seeing. But on the basis of this kind of alteration we register two things: one, the alteration itself, i.e. the impression, the other the thing which produced the alteration in us, i.e. the object seen. Similarly too with the other senses. Hence just as light shows up both itself and all the things in it, so too the impression, as the prime mover of the animal's knowledge, must in the manner of light both show up itself and be capable of revealing the self-evident object that caused it. (7) But because it does not always reveal what is truly there, but often deceives us and is at variance with the things which transmitted it, like incompetent messengers, a necessary consequence is that we cannot allow every impression to be a criterion of truth, but just, if any, the true impression. (8) Then since, once again [cf. **41C 8**], there is no true impression of such a kind that it could not turn out to be false, but for every apparently true impression an indiscernible false one is found, the criterion will turn out to consist in an impression which spans true and false. But the impression which spans both of these is not cognitive, and, not being cognitive, will not be a criterion either. (9) Given that no impression is criterial [or 'judgemental'], reason could not be a criterion either, since it is derived from impression. This is plausible. For the object being judged must first appear to it, and nothing can appear without irrational sensation. (10) Therefore neither irrational sensation nor reason is a criterion. [continued at **69D**]

B Cicero, *Academica* 2.40–1

[Speaker: the Antiochean Lucullus] (1) First you can familiarize yourselves with the basic principles, so to speak, of their [the Academics'] whole philosophy. (2) They start by constructing a sort of expertise concerning what we are calling 'impressions', defining their power and their kinds, including a description of the kind that can be cognized and grasped. Their account is as full as that given by the Stoics [cf. **39G; 40E**].

(3) Then they expound the two theses which virtually embrace this whole issue: when impressions are such that other impressions too can be just like them and not differ at all, it is impossible that some of them should be cognitive while others are not; but they count as not differing at all not only if they are alike in every respect, but also if they are impossible to tell apart. (4) Having posited these theses, they embody their entire case in the conclusion of a single argument. That conclusion is established in the following way. 'Of impressions, some are true, some false. A false impression is not cognitive. But every true impression is such that a false one just like it can also occur. And where impressions are such that there is no difference between them, it cannot turn out that some of them are cognitive but others not. Therefore no impression is cognitive.' (5) Of the premises which they adopt in order to reach their conclusion, they take two to be conceded to them, since no one raises an objection. These are, first, that false impressions are not cognitive; and second, that when impressions do not differ at all it is impossible that some of them should be cognitive, others not. (6) But the other premises they defend with a long and wide-ranging disquisition. Here again there are two of them: first, that of impressions some are true, others false; second, that every impression arising from something true is such that it could also arise from something false.

C Sextus Empiricus, *Against the professors* 9.139–41

(1) If, then, there are gods, they are animals. And if they are animals, they have sensation, since every animal is thought of as an animal in virtue of its sharing in sensation. (2) But if they have sensation, they are also affected by bitter and sweet. For it is not the case that while registering sense-objects through some other sense they do not do so also through that of taste. (3) Hence simply to strip god of this or any other sense is quite unconvincing, for if man has more senses than god he will be superior to god, whereas, as Carneades said, god ought to have, as well as these five senses which we all have, the additional evidence of further senses, so as to be able to register more things, rather than be deprived of the five. (4) Therefore we must say that god has some sense of taste, through which he registers taste-objects. But if he registers through the sense of taste, he is affected by sweet and bitter. And if he is affected by sweet and bitter, he will be pleased by some things and displeased by others. But if he is displeased by some things, he will be vulnerable to distress and to change for the worse. If so, he is perishable. (5) Hence if there are gods, they are perishable. Therefore there are no gods.

D Cicero, *On the nature of the gods* 3.43–4

[Speaker: the Academic Cotta] (1) 'You count Zeus and Posidon as gods. Therefore their brother Orcus too is a god. And so are Acheron, Cocytus and Pyriphlegethon, who are said to flow in the underworld. Then Charon and Cerberus are to be considered gods. But this last claim must be rejected. Therefore Orcus is not a god either. What, then, do you say about his brothers?' (2) Carneades' purpose in saying this was not to get rid of the gods – for what could be less fitting for a philosopher? – but to convict the Stoics of failing to explain anything about the gods.

E Sextus Empiricus, *Against the professors* 9.182–4

(1) There are also some arguments posed by Carneades in the manner of the Sorites. They were written up by his colleague Clitomachus, who took them to be very weighty and effective, and they take the following form. (2) 'If Zeus is a god, . . . Posidon too, being his brother, will be a god. But if Posidon is a god, the [river] Achelous too will be a god. And if the Achelous is, so is the Nile. If the Nile is, so are all rivers. If all rivers are, streams too would be gods. If streams were, torrents would be. But streams are not. Therefore Zeus is not a god either. But if there were gods, Zeus too would be a god. Therefore there are no gods.' (3) Again, 'If the sun is a god, day too would be a god (for day is nothing but the sun above the earth). And if day is a god, so will the month be (for it is a compound of days). And if the month is a god, the year too would be a god (for the year is a compound of months). But not the last. Therefore not the first either.'

F Cicero, *On divination* 2.9–10

[Speaker: Cicero, against Stoic theory of divination] (1) I am motivated by the question which Carneades in particular used to ask, namely what things were the objects of divination. Things perceived by the senses? But they are what we see, hear, taste, smell and touch, so they surely include nothing for us to sense by foresight or by stimulation of the mind, rather than just naturally . . . (2) Nor, again, is divination needed in those things which are the subject-matter of expertise. For when people are sick, it is not soothsayers or fortune-tellers that we normally summon, but doctors. Nor are those who want to play the harp or the flute taught to handle them by seers, but by musicians. The same principle applies in literature, and in everything else that is the subject-matter of some discipline.

G Cicero, *On fate* 26–33 (continuing **20E**)

(1) This being so, why should it not be the case that every proposition is either true or false, without our conceding that everything that happens happens by fate? (2) 'Because', comes the reply, 'there cannot be things which are going to be true if they do not have causes of their future being. So things which are true must necessarily have causes. Thus when they come about it will have been by fate.' (3) That is the end of the matter, if I

ave to concede to you that either all things come about by fate, or something can happen without a cause. (4) Can the proposition 'Scipio will capture Numantia' not be true unless it is going to be brought about by an eternal chain of causes? Could it have been false if it had been said six hundred centuries earlier? (5) If the proposition 'Scipio will capture Numantia' had not been true then, neither would the proposition 'Scipio captured Numantia' be true, now that Numantia has fallen. So is it possible for anything to have come about of which it was not previously true that it would come about? For just as we call 'true' those past things of which it was at an earlier time true that they were being actualized, so we will call 'true' those future things of which it will later be true that they are being actualized. (6) Nor, if every proposition is either true or false, does it automatically follow that there are immutable eternal causes to prevent anything from turning out in any way other than that in which it will turn out. The truth of statements like 'Cato will come into the senate' is brought about by contingent causes, not by causes bound up in nature and the world. (7) And yet that something will come about, when true, is as immutable as the truth that something has come about. Nor is that any reason for living in terror of fate or necessity. (8) For it has to be admitted: if the proposition 'Hortensius will come to Tusculum' is not true, it follows that it is false. (Your people [the Epicureans] want neither, but that is impossible.) (9) [= **55S**, on the Lazy Argument] (10) Carneades rejected this whole kind of approach, and thought that this argument [the Lazy Argument] was not worked out with sufficient care. He therefore pressed his attack in another form, quite without trickery. Here is his inference: 'If all things come about through antecedent causes, all things come about through interconnexion in a natural chain. If that is so, all things are the product of necessity. If that is true, nothing is in our power. But there is something in our power. But if all things come about through fate, all things come about through antecedent causes. Therefore it is not the case that whatever happens happens through fate.' (11) You cannot get a tighter argument than this. For if someone wanted to repeat it in the form 'If every truth about the future has been true from eternity, so that its coming about in the way in which it will come about is certain, all things must necessarily come about through interconnexion in a natural chain', he would be talking nonsense. For it makes a great difference whether things which are going to be true are the product, from eternity, of a natural cause, or whether the truth of things which are going to be can be understood even without their eternal embodiment in nature. (12) That is why Carneades used to say that not even Apollo could foretell the future, apart from things whose causes were embodied in nature in such a way as to render their coming about necessary. (13) For by inspecting what could even the god himself tell that Marcellus

464

who was three times consul would die at sea? This is something that was true from eternity but did not have causes working to bring it about. (14) Thus he held that Apollo did not even know those *past* facts of which no signs survived as traces. How much less could he know the future? For knowledge of the future required knowledge of the causes working to bring each thing about. (15) Therefore Apollo could have foretold neither the story of Oedipus – for there were no pre-existent causes in nature necessitating his killing his father – nor anything else of the sort.

☐ Although its role was essentially critical, the Hellenistic Academy did make many substantive contributions to current philosophical debates. Under Carneades these became often more constructive in tone than they had been under Arcesilaus, thanks to Carneades' practice of *defending* philosophical theses for his own dialectical purposes (**68** commentary; **64G 5**; **69D–E, H, L**). Indeed, his successors in the Academy, especially under the headship of Philo, went so far as to adopt some of these theses as their own, thus incurring the complaint from the radical sceptic Aenesidemus that they had become barely distinguishable from their Stoic opponents (**71C 5–9**; see **68** commentary).

In epistemology the sceptical Academics' contribution is twofold in nature. On the one hand, they marshall arguments to show that there is no possible criterion of truth. These are already well represented in **40** and **41C**, but **A–B** in the present section convey better the systematic nature of the campaign, which, although primarily motivated by a Stoic target, aims equally at all other doctrines of the criterion. On the other hand, as we saw in **68–9**, Arcesilaus and Carneades also offered surrogate principles of conduct in place of the criterion, one of which, the 'convincing', was to win much favour with Carneades' doctrinaire successors in the Academy.

The themes of some other individual critiques of Stoic theses can be briefly noted. Change: **28A–C**. Mixture: **48E**. The gods: **C–E**. Teleology and providence: **54P, R**. Divination: **F**. Justice: **57H, 68M**. The ethical end: **64**. The Academics' insistent use of paradoxes like the Sorites (as at **D–E**) and the Lying Argument also had a considerable impact on Stoic logic (**37B–I**; cf. the reference to Arcesilaus at **37B 6**). For evidence of a debate with the Epicureans over friendship, see **22O 4**.

The topic on which Carneades' own positive ideas have rightly aroused most interest is that of free will and determinism, which exercised both the Epicureans (**20**) and the Stoics (**38; 55; 62**). We have seen at **20E 4–7** that he offered the Epicureans some positive suggestions which he thought would strengthen their anti-determinism into an adequate counterweight to Stoic determinism. The object of these was no doubt his regular one of producing a stalemate between two opposed doctrines in the interests of suspension of judgement (cf. **68**), and we should heed Cicero's warnings not to take Carneades' dialectical defence of some position as signalling his own acceptance of it (**64G 5**; **69L**; cf. **D**; **68M**). Nevertheless, his suggestion is important and sophisticated enough to deserve discussion in its own right. It is elaborated in **G**.

We may start by separating three guises in which predetermination, or 'fate', was viewed. First, causal determinism: any event is preceded by *causes* sufficient to bring it about. Second, logical determinism: it is already *true* that the event in question will occur. Third, epistemic determinism: it is already *known* (e.g. by a god or seer) that the event will occur. On all three grounds, the determinist may claim that the event definitely will occur. He will normally claim also that the event *must* occur, but Chrysippus (**38E**; **62C**), at least, hoped to avoid this corollary.

Both Chrysippus and Epicurus treated causal and logical determinism as effectively equivalent, or at least as inter-entailing: cf. **20E** 1–3, **H–I**; **38G**. Both agreed that causal determinism and the logical principle of bivalence (that every proposition is either true or false) stand or fall together: Chrysippus accepted both, Epicurus rejected both. Epistemic determinism was not treated separately, but was assumed at least to entail the other two varieties (**20G**; **52C** 4; **55P**).

Carneades' major innovation is the separation of these three varieties of determinism. The epistemic kind, he implicitly concedes, entails the causal and logical kinds, and the causal kind entails the logical kind. But, crucially, the logical kind does not entail either the causal or the epistemic kind (**G** 4–6, 11–15). In the light of these distinctions, Carneades will maintain that causal and epistemic determinism are false, while logical determinism is in a way true, but harmless.

His objection to causal determinism is contained in the argument at **G** 10, which relies on the premise that some actions are 'in our power' (i.e. in our power to perform or not perform, rather than in the attenuated Stoic sense of merely 'brought about by our own agency', cf. **62G**). The premise may have been intuitive, or may have been inferred from the universal existence of moral attitudes (cf. **62C** 4). His positive alternative, alluded to at **G** 3, is fully set out, admittedly in Epicurean dress, at **20E** 4–7: the very proper principle that nothing happens without a cause need not in turn imply the subjection of our actions to everlasting causal chains, because volitions are 'in our power'. This fact of the autonomy of volition is itself caused – so that the principle is not violated – but not by antecedent causes, such as might go to make up a causal chain. The cause is simply the intrinsic nature of volition itself. Consequently our actions have, in volitions, causes which are not historically or naturally necessary, but 'contingent' (**G** 6).

Once causal determinism is eliminated, epistemic determinism falls with it (**G** 12–15). This is because knowledge requires evidence, and in the absence of predetermining causes there is no possible evidence that a hypothetical future event will indeed occur. The mere fact of its being *true* now that the event will take place is not, in any appropriate sense, open to inspection. (Cf. also Carneades' objections to divination in **F**.)

This leaves him with the threat of logical determinism to contend with. The Epicurean solution of simply denying bivalence (**20H–I**) is quickly dismissed (**G** 8). Instead, Carneades' main thesis is that the present truth value of propositions about future events is no more than a matter of tense logic: **G** 5. Chrysippus (see **38** commentary) had held such propositions to have their present truth value in virtue of the present existence or non-existence of causes sufficient to bring about the events predicted. Carneades suggests instead that it is the future events themselves, or their non-occurrence, which make the predictions true or false. This is reinforced by insistence upon the *symmetry* of past and future at **G 5**, cf. **G 14**. (We may indeed wonder how Chrysippus would account for the present truth of facts about the past: are they true in virtue of their present *effects?*)

Despite this reductive treatment of logical predestination, Carneades accepts that true propositions about future events are *immutably* true: **G 7**. How then can I be free to perform or not perform an action, if it is now immutably true that I will perform it? Here we must speculate as to the precise nature of Carneades' solution.

First, it is hard to deny his immutability thesis, because if it were to become false that I will perform the action it would *eo ipso* follow that it had been false all along, so that there would have been no *change* of truth value. (Of course, the prediction will normally cease to be true after the event has occurred, but the determinist can happily accept that: he is only interested in the immutability of its truth value *up to* the time of its fulfilment.) But once we read the immutability in these terms, and bear in mind Carneades' appeal to the symmetry of past and future, we can interpret him as follows. By performing the action, just as I cause it to become consistently true hereafter that I have performed it, so too *I cause it to have been* consistently true hitherto that I would perform it. In other words, it is my action which causes all assertions of my performance of it, however tensed, to be true. That the truth value of the prediction cannot change prior to its fulfilment is no more a threat to my freedom of choice than the fact that the truth that I did perform the action cannot change after the performance. In both cases, the stable truth value is the *result* of my action, not its cause. (For the attribution of a similar, though less articulated, position to Cleanthes, see **38** commentary.)

The Pyrrhonist revival

71 Why to suspend judgement

A Diogenes Laertius 9.106–7

(1) Aenesidemus, in the first of his *Pyrrhonist discourses*, says that Pyrrho determines nothing in doctrinaire fashion, because of the opposition of arguments, but follows appearances. He says the same in his *Against wisdom* and *On inquiry* . . . (2) Hence according to the Sceptics it is what appears that serves as a criterion, as Aenesidemus also says . . . (3) As end the Sceptics name suspension of judgement, upon which freedom from disturbance follows like a shadow, as the followers of Timon and Aenesidemus put it.

B Diogenes Laertius 9.78

Pyrrhonist discourse is a kind of recollection of appearances, or of ideas of any kind, on the basis of which they are all brought into confrontation with each other and, when compared, are found to present much disparity and confusion. This is what Aenesidemus says in his *Outline introduction to Pyrrhonism*.

C Photius, *Library* 169b18–170b3

(1) I read Aenesidemus' eight *Pyrrhonist discourses*. The overall aim of the book is to establish that there is no firm basis for cognition, either through sense-perception, or indeed through thought. (2) Consequently, he says, neither the Pyrrhonists nor the others know the truth in things; but the philosophers of other persuasions, as well as being ignorant in general, and wearing themselves out uselessly and expending themselves in ceaseless torments, are also ignorant of the very fact that they have cognition of none of the things of which they think that they have gained cognition. (3) But he who philosophizes after the fashion of Pyrrho is happy not only in general but also, and especially, in the wisdom of knowing that he has firm cognition of nothing. And even with regard to what he knows, he has the propriety to assent no more to its affirmation than to its denial. (4) The whole scheme of the book is directed towards the purpose I have mentioned. In writing the discourses

Aenesidemus addresses them to Lucius Tubero, one of his colleagues from the Academy, a Roman by birth, with an illustrious ancestry and a distinguished political career. (5) In the first discourse he differentiates between the Pyrrhonists and the Academics in almost precisely the following words. He says that the Academics are doctrinaire: they posit some things with confidence and unambiguously deny others. (6) The Pyrrhonists, on the other hand, are aporetic and free of all doctrine. Not one of them has said either that all things are incognitive, or that they are cognitive, but that they are no more of this kind than of that, or that they are sometimes of this kind, sometimes not, or that for one person they are of this kind, for another person not of this kind, and for another person not even existent at all. Nor do they say that all things in general, or some things, are accessible to us, or not accessible to us, but that they are no more accessible to us than not, or that they are sometimes accessible to us, sometimes not, or that they are accessible to one person but not to another. (7) Nor indeed, do they say there is true or false, convincing or unconvincing, existent or non-existent. But the same thing is, it might be said, no more true than false, convincing than unconvincing, or existent than non-existent; or sometimes the one, sometimes the other; or of such a kind for one person but not for another. (8) For the Pyrrhonist determines absolutely nothing, not even this very claim that nothing is determined. (We put it this way, he says, for lack of a way to express the thought.) (9) But the Academics, he says, especially those from the present-day Academy, are sometimes in agreement with Stoic beliefs, and to tell the truth turn out to be Stoics fighting with Stoics. Moreover, they are doctrinaire about many things. For they introduce virtue and folly, and posit good and bad, truth and falsity, convincing and unconvincing, existent and non-existent. They give firm determinations for many other things too. It is only about the cognitive impression that they express dissent. (10) Thus the followers of Pyrrho, in determining nothing, remain absolutely above reproach, whereas the Academics, he says, incur a scrutiny similar to that faced by the other philosophers. (11) Above all, the Pyrrhonists, by entertaining doubts about every thesis, maintain consistency and do not conflict with themselves, whereas the Academics are unaware that they are conflicting with themselves. For to make unambiguous assertions and denials, at the same time as stating as a generalization that no things are cognitive, introduces an undeniable conflict: how is it possible to recognize that this is true, this false, yet still entertain perplexity and doubt, and not make a clear choice of the one and avoidance of the other? (12) For if it is not known that this is good or bad, or that this is true but that false, and this existent but that non-existent, it must certainly be admitted that each of them is incognitive. But if they receive self-evident cognition by means of sense-perception or thought, we must say that each is cognitive. (13) These similar considerations are set out by Aenesidemus of Aegae at the beginning of his discourses, to indicate the difference between the Pyrrhonists and Academics. He goes on in the same discourse, the first, also to report in summary outline the entire way of life of the Pyrrhonists.

D Anonymous commentary on Plato's *Theaetetus*, 60.48–61.46

(1) Since Theaetetus, when asked what knowledge is, replied '. . . and as it appears to me at present . . .', Socrates [*Theaetetus* 151e] welcomes his lack of hesitancy in saying what appears to him and what he believes knowledge to be. For what he is saying is not the Pyrrhonian dictum, namely that one would not determinately assert any doctrine but just says that it appears to one. (2) For according to Pyrrho, what is the criterion is neither reason, nor a true impression, nor a convincing impression, nor a cognitive impression, nor anything else of the kind, but what now appears to him. (3) Whether it is or is not such as it appears he does not assert, because he thinks that the arguments for the opposing views are of equal strength, and he makes the impressions on a par with each other, leaving no difference between them in respect of their being true or false, convincing or unconvincing, self-evident or obscure, or cognitive or incognitive, but holds that they are all alike. (4) He does not even assert as a doctrine the consequence – to live his life in accordance with whatever impression befalls him at each time, not on the grounds that it is a true impression, but because it now appears to him.

☐ Our story of Hellenistic philosophy closes, as it opened, with Pyrrhonian scepticism. As the New Academy under the headship of Philo of Larissa in the early first century B.C. drifted away from its sceptical stance (see **68** commentary), one disillusioned member, Aenesidemus, founded a breakaway movement, under the title 'Pyrrhonists' (see especially **C**). This was the group which in time – probably not before the mid-first century A.D. – became known as the 'Sceptics', literally 'searchers'. Another title was *ephektikoi*, 'suspenders of judgement'. The eventual outlook of the school is well presented in the surviving works of Sextus Empiricus, who wrote in the second century A.D. However, since our coverage is focused on the Hellenistic period, we will concentrate here on Aenesidemus himself, with just occasional help from Sextus' *Outlines of Pyrrhonism*.

Academic scepticism had arisen as an essentially epistemological stance – the safeguarding of intellectual integrity against the temptation to hazard opinions. Although the Academy did develop certain strategies relating to the practical conduct of life (see **69**), and even, under Philo, the makings of an ethical system, these were subordinate to its scepticism rather than at the root of it. Aenesidemus' idea, by contrast, was to develop the philosophical basis for the celebrated tranquillity manifested by Pyrrho (**A**, **C 3**; cf. **2** for Pyrrho himself), so that from the outset his philosophy was shaped by a moral motive.

Developing the picture presented in the writings of Pyrrho's disciple Timon (**1–3** *passim*), Aenesidemus defended the great man's lifestyle against the derogatory tradition which had in the mean time grown up. Suspending judgement had not, he claimed, led Pyrrho into reckless behaviour (**1A 4**). He had lived his life, as any Pyrrhonist would, in non-committal conformity with appearances: **A 1–2** (cf. **1H**).

What are Pyrrhonian 'appearances'? First, although in a narrower sense they are confined to sensory appearances (cf. **72A**), the commoner usage is one which involves no such restriction (cf. **72E 4**, **K 16**). Second, although there has been some controversy so far as concerns Sextus' later account (*Outlines of Pyrrhonism*, especially 1.19–20), there is good reason to believe that Aenesidemus, at any rate, meant 'appearances' in a sense which eliminated any epistemic component. That is, when a Pyrrhonist says 'It appears to me to be raining', he is not expressing any kind of belief that it is raining, but is just describing from a neutral stance the impression currently affecting him. This is clearly the distinction made in **D**, from an Academic work written possibly as early as the first century B.C. and, if so, reflecting 'Pyrrhonism' as it was presented at that date. Pyrrho, on this story, was able to act in accordance with impressions *without taking them to be true* (**D 4**).

It may seem puzzling why a Pyrrhonist should open his umbrella at all if he does not even take his impression that it is raining to be true. Sextus, at least, would reply that his actions are either instinctive, e.g. drinking when thirsty, or conditioned by the customs and educational processes of his own society, and can therefore be performed automatically without the intervention of assent (*Outlines of Pyrrhonism* 1.21–4). This might be read as an attempt to accommodate the fact that even though inwardly the Pyrrhonist insulates himself from assent in a way which results in supreme tranquillity, to all outward appearances he leads a quite conventional life. Since, however, Pyrrho himself had not led an outwardly conventional life (cf. **1A–C**), we may take his own acquiescence in appearances to have been rather more restricted in scope than this, and it must be left an open question how conventional Aenesidemus intended the Pyrrhonist lifestyle to be. (One might compare the influence of Socrates' personal example, which could encourage on the one hand respectable citizens like Xenophon and Plato, on the other hand the outrageously anti-social Cynics.) Minimally, we can ascribe to Aenesidemus the position that ordinary acts of self-maintenance and self-preservation may be performed automatically, without assent.

The reward for eliminating assent is tranquillity ('freedom from disturbance', **A 3**). Why so? One answer, based again on Sextus, might go as follows. Actually believing that it is raining, that rain makes you wet, cold and ill, and that getting ill is bad, wrecks your tranquillity by making you *care* about keeping dry. A Pyrrhonist, for whom opening his umbrella is little more than a reflex action, lacks these beliefs, and so is free from any such anxiety. Extend this to the entire range of human actions, and sublime tranquillity will ensue. In Aenesidemus' case, however, we might expect his defence of the position to rest more directly on appeal to Pyrrho's personal example (see **2**), in which he seems to have taken a greater interest than Sextus does.

We have spoken so far of the ordinary conduct of life. But Pyrrho was also admired, at least by Timon, for refusing to be seduced into any kind of theoretical stance on any issue (**2B–C**). The Greek word for such a stance is *dogma*, and for one who takes it *dogmatikos*. We translate these respectively as 'doctrine' and 'doctrinaire' (cf. **66I–J**; **72K 5**; 'dogma', often preferred as a translation, has misleading associations of pig-headedness). Opposition to doctrinaire theses is one of the hallmarks of Aenesidemus' philosophy (cf. **A 1**, **B**), and the Academics were among his first targets, for their alleged inconsistency in trying to combine numerous doctrinaire stances with a residual denial of cognitive certainty (**C 5**, **9–13**; cf. **68N 2**). Doctrinaire belief creates a permanent state of inner torment (**C 2**); since any subject of inquiry turns out to present conflicting impressions (**B**), to adopt this or that position in relation to it is to condemn yourself to being permanently troubled by it. The alternative approach, called 'Pyrrhonist discourse' (**B**, cf. **A 1**), involves methodically exposing the conflicts, precisely *in order to* suspend judgement and thus remain untroubled (**A 3**). How this is done will be the topic of **72**.

But how can Aenesidemus at **C 11** claim for his philosophy the virtue of self-consistency? Is it not itself a doctrinaire position, laying down a partisan end and recommending a specific lifestyle? This time there is no sign of at least one defensive strategy later adopted by Sextus, that of claiming an allegedly non-doctrinaire (because uncontroversial) end, freedom from disturbance, and describing suspension of judgement as a means of achieving it which has been stumbled upon by pure accident (*Outlines of Pyrrhonism* 1.12, 25–30). Aenesidemus' end is suspension of judgement itself (**A 3**), and he even apparently recommends it as pleasurable (**1F 5**). One might, then, wonder how he can avoid disrupting his own tranquillity by *caring* about achieving his own partisan end (contrast **72L 7**), or being troubled by the arguments in favour of various rival ends.

However we try to read Aenesidemus' fragments, a degree of this tension will probably remain (see further, **72** commentary). To judge from **C 8** (cf. also **D 4**), his ground for the consistency claim lies in the policy of bringing his sceptical utterances within their own and each other's scope. This is clearly a delicate procedure, since it involves simultaneously making and withdrawing an assertion. Sextus likes the parallels of fire, which destroys both the combustible material and itself, and of a ladder which you climb up and then throw away; but these suffer from the weakness of seeming to make the two actions successive, where they should be simultaneous. Aenesidemus seems to prefer the defence that language is ill-fitted for expressing his idea: **C 8**. You can adopt a non-assertive frame of mind; what you cannot straightforwardly do is *assert* that you are adopting it.

There is, admittedly, one puzzling exception to this strategy. At **C 2–3** Aenesidemus tells us that unlike other philosophers the Pyrrhonist *knows* that he has firm cognition of nothing. This sounds like the kind of negative dogmatism associated with the name of Socrates (**68A 3**), and notionally approved by the Stoic Antipater (**68N 1**), but repudiated as inconsistent by Metrodorus of Chios (**1D**), by Arcesilaus (**68A 3**), and by Carneades (**68N 1**). Since Pyrrho himself had a strong tendency towards negative dogmatism (see **1** commentary), it might be thought that Aenesidemus is here following his lead. But that would run directly counter to the more sophisticated policy noted above. It seems safer to take refuge in the fact that the verb which he uses at **C 3** is the ordinary Greek verb for 'know', not the technical term for infallible 'cognition' (on which see **40**) used elsewhere in the same text, and that its usage here is such a weak one that it does not even entail assent. Perhaps, then, all that **C 2–3** amounts to is that, unlike other philosophers, the Pyrrhonist *is not under the illusion that he has cognition*. (For a similar usage, cf. **69K**.)

The other tactic familiar from Sextus (e.g. **68I 4**; cf. **1H 1**), which Aenesidemus might be expected to use, is that of warning us to prefix 'It appears that . . .' to all his utterances. Aenesidemus certainly treated descriptions of what (non-epistemically) appears as a basis for ordinary action. Whether he also anticipated Sextus in using them as a means of insulating himself from his own philosophical pronouncements is less clear. The only apparent instance in our texts of this tactic is at **72I 2**, and there we argue that a rather more restricted purpose is in view. But since it had already been to some extent sanctified by Timon as an interpretation of Pyrrho (**1H 2–3**; **2E**), it is hard to doubt that Aenesidemus too felt able to make use of it.

Aenesidemus' position on the ethical end is also puzzling. If we are to avoid an outright contradiction between **A 3**, where suspension of judgement is the end, and **72L 7**, where he argues that there is no end, it seems that we must take his own end to be somehow exempted from the latter text's attack on 'any end which any philosophical persuasion might believe in'. A persuasion (*hairesis*) is, strictly understood, adherence to a doctrinal system (Sextus, *Outlines of Pyrrhonism* 1.16), and Aenesidemus might maintain that suspension of judgement runs directly counter to this. Hence far from being itself doctrinaire, Aenesidemus' end is the antidote to doctrine. See further, **72** commentary.

72 How to suspend judgement

A Sextus Empiricus, *Outlines of Pyrrhonism* 1.31–9

(1) Broadly speaking, this [suspension of judgement about everything] comes about because of the setting of things in opposition. We oppose either appearances to appearances, or ideas to ideas, or appearances to ideas. (2) We oppose appearances to appearances when we say 'The same tower seems round from a distance but square from near by.' (3) We oppose ideas to ideas when someone establishes the existence of providence from the orderliness of the things in the heavens and we oppose to this the frequency with which the good fare badly and the bad prosper, thereby deducing the non-existence of providence. (4) We oppose ideas to appearances in the way in which Anaxagoras opposed to snow's being white the consideration: snow is frozen water, and water is black, therefore snow is black too. (5) On a different scheme, we oppose sometimes present things to present things, as in the cases just given, but sometimes present things to past and future things. For example, when

someone presents us with an argument for a thesis which we cannot refute, we reply, 'Just as before the founder of the school you follow was born the school's thesis did not yet seem sound, but was an objective natural fact, likewise it is possible that the very opposite thesis to the one you have just argued is an objective natural fact but does not yet appear so to us. Hence it is premature to assent to the thesis which appears powerful to us at the present moment. (6) To give us a more accurate impression of these oppositions, I shall add the modes through which suspension of judgement is deduced. But I shall make no assertions about either their number or their cogency: it is possible that they are both unsound and more numerous than those which I shall be listing. (7) Well, the familiar tradition among the older Sceptics is of modes, ten in total, through which suspension of judgement seems to be deduced. They also use the terms 'arguments' and 'outlines' as equivalents to 'modes'. They are as follows. (8) *1*, the mode depending on the disparity between animals; *2*, that depending on the difference between men; *3*, that depending on the different structures of the sense-organs; *4*, that depending on situations; *5*, that depending on positions, distances and locations; *6*, that depending on admixtures; *7*, that depending on the quantities and configurations of the objects; *8*, that derived from relativity; *9*, that depending on regularity or rarity of meeting; *10*, that depending on ways of life, customs, laws, legendary beliefs, and doctrinaire opinions. We adopt this order arbitrarily. (9) There are three modes superordinate to these: that derived from the judging subject, that derived from the object of judgement, and that derived from both. Modes *1–4* fall under that derived from the judging subject, since the judging subject is either an animal or a man or a sense, and in some situation. Modes *7* and *10* are referred to that derived from the object of judgement. And modes *5*, *6*, *8*, and *9* are referred to that derived from both. (10) Then again, these three are referred to the mode of relativity. Hence the mode of relativity is the most generic, the three are species, and the ten are sub-species. We say this about their number in accordance with what is plausible.

B Sextus Empiricus, *Outlines of Pyrrhonism* 1.40–61

(1) The first argument we mentioned was the one according to which depending on the difference between animals the same objects do not produce the same impressions. We infer this from their different modes of generation and the variety of their bodily make-up. (2) The point about modes of generation is that some animals are generated asexually, some sexually; and of those generated asexually some are generated from fire, such as the tiny creatures that appear in ovens, others from putrescent water, such as mosquitoes . . . Of those generated sexually, some have homogeneous parents, like the majority of animals, others

have heterogeneous parents, as mules do . . . It is likely, then, that the generative dissimilarities and divergences should produce great contrasts in the way the animals are affected, bringing in their wake incompatibility, incongruity and conflict. (3) Another potential source of conflict among impressions depending on the disparity between animals is the difference in the principal bodily parts, especially those whose natural function is to discriminate and to perceive. People with jaundice say that those things are yellow which appear white to us, and people with bloodshot eyes call them blood-red. Since, then, with animals too, some have yellow eyes, some bloodshot, some white, some of other colours, it is likely, I think, that they register colours in different ways . . . (4) The same argument applies to the other senses. How could the tactile processes of shelled, fleshy, prickly, feathered, and scaly creatures be called similar? How could hearing be called alike in creatures with the narrowest auditory ducts and those with the widest, or in those with hairy and those with bare ears, considering that even our own auditory processes are different when we block our ears from when we leave them alone? . . . (5) Just as the same food when digested becomes here a vein, here an artery, here a bone, here a sinew, and so on, revealing different capacities depending on the differences in the parts which absorb it . . ., so too it is likely that external objects are perceived differently according to the different structures of the animals undergoing the impressions. (6) A more self-evident understanding of the matter can be obtained from animals' choices and avoidances. Perfume seems delightful to men but unbearable to beetles and bees. Olive oil is beneficial to men, but is sprinkled to exterminate wasps and bees. Sea water, if drunk, is unpleasant and poisonous to men, but delicious and drinkable for fish. Pigs get more pleasure from wallowing in foul-smelling sewage than in clear pure water . . . If the same things are unpleasant to some animals but pleasant to others, and pleasant and unpleasant depend on impressions, the animals are receiving different impressions from objects. (7) If the same things appear unalike depending on the difference between animals, we will be able to say how the object is perceived by us, but will suspend judgement as to how it is in its own nature. For we ourselves will not be able to adjudicate between our own impressions and those of other animals: we are ourselves parties to the disagreement, and hence in need of an adjudicator, rather than capable of judging for ourselves. (8) Besides, we cannot judge our impressions superior to those found in irrational animals either without proof or with proof. For in addition to the possibility that proof does not exist, as we will note later, the so-called proof must itself be either apparent to us or non-apparent. If it is non-apparent, we will not propound it with confidence. But if it is apparent to us, since our inquiry is about what is apparent to animals and proof is apparent to us, who are animals, it will itself in so far as it is apparent be subject to inquiry as to its truth . . . (9) If, then, impressions differ depending on the divergences between animals, and there is no way of adjudicating between them, it is necessary to suspend judgement about external objects.

C Sextus Empiricus, *Outlines of Pyrrhonism* 1.79–91

(1) Such [see **B**] is the first mode of suspending judgement. The second, as we said, is that derived from the difference between men. For even if one hypothetically grants that men are more credible than the irrational animals, we will find inducements to suspend judgement even so far as concerns our own differences. (2) Now man is said to have two constituents, namely soul and body, and we differ from each other in respect of both. In respect of the body, we differ both in form and in our individual mixtures. For the body of a Scythian differs from the body of an Indian in form. This divergence is, it is said, the result of different predominance of humours. And in accordance with different predominance of humours impressions also differ, as we established in the first argument . . . (3) Such are the differences of our individual mixtures that some men digest beef more easily than rock-fish, and get an upset stomach from a drop of Lesbian wine. There was reportedly an old Attic woman who could swallow thirty drams of hemlock without ill-effect. Lysis also used to take four drams of opium without upset. Demophon, Alexander's butler, shivered in the sun or in the bath but felt warm in the shade . . . (4) Since (if we may make do with listing a few of the many cases recorded by the doctrinaire writers) the divergence between men with regard to their bodies is so great, it is likely that they also differ from each other with regard to their actual souls. For the body is a sort of outline sketch of the soul, as is also shown by the science of physiognomics. (5) But the strongest indication of men's great and limitless mental differences is the disagreement between what the doctrinaire thinkers say, especially about what to choose and what to avoid . . . (6) Since, then, choice and avoidance lie in pleasure and displeasure, and pleasure and displeasure lie in sensation and impression, when some people choose what others avoid the natural consequence is for us to infer that they are not moved in even similar ways by the same things, since if they were they would have the same choices or avoidances. (7) But if the same things move us differently depending on the difference between men, that too might reasonably induce us to suspend judgement. Perhaps we are capable of saying how each object appears, with respect to each human difference, but not of asserting what its power is, with respect to its own nature. (8) For we will trust either all men, or some. If all, we will be attempting the impossible and accepting

contradictories. If some, let them tell us whose view we are to assent to. The Platonist will say Plato's, the Epicurean Epicurus', and the others likewise. And by this inarbitrable dispute they will once again bring us round to suspension of judgement. (9) Anyone who says that we should assent to the *majority* opinion is accepting a childish idea. Nobody is capable of approaching all the men in the world and calculating what is the majority opinion. It is possible that in some tribes unknown to us things rare among us are found in the majority of people, while attributes which belong to the majority of us are rare . . . (10) Certain self-satisfied people, the doctrinaire thinkers, say that in judging things they should rate *themselves* above other men. We know the absurdity of this evaluation. They are, after all, themselves parties to the disagreement, and if their way of judging between appearances is to give themselves precedence they are, by entrusting the judgement to themselves, begging the question. But even so, in order to achieve the suspension of judgement by focusing the argument on a single man, such as their dream-figure the wise man, we adopt the third mode.

D Sextus Empiricus, *Outlines of Pyrrhonism* 1.91–8

(1) This ['the third mode', cf. **C 10**] is how we label the mode which derives from the difference between the senses. That the senses are at variance with each other is pre-evident. (2) Pictures seem to the sense of sight to have concavities and convexities, but not to the touch. Honey seems pleasant to the tongue on some things, but unpleasant to the eyes, so that whether it is absolutely pleasant or unpleasant is impossible to say. Likewise perfume: it delights the sense of smell, but displeases that of taste . . . (3) Hence what each of these is like as regards its nature we will be unable to say. What we can say is how it appears on each occasion. (4) . . . Each of the sense-objects which appear to us seems to make a complex impression on us. For example, the apple strikes us as smooth, pleasant-smelling, sweet and yellow. Consequently it is not evident whether it really has these and only these qualities; or whether it has a single quality, but appears different according to the different structures of the sense-organs; or whether it has more qualities than those apparent but some of them do not strike us. (5) The idea that it has a single quality can be worked out on the basis of our earlier remarks . . . [see **B 5**] (6) Our argument for the apple's having more qualities than those apparent to us is as follows. Let us imagine someone who from birth has had the senses of touch, smell and taste, but has lacked hearing and sight. He will start out believing in the existence of nothing visible or audible, but only of the three kinds of quality which he can register. It is therefore a possibility that we too, having only our five senses, only register from the qualities belonging to the apple those which we are capable of registering. But it

may be that there objectively exist other qualities, and that these are the objects of further sense-organs which we do not share, so that we do not register the corresponding sense-objects either. (7) Someone will reply that nature made the senses co-extensive with the range of sense-objects. What *kind* of nature, in view of the great inarbitrable disagreement among the doctrinaire thinkers about natural existence? For anyone arbitrating the very question whether nature exists would, if he were a layman, according to them be unreliable. But if he is a philosopher, he will be a party to the disagreement, and himself subject to judgement, not a judge.

E Sextus Empiricus, *Outlines of Pyrrhonism* 1.100–13

(1) In order also to be able to end up suspending judgement by focusing the argument on each individual sense, or even without reference to the senses, we adopt in addition the fourth mode. This is the one which we say depends on 'situations', a word which we use for 'dispositions'. We say that it is observed in the natural or unnatural state, in being awake or asleep, and depending on age, on motion or rest, on hating or liking, on want or satiety, on intoxication or sobriety, on predispositions, on confidence or fear, or on depression or elation. (2) For example, things strike us differently depending on whether our state is natural or unnatural, because those who are deranged or possessed seem to hear the voices of spirits, while we do not . . . And the same honey appears sweet to me but bitter to those with jaundice. (3) If someone says that it is an intermingling of certain bodily humours that produces, in those in an unnatural state, improper impressions deriving from objects, we must reply that since the healthy also have mixtures of humours, it is possible that external objects are in their nature such as they appear to people in the so-called 'unnatural' state, and that these mixtures make them appear different to the healthy. For to assign a power of distorting objects to one set of mixtures, while denying it to the other set, is artificial. Indeed, just as the healthy are in a state which is natural for the healthy but unnatural for the sick, so too the sick are in a state which is unnatural for the healthy but natural for the sick. So we should have faith in the sick too, as being, relatively speaking, in a natural state. (4) . . . The point about 'depending on age' is that the same air seems chilly to the aged but mild to the youthful, and the same colour dull to the elderly but strong to the youthful . . . Things appear different 'depending on motion or rest' because things which we see as stationary when we are standing we think are moving when we sail past them . . . 'Depending on intoxication or sobriety': things we think infamous when sober appear not at all infamous to us when we are drunk. 'Depending on predispositions': the same wine appears dry to those who have just eaten dates or dried figs,

but sweet to those who have been tasting nuts or chick-peas . . . (5) Given that there is also such a great disparity depending on dispositions, and that men are differently disposed on different occasions, while it is perhaps easy to say how each object appears to each person, it is by no means easy to say what the object is like. For the disparity is inarbitrable: its arbitrator is either in some of the dispositions we have mentioned, or in no disposition whatsoever. Now to say that he is in absolutely no disposition – neither healthy nor sick, neither moving nor stationary, of no age, and likewise lacking the other dispositions – is completely incoherent. But if he is going to arbitrate our impressions while himself in some disposition, he is a party to the disagreement, and in any case he is not a neutral judge of external objects, his viewpoint being obscured by the dispositions he is in.

F Sextus Empiricus, *Outlines of Pyrrhonism* 1.118–20

(1) The fifth mode is the one depending on positions, distances and locations. For according to each of these factors too the same things appear different. (2) For example, the same colonnade seen from one end appears tapering, and seen from the centre appears completely symmetrical. The same ship appears small and stationary from far off, large and moving from near by. The same tower appears round from far off but square from near by. These are examples depending on distances. (3) Examples depending on locations are that the light of a lantern appears dim in sunlight but bright in the dark, and that the same oar appears bent in water but straight when out of the water . . . (4) Examples depending on positions are that the same picture appears flat when lying on its back but at a certain angle seems to have concavities and convexities; and that pigeons' necks seem differently coloured depending on the angle of inclination.

G Sextus Empiricus, *Outlines of Pyrrhonism* 1.124–8

(1) The sixth mode is the one based on admixtures, by which we deduce that since no object strikes us entirely by itself, but along with something, it may perhaps be possible to say what the mixture compounded out of the external object and the thing perceived with it is like, but we would not be able to say what the external object is like by itself. (2) That nothing external strikes us by itself, but always along with something, and that, depending on this, it is perceived as different, is I think pre-evident. Our colour appears one way in warm air, another in the cold, and we would not be able to say what our colour is like in its nature, but just how it is perceived along with each of these accompaniments. The same sound appears one way when accompanied by a rarefied atmosphere, another way when accompanied by a dense atmosphere.

Smells are more pungent in a bath-house or in sunshine than in chilly air. And the body is light when immersed in water, but heavy when in air. (3) To pass on from external admixture, our eyes have membranes and liquids in them. Hence visible objects, since they are not seen without these, will not be accurately grasped. For what we are registering is the mixture, and that is why jaundice-sufferers see everything as yellow and those with bloodshot eyes see everything as blood-red . . . (4) Nor does the mind [register external objects accurately], especially since its guides the senses make mistakes. It may also be that it itself adds some admixture of its own to the reports of the senses. For we see certain fluids belonging to each of the regions in which the doctrinaire thinkers believe that the commanding-faculty is located – be it the brain, the heart, or whatever part of the animal one may care to put it in. (5) So according to this mode too we see that, being unable to say anything about the nature of external objects, we are forced to suspend judgement about it.

H Sextus Empiricus, *Outlines of Pyrrhonism* 1.129–32

(1) The seventh mode, as we said, is the one which depends on the quantities and configurations of the objects. By 'configurations' we mean quite generally their composition. This is another mode according to which we are clearly forced to suspend judgement about the nature of things. (2) For example, filings of goatshorn, when perceived simply and not in composition, appear white, but composed in the actual horn they are perceived as black . . . Isolated grains of sand appear rough, but composed as a heap they produce a smooth sensory effect . . . (3) Wine drunk in moderation invigorates us, but taken in larger quantities incapacitates the body. And food likewise displays different powers depending on the quantity. Often through heavy consumption it purges the body with indigestion and diarrhoea. (4) Here too, then, we will be able to describe the quality of powdered horn and of the composite of many filings . . ., and in the cases of the sand . . . and the wine and the food to describe their relative qualities. But we will not be able to describe the nature of the things in itself, thanks to the disparity among impressions which depend on composition.

I Sextus Empiricus, *Outlines of Pyrrhonism* 1.135–40

(1) The eighth mode is the one derived from relativity, on the basis of which we deduce that, since all things are relative, we will suspend judgement about what things exist absolutely and in nature. (2) It must be recognized that here, as elsewhere, we use 'are' loosely, to stand for 'appear', so that what we say is tantamount to 'all things are relative in appearance'. (3) This has two senses. One is in relation to the judging

subject, since the external object being judged appears in relation to the judging subject. The other is in relation to the things perceived with it, like right in relation to left. (4) That all things are relative we have also argued earlier: so far as concerns the judging subject, that each thing is relative in appearance to the particular animal, the particular man, and the particular sense, and also to the particular situation; so far as concerns the things perceived with them, that each thing is relative in appearance to the particular admixture, the particular location, the particular composition, the particular quantity, and the particular position. (5) It can also be specifically deduced that all things are relative, as follows. Are differentiated things different from relative things, or not? If not, they too are relative. But if they are different, since everything different is relative, being called different in relation to that from which it differs, differentiated things are relative. (6) Also, of existing things, some are *summa genera* according to the doctrinaire thinkers, others *infimae species*, and yet others genera and species. And all of these are relative. Therefore all things are relative . . . (7) Even someone who denies that all things are relative *eo ipso* confirms that all things are relative. For by his means of opposing us he shows that 'All things are relative' is relative to us, and not universal. (8) It remains to add that, in view of our proof that all things are relative, it is clear that we will not be able to say what each object is like in its own nature and absolutely, but just how it appears in its relativity. It follows that we should suspend judgement about the nature of things.

J Sextus Empiricus, *Outlines of Pyrrhonism* 1.141–4

(1) Here now is some explanation of the mode which we listed as ninth, the one depending on regularity or rarity of meeting. (2) The sun is much more astonishing than a comet, but because we see the sun regularly but the comet rarely, we are so astonished at the comet as to think it a portent, but not at the sun. If, on the other hand, we imagine the appearance and setting of the sun as rare, and the sun as all at once illuminating the whole world, then suddenly casting it all into shade, we might expect to witness immense astonishment at it . . . (3) Also, rare things seem precious, whereas familiar and plentiful things do not. If we imagine water as a rarity, how much more precious it would appear to us than all the things that are thought precious. Or if we imagine gold simply scattered over the earth like stones, to whom could we expect it to be precious or worth hoarding? (4) Since, then, the same things seem astonishing or precious at some times but not at others, depending on regularity or rarity of confrontation, we reason that we will perhaps be able to say how each of them appears with regular or rare confrontation, but cannot baldly state what each of the external

objects is like by itself. Hence this is another mode that leads us to suspend judgement about them.

K Sextus Empiricus, *Outlines of Pyrrhonism* 1.145–63

(1) The tenth mode, which is also the most relevant to ethics, is the one depending on ways of life, customs, laws, legendary beliefs, and doctrinaire opinions. (2) A 'way of life' is a choice of lifestyle or of a certain behaviour adopted by one or many people, such as Diogenes [the Cynic] or the Spartans. (3) A law is a written agreement within the body politic, infringement of which incurs punishment. A custom, or convention (which is the same thing), is the acceptance of a certain behaviour in common between many people, infringement of which does not necessarily incur punishment. For example, not to commit adultery is a law, whereas not to have sexual intercourse in public is (for us) a custom. (4) A legendary belief is the acceptance of unhistorical and fictional events. A good example is the legends about Cronos, which induce many people to believe them. (5) A doctrinaire opinion is the acceptance of something which seems to be confirmed through analogical reasoning or through some proof, for example that as elements of existing things there are atoms, homogeneous substances, minima, or whatever. (6) We oppose each of these sometimes to itself, sometimes to each of the others. (7) For example, we oppose custom to custom as follows. Some Ethiopians tattoo their babies, but we do not. Persians think it proper to wear lurid ankle-length clothing, while we think it improper. And Indians have sexual intercourse in public, while most other races think it shameful. (8) We oppose law to law as follows . . . In Scythian Tauri, there was a law that foreigners should be sacrificed in propitiation of Artemis, while here human sacrifice is banned. (9) We oppose way of life to way of life when we oppose that of Diogenes to that of Aristippus, or that of the Spartans to that of the Italians. (10) We oppose legendary belief to legendary belief when we observe that in some places legend makes Zeus the father of men and gods, but in other places Ocean, quoting 'Ocean who begat the gods, and Tethys their mother' [Homer, *Iliad* 14.201]. (11) We oppose doctrinaire opinions to each other when we observe that some people declare that there is one element, others infinitely many; some say that the soul is mortal, others immortal; some say that our affairs are governed by divine providence, others that they are unprovidential. (12) We also oppose custom to the other things. For example to law, when we say that among the Persians intercourse beween males is customary, whereas among the Romans it is prohibited by law . . . (13) Custom is opposed to way of life when most men go indoors to have intercourse with their wives, while Crates [the Cynic] did it with Hipparchia in public . . . (14) Custom is opposed to

legendary belief when the legends say that Cronos ate his own children, while our custom is to take care of children. And it is conventional among us to revere the gods as good and impervious to harm, whereas the poets introduce gods who sustain wounds and bear grudges against each other. (15) Custom is opposed to doctrinaire opinion when our custom is to pray for blessings from the gods, whereas Epicurus says that divinity pays no attention to us . . . (16) We could have taken many more examples of each of the oppositions mentioned, but this will suffice as a summary. It just remains to add that since this mode too reveals such a great disparity among things, we will not be able to say what each object is like in its nature, but just how it appears in relation to this way of life, to this law, to this custom, and so on for each of the others. Therefore this is another mode which makes it necessary for us to suspend judgement about the nature of external objects. (17) That then is how, by means of the ten modes, we end up suspending judgement.

L Photius, *Library* 170b3–35 (continuing **71C**)

(1) In the second [of his *Pyrrhonist discourses*] he [Aenesidemus] starts to expound in detail the arguments which he has summarily listed, analysing truths, causes, affections, motion, generation and destruction, and their opposites, and exposing by tight reasoning (or so he thinks) the impossibility of fathoming or grasping them. (2) His third discourse is also about motion and sense-perception and their peculiar features. Working elaborately through a similar set of contradictions, he puts them too beyond our reach and grasp. (3) In the fourth discourse he says that signs, in the sense in which we call apparent things signs of the non-apparent, do not exist at all, and that those who believe they do are deceived by an empty enthusiasm. And he raises the customary series of difficulties about the whole of nature, the world, and the gods, contending that none of these falls within our grasp. (4) His fifth discourse too holds out an aporetic guard against causes, refusing to concede that anything is cause of anything, saying that the causal theorists are mistaken, and enumerating some modes according to which he thinks that, by being attracted to causal theory, they have been steered into such an error. (5) His sixth discourse turns to good and bad things, objects of choice and avoidance, and also preferred and dispreferred things, subjecting them to the same quibbles, so far as he is able, and shutting them off from our grasp and knowledge. (6) The seventh discourse he marshalls against the virtues, saying that those who philosophize about them have uselessly invented their doctrines, and that they have misled themselves into thinking that they have attained the theory and practice of them. (7) The eighth and last launches an attack on the end, allowing the existence of neither happiness nor pleasure nor

prudence, nor any other end which any philosophical persuasion might believe in, but asserting that the end which they all celebrate simply does not exist.

M Sextus Empiricus, *Outlines of Pyrrhonism* 1.180–5

(1) Aenesidemus presents eight modes in accordance with which he thinks that he criticizes every doctrinaire causal theory and exposes it as defective. (2) The first, he says, is one according to which the whole class of causal theory, dealing as it does with non-apparent matters, does not have agreed attestation from things apparent. (3) The second is one according to which often, although the object of investigation has a plentiful variety of causal explanations available, some people choose a single kind of causal explanation for it. (4) Third is one according to which, when dealing with things which come about in an order, they expound causal explanations for them which display no order. (5) According to the fourth mode, they take the way apparent things come about and think they have grasped how non-apparent things come about. For although the non-apparent things *may* be effected in a way similar to apparent things, it is also possible that they are not, but in their own distinctive way. (6) According to the fifth, practically all base their causal theories on their own hypotheses about the elements, and not on some common and agreed methods. (7) According to the sixth, they often adopt findings obtained by their own hypotheses while rejecting equally convincing findings to the opposite effect. (8) According to the seventh they often expound causal explanations which conflict not only with things apparent but also with their own hypotheses. (9) According to the eighth, the things thought to be apparent and the things subject to inquiry are often equally problematic, so that their demonstrations have their premises and their conclusions equally problematic. (10) It is not impossible, he says, that some people's errors in causal theory also accord with some mixed modes, dependent on those just listed.

N Sextus Empiricus, *Against the professors* 9.237–40

[Reporting arguments of Aenesidemus against cause] (1) Again, if some cause exists, either it is the complete cause of something, using nothing but its own power, or it needs the matter affected as an auxiliary means to this, so that the effect is to be thought of in relation to the conjunction of both. (2) And if it is its nature to be a complete agent by use of its own power, it ought, since it permanently has itself and its own power, to produce the effect at all times, and not to act in some cases but be inactive in others. (3) If on the other hand it is, as some of the doctrinaire writers say, not absolute and independent but relative, since it and the thing affected are viewed in conjunction with each other, a worse result will emerge. (4) For if the thing acting and the thing affected are thought of in conjunction with each other, there will be one conception, but with two names, 'the thing acting' and 'the thing affected'. Consequently, the productive power will reside no more in it than in the thing said to be affected. For just as it cannot act at all without the thing said to be affected, so too the thing said to be affected cannot be affected without its presence. (5) It follows that the power productive of the effect no more exists objectively in it than in the thing affected.

☐ There can be little doubt that Aenesidemus made a pioneering contribution to the Sceptical methodology which we find in the works of Sextus Empiricus, especially with his massive compilation under the heading 'The ten modes' (often rendered 'tropes'). These are, more fully, ten modes of suspending judgement (cf. **A 6–7**), i.e. ten methods of achieving the result which Aenesidemus had set up as the Pyrrhonist's end (**71A 3**). In **A–K** our excerpts are taken from Sextus' own exposition of the modes, which is in most ways the best. Sextus himself elsewhere (*Against the professors* 7.345) names Aenesidemus as their author. Much of the actual material was admittedly traditional – it is indeed an important part of the methodology that the doctrinaire writers should themselves be the source of the material that is to prove their undoing (cf. **C 4**) – but Aenesidemus is beyond doubt the genius who shaped it for this new task.

Some sources mention only eight or nine modes, and in partly different orders. This should not be read as a conflict of evidence, in any normal sense. To have insisted on any one specific list of the modes would have run counter to the true spirit of Pyrrhonist scepticism. Hence both the number and the order given by Sextus are to be understood as arbitrary and open to variation: **A 6, 8**.

Broadly speaking the modes, like all Aenesidemus' arguments, are aimed at dissuading us from ever adopting a partisan stance with regard to any issue whatever (although the modes themselves concentrate largely on sensory matters). This is achieved by exposing the irresoluble conflict that exists between the opposing grounds of belief (**A 1–6**).

If there is a single unifying theme in the modes, it is perhaps that of inarbitrability. There is not, and could not be, a privileged viewpoint from which any case of conflict could be resolved; therefore the only proper reaction is to suspend judgement (cf. also **40T**). Sextus at **A 10** suggests that the unifying theme is *relativity*. We will see that this is broadly correct, but only because relativity and inarbitrability here come out as virtually equivalent.

It will be noticed that the first four modes (**B–E**) proceed in a careful dialectical sequence. (*1*) No one animal's viewpoint is privileged over those of others. (*2*) Even if man's viewpoint were privileged, no *one* man's is. (*3*) Even if one man's viewpoint were privileged, no one of his senses is. (*4*) Even if one of his senses were privileged, no one set of viewing conditions is. Modes 5–7 then supplement mode 4 with various further relativities to which sense-perception is subject (**F–H**).

Mode *8* (**I**) moves to a generalization about relativity: *all* things are relative. It is tempting to read this as a version of the familiar sceptical inference from a thing's being relative in character (e.g. sweet, good) to its being nothing in itself, i.e. unreal (the inference ably countered by the Epicurean Polystratus at **7D**). It would then easily follow that the thing was unknowable too. This reading, however, faces several difficulties. First, the conclusion at **I 8** concerns only the undiscoverability of things' natures, and their unreality plays no apparent part in the argument. Indeed, if there *were* good grounds for taking things to be nothing in themselves, that would steer us less towards suspension of judgement than towards a rather firm conclusion, namely that they have no intrinsic nature. Second, the thesis is said at **I 4** to embrace modes *1–7*, which are likewise about things' undiscoverability, and do not arrive at this via their unreality. Third, the arguments at **I 5–6** would come out as ludicrous: it is not even superficially plausible that gold is *nothing* in itself just because it stands in *some* relation to other things.

A more palatable alternative is to understand the slogan 'All things are relative' in the light of the corrective gloss at **I 2**. The expression there which in order to hedge our bets we have translated 'All things are relative in appearance' (cf. also **I 4**) is ambiguous between 'All things appear (to be) relative' and 'All things appear relatively.' The latter seems greatly preferable. It much more straightforwardly yields the undiscoverability conclusion at **I 8**. It makes the claim in **I 4** that modes *1–7* fall under this heading entirely correct. And it even endows the argument at **I 5–6** with some prima facie plausibility. If gold appears to us as a 'differentiated' (= absolute: cf. **29C**) thing, that is only in virtue of its appearing to us in a certain relation with relative things; and the appearance of the nature of gold to us inextricably involves a relation to the genus of metals. These then are two ways in which it is unimaginable that one thing's intrinsic nature might strike us entirely in itself and without relativity to other things. And although that leads to no ontological conclusion, it does raise a good epistemological question, whether one's grasp of a thing could ever be independent of one's way of perceiving the world in general.

Mode *9* (**J**) makes a rather peripheral point: the degree to which things impress us is less a function of their nature than of their unfamiliarity to us. Of course, the surprisingness and preciousness mentioned there are not properties commonly held to be part of a thing's nature. But we may easily be tempted to *infer* a thing's nature from them, e.g. that a comet is a portent (**J 2**), or that gold is good (cf. **J 3**).

Mode *10* (**K**) is sometimes said to be about value judgements, but **K 10, 11** and **15** scarcely fit this reading. It may be more accurate to say that whereas the first nine modes are about the way things *naturally* appear, the tenth is about conflicts between the various *cultural* viewpoints which men adopt. These viewpoints are not necessarily themselves offered as a further variety of 'appearance', but they do at any rate govern the way things appear to us (**K 16**).

According to **A 9–10** the ten modes are interrelated as shown in the diagram.

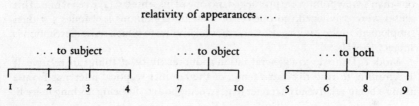

If relativity appears both as the supreme genus and, in mode *8*, among the species, that is in virtue of the 'specific' applications of relativity in **I 5–8**. Mode *10* is perhaps the only one that fits the schema less than comfortably: 'relativity of appearances to their (cultural) *context*' would describe it better.

The upshot is that *all* appearances are determined by relativity to factors over and above the intrinsic nature of the appearing object, and that there is therefore no uncontaminated viewpoint from which the conflicts between them can be arbitrated. Consequently we are compelled to suspend judgement about the nature of things.

Beyond the modes, Aenesidemus seems to have developed a huge battery of anti-doctrinaire arguments, the range of which can be just glimpsed from **L–N**. Favourite targets include theories of signs (**L 3; 36G 6**; cf. **18; 42**) and of cause (**L 1, 4, M, N**; cf. **55**). For further examples of his school's critiques, cf. **23F, 36C 6, 40T, 50F, 67B**.

The texts may occasionally give the impression that Aenesidemus was arguing for the specifically negative conclusion that the object of inquiry does not exist. On closer scrutiny, however, they turn out to divide up as follows. Alleged objective things or states of affairs, such as truth, cause, motion, generation, nature, god and good, are shown to be *beyond our cognition*. This squares well with the strategy of the ten modes (it is perhaps the allegedly extremist position attacked at **68R**), and implies the result that we should suspend judgement about whether there are such things, not actively deny them. On the other hand, positive epistemological or moral doctrines are apparently shown to be *false*: at **L 3** he is reported as concluding that signs do not exist, and at **L 7** that no ethical end exists.

Despite the frequent tendency of sources to exaggerate the negativity of sceptics' conclusions, it seems not implausible that here the reporting is correct. Pyrrhonist neutrality is achieved by close attention to the inarbitrability principle which underlies the modes. But if a doctrinaire philosopher comes up with a second-order doctrine, a theory of signs to provide secure access to the hidden nature of things, to react by merely suspending judgement about whether there are such signs may seem altogether inadequate to safeguard your neutrality. It is safer to come down firmly *against* the possibility of learning the nature of things – just as all the modes also do, and indeed as Pyrrho himself had done, according to Timon (**1F**). No doubt Aenesidemus felt he could do this without committing himself to a knowledge claim, or even assenting to it or asserting it as a truth (cf. **71C 6**): he could simply say that this is the way things appear to him (non-epistemically: see **71** commentary).

His position on the 'end' might be treated similarly. We have already tentatively suggested (**71** commentary) that he would see his own end, suspension of judgement, as exempt from his attack on doctrinaire ends in **L 7**. Just, then, as he wants it to appear to us that things' natures are undiscoverable, in order that we may be freed of all doctrinaire belief about them, so too he wants it to appear to us that suspension of judgement is the end, precisely in order that we may be freed of doctrinaire commitment to any end.

The strategy described above seems to affect all Aenesidemus' work. There is no sign of his following Carneades' method (see **68**; **70**) of defending both sides in a dispute in order to induce suspension of judgement. If anything, he seems closer to the directly polemical method we have ascribed to Arcesilaus (**68** commentary; cf. especially **68I**). All his recorded arguments are one-sided attacks on doctrinaire theses. His aim throughout is to show, not that there are two sides to every doctrinal issue, but that there is no basis for contemplating a doctrinal stance on any issue in the first place.

(One part of the evidence which has proved too intractable to cover in this book consists of a number of passages linking Aenesidemus doctrinally with the views of the Presocratic Heraclitus. Suffice it to say that this *may* be adequately explained as a specifically anti-Stoic campaign on Aenesidemus' part. Heraclitus was regarded by the Stoics as an important forerunner, and it has been plausibly suggested that Aenesidemus was trying to embarrass them by developing the un-Stoic aspects of Heraclitus' thought.)

Apart from the texts excerpted above, there is undoubtedly a good deal of Aenesidemus' argumentation embedded in the text of Sextus; at *Against the professors* 8.440 ff. and 9.218 ff. the debt is made explicit. A cardinal feature of Aenesidemus' arguments was clearly the dilemmatic method exemplified at **N**, a method ubiquitous in Sextus' writings too.

Indexes

GLOSSARY

Italicized terms are Greek except where Latin (Lat.) is indicated. The references to texts are selective, being intended to direct readers only to the primary evidence for each of the terms listed. A fuller set of references will be found in the *Index of topics*.

accident = *sumptōma*: 7
additional premise = *proslēpsis*: 36
affinity = *oikeion, oikeiōsis*: 21B–C, 22M; also 'appropriation'
agreement = *homologia*, in agreement = *homologoumenōs*: 63
alienation = *alloiōsis*: 57
ambiguity = *amphibolia*: 37P–Q
AN: see 'in accordance with nature'
analogy = *analogia*: 15F, 39D, 60D–E
antecedent cause = *proēgoumenon aition*: 55F
appearance = *phainomenon*: 1H, 71
appellative = *prosēgoria*: 33M
appropriate = *oikeios*, appropriation = *oikeiōsis*: 57; also 'affinity'
argument = *logos*: 36–7; also 'account', 'discourse', 'language', 'principle', 'rationale', 'reason'
assent = (noun) *sunkatathesis*, (verb) *sunkatatithesthai*: 40, 41A, 53S, 69G–K
atom = *atomos*: 8
attribute = *sumbebēkos*: 7, 51B
auxiliary cause = *sunergon (aition)*: 55I
attest = *epimarturein*, attestation = *epimarturēsis*: 18

be = *huparchein*: 34D, 40E, H; also 'belong'
belong = *huparchein*: 51B; also 'be'
benefaction = *ōphelēma*: 33J
benefit = (noun) *ōpheleia*, (verb) *ōphelein*: 60G, I
blend = *krama*: 14C; blending = *krasis*: 48
breath = *pneuma*: 47, 53

case = *ptōsis*: 33, 55C
cause = *aition* (occasionally *aitia*): 55, 72M–N
changing argument = *metapiptōn (logos)*: 37A, J, K
character = *diathesis*: 47S, 60J, L, 61

choiceworthy = *hairetos*: 21, 33J, 60O
CN: see 'contrary to nature'
co-affection = *sumpatheia*: 14A, 15A; also 'interaction'
co-elimination = *sunanaskeuē*: 18
co-fated = *suneimarmenos*: 55S, 62F
cognition = *katalēpsis*, cognitive = *katalēptikos/katalēptos*, cognize = *katalambanein* (also 'grasp'): 39–41, 68–9, 71C
cohesion = *sunartēsis*: 35B
collision = *antikopē*: 11
combination = *sunthesis*: 15F, 39D
commanding-faculty = *hēgemonikon*: 53
commonly qualified = *koinōs poios*, common quality = *koinē poiotēs*: 28
complete cause = *aition autoteles*: 55I, R, 62C
concept = *ennoēma*: 17C, 30
conception = *ennoia*: 39E–F
conclusion = *epiphora, sumperasma*: 36
concomitance = *parakolouthēsis*: 54Q; concomitant = *parakolouthoun*: 7B
conditional = *sunēmmenon*: 35A–C
conflagration = *ekpurōsis*: 46
conflict (verb) = *machesthai*: 35
confrontation = *periptōsis*: 15F, 39D
conjunctive (proposition) = *sumpeplegmenon*: 35A, D
consequentiality = *akolouthia*: 59; also 'following'
constitution = *sustasis*: 29F, 57
contest = *antimarturein*, contestation = *antimarturēsis*: 18
contradictory = *antikeimenon*: 34G, 35E
contrary to nature/*CN* = *para phusin*: 58
convincing = *pithanos*: 39G, 42I–J, 68S, 69D–F; also 'plausible'
criterion = *kritērion*: 17, 40, 70A, 71A; also 'discriminatory faculty'
cut = *temnein*, cutting = *tomē*: 37B, G

489

Glossary

deduce = *sunagein*, deduction = *sunagōgē*, deductive = *sunaktikos*: 36
define = *horizein*; also 'determine'
definite = *hōrismenos*: 34H
definition = *horismos*: 19, 32
delineation = *tupos*: 17E
demonstration = *apodeixis*: 36B, 42
demonstrative reference = *deixis*: 34H–J
designing fire = *pur technikon*: 46A
determine = *horizein*: 1G, 71A, C; also 'define'
development = *apogegennēmenon*: 20B–C
dialectic = *dialektikē*, dialectician = *dialektikos*: 31
differentiated = *kata diaphoran*: 28M–N, 29C, 72I
dimension = *diastēma*: 51A; also 'distance', 'interval'
disconnexion = *diartēsis*: 36C
discourse = *logos*: 71A–C; also 'account', 'argument', 'language', 'principle', 'rationale', 'reason'
discriminatory faculty = *kritērion*: 15A, 17D; also 'criterion'
disjunctive (proposition) = *diezeugmenon*: 35A, E
disposed = *pōs echōn*: 29
dispreferred = *apoproēgmenos*: 58
distance = *diastēma*: 50F; also 'dimension', 'interval'
disturbance = *tarachē*, freedom from disturbance = *ataraxia*: 1F, 2, 21, 25, 71
disvalue = *apaxia*: 58
division = *diairesis*: 32C
doctrine = *dogma*, doctrinaire = *dogmatikos*, hold doctrines = *dogmatizein*: 22Q 6, 66I–J, 68N, 71, 72K

effect = *apotelesma*: 55
element = *stoicheion*: 47
elimination = *anaskeuē*: 18, 42G–H, J
end = *telos*: 21A–B, 63–4, 71A
expertise = *technē*: 42
explanation = *aitia*: 55A; also 'responsibility', 'cause'
expression = *lexis*: 37P; also 'speech'
extension / that which has extension = *to diastaton*: 45E–F, 49E
extremity = *akron*: 9–10, 50C

familiar (to us) = *par' hēmin*: 18C, G, 42G
fate = *heimarmenē*: 20, 38, 54B, U, 55J–S, 62, 70G
feeling = *pathos*: 17; also 'passion'
figment = *phantasma*: 30A, C, 39A–B
focusing = *epibolē*: 15, 17A–B
follow (from) = *akolouthein, hepesthai*,

following = *akolouthia* (also 'consequentiality'): 35, 38, 53T
fusion = *sunchusis*: 48C

good feeling = *eupatheia*: 65F
grasp = *katalambanein*; also 'cognize' (q.v.)
ground-rule = *thema*: 36H–J
Growing Argument = *auxanomenos logos*: 28

happiness = *eudaimonia*: 21, 23F, 63
honourable = *kalos*; cf. 'rectitude'

image = *eidōlon*: 15, 23
impassivity = *apatheia*: 2F
impression = *phantasia*: 15–16, 39–40, 70A–B
impressor = *phantaston*: 39B
impulse = *hormē*: 33I, 53, 57
in accordance with nature / AN = *kata phusin*: 58
inarbitrable = *anepikritos*: 1F, 72
incognitive = *akatalēptos*: 39–40, 68
incorporeal = *asōmatos*: 7B, 14A, 27
indefinite = *aoristos*: 34H, K
indemonstrable = *anapodeiktos*: 36
indifferent = *adiaphoros*: 1F, 58
indiscernible = *aparallaktos*, indiscernibility = *aparallaxia*: 28O, 40, 42H, 52, 70A
inferior = *phaulos*
in our power = *eph' hēmin*: 62
interact = *sumpaschein*: 45C; interaction = *sumpatheia*: 47L; also 'co-affection'
inter-entailment (of virtues) = *antakolouthia*: 55D, 61F
interval = *diastēma*: 49B; also 'dimension', 'distance'
invalid = *aperantos*: 36

joining = *harmē*: 48C, 51C
joint-cause = *sunaition*: 55I
juxtaposition = *parathesis*: 48

kinetic = *en kinēsei*: 21; also 'in process' (see 'process')

language = *logos*: 33, 53U; also 'account', 'argument', 'discourse', 'principle', 'rationale', 'reason'
limit = *peras*: 9–10, 24C, 50C–E
Lying Argument = *pseudomenos (logos)*: 37

Master Argument = *kurieuōn (logos)*: 38
matter = *hulē*: 44
mind = *psuchē*: 14, 53 (also 'soul'); (Lat.) *mens, animus*: 14
minimum = *elachiston*: 9
mode = *tropos*: 36, 72
moderation = *sōphrosunē*: 61

Mowing Argument = *therizōn (logos)*: 31M, 38I

name-bearer = *tunchanon*: 19K, 33B
nature = *phusis*: 43A; also 'physique', 'substance'
natural philosophy = *phusiologia*: 25
no more = *ou mallon*: 1F–G, 58A, 71C
non-contestation = *ouk antimarturēsis*: 18
non-evident = *adēlos*: 18, 36B, 68R
Not-someone Argument = *outis (logos)*: 30E

opinion = *doxa*: 16, 21, 41, 68–9
outline account = *hupographē*: 32

PAN: see 'primary things in accordance with nature'
parody = *parabolē*: 54D, F
partition = *merismos*: 32C
passion = *pathos*: 65; also 'feeling'
PCN: see 'primary things contrary to nature'
peculiar characteristic = *idion*: 32B–C, E
peculiarity = *idiōma*: 40E
peculiarly qualified = *idiōs poios*, peculiar quality = *idia poiotēs*: 28
pervade = *diēkein*: 44–8
physique = *phusis*: 53A–B; also 'nature', 'substance'
plausible = *pithanos*: 37A, M; also 'convincing'
precept = (Lat.) *praeceptum*: 66I–J
preconception = *prolēpsis*: 17, 23E, 39E, 40A, G, R–T
predicate = *katēgorēma*: 33, 55A–C
pre-evident = *prodēlos*: 36B
preferred = *proegmenos*: 58
preliminary cause = *aition prokatarktikon*: 55F, I, R
premise = *lēmma*: 36; see also 'additional premise'
primary things in accordance with nature / PAN things = *prōta kata phusin*: 58
primary things contrary to nature / PCN things = *prōta para phusin*: 58
principle = *archē*: 44; = *logos*: 46F (see also 'seminal principles'); also 'account', 'argument', 'discourse', 'language', 'reason', 'rationale'
printing = *tupōsis*: 39A, F
process = *kinēsis*: 28N, 60J
progress = (noun) *prokopē*, (verb) *prokoptein*: 59I, 61T
proper function = *kathēkon*: 59, 66
proposition = *axiōma*: 34–5
providence = *pronoia*: 54
prudence = *phronēsis*: 21, 61
pursuits = *epitēdeumata*: 26H, 60J, L

qualified = *poios* 28: see also 'peculiarly qualified', 'commonly qualified'
quality = *poiotēs*: 12D, 28; see also 'peculiar quality', 'common quality'
quiescent (become) = *hēsuchazein*: 37F, H, S

rationale = *logos*; also 'account', 'argument', 'discourse', 'language', 'principle', 'reason'
reason = *logos*: 16A–B, 39E, 53V; also 'account', 'argument', 'language', 'principle', 'rationale'
reasonable = *eulogos*: 40F, 42J, 59B, 69B
rectitude = *to kalon* (Lat. *honestum*); cf. 'honourable'
redundancy = *parolkē*: 36C
relative = *pros ti*: 7D, 29C, 72I
relatively disposed = *pros ti pōs echōn*: 29
repulsion = *aphormē*
resistance = *antitupia*: 7C, 45F
responsibility = *aitia*: 20; also 'cause', 'explanation'
revelatory = *ekkaluptikos*: 36C
right action = *katorthōma*: 59K–O, 69B
room = *chōra*: 5, 49B

sayable = *lekton*: 33
science, scientific knowledge = *epistēmē*: 31B, 41–2, 61D, H
seen by reason = *logōi* (or *dia logou*) *theōrētos*: 11D–E, 23G
self-evidence = *enargeia*, self-evident = *enargēs*: 18A, 40K, 68U
seminal principles = *spermatikoi logoi*: 46A
sensation, sense, (sense-)perception = *aisthēsis*: 1F, 15–16, 39, 40L, N, Q, 43G, H, M, 72D
sensory recognition = *epaisthēsis*: 16B–C
sign = *sēmeion*: 18C, 35C, 42, 51H, 53T
signification = *sēmainomenon*, signifier = *sēmainon*: 33
similarity = *homoiotēs*: 15F, 18F–G, 39D, 42G–H
solid body = *steremnion*: 15–16, 23E
something = *ti*: 27
soul = *psuchē*: 14, 53; also 'mind'
sound (in logic) = *hugiēs*: 35
speech = *lexis*: 33; also 'expression'
spirit = (Lat.) *anima*: 14
state = *schesis*: 28N, 60J
state of affairs = *pragma*: 33
static = *katastēmatikos*: 21
subconditional = *parasunēmmenon*: 35A
subsist = *huphistasthai*: 27, 51A
substance = *phusis*: 5A, D, 7B (also 'nature', 'physique'); = *ousia*: 28, 44
substrate = *hupokeimenon*: 28
suppose = *hupolambanein*, supposition = *hupolēpsis*: 41

suspend judgement = *epechein*, suspension of judgement = *epochē*: **1A, 68–9, 71–2**
sustain = *sunechein*, sustaining power = *sunektikē dunamis*: **47**; sustaining cause = *sunektikon aition*: **55H–I**
swerve = (noun) *parenklisis*, (verb) *parenklinein*: **11H, 20**

target = *skopos*: **63–4**
tenor = *hexis*: **47, 53A, 60J, L**
tension = *tonos*, tensile = *tonikos*: **47J**; tensility = *eutonia*: **47G**
thoroughly explored = *diexōdeumenos*: **69E**
through and through = *di' holōn* (or *di' holou*): **48**
to-be-taken = *lēptos*: **58C**
transition = *metabasis*: **23E–F, 39D**; also 'traversal'

traversal = *metabasis*: **9A**; also 'transition'

undiverted = *aperispastos*: **69E–F**
unified = *hēnōmenos*, unify = *henoun*: **28M, 48C**
unsound = *mochthēros*: **36**
utterance = *phōnē*: **33, 53U**

valid = *perantikos*: **36**
value = (noun) *axia*: **58**
vary (pleasure) = *poikillein*: **21**
Veiled Argument = *enkekalummenos (logos)*: **37L**
virtuous = *spoudaios*
void = *kenon*: **5–6, 49**

world = *kosmos*: **13, 44F, 54**
world-order = *diakosmēsis*: **44F**
wrong action = *hamartēma*: **59K–O**

INDEX OF SOURCES

All passages, unless otherwise indicated, are referred to by their book number, if there is more than one book of the work, and by chapter and/or section numbers within the book. If the book is regularly printed with two systems of section divisions, the smaller section numbers are used, e.g. Cicero, *On ends* 1.36 = book 1, smaller section 36. This reference is followed by the equivalent notation used in our book. Numbers in square brackets refer to portions of text which appear in volume 2 only. The texts in volume 2 on which our volume 1 translations are based follow the editorial conventions, but not necessarily the readings, of the editions listed below (see further, vol. 2, introductory note). The following abbreviations are used: OCT = Oxford Classical Text; *CAG* = *Commentaria in Aristotelem Graeca* (Berlin 1882–1909).

AETIUS. Greek doxographer, c. A.D. 100. His text has been conjecturally reconstructed out of later doxographical material, transmitted under the names of Plutarch, Stobaeus and others, by H. Diels, *Doxographi Graeci* (Berlin 1879), to which we refer by chapter and section.
prooem. 2 = **26A**; [1.7.37 = **23M**]; 1.7.33 = **46A**; 1.10.5 = **30B**; 1.11.5 = **55G**; 1.20.2 = **5C**; 1.28.4 = **55J**; 4.3.11 = **14C**; 4.11.1–4 = **39E**; [4.11.4–5 = **30J**]; 4.12.1–5 = **39B**; 4.21.1–4 = **53H**; 4.23.1 = **53M**
ALEXANDER of Aphrodisias. Peripatetic philosopher and commentator on Aristotle, fl. A.D. 200. References here are to page plus line number of the editions cited below.
On Aristotle's Prior Analytics [*In Ar. An. pr.*, M. Wallies, *CAG* II i, 1883]
177,25–178,1 = **38F**; 180,33–6, 181,25–31 = **52F**; 183,34–184,10 = **38B**; 278,11–14 = **36J**
On Aristotle's Topics [*In Ar. Top.*, M. Wallies, *CAG* II ii, 1891]

1,8–14 = **31D**; 42,27–43,2 = **32E**; 301,19–25 = **27B**; 359,12–16 = **30D**
On fate [*De fato* = *Fat.*, I. Bruns, *CAG* Supplementum Aristotelicum II ii, 1892]
176,14–24 = **38H**; 181,13–182,20 = **62G**; 185,7–11 = **62H**; 191,30–192,28 = **55N**; 196,24–197,3 = **61M**; 199,14–22 = **61N**; 205,24–206,2 = **62I**; 207,5–21 = **62J**
On mixture [*De mixtione* = *Mixt.*, I. Bruns, *CAG* Supplementum Aristotelicum II ii, 1892]
216, 14–218,6 = **48C**; 223,25–36 = **47L**; 224, 14–27 = **47I**; [224,32]225,1–2[3] = **45H**
On soul II [*De anima libri mantissa* = *Mantissa*, I. Bruns, *CAG* Supplementum Aristotelicum II i, 1887]
118,6–8 = **29A**; 164,3–9 = **64B**
ALEXANDER LYCOPOLIS. Platonist philosopher, 3rd cent. A.D.
Contra Manichaeorum opiniones disputatio [A. Brinkmann, Teubner ed., 1895; cited here by page plus line number]
19,2–4 = **46I**
AMMONIUS. Platonist philosopher and commentator on Aristotle, 5th–6th cent.

A.D. References here are to page plus line number of the editions cited below.

On Aristotle's De interpretatione [In Ar. De int., A. Busse, *CAG* IV v, 1897]
17,24–8 = **33N**; 38,17–20 = **37O**; 43,[5]9–15 = **33K**; [44,19–45,7 = **33q**]; 131,[20]24–32 = **38I**

On Aristotle's Prior analytics [In Ar. An. pr., M. Wallies, *CAG* IV vi, 1899]
8,20–2 and 9,1–2 = **26E**

ANDRONICUS of Rhodes. Peripatetic philosopher, 1st cent. B.C., to whom is traditionally attributed

On passions [De passionibus, A. Glibert–Thirry, Leiden 1977]
1 = **65B**

ANONYMOUS Academic treatise (Oxyrhynchus Papyrus 3008) [P. Oxy. 3008, P. Parsons, *The Oxyrhynchus Papyri* XLII, 1973]
27C

ANONYMOUS commentary on Plato's *Theaetetus*. Fragmentary papyrus, by Academic author of uncertain date [Anon, *In Plat. Theaet,* H. Diels / W. Schubart, *Berliner Klassikertexte* 2, Berlin 1905]
5.18–6.31 = **57H**; 22.39–47 = **19F**; 60.48–61.46 = **71D**; 70.5–26 = **28B**

ANONYMOUS Epicurean treatise on the senses (Herculaneum Papyrus 19/698) [W. Scott, *Fragmenta Herculanensia,* Oxford 1885]
cols. 17, 18, 22, 23, 25, 26, fr. 21 = **16C**

ANONYMOUS Epicurean treatise on theology (Oxyrhynchus Papyrus 215). Perhaps by Epicurus himself. [P. Oxy. 215, B.P. Grenfell / A.S. Hunt, *The Oxyrhynchus Papyri* II, Oxford 1889]
1.[3]4–24 = **23I**

ANONYMOUS Stoic treatise (Herculaneum Papyrus 1020) [Anon. Stoic. (P. Herc. 1020), H. von Arnim, *Hermes* 25, 1890]
col. 4 + col. 1 = **41D**

APULEIUS. Roman novelist and Platonist philosopher, 2nd cent. A.D., to whom is traditionally attributed

De interpretatione [De int., P. Thomas, Teubner ed., 1908; cited here by page plus line number]
184,16–23 = **36D**; 191,5–10[21] = **36I**

ARISTOCLES. Peripatetic philosopher, (?) 1st cent. A.D., quoted *in extenso* by Eusebius (q.v.)

ARIUS DIDYMUS. Alexandrian doxographer, late 1st cent. B.C., quoted *in extenso* by Eusebius (q.v.)

ATHENAEUS. Greek author, c. A.D. 200. Wrote enormous collection of learned chit-chat over dinner:

Deipnosophistae [G. Kaibel, Teubner ed., 1887]
267B = **67Q**; 337A = **21**; 354E = **40F**; 546F = **21M**; 561C = **67D**; 588A = **25F**

AUGUSTINE of Hippo. Bishop, theologian, philosopher, saint, A.D. 354–430; wrote in Latin.

Against the Academics [Contra Academicos = Acad., W.M. Green, *Corpus Christianorum* xxix, Turnholt 1970]
2.11 = **68P**

City of God [De civitate dei = Civ. dei, B. Dombart/A. Kalb, *Corpus Christianorum* xlvii, Turnholt 1955]
8.7 = **32F**

AURELIUS, MARCUS. See Index of Philosophers. [J. Dalfen, Teubner ed., 1979]
2.14 = **52H**; 5.16 = **63K**; 8.14 = **61P**

BOETHIUS. Roman philosopher and commentator, c. A.D. 480–524.

On Aristotle's De interpretatione [In Ar. De int., K. Meiser, Leipzig 1877–80]
234,22–6 = **38C**

CALCIDIUS. Christian translator and commentator on Plato's *Timaeus,* c. 4th cent. A.D. [J.H. Waszink, London and Leiden 1962]
144 = **54U**; 220 = **53G**; 292 = **44D**; 293 = **44E**

CHRYSIPPUS. See Index of Philosophers.

Logical questions III *[Quaestiones logicae* III = *Quaest. log.* III, W. Crönert, *Hermes* 36 (1901)], extant only in papyrus fragments (Herculaneum Papyrus 307)
9.7–12 = **37G**

CICERO. Roman orator, statesman and philosopher, 106–43 B.C. In the last years of his life he wrote an extensive series of books, mainly dialogues, presenting in Latin the principal positions of the leading Hellenistic schools, from the professed standpoint of a New Academic. Cicero was personally acquainted with some of the philosophers to whom he refers, e.g. Antiochus, Philo of Larissa, Posidonius.

Academica [Acad., O. Plasberg, Teubner ed., 1922], a confrontation between Stoic epistemology and Academic scepticism.
1.13 = **68B**; 1.39 = **45A**; 1.40–1 = **40B**; 1.41–2 = **41B**; 1.43–6 = **68A**; 2.7–8 = **68S**; 2.16 = **68C**; 2.17–18 = **68U**; 2.21 = **39C**; 2.22 = **40M, 42B**; 2.28–9 = **68N**; 2.30–1 = **40N**; 2.32 = **68R**; 2.36 = **42F**; 2.37–8 = **40O**; 2.40–1[2] = **70B**; 2.57 = **40I**; 2.59 = **69F**; 2.60 = **68Q**; 2.66–7 =

7.108–9 = **59E**; 7.115 = **65F**; 7.121–2 = **67M**; 7.124 = **67P**; 7.127 = **61I**; [7.128 = **64o**]; 7.130 = **66H**; 7.131 = **67U**; 7.132 = **43B**; 7.134 = **44B**; 7.135 = **45E, 50E**; 7.135–6 = **46B**; 7.136–7 = **47B**; 7.138–9 = **47O**; 7.137[–8] = **44F**; 7.141 = **46J**; 7.142 = **46C**; 7.143 = **53X**; 7.147 = **54A**; 7.148–9 = **43A**; 7.150–1 = **50B**; 7.151 = **48A**; 7.157 = **53N**; 7.160 = **58G**; 7.160–1 = **31N**; [7.165 = **58l**]; 7.171 = **69C**; 7.177 = **40F**; 7.180 = **31Q**; 7.182–4 = **31O**; 7.187 = **37R**; 7.192–8 = **37B**; 7.199–200 = **32I**; 8.48 = **32A**; 9.23 = **3H**; 9.25 = **3I**; 9.40 = **3J**; 9.60 = **1E**; 9.61–2 = **1A**; 9.63–4 = **1B**; 9.64 = **2C**; 9.65 = **2D**; 9.66–7 = **1C**; 9.76 = **1G**; 9.78 = **71B**; 9.104–5 = **1H**; 9.106–7 = **71A**; 9.111 = **3A**; 10.2 = **3K**; 10.6 = **25G**; 10,22 = **24D**; 10,31 = **17A, 19I**; 10.31–2 = **16B**; 10.32 = **15F**; 10.33 = **17E**; 10.34 = **18B, 19J**; 10.117–20 = **22Q**; 10.121 = **21K**; 10.136–7 = **21R**

DIOGENES OF OENOANDA. Epicurean philosopher who had his works inscribed on stone in a public colonnade in central Turkey, 2nd cent. A.D.

Fragments [C.W. Chilton, Teubner ed., 1967]

[7.1.4–2.11 = **15g**]; 10.2.11–5.15 = **19C**; 25.2.3–11 = **22P**; 26.1.2–3.8 = **21P**; 32.1.14–3.14 = **20G**; 38.1.8–3.14 = **21V**

New fragments 1–4 [M.F. Smith, *AJA* 74 (1970)]; new fragments 5–16 [M.F. Smith, *AJA* 75 (1971)]

[1.2.7–3.14 = **15g**]; 5.3.3–14 = **15E**; 21.1.4–14, 2.10–14 = **22S**

DIOGENIANUS. Critic of Chrysippus with Epicurean leanings, quoted *in extenso* by Eusebius (q.v.)

EPICTETUS. See Index of Philosophers [H. Schenkl, Teubner ed., 1916].

Discourses [*Dissertationes = Diss.*]

1.1.7–12 = **62K**; 1.6.12–22 = **63E**; 1.7.1 = **37J**; 1.7.2–5, 10 = **31R**; 1.7.10–21 = **37J**; 1.12.20–1 = **65V**; 1.17.7–8 = **31S**; 1.22.1–3, 9–10 = **40S**; 2.6.9 = **58J**; 2.10.1–12 = **59Q**; 2.19.1–5 = **38A**; 2.23.44–6 = **31T**; 3.2.1–5 = **56C**; 3.3.2–4 = **60F**; 4.8.12 = **31J**; 4.12.15–19 = **66F**; fr.9 = **65Y**

Manual [*Enchiridion = Ench.*]

5 = **65U**; 53 = **62B**

EPICURUS. See Index of Philosophers. The following works are preserved in Diogenes Laertius (q.v.) book 10 whose chapter numbers are used in citations from them:

Letter to Herodotus [*Ep. Hdt.*], epitome on

physics

37–8 = **17C**; 38–9 = **4A**; 39–40 = **5A**; 40–1 = **8A**; 41–2 = **10A**; 42–3 = **12B**; 43–4 = **11A**; 45 = **13A**; 46–7 = **11D**; 46–53 = **15A**; 54–5 = **12D**; 55–6 = **12A**; 56–9 = **9A**; 60 = **10C**; 61–2 = **11E**; 63–7 = **14A**; 68–73 = **7B**; 73–4 = **13C**; 75–6 = **19A**; 76–7 = **23C**; 82 = **17D**

Letter to Pythocles [*Ep. Pyth.*], epitome on celestial phenomena

85–8 = **18C**; 88 = **13B**

Letter to Menoeceus [*Ep. Men.*], epitome on ethics

122 = **25A**; 123–4 = **23B**; 124–7 = **24A**; 127–32 = **21B**; 133–4 = **20A**; 135 = **23J**

Two anthologies of individually numbered maxims are also extant:

Key doctrines [*Ratae sententiae = RS*, in Diogenes Laertius 10.139–54]

1 = **23E** 4 [and **23G**, vol. 2]; 3–4 = **21C**; 7 = **22C** 1; 8–10 = **21D**; 11–13 = **25B**; 17 = **22B** 3; 18 = **23E** 1; 19–21 = **24C**; 23 = **16D**; 24 = **17B**; 25 = **21E** 2; 27–8 = **22E**; 30 = **21E** 3; 31–5 = **22A**; 36–7 = **22B** 1–2; 40 = **22C** 2

Vatican sayings [*Sententiae Vaticanae = SV*, P. von der Mühll, Teubner ed. of Epicurus, 1922]

17 = **21F** 1; 21 = **21F** 2; 23 = **22F** 1; 25 = **21F** 3; 27 = **25I** 1; 28 = **22F** 2; 29 = **25D** 1; 31 = **24B**; 33 = **21G** 1; 34 = **22F** 3; 39 = **22F** 4; 40 = **20D**; 41 = **25I** 2; 42 = **21G** 2; 45 = **25E**; 51 = **21G** 3; 52 = **22F** 5; 54 = **25D** 2; 58 = **22D** 1; 59 = **21G** 4; 63 = **21H** 1; 66 = **22F** 6; 70 = **22D** 2; 71 = **21H** 2; 73 = **21H** 3; 78 = **22F** 7; 79 = **22D** 3; 81 = **21H** 4

There are also papyrus fragments of Epicurus' 37-book magnum opus *On nature* [*Nat.*, G. Arrighetti, *Epicuro, opere*, ed. 2, Turin 1973]

31.10.2–12 = **19D**; 31.13.23–14.12 = **19E**; 34.21–2 = **20B**; 34.25.21–34 = **20j**; 34.26–30 = **20C**

EROTIANUS. Greek grammarian, late 1st cent. A.D.

Vocum Hippocraticarum conlectio [J. Klein, Leipzig 1865; cited here by page plus line number]

34.10–20 = **19G**

EUSEBIUS. Bishop, theologian, historian, c. A.D. 260–340

Evangelical preparation [*Praeparatio evangelica = Pr. ev.*, K. Mras, Berlin 1954–6]

4.3.1 = **55P**; 6.8.25–9 = **62F**; 14.6.4–6 = **68F**; 14.6.12–13 = **68G**; 14.18.1–5 = **1F**;

inst., S. Brandt, Vienna 1890]
5.14.3–5 = **68M**; 7.23 = **52B**
LUCIAN. Greek satirist, 2nd cent. A.D.
Philosophers for sale [*Vitarum auctio* = *Vit.
auct.*, M.D. MacLeod, OCT, 1974]
22 = **37L**
LUCRETIUS Early to mid-1st cent. B.C. Roman
author of didactic poem on Epicurean
physics
De rerum natura [C. Bailey, Oxford 1947]
1.159–73 = **4B**; 1.225–37 = **4C**; 1.334–
90[97] = **6A**; 1.419–44 = **5B**; 1.445–82
= **7A**; 1.503–98 = **8B**; 1.599–634 = **9C**;
1.[665]670–71 = **4D**; 1.746–52 = **9B**;
1.958–97 = **10B**; 2.1–61 = **21W**; 2.80–
124 = **11B**; 2.142–64 = **11C**; 2.216–50 =
11H; 2.251–93 = **20F**; [2.303–7 = **4e**];
2.381–407 = **12F**; 2.478–531 = **12C**;
2.730–833 = **12E**; 2.1052–1104 = **13D**;
3.136–76 = **14B**; 3.[258]262–322 = **14D**;
[3.350–69 = **14j**]; 3.417–62 = **14F**; 3.624–
33 = **14G**; 3.806–29 = **14H**; 3.830–911 =
24E; 3.966–1023 = **24F**; 3.1087–94 =
24G; 4.230–8 = **15B**; 4.256–68 = **15C**;
4.353–63 = **16G**; 4.[364]379–86 = **16H**;
4.469–521 = **16A**; 4.622–32 = **21S**;
4.722–822 = **15D**; 4.823–57 = **13E**;
4.877–91 = **14E**; 5.146–55 = **23L**; 5.156–
234 = **13F**; 5.509–33 = **18D**; 5.837–77 =
13I; 5.925–38, 953–61 = **22J**; 5.1011–27 =
22K; 5.1028–90 = **19B**; 5.1105–57 = **22L**;
5.1161–1225 = **23A**; 6.1–28 = **21X**; 6.68–
79 = **23D**; 6.703–11 = **18E**

MARCIAN. Roman jurist, 3rd cent. A.D. [T.
Mommsen / P. Krüger, *Corpus iuris civilis*
I, ed. 11, Berlin 1908]
1 = **67R**

NEMESIUS. Bishop and Platonist philosopher,
fl. c. A.D. 400
De natura hominis [C.F. Matthaei, Halle 1802;
cited here by page plus line number]
70,6–71,4 = **47J**; 78,7–79,2 = **45C**; 81,6–10
= **45D**; 164,15–18 = **47D**; 212,6–9 =
53I; 291,1–6[8] = **53O**; 309,5–311,2 =
52C
NUMENIUS. Platonist philosopher, 2nd cent.
A.D., quoted *in extenso* by Eusebius (q.v.)

OLYMPIODORUS. Platonist philosopher and
commentator, 6th cent. A.D.
On Plato's Gorgias [*In Plat. Gorg.*, L.G.
Westerink, Teubner ed., 1970]
12.1 = **42A**
ORIGEN. Christian theologian and philosopher,
early 3rd cent. A.D.

Against Celsus [*Contra Celsum* = *Cels.*, M.
Borret, Paris 1967–76]
1.24 = **32J**; 4.14 = **46H**; 4.68, 5.20 = **52G**;
7.15 = **36F**
On principles [*De principiis* = *Princ.*, P.
Koetschau, Leipzig 1913]
3.1.2–3 = **53A**

PHILO of Alexandria. Jewish exegete of the
Old Testament, with Platonic and Stoic
leanings, c. 30 B.C.–A.D. 45 [L. Cohn / P.
Wendland / S. Reiter, 1896–1930]
Allegories of the laws [*Leg. alleg.*]
1.30 = **53P**; 2.22–3 = **47P**
On the cherubim [*Cher.*]
14–15 = **59H**
God's immutability [*Quod deus sit immutabilis*]
35–6 = **47Q**
On the indestructibility of the world [*De
aeternitate mundi* = *Aet. mundi*]
[47]48[–51] = **28P**; 52, 54 = **52A**; 76–7 =
46P; 90 = **46M**
Questions and answers on Genesis [*Quaestiones
et solutiones in Genesim*]: extant only in
Armenian.
2.4 = **47R**
On every virtuous man's being free [*Quod omnis
probus liber sit*]
97 = **67N**
PHILODEMUS. Epicurean philosopher, 1st cent.
B.C. Extensive papyrus remains of his
works were found at Herculaneum.
On piety [*Piet.*, T. Gomperz, Leipzig 1866]
112.[1]5–12[18] = **23H**
On signs [*De signis* = *Sign.*, P. and E. De
Lacy, *Philodemus, On methods of inference*,
ed. 2, Naples 1978]
1.2–4.13 = **42G**; 6.1–14 = **42H**; 7.26–38 =
42J; 11.32–12.31 = **18F**; 34.29–36.17 =
18G
Against the sophists [*Adversus sophistas*, F.
Sbordone, Naples 1947]
4.9.14 = **25J**
PHOTIUS. Patriarch of Constantinople, 9th
cent. A.D.
Library [*Bibliotheca* = *Bibl.*, R. Henry, Paris
1959–74]
169b18–170b3 = **71C**; 170b3–35 = **72L**
PLOTINUS. Platonist philosopher and author of
Enneads, A.D. 205–70 [P. Henry / H.R.
Schwyzer, OCT, 1964–82]
[2.4.1. = **44g**]
PLUTARCH. Greek biographer and Platonist
philosopher, later 1st to early 2nd cent.
A.D. Our citations, as in all editions, refer
to page and letter divisions in the edition
of Stephanus (1572).

commentator on Aristotle, 4th–5th cent. A.D.
On Aristotle's Metaphysics [*In Ar. Met.*, G.
Kroll, *CAG* VI i, 1902; cited here by page
plus line number]

THEMISTIUS. Greek orator and commentator
on Aristotle, 4th cent. A.D.
On Aristotle's Physics [*In Ar. Phys.*, H.
Schenkl, *CAG* V ii; cited here by page plus
line number]

Collections of fragments

A good many of the texts translated in this volume also appear in at least one other published
collection of fragments. We have not systematically tried to cross-refer to these collections,
except for the following works. (Even with these we often omit the cross-reference if the
coincidence is only partial.)

In some cases an editor or work is named:

Caizzi = F. Decleva Caizzi, *Pirrone,
testimonianze* (Naples 1981)
FDS = K. Hülser, *Die Fragmente zur
Dialektik der Stoiker* (forthcoming; cited
in vol. 2 only)
Giannantoni = G. Giannantoni, *Socraticorum
reliquiae* (Naples 1983)
SVF = H. von Arnim, *Stoicorum veterum
fragmenta* (Leipzig 1903–5)
Usener = H. Usener, *Epicurea* (Leipzig
1887)

In other cases we name a philosopher,
followed by a fragment number. The
reference is to the following collections:

Panaetius: M. van Straaten, *Panaetii Rhodii
fragmenta*, ed. 3 (Leiden 1962)
Posidonius: L. Edelstein / I.G. Kidd,
Posidonius, vol. 1, *The fragments*
(Cambridge 1972)
Timon: H. Lloyd-Jones / P. Parsons,
Supplementum Hellenisticum, Berlin and
New York, 1983

Pre-Hellenistic Philosophers

A few texts from pre-Hellenistic philosophers are included in vol. 2 for comparative
purposes. These are:

ARISTOTLE
PLATO

INDEX OF PHILOSOPHERS

All dates are B.C. unless A.D. is indicated. Many ancient philosophers who feature in this volume purely or primarily as sources will be found in the Index of sources.

ACADEMY. School founded by Plato (*q.v.*), which turned to scepticism in the Hellenistic period (*see* New Academy). Location of school, 3–5; history in Hellenistic period, 5; defunct in 1st cent. A.D., 15

AENESIDEMUS. Ex-Academic, founder of neo-Pyrrhonist movement in 1st cent. B.C. His rift with Academy, 449, 465, 469–70, 472; compared with Arcesilaus and Carneades, 488; his philosophy, 468–88 *passim*; on Pyrrho, 13, 16, 468; contribution to Pyrrhonist methodology, 485, 488; reliance on Timon, 23; on pleasure, 15; scepticism, 17; on appearance, 18, 468, 471, 473, 476–7, 479–81, 483, 486–7; against signs, 217, 483; on the end, 468, 472, 483–4, 487; on tranquillity, 468, 471; on suspension of judgement, 468–88; his ten modes, 473–83, 485–7; against cause, 483–5; alleged Heracliteanism of, 488

ALEXANDER of Aphrodisias. *See Index of sources*

ALEXINUS. Late 4th- and early 3rd-cent. dialectician, reputedly eristic. Criticized Zeno's theological syllogism, 325, 331

ANAXAGORAS. Physical theorist, mid-5th cent. Alleged scepticism, 438

ANAXARCHUS. Sceptically inclined Democritean, 4th cent. Philosophy and temperament, 14, 17; relation to Pyrrho, 13

ANSELM, ST. A.D. 1033–1109. Ontological Argument, 332

ANTIOCHUS of Ascalon. Member of New Academy, who in 87 formed a breakaway movement, the 'Old Academy', claiming to revert to authentic Platonism, 449; studied with Philo of Larissa, 449; his debate with Philo, 439, 444; his rift with Philo, 449; influenced by Carneades, 460; reporter of Carneades, 461; opponent of Academic scepticism, 252, 442; read Stoicism into Plato, 444; on things in accordance with nature as part of final good, against Stoics, 405–6; heir to Stoic epistemology, 249, 252, 449; on Epicurean scientific method, 94–7; used Carneades' division of goods, 403. (Note: Ciceronian passages where an Antiochean spokesman is invoked merely as a representative of Stoicism are not recorded here, and are treated as 'Stoic' in the Index of topics. They are readily identifiable by the

introductory glosses to our translations.) ANTIPATER of Tarsus. Head of Stoic school from c. 152 to c. 129. On definition, 190, 194; on single-premise arguments, 216, 219; on analysis of syllogisms, 218, 220; on Master Argument, 231; on criterion of truth, 241–2; on scepticism as exempt from its own scope, 442, 472; criticized for arguing against scepticism, 444; on divination, 261; no action without assent, 317; on division of ethics, 344; on selective value, 355; formula for end, 357, 359, 401, 407–8; controversy with Carneades concerning end, 402, 409–10

ANTIPATER of Tyre. Stoic, 1st cent. B.C. On world's commanding-faculty, 284

APOLLODORUS of Seleucia, Stoic, late 2nd cent. On division of philosophy, 158; on 'predicate', 197; on criterion of truth, 241; definition of body, 272; on time, 305; on division of ethics, 344

ARCESILAUS. Sceptical head of New Academy, from c. 273 to c. 242. His Platonism, 5, 438–9, 441, 445–6; his school called the 'Middle' Academy by some, 439, 441, 448; published no books, 439, 449; Timon on, 23; Aristo on, 439–40; arguments with Aristo, 445; his alleged debt to Pyrrho and Diodorus Cronus, 439–41, 445–6; called a Pyrrhonist by some, 440; studied with Theophrastus, 440; studied with Polemo, 445; his standing in the Academy, 445; acknowledged a debt to Socrates, Plato, Parmenides and Heraclitus, 440–1, 446; taught Chrysippus, 186; attacked by Chrysippus, 222, 224; opposition to Zeno, 438–40, 442–3, 445; agreed with Zeno about infallibility of wise man, 454; exchange with Cleanthes, 451; grounds of his scepticism, 438, 446–8; allegation that his scepticism was a sham, 440, 441, 445–6; on opinion, 454; criticism of cognition, 242–3, 249, 251, 254–5, 257–8, 439–40; on suspension of judgement, 258, 438–9, 441, 443, 453, 456; view of dialectic, 189, 439; argumentative method, 441–2, 448; use of paradoxes, 465; possible use of Sorites, 251, 465; on indiscernibility, 446; on the 'reasonable', 451, 456–7, 459; reply to 'inactivity' argument, 456–7; on mixture, 292; on wise man, 454; on proper function, 454, 457; compared with Aenesidemus, 488

Index of philosophers

ARCHEDEMUS. Stoic, 2nd cent. On division of philosophy, 158; on universals, 180; on the present, 305, 307; on predicates and sayables, 333; on division of ethics, 344; formula for end, 363, 366
ARISTIPPUS. *See* Cyrenaic school
ARISTO of Chios. Unorthodox 3rd-cent. Stoic, pupil of Zeno of Citium. Arguments with Arcesilaus, 445; heterodox view on indifferents, 3, 19, 355-6, 358-9, 406, 428; on division of philosophy, 160, 186, 190; did not use the theory of four genera, 178-9; formula for end, 356, 359; on unity of the virtues, 177-9, 377-8, 384; on precepts and doctrines, 426, 429; on relativity of 'native land', 'home', etc., 431; linked with Pyrrho, 15, 16, 19
ARISTOTLE. 384-322. Founder of Peripatetic school (*q.v.*). Compared with Hellenistic philosophers, 1-6; Timon on, 23; on void, 29-30, 50, 296-7; on indivisibles, 41-4, 49, 51-2, 301; denied infinity of universe, 46; on motion towards centre, 50; on god, 63, 146; on teleology, 65, 278, 332, 340; on soul, 70, 319-21; on regress of proofs, 89; on mixed actions, 109; restrictions on bivalence, 111-12, 206; on pleasure, 121-3; on friendship, 137-8; on political connotations of 'honourable', 138; on a 'complete life', 154, 399; on matter, 168, 172, 271-2; on nature of shape, 169; on particulars, 180; on universals, 181; *Topics*, 185; on rhetoric, 189; on dialectic, 185, 189; on definition and outline account, 101, 190, 193-4; on division, 191, 193; on peculiar characteristic, 194; on meaning, 198; on case, 201; logic of terms, 218; *per impossibile* proof, 219; on sophisms, 230; on contemplation, 259; paradigmatic use of mathematics, 264, 301; on 'first philosophy', 267; on hallmark of existence, 270, 273; on first mover, 271; on definition of body, 273; on interaction, 273; on celestial physics, 273, 286-7; on cosmic cycle, 279; on *hexis* and *diathesis*, 285-6; on elements, 286-7; on mixture, 292-4; on time, 306-7; on animal motion, 321-2; on homogeneous substances, 334; ethics not an exact science, 374; allegedly a determinist, 386; partial dependence of happiness on luck, 398, 428; moral life as self-fulfilment, 399; functional view of human good, 400; on influence of environment, 416; doctrine of the mean, 428; rhetorical method, 441-2; on justice, 442
ARNOLD, Matthew. A.D. 1822-88. Epicurus' theology compared to, 148

ATHENAEUS of Attaleia. *See* Pneumatic school
AUGUSTINE. *See Index of sources*
AURELIUS, MARCUS. Roman emperor A.D. 161-80, and Stoic philosopher; wrote *Meditations*, addressed to himself (*see Index of sources*); much influenced by Epictetus (*q.v.*). On cyclical recurrence, 310, 313; on moral error, 381-2, 385; ethical teleology, 397

BENTHAM, Jeremy. A.D. 1748-1832. Epicurus' ethics compared to, 134
BION of Borysthenes. Author of Cynic diatribes, early 3rd cent. Arcesilaus' alleged fear of him, 440
BOETHUS of Sidon. Stoic, 2nd cent. On criteria of truth, 242, 253; denied conflagration 277
BRYSON. Philosopher of disputed identity, who taught Pyrrho, 13

CALLIPHO. Philosopher of uncertain date and allegiance. On highest good, 455
CARNEADES. Fourth head of New Academy, in mid-2nd cent.; retired in 137, died in 129. Said to have initiated a new phase in the Academy, 448; maintained Arcesilaus' philosophy, 439, 448; modified Arcesilaus' philosophy, 448, 453; wrote nothing, 449; argumentative method, 442, 448, 488; speeches in Rome, 442; on scepticism as self-applicable, 442; applied scepticism only to philosophical questions, 443, 460; systematic critique of doctrinaire theses, 447-8; defended philosophical positions, but only for dialectical purposes, 110, 404, 408, 455, 465; opponent of Stoics, 192; criticism of cognitive impression, 244, 251, 460-1; criticism of criteria of truth, 451, 459-61, 465; on truth value of sense-impressions, 178, 451-2, 459-61; senses as messengers, 250, 461; on truth, 463-7; on the 'convincing', 448, 451-3, 457-60; on opinion and assent, 453-6, 460; said by some to sanction qualified opinion, 453-5; on Sorites, 224, 462-3, 465; criticism of Stoic teleology, 329, 332; criticism of Stoic theology, 462-3, 465; not an atheist, 463; criticism of divination, 463-5; on causes, 463-7; on determinism and free will, 105, 110, 463-7; on the Lazy Argument, 464; criticism of Stoic end, 402, 407-10; division of views on final good, 403, 448; on the wise man, 454-6
CASSIUS the Sceptic. Pyrrhonist and doctor, 1st or 2nd cent. A.D. Criticized Zeno's *Republic*, 430

CRANTOR. Academic, and the first Platonic commentator, late 4th and early 3rd cent. Close friend of Arcesilaus, 440

CRATES of Thebes. Late 4th and early 3rd cent.; Cynic, pupil of Diogenes of Sinope. Teacher of Zeno of Citium, 3; had sex in public, 482

CRATES of Athens. Successor to Polemo and Arcesilaus' predecessor as head of the Academy, early 3rd cent., 439, 445

CRINIS. Stoic, late 2nd cent., noted mainly for his definitions. 'Partition', 191; 'subconditional', 208; 'argument', 212

CRITIAS. 5th-cent. Sophist, playwright, and associate of Socrates. Alleged atheism of, 144

CYNIC SCHOOL. School of 'Doglike' philosophers, so called because of their Bohemian lifestyle, based on an extreme form of Socratic ethics. Their founder or figurehead was Diogenes of Sinope (*q.v.*). *See also* Crates, Monimus. Philosophy, 3; influence on Zeno and Stoicism, 3, 435; influence on Pyrrho and Timon, 16, 20; Epicurus on, 133, 139; influence on Stoic view of passions, 419; animal behaviour as a criterion of naturalness, 436

CYRENAIC SCHOOL. Founded by Aristippus of Cyrene, and influential in later 4th and early 3rd cent. Main doctrines: hedonism, and the unknowability of anything beyond one's own feelings. On pleasure and pain, 113, 118, 121, 123, 404; hedonist lifestyle of Aristippus, 482

DAMASCIUS. Neoplatonist, 5th cent. A.D. Doctrine of divisible leaps, 303

DEMETRIUS of Laconia. Epicurean, c. 100 B.C. Exegesis of Epicurus on attributes and time, 34–7; reinstates method of division, 101

DEMOCRITUS. Co-founder with Leucippus of atomism, mid to late 5th cent. Epicurus started out as his follower, 5; compared with Pyrrho, 16; attitude of Pyrrho and Timon to, 14, 17, 23–4; on generation and destruction, 26; on indivisibility, 41; on size of atoms, 56; scepticism, 57, 83, 86, 438, 443; committed to determinism, 106–9, 386; ethics, 121; on gods, 145, 327; cone puzzle, 299, 301–3

DESCARTES, René. A.D. 1596–1650. Mind–body dualism, 110; Epicurean defence of hedonism compared to, 122

DIAGORAS. 5th-cent. atheist, 144

DIALECTICAL SCHOOL. Specialists in logic and methods of argument, active and

influential c. 320–250. *See also* Diodorus Cronus, Panthoides, Philo the Dialectician. Main precursors of Stoic logic, 189, 205 n.; on Mowing Argument, 186; interest in sophisms, 186, 189, 220–1, 229–30

DIODORUS Cronus. Leader of the Dialectical school (*q.v.*), died c. 284. Teacher of Zeno of Citium and Philo the Dialectician (*qq.v.*). Influence on Stoicism, 189; on indivisible magnitudes, 44, 51–2, 301, 303; on tense logic, 51; on meaning and ambiguity, 101, 227–30; on conditionals, 209–10; on Master Argument and modality, 230–2, 234–6

DIOGENES of Babylon. Head of Stoic school in early to mid-2nd cent.; died c. 152. Visited Rome in 155 with Carneades, 185; on division of philosophy, 158; on dialectic, 185; on rhetoric, 189; on language and meaning, 195, 197; on nouns and verbs, 198; on conditionals, 208; on divination, 261; doubts about conflagration, 277; defence of Zeno's theological syllogism, 324; on division of ethics, 344; formula for end, 357, 359, 401, 407–8

DIOGENES of Oenoanda. *See Index of sources*

DIOGENES of Ptolemais. Stoic, known only for his view that ethics is the first division of philosophy, 158

DIOGENES of Sinope. Fl. mid-4th cent. Founder figure of Cynic school (*q.v.*). Compared with Pyrrho, 16; his distinctive lifestyle, 482

DIONYSIUS of Cyrene. Stoic, late 2nd cent. On the reasonable, 263

EDDINGTON, Sir Arthur. A.D. 1882–1944. On indeterminism and free will, 111

ELEATICS. The school consisting of Parmenides, Zeno of Elea and Melissus (*qq.v.*). On motion, 32

ELIOT, George. A.D. 1819–80. Epicurus' theology compared to, 148

EMPEDOCLES. Philosophical poet, mid-5th cent. Originator of four-element theory. On 'reciprocal replacement', 32; on origin of species, 62–4; allegedly a determinist, 386; allegedly a sceptic, 438

EPICHARMUS. Sicilian comic playwright with a philosophical bent, early 5th cent. Originator of Growing Argument, 166–7, 172–3

EPICTETUS. A.D. c. 55–c. 135. Major Stoic philosopher, whose lectures (*see Index of sources*), recorded by his pupil Arrian, concentrate particularly on ethics and theology. On importance of reason, 185–6; on dialectic, 187, 190, 226; on use of impressions, 241, 322, 359, 391–2, 395; on preconceptions, 248–9, 253; on what is in our power, 249, 391–2; developed providence doctrine, 333; on division of ethics, 344, 346; on roles, 364, 368, 425, 428; on natural inclination to good, 370, 375; on adaptation to world, 396, 400–1; passions rest on errors of judgement, 418, 421

EPICUREAN SCHOOL. Founded by Epicurus (*q.v.*). Location, 4; attitude to founder, 6

EPICURUS. 341–271, founder of Epicureanism. *See also Index of sources.* Life and school, 3–4; Timon on, 23; outline of system, 6–7; physics, 25–78; epistemology, 78–101; ethics, 102–57. *For details, see Index of topics*

ERETRIAN SCHOOL. *See* Menedemus

EUCLEIDES of Megara. Associate of Socrates and Plato, and founder of the Megarian school (*q.v.*); c. 450–c. 380. Timon on, 22

EUDOXUS. Mid-4th cent., pupil of Plato, astronomer, and hedonist. On pleasure, 122

EUDROMUS. Stoic, probably 2nd cent. Known only for his orthodoxy concerning the division of philosophy, 158

FAVORINUS. Academic, friend of Plutarch, late 1st to early 2nd cent. A.D. On history of definition, 190; on Academic method, 444–5

FEUERBACH, Ludwig. A.D. 1804–72. Epicurus' theology compared to, 148

HECATO. Early 1st cent. B.C., pupil of Panaetius and associate of Posidonius (*qq.v.*) in the Rhodian group of Stoics. Formula for the end, 395

HERACLITUS. Major Presocratic philosopher, fl. c. 500–480. Important forerunner of Stoicism, 488; legacy to Stoic fire doctrine, 273, 278; on interdependence of opposites, 332; allegedly a determinist, 386; his doctrines apparently invoked by Aenesidemus, 488

HERILLUS. 3rd cent. B.C. Stoic from Carthage, pupil of Zeno of Citium. Linked with Pyrrho, 15; on 'subordinate end', 359

HERMARCHUS. Succeeded Epicurus as head of Epicurean school in 271. On the origins of law, 129–32, 135–6

HIEROCLES. Stoic, fl. c. A.D. 100. *Cf. Index of sources.* On animal development,

313–14, 321, 347; on appropriation, 347–50, 352–3

HIERONYMUS. Former Peripatetic who founded his own school; c. 290–c. 230. Absence of pain as final good, 404

HUME, David. A.D. 1711–76. On indivisible magnitudes, 42; insulated ordinary life from scepticism, 460

KANT, Immanuel, A.D. 1724–1808. Stoic ethics compared with, 398–9

LACYDES. Head of Academy after Arcesilaus, from c. 242. Maintained Arcesilaus' philosophy, 439; acquaintance of Timon, 23; taught Chrysippus, 186

LEUCIPPUS. Co-founder with Democritus of atomism, mid-5th century. *See* Democritus

LOCKE, John. A.D. 1632–1704. His conceptualism compared to Stoic theory of universals, 181

LUCRETIUS. *See Index of sources*

MEGARIAN SCHOOL. Founded by Eucleides, later headed by Stilpo (*qq.v.*). Noted for a blend of Socratic and Cynic ethics, and eristic argument. Timon on, 22; Chrysippus on, 187

MEINONG, Alexius. A.D. 1853–1920. On subsistence, 164

MELISSUS. Follower of Parmenides (*q.v.*), late 5th cent. On change, 27; on void, 32

MENEDEMUS of Eretria. Late 4th and early 3rd cent. Pupil of Stilpo (*q.v.*), and founder of the Eretrian school, noted for eristic tendencies. On unity of virtues, 377, 383; his school's influence on Arcesilaus, 439–40

METRODORUS of Chios. 4th cent. Democritean sceptic, 17; made scepticism applicable to itself, 14, 472

METRODORUS of Lampsacus. Epicurean, close associate of Epicurus, c. 331–278. On sex, 116

METRODORUS of Stratonicia. New Academic, pupil and interpreter of Carneades, late 2nd and early 1st cent.; strongly influenced Philo of Larissa's positive interpretation of Carneades, 448, 454; took Carneades' approval of opinion as official doctrine, 454

MILL, John Stuart. A.D. 1806–73. Epicurus' ethics compared to, 134

MNESARCHUS. Joint head of Stoic school after the death of Panaetius c. 110. On substance and quality, 168, 173

Index of philosophers

Index of philosophers

virtue, 383; virtue as an expertise, 383; on unity of virtues, 384; did not fear death, 418; forerunner of Stoic view that wise man is free of passions, 419; disavowed knowledge, 438, 472; his dialectical method taken over by Arcesilaus, 441, 445
SPEUSIPPUS. Plato's nephew and successor as head of the Academy; c. 407–339. Systematized Platonic thought, 445
SPHAERUS. Stoic, mid to late 3rd cent. Chief Stoic specialist on definitions, 191–2; on the cognitive and the reasonable, 243–4, 251, 457 n.
STILPO. Head of Megarian school (q.v.), late 4th and early 3rd cent. Teacher of Zeno of Citium. Possible relation to Pyrrho, 13
STOIC SCHOOL. The major school of the Hellenistic age. Founded by Zeno of Citium, 2–3; location, 4–5; attitudes to founder, 5–6; outline of system, 7; division of philosophy, 158–62; ontology, 162–83; logic and semantics, 183–236; physics, 266–343; ethics, 344–437. For details, see Index of topics. ('Early Stoicism' refers to the school's first phase, c. 300–c. 130. Panaetius and Posidonius (qq.v.) are sometimes thought sufficiently innovative to constitute a separate phase, 'Middle Stoicism'. 'Roman Stoicism' is the phase represented by Seneca, Epictetus, Marcus Aurelius, and Hierocles (qq.v.).)
STRATO of Lampsacus. Third head of Peripatetic School, from c. 287 to c. 269. Concentration on physics, 2; on hot and cold, 287 n.

THEODORUS the Atheist. Member of Cyrenaic school (q.v.), late 4th and early 3rd cent. Arcesilaus' alleged fear of him, 440
THEOPHRASTUS. Head of Peripatetic school after Aristotle, from 322 to c. 287, and founder of botany. Teacher of Arcesilaus, 440; shared Aristotle's view of philosophy, 2; on god, 63, 146; on division, 191; on hot and cold, 287 n.
TIMON of Phlius. Follower of Pyrrho (q.v.), c. 325–c. 235. Publicist for Pyrrho, 13–24, 471, 472; criticisms of other philosophers, 22–4; own philosophy, 24; called Arcesilaus a Pyrrhonist, 440; on tranquillity, 468

XENOCRATES. Second successor of

Plato, head of Academy from 339 to 314. On indivisible magnitudes, 44; on division of philosophy, 160; on incorporeality of soul, 272; systematized Platonic thought, 445
XENOPHANES. Late 6th-cent. poet and philosopher. Timon's admiration for, 22, 24

ZENO of Citium. Founder of Stoicism, 334–262. Early life, 2–3; studied with Polemo, 445; influence of Dialectical school on, 189, 446; interest in hands, 185, 242, 250, 253–4; wrote against Plato's Republic, 186; his own youthful work, the Republic, 429–30, 434–6; against conventional conceptions of freedom, 432, 436; Timon on, 23; on division of philosophy, 158; did not have the theory of four genera, 178–9; on universals, 179; on dialectic and rhetoric, 185–6, 189; interest in Mowing Argument, 186; innovations in epistemology, 242; criticized by Arcesilaus, 242–3, 251, 257; on opinion, 242, 254, 257–9, 454; on cognition, 242, 250, 253–4; on assent, 242, 253–4; on impressions, 253; on knowledge, 254; on sense-perception, 254; on expertise, 259; god identified with world, 266; on matter and god, 172, 273; on substance, 269; only body has interactive powers, 272–3; on cosmic primacy of fire, 273, 275; on conflagration, 276; on elements, 280; on mixture, 292–3; on centripetal motion, 296; argument from microcosm to macrocosm, 287, 325; theological syllogisms of, 189, 324–5, 331–2, 374; on cause, 333, 341; on fate, 342–3, 386, 389; on division of ethics, 344; on preferred and dispreferred, 19, 355, 358; on proper function, 360; on good and bad men, 364; on interrelation of the virtues, 178, 377–8; on happiness, 394, 399; formula for the end, 394–5, 400; taken, probably wrongly, by Galen to allow irrational parts to soul, 412–14, 422
ZENO of Elea. Eleatic philosopher, mid-5th cent. Timon on, 23; on size and existence, 29; on motion and infinite division, 41–2, 51, 303
ZENO of Sidon. Epicurean, c. 155–75; head of school, teacher of Philodemus. On signs, 96
ZENO of Tarsus. Stoic, succeeded Chrysippus as school head c. 206. On division of philosophy, 158; on division of ethics, 344

INDEX OF TOPICS

Ac. = Academics; Ep. = Epicureans; Pyr. = Pyrrhonists (early *and* late); St. = Stoics

Index of topics